SOFTWARE ENGINEERING

WORLDWIDE SERIES IN COMPUTER SCIENCE

Series Editors **Professor David Barron, *Southampton University, UK***
Professor Peter Wegner, *Brown University, USA*

The Worldwide Series in Computer Science has been created to publish textbooks which both address and anticipate the needs of an ever evolving curriculum thereby shaping its future. It is designed for undergraduates majoring in Computer Science and practitioners who need to reskill. Its philosophy derives from the conviction that the discipline of computing needs to produce technically skilled engineers who will inevitably face, and possibly invent, radically new technologies throughout their future careers. New media will be used innovatively to support high quality texts written by leaders in the field.

SOFTWARE ENGINEERING
An Engineering Approach

James F. Peters
University of Manitoba

Witold Pedrycz
University of Alberta

John Wiley & Sons, Inc.
New York · Chichester · Weinheim · Brisbane · Singapore · Toronto

ACQUISITIONS EDITOR Bill Zobrist
MARKETING MANAGER Katherine Hepburn
SENIOR PRODUCTION EDITOR Robin Factor
ILLUSTRATION EDITOR Sigmund Malinowski
SENIOR DESIGNER Kevin Murphy
COVER ART M.C. Escher/Cordon Art b.v.

This book was set in New Times Roman by The PRD Group, Inc. and printed and bound by R.R. Donnelley & Sons Company. The cover was printed by Lehigh Press.

This book is printed on acid-free paper. ∞

Library of Congress Cataloging-in-Publication Data
Peters, James F.
    Software engineering : an engineering approach / James F. Peters and Witold Pedrycz.
        p. cm.
    Includes bibliographical references and index.
    ISBN 0-471-18964-2 (alk. paper)
    1. Software engineering.   I. Pedrycz, Witold, 1953–   .
II. Title.
QA76.758.P45   1999
005.1—DC21   99-16026
                                                      CIP

Printed in the United States of America

10 9 8 7 6 5 4 3

PREFACE

Most instrumental in triggering the revolution in one-person programming has been the evolution of a fitting, general-purpose framework, which we call "vanilla."
—DAVID HAREL, 1992

The world of software engineering continues to evolve at a rapid pace. Software engineering provides a rich variety of frameworks, methods, and technologies in aid of the activities typically found in software projects. These activities tend to overlap much like the hands drawing each other in Escher's sketch called Drawing Hands. Each activity supplies a new level of detail and refinement to a software design that is part of an earlier software development cycle. Similarly, each hand in Escher's drawing refines and adds detail to a sketch done earlier. Notice, also, that part of the arm being sketched in Escher's drawing is hidden from view. What is visible in the drawing is suggestive of what is not seen. Similarly, the discovery of the benefits of hiding the details of a software design has led to the development of software that is more understandable. The idea of information hiding was introduced by David Parnas in 1972. This idea is realized in design of software with a modular structure. In effect, the artist's trick of suggesting what lies behind the visible carries over into software design. The visible part of a software architecture is designed to suggest what lies behind a visible structure.

New releases of existing software products, as well as releases of new software products and technologies, occur often each year. The advent of new programming languages such as Java, web browsers, markup languages, and visual integrated development environments has changed our way of thinking about software and its role in contemporary society. It is also the case that software engineering itself is maturing. Increasingly, software engineering is viewed as the application of engineering methods and technologies to plan, specify, design, implement, validate, test, measure, maintain, and evolve software systems. The evolution of software systems occurs in response to suggestions from project stakeholders, changing requirements, new knowledge of software behavior and environments, and the need to optimize the performance of software.

The need to develop software of a high caliber is extremely great. We are provided with a number of new powerful tools that help organize the development process and support the software process to a great extent. Interestingly, some of the fundamentals of software development remain the same as they were 30 years ago, and the challenges confronting software engineers today are similar to what they were when software engineering was in its infancy. After 30 years, we are still struggling to develop reliable software systems. We are at a similar position right now with some problems being even harder to overcome than in the past. Software artifacts are highly abstract. It is fair to say that they are among the most abstract of contemporary human constructs. Software artifacts are not governed by any laws of physics. In particular, they do not age, do not occupy space, do not wear out, and do not exhibit continuity.

The intent of this book is to provide a highly readable and systematic introduction to software engineering. Its principal objective is to create a balanced text that avoids verbosity in the exposure of the material and stays away from overly formalized and difficult to understand mathematical techniques. We view this book as the first attempt to write an extensive and coherent text aimed at meeting the needs of the software engineering community. The inclusion of selected classical articles from the software engineering literature is intended to save the reader time in gaining access to a somewhat scattered collection of readings, and more importantly, to make chapter discussions more pertinent to current trends in software engineering. We are convinced that these readings are also important to create a complete image of software engineering and fully reflect its essence and culture. Similarly, the role of software standards is essential in a systematic design; the inclusion of a selected IEEE software standard on preparing software requirements helps reinforce this important point of view.

Although this book includes an abundance of programming examples and suggestions on how to develop a computer program, the focus of this book is not on programming. For us, this disclaimer is intended to emphasize that software development embraces a number of processes besides programming. The engineering approach to software development implies a certain way of thinking and promises a lot. Essentially, this engineering approach has easily identified threads common to system engineering, namely, designing and measuring (evaluating) with the overriding goal of coming up with an analysis of several alternative features of a system. This approach cultivates a perception of the role of knowledge representation in software development. Knowledge representation of such things as software structures, data flow, control flow, and system performance is expressed concisely in various symbolic forms such as formulas and graphs. The end result in cultivating the engineering side of software engineering is a clear-cut, practical approach to the development of software systems.

The present book is the first comprehensive and complete text on a quantitative approach to software engineering. This book provides the reader with well-defined and carefully described software practices based on industry standards. It presents practical approaches to specifying, designing, and testing software, as well as the foundations of software engineering. Frameworks, methods, and technologies in aid of the activities typically found in software projects are thoroughly presented. This book includes a complete case study representing all of the major phases in software development. This text provides students with a holistic look at software design by encouraging them to view the process as an interplay between hardware and software. Students will also find the latest information in the field, frequent references to related web sites, a glossary of technical terms and acronyms, and supplementary material at the authors' web site.

What makes this book different from other texts currently available on the market? In our opinion, there are a number of distinct features:

- Carefully balanced and highly coherent introduction to software engineering, emphasizing equally important analysis and design aspects of the technology.
- Self-containment of the book.
- Well-thought-out organization of the material, allowing for easy use of the book.
- A strong design slant of the overall exposure.
- A broad range of problems at the end of each chapter.
- A wealth of current WWW sources referred to in the book.
- Statecharts used in selecting software architectures and in designing software.
- Specific applications (such as air traffic control in Java).
- Modularity and information hiding from David Parnas a recurrent theme in book.
- Charting techniques useful in managing and controlling software development.
- The "what" and the "how" of software engineering.
- Cleanroom approach, which works well in designing software.
- Detailed glossary of technical terms and acronyms.
- Humphrey's ETXVM architecture in designing project-specific processes.
- Designing with maintenance in mind paradigm.
- C++ and Java examples.

Here is a brief review of each chapter in order to underline the main topics and provide the reader with a better insight into the coverage of the book.

- Chapter 1 (Software Engineering Landscape) gives an overview of some of the basic features of an engineering approach to software development. This chapter calls attention to the conceptual problem in specifying, designing, and testing software. The use of visual formalisms and the idea of a vanilla framework in solving this problem is also presented.

- Chapter 2 (Software Process) looks at the software process, evolution of the components of a software system during its lifetime, and various models of the software life-cycle. The Humphrey ETXM process architecture, feedback system, Boehm Win-Win, and Microsoft synchronize-and-stabilize models are included in this chapter.

- Chapter 3 (Software Configuration Management) gives an overview of how to manage and control project documents. Three CFM tools are presented.

- Chapter 4 (Software Project: Planning) illustrates the planning of a project in which a training program for air traffic controllers (tATC) is developed.

- Chapter 5 (Requirements Engineering) tackles requirements engineering in terms of two basic tasks: problem analysis leading to an understanding of the basis for a software system, and the preparation of a software requirements specification.

- Chapter 6 (Software Project: Requirements) illustrates the development of requirements for a tATC system. Process descriptions are given using dataflow diagrams and statecharts.

- Chapter 7 (Software Design: Architectures) surveys possible architectures and architectural elements that can be used in designing a software system.

- Chapter 8 (Design Elaboration) presents methods of elaborating a software design in the transition from design to zero-defect code.

- Chapter 9 (Design Elaboration: Mobile Computing) tackles design elaboration in the context of mobile computing, and the development of Java programs.

- Chapter 10 (Software Project: Design) brings together techniques in planning, specifying, designing, and verifying a tATC system. A methodology for choosing a software architecture is given in this chapter. Sample Java code for parts of a tATC system is also given.

- Chapter 11 (Software Design: Validation and Risk Analysis) considers approaches to validating a software design and risk analysis.

- Chapter 12 (Software Testing) focuses on approaches to testing software products.

- Chapter 13 (Software Measures) concentrates on various ways of measuring complexity of software systems and quantifying its effects on software design, verification, and maintenance.

- Chapter 14 (Software Cost Estimation) covers several cost estimation methods: the function points method, COCOMO models, and Delphi approach.

- Chapter 15 (Software Reliability) introduces methods of assessing the reliability and availability of software products.

- Chapter 16 (Human Factors) focuses on the user's as well as the developer's points of view in considering the human factors in software development.
- Chapter 17 (Software Reengineering) examines reengineering, its methodology and economics.
- Chapter 18 (Software Maintenance) carries software engineering full-circle back to designing with maintainability in mind.

A roadmap of possible paths through this book is shown in Figure 0.1. The material in this book can be used in several different ways depending on the audience and its objectives. We are convinced that the coverage of the material will appeal to a broad spectrum of readership. In the following, we outline a number of choices in Figure 0.1. In any case, try not to be biased. You can still travel on your own and use the material that best suits your needs. The book

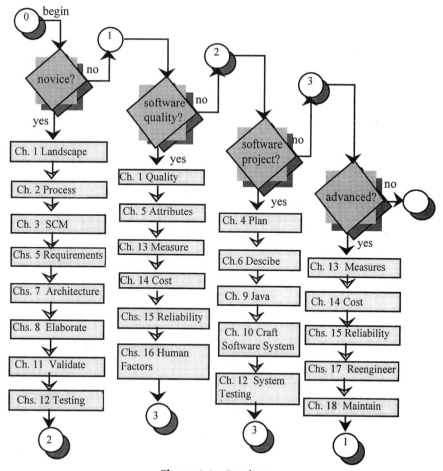

Figure 0.1 Roadmap.

can be equally useful to novice and advanced students and professionals in software engineering. One can find this material instrumental in a new curriculum of software engineering, where the book can serve as an introductory text as well as a reference material in more specialized courses including software quality, software reliability, software measures, software architectures, software testing, and so on.

- *Beginning undergraduate students.* We can envision two types of courses. The short, one-term course, being essentially an introduction to software engineering, can be built using Chapters 1 to 3, 5 to 8, and 11 to 12 (path 0 in Figure 0.1). Also of interest in this context is the software project in path 2 of Figure 0.1.

- *Advanced undergraduate students.* The longer, two-term course could start with the material covered in Chapter 1, with the second half of the course developed around the ideas of software quality, measures, cost estimation, reliability, reengineering, and maintenance (path 2 in Figure 0.1).

- *Practitioners and researchers.* Practitioners and researchers can use this book in a different way by quickly browsing through the basic material and concentrating on more advanced topics. Paths 1, 2, and 3 in Figure 0.1 could be of particular interest in highlighting some recent trends in software engineering.

We would like to thank the long-suffering students in the undergraduate systems engineering principles course at the University of Manitoba, who have used drafts of this book over the past several years. Many problems, examples, suggestions, explanations, and processes have grown out of discussions with these students. In addition, we would like to thank the following persons in the Faculty of Engineering at the University of Manitoba: Ewa Pedrycz for helping develop the web page for this book, Sheela Ramanna for her insights and suggestions as well as her help in editing and correcting the entire book; Technicians Gord Toole, Ken Biegan, Al McKay, Mount First, Ken Podaima, and Guy Jonatschick for their help in managing the systems used in developing these materials; and Steve Onyshko, Rob Menzies, and Donald Shields for their help in creating an environment which made the writing of this book possible. We also gratefully acknowledge the many discussions and interactions with Andrzej Skowron in the Institute of Mathematics at Warsaw University, Poland; Zbigniew Suraj at the Institute of Mathematics, Pedagogical University, Rzesqów, Poland; Witold Kinsner, Steve Onyshko, Howard Card, Bob McCleod, Dave Blight, Rob Menzies, and Mirek Pawlak in the ECE Department at the University of Manitoba; Dario Maravall and Luis Baumela at the Polytechnic University of Madrid; David Schmidt, William Hankley, Dave Gustafson, Austin Melton, Rod Howell, Elizabeth Unger, Maria Zamfir, and Virg Wallentine at Kansas State University; Richard McBride at the University of South Dakota; Gene Kemper at the University of North Dakota; B.V. Saroja at Osmania University, India; Keith Pierce at the University of Minnesota-Duluth; Verner Hogatt, John Dutton, and Gareth Williams at California State

University at San Jose; Bob Dumonceaux, Chuck Lavine, Jerry Lenz, Melchior Freund, Gordon Tavis, and Noreen Herzfeld-Gass at St. John's University; Leon Schilmoeler at 3M Corporation; Hamid Sallam at Mankato State University; Paul Willis and John Kelly at the Jet Propulsion Laboratory/Caltech; Hal Berghel, Roy Fuller, and Greg Starling at the University of Arkansas; E. Roventa at York University; K. Hirota at the Institute of Technology, Japan; T. Furuhashi at Nagoya University, Japan; Shusaku Tsumoto at the Tokyo Medical and Dental University; and Fernando Gomide at the University of Campinas, Brazil. We would like to express our gratitude to the reviewers of this book for their many constructive and helpful comments and suggestions. We wish to gratefully acknowledge the funding we have received from the Natural Sciences and Engineering Research Council of Canada (NSERC), John Wiley & Sons, and the Research Grants Committee at the University of Manitoba, which has supported the development of materials for this book. We would also like to thank Regina Brooks and Bill Zobrist at John Wiley & Sons in New York for their help in developing this book.

James Peters
Winnipeg, Manitoba

Witold Pedrycz
Edmonton, Alberta

CONTENTS

CHAPTER 1
Software
Engineering Landscape

**I often say when you can measure what you
are speaking about, and express it in numbers,
you know something about it.**
—LORD KELVIN, 1883

Aims

- Explore features of the software engineering landscape
- Consider the vanilla frameworks approach
- Begin measuring the quality of software
- Consider incremental software development
- Begin measuring capability maturity levels

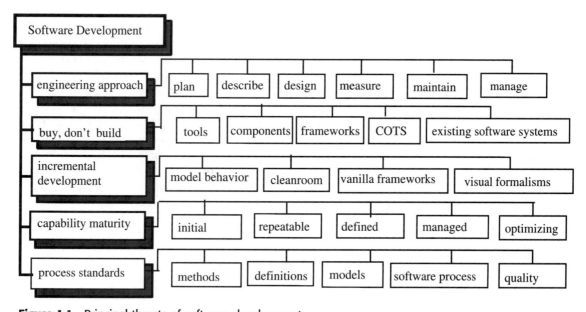

Figure 1.1 Principal thrusts of software development.

1.1 INTRODUCTION

The software engineering landscape is rich and varied. The structure and extent of this landscape is described relative to a number of dominant features shown in Figure 1.1. One of the dominant features of this landscape is an engineering approach to workable frameworks for planning, conceptualizing, and designing software. Buying rather than building parts of software systems is recommended. It makes more sense to tap into the resources provided by Commercial Off-the-Shelf (COTS) products rather than "rebuilding the wheel." COTS vendors now supply a variety of software tools, components, libraries, and complete software development environments. The benefit of starting out in software engineering at this point in time is that life is made easier by the availability of lots of tools and existing software libraries useful in starting new software projects. Instead of building new software systems from scratch, it is now possible to buy off-the-shelf "parts" and, sometimes, complete packages to satisfy a client's needs. It is now just as important to know what software is already available as it is to know how to put together a new software system.

There is an incremental development feature of the software engineering landscape in Figure 1.1. Developing software incrementally makes more sense than trying to do everything at once. It is easier to describe, design, test, and correct a software increment with some of the desired features of a planned system. Once a software increment has been synchronized relative to a set of requirements and the increment has proved to be stable, it is then possible to refine and add features to the increment. The synch-and-stabilize approach has been used quite effectively by Microsoft (Cusumano & Selby, 1997).

The software engineering landscape includes an assessment of the maturity of software development organizations. This assessment is aided by the Capability Maturity Model (CMM), which is a prescription for continuous improvement of a software development organization relative to the identification of software process capability maturity levels. This model was developed by the Software Engineering Institute at Carnegie Mellon University (Carnegie Mellon University, 1995). The aim of CMM is to help software organizations improve the maturity of software processes. CMM facilitates the evolution of software process from an initial ad hoc, chaotic level to rigorous, disciplined levels. In effect, CMM encourages continuous improvement of the software process.

The profusion of competing software products and tools has necessitated the introduction of standards. A *software standard* prescribes mandatory methods, rules, requirements, and practices to be employed during software development. Standards make it possible to measure the size, content, value, or quality of a software entity.

Another important feature of the landscape is the software process. A *software process* consists of those activities, methods, and practices useful in developing a software product. The activities associated with a software process include describing and preparing blueprints identifying the structure of the data and control elements of a system, coding, checking, and deploying software. In other words, the total set of activities needed to transform a user's requirements into software is termed a software engineering process (Humphrey, 1989).

1.2 THE NUGGETS OF SOFTWARE ENGINEERING: COMPONENTS

The software engineering landscape includes what are known as components and frameworks. A *component* is a tested, special-purpose software unit (e.g., a Java class, thoroughly tested, judged to be highly reliable) which is useful, adaptable, portable, and interoperable. Searching for a software component is comparable to panning for gold. Just as gold tends to accumulate in riverbeds after a good rain washes the gold off mountain slopes, components have accumulated after many years of product development by software engineers. The main goal of component-based software development is to let developers use and reuse code that is written in any language and that runs on any platform (Kiely, 1998).

Borrowing from the term *software*, components are also called componentware (CW). Component-based programming has been called megaprogramming (Boehm, 1990). Components come from reuse libraries such as RAPID (Ruegsegger, 1988) or from COTS software such as GRACE (Berard, 1986). The main thrust of componentware technology in software engineering is to design "plugable," individual software units—these are units that can be plugged into an application easily to enhance the operation of an application. Revenue projections in billions of U.S. dollars for componentware and services associated with the use of componentware have been made by the Gartner group (Kiely, 1998). A graph comparing component software and services projections extending to 2001 is given in Figure 1.2.

A *framework* is a combination of components (e.g., class library) that simplifies the construction of applications and that can be plugged into an application. The pursuit of componentware by software engineers can be traced to the goals of increased software productivity and quality.

A natural result of the decomposition of software systems into reusable components is the development of interfaces that make it possible to "wire" components to applications. A *software interface* is a program that makes it possible for components to interact and interoperate with each other. JavaBeans from Sun Microsystems, and the Distributed Component Object Model (DCOM) and ActiveX from Microsoft, are examples of emerging component interface technologies. JavaBeans is a component architecture that helps software developers write Java classes, which can be treated as components of larger systems assembled by users. A *bean* is a reusable software component that can be manipulated visually

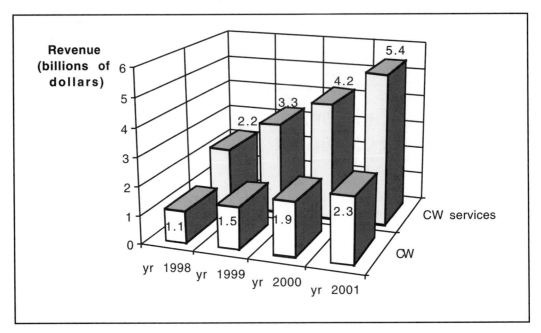

Figure 1.2   ComponentWare (CW) revenue projections.

in a builder tool (Brookshier, 1997). A bean exports properties, generates events, and implements Java methods (Arnold & Gosling, 1998).

JavaBeans provides a platform-neutral interface for creating and using Java components. ActiveX makes it possible to transform available software components into components that execute in a browser's address space. It has been observed that some components run on a single platform (ActiveX) or with applications written in a specific language (JavaBeans) (Kiely, 1998). Another example of a software interface is MathLink from Wolfram Research. MathLink makes it possible to link Mathematica with Microsoft Word and Excel as well as Xmath from the MATRIXx family. In the case of the link between MathLink and Excel, for example, it is possible to enhance the table-building features of Excel with the numerical, graphical, and programming capabilities of Mathematica.

A *software product* is a computer program combined with those items that make it intelligible, usable, and extendible (Brooks, 1975). Computer programming has reached an advanced stage aided by object orientation, integrated development environments, and a variety of helpful tools. Personnel, equipment, and workplaces are examples of *software resources* needed to develop software. The processes, requirements, products, and resources of a software engineering landscape are examples of what are known as *software entities*.

1.3 AN ENGINEERING APPROACH

An engineering approach to software engineering is characterized by a practical, orderly, and measured development of software. The principal aim of this approach is to produce satisfactory systems on time and within budget. There is good reason for tackling the problem of planning, developing, evaluating, and maintaining software using the engineering approach. Quite simply, this approach is needed to avoid chaos in developing software. The engineering approach is practical because it is based on proven methods and practices in software development. The approach is orderly in cases where the sequencing and definition of software engineering team activities and products is mapped to software process models tailored to fit client needs. The benefit of this mapping is that it facilitates the management of the software process. Finally, this approach is measured. During each phase of the software process, software metrics are applied to the products that have been produced. The goal of this part of the engineering approach is to gauge the quality, cost, and reliability of what has been produced. A better understanding of software results from measuring it. This is really a quite crucial part of the approach, since software measurements serve as indicators telling us whether to go forward or backward in the software process. Put simply, software engineering requires the application of a systematic, disciplined, quantifiable approach to software development, operation, and maintenance.

To be successful, development of software systems requires an engineering approach. The need for an engineering approach to developing software was first suggested at a NATO conference in 1968 (Naur & Randell, 1969). In its classical sense, the term *engineering* refers to the application of scientific principles in the design, manufacture, and operation of structures and machines. An engineering approach to software development is characterized by the application of scientific principles, methods, models, standards, and theories that make it possible to manage, plan, model, design, implement, measure, analyze, maintain, and evolve a software system. Ideally, software engineering results in the economical production of quality software. It has been observed that software development requires the establishment of measurable targets, the quantification of software quality, and the measurement of the components contributing to the cost of a software product (Fenton, 1991).

In plain language, a measurement results from the act of determining the size or extent of a thing relative to a standard (Sykes, 1982). Measurement activities during software development are defined in terms of the attributes of software entities (Fenton, 1991; Melton, 1996), (Fenton and Melton 1996). In the context of software development, a *software measurement* is an association of numbers or symbols with attributes of software entities. Again, in plain language, an *attribute* is a quality ascribed to a person or a thing. An attribute of a software entity is a capability, performance level (e.g., timing, throughput), or property (e.g., complexity, reliability, human engineering). Multithreading of some Java applets, conciseness of Occam programs, verboseness of COBOL programs, and the cryptic character of Berkeley Unix shell programs are examples of software singularities. An *applet* is a mini-application that runs inside a web browser page. Applets can perform tasks and interact with users on web browser pages without using resources from a web server after an applet has been downloaded (Arnold & Gosling, 1998).

In measuring software process work products, the focus is on the cost, reliability, and quality of a product. Any tangible item that results from a project task is called a *work product*. Interest in measuring software is motivated by a need to gain a better understanding of how software is structured and behaves. Measuring activities typically occur early in a software process in connection with problem definition and project planning. Software measurement activities are motivated by the need to determine the extent to which a particular software process minimizes the essential as well as the accidental difficulties of software.

1.4 SOFTWARE DEVELOPMENT PROBLEMS

Two principal software development problems have been identified (Brooks, 1987):

1. *Conceptual problem.* Specifying, designing, testing the conceptual construct underlying a software system.
2. *Representation problem.* Representing software and testing the fidelity of a representation.

The conceptual problem is considered hard because the essence of a software entity is a construct of interlocking concepts. These concepts can be found in the data sets, relationships among data items, algorithms, and invocations of functions within a program. By contrast, the representation problem is considered easier because it concerns accidental features of software. The distinction between the accidental and essential features of an object was introduced by Aristotle in a book called Topics written about 340 B.C. (Barnes, 1984). A feature of a thing is considered *accidental* if the thing can persist with or without the feature. Examples of accidental features of software are its language (high level or machine level), its graphical representation, or its composition (modular or not). These features can be changed without changing the essence of the software. Notice, for instance, that object orientation can be considered an accidental feature of a software design. This form of software design is characterized by objects where each object is an instance of class. The functionality of an object-oriented program persists even if it is rewritten in a non-object-oriented way (without user-defined classes). Again, for example, the underlying conceptual construct of a program remains the same if it contains one block (just a single, main method) or is modularized (details are hidden inside modules). Program functionality also does not change if a program is made more understandable when it is written in a high-level language such as C++ or Ada as opposed to assembly or machine language.

A feature of a thing is *essential* if a thing cannot persist without the feature. Complexity and abstractness are examples of essential difficulties of software entities. Complexity can be measured relative to the number of conditional predicates in a program. Complexity can also be measured based on statement types, operator count, nesting levels, information flow, and statement count. Further, complexity can be measured by determining the requirements for resources (e.g., count and type of people, computers, physical facilities), space (e.g., sizes of areas for development teams or memory or disk space for program installation and operation), and time (e.g., duration of each of the processes during software development or average computation time for a program). Basically, the more complex a software entity, the harder it is to realize. Abstractness is considered another essential difficulty of software requirements, function, or usage, or of architecture specification. In particular, the logic (construction and application of a set of rules) underlying a software process model is abstract.

1.4.1 Overcoming Accidental Difficulties of Software

The basic problem with software development is deciding what we want to say, not saying it (Brooks, 1987). It has been pointed out that a number of innovations in software engineering target accidental difficulties in building software. Other innovations work toward solving the problem of essential software difficulties. These innovations are summarized in Table 1.1. The approaches to solving

TABLE 1.1   Innovations in Software Engineering

Ways to Combat Essential Difficulties	Solving Accidental Difficulties
1. Buy, don't build (COTS approach)	8. High-level programming languages
2. Refining requirements iteratively and interactively with a client using prototypes	9. Object-oriented (OO) programming
	10. Artificial intelligence (AI)
3. Incremental software development	11. Expert systems
4. Cultivating talented designers	12. Automatic programming
5. Vanilla frameworks	13. Visual programming
6. Modeling software systems	14. Program verification
7. Analyzing software systems	15. Hardware improvements

the accidental difficulties (methods 8 through 15 in Table 1.1) are primarily concerned with representation (how we view software). However, advances have been made since the 1980s that suggest that some of the solutions to accidental software difficulties also helped combat the essential difficulties of software. The discussion concerning approaches to solving the accidental difficulties of software will be limited to programming languages, object-oriented programming, and COTS. Exploration of the remaining six approaches in Table 1.1 (approaches 10 to 15) are part of the problem set for this chapter. In the next section, the ways to combat the essential difficulties of software will be explored.

High-level programming languages such as Ada, COBOL, FORTRAN, C, and, Pascal simplified the coding of complex systems. These languages eliminated the need for a programmer to code operations, data types, control structures, and communication at the level of bits, registers, memory addresses, and input/output channels. Thanks to high-level programming languages, it became possible to conceptualize software at a more human level. Programming became more "comfortable." Object-oriented (OO) programming was made possible with languages such as Smalltalk, C++, and Java. The OO approach facilitates the introduction of new data types, modularization, and information hiding. *Information hiding* is a design approach where software is decomposed into modules that hide design decisions (Parnas, 1972a). A *module* is a logically separate part of a program. Each module hides design decisions about the characteristics and contents of data structures, and exports operations needed by a user to use "the program correctly, *and nothing more*" (Parnas, 1972b). A principal advantage to information hiding is that it simplifies software design.

A class can be thought of as a module with visible operations on an encapsulated data structure (Shumate, 1994). An object is an instance of a class. In an OO approach to software design, attention shifts from designing classes to invoking operations in existing "off-the-shelf" classes as much as possible. The details of the implementation of a class remain hidden. In effect, classes and related objects provide a working realization of the information hiding paradigm. A simplified software design results. In some sense, this simplification does contribute to more understandable code. For this reason, OO software design grapples with conceptual constructs underlying software being built, not just software representation.

The OO approach also spills over into the left-hand side of Table 1.1, since this approach facilitates reuse. Instead of building software, it is cheaper to buy it. What may not have been apparent in the late 1980s is the contribution OO programming has made to COTS software. Not only are software tools and environments available off-the-shelf, but also class libraries and application frameworks have become available for use by developers in new applications.

Consider, for example, the case where the requirements for a web browser application call for the display of digital alarm clock that also displays the day of the week and date. The sample solution in Figure 1.3 was produced by a Java class that is part of a COTS Java class library (Davis et al., 1996).

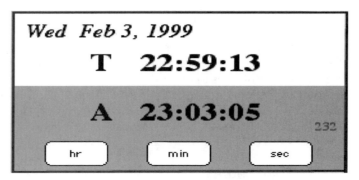

Figure 1.3 Digital alarm clock.

1.4.2 Tackling the Essential Difficulties of Software

The challenge for software engineering is finding ways to capture the conceptual construct of complex systems (Harel, 1992). A number of approaches to specifying, designing, and testing the conceptual construct underlying software being built have been suggested. A summary of these approaches is given in Figure 1.4. Iterative and interactive refinement of requirements with the help of rapid prototyping is seen as a means of attacking the conceptual essence of software

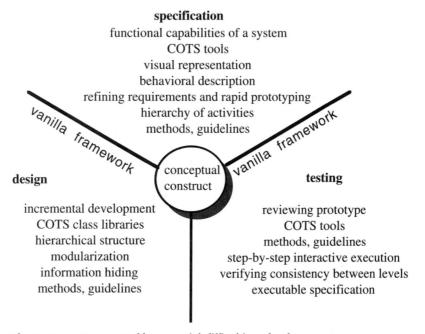

Figure 1.4 Ways to tackle essential difficulties of software.

(Brooks, 1987). A software prototype simulates selected interfaces and performs one or more of the main functions of a system. The advantage to software prototyping is that it tends to reveal a specified conceptual structure so that a client can test it for consistency and usability. A second way to attack the essential difficulties of software is to develop software incrementally (Mills, 1971). These two promising ways to attack the essential difficulties of software are incorporated into what is known as a vanilla framework in Figure 1.4.

1.4.3 Vanilla Frameworks

The basic idea underlying the approaches to solving the essential difficulties of software is the vanilla framework. A vanilla framework is an evolving, general-purpose conceptual system that helps bridge the gap between a high-level solution to a problem and its implementation in software. Such a framework provides a convenient means of structuring and combining data and control structures into an algorithmic whole. Using vanilla frameworks in software engineering is motivated by the need to free a programmer from thinking at an inappropriate level of detail. This is a carry-over from the high-level programming language paradigm, where one designs with natural language constructs like "while" and "if" instead of assembly language instructions that test the values in registers. In the case of a vanilla framework, a designer maps ideas for solving problems to a high-level medium that captures conceptual constructs. A top-down approach is taken in developing software using this framework. A system's essential complexity is not hidden, but is harnessed and managed by capturing the conceptual structure of a software system in a natural way. A layered approach is taken in specifying a system. The idea is to construct a functional hierarchy (layered description of system activities) interwoven with controlling activities. Hierarchies of conceptual constructs in a design are captured with visual formalisms. A visual formalism provides a notation with size, shape, and color to represent software structure and function. A good visual notation is helpful in conceiving good algorithms and in communicating algorithms *and* ideas to others (Harel, 1992).

The vanilla framework approach takes its cue from the early work of Parnas and others on modularization and information hiding. A software system model is viewed as a hierarchy of activities that capture the functional capabilities of the system. Overlapping of system elements is possible. Data elements and data stores are associated with inputs and outputs that flow between activities on various levels (Harel, 1992). Behavioral description is part of a vanilla framework. The control activities of software constitute its behavior. This form of software description has been singled out because of the demands of what are known as reactive systems. Such a system is designed to maintain permanent interaction with its environment. It is always input ready. Reactive systems wait for events coming from their environment and respond instantaneously to inputs from the environment. Examples of reactive systems are human–computer user interfaces and real-time process controllers.

1.5 MEASURING SOFTWARE QUALITY

The engineering approach to software development has led to the creation of requirements engineering (Davis, 1993), software factories (Cusumano, 1991), cleanroom engineering (Mills et al., 1987), IEEE software engineering standards (IEEE, 1997), and software process maturity frameworks (Humphrey, 1989). *Requirements engineering* is the systematic use of verifiable principles, methods, languages, and tools in the analysis and description of user needs and the description of the behavioral and nonbehavioral features of a software system satisfying user needs. In effect, requirements engineering has two principal stages: detection (problem solution and analysis stage) and behavioral and nonbehavioral specification (software description stage). The principal by-products of requirements engineering are a Software Requirements Specification (SRS) and a set of what are known as nonbehavioral requirements for a software product. An SRS provides a blueprint for the complete design of a software product. An SRS results from intensive analysis of a problem provided in a software plan. Problem analysis makes it possible to develop an SRS, which provides a complete description of the functionality (behavior) of a software product with sufficient, understandable detail to enable a designer to develop a corresponding computer program. Behavioral descriptions reveal data flows and entry and exit conditions for each software task, as well as properties of software to be verified.

The nonbehavioral requirements define the required attributes that a software product should exhibit. In other words, the nonbehavioral requirements deal with the product quality, the required degree of each of the quality attributes that a software product must possess, and attributes to be measured. Quality itself is identified with the degree to which a system, component, or process satisfies specified requirements (IEEE, 1997). An attribute of a software product is a measurable characteristic of the software such as human engineering, reliability, or maintainability. The measurement of software is performed relative to a hierarchy of attributes. That is, software quality is assessed in terms of high-level attributes called factors, which are measured relative to lower-level attributes called criteria. A software *factor* is a user-oriented view of product quality (McCall, 1994). By contrast, *criteria* are software-oriented characteristics that indicate product quality (Bowen et al., 1985). Software factors and criteria tend to have a cause–effect relationship (Peters & Ramanna, 1998). The correspondence between criteria and factors is given in Table 1.2.

1.5.1 Software Quality Measurement Method

Typically, software quality is measured with a weighted sum of criteria measurements (Bowen et al., 1985). To measure a quality factor of a software entity, the following steps are used.

TABLE 1.2   Quality Factors and Criteria

Quality Factors (Effect)	Criteria (Cause)
Correctness: extent that software satisfies its requirements	Traceability, completeness, consistency
Reliability: frequency of occurrence of software problems	Error tolerance, consistency, accuracy, simplicity
Maintainability: effort required to locate and fix a software error	Consistency, conciseness, simplicity, modularity, number of comments, complexity, understandability, modularity, scalability
Testability: effort required to ensure that software performs its intended functions	Simplicity, modularity, instrumentation, self-descriptiveness
Efficiency: amount of resources that software requires	Execution efficiency, storage efficiency
Integrity: extent of control of accidental modification or access	Access control, access audit
Usability: effort required to learn, operate, prepare input, and interpret output of a software system	Operability, training, friendliness, efficiency, understandability, durability, human engineering, productivity, system maintenance, syntax flexibility, adaptability, ease of learning, familiarity, error recovery, helpfulness, communicativeness
Portability: effort required to transfer software between platforms	Software system independence, machine independence, self-descriptiveness, modularity
Interoperability: effort required to couple software systems	Communications commonality, data commonality
Reusability: extent to which software modules can be used in different applications	Self-descriptiveness, modularity, portability, platform independence

Method to Measure Software Quality

Step 1. Select criteria used to measure a software factor.

Step 2. Select a weight w for each criterion (usually $0 \leq w \leq 1$).

Step 3. Select a scale of values for criteria scores (e.g., $0 \leq$ criterion score ≤ 10).

Step 4. Select a minimum and maximum target value for each criterion score.

Step 5. Select a minimum and maximum target value for the factor score.

Step 6. Give each criterion a score.

Step 7. Compute a weighted sum.

Step 8. Compare the weighted sum with the preset min-max factor scoring range.

Step 9. If the weighted sum is outside the min–max scoring range, compare each individual criterion score with the preset min–max criterion score range to direct software improvement activities.

The weighting formulas for each factor in the quality measurement framework have the form $w_1c_1 + w_2c_2 + \ldots + w_nc_n$, where $w_1, \ldots, w_n$ are weights and $c_1, \ldots, c_n$ are criteria measurements. A weighting formula measures the aggregative effect of weighted criteria.

1.5.2 Example: Measuring Software Reusability

To measure the reusability of a software entity, the first three steps of the software quality measurement method are illustrated in Table 1.3 relative to two hypothetical software products called Steersman and Ucontrol (for controlling some device). *Self-descriptiveness* is associated with software that can be read and understood because of its syntax, its use of natural language. Consider Pascal or COBOL programs, which tend to be self-descriptive, whereas FORTRAN or Java are not considered self-descriptive. *Modularity* is defined relative to the degree to which a system or computer program is composed of discrete components such that a change to one component has minimal impact on other components. C++, Occam, and Java programs usually have high modularity. *Portability* refers to the ease with which software can be transferred from one hardware or software environment to another. *Platform independence* pertains to software that does not rely on features unique to a particular type of computer, and therefore executes on more than one type of computer. Java applets tend to be quite portable as well as platform independent. By contrast, COBOL programs are neither very portable nor platform independent. The selection of criteria and weights on the criteria (in Table 1.3) are determined by a planning team in creating a guide to software development for a particular project.

Criterion scores in Table 1.3 are assigned by experienced software developers. Although criterion scores are not known during the planning stage, target values for software quality factors can be identified. The selection of a target value for a quality factor provides software development teams with a measurement scale. Such a scale provides the basis for judgements about the acceptability of a

TABLE 1.3 Sample Reusability Criteria

Reusability Criterion	Steersman Score	Ucontrol Score	Weight
self-descriptiveness (SD)	5	1	$w_1 = 0.8$
modularity (M)	5	7	$w_2 = 0.9$
portability (P)	9	3	$w_3 = 0.2$
platform independence (PI)	1	9	$w_4 = 1$

TABLE 1.4   Sample Reusability Estimates

Reusability of Steersmn	Reusability of Ucontrol
reusability $= w_1 (SD) + w_2(M) + w_3(P) + w_4(PI)$ $= (.8)(5) + (.9)(5) + (.2)(9) + 7$ $= 4.0 + 4.5 + 1.8 + 1$ $= 11.3$	$w_1 (SD) + w_2(M) + w_3(P) + w_4(PI)$ $= (.8)(1) + (.9)(7) + (.2)(3) + 9$ $= 0.8 + 6.3 + 0.6 + 9$ $= 16.7$

software entity. To complete the evaluation of reusability of Steersman and Ucontrol, compute

$$reusability = w_1 (SD) + w_2(M) + w_3(P) + w_4(PI)$$

A summary of the computations for the two application programs is given in Table 1.4. Using this formula, Ucontrol fairs better than Steersman. Ucontrol gets a reusability score of 16.7, whereas Steersman gets a score of 11.3. A comparison of the individual weighted criteria scores for the two software products is shown in Figure 1.5.

From Figure 1.5, it is apparent that by increasing the platform independence of Steersman, this software product will score higher than Ucontrol. For example, if Steersman eventually achieves a platform independence score of 6, its new

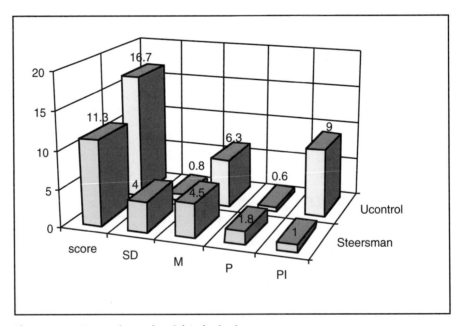

Figure 1.5 Comparison of weighted criteria scores.

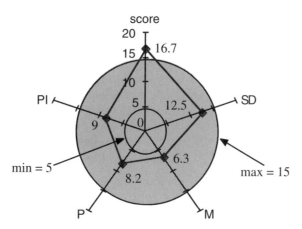

Figure 1.6 Sample Kiviat diagram after some improvements.

reusability score is 16.3, which is almost the same as Ucontrol. In other words, a graph like the one in Figure 1.5 suggests ways that developers might improve a software product to achieve targeted project goals. The preset min–max factor scoring range provides an indication of which software entity has insufficient (or better than expected) quality. If we assume that the minimum for each of the weighted criteria is 5, and targeted maximum for each of the weighted criteria is 15, we can construct what is known as a Kiviat diagram (Figure 1.6).

A Kiviat diagram depicts measurements relative to minimum and maximum values. Such a diagram has the shape of a wheel with spokes. The radius of the inner hub equals a selected minimum, while the rim of the wheel has a radius equal to a selected maximum. There is a spoke for each measured criterion in a Kiviat diagram that depicts quality measurements. Ideally, criteria measurements should fall between the rim and hub of a Kiviat diagram. The beauty of this very simple form of metric is that it shows how each measurement compares with the targeted min–max values, and where further improvement is needed. The Kiviat diagram in Figure 1.6 reflects the fact that improvements have been made to the Ucontrol software system to achieve higher scores for the weighted SD (self-descriptive) and P (portability) criteria.

Target levels for software quality factor scoring can be negotiated beforehand with a client. This is common practice in software factories (Cusumano, 1991). For example, if the target reusability scores are preset in the [15, 18] range, then the Ucontrol package score in Figure 1.6 would be accepted (its reusability score of 16.3 falls within the preset min–max range), but further improvement of the Steersman package would have to be made since its score of 11.3 falls below the preset minimum. The assignment of minimum and maximum values of criterion scores provides a scale against which the scores of individual criteria can be judged. The scoring of a software quality factor can be judged relative to minimum and maximum factor values identified by a software quality assurance team. For example, if self-descriptiveness criterion scores are required to be in the range [3.5, 6], further efforts to improve the SD score might be postponed. In the case where the modularity score of 1.8 falls below a preset minimum (e.g., M = 5), the Steersman package would be modularized further to increase its reusability factor score. Notice that other criteria besides the ones given in Table 1.3 might be considered in measuring the reusability of software (e.g., interoperability).

1.6 BUY, DON'T BUILD

Software development can often mean reusing, extending, or refining an existing software product. In this approach to software development, it is advantageous to buy rather than build a software product from scratch. This approach has also been characterized as one of the promising approaches to reckoning with and partially solving the essential difficulty of software (Brooks, 1987). There is an abundance of examples of the benefits of this approach. For example, in developing platform-independent, graphical user interfaces executable with a web browser, time and effort can be reduced by using the Java Abstract Windowing Toolkit (AWT) rather than reinventing the methods found in AWT (Zukowski, 1997). It is quite natural to find software developers looking for ways to reuse software blueprints relative to a variety of products, and to attempt to mimic the successes that have been experienced in engineering hardware products. It is also quite natural to consider how existing software products can be incorporated into new products or how they can be modified, improved to produce a new product. As a result, software factories have been introduced. A software factory combines the tools and skills of software engineering with skillful management of product, process, and organizational development. The software factory approach is applied across a series of similar projects. The benefits of this approach have been significant: repeated use of similar software process plans and software engineering guides, quality analysis and control, skills standardization, system reusability of software entities applied to the development of similar products, and incremental improvement of product designs and performance (Cusumano, 1991).

1.7 INCREMENTAL DEVELOPMENT

Incremental development of software systems has been identified as one of the ways to reckon with the essential difficulties of software (Brooks, 1987). The incremental approach to software development also provides one of the principal means of managing the problem of continual changes in system requirements and resources. The increments should be small, and carefully selected with an eye to future increments.

1.7.1 Humphrey's Rules

This incremental approach to software development has been formulated by Watts Humphrey as a set of rules for software management teams to follow during the requirements and design phases of a software process (Humphrey, 1989). Humphrey's rules are included in Table 1.5, which identifies the applicable software development phase as well as the event that causes a rule to be invoked.

Rule 1 in Table 1.5 provides an essential ingredient in providing stability during software development. By freezing an incremental step in the software requirement process, a designer can proceed with the confidence that incremental steps during implementation will dovetail the parts of the frozen increment. This is implicitly an evolutionary model of software management where feedback from the design phase induces changes in the requirements. This is also the secret of the cleanroom approach to software development introduced by Harlan Mills (Mills, 1987).

TABLE 1.5 Approaches to Incremental Development

Phase	Stimulus	Response	No.	Humphrey's Rule
Requirements	Incremental step in software requirements completed	Freeze requirements	1.	Freeze requirements for each incremental step before starting design
Requirements and design phases	Ready to increment	Select increment to support future increments	2.	Select each increment to support succeeding increments and/or improve requirements [design] knowledge
Design	Receive stable requirements definition for a product	Choose small increment to implement	3.	Implement a software product in small, incremental steps
Design	Requirements change occurs	Defer change	4.	Whenever requirements change during implementation, defer change to a subsequent increment
Design	Nondeferrable requirements change arises	Stop work, revise SRS	5.	If changes cannot be deferred, stop work, modify requirements, revise plan, and start again on the design

Enforcing rules 1 and 4 assures a function satisfies its requirements specification, since each incremental requirement is not changed during the implementation of the requirement by a designer. Incremental steps during the design phase of a software process are called *builds*. The aim of each build is to produce running code as soon as possible. Notice that there is no point in continuing an implementation that reveals a nondeferrable change in system requirements. Rule 5 recommends that further implementation be stopped until the requirements have been modified and the software plan has been revised. Rule 2 applies to both requirements and design phases during software development. Rule 2 says increments in requirements should aid our understanding of future increments. Rule 3 suggests that a software increment should be small.

1.7.2 Cleanroom Engineering

> Redefining software development as an
> engineering design process, with an
> independent engineering test process, changes
> the entire prospective.
> —HARLAN MILLS, 1994

Cleanroom Engineering (CE) consists of the scientific application of methods and tools to assess and control the quality of incrementally developed software products and to certify the fitness of software products for usage at the time of delivery. The principal characteristics of cleanroom engineering are incremental development and independent quality assessment through verification-based inspection of increments and statistical testing (Dyer, 1992; Linger & Trammel, 1996). CE achieves quality control over software development by strictly separating the design and testing processes. Activities associated with software design and testing belong to a pipeline of incremental software development. Pipelining software development activities makes it possible, for example, for work to begin on the description of the next increment immediately after a completed description for the current increment has been forwarded to designers. The incremental development of software modules makes the software process easier to control. Each new software increment is separately tested. The basic steps associated with the CE approach are given in Figure 1.7.

Verification-based inspection of an increment hinges on the specification of a correctness condition that the increment must satisfy. *Think about it before developing it,* is the moral here. The "it" in the moral refers to the correctness condition for an increment leading to a software product. Correctness conditions tend to channel development effort, giving them focus. A correctness condition also provides a yardstick in checking to what extent an increment satisfies a condition. It has been shown that the verification step in the cleanroom approach is remarkably effective in eliminating defects and contributes to quality improvements (Linger & Trammel, 1996). A full explanation of function verification is given in Linger (1979). Statistical testing begins after delivery of verified software

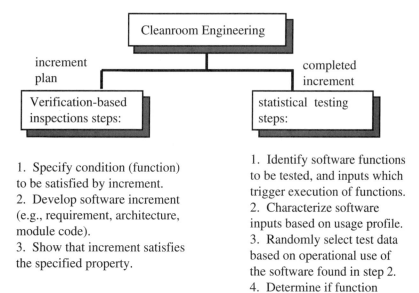

Figure 1.7 Steps in cleanroom approach.

increments to a certification team. The basic idea in statistical testing is to create a usage model that defines all possible software usage scenarios. This is done to identify stress situations (instances where the functionality of an increment must be tested). Then test data are randomly generated based on usage models. In effect, the input data for every test case provide a means of checking a possible use of the software, making sure that the software performs correctly in stress situations identified in usage models.

The practice of cleanroom engineering consists of 14 principal processes used in measuring the performance of a software team. These processes and the work products resulting from each of these processes are summarized in Table 1.6. Cleanroom management processes are carried out concurrently with all of the remaining cleanroom engineering processes. The fulcrum of cleanroom engineering is project planning, which establishes or revises a Cleanroom Engineering Guide (CEG) and Software Development Plan (SDP). The structure of the CEG is shown in Figure 1.8.

The CEG is successively refined for use by cleanroom teams, product lines, and specific projects. The CEG is also tailored relative to standards from ISO and IEEE, specific technologies such as Windows NT, and programming languages such as Java or Ada. The SDP complements the CEG. The main goals of the SDP are to facilitate performance tracking, and quantitative process management, and initiate tasks such as requirements analysis. The SDP defines the bases for software process management, and serves to define the organization, schedules, tracking, evaluation, and control of software process work products.

TABLE 1.6   Cleanroom Processes and Work Products

Process Type	Process	Work Product
Management (present during all phases of a software development process)	1. Project planning	Cleanroom engineering guide Software development plan
	2. Project management	Project record
	3. Performance improvement	Performance improvement plan
	4. Engineering change process	Engineering change log
Specification (requirement phase)	5. Requirements analysis	Software requirements
	6. Function specification process	Function specification
	7. Usage specification process	Usage specification
	8. Architecture specification	Software architecture
	9. Increment planning process	Increment construction plan
Development (design phase)	10. Software engineering	Reengineering plan Reengineering software
	11. Increment design process	Increment design
	12. Correctness verification	Increment verification report
Certification (statistical control phase)	13. Usage modeling and test planning process	Usage models Incremental test plan Statistical test cases
	14. Statistical testing and certification process	Executable system Statistical testing report Increment certification report

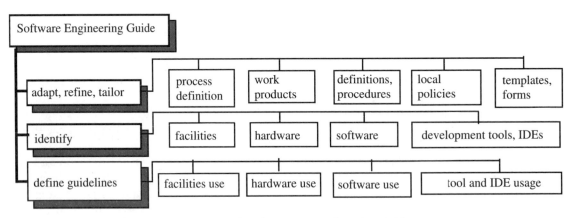

Figure 1.8   Structure of a Cleanroom Engineering Guide.

1.8 CAPABILITY MATURITY MODEL

The Capability Maturity Model describes software process management maturity relative to five levels (Figure 1.9).

1.8.1 Measuring the Maturity Levels: Checklist Method

Each of the maturity levels of the Capability Maturity Model (CMM) can be measured. This can be done by constructing a checklist of items that characterize each maturity level. The degree to which an item is present in an organization is then measured. Then the sum of the degree-estimates are computed. This sum provides a gauge of the extent that an organization manifests a particular maturity level. This measurement process can be automated, and provide a means of simulating (and tracking) the changing maturity levels of an organization. In this section, an approach to measuring capability maturity is illustrated relative to the initial level.

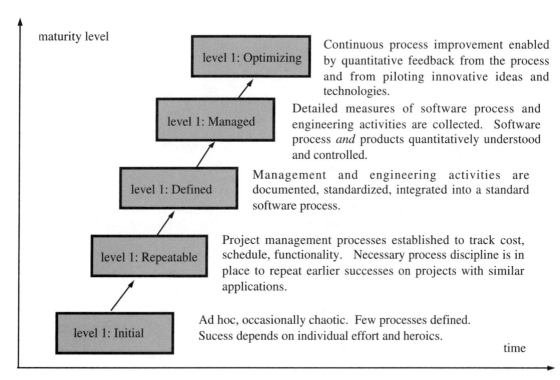

maturity level

level 1: Optimizing — Continuous process improvement enabled by quantitative feedback from the process and from piloting innovative ideas and technologies.

level 1: Managed — Detailed measures of software process and engineering activities are collected. Software process *and* products quantitatively understood and controlled.

level 1: Defined — Management and engineering activities are documented, standardized, integrated into a standard software process.

level 1: Repeatable — Project management processes established to track cost, schedule, functionality. Necessary process discipline is in place to repeat earlier successes on projects with similar applications.

level 1: Initial — Ad hoc, occasionally chaotic. Few processes defined. Sucess depends on individual effort and heroics.

time

Figure 1.9 Software process management maturity levels.

The *initial level* of the CMM is characterized by chaos. An organization with an initial maturity level is disorganized, and relies on heroics of individuals to push through a software project. There is a lack of planning and the development of a clear-cut guide that software development teams can follow. Few details of a software process have been defined at this level. Good results are considered miraculous. The checklist in Table 1.7 gauges whether or not an organization is functioning at the initial maturity level. A high initial maturity level score serves as an indicator of a fledgling software development organization, one with potentially chaotic behavior. The sample score of 0.78 points to an organization in need of basic improvements, starting with a complete software development plan and software engineering guide.

Notice that the checklist in Table 1.7 could be expanded to include other indicators of the initial maturity level (e.g., scheduling conflicts, lack of follow-through). Scores on individual initial maturity level checklist items point to weaknesses (high scores) or strengths (low scores), and serve as indicators of where an organization needs improvement. Using this approach, the scoring of a checklist for each of the other maturity levels of the CMM is completed as a straightforward means of gauging overall capability maturity of an organization.

1.8.2 Architecture of Capability Maturity Levels: Key Process Areas

Measuring the maturity level of an organization can be carried out in terms of what are known as Key Process Areas (KPAs). A KPA identifies a cluster of related

TABLE 1.7 Initial Maturity Level Checklist

Item (10 items in checklist)	Degree of (0 ≤ assessment ≤ 1) (sample measurements)
Absence of software development plan	0.7 (partial plan present)
Absence of engineering guide	1.0 (no guide)
Absence of agreed-upon process model	1.0 (no process model agreed-upon)
Absence of covenant (confidentiality)	0.0 (covenant has been signed by team)
Absence of senior management involvement	0.4 (some senior mgmt. involvement)
Continually changing requirements	0.8 (indication of chaos)
Inexperience of team (poor staffing)	1 (highly inexperienced team)
Absence of (availability of) prototypes	1 (no prototypes available or in use)
Increasing size of software system	1 (no control on size)
Inadequate support	0.9 (very little commitment to project)
Initial maturity level score =	$\dfrac{\sum\limits_{i=1}^{10} InitialLevelIndicator_i}{10} = \dfrac{7.8}{10} = 0.78$

TABLE 1.8 Key Process Areas

Maturity Level	Key Process Areas	Brief Explanation
Repeatable	Requirements management (RM) Software project planning (PP) SW project tracking, oversight (PT) SW subcontract management (SM) SW quality assurance (QA) SW configuration management (CM)	Plan, manage, analyze requirements Project and increment planning Track production versus plans, targets Select, manage qualified contractors Product verification, certification Engineering change
Defined	Organization process focus (PF) Organization process definition (PD) Training program (TP) Integrated SW management (IM) Software product engineering (PE) Intergroup coordination (IC) Peer reviews (PR)	Organization responsibilities identified Develop, maintain software assets Develop team skills, knowledge Integrate SW and management activities Well-defined engineering process Intergroup activities Identifying defects early, objectively
Managed	Quantitative process management (QP) Software quality management (QM)	Control process performance Develop, maintain SW process assets
Optimizing	Defect prevention (DP) Technology change management (TM) Process change management (PC)	Identify, track sources of defects Identify beneficial new technologies Continually improving performance

activities to be performed collectively to enhance process capability. An overview of the KPAs for each level of the CMM is given in Table 1.8.

No KPAs are associated with level 1 (initial) of the CMM, which is characterized by an absence of well-defined methods for managing the software process. Hence, no KPAs for level 1 are given in Table 1.8. Level 2 (repeatable process) of the CMM is characterized by a commitment to discipline in carrying out a software development project. This discipline is achieved by reaching agreement concerning project plans, estimates (e.g., person-months, resources, skills), and reviewing and tracking systems. By putting these support items into place, it becomes possible to assure software product quality (comparing work product features with project requirements and plans), and to repeat the software process in an effective way. Six KPAs are associated with level 2 (repeatable).

Key Process Areas of Level 2 (CMM Repeatable Process)

- Requirements Management (RM) establishes a common understanding between client and software development teams concerning client requirements.

- Software Project Planning (PP) establishes a plan for a software project and software process management.

- Software Project Tracking and Oversight (PT) establishes visibility of software process activities to facilitate identifying deviations from software project planning.
- Software Subcontract Management (SM) selects and manages software subcontractors.
- Software Quality Assurance (QA) provides independent review of technical and planning work, assurance that work has been done according to plan, and that conclusions fit work accomplished (Humphrey, 1989).
- Software Configuration Management (CM) establishes, oversees engineering change, maintains products of a software process.

Level 3 (Defined Process) of the capability maturity model ushers in standards to guide the structuring and evaluation of a software project. A software standard is a set of rules prescribing mandatory requirements to be carried out in a disciplined, uniform approach to software development (IEEE, 1997). Put another way, a software standard provides a basis for comparison in assessing the size, content, value, or quality of a software entity or activity (Humphrey, 1989). Seven KPAs are associated with level 3.

Key Process Areas of Level 3 (CMM Defined Process)

- Organizational Process Focus (PF) establishes organizational responsibility for improving software process activities and capabilities.
- Organizational Process Definition (PD) develops and maintains a set of software process assets (tools, measures, standards) to improve process performance.
- Training Program (TP) designed to develop needed skills and knowledge of team members.
- Integrated Software Management (SM) unifies software engineering and management activities tailored to software process standards and process assets.
- Software Product Engineering (PE) establishes a well-defined software process that integrates all software engineering activities to produce correct, consistent software products effectively and efficiently (Linger et al., 1996).
- Intergroup Coordination (IC) establishes collaboration between teams of different software projects.
- Peer Reviews (PR) provide software inspections that check for errors at the earliest possible time during a software development cycle.

Software inspections are carried out relative to checklists and software standards. These checklists and standards are sometimes tailored to specific software projects. Tailoring results from discussions of the particular features of the worldly level and atomic-level process models for a software project. Checklists deal with entry and exit conditions, verification items, software quality, reliability, and cost measurements for software development tasks. Checklists also cover software inspecting planning and necessary preparation and reporting procedures.

Level 4 (Managed Process) of the capability maturity model is associated with two principal activities: data gathering and analysis and managing software quality. The two KPAs for level 4 are Quantitative Process Management (QP) and Software Quality Management (QM).

Key Process Areas of Level 4 (CMM Managed Process)

- Quantitative Process Management (QP) controls software process performance quantitatively based on software data gathering and analysis.
- Software Quality Management (QM) provides a quantitative assessment of software product quality relative to software quality goals.

Gathering software data is carried out to foster understanding, evaluation, control, and prediction in a software engineering effort. Software data (e.g., lines of code, defects, errors, failures, problems, software usage sequences, measures of quality, reliability, cost) provide a basis for determining software increment development rates and software process trends. In addition, trend analysis and development rates are essential to the decision-making process for a software project. Quantitative assessment of software product quality can be achieved by comparing quality measurements with software quality requirements. This can be done, for example, by periodically plotting quality measurements (e.g., human engineering, efficiency, maintainability) relative to min–max measurements in a Kiviat diagram.

Level 5 (Optimizing Process) of the capability maturity model is the highest level in a managed software process. The optimizing process is associated with defect prevention, automation of the software process wherever possible, and methods for improving software quality and team productivity, and shortening development time. The three KPAs of level 5 are Defect Prevention (DP), Technology Change Management (TM), and Process Change Management (PC).

Key Process Areas of Level 5 (CMM Optimizing Process)

- Defect Prevention (DP) identifies causes of defects and carries out procedures to prevent defects from recurring.
- Technology Change Management (TM) identifies and transfers beneficial software technologies (tools, methods, processes) into a software development effort in an orderly way.
- Process Change Management (PC) aims at continually improving software quality and productivity, and decreasing cycle time for software product development.

1.9 SOFTWARE STANDARDS

Many organizations are sources of software engineering standards. The Institute for Electrical and Electronic Engineers (IEEE), International Standards Organization (ISO), American National Standards Institute (ANSI), U.S. Department of Defense (DoD), British Standards Institute (BS), Institute of Electrical Engineers in the UK (IEE), Common Request Object Broker Architecture (CORBA), and the Object Management Group (OMG) are sources of software standards.

IEEE regularly publishes software development standards. For example, IEEE Std. 380-1993 (Recommended Practice for Software Requirements Specification) describes the content and quality of a good software requirement specification. This standard provides uniform procedures for describing the behavioral (functional) and nonbehavioral (quality) aspects of a software product. Currently, a concerted effort is being made to develop international standards for software development and configuration management. This effort is sponsored by the ISO and North Atlantic Treaty Organization (NATO). The NATO Std. 4591 is hardware oriented. ISO standards cover design and description (ISO 6593), documentation (ISO 9127), and software quality management (ISO 9000 series). ANSI works closely with IEEE in developing industrial software development standards. The DoD publishes military standards for software. Prominent among these is the software life-cycle model for embedded systems (DoD Std. 2167, 1988). The British Standards Institute and IEE are also rich sources of standards concerning every aspect of software development.

The OMG is an international trade organization founded in 1989 and now has over 600 members (see *http://www.omg.org*). It is one of the largest consortiums in the software industry. CORBA was created by the OMG. CORBA defines the standard capabilities that allow objects to interact with each other. Standards lend themselves to process management, since they provide a basis for a consistent method of reviewing the work of software development teams.

1.10 SUMMARY

The cure for boredom is curiosity.
There is no cure for curiosity.
—DOROTHY PARKER

This chapter offers a "stroll" over the software engineering terrain. It provides a glimpse of some of its basic features, methods, and problems. A principal feature of this landscape is the conceptual scheme that underlies the design of each piece of software. The data sets, and relationships among data items, algorithms, and function calls within a program, reflect a conceptual scheme.

This feature of the landscape is also its central problem. It is necessary to specify, design, and test conceptual constructs in software being built. This is considered difficult because the essence of a software entity is a construct of interlocking concepts. Two features of software make it difficult to specify, design, and test its conceptual construct. First, software is basically abstract. Its conceptual scheme is difficult to visualize. Abstractness is an inherent, "essential" feature of software. A second feature of software that makes its engineering difficult is its complexity. A number of ways of solving the conceptual problem of software have been suggested. Harlan Mills has suggested that software be developed incrementally. Software increments are easier to understand, describe, design, test, and debug than complete systems. David Parnas has suggested that modularity and information hiding are helpful in designing software. The idea behind this is to focus on design concepts (what a function does), and hide the details of the implementation. Fred Brooks has pointed out the benefits of iterative and interactive refinement of requirements with the help of rapid prototyping. Prototypes are helpful because they make it possible to study selected software behaviors during the early stages of a project. David Harel has made a number of suggestions on how one might tackle the essential difficulties of software. Central to Harel's approach is the notion of a vanilla framework. This is a general-purpose framework that is rooted in modularization and information hiding, and that supports executable specification, a hierarchical view of the functional and behavioral description of software, rapid prototyping, and a visual specification. The basic idea in a vanilla framework is not to hide complexity but to manage and control complexity of software. In a vanilla framework supported by a system like Rhapsody from i-logix, it is to create an executable model of a system that clearly and precisely represents the intended functions and behavior of a system being specified. Rhapsody is an object-oriented, visual programming environment (see *http://www.ilogix.com*).

Software development works well when it is treated as an engineering discipline. The software process is repeatable to a degree if basic project management practices are in place. This process achieves the defined level when it is standardized. The managed level of the software process is achieved through quantization and training. Quantified management of a software process entails measurements of risk and project team performance as well as software process definition, maintenance, and an active training program. The optimizing level of the Capability Maturity Model (CMM) is characterized by continuous process improvement. Knowing this is all well and good. Quantifying this knowledge introduces measurements (numbers), which can be plotted and compared for a better understanding of the landscape. Measurements provide valuable feedback to planners, facilitate control and engineering of software changes, and help identify where improvements can be made in the software process and its products. To design good software, it is necessary to understand how software will be used and how it will change over time. For this reason, the cleanroom engineering approach is tied to the development of software usage models. A usage model helps a developer gauge how a piece of software (an increment) will be used, and to assess the risks associated with usage.

1.11 PROBLEMS

1. Do the following:
   (a) Identify a computer program or tool familiar to you (e.g., plotting package, word processor, spreadsheet).
   (b) Select criteria used to measure the usability quality factor.
   (c) Select a weight w for each criterion in part (b), where $0 \leq w \leq 1$.
   (d) Select a scale of values for criteria scores, where $0 \leq$ criterion score ≤ 10.
   (e) Select a minimum and maximum target value for each criterion score in part (d). For simplicity, select the same min–max range for each of the criteria.
   (f) Select a minimum and maximum target value for the usability factor score.
   (g) Construct a quality criteria evaluation table relative to the usability quality factor, giving a score for each criterion in part (b).
   (h) Compute the usability factor score.
   (i) Draw a Kiviat diagram depicting the criteria scores relative to the min–max range from part (e).
   (j) Compare the score in part (h) with the min–max range in part (f).
   (k) Compare the scores in Part (g) with min–max ranges in part (e).
   (l) Based on parts (i) and (j), give an assessment of what improvement to make in the selected software.

2. Do the following:
   (a) Write a computer program to automate the measurement process in no. 1.
   (b) Simulate software quality assessment with three separate criteria scorings relative to a factor score that falls below a specified min–max range.
   (c) Plot the criteria scores for each of the three runs in part (b).
   (d) Comment on the changes you found necessary to improve the usability quality factor score of the selected software.

3. Do the following:
   (a) Identify a product-producing organization familiar to you. The product(s) produced by the organization need not be software.
   (b) Construct a repeatable-maturity level table (including your assessments from 1 to 10 of the features associated with the initial level).
   (c) Write a computer program that automates the table-building process in part (b).
   (d) Simulate the repeatable-maturity level with 3 sets of changes to the scoring of the features associated with the repeatable maturity level (give an explanation of how increases or decreases in the scoring of the features were caused).
   (e) Plot the results of the simulation in Part (d).

4. Do the following:
   (a) Select a min–max range common to the repeatable maturity level criteria.
   (b) Based on the output from part 3(d), construct a Kiviat diagram.
   (c) Comment on the combined measurements in the diagram in part (b).

5. Do the following:
   (a) Repeat parts 3(b) through 3(e) relative to the defined maturity level of the capability maturity model and the organization identified in 3(a).
   (b) Repeat parts 4(a) through 4(c) relative to the measurements in part (a).

6. Do the following:
   (a) Repeat parts 3(b) through 3(e) relative to the managed maturity level of the capability maturity model and the organization identified in 3(a).
   (b) Repeat parts 4(a) through 4(c) relative to the measurements in part (a).

7. Do the following:
   (a) Repeat parts 3(b) through 3(e) relative to the optimizing maturity level of the capability maturity model and the organization identified in 3(a).
   (b) Repeat parts 4(a) through 4(c) relative to the measurements in part (a).

8. Construct a table that correlates KPAs in the capability maturity model with cleanroom processes.

9. Explain how the CMM encourages continuous improvement of the software process.

10. Construct a 4-column table giving the accidental and essential features of a software package that you use (e.g., Windows 95), and loss (to society) resulting from the estimated cost of each feature.

11. Do the following:
    (a) Construct the following table, which compares essential difficulties of software with the key process areas in the CMM.

Essential Difficulty	KPA	How KPA Solves Essential Difficulty

    (b) Construct the following table, which compares the essential difficulties in software with the processes in the cleanroom engineering model.

Essential Difficulty	Cleanroom Process	How Cleanroom Process Solves Essential Difficulty

12. A number of approaches to solving the accidental difficulties of software are listed in Table 1.1. Do the following.
    (a) Define each approach.
    (b) For each approach, indicate how the approach has helped in software development.
    (c) Which of the approaches also help combat the essential difficulties of software? Why?

1.12 REFERENCES

Arnold, K., Gosling, J. *The Java Programming Language,* 2nd ed. Addison-Wesley Longman, Reading, MA, 1998.

Barnes, J., Ed. *The Complete Works of Aristotle,* Princeton University Press, 1984, pp. 169–170. See Aristotle, Topics, Sections 5 and 6 for an explanation of the terms *accident* and *essence.*

Berard, E.V. Creating reusable Ada software. *Proceedings of the National Conference on Software Reusability and Maintainability,* Sept. 1986.

Boehm, B., DARPA Software Strategic Plan. Proceedings of ISTO Software Technology Meeting, 27–29 June 1990.

Bowen, T.P., Wigle, G.B., Tsai, J.T. *Specification of Software Quality Attributes: Software Quality Evaluation Guidebook.* Technical Report RADC-TR-85-37, vol. II (of three), Rome Air Development Center, Griffiss Air Force Base, NY 13441-5700, Feb. 1985.

Brooks, F.P. No silver bullets: Essence and accidents of software engineering. *IEEE Computer.* April 1987, pp. 10–19.

Brooks, F.P. *The Mythical Man-Month.* Addison-Wesley, Reading, MA, 1975.

Brookshier, D. *JavaBeans Developer's Reference.* New Rider's Publishing, Indianapolis, IN,1997.

Carnegie Mellon University (CMU), Software Engineering Institute. *The Capability Maturity Model: Guidelines for Improving the Software Process.* Addison-Wesley, Reading, MA, 1995.

Cusumano, M.A. *Japan's Software Factories.* Oxford, Oxford University Press, 1991.

Cusumano, M.A., Selby, R.W. How Microsoft builds software. *Communications of the ACM.* **40**(6):53–61, 1997.

Davis, A.M. *Software Requirements: Objects, Functions, and States.* Prentice-Hall, Englewood Cliffs, NJ, 1993.

Davis, O., McGinn, T., Bhatiani, A. *Instant Java Applets.* Ziff-Davis Press, Emeryville, CA, 1996.

Dyer, M. *The Cleanroom Approach to Quality Software Development.* Wiley, New York, 1992.

Fenton, N.E. *Software Metrics: A Rigorous Approach.* Chapman & Hall, London, 1991.

Fenton N., Melton, A. Measurement theory and software measurement. In: *Software Measurement,* A. Melton, Ed. International Thomson Computer Press, London, 1996.

Halstead, M.H. *Elements of Software Science.* Elsevier / North Holland, New York, 1977.

Hamilton, S. Inside Microsoft research. *IEEE Computer.* **31**(1):51–58, 1998.

Harel, D. Biting the silver bullet: Toward a brighter future for system development. *IEEE Computer.* **25**(1):8–24, 1992.

Hoare, C.A.R. *Communicating Sequential Processes.* Prentice-Hall, Englewood Cliffs, NJ 1985.

Hoare, C.A.R. Communicating sequential processes. *Communications of the ACM.* **21**(8):666–677, 1978.

Humphrey, W.S. *Managing the Software Process.* Addison-Wesley, Reading, MA, 1989.

IEEE Std. 610.12-1990, *IEEE Standard Glossary of Software Engineering Terminology* (replaces IEEE Std 729-1983), IEEE Standards Collection Software Engineering, ISBN 1-55937-898-0. IEEE, Piscataway, NJ, 1997.

Kiely, D. Are components the future of software? *IEEE Computer.* **31**(2):10–11, 1998.

Kolence, K.W. *An Introduction to Software Physics.* McGraw-Hill, New York, 1985.

Linger, R.C. Cleanroom software engineering for zero-defect software. *Proceedings of the 15th International Conference on Software Engineering,* 1993, pp. 17–21.

Linger, R.C., Mills, H.D. A case study in cleanroom software engineering. *Proceedings of the 12th Annual International Computer Software and Applications Conference,* 1988.

Linger, R.C., Paulk, M.C., Trammel, C.J. *Cleanroom Software Engineering Implementation of the Capability Maturity Model (CMM) for Software.* Technical Report CMU/SEI-96-TR-023, Software Engineering Institute, Carnegie Mellon University, Pittsburgh, PA 15213, 1996. URL: *http://www.rai.com.*

Linger, R.C., Trammel, C.J. *Cleanroom Software Engineering Reference Model.* Technical Report CMU/SEI-96-TR-022, Software Engineering Institute, Carnegie Mellon University, Pittsburgh, PA 15213, 1996.

McCabe, T.J. A complexity measure. *IEEE Transactions on Software Engineering.* **2**(4):308–320, 1976.

McCall, J.A. Quality factors. In: *Encyclopedia of Software Engineering.* Vol. 2, J.J. Marciniak, Ed. Wiley, New York, 1994, pp. 959–969.

Melton A., Ed. *Software Measurement.* International Thomson Computer Press, London, 1996.

Mills, H.D. Top-down programming in large systems. In: *Debugging Techniques in Large Systems,* R. Ruskin, Ed. Prentice-Hall, Englewood Cliffs, NJ, 1971.

Mills, H.D., Dyer M., Linger, R.C. Cleanroom software engineering. *IEEE Software.* Sept. 1987, pp. 19–25.

Musa, J.D., Iannino, A., Okumoto, K. *Software Reliability: Measurement, Prediction, Application.* McGraw-Hill, New York, 1990.

Naur P., Randell, B. Eds. *Software Engineering: Report on a Conference Sponsored by the NATO Science Committee, October 1968,* pp. 7–11. Science Affairs Division, NATO, Brussels.

Oman, P.W. Using automated software quality models in industry. *Proceedings of the Annual Oregon Workshop on Software Metrics,* Coeur d'Alene, Idaho, May 1997, pp. 1–23.

Parnas, D.L. A technique for software module specification with examples. *Communications of the ACM.* **15**(5):330–336, 1972a.

Parnas, D.L. On the criteria to be used in decomposing systems into modules. *Communications of the ACM.* **15**(12):1053–1058, 1972b.

Peters, J.F., Ramanna, S. A rough sets approach to assessing software quality: Concepts and rough Petri net models. In: *Rough-Fuzzy Hybridization: New Trends in Decision Making,* S. Pal, A. Skowron, Eds. Springer-Verlag, Singapore, 1998.

Reugsegger, T. Making reuse pay: The SIDPERS-3 RAPID Center. *IEEE Communications* **26**(8):816–819, 1988.

Shumate, K. Design. In: *Encyclopedia of Software Engineering.* J.J. Marciniak, Ed. Wiley, New York, 1994.

Sykes, J.B. *The Concise Oxford English Dictionary of Current English.* Clarendon Press, Oxford, 1982.

Zukowski, J. *Java AWT Reference.* O'Reilly & Associates, Sebastopol, CA, 1997.

CHAPTER 2
Software Process

Software defines a process, process models reflect one.
—M. M. LEHMAN, 1994

Aims

- Explore the structure of the software process
- Distinguish types of universal software process models
- Map universal process models onto worldly level models
- Map worldly level process tasks onto atomic-level models
- Identify common practices in engineering software systems
- Specify steps in getting started

Figure 2.1 Levels and architecture of the software process.

2.1 INTRODUCTION

In developing software, an engineer engages in a sequence of activities that produce a variety of documents culminating in a satisfactory, executable program. These engineering activities comprise what is known as the *software process* (a sequence of steps with feedback resulting in the production and evolution of software). The software process can be viewed hierarchically. Three levels in this hierarchy are identified in Figure 2.1. During the 1970s and 1980s the software process was modeled at the universal level. The idea was to provide a software process model suitable for any project. A universal-level model can then be decomposed into a worldly level model which is project specific. At the worldly level, the particular needs, plans, methods, and guides for a particular project are identified. The worldly level model specifies procedures to carry out project plans. These procedures will prescribe sequences of tasks to be performed.

The tasks identified at the project level can then be decomposed into detailed sequence steps (algorithms). This is atomic level where the software process becomes task specific.

A traditional view of the software process is a linear sequencing of product development activities Dowson (1993). In more recent years, product development has been characterized by an overlapping of activities needed to specify, design, and test conceptual constructs of software being built. Feedback from these activities increases our understanding of what is needed to produce a product. Feedback from experience with prototypes can cause the shape and conceptual construct of software to change. The collection of activities (possibly overlapping) making up a software process forms a feedback system like the one shown in Figure 2.2.

Feedback has four principle forms:

- *Software entity measurements.* Numbers derived from results produced by effector processes.
- *Corrective.* Feedback due to software errors, faults, failures.
- *Change.* Modify software to eliminate defects.
- *Improvement.* Enhance software (e.g., increasing number of operations performed).

Software entity measurements quantify effector process performance, software quality, reliability, cost, and risk associated with a software project. A *software defect* is a product anomaly (e.g., omission of a required feature or imperfection in the software product). A *software error* is an observed difference between a computed and a required value or condition. For example, an error might result from a misinterpretation of a specific software requirement or faulty logic in the translation of a requirement. Software contains a *fault* whenever it has an incorrect step, process, or data definition. A *software failure* occurs whenever software is unable to perform its required function. Feedback is an essential feature of a software process. Evolution of a software system depends on feedback to correct faults, implement changes, and improve the usefulness of the system. The documents in a software process represent decisions (results of reasoning in form of

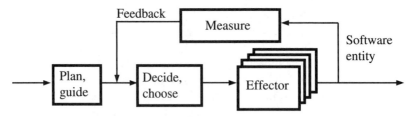

Figure 2.2 Software process as a feedback system.

plans, component architectures, control logic, interfaces, proofs of concept, and so on). A purely descriptive representation of the activities during software development is called a software process model. The feedback software process model in Figure 2.2 is derived from IEEE Std. 1074-1995 (IEEE Standard for Developing Software Life Cycle Processes) and Wiener (1948).

An *effector* is a process that performs some task, verifies its work, and exits whenever its exit condition has been satisfied. The box labeled "Decide, Choose" in Figure 2.2 represents a process (call it "decider") that determines if the entry condition for a task has been satisfied and chooses an appropriate effector to carry out a task. The decider relies on the availability of a plan and software engineering guide to make its evaluation. The box labeled "Measure" in Figure 2.2 represents a process that measures the results produced by an effector.

2.2   ETVXM ARCHITECTURE

The combination of these three boxes (decider, effector, measure) in Figure 2.2 define an Entry, Task, Verify, Exit, Measure (ETVXM) process architecture with feedback. Feedback to a decider process in Figure 2.2 provides the basis for iterative refinement of project requirements and design. The connection between feedback and an ETVXM process are shown in Figure 2.3. The basic structure of the predesign and design effector processes is shown in Figures 2.4 and 2.5.

The ETVXM architecture was introduced by Watts Humphrey in 1989. The feedback system in Figure 2.3 is a simplified universal-level model of the software process. The cluster of effector boxes in Figure 2.3 represents various possibly

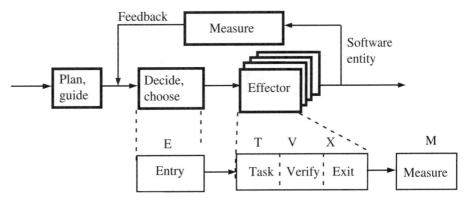

Figure 2.3   Correspondence between feedback and an ETVXM process.

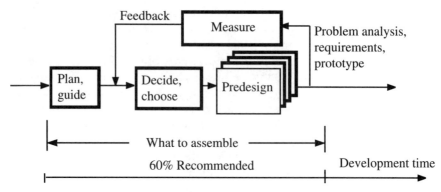

Figure 2.4   Predesign effector process.

concurrent software development subprocesses in the software process. Effector processes as well as the other processes in a software process feedback system are implemented by software engineering teams. Each subprocess is also a mini-feedback system. Examples of effector subprocesses viewed at the universal (macro) level are shown in Figures 2.4 and 2.5.

Each *effector process* consists of a principal activity that produces a software entity (e.g., description of a software increment, executable prototype, architecture) that must be measured. Measurements provide feedback, which ripples backward. Feedback (measurements, testing, assessments) from effectors must be compared with the project blueprint (plan) and software engineering guide to check for discrepancies and possible ways to improve the product. The software project plan and software engineering guide provide ''yardsticks'' in evaluating these software entities. The decider compares feedback measurements with target values in the project plan. Example measurements such as the number and types of choices in menus in a graphical user interface can be obtained from project

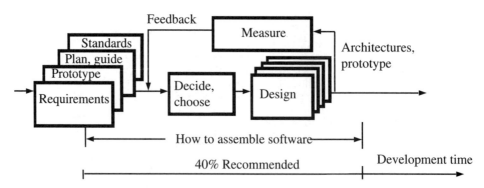

Figure 2.5   Design effector process.

plan checklists. As a result, a decider process modifies (induces changes) in a predesign effector process to improve performance, and to achieve a more desirable result. Notice that there is a feed-forward flow of information (plans, guides, measurements, effector-process results) in a feedback system for a software process. Results obtained from a feedback subsystem are ''fed'' forward to other feedback subsystems in a software process. This is the case in the feedback system with the requirements effector process in Figure 2.4, which feeds forward software requirements and prototypes to a design effector process like the one shown in Figure 2.5.

The design effector process in Figure 2.5 begins its work as soon as the results obtained from a predesign effector process have been certified. Certification of requirements is the initial entry condition for a design effector process. The decider in Figure 2.5 relies on a project plan, engineering guide, initial performance measurements from prototypes, requirements, and software development standards to evaluate design documents produced by the design effector process. The percentages of time devoted to predesign (60%) and design (40%) in Figures 2.4 and 2.5 are recommended, *not* actual. Errors in predesign portion of a software engineering effort are less costly to correct than they are in later stages of a software project. Errors in a project plan, guide, requirements, quality plan, software increment plan, risk analysis, problem analysis, budgeting, project description (its behavioral requirements) and nonbehavioral (quality) requirements are easier and less time-consuming to correct. The likelihood of error in later stages of a software process tends to diminish in proportion to the effort devoted to project predesign. Design is easier and less error prone if it is clearer what is expected. There is evidence that the cost of repairing errors is significantly less during predesign stages than it is in later stages (coding, testing, maintenance) of a software process. Evidence of this can be seen in the distribution of the cost of repairing errors during each of the software process phases shown in Figure 2.6. The chart is derived from several studies reported in Davis (1993).

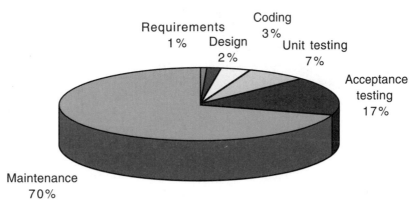

Figure 2.6 Cost to detect and repair errors.

2.3 PROFILES OF A SOFTWARE PROCESS

An effective software process consists of a collection of interconnected feedback systems like the one in Figure 2.2. There are two kinds of effectors in a software process: what-effectors and how-effectors. A what-effector in a software process determines the basic features of a software product and what must be done to satisfy the requirements of a client. A how-effector determines the structure and content of a software product and how to assemble the necessary components to produce a product matching project requirements. A preliminary overview of the two types of effectors in a feed-forward scheme is given in Figure 2.7. The → notation in the figure reads "leads to."

Decisions about the form of a system make it possible to choose appropriate architectures, control structures, data types, and inputs and outputs in deciding *how* a system will be constructed, and lead to the implementation of an operational system.

2.3.1 Software Verification and Validation

Verification and validation (V&V) is associated with each of the activities in a software process. Validation occurs whenever a system component is evaluated

What (Management processes: statement of need)   →
What (Management processes: project plant)   →
What (Management processes: software engineering guide)   →
What (Management processes: results from similar projects)   →
What (Software process standards)   →
What (Requirements engineering standards)   →
What (Software design standards)   →
What (Software design standards)   →
What (Other standards, e.g., documentation, testing, productivity)   →
What (Measures, measurement scales, min–max values)   →
What (Problem analysis, prototype)   →
What (Sources of risk and risk analysis)   →
What (Behavioral requirements specification)   →
What (Nonbehavioral requirements—required software quality)   →
What (Select software increment)   →

Figure 2.7.A Sample what-effectors.

How (Design of software architecture)   →
How (Design of software architectural elements and interfaces)   →
How (Prototype with architectural features)   →
How (Architectural validation [check requirements], verification)   →
How (Design of software component interfaces)   →
How (Validate and test interface prototype)   →
How (Algorithm design)   →
How (Prototype with algorithmic features)   →
How (Algorithm validation [check requirements], verification)   →
How (Data structures design)   →
How (Prototype with data structure features, e.g., file-handling)   →
How (Data structure validation [check requirements], verification)   →
How (Design elaboration [pursue details])   →
How (Prototype with design elaboration improvements)   →
How (Detailed design validation [check requirements], and verification)   →
How (Design usability models)   →
How (Implement design)   →
How (Certify implementation)   →

Figure 2.7.B Sample how-effectors.

to ensure that it satisfies system requirements. Verification consists in checking whether the product of a particular phase satisfies the conditions imposed at the beginning of that phase. For example, in the case of the Sojourner robot aboard the lander of the Pathfinder spacecraft, which landed on Mars on July 4, 1997, the V&V process is illustrated in terms of the software controlling the arm holding the APXS (alpha photon x-ray spectrometer) sensor (Figure 2.8).

The APXS arm must be pressed against a rock sample to make it possible to bombard the sample with alpha particles to determine what elements make up the sample. An example of a lander system requirement is that the robot be able to navigate the Martian surface to align the APXS with and press against a designated rock sample. Successive products (e.g., lander length = 62 cm needed for navigation between Martian rocks, sensor on extendable arm for APXS, program to control APXS arm) must satisfy system requirements. Verifying a product for a lander software process stage (e.g., design stage) means checking that the product satisfies constraints put on that product at the beginning of the stage. For example, at the beginning of the design stage for the APXS controller, a pressure constraint on the extendable arm requires that the APXS maintain a steady pressure against a rock sample and that this pressure not exceed 0.012 lbs even if the robot experiences minor vibrations from the Martian

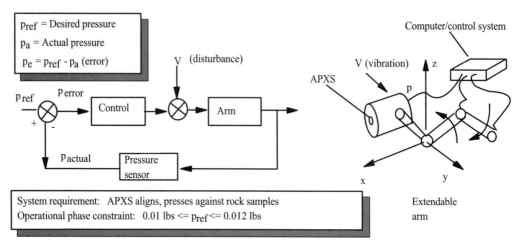

Figure 2.8   V&V applied to Sojourner robot arm controller.

surface. The APXS controller is verified by making sure that it satisfies this pressure constraint.

2.3.2   Software Evolution

A software process becomes an effective means of evolving software, making it responsive to client needs and changes in its environment, whenever it includes feedback. Much like salmon moving upstream in the springtime, feedback in a software process has a ripple effect where information concerning faults and changing requirements makes its way backward to earlier stages in the cycle. Responses to feedback cause software products to evolve. Evolution in a software process can be characterized by genotypes and phenotypes (Fogel, 1995). The plans, criteria, requirements, architectures, and control structures of software can be compared with genotypes in biology. A genotype provides information (underlying genetic coding) about a member of a population (e.g., design document for a computer program). The operational products (manner of responses of processes in execution) are analogous to phenotypes of organisms. A phenotype characterizes the behavior of a population member. Software process products make up the genotypic (information) state space of an evolving software system. Executing processes constitute the phenotypic (behavioral) state space of software system. Let $s1, s2, s3, \ldots$ and $p1, p2, p3, \ldots$ be successive software genotypes and process phenotypes, respectively. The interactions between software genotypes and phenotypes are shown in Figure 2.9.

DNA (deoxyribonucleic acid) provides the building blocks (pieces of coding information) of a gene. The information in software documents is analogous to DNA, and is carried over into revised documents during software evolution. Both genes and processes (genotypes and phenotypes) evolve. In the context of evolving software systems, feedback from operation systems as well as information in existing software documents contribute to the development of a new software release (e.g., Microsoft Word 5.0 eventually leads to Word 6.0). In practical terms, the phases of a software process can be mapped to what is known as evolution patterns containing parallel activities (Nguyen et al., 1997). Let the symbol ‖ symbolize parallel. Then a software evolution pattern can be formulated as a collection of parallel activities as follows:

software evolution pattern = where ‖ why ‖ what ‖ when ‖ how ‖ by-whom

The framework for an evolution pattern is given in Figure 2.10. The when-part identifies the sources that cause a software change (in the what-part). A partial list of the major causes of software changes are identified in the why-part. The how- and by-whom-parts indicate corrective actions and either who performs them (an engineer) or who approves them (e.g., client, user). Many evolution patterns are possible, but not all are implemented. A software pattern is instrumented by a cost measure that determines the gain or loss of productivity as a result of carrying out the pattern. For example, let pg, MM (156 hours), max equal the number of pages, number of man months required to implement an evolution pattern, and maximum cost, respectively. Then an evolution pattern would be carried out if

$$\frac{pg}{MM} \leq \max$$

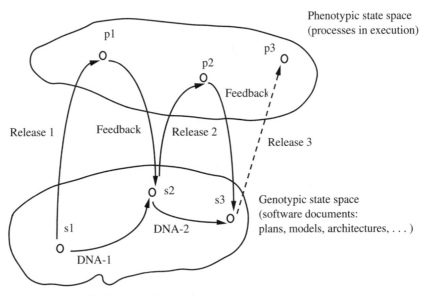

Figure 2.9   Evolution of software documents.

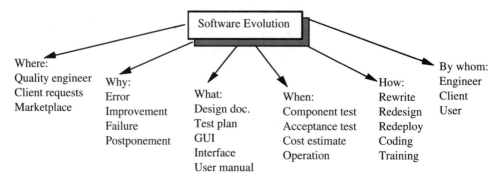

Figure 2.10   Framework for an evolution pattern.

Assuming that a project manager allows up to 25 MM, and a threshold value (value of max) of 0.5, estimated page counts below 12 would trigger the evolution pattern (Figure 2.11).

2.3.3   Software Life-Cycle Processes

A Software Life-Cycle (SLC) is the period of time beginning with a concept for a software product and ending whenever the software is no longer available for use. A Software Life-Cycle Model (SLCM) represents the activities, their inputs and outputs (documents, tables, measurements) and their interactions during the life-cycle. A software life-cycle begins by selecting an SLCM and mapping activities to the chosen SLC model as shown in Figure 2.12.

A summary of the SLC mapping guidelines is given in Table 2.1. A software life-cycle becomes specific as a result of choosing a particular life-cycle model

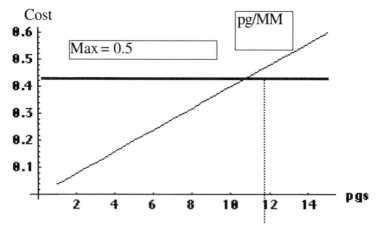

Figure 2.11   Cost restriction on an evolution pattern.

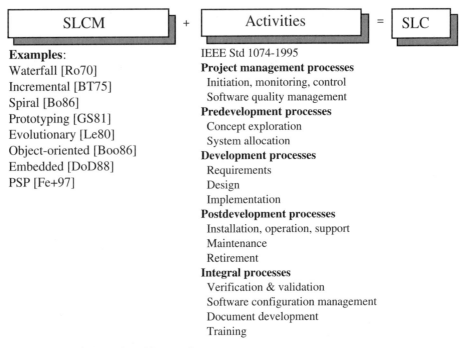

Figure 2.12 Life-cycle with sample SLCMs.

and mapping project activities to that model. The formula shown in Figure 2.12 characterizes software life-cycles and is derived from IEEE Std. 1074.1-1995 (IEEE Standard for Developing Software Life Cycle Processes). This document provides a standard for life-cycle activities shown in Figure 2.12. This provides a standard for a universal-level software life-cycle model. It does *not* provide either a world-level (project specific) process model nor does it treat the issue of atomic-level (task specific) modeling of a software process. These are more detailed process models needed by software engineering teams relative to specific software project needs and limitations. The worldly and atomic levels of the software process represent mappings of a standard model onto specific software projects and tasks. The IEEE Std. 1074.1-1995 standard provides a useful framework in structuring a particular software process. The standard universal-level predevelopment and development processes (and associated activities) are described in this section.

2.4 PREDEVELOPMENT PROCESS

Predevelopment in a software life-cycle consists of two major processes: concept exploration and system allocation. Each of these processes has activities that respond to inputs shown in Table 2.2.

TABLE 2.1   SLC Mapping Guidelines

Step	Actions
1. Select software life-cycle model	(a) Identify available SLCMs (b) Identify project attributes (e.g., rapid prototyping, purchased applications, reverse engineering, object orientation) (c) Identify project constraints (risks, contractor–vendor relationships, lines of authority, available hardware, software)
2. Compare activities to SLCM	Construct checklist so that all activities are mapped, and SLCM requirements are satisfied
3. Place activities in time sequence	Map activities to general time schedule (i.e., MM) without specific dates
4. Check information flow	Construct information flow tables (inputs and outputs for each activity)
5. Assign information to documents	Identify documents SLCM delivers
6. Assign actual dates, durations	Assign actual dates (durations) to schedule
7. Reconcile external constraints	Make possible adjustments of mapped activities relative to external constraints based on personnel resources, interfaces, and time available for project
8. *Evolve* the schedule and SLC	Let the schedule evolve over time based on new factors that occur

The system allocation process is the bridge between concept exploration and the software development process. System allocation has three main activities: analyze functions, identify the architecture, and derive the hardware and software requirements of the system to be developed. As a result of the functions analysis activity, a statement of need is produced. This statement of need provides a functional description of the system. It identifies the inputs to the system, the functions to be applied to the inputs, and the required outputs. The system functions are derived from the system requirements resulting from concept exploration (its statement of need). The architecture of a system is its organization—hardware, software, and interfaces—which establishes a framework for the development of the system. An example is the APXS sensor, pressure sensors and extendable arm (hardware), controller to regulate positioning and pressure exerted by the extendable arm (software), and interfaces between sensors, computer, and arm on the Mars Sojourner robot. It is the identification of the system architecture that makes it possible to derive a complete functional description of the system. The functional description is divided into software requirements, hardware requirements, and system interface requirements. The software requirements provide high-level input to the beginning activities of the software development process. Other possible inputs to development process

TABLE 2.2   Concept Exploration Activities

Input	Activity	Output
Changing software needs, customer requests, ideas within development group, marketing findings, system feedback data	Identify ideas, needs	Statement of need
Development resources, and budget, market data, statement of need	Formulate potential approaches	Constraints, benefits, and potential approaches (e.g., feasibility study)
Statement of need, constraints, benefits, potential approaches	Feasibility study	Analysis of risks, recommendations
Previous reports, recommendations	Refine, finalize idea, need	Revised statement of need

are preliminary system models and prototypes resulting from predevelopment activities.

2.5   SOFTWARE DEVELOPMENT PROCESS

Three principle processes are identified in the IEEE 1074-1995 standard during the software development phase:

- *Requirements.* Decide what a system must do, its activities, risks, and testing plan.
- *Design.* Determine how a system computes, its specific functions and structure.
- *Implementation.* Produce source code, documentation, and tests; validate and verify.

The requirements process focuses on *what* a software system should do, and provides an engineering description of the objects, functions, and states of a software system. During the requirements process, priorities, software integration and interface needs, dataflow models, detailed analysis of risks, and test and installation plans are developed. Formal models exhibiting the structure of software systems (inputs, outputs, and connections between activities) are usually an outcome of the requirements process. This is usually accomplished with a variety of software tools, which are evaluated on a regular basis (Nahouraii, 1996). The design phase focuses on how software requirements can be realized. In this case, the principal concerns are the functions and structure of the system being developed. This means that software architectures, specific interfaces, and algorithms are selected. Selections are validated to ensure that they satisfy requirements specifications. The products of design activities must also be verified relative specific constraints identified at the beginning of the design phase. Finally, during the implementation process, source code is produced. Source code must be validated to ensure that it satisfies requirements specifications, and it must be verified relative to design constraints. Test data is generated during the execution of the resulting source code. The operation system is documented (e.g., results of testing, software cost, software quality measurements, user manuals).

2.6 SOFTWARE LIFE-CYCLE MODELS

> **Software development is an exploratory and self-correcting dialogue, complete with stuttering, hemming and hawing, and Freudian slips.**
> **—JAMES BACH, 1999**

The modeling of software processes has reached a mature stage based on extensive knowledge and experience with a variety of large-scale software projects. A software process model prescribes a framework for principal project activities, inputs, outputs, and constraints. Software processes have been studied intensively since the introduction of the waterfall model as a framework for sequencing activities associated with software development (Royce, 1970).

2.6.1 Waterfall, Incremental, and Spiral Models

The waterfall model is the oldest of these models (Figure 2.13). In its original form, the waterfall model described a sequence of activities in a software lifecycle that began with concept exploration and concluded with maintenance and eventual replacement. Concept exploration and requirements focus on *what* we know about the basic features of the solution to a problem. This means identifying and describing the basic activities and attributes of a system. The results of each waterfall activity provides feedback to earlier phases. Once the solution to a problem has been worked out, software developers shift their attention to determining *how* the system is put together so that it functions correctly and has required qualities. In the final stages of the waterfall, the focus is on the operation of the system. Each of the activities in the waterfall provides feedback to developers responsible for earlier activities. Ideally, this feedback provides impetus for the improvement and evolution of the software. Notice that the waterfall model

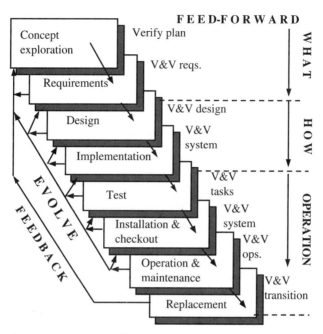

Figure 2.13 Waterfall software process model.

caters to what is known as forward engineering of software products. This means starting with a high-level conceptual model for a system. After a description of the conceptual construct for a system has been worked out, the software process continues with the design, implementation, and testing of a physical model of the system.

A principal advantage of the waterfall model is that it provides for baseline management, which identifies a *fixed* set of documents produced as a result of each phase in the life-cycle. Except for feedback, the waterfall model does not make it clear how one might go about discovering the intentions of designers of legacy systems. A *legacy system* is a collection of hardware and software that has accumulated over the years. The process of identifying and analyzing the components and relationships between components of a legacy system is called reverse engineering. The waterfall model is lacking in prescribing how one reverse engineers an existing system. Another drawback in the waterfall model is that a client must wait until the installation and checkout phase to see how a system works. The development of a large, complex system requires considerable time and effort. Absent from the waterfall model are the notions of rapid proto-typing and incremental development. A prototype is an executable model that accurately reflects a subset of the properties of a system being developed. Pro-toypes make it possible for clients and developers to see how a software increment works in the early stages of a software process. It is also the case that prototypes aid the understanding of a system. Making changes to prototypes of software increments is easier than trying to change a complete system.

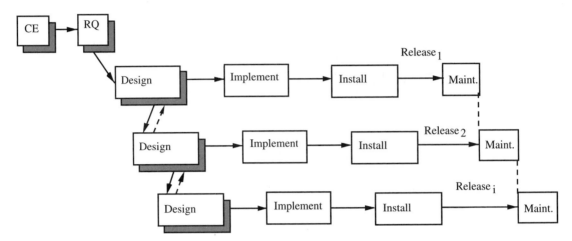

Figure 2.14   Incremental life-cycle model.

To remedy the weaknesses of the waterfall model, the evolutionary (Lehman, 1994, 1997) and prototyping (Connell & Shafer, 1989) life-cycle models were introduced. The incremental life-cycle model (European Space Agency, 1991) is similar to the waterfall model (Figure 2.14). The system and software concepts and requirements are first identified, and then the remaining activities of software development are repeated each time there is a new release of the software. The incremental model makes the unrealistic assumption that the system as well as software requirements remain stable. However, requirements tend to evolve due to changes in technology and experience (feedback concerning an operational version of the system).

The spiral life-cycle model introduced by Boehm in 1986 combines the good features of baseline management (document associated with cycle phases) in the waterfall model, overlapping phases found in the incremental model, and early versions of a system from the prototyping model (Figure 2.15). The basic assumption in the spiral model is that the form of software development cannot be completely determined in advance. Prototyping, risk analysis, simulation, modeling, financial analysis (cost estimates), and benchmarks (results simulations and experiments with prototypes) are needed before committing to detailed design of a software system. An iterative and interactive development of system requirements is made possible by gaining experience with the behavior and shortcomings of product prototypes. Prototyping is seen as a means of reducing risk, discovering potential problems before committing to a full-fledged system. Boehm characterized his model as a process model generator (Boehm, 1989). Each cycle of the spiral model in Figure 2.15 has four principal activities.

- Elaborate software entity objectives, constraints, and alternatives.
- Evaluate alternatives relative to objectives and constraints, and identify major sources of risk.

- Elaborate the definition of software entities for a project.
- Plan the next cycle. Terminate a project if it is too risky. Secure management commitment.

2.6.2 System Risk Assessment

A risk is a potential problem in a system. In software engineering, a risk is identified with likelihood of a specified hazardous (or undesirable) event occurring within a designated time or in designated circumstances. Risk analysis is needed in choosing product development paths that have the best chance of success within a reasonable time. Risk assessment establishes whether a perceived risk level is less than or equal to a tolerable risk level. A partial summary

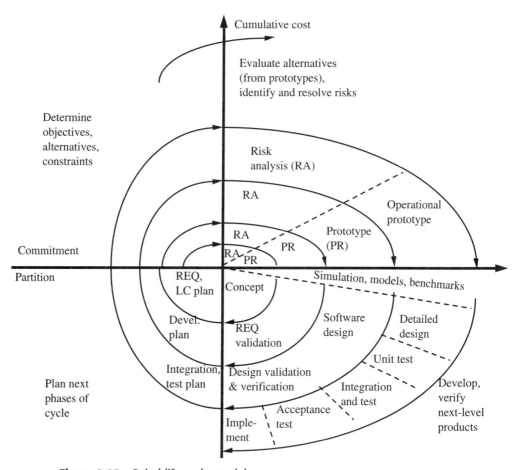

Figure 2.15 Spiral life-cycle model.

TABLE 2.3   Risk Assessment Table

Source	Type of Risk (Example)	Risk Level
procurement/lease data	cost (possibility of overrun)	medium
	resource (possibility of equipment shortage)	high
	liability (what if equipment, tool fails?)	low
system constraints	technical (product feature unobtainable)	low
	technical (product feature hazardous)	medium
	legal (product feature violates patent)	high
	economic (product feature too costly)	high
	operational (product lifespan too short)	low
statement of need	technical (feature unrealizable)	low
(pre-development)	technical (resources inadequate)	medium
prototype	technical (causes system to self-destruct)	high

of the forms of the sources and forms of risk (IEEE Std. 1074-1995) is given in Table 2.3.

Risk assessments are computed in terms of two factors: the probability that an undesirable event might occur and the consequent estimated loss (Fairley & Rook, 1997).

Factors to Consider in Risk Assessment

- Probability p that an undesirable event might occur ($0 <= p <= 1$)
- Estimated loss L (e.g., cost of software failure, number of lives lost) with the occurrence of the undesired event.

Probabilities are computed in terms of events. An *event* (some observable, random occurrence) is the result of a trial that can but need not occur. An event is random if its occurrence and nonoccurrence are equally likely (e.g., rolling a die to obtain or not obtain a 7). A trial is the result of n equally likely events where m of the events favor the occurrence of an event E. The probability pr(E) is computed as follows:

$$pr(E) = \frac{m}{n} = \frac{\text{number of favorable events}}{\text{number of possible events}}$$

The loss associated with an undesirable event is called risk impact computed. Let E_u be the event that an undesirable event occurs. In cases where loss L can be quantified, a measure of risk known as *risk exposure* can be computed:

$$risk \text{ exposure} = pr(E_u) * L$$

2.6.3 Example: Risk Exposure for the Soujourner Robot

The Sojourner robot was part of a NASA spacecraft mission to explore the Martian surface. This robot must operate in $-58°C$ Martian surface temperatures. What is the risk that the software commanding the robot steering system will fail if a Sojourner impact sensor freezes? Assume that a Sojourner command module failure is hazardous. In this case, risk assessment would determine if the Sojourner command module can still function adequately for robot navigation even with the loss of one or more of its impact sensors. Assume that the probability of command module failure is 0.35 (number of commanding instruction failures due to sensor loss relative to the total number of commanding instructions requiring sensor input). Also assume that a command module failure results in a loss of \$45,000 (hypothetical cost related to MM required to modify the command module so that the robot functions without the malfunctioning sensor). Then risk exposure is computed as follows:

$$risk \text{ exposure} = 0.35 * 45000 = 1575$$

The driving force behind the spiral model is a divide-and-conquer strategy for minimizing risk (software development is in measured steps resulting assessments of risk gained from successive system prototypes). This approach has the unwanted side effect of increasing development costs. The original spiral model has been succeeded by the Win Win spiral model (Boehm et al., 1998).

2.6.4 Win Win Spiral Model

The Win Win model has a provision for system stakeholders to negotiate mutually satisfactory (win-win) specifications. Customers, developers, maintainers, interfacers, testers, reusers, and the general public are examples of stakeholders. The new features of the spiral model are grafted onto the original spiral model as shown in Figure 2.16.

The shaded areas in Figure 2.16A indicate where the objectives, constraints, and alternatives come from during a project. The nonshaded areas in Figure 2.16A are in the original spiral model. Two major difficulties in the original spiral model led to the introduction of the Win Win model.

- Origin of objectives, constraints, and alternatives were unclear in the spiral model.
- Across an organization's projects, the spiral model lacked anchor points to correlate the completion of spiral cycles and an organization's major milestones.

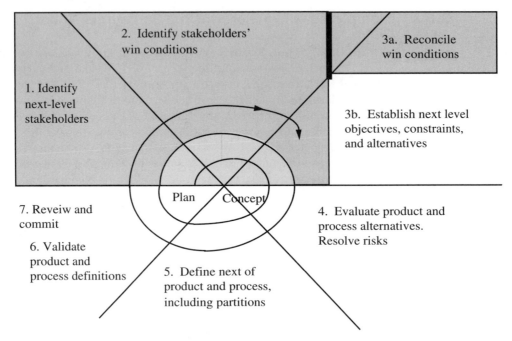

Figure 2.16.A Win win spiral model.

As excellent presentation of the Win Win model is given by Boehm in a lecture available on the web *(http://sunset.usc.edu/classes/cs577a_98/lectures/04)*. This lecture includes a Win Win negotiation model (Figure 2.16B). An industrial-grade Win Win groupware tool is being developed. This tool facilitates negotiation of mutually satisfactory system specifications by distributed stakeholders. A very

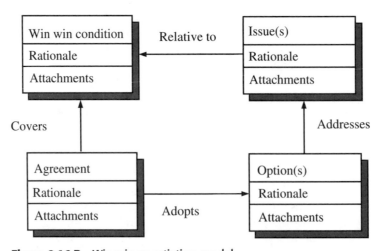

Figure 2.16.B Win win negotiation model.

detailed description of this tool is also available on the web. Try the following web page for more details about the Win Win spiral model.

```
http://www.sea.uni-linz.ac.at/systtechnik/
lehranstaltungen/st old srv/introwinwin/
```

An agreement with project stakeholders is accompanied by a rationale in Figure 2.16B. The agreement covers a Win Win condition. During negotiation, stakeholders adopt an option relative to an agreement. Associated with each option is an issue relative to the Win Win condition.

For further information about Win Win, try using the keywords "WinWin groupware" using the web search tool found at *http://www.yahoo.com*. Apart from a helpful discussion concerning negotiation with key stakeholders, the Win Win spiral model does not specifically address the issue of how developers specify, design, and test the conceptual construct of software being developed. It is clear that incorporation of the Win Win approach in the software process provides the basis for a unified effort in tackling the essential difficulties of software.

2.6.5 Evolutionary Model

The evolutionary SLCM consists of planned development of multiple releases of a product (the product evolves). Five properties of software systems motivating evolutionary SLCMs have been identified (Lehman & Belady, 1985). These properties are summarized in Table 2.4.

The evolutionary life cycle model entails continual overlapping of development activities (Figure 2.17), which produce a succession of software releases.

TABLE 2.4 Properties of Software Evolution

Property of Software System	Basis
Continuing change, degradation	Software systems continually change and degrade, becoming less and less useful
Increasing complexity	Due to continual changes, software complexity increases
Program evolution	Programs, programming processes, and measures of project and system attributes are statistically self-regulating with determinable trends and invariances
Invariant work rate (large projects)	Rate of activity in large software projects is statistically invariant (e.g., a property such as the average number of changes per cycle is approximately the same)
Incremental growth limit (large projects)	During the life of a large software system, the volume of modifications in successive releases is statistically invariant

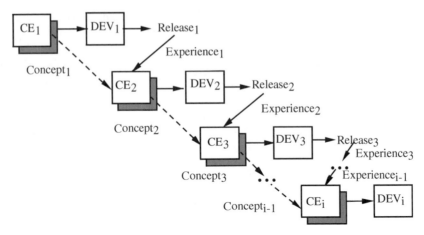

Figure 2.17   Evolutionary software life-cycle.

Each release reflects the knowledge and experience gained from earlier releases. The disadvantage of the evolutionary model is that it can be costly if it is assumed that a current release is made with the assumption that it will be succeeded by an improved version of the software later. In addition, reported studies of the evolutionary model have focused on large software systems.

2.6.6   Prototyping Model

The prototyping approach to software development focuses on producing software products quickly. Software prototypes are produced with limited functionality and performance to make it possible for developers and clients to check the functions of preliminary implementations of systems models before committing to a final system (Figure 2.18). The prototyping approach solves the waiting

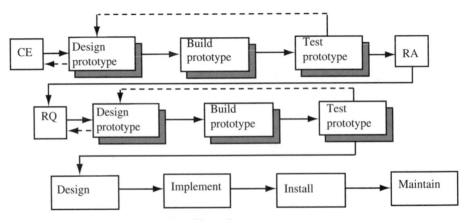

Figure 2.18   Prototyping software life-cycle.

problem in the waterfall model (it is not necessary to wait until the end of the development cycle for a working version of the software). Prototyping is iterated to obtain feedback from clients, and changes in system concepts (CE stage) requirements (RQ stage) are made before entering the design stage. Prototypes usually focus on high-risk functional, performance, and user requirements. Unfortunately, prototypes also usually ignore (because they are incomplete) quality, reliability, maintainability, and safety requirements (European Space Agency, 1991). This means it is difficult to obtain complete validation results (guarantees that prototypes satisfy requirements).

2.6.7 Object-Oriented Model

The object-oriented (OO) life-cycle model describes software development in terms of the identification of objects used to construct object networks as in Löhr-Richter and Reichwein (1997), and Sutcliffe (1997) (Figure 2.19). The OO model prescribes software development in terms of a synergy between abstraction, modularity, encapsulation, hierarchy, typing, concurrency, and persistence. Abstraction hides details, and provides simplified descriptions of a system (e.g.,

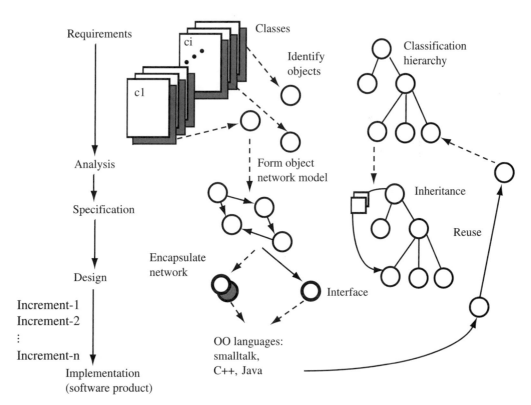

Figure 2.19 OO life-cycle model.

principal connections between activities rather than all connections). Collections of applicable classes are identified. Then instances of classes (objects) are selected for construction of object networks. Three kinds of abstraction are common: entity, action, and virtual machine. For example, in a robot, entity abstraction is illustrated in terms of the perception subsystem described as a C++ class.

```
typedef float Location;
//Perception subsystem of a mobile robot
typedef unsigned int Location;
class Perception {
public:
  ImpactSensor(Location);
  PressureSensor(Location);
  void calibrate();
  ...
private:
  ...
};
```

The Perception class makes it possible to introduce a collection of objects (instances of perception systems for robots).

```
Location loc1, lo2, loc3;
Perception robot1, robot2, robot3;
```

Then calibrations for each perception subsystem can be computed.

```
loc1 = robot1.calibrate();
loc2 = robot2.calibrate();
loc3 = robot3.calibrate();
```

Encapsulation hides the details of the implementation of an object. Modularization consists in partitioning a software system into modules that can be compiled separately, and identifying connections with other modules. In a hierarchical approach to software development, abstractions are ordered in terms of superclasses (classes which reference other classes) and subclasses (classes contained in superclasses). Typing identifies the structural or behavioral properties that a collection of entities share. Concurrency permits more than one thread of control to be active at the same time (Concurrent C++ and Ada are examples of concurrent programming languages with object orientation). Persistence in a software system means that the state and class of an object are preserved across time and space. The development phase of the OO model culminates in implementation coded in an OO language such as C++, Ada, or Java.

Two principal advantages to the OO approach are that it simplifies software development because it hides complexity, and the development of classes sup-

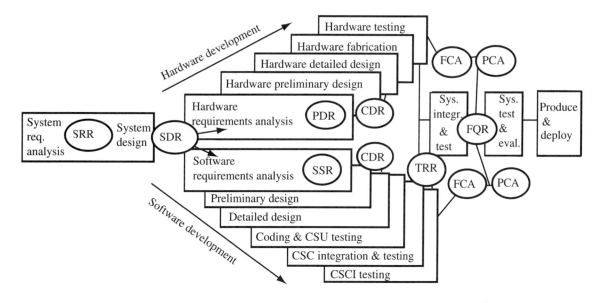

Figure 2.20 H/W system life-cycle model.

Legend :
SDR = System Design Review
SSR = System Specification Review
CDR = Critical Design Review
FCA = Functional Configuration Audit
FQR = Formal Qualification Review
CSCI = Computer Software Configuration Item

SRR = System Requirements Review
PDR = Preliminary Design Review
TRR = Test Readiness Review
PCA = Physical Configuration Review
CSC = Computer Software Component
CSU = Computer Software Unit

ports multiple instances of objects as well as encapsulation, which leads to reuse. There is a drawback to the OO approach in safety critical applications, which require a design by contract in the construction of reliable software (i.e., interfaces between modules of a software system are governed by precise specifications). Design by contract covers mutual obligations (preconditions), benefits (postconditions), and consistency constraints (invariants). Neither Ada nor Java have built-in support for design by contract (Jezequel & Meyer, 1997).

2.6.8 Embedded System Process Model

The U.S. Department of Defense system life-cycle model DoD-Std-2167 (1988) describes how an embedded computer system should be developed (Figure 2.20). *An embedded computer system* is an electromechanical system governed by one or more computers (e.g., rocket guidance systems). This form of a computer system contrasts with stand-alone computers that primarily supported data processing and conventional information systems. The computer in an embedded system performs some of the requirements of that system, making it possible for the system to carry out its functions. Examples of embedded computer systems are recent models of most automobiles, avionics systems for civilian and military aircraft, rocket guidance systems, satellites, spacecraft, and robotic devices.

2.6.9   Example Embedded System: Mobile Robot

An example of an embedded system is shown in Figure 2.21. An embedded computer system (ECS) is distinguished from an automatic data processing system by how it is developed, acquired, and operated (Manley, 1994). An ECS has three main features.

- An ECS is physically incorporated into a larger system with a primary function that is not data processing.
- An ECS is an integral part of a larger system from a design, procurement, and operations viewpoint.
- The output of an ECS usually includes system performance information, control signals, and computer data (e.g., frequency of stimulations of sensors).

A sample near-infrared proximity detector circuit connected to input/output ports on a microprocessor is shown in Figure 2.22. The layout in Figure 2.22 is derived from a description of a proximity detector to implement "following" behaviors in mobile robots (Jones & Flynn, 1993). This is a good example of an embedded computer system. A near-infrared proximity detector (symbolized IR) is sensitive to infrared wavelengths in the range just below visible light (about

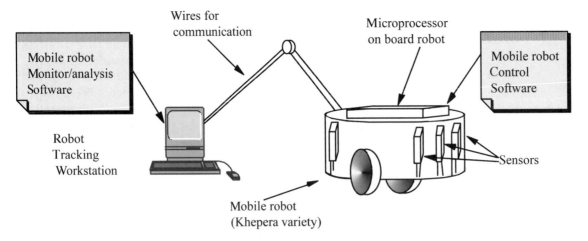

Figure 2.21   Sample embedded computer system.

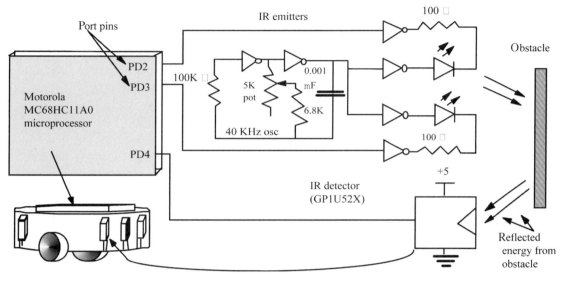

Figure 2.22 Sample infrared detector layout.

880 nanometers wavelength where 1 nm equals 10^{-9} meter). Infrared radiation is long-wave radiation emitted by hot bodies with wavelengths ranging from the red end of the spectrum at about 730 nm to about 1 mm. Assume the emitter in Figure 2.22 is a device (e.g., a light-emitting diode made from gallium arsenide) that emits near-infrared energy at 880 nm. The IR detector in the figure responds to a carrier frequency of 40 kHz, and is turned on and off at regular intervals (e.g., on for 600 μs, off for 600 μs, where 1 μs (one microsecond) equals 10^{-6} second). A computer program running on the microprocessor is responsible for turning the IR emitter on and off at regular intervals. The IR detector in Figure 2.22 outputs a low signal when it detects reflected energy and a high signal whenever no reflected energy is detected. In other words, an obstacle is detected if the IR detector is low when it is turned on. The emitter circuit is constructed with two inverters (diamond symbols), a capacitor (double bars), a resistor, and a potentiometer in the sample circuit in Figure 2.22. The IR emitter/detector circuit is connected to input/output ports on a microprocessor, which runs obstacle-avoidance software to respond to detected obstacles by controlling robot motors, moving the robot to avoid a collision with objects providing *reflected* radiation. This form of detector circuit is used to design rug warrior robots (Jones & Flynn, 1993).

Microwave oven control systems, fuzzy rice cookers, programmable CD players, the Mars Pathfinder spacecraft, the Mars Sojourner robot, satellite command and control systems, rocket guidance systems, aircraft control systems, weapon control systems, and automatic teller machines are other examples of embedded systems. The DoD model provides a detailed view of the parallel activities needed to design and implement a hardware–software system. Its baselines (documents and reviews) make it possible to manage a large project, and maintain a flow of information in the codesign effort. However, there are features missing in the model: interprocess communication modeling, and development of formal structural and logical descriptions of the software. In the case where a system has more than one computer (e.g., U.S. space shuttle, which has five interacting computers), modeling and analyzing interprocess communication is necessary. Formal structural and logical descriptions of software are needed to facilitate validation and verification in safety critical applications.

2.7 SYNCHRONIZE AND STABILIZE MODEL

The synchronize and stabilize model is used by Microsoft to develop software (Cusumano & Selby, 1997). This model has three phases: planning, design, and stabilization. The details and sequencing of tasks in these phases is given in Figure 2.23. During a project, what project team members are doing is continuously synchronized. A product is developed incrementally using rapid prototyping and automated regression testing. Test cases for a software increment that previously executed correctly are rerun and compared during regression testing to detect errors. As a project proceeds, software increments are periodically stabilized. An increment is considered stable if no severe bugs are found. The synchronize part of this model resembles the Win Win approach to some extent, since the objectives and constraints of a product are determined in consultation with program managers and developers. Program managers write a functional specification in consultation with developers. This specification gives an outline of product features in sufficient depth to make it possible to organize project schedules and to establish project teams. At Microsoft, developers work with daily builds. A build is the act of putting together a software increment to determine what functions work and what problems exist by compiling the source code for the increment and verifying the prototype with regression tests. The overlapping of the phases in Figure 2.23 is suggestive of a technique that has widespread usage. The software process is seen as an iteration among overlapping activities: product specification, software design, frequent prototyping of software increments, and testing. Experience with daily builds can result in improvements in the specification and design of a product.

A drawback to the synch and stabilize model is its reliance on testing and debugging to determine when an increment is stable. Consideration of the proof of the functional correctness of an increment has not been reported. Another drawback to the synch and stabilize model is its arbitrary partition of the design phase into three subprojects each with one-third of the features of a product. For a large, complex system, smaller partitions of the design phase will probably be necessary.

Planning phase : Define product vision, specifications, schedule.

- **Vision statement** : Product & program management use extensive client input to identify & priority-order product features
- **Specification document**: Based on vision statement, program management & development group defines feature functionality, architectural issues, component interdependencies
- **Schedule and feature team formation:** Based on specification document, program management coordinates schedule and feature teams: 1 manager, 3–8 developers, 3–8 testers working in parallel with developers.

Design phase: Feature development, 3 or 4 sequential subprojects with milestones.

- **Subproject 1**: First 1/3 of features (critical features, shared components).
- **Subproject 2**: Second 1/3 of features.
- **Subproject 3**: Final 1/3 of features (less critical features).

Stabilization phase: Comprehensive internal & external testing, final product stabilization, and release.

Program managers coordinate and monitor client feedback. Developers perform final debugging and code stabilization. Testers recreate and isolate errors.

- **Internal testing**: Thorough testing of complete product within the company.
- **External testing**: Thorough testing of complete product outside the company by "beta" sites.
- **Release preparation**: Prepare final release of "golden master" disks and documentation for manufacturing.

Figure 2.23 Synchronize and stabilize model.

2.8 CLEANROOM PROCESS MODEL

Each of the software process models up to this point are examples of what are known as universal-level process models. A *universal-level process model* describes the basic process components (tasks to be performed at each stage in a software development effort, task sequencing, by-products of the stages in a development process), and provides the basis for a general framework for developing software. The process model in Figure 2.24 is considered universal, since it describes

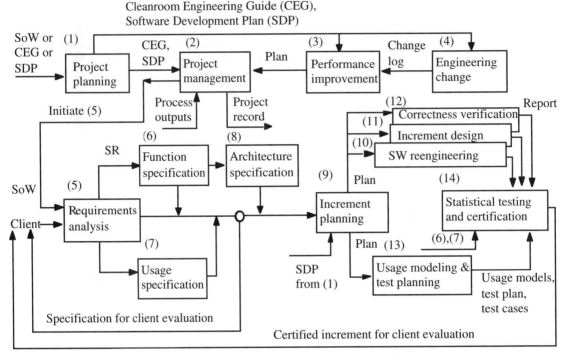

Figure 2.24   Universal-level cleanroom process model.

process flow in the cleanroom engineering approach to software development for any project.

Cleanroom engineering starts during software process management (processes 1 to 4). It should also be noticed that in a fully mature software management organization, project planning, project management, performance improvement, and engineering change are also at work during the specification, development, and certification phases of a project. Each cleanroom process has an Entry, Task, Verification, Exit, Measurement (ETVXM) structure:

- *Entry.* Conditions to satisfy before beginning task.
- *Feedback.* Input to task from other processes, output from task to other processes.
- *Task.* What is to be done, by whom, how, and when.
- *Verification.* Confirmation of work done, checking work products against specification.
- *Exit.* Results produced, their format, and criteria to satisfy before terminating a task.
- *Measurement.* Required task measures (activities, resources, time), output (number, size, quality), and feedback (number, size, quality).

Tasks also include feedback (from other processes as well as outputting task results to other processes). For example, the project planning process has the architecture shown in Figure 2.25. The architecture of the planning process shown in Figure 2.25 provides the framework for what is known as a universal-level process model for cleanroom project planning.

2.8.1   Cleanroom Specification Process

During a software development project, the cleanroom management process is concurrent with a specification process, which begins with a requirements process. The architecture of a universal-level model of the cleanroom requirements process is given in Figure 2.26. Specifically, the task of the requirements process in Figure 2.26 is to define software function (principal actions performed by software) and usage (typical usage scenarios), hardware and software configurations as well as environments, necessary interfaces, operational constrains, dependencies, and goals for reliability, capacity, and performance (quality features of the software).

The main aim of the function specification process is to define the functional behavior of software (what the software does) in all possible circumstances, to construct a behavioral specification that satisfies the software requirements, and to obtain client acceptance of the specified function. The usage specification process focuses on identifying and classifying software users, usage scenarios, and environments. The usage process also develops software usage models and obtains agreement from clients concerning the specified usage. The key point

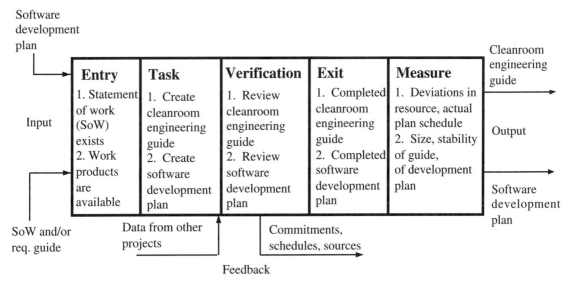

Figure 2.25   Architecture of cleanroom project planning process.

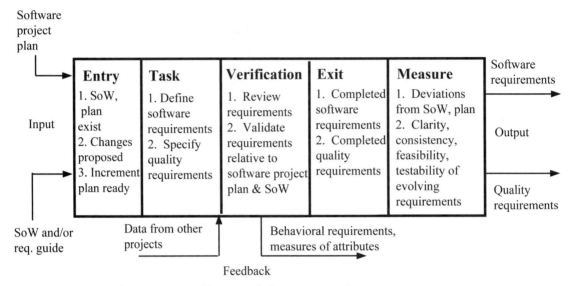

Figure 2.26   Architecture of cleanroom requirements process.

to notice is that the usage specification process defines the scope of software testing and establishes the basis for incremental usage model development (Linger & Trammell, 1996). The main thrust of the architectural specification process is the description of structure (architectural components and connections) and execution profile of the software. The input to this process is a black box structure (feed-forward description from the function specification process). A black box specification is in the form of a table providing current stimuli (hardware, software, user interface inputs), input sequences, conditions for performing activities defined for a function, details of interaction as well as responses (outputs), and exit conditions. The output of the architecture process is a state box structure. A state box specifies high-level procedures for operations on inputs to states specified in a corresponding black box description. The cleanroom increment planning process creates an increment construction plan. This plan provides the project management team with a rationale for assigning tasks, tracking team performance, and monitoring and controlling product quality.

2.8.2   Cleanroom Usage Modeling

A usage model is a formal representation of software usage. The principal goals of the cleanroom usage modeling and test planning are as follows:

- Create usage models for software testing based on the usage specification.
- Establish a test plan for a software increment.
- Obtain client agreement concerning usage models and test plan.

- Generate test cases, and prepare the testing environment (determine hardware configuration and software needed to test a software increment).

Sequences of outcomes (results) of experimental usage can then be simulated and studied. For example, let X_i be the outcome of the ith trial of some experiment with a software increment for the training program for air traffic controllers. The experiment might be, for instance, clicking a mouse to select an action in a pulldown menu. The results of this experiment are in the set {menu display, nothing happens, system halts}. Then define the variable X_1 as follows:

$$X_1 = \begin{cases} 1, \text{ if mouse click displays main menu} \\ 0, \text{ if mouse click fails to display menu} \\ -1, \text{ if system halts after mouse click} \end{cases}$$

(sample random variable for testing)

Next try defining variables relative to experiments for software to manage and control a menu bar for a GUI for an air traffic control system. A sample sequence of sample variables is shown in Figure 2.27. The possible values of the usage

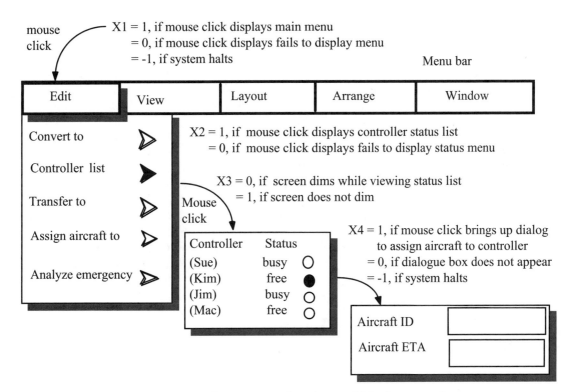

Figure 2.27 Sample sequence of random variables for ATC software usage.

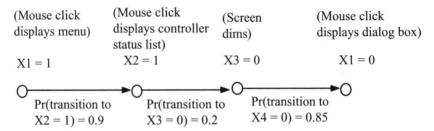

Figure 2.28   Sample usage transition graph.

variables are called states. It is assumed that mouse click actions represented by X_1, X_2, X_3, and X_4 in Figure 2.27 depend only on the event associated with previous mouse click. A probability is assigned to each event associated with a mouse click. State sequences can constructed representing successions of software usage actions. These state sequences (and corresponding probabilities) can be represented as directed graphs. The nodes of a usage graph represent usage states; the arcs, transitions between usage states. Each arc is labeled with the probability that a transition to the next state in the sequence will occur. A sample directed graph derived from the example in Figure 2.27 is shown in Figure 2.28.

In a usage-directed graph, probabilities are assigned to transitions between states, and highlight the probability of a transition to a usage state that results in failure. Transition probabilities define *expected* software use. User estimates and experience with similar software systems provide insight into how to assign usage transition probabilities. Notice that many other possible state sequences besides the one in Figure 2.28 are possible. Test cases are devised relative to highly likely usage sequences. Good sources of examples of software usage models can be found in Dyer (1992).

In the cleanroom engineering process model, software increments follow each other in a pipeline. More than one increment can be in the pipeline at the same time. There are usually four cleanroom teams: management, specification, development, and certification. It is common for each team to have between five and eight members. Teams will overlap during small projects. During large projects, hundreds of team members may be present (Linger & Trammel, 1996). Cleanroom engineering complements and reinforces the process management maturity process during software development. For more details about cleanroom, see *http://www.clearlake.ibm.com/MFG/solutions/cleanrm.html.*

2.9 SPECIALIZING UNIVERSAL SOFTWARE PROCESS MODELS

To be useful to a practicing engineer, a universal process model needs to be reduced to a level that guides the sequencing of tasks for a software increment, and reveals specifics about what is needed (inputs, entry conditions, necessary work products) to start work, how and when results will be measured, and the anticipated results to be produced by a process. This is what is known as the worldly level of software process modeling (Humphrey, 1989). A *worldly level process model* specifies software project tasks to be performed by a process, guides the sequencing of tasks, entry and exit conditions for tasks, what should be verified and measured by a process, necessary feedback (to and from a process), and the results produced by a process. In effect, a world process model has the appearance of a procedure that guides the sequencing of tasks needed to obtain what is known as a work product.

Once a universal-level model for a software process has been selected, it is necessary to map that model onto a worldly level model for a specific project. This is done to specify clearly project tasks of specific effector processes needed for a particular software project. A worldly level model is also needed to do the following:

- Guide sequencing of project tasks.
- Specify necessary entry and exit conditions.
- Specify what should be verified by an effector process.
- Obtain feedback—measurements to be obtained from the output of an effector process.

In effect, a *worldly level model* will describe an effective procedure for obtaining software products. This form of process model will constitute a network of connected feedback systems needed to carry out a project. Worldly models are project specific but necessarily sparing in detail to gain clarity and to encourage practical interpretations of the general descriptions of project tasks. To be useful to software engineers, the effector processes in a worldly model must be mapped to an atomic-level process model. By contrast with a worldly model, an atomic model is very detailed. An *atomic-level model* is task-centered and describes the inner workings (steps) of an effector task in detail. An atomic model gives details concerning

- Specific algorithms to implement an effector process.
- Measures to use in making measurements.
- Descriptions of required input to an effector process.
- Descriptions of verification techniques to be carried out by an effector process.
- Descriptions of exit conditions for an effector process.
- Specific connections of each feedback subsystem to other feedback systems in an atomic-level software process.
- Prescription of required results to be obtained by an effector process.
- Software development standards to follow.

In sum, an atomic-level model gives detailed steps in an effective procedure to obtain a software product.

2.10 EXAMPLE: WORLDLY AND ATOMIC MODELS

To see the progression from a universal to a worldly level software process model, consider the problem of developing software for training air traffic controllers Peters et al. (1998) and Ip et al. (1998). In other words, try putting together a worldly process model as part of a project to develop a program to train air-traffic controllers (tATC). Suppose that one of the increments in this project is identify the risks involved in developing a web-version of a tATC.

The work products of risk process for the tATC are a completed Taxonomy-Based Questionnaire (TBQ) and assessment of all risks listed in a Statement of Work (SoW). A TBQ relies on a taxonomy (classification) of software development risks into three levels consisting of class, element, attribute. A risk class is a major grouping of software risks. Members of a risk class are called elements. Measurable characteristics of a risk element are called attributes. Examples of a software risk class are product engineering, development environment, and program constraints. Examples of product engineering elements are requirements such as need for a Graphical User Interface (GUI), pulldown menus, movable icons, and so on. The taxonomy is completed by identifying attributes of elements. Take, for instance, the attributes of a GUI for an air traffic control trainer: airspace display size, feasibility of simulating airspace emergency conditions with a web presentation of near-collision of aircraft. A TBQ consists of questions about each risk attribute designed to elicit the range of risks potentially affecting a software product.

Verification of the risk-compilation tasks for a tATC will be carried out by cross-checking the new measurements with similar studies to check for inconsistencies, and to compare measured risks with projected risk measurements. The effectiveness of the process will be measured by reviewing the risk assessment work product, determining to what degree the requirements of the SoW have been satisfied, and to what extent the risk report deviates from the SoW. Task sequencing and data flow in a worldly process model for assessing risk for a web-based ATC training program are given in Figure 2.29. Notice that the sequencing of tasks in the risk assessment process model in Figure 2.29 can be refined further. Task sequencing is in the form of a pipeline. Once the SoW for web risk analysis been transmitted to the TBQ survey team, it is possible to begin a new SoW for a different set of risks (e.g., Visual Basic program instead of a Java program with eventual web browsing). In other words, while the first SoW is making its way through the pipeline, another SoW can be started. Notice, also, that risks r1 through r10 can be measured concurrently. Different sequences are possible, too.

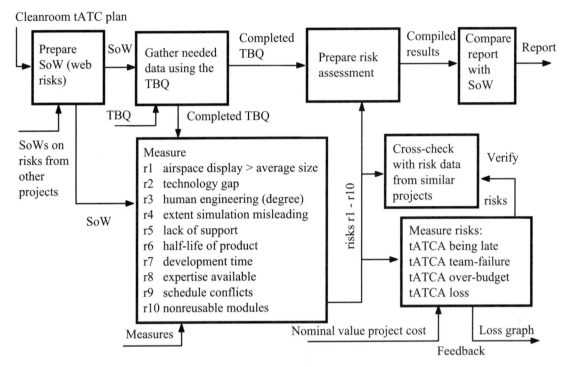

Figure 2.29 Risk assessment worldly level process model.

A worldly model must be brought down to an atomic, project-specific level to be useful for a particular software project. An *atomic-level process model* specifies precise input and output definitions, project specific entry and exit conditions, detailed steps to be followed by tasks (algorithms), information flows (specific feedback into and out of a process), procedures to follow in verifying and measuring process products and performance, and project-specific results produced by a process. In other words, by contrast with a worldly model, which hides details (algorithms, measures to use), an atomic model is tailored to the workings (input, entry conditions, algorithm, exist conditions, measures) for specific tasks. By way of illustration of an atomic-level process model, consider the problem of measuring the risk in terms of tATC loss and the nearness of the risked cost to the nominal value of project cost taken from a cleanroom plan.

The loss due to cost overrun in developing a software product can be estimated using the Taguchi method (Ross, 1996). The idea is to compare a nominal (budgeted) value m for a software product to an actual value x spent in developing a product. In effect, m equals the estimated cost of a software product, which has been determined by software project planners. The x-value is the amount of risked over-budget, if the software design team is late in completing the product. Then the Taguchi loss function is

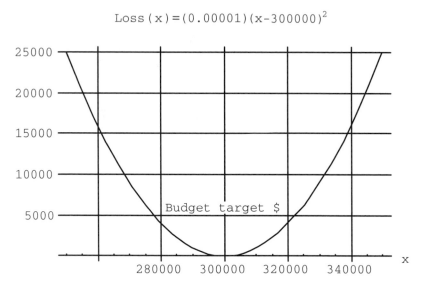

$$\text{Loss}(x) = (0.00001)(x-300000)^2$$

Figure 2.30   Plot of loss estimates.

$$loss(x) = k(x - m)^2$$

The constant k in the Taguchi loss function depends on the cost of actual budget limits and the width of the interval over which the risked value and nominal value are computed. For instance, a value of $0.00001 per (feature of product) relative to a project budget of $300,000 (the target value in the cleanroom plan) produces the graph in Figure 2.30. The plot indicates that loss begins rising sharply when project cost is approximately $30,000 over budget. This approach to estimating risked loss for a software product leads to the atomic process model shown in Figure 2.31.

The architecture of the worldly model for the cleanroom software project planning process in Figure 2.25 provides a straightforward framework for estab-

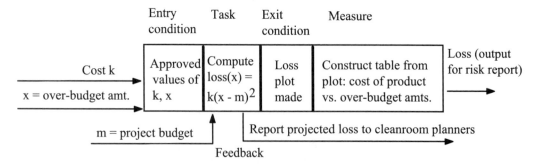

Figure 2.31   Atomic process model for estimating loss risk.

TABLE 2.5 Architectural Components of Cleanroom Management Processes

Element	Entry	Task	Verify	Exit	Measure
1 Plan	See Fig. 27	See Fig. 27	See Fig. 27	See Fig. 27	See Fig. 27
2 Manage	plan, guide agreed upon, and work products available	customer, peer interaction, form, staff, train teams, initiate, monitor performance	Review level of interaction and team performance	complete mgmt, specification, development, certification teams, and project record.	Deviations of team sizes and staff from project plan & project guide
3 Improve	input (software increment, work product) received)	evaluate team performance & new methods, devel. improve. plan	Check results against plan.	Evaluation, improvement plan completed.	Degree of deviation of team results from plan.
4 Engineer Process Change	Increment verification report, statistical testing report, entry work products available.	Identify needed changes, establish Engineering Change Log	Evaluate correctness and consistency of changes relative to configuration management plan.	Engineering Change Log completed.	Status of changes (approved, rejected, scheduled, in progress, completed)

lishing an atomic model of the planning process for a specific project. The chief advantage to an architectural model for a cleanroom process like the mode for planning in Figure 2.25 is that it makes it easier to represent and manipulate a process at a very detailed, atomic level. This is extremely important in harnessing, understanding, and controlling cleanroom processes or any other software processes. At the atomic level, each software project would have its set of detailed architectures for each cleanroom process. The details like feedback from other projects would be tailored to the particular data available for project planning. The software development plan and Statement of Work (SoW) would be defined anew for each project. A summary of the architectural components of the remaining cleanroom management processes is given in Table 2.5. The principal aim of the project management (process 2) is to facilitate delivery of software on schedule and within a prescribed budget. The activities of this project management model resemble the synchronize feature of the Microsoft synch and stabilize model and the risk analysis feature of the Win Win model.

2.11 SUMMARY

This chapter explores a variety of universal software process models. These models provide very general frameworks for software development. Each universal model implicitly represents the policies and interlocking activities considered vital in the successful development of software systems. These models become useful if they are interpreted in the context of specific software projects. The selection of a universal software process model is guided by what appears to be a comfortable fit between specific project goals and constraints. This selection will depend on a number of factors (e.g., estimates of software product size, available resources, organizational maturity level, and budget). The essential feature in successful life-cycle models is quantitative forms of feedback, which make it possible for a software process to evolve, to adapt to changing environments and technologies, and to achieve the optimizing level in the Capability Maturity Model described in Paulk et al. (1997).

2.12 PROBLEMS

1. Let Pr(E) be the probability of that an undesirable event occurs during program execution, and assume that values of Pr(E) occur randomly (no particular pattern) over the interval [0, 0.85]. Assume that the loss due to the occurrence of E is quantifiable in terms of MM ranging from 5 to 50,000. Give a 3D graph showing possible values of loss exposure.

2. Give an example of corrective feedback for a fast-food restaurant that intermittently serves burgers containing tiny metal fragments. Assume that the average diameter of the metal fragments is 0.01 cm.

3. Assume that you receive a questionnaire asking for suggested improvements in Netscape (to improve the usefulness of Netscape in adding Hypertext links to a web page). Give an example of improvement feedback.

4. The designer of the questionnaire in no. 3 had the following set of requirements to satisfy:

Questionnaire Feature	Requirement
Keywords: Netscape, optional, copyright, local, global	Boldface
Source of questions	Identify
Rationale for questions	Identify
Automate questionnaire	Supply questionnaire on web

Assume that the evolutionary life-cycle model is used to develop the web page version. Assume that the implementation phase requires a spell check to be performed on the text for the questionnaire. During the implementation of the questionnaire on the web, the following questions appeared:

```
Does Netscape satisfy your local needs?
Would it be helpful to display an optional list of
links embedded in each web page?
```

(a) Validate the questions (give steps, results).
(b) Verify the questions (give steps, results).

5. Let s-design be a document that tells how to create a jigsaw puzzle using a photograph, a bottle of glue, a saw, a sheet of wood big enough to hold the photo, and electronic parts and sensors. A requirement for the finished product is that at least one puzzle piece be equipped with a pressure sensor that cause a beeper to sound whenever that piece is pressed against another puzzle piece. Assume that there are many sheets of wood of variable thickness to choose from. Also assume the finished thickness is ⅛ of an inch.
   (a) Give a sample version of s-design (specify steps, test plan, quality measure).
   (b) Give examples of information in s-design that can be characterized as DNA coding (information that can be incorporated into successive generations of the design document). Hint: a test plan should include boundary conditions like minimum (maximum) thickness of wood so that cutting is possible with a given saw. A quality measure should give a method or means of measuring acceptability of picture (e.g., roughness of cut).

6. Using the example in no. 5, give a specific sequence of phenotypes for finished puzzles p1, p2, p3, . . . pi so that each new phenotype results in an improved process behavior. Hint: carry through the requirement in no. 5 in successive, improved ways.

7. Give an example of a succession of genotypes for designs of puzzles s1, s2, s3, . . . si based on inheritance of DNA (information coding from previous generations) and feedback resulting from the operation of the phenotypes p1, p2, p3, . . . pi.

8. Give examples of quantitative measures of productivity of the design processes leading to the sequence s1, s2, s3, . . . si.

9. At the predevelopment stage for a company about to launch the development puzzles described in no. 5:
   (a) List resources needed to launch the project (this is an open-ended question but it should have a reasonable response).
   (b) List inputs, functions, outputs to be performed by a puzzle.
   (c) List methods to be used to control the development process (e.g., preliminary schedule).
   (d) List methods to measure the quality of the design stage in the development process.

10. Give an example of a complete evolution pattern for the production of the puzzles in no. 5.

11. Let fn be the number of functions performable by a software package, and let MM be the number of man-months required to produce a new version of the software.

(a) Give an example of two releases of a software package (e.g., Microsoft Word 5.0 and Microsoft Word 6.0).

(b) Determine the value of fn, MM for the package identified in (a).

(c) Estimate the productivity of the organization that produced the software in (a).

12. Modify the incremental life cycle model so that the requirements documents can evolve.

(a) Give a sketch of the revised model.

(b) Instrument the revised model to make it possible to measure to what extent the evolution of requirements documents lead to improvements in product design.

(c) Indicate the specific sources of feedback in the revised model.

13. List the drawbacks to the evolutionary software life-cycle model in terms of small software projects (producing programs with less than 300 lines).

14. Modify the evolutionary software life cycle model so that it can be used with small software projects that increase in complexity over time.

(a) Give a sketch of the new model.

(b) List the documents that would evolve in the design process.

15. Compare the features of C++ and Java, and for each language give an example of (a) class, (b) object, (c) encapsulation, and (d) typing.

16. Construct a risk assessment table for a project to develop software to control the movements of a mobile robot like that shown in Figure 2.21. Assume that the software will perform the following functions: avoid (to avoid obstacles), and wander (to allow robot to move freely whenever no obstacles are detected).

17. Estimate risk exposure for a mobile robot in terms of the undesirable event that the mobile robot controller software has a logical error that causes the robot to fail every time it detects an obstacle 10 cm away from the robot. Give this estimate in terms of

(a) Robot world 3 m × 3 m bounded by walls and with no other obstacles. Assume the robot starts in the center of its world.

(b) Robot world 3 m × 3 m bounded by walls with one stationary object located in the center of the robot world.

18. Do the following.

(a) Give a feedback system model of project management. This is a universal model that specifies the collection of effector processes needed to manage a software project. A good way to start is to identify the effectors needed at the repeatable level of the capability maturity model.

(b) Incrementally give a worldly level interpretation of the project management model in part (a) relative to developing a training program for air traffic controllers.

(c) Link activities in the worldly model in part (b) to atomic processes.

(d) Give the steps in atomic process models identified in part (c).

    (e) Give method for verifying the results produced by the worldly model in part (b).

    (f) Give method for verifying the results produced by the atomic models in part (c).

    (g) Give exit conditions for the worldly model in part (b).

    (h) Give exit conditions for the atomic models in part (c).

    (i) Give a method for measuring the results produced by the worldly model in part (b).

    (j) Give a method for measuring the results produced by the atomic models in part (c).

19. How does the notion of vanilla frameworks in tackling the essential difficulties of software correlate with the selection of a universal software process model?

20. How does the notion of vanilla frameworks correlate with the selection of a worldly level software process model?

21. How does the notion of vanilla frameworks correlate with the selection of an atomic-level software process model?

22. How does the notion of software process evolution correlate with the feedback system model of the software process?

23. Compare the features of a vanilla framework with those in the synch and stabilize software process model. What elements in a vanilla framework are missing in the synch and stabilize model?

2.13 REFERENCES

Boehm, B.W., Ed. *Software Risk Management.* IEEE Computer Society Press, Piscataway, NJ, 1989, p. 434.

Boehm, B., Egyed, A., Kwan, J., et al. Using the WinWin spiral model: A case study. *IEEE Computer.* **31**(7):33–45, 1998.

Connell, J.L., Shafer, L.B. *Structured Rapid Prototyping.* Yourdon Press, NY, 1989.

Cormier, S., Dack, N., Kaikhosrawkiani, F., Orenstein, O. *ATC Trainer Prototype.* Report, Department of Electrical and Computer Engineering, University of Manitoba, Nov. 1997.

Cusumano, M.A., Selby, R.W. How Microsoft builds software. *ACM Communications.* **40**(6):53–61, 1997.

Davis, A.M. *Software Requirements: Objects, Functions, and States.* Prentice-Hall, Englewood Cliffs, NJ, 1993.

Department of Defense (DoD) standard 2167A, Defense System Software Development. Washington, D.C., U.S. Department of Defense, 29 Feb. 1988.

Dowson, M. The structure of the software process. In *Software Engineering: A European Perspective,* R.H. Thayer, A.D. McGettrick, Eds. IEEE Computer Society Press, Piscataway, NJ, 1993, pp. 55–60.

Dyer, M. The Cleanroom Approach to Quality Software Development. John Wiley & Sons, NY, 1992.

European Space Agency. *ESA Software Engineering Standard* PSS-05-0. Issue 2, Feb. 1991, pp. 1–12.

Fairley R., Rook, P. Risk management for software development. In *Software Engineering,* M. Dorfman, R.H. Thayer, Eds. IEEE Computer Society Press, Los Almitos, CA, 1997, pp. 387–400.

Fogel, D.B. *Evolutionary Computation.* IEEE Press, Piscataway, NJ, 1995.

Humphrey, W.S. *Managing the Software Process.* Addison-Wesley, Reading, MA, 1989.

IEEE Std 1074-1995, IEEE standard for developing software life cycle processes. In *IEEE Standards Collection Software Engineering.* IEEE Press, Piscataway, NJ, 1997.

Ip, S., Lao, N., Thang, P., et al. *Simulation of Interacting Aircraft.* Report, Department of Electrical and Computer Engineering, University of Manitoba, 1998.

Jezequel J.M., Meyer, B. Design by contract: The lessons of Ariane. *IEEE Computer.* **30**(1):129–130, 1997.

Jones, J.L., Flynn, A.M. *Mobile Robots: Inspiration to Implementation.* A.K. Peters, Wellesley, MA, 1993.

Lehman, M.M. Process modelling—where next? In *Proceedings of the 19th International Conference on Software Engineering,* Boston, 1997, May, pp. 549–552.

Lehman, M.M. Software evolution. In *Encyclopedia of Software Engineering,* J.J. Marciniak, Ed. Wiley, New York, 1994, pp. 1202–1208.

Lehman, M., Belady, L. *Program Evolution: Processes of Software Change.* Academic Press, New York, 1985.

Linger, R.C., Trammel, C.J. Cleanroom Software Engineering Reference Model. Report CMU/SEI-96-TR-022, SEI. Pittsburgh, PA, 1996.

Löhr-Richter, P., Reichwein, G. *Object Orientation as a Promising Perspective for Life Cycle Models.* Report, TU Braunschweig, Germany, 1997.

Manley, J.H. Embedded systems. In: Marciniak, J.J. (Ed.), *Encyclopedia of Software Engineering.* John Wiley & Sons, NY, 1994.

Nahouraii, E. An international perspective on tools assessment (panel discussion). *Proceedings of the Fourth International Symposium on Assessment of Software Tools,* May 1996, pp. 88–96.

Nguyen, M.N., Wang, A.I., Conradi, R. Total software process model evolution in EPOS Experience Report. *Proceedings of the 19th International Conference on Software Engineering,* Boston, 1997, pp. 390–399.

Paulk, M.C., Curtis, B., Chrissis, M.B., Weber, C.V. The capability maturity model for software. In *Software Engineering,* M. Dorfman, R.H. Thayer, Eds. IEEE Computer Society Press, Los Almitos, CA, 1997, pp. 427–443.

Peters, J.F., Agatep, R., Cormier, S., et al. Air traffic control trainer software development: Multi-agent architecture and Java prototype. *Proceedings of the IEEE Canadian Conference on Electrical and Computer Engineering,* Waterloo, Ontario, May 1998.

Ross, P.J. Taguchi Techniques for Quality Engineering, NY, McGraw-Hill, 1996.

Royce, W.W. Managing the development of large software systems. In Proc. IEEE Western Conference (Wescon), 1970, pp. 1–9.

Sutcliffe, A.G. Object-oriented systems development: Survey of structured methods. In *Software Engineering*, M. Dorfman, R.H. Thayer, Eds. IEEE Computer Society Press, Los Almitos, CA, 1997, pp. 160–169.

Wiener, N. *Cybernetics: Or Control and Communication in the Animal and the Machine.* Cambridge, MIT Press, 1948.

CHAPTER 3
Software Configuration Management

**Knowledge is of two kinds: We know a subject
ourselves, or we know where we can find
information about it.**

—SAMUEL JOHNSON, 1775

Aims

- Consider SCM process model
- Identify SCM activities
- Use SCM to prevent conflicts and facilitate recovery of information
- Review common SCM tools
- Begin using PERT and Gantt charts

SCM Activities

1. Establish baselines*

   1.1 Assign unique identifier to Configuration Item (CI).
(example CIs: project plan, project software engineering
guide, needs statement, requirements description,
architectural description, source code, test plan)

   1.2 Create baseline document

2. Identify different internal releases (i.e., successive variants of same product baseline)

3. Ensure complete, current technical product documentation

4. Enforce standards

   Software quality assurance (SQA)

5. Use SCM to promote each CI from one development phase or test to another

6. Use SCM to identify customer involvement in internal (development) baselines

------

*baseline = a work product that has been formally reviewed and

agreed upon that serves as the basis for further development, and

can be changed only through formal change control procedures.

Baseline document = a software document or set of documents
that completely describes a CI.

From IEEE std 1042-1987

Figure 3.1 CM activities.

3.1 INTRODUCTION

A dominant feature of each phase of the software process is the production of a set of documents that serve as a guide in succeeding product development phases. Based on feedback and change requests, new versions of the documents are produced. This is a normal part of the evolution of a software product. It becomes very important to manage these documents, to provide an orderly way of governing the development of work products resulting from a software process. Software Configuration Management (SCM) manages all software entities (Figure 3.1). Configuration management is viewed as a communicator (Berlack, 1994). SCM communicates a client's requirements and ensures that system requirements can be traced to the final product. SCM provides mechanisms for managing all changes in efficient, cost-effective, and timely manner. SCM also puts into place a framework for maintenance and support of a product.

An entity that is designated for configuration management and treated as a single entity in the CM process is called a configuration item. Software is viewed as a collection of Software Configuration Items (SCIs). In early stages of a software process, an SCI takes the form of a problem definition and analysis, software specification, planning document, manual for support software, report from an earlier project, or software engineering guide. In later stages of a software process, an SCI will have various software representations. Examples of configuration items managed in a software engineering process are summarized in Table 3.1.

Change management is defined relative to baselines. A *baseline* is a work product that signals a point of departure from one activity and the start of another activity. For example, in writing a paper, the completion of an outline of the paper with a number of sections or chapters signals the completion of an initial stage in the writing process, and the start of the next stage. A baseline

TABLE 3.1 Sample Configuration Items

Configuration Item	Examples
Management plan	Process plan, SE guide, SCM plan, test plan, maintenance plan
Specification	Requirements, design, testing specification
Design	Source code
Testing	Test design, case, procedure, data, generation
Support software	Planning documents
Data dictionary	Software requirement specification
Code	Source, executable, requirement
Libraries	Component, reuse libraries
Databases	Audit database
Maintenance	Listing, detailed design descriptions, measures

TABLE 3.2 Basic Elements of SCM

SCM Element	Method
Software configuration item identification	Define baseline components
Software configuration control	Mechanism for initiating, preparing, evaluating, approving, or disapproving all change proposals
Software configuration auditing	Mechanism for determining the degree that the current state of a software system reflects its baselines (requirements and planning documents)
Software configuration status accounting	Mechanism for maintaining a record of how a system has evolved, and the state of a system relative to published documents and written agreements

for each section of a paper would be an outline indicating the main features of the section. The completion of the writing for a section of paper represents another baseline in a writing project.

Change management is accomplished by identifying each baseline document and tracking all subsequent changes made to that baseline. A baseline document (e.g., SE guide, CM plan, specification) establishes one of the configuration identifications of a configuration item. The goal of SCM is to ensure that configuration of a software process product is accurately known at any particular time. For example, change management for software process plans is accomplished by identifying each baseline planning document, the time of its creation, and all subsequent changes made to it. Software specification, design, source code, and testing are other examples of items subject to this change management. The four basic components of SCM are summarized in Table 3.2.

3.2 SOFTWARE CONFIGURATION IDENTIFICATION

Effective software configuration management begins with the definition of baselines. Recall that a baseline is a work product marking the completion of one activity and the beginning of another activity during a software process. A baseline can be thought of as snapshot of a collection of system components such as object diagrams in a software requirements specification. Software configuration identification consists in supplying two kinds of labels for baselines:

• Label to identify a baseline (e.g., GUI_req for Graphical User Interface requirement).

- Label to identify an update to baseline (e.g., GUI_req.2 for 2nd update to GUI_req).

3.3 SOFTWARE CONFIGURATION CONTROL

Software configuration control focuses on managing changes to baseline documents. A description of this control process is given in Figure 3.2. After an SCI has been established, the control process in Figure 3.2 begins with a change initiated by either a software user, buyer, or marketing agent (step 1). The control process has five basic steps summarized in Table 3.3. The initiation of change (step 1 in Table 3.3) is associated with an Engineering Change Proposal (ECP).

An ECP provides a description of a proposed change, and identifies the originator, rationale, and baselines affected by a proposed change. A sample

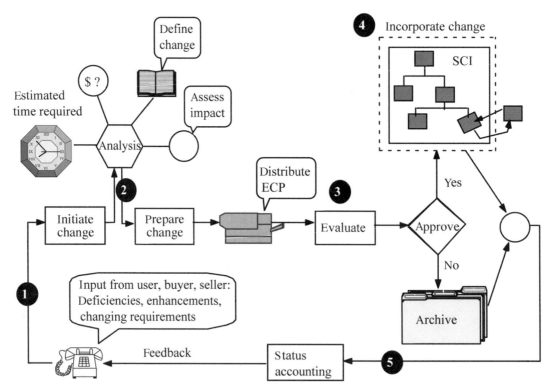

Figure 3.2 Software configuration control process.

TABLE 3.3   Basic Steps of Control Process

Step	Action	Process
1	Initiate change	Requests for changes to software configuration item (SCI) are initiated by team members and/or project clients.
2	Analysis	Requested changes are analyzed relative to definition of change, time, cost, and schedule impact of changes.
3	Prepare change	Results of proposed changes to each SCI are distributed to team members.
4	Evaluation	Proposed changes to an SCI are evaluated. Automated tool support is used to carry out changes, document version maintenance, and recording changes. Rejected changes are archived for future reference.
5	Feedback	The results of evaluation of a change request become feedback to software developers and clients.

ECP is given in Figure 3.3. The ECP documents a proposed change to a software configuration item. An ECP also provides an indication of the project baselines and drawings affected by a proposed change. This information facilitates analysis of the ECP. A knowledge of the project baselines and drawings affected by a change will serve as an aid in estimated the time and cost of carrying out a change. An assessment of the impact of a change on a project is aided by what a proposer says about the "need for change." In the case where the cost of making a change is high, a strong justification for a change helps provide a basis for deciding to implement a change. It is not enough to respond with "very

Engineering Change Proposal	Submission date		Form number	
Originating organization name and address	Justification code	Priority	ECP number / type	
Baselines affected by change:			Drawings affected by change:	
Description of change:				
Need for change:				
Estimated delivery schedule		Estimated costs / savings resulting from change:		
☐ Approval ☐ Disapproval	Signature(s):		Decision date:	

Figure 3.3   Sample engineering change proposal from.

much needed'' in filling in the ECP. It is necessary to provide a clearcut rationale for a change.

Step 2 of the control process provides a formal definition of the proposed change and the impact of this change relative to time and cost. In Step 2, ECPs are reviewed and evaluated. After analyzing a proposed change, the results of the proposed change are distributed to team members. This is the change preparation step in the control process (step 3). Usually automated tools called Program Support Libraries (PSLs) support the control process. These tools come into play in step 4 of the control process. A PSL provides a repository of versions of each work product document in a software project. It is common for a PSL to provide library access control, version maintenance, change recording, and document reconstruction. Notice that rejected changes are archived for future reference. A change request rejected today may provide the basis for a future (possibly revised) change request. Finally, in step 5 of the control process, the status accounting of a configuration item is reported to originators of change requests and to team members.

3.4 SOFTWARE CONFIGURATION AUDITING

A software configuration audit verifies that what has been designed has in fact been built and that tests applied to a software configuration item prove that requirements for an SCI have been satisfied. Two types of auditing are performed:

- *Functional Configuration Audit (FCA).* An FCA ensures that the actual performance of a CI conforms to its requirements given in the SRS. A description of how tests to a CI were performed, how they were conducted, and how reports were prepared and witnessed is provided by a FCA.
- *Physical Configuration Audit (PCA).* A PCA ensures that all documentation delivered with software accurately represents software content. A PCA provides a complete review of a software product specification, minutes of corrective actions needed prior to an audit, design descriptions for proper symbols, labels, and data descriptions, review of software manuals, source code, and labeling of proprietary information in documentation.

3.5 SOFTWARE CONFIGURATION STATUS ACCOUNTING

Software configuration status accounting provides a basis for communicating the state of a software product's development to a project team, to a company, and to a client. All changes that were made to a baseline document and all changes in process are recorded by status accounting for a project. Status accounting consists in recording and reporting information needed to manage a configuration effectively. This information includes the following items:

- List of approved configuration identification
- Status of proposed changes to a configuration
- Implementation status of approved changes

3.6 DYNAMICS OF SCM

Effective management of baseline changes requires a scheme for identifying the structure of a software product. This structure has two main features. First, the steps of each phase of a particular software process are identified. Second, each work product (baseline) associated with each step is identified. Each baseline has its own document, which is tracked by SCM. A label is assigned to each baseline (e.g., baseline A for the requirements phase shown in Figure 3.4). The status of changes to baseline documents (e.g., minor, major, temporary) will be recorded. Each new configuration of a baseline will be verified. A sample model of change management during a software process is given in Fig. 3.4.

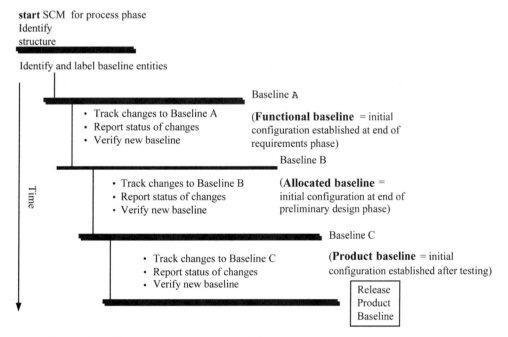

Figure 3.4 Change management model.

3.7   TOOLS OF SCM

Software configuration management tools make it possible to establish, control, and maintain repositories of software project documents and drawings. There are a number of different types of software repositories:

- *Master library.* A collection of approved and released code as well as released software documents distributed to a client or to the marketplace.
- *Production library.* A collection of software artifacts (e.g., plans, SRS, architectural descriptions, charts, drawings, test results) produced during a project.
- *Software development library.* A collection of source code (e.g., classes, functions, programs) produced during a project.
- *Software archive.* A collection of source code and related document at the close of a project. All released documentation and software in the master library should be backed up in the software archive.

Repositories can created and managed with the help of commonly available tools.

3.7.1   Source Code Control System

The source code control system (sccs) is a suite of Unix operating system programs for tracking and control of versions of text files (Rochkind, 1975). The idea for get and put in Unix comes from sccs (Kernighan & Pike, 1984). The sccs system was introduced by Rochkind to maintain large programs in a production environment. If you are on a Unix system, here are the steps to follow to start using sccs:

- Create a subdirectory SCCS. Let plan be an existing text file for a project plan. To install plan in the SCCS subdirectory, type

```
% sccs admin ifile SCCS/s.plan
```

- To archive a C++ program named hello.cpp in the SCCS directory, type

```
% sccs admin ifile SCCS/s.hello.cpp
```

- Reclaim a file for some purpose (e.g., to compile it). To reclaim a file named hello.cpp for compiling or printing but not editing, type

```
% sccs get hello.cpp
```

- Extract the latest version of a file for editing. To extract a file named plan for editing, type

```
% sccs edit plan
```

This command line extracts the file named plan from the SCCS subdirectory, makes a note of who is editing this file, and locks the SCCS file to prevent parallel editing by another user to edit the same file.

- Putting back a changed file. To put back a changed file (for example, a file named plan, which has been edited), type

```
% sccs delta file
comments? The section named ''Required Gantt charts'' changed on 12/22/98 (jfp).
```

The delta command makes the current version of the file named plan the latest version. It also unlocks the SCCS file to permit other users to edit this file. Finally, it also prompts for comments about the latest version of the file.

- To learn more about sccs, type

```
% man sccs
```

A good reference for sccs is Foxley (1985). An overview of Unix is given in Peters (1988).

3.7.2 Revision Control System

The revision control system (rcs) is another suite of Unix operating system programs for tracking and control of versions of text introduced in 1982 by Walter Tichy. This archival control system is considered easier to use than sccs. After a subdirectory named RCS has been set up, check-in (ci) and check-out (co) commands are used to store and extract files. To begin using rcs, try the following steps:

- First set up a subdirectory named RCS by typing

```
% mkdir RCS
```

- Let plan.html be the name of a hypertext file for project planning. To add plan.html to the RCS subdirectory, type

```
% ci plan.html
RCS/plan.html, v ← plan.html
enter description, terminated with single '.' or end of file:
>> project plan created on 12/22/98 by jfp
>> .
initial revision: 1.1
%
```

- To extract a file named plan.html from the RCS subdirectory (and lock it for editing), type

```
% co-1 RCS/plan.html, v
RCS/plan.html, v → help.html
revision 1.1 (locked)
done
%
```

- After editing the plan.html extracted from the RCS subdirectory, store the edited file back by typing

```
% ci plan.html
RCS/help.html, v ← help.html
New revision: 1.2; previous revision: 1.1
Enter log message, terminated with a single '.' or end of file:
>> Revision 1.2 of project plan contains a new description of development tools.
>> Revision on 12/26/98 by sr
>> .
done
```

- The rlog command can be use to check what rcs has done so far. To see this, try typing

```
% rlog RCS/plan.html, v
RCS file: RCS/help.html, v
Working file: help.html
Head: 1.2
Branch:
Locks: strict
Access list:
Symbolic names:
Keyword substitution: kv
Total revisions: 2; selected revisions: 2
Description:
Version 1.2 of project plan contains a new description of development tools.
Revision on 12/26/98 by sr
--------------------------
```

```
revision 1.2
date: 1998/12/26 15:33:22; author: rather; state: Exp; lines: +10-10
----------------------------
revision 1.1
date: 1998/12/22 15:28:10; author: paxton; state: Exp;
Initial revision
```

Notice that rcs automatically adjusts the version number each time a file is extracted for editing. To learn more about rcs, use the Unix man command to see the rcs manual. See *http://www.ecst.esuchico.edu/~murphy/gradinfo/210/config13.txt* for an example of how to use rcs.

3.7.3 Concurrent Version System

The concurrent revision system (cvs) for Unix systems is downloadable from *http://www.mozilla.org*. This is part of what is known as the Mozilla project at Netscape. A PC version of cvs called WinCVS is downloadable from *http://www.cyclic.com*. Unlike rcs, the cvs system supplies navigation windows with user-friendly menus and help button. To start a cvs repository using WinCVS, do the following.

- First set up a subdirectory named RCS by typing

```
CVSROOT: \home\cvs_repository
TCL is available, shell is enabled: help (select and press enter)
Cvs init
```

- Now select a folder to import. This action is illustrated using a projects directory for a traffic navigation system (Figure 3.5).
- Assume that class files in the traffic control system directory in Figure 3.5 are to be imported. Type

```
Cvs import -I ! -I CVS - W ''-I*.class - W''
```

Both cvs and rcs use a checkout system to retrieve files for revision. In cvs, there are a number of options that can be selected whenever a repository filed is checked out. See, for example, the options for a checkout file named TrafficControl in a directory named CVS_WORKING in Figure 3.6.

A commit command is used by cvs to check in a new version of a file. For example, assume that car.java is a program that has been checked out, edited, and then is ready to be checked back into the cvs repository. A sample cvs commit window is given in Figure 3.7. Both cvs and rcs automatically update the version of numbers of edited files. The cvs example in this section appears in Minuk (1998).

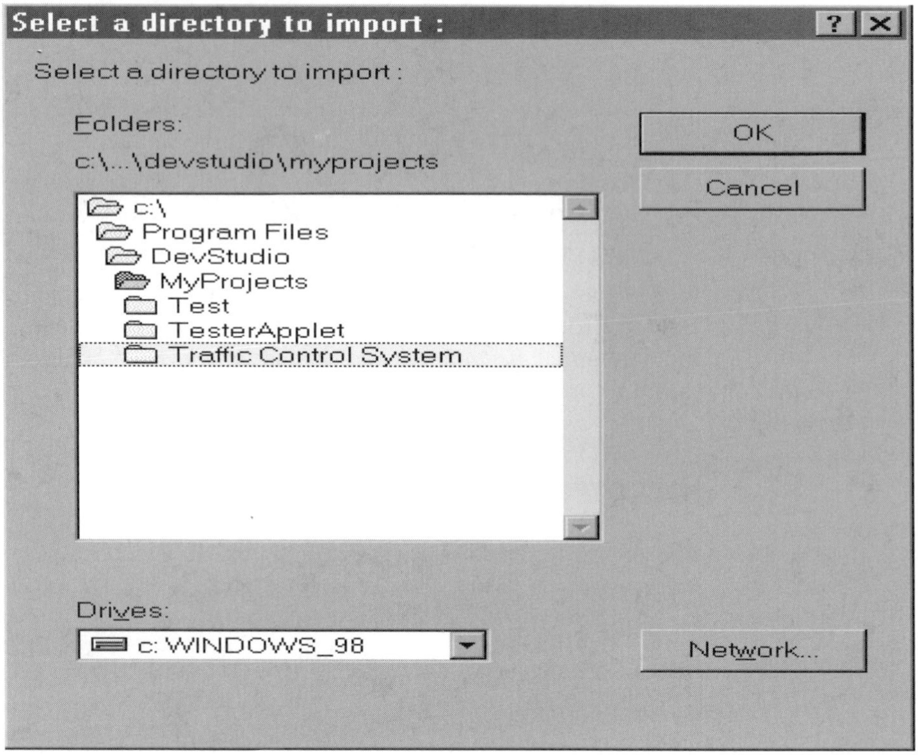

Figure 3.5 Selecting a folder for a cvs repository.

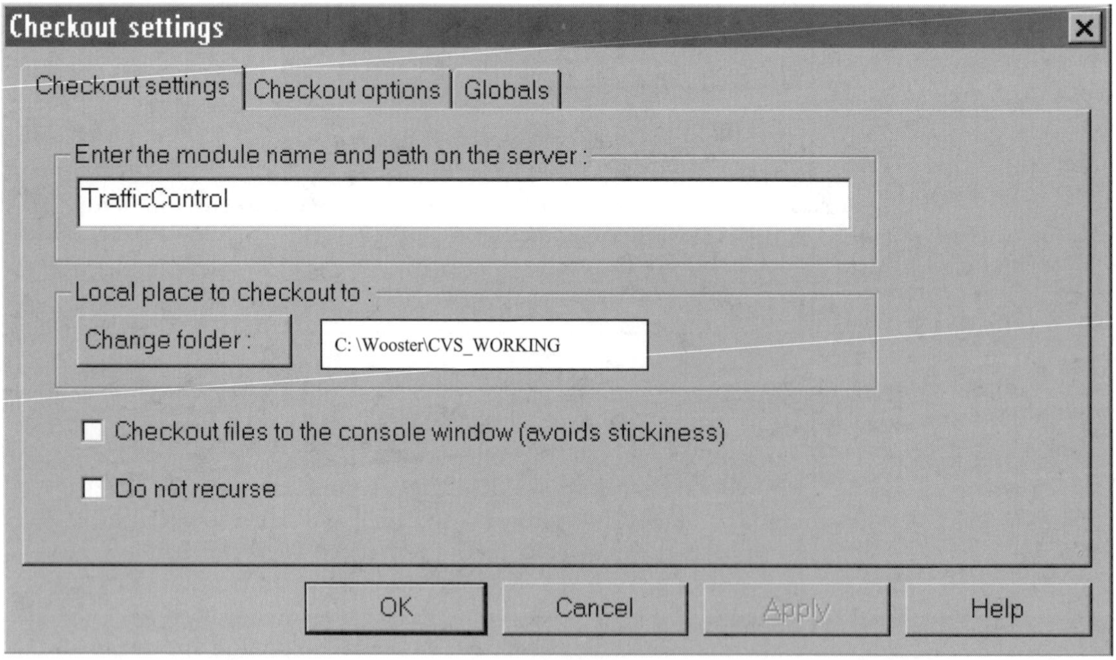

Figure 3.6 Sample checkout window.

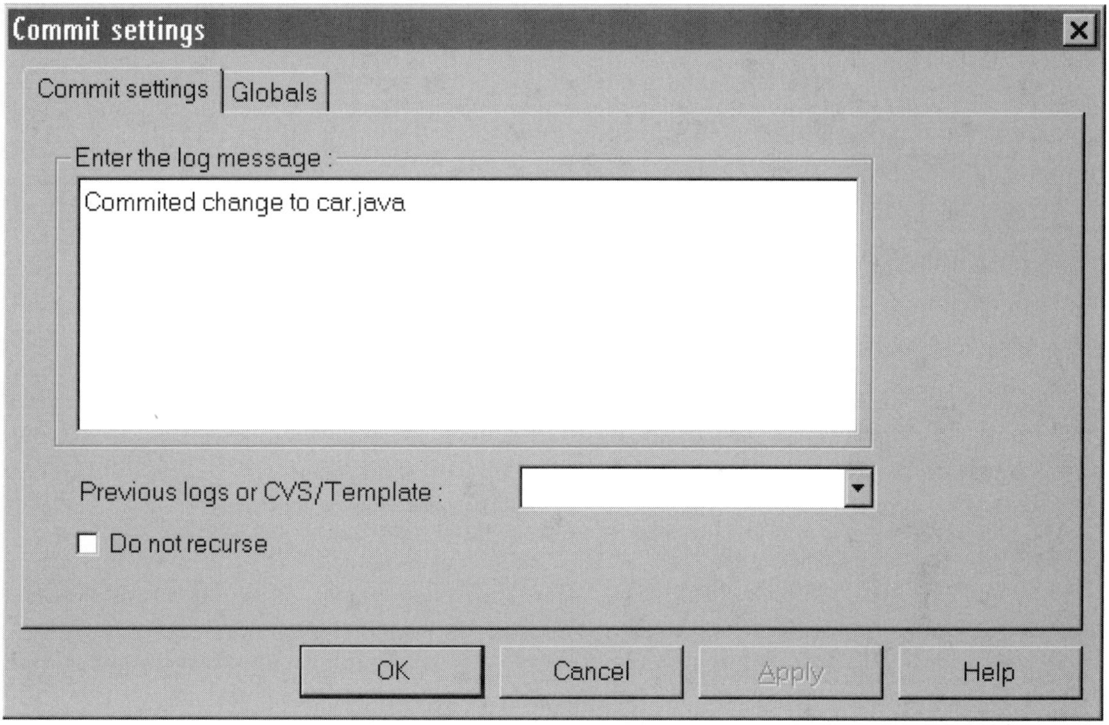

Figure 3.7   Sample cvs commit window.

3.8   TOOLS FOR SCM AUDITING

Well-planned projects take advantage of tools such as the Project Evaluation Technique/Critical Path Method (PERT) network diagram and Gantt time-allocation charts. Audit trail reports reflect back to milestones (completion times, activities, work products) in planning charts. Planning charts give a project management team tools for tracking the progress of developers during a project. They have become an accepted part of SCM auditing (IEEE Std. 1042-1987). A brief introduction to these charting techniques is given in this section.

3.8.1   PERT Charts

A PERT network diagram displays task sequences required for a project. A path through a network is any sequence of activities from the beginning to the end

of a project (Figure 3.8). A PERT network helps display interrelationships between tasks. PERT charts also make it possible to described varying task schedules.
The notation $\xrightarrow{\text{min,avg,max}}$ specifies the estimated minimum, average, and maximum
times required to complete a task. Task durations are typically measured
in days. So, for example, $\xrightarrow{38,44,48}$ represents a minimum of 38 days, an average
of 44 days, and a maximum of 48 days to complete task d in Figure 3.8. A
boldfaced arrow indicates what is known as a critical path (a network path where
the sum of the maximum times between tasks is longer than any other network
path). The task sequence a, c, f, g forms a critical path in the PERT chart in
Figure 3.8. PERT charts have been credited with saving time and cost in the
design of the Polaris submarine system (Hurst, 1983). A sample PERT chart
representing a partial, high-level view of a network of activities in developing a
module in a software system is shown in Figure 3.9. The network of tasks connected by nodes 1, 2, 4, 6, 7, and 8 in Figure 3.9 form a critical path, since the
sum of the maximum times for the activities in this network is largest. This is
the path that would be carefully watched by project auditors. This could change,
since the PERT chart in Figure 3.9 is incomplete. For example, validation of
the architecture for the module being developed is missing. Also, notice
that a different critical path may result from changes in the duration estimates
for tasks.

The milestones in the PERT chart in Figure 3.9 are superficial. To be useful,

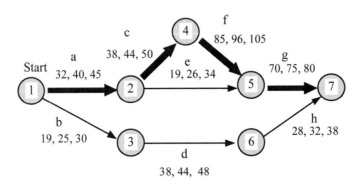

Explanation of Notation

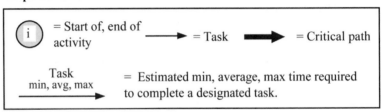

Figure 3.8 Typical PERT network.

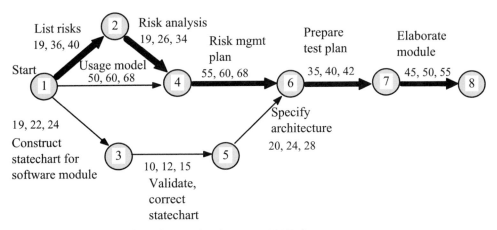

Figure 3.9 Sample software development PERT chart.

PERT charts are tiered. Selected activities in a PERT chart will be associated with separate task schedules in lower-level PERT charts that give a more accurate picture of what must be done to complete a particular task. In other words, milestones in a PERT charts will be visible at different levels of detail. This makes it possible for managers to summarize more detailed task schedules and track subtasks leading to the completion of a major activity in a high-level PERT chart (Marciniak, 1994).

3.8.2 Gantt Charts

A Gantt chart provides another means of depicting task schedules for a software development project. This form of task scheduling was introduced in 1903 by Henri Gantt to plan and control military campaigns. Horizontal bars are used to depict tasks or activities, and indicate starting (beginning of bar) and completion times (end of bar). A partial Gantt chart for scheduling risk analysis and risk management during a software development project is shown in Figure 3.10.

It is helpful to indicate the starting dates for the beginning and ending of an activity. For example, in Figure 3.10, risk monitoring begins on 10/1 (immediately after the sources of risk have been identified) and ends on 6/30. This form of scheduling serves as an aid in tracking project activities relative to the schedule in a Gantt chart. The disadvantage to a Gantt chart is that it does not show dependencies. Notice, for example, that it is not immediately apparent from the chart in Figure 3.10 that risk monitoring is dependent on identifying sources of risk. This problem can be solved by annotating the bars in a Gantt

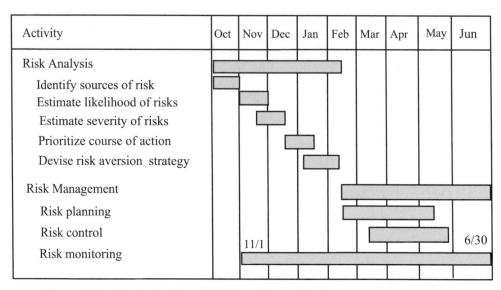

Activity	Oct	Nov	Dec	Jan	Feb	Mar	Apr	May	Jun

Risk Analysis

   Identify sources of risk

   Estimate likelihood of risks

   Estimate severity of risks

   Prioritize course of action

   Devise risk aversion strategy

Risk Management

   Risk planning

   Risk control

   Risk monitoring

11/1   6/30

Figure 3.10   Gantt chart for scheduling risk analysis/management.

chart (noting task dependencies), and by supplementing this form of scheduling with PERT charts.

3.9 SUMMARY

An archive of baseline documents establishes a project history, and serves as a repository for ideas, plans, guides, schedules, charts, methods, specifications, design documents, prototypes and their refinements, test plans, test cases, test specifications, test results, faults, fault recovery procedures, and maintenance records. In the case of object-oriented design, evolving class libraries can be archived. Such archives provide valuable information and a variety of reusable artifacts for other projects. These archives make it possible to construct PERT and Gantt charts that reflect past experience and knowledge of elapsed times and sequencing of project activities. A knowledge of what worked best in the past in sequencing project activities makes it possible to construct realistic worldly and atomic software process models for a project. It is also the case that a review of project archives will reveal sources of risk in undertaking new projects. For example, certain features chosen for an early software increment of a system being developed may have resulted in excessive change requests and unsatisfactory results. This would be revealed in a review of a project archive. In new projects, features identified as sources of high risk can be scheduled for later increments in a project.

3.10 PROBLEMS

1. Prepare a configuration management plan for a project to develop a vehicular traffic navigation system (VTNS) for a highway named 1A passing through the business district of a city named Lake Wobegon with a population of 500, 000. You can assume that 1A is equipped with towers having sensors to monitor traffic flow, and that all vehicles traveling on 1A are equipped with transmit-receive equipment used to communicate with a traffic navigation control center. Do the following:
    (a) Create a VTNS needs assessment. Use an SCM tool to archive the assessment.
    (b) Create a VTNS plan based on the needs assessment. Archive the plan.
    (c) Identify project team to prepare project requirements.
    (d) Select a universal software process model to follow in developing VTNS software.
    (e) Construct a worldly model of the VTNS project. Archive identified procedure.
    (f) Create a VTNS engineering guide indicating standards to follow and resources to use. Archive the guide.
    (g) Identify the sources of risk for this project. Archive the sources of risk.
    (h) Identify the features to be included in the design of the first prototype of the VTNS. Archive the identified features.

2. Give examples of change requests and configuration control of the requests relative to the archived items in no. 1.

3. Assume that the Win Win spiral model has been selected as the universal-level software process to follow during the VTNS project.
    (a) Give a PERT network detailing the sequences of activities and timing estimates leading to a project plan.
    (b) Identify the critical path in the network devised in part (a).

4. Give a Gantt chart for scheduling project planning for the VTNS project.

5. Compare and contrast the PERT and Gantt charts in nos. 3 and 4.

6. Repeat nos. 3 and 4 relative to the selection of the synch and stabilize process model to follow during the VTNS project.

7. Using the web, do the following:
    (a) List available SCM tools. Distinguish between public domain and commercial tools.
    (b) Give an example using at least one tool not covered in this chapter.

8. Do the following:
    (a) Comment on the features of cvs that make it superior to sccs and rcs.

(b) Comment on features of sccs that make it superior (or inferior) to rcs.

(c) Comment on features of sccs that make it superior (or inferior) to cvs.

3.11 REFERENCES

Berlack, H.R. Configuration management. In *Encyclopedia of Software Engineering*, J.J. Marciniak, Ed. Wiley, New York, 1994.

Bersoff, E.H. Elements of software configuration management. In *Software Engineering*, M. Dorfman, R.H. Thayer, Eds. IEEE Computer Society Press, Los Alamitos, CA, pp. 320–328, 1997.

Foxley, E. *Unix for Super Users*. Addison-Wesley, Reading, MA, 1985.

Hurst, E.G. PERT/CPM. In *Encyclopedia of Computer Science and Engineering*, A Ralston, E.D. Reilly, Eds. Van Nostrand Reinhold, New York, 1983.

IEEE Guide to Software Configuration Management. IEEE Std. 1042-1987. In *IEEE Standards Collection Software Engineering*, ISBN 1-55937-898-0. IEEE, Piscataway, NJ, 1997.

Kernighan, B., Pike, R. *The Unix Programming Environment*. Prentice-Hall, Englewood Cliffs, NJ, 1984.

Marciniak, J.J. Acquisition management. In *Encyclopedia of Software Engineering*, J.J. Marciniak, Ed. Wiley, New York, 1994.

Minuk, B. *Concurrent Version System: A Systems Engineering Report*. Department of Electrical and Computer Engineering, University of Manitoba, December 1998.

Peters, J.F. *Unix Programming: Methods and Tools*. Oxford University Press, New York, 1988.

Rochkind, M. The source code control system. *IEEE Transactions on Software Engineering*, vol. SE-1, no. 4, April 1975, 225–265.

CHAPTER 4

Software Project: Planning

"Begin at the beginning," the King said,
gravely, "and go on till you come to the end:
then stop."
—LEWIS CARROLL, 1865

Aims

- Identify the main features of a project plan
- Begin a project plan for the tATC project
- Establish a project-specific software process model
- Establish an atomic-level planning process

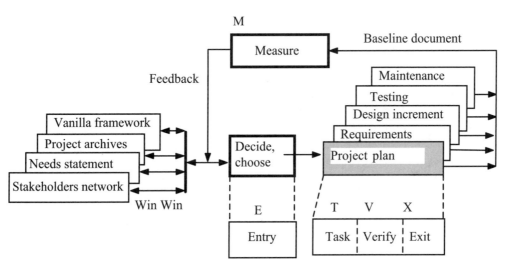

Figure 4.1 Software process model.

4.1   INTRODUCTION

In developing software, an engineer engages in a sequence of activities that produce a variety of documents culminating in a satisfactory, executable program. Central to any software development effort is an effort to specify, design, and test the conceptual construct of the software being built. For the development of a training program for air traffic controllers, a feedback system model for the software process has been chosen. This model is a composite of features from other well-known models. Each iteration through the feedback system in Figure 4.1 includes interaction with distributed stakeholders as in the Win Win spiral model (Boehm et al., 1998). Recall that project stakeholders include customers, developers, maintainers, interfacers, testers, reusers, and the general public. Starting with project planning, there is repeated interaction with stakeholders concerning features of the project plan and its refinements. This interaction continues during the lifespan of a project. Also included in Figure 4.1 is a vanilla framework. Recall that this is a general-purpose framework making it possible to conceive an idea for solving an algorithmic problem and to map the idea into an appropriate high-level medium (Harel, 1992). The identification of a vanilla framework for a project is considered crucial in tackling the essential difficulties of software. This part of the feedback system model is aided by choosing a toolset that supports a vanilla system design approach. This chapter gives an overview of the main features of a software project plan. Some of these features are illustrated in the preparation of a project plan for developing training software for air traffic controllers.

Each of the overlapping entry-effector processes in Figure 4.1 has a Humphrey ETVXM architecture (Humphrey, 1989). The software process begins with a decider process, determining if the entry conditions for starting the process have been satisfied. In the universal feedback system model for a software process in Figure 4.1, the entry condition for a project calls for the availability of a network of stakeholders, needs statement, project archive, and vanilla framework. The ETVXM architecture provides an orderly transition from state to state during a software project. An effector task is completed only after it has been verified (the V part of the model). Verifying the output of a task usually means testing a prototype of some increment of a system being developed. Even in the planning stages of a process, simple prototyping is possible based on results from past or similar projects. A prototype clarifies what is possible and helps identify the sources of risk associated with a new software system. Exit conditions must be satisfied to continue the iteration through the development loop in Figure 4.1. Checklists can be used to compare expected features against completed features of a work product output by a task. This is the X part of Figure 4.1. Finally, the results produced by an effector process are measured. This provides feedback used in consulting stakeholders and in deciding whether another iteration is necessary to add refinements to a software increment.

4.2   GETTING STARTED

The feedback system model in Figure 4.1 has features that are attractive, but it lacks sufficient detail to be useful. For this reason, a worldly level model of the software process should be introduced. Recall that a world-level process model is project specific. This is done by decomposing each effector process in the universal-level model in Figure 4.1 into mini-feedback systems. The first decomposition usually leads to a universal-level model of an effector process. For example, the planning effector can be mapped to a universal model of planning. Each of the effectors in the planning model can then be mapped to project-specific process models. Each effector at the worldly level of a software process is fleshed out with project details. Specific entry conditions are given for a particular project and are identified for each effector. A procedure is associated with each task. Each procedure provides a sequence of activities required for some part of a project. Its verification and exit blocks are designed relative to a project. Measurements of baseline documents and all outputs from effector processes are tailored to the needs of a project.

The decomposition starts with project planning. The flow diagram for project planning is given in Figure 4.2. The box labeled "Needs statement" in Figure 4.2 represents the process that launches a software project. Meetings with clients, consultants, and managers in a stakeholders network have resulted in a summary of the main features and restrictions needed in a software system. The effector processes are patterned after IEEE Std. 1058.1-1987 (IEEE Standard for Software Project Management Plans), which provides a standard for project management planning. Each of the effectors in Figure 4.2 maps to a set of overlapping subeffectors. The connections between each planning effector and its subeffector process are shown in Figure 4.3. A Software Project Management Plan (SPMP) will have a title, unique identifier, revision chart, preface, table of contents, list of figures, list of tables, five main parts shown as effectors in Figure 4.2, an index, and possible appendices. A revision chart can be maintained using configuration management data. During a project, the parts of a plan will be refined, and the

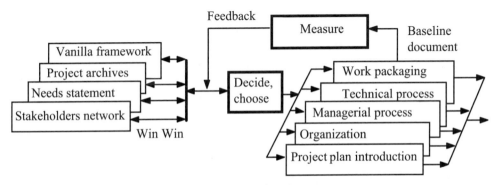

Figure 4.2   Feedback system for project planning.

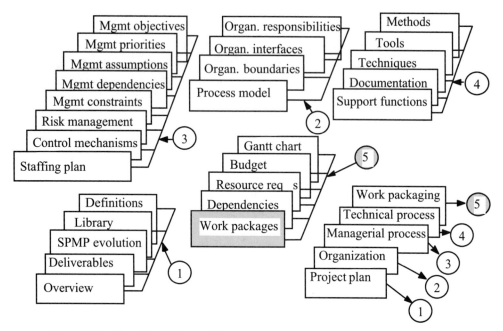

Figure 4.3   Planning effector subprocesses.

plan will evolve. Each baseline document associated with a part of the plan becomes a configuration item, which can be controlled. A revision chart reflects the status of a configuration item, its stability, and its change history.

In the IEEE standard, there are five main parts to an SPMP (reflected in the block diagram in Figure 4.3.):

1. *Introduction.* Overview, deliverables, SPMP evolution, library, definitions.
2. *Organization.* Process model, organization boundaries, interfaces, responsibilities.
3. *Management process.* Objectives, priorities, assumptions, dependencies, constraints, risk management, control mechanisms, and staffing plan.
4. *Technical process.* Methods, tools, techniques, documentation, support functions.
5. *Work packaging.* Work packages, dependencies, resource requirements, budget, resource allocation, and schedule. The schedule can be in the form of a Gantt chart and/or PERT chart.

4.2.1   Introduction to SPMP

The introduction to an SPMP begins with a project overview. This is high-level view of project objectives, specific products to be delivered, major work activities, work products and milestones, required resources, master schedule, and budget. The relationship of the current project to other parallel or past projects is described. In addition, in keeping with the Win Win spiral model, an overview of the network of stakeholders associated with the project is given. This overview includes a description of methods of communication with stakeholders. Project deliverables include a list of all items to be delivered to a customer, delivery dates, delivery locations, and quantities required to satisfy the terms of the project. Project evolution is identified with plans for producing scheduled and unscheduled updates to the SPMP. Methods of disseminating the updates are also considered. The project library consists of all documents and other sources of information referenced in the SPMP. Finally, definitions of key terms and explanations of acronyms are given. This last activity in preparing an introduction to a project plan is important, since it identifies the terms and acronyms required to interpret and understand the SPMP.

4.2.2 Project Organization

Project organization begins with the selection of a process model. This model defines the relationships among major project functions and activities by scheduling milestones, baselines, reviews, work products, deliverables, and sign-offs throughout a project. Usually, a process model is described with a combination of graphical and textual notations. The feedback system model is an example. Notice that a project plan presents a project-specific process model, not a universal-level model. This is a worldly level model that specializes the parts of a universal model.

Also included in a project organization is a collection of charts describing lines of authority, responsibility, and communication with project stakeholders. Organizational boundaries are described relative to a parent, customer, and subcontractor organizations that interact with the project. Project interfaces are derived from the application of configuration management, quality assurance, and verification and validation of work products. Finally, the identity of those responsible for major project functions and activities is established.

4.2.3 Project Managerial Process

The managerial process begins by identifying management objectives, priorities, project assumptions, dependencies, constraints, risk management techniques, monitoring and control mechanisms, and a staffing plan. Notice that this section is aided by the work that has been done with the Win Win spiral model, since its focus is on process management. The key to this process is to establish a basis for iterative and interactive refinement of project baseline documents with the help of project stakeholders. In the context of the tATC project, this means visiting a nearby airport and talking to air traffic controllers. Initially, a visit to a nearby airport would be part of an orientation concerning the needs of air traffic controllers.

The managerial process begins with a statement of project philosophy, goals, and priorities for management activities during a project. This philosophy could begin with the following preamble to set the tone of the plan:

Project Philosophy

Project objectives, constraints, and alternatives are rooted in interaction with stakeholders.

Topics to include in project priorities are frequency and mechanisms for reporting, primary elements of requirements, schedule, budget, and risk management procedures. Next, sources of risk are identified. These include contractual, technology, product size and complexity, personnel acquisition and retention, and risks in obtaining customer acceptance of a product. Identifying these risks helps in allocating resources and channeling development team efforts.

4.2.4 Technical Process

This is section 4 of a standard SPMP. This is the part of the plan that identifies the methods, tools, and techniques to be used by project teams. This is also the place where a plan for software documentation is given. In addition, a number of support functions are specified. These support functions include quality assurance, configuration management, and verification and validation methods. Plans for these support functions are developed with enough details to guide software development team activities. The documentation plan provides a blueprint for presenting software products:

- *Documentation requirements.* How to get started, major functions, Internet usage.
- *Milestones.* Special features included in a product.
- *Reviews.* Results of external reviews.

4.2.5 Work Packages

A description of project work packages is given in part 5 of a project plan. A work package is a specification of the work to be accomplished in completing a task. A work package defines work products for a project. Each work product is a tangible item resulting from a project activity. Examples of work products are customer requirements, project plan, functional specification, design document, source code, user manuals, installation instructions, test plans, maintenance procedures, meeting minutes, schedules, budgets, and problem reports. A work package is usually accompanied with a diagram giving a breakdown of project activities into subactivities and tasks. This diagram can be used to show relationships between work packages for a project. This is the part of a project plan that supplies atomic-level process models. The specific steps to follow in completing a task are given. These details are needed to assure an orderly progression in the work done by project teams.

4.3 CASE STUDY: tATC PROJECT

The mapping of the universal model onto a worldly model will be carried out relative to the project planning task for a software project set up to develop a training program for air traffic controllers (call it tATC). Air traffic controllers at airports are chiefly concerned with the movement of aircraft in the neighborhood of an airport. Controllers decide on movements of aircraft within designated zones, and they track the movement and status of aircraft. This specialization of the feedback system model of the software process is based on studies reported in Peters and others (1998) and Ip and others (1998).

4.3.1 NEEDS STATEMENT

The beginning of a needs statement needed to derive a worldly level model for project planning for a training program for air traffic controllers is given in this section. Enough detail is given in this needs statement to define many of the effector processes for project planning.

Needs Statement (NS)

NS-1. *Introduction*

The formulation of a needs statement for a training program for air traffic controllers (tATC) is based on discussions with air traffic controllers at a local airport serving a city with a population of 750,000 people. The tATC should include the following main features:

Main Features of the tATC
- Training for air traffic controllers through a program that simulates air traffic control problems and that allows trainees to respond and correct problems.
- Incorporation of a display subsystem commonly used by controllers.

- Incorporation of a drive plan view display used by controllers at enroute centers to handle aircraft flying between airports at higher altitudes.
- Provide an organized scratchpad useful in tracking the location of aircraft and to track who is controlling each aircraft.
- Assist controllers in making decisions in managing air traffic.

NS-2. *Needed Features in tATC Prototype*

The first version of the tATC will be limited to local airport aircraft control, and should not include training for enroute air traffic control. The tATC prototype will have the following features:

- Display of weather information. The tATC warns an ATC of significant changes in weather conditions that may affect air traffic flow.
- Aircraft entering an airspace zone or that are preparing to take off are identified.
- Aircraft leaving an airspace are assigned to an enroute center and re-moved from the list of aircraft displayed by the tATC
- Identification of direction of runway, aircraft using runway queue, ground conditions, and changes to runway conditions (updated by the controller and/or ground crews).
- The tATC will be run by a web browser.
- The tATC will support drag-and-drop as well as click-and-see techniques for navigating a web browser document.
- All drag-and-drop operations are accomplished within 100 milliseconds during interactive tATC sessions.
- The tATC will support quick and easy retrieval and input of air traffic control data through a graphical user interface.
- The tATC will support up to 20 simultaneous users.
- Each controller workstation has a high-resolution 2048 × 2048 pixel display on a 20-inch color monitor.
- Transactions during tATC sessions are logged in a relational database.
- The tATC will enforce standards imposed by national standards for air traffic control (e.g., U.S. Federal Aviation Administration or FAA standards).
- The tATC enforces a What-You-See-Is-What-You-Get (WYSIWYG) display. In other words, no information is hidden from a trainee.
- The tATC maintains a knowledge base about all aircraft relative to airport tower, airport runways, and weather.
- The tATC controls the flow of information (e.g., characteristics of aircraft in a controlled zone) in the air traffic control system. The trainee controls the flow of aircraft entering, leaving, or navigating airspace zones.

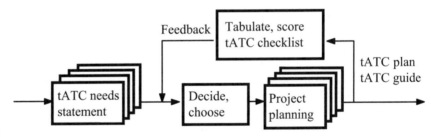

Figure 4.4 Worldly project planning model for tATC (first cut).

- The tATC simulates the optional use of sensors such as radar, meteorological instruments, and information gathered from pilots and ground crews.

4.3.2 WORLDLY LEVEL PROJECT PLANNING MODEL FOR ATC

The construction of a worldly model for project planning can be done in steps (incrementally). First, the universal model for project planning is specialized relative to the tATC (specific needs, plan, guide, checklist, scoring). This is shown in Figure 4.4. Next, each of the effector process boxes in the worldly project planning model boxes can be "uncovered" (decomposed into sequences of tasks with associated entry and exit conditions, and indications of what should be verified, and what should be measured). We illustrate the opening of the project planning box in terms of an effector processes for developing an tATC mission plan, organizational plan, and work products plan, which are part of the tATC plan. The second version of the worldly model for project planning is given in Figure 4.5.

The worldly model in Figure 4.5 can be expanded to include sequencing of the remaining effector processes needed to construct a complete software development plan for the tATC. Notice that concurrent processing is possible. The tasks performed by the tATC mission planning effector process in Figure 4.5 can be performed concurrently with other project planning effectors processes (e.g., standards planning). Notice also that each effector process box

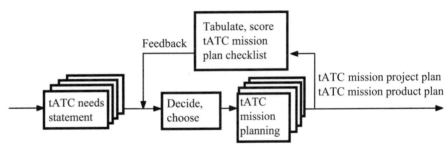

Figure 4.5 Worldly project planning model for tATC (second cut).

needs to be expanded to complete the development of the worldly model. This expansion is needed to specify the entry, added task sequencing, and exit conditions, as well as what each task must verify and what features of task output need to be measured. This expansion process is illustrated relative to mission planning for the tATC, which has two main tasks. These tasks are defining the overall mission, end (termination) points, and measurable features of the tATC software product and defining the overall mission, goals, and objectives the tATC software development project. The entry condition for both of these tasks is the availability of a completed needs statement. For example, the product-defining task must verify that a report has been prepared containing the product mission statement, quantifiable end points, and quantifiable features. The product mission is to develop an air traffic control training program that runs on the web. One of the product end points is the completion of a version of the tATC that conforms to national air traffic control standards. The quantifiable features of the training program of defined in terms of a description of the basic features of the main modules for the tATC. The main tATC modules are weather, airspace, aircraft, airport, and scoring. To complete the mission product plan, it is necessary to give more details concerning each of these modules. This leads to a decomposition of mission planning activities down to the atomic level. The exit condition for the product-defining task is that the mission product report is complete. The output of the product-defining task is measured relative to a checklist extracted from the tATC needs statement. Similar entry, verification, exit, and measurement requirements are imposed on the tATC project-defining task. The worldly model for the mission planning part of the tATC project planning model has the form shown in Figure 4.6.

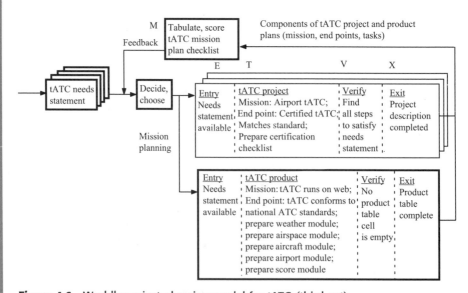

Figure 4.6   Worldly project planning model for tATC (third cut).

4.4 ATOMIC-LEVEL MODELS FOR ATC

An atomic model provides the details needed by software engineering teams to implement a worldly model. Atomic models have the following features:

- An algorithm (steps, operations, measurements) to follow in preparing tables (e.g., Microsoft Excel to build a table, produce graphs), sketches (e.g., drawings with Microsoft Draw for Windows environments or Claris-Draw for Macs), or photos (e.g., for retouching, cutting out segments of photos with Adobe PhotoShop or Color It).
- A standard to build or apply measures, or to formulate steps needed to produce prototypes. In the case where a worldly mission planning model for the tATC references a product table, then include a link to an atomic model giving the details such as the tool to use (e.g., Excel).
- Methods for computing numeric values for end points such as minimum number of aircraft that can be displayed, maximum size of airspace zones displayed, minimum and maximum size of icons for aircraft, and so on.

4.4.1 WIRING A WORLDLY MODEL TO AN ATOMIC MODEL

Effector processes in a worldly model can be linked to atomic-level processes in cases where the completion of a task requires an algorithm (precise steps to complete the task), the application of tools. The symbol for an atomic model is given in Figure 4.7. The inclusion of links to atomic-level process models is important to give a complete picture of the context for a worldly model, and to make it clear where engineers should look to find information on how to perform a worldly model task. A Worldly, model can be "wired" to an atomic model by connecting the tail of the arrow in Figure 4.7 to a task in the worldly model. For example, the tATC mission product task in Figure 4.6 is wired to five atomic models: weather, airspace, aircraft, airport, and score in Figure 4.8.

The atomic models referenced in Figure 4.8 give the necessary details concerning the preparation of the tATC product report in the Mission Plan. A worldly model link to an atomic model is analogous to a procedure call. The atomic model symbols in worldly model are just stubs referencing empty process structures. The details of these atomic models need to be worked out. Reasoning at the atomic process level begins at the point where we begin "fleshing out"

Figure 4.7 Atomic model symbol.

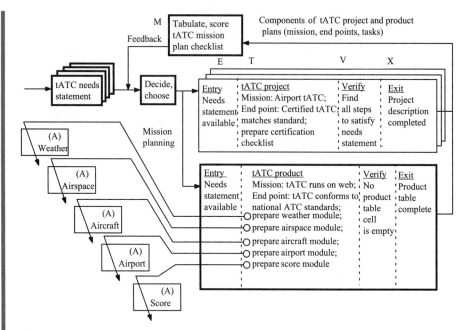

Figure 4.8   Wiring a worldly model task to atomic models.

an atomic model stub referenced in a worldly model. This fleshing out of an atomic model stub supplies the details (steps, sketches, diagrams, tables, plans, feedback from earlier projects, work product descriptions, quality requirements, quality measures, target quality measurement ranges) needed to complete a worldly level task. The beauty of this unfolding of worldly model tasks is that it has desirable side effects. First, it leads to details (steps, methods, prototypes) that contribute to an understanding of the necessary software engineering procedures needed to produce a product. Second, the unfolding of a worldly model into atomic processes provides reusable artifacts. In other words, all of the work that goes into the complete development for one worldly model and its associated atomic models provides mechanisms and methods that can be reused in similar software development projects. At the worldly model level, it is necessary to reference atomic models that mission planners indicate must be developed to clarify the mission product task. Eventually, a complete worldly model for project planning for the tATC is constructed.

4.4.2   AIRSPACE PLANNING ATOMIC MODEL

The airspace and aircraft atomic models linked to the product planning task of the tATC worldly model in Figure 4.8 each give software engineers information needed to develop the training program for air traffic controllers. The basic features of a *sample* airspace planning atomic process model are given in

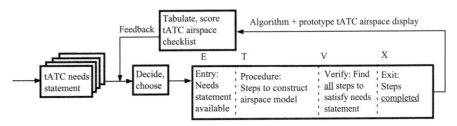

Figure 4.9 Atomic process to construct tATC airspace.

Figure 4.9. The airspace atomic model gives the steps of a plan to develop the airspace to be displayed.

Steps in Airspace Atomic Process Model

Step 1. Use a drawing tool to create a model of the airspace to be viewed by controllers (see Table 4.1).

Step 2. The airspace is to display two runways (see Table 4.1).

Step 3. Provide a view of airport runways as seen by airborn aircraft.

Step 4. A button should be added to the display to make it possible for trainees to start and stop a simulation of aircraft entering and leaving displayed airspace. This is a click-and-see feature of the tATC.

4a. Click (starts simulation): aircraft begin entering displayed airpace.

4b. Click (pause in simulation): display freezes, screen captures can be made.

Step 5. Use a table-building tool to tabulate information about airspace features (number of runways) and tools (name, platform) to be used (see Table 4.1).

Step 6. Give prototypes of displayed airspace for evaluation. A sample prototype of an airspace display is given in Figure 4.10.

The sample airspace shown in Fig. 10 was created by a software engineering team working on a similar software development project (Cormier et al., 1997; Ip et al., 1998; Peters et al., 1997).

TABLE 4.1 Aircraft Prototype Data

Tool	Platform	Airspace	Feature
Microsoft Draw	Windows 95	Runways	2
Claris Draw	Mac OS	Terrain	10 defined areas
Mathematica ≪Miscellaneous 'WorldData'	Windows, Mac, Unix	Macro-view of geographic area	Enroute airspace view

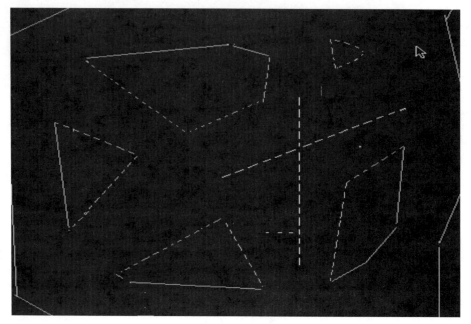

Figure 4.10   Sample prototype of airspace.

4.4.3   AIRCRAFT DISPLAY PLANNING ATOMIC-LEVEL MODEL

The aircraft atomic model referenced in the tATC worldly process model gives the basic features of displayed aircraft. A sample atomic process to construct tATC aircraft displays is given in Figure 4.11. The steps in the aircraft atomic process model (see Figure 4.11) are given next.

Steps in Aircraft Display Atomic Process Model

Step 1.   Each aircraft can be displayed moving at the center of two concentric circles.

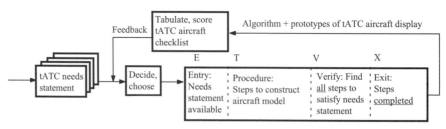

Figure 4.11   Atomic process model to construct tATC aircraft displays.

TABLE 4.2   Aircraft Prototype Data

Aircraft	Radius	Label	Feature
Inner circle	Minimum	None	Spin area
Outer circle	Maximum	None	Buffer zone
Direction arc	Inner circle	None	Planned direction
Change arc	Sensor	Distance	Changed direction
Flight coordinates		Flight no. (x, y)	Identify aircraft
Altitude		Meters	Planar position
Speed		Kilometers	Above ground
Status		Safe	Air speed
			(True, false)

Step 2. Associate with each aircraft a circular "slice" of airspace containing aircraft. This is the inner of the circles in step 1. See Table 4.2 for radius.

Step 3. Associate with each aircraft a circular "slice" of airspace representing a danger zone. The space between the leading edge of this circle and the leading edge of the inner circle (step 2) must be protected and monitored by a tATC trainee.

Step 4. The identity, coordinates, altitude, air speed, and status of each aircraft are to be displayed. This text of this information appears between the inner and outer concentric circles surrounding a displayed aircraft.

Step 5. Associate with each air craft an arc indicating direction of flight corresponding to a flight plan. This direction is represented by a flight-plan-arc drawn from the center of the aircraft to the edge of the inner circle in step 2.

Step 6. Associate with each aircraft an arc indicating direction of flight corresponding to a change in the flight plan (needed to avoid a collision or to solve a flight control problem). This direction is represented by change-of-direction-arc drawn from the center of the aircraft to the edge of the outer circle in step 3.

Step 7. Associate with each change-of-direction-arc a number representing range of an aircraft sensor (e.g., its collision-avoidance radar). This number appears at the end of the change-of-direction arc.

Step 8. Aircraft icon, concentric circles, aircraft flight information, aircraft status (safe, unsafe), and direction arcs move together across a displayed airspace.

Step 9. Prepare prototypes of aircraft displays. A sample aircraft prototype is given in Figure 4.12.

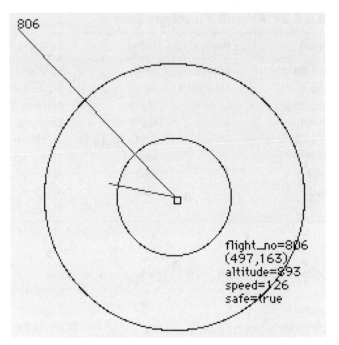

806

flight_no=806
(497,163)
altitude=893
speed=126
safe=true

Figure 4.12   Prototype of aircraft display.

Step 10. The tATC has built-in collision-impending detection mechanisms. In the case where aircraft are in danger of colliding (one aircraft enters the airspace between the inner and outer concentric circles surrounding another aircraft), the outer circle of both aircraft will change color (e.g., from green to amber).

Step 11. Construct a table with the data needed to construct prototypes of the tATC (see Table 4.2).

The aircraft prototype display shown in Figure 4.12 was created by a team working on a similar software development project (Ip et al., 1998). The details of each of the remaining atomic processes (weather, airport, scoring) linked to the tATC worldly process model in Figure 4.8 still need to be examined. The weather atomic model gives the details needed to develop displays of weather information during a simulation of air traffic control. The airport atomic model gives the details about the information and menu choices associated with simulated features of an airport tower, runways, ground crew, emergencies, runway conditions, and so on. Finally, it is also necessary to give the details needed to develop a scoring module for the tATC. The scoring module keeps track of the responses of a trainee to simulated normal as well as emergency conditions during an air traffic control training session. This module tabulates responses, gathers statistics, and produces graphs needed to evaluate the performance of an air traffic control trainee.

4.5 SUMMARY

The basic features of software project planning are explored in two contexts in this chapter. First, planning is seen as part of a software process. A feedback model of the software process is considered. This process model includes three features derived from other well-known approaches: vanilla framework, Win Win stakeholders, and Humphrey ETVXM architecture. In a project plan, a vanilla framework provides a generic approach to specifying, designing, and testing the conceptual construct of software to be developed. This framework underlying the approach serves as an instrument in guiding the efforts of project teams. The importance of stakeholders as sources of project objectives, constraints, and priorities is highlighted in the Boehm Win Win spiral model. The stakeholders network paradigm is incorporated into the feedback model to highlight the importance of an interactive and iterative approach in project planning and in developing software products. The Humphrey ETVXM architecture induces an orderly progression through the steps of procedures required for each project task. Second, the IEEE standard for project planning paves the way to a detailed view the structure and content of a plan. A case study is also given. The needs statement and worldly and atomic-level process models for project planning for air traffic control training software are presented.

4.6 PROBLEMS

1. Create a graphical representation of an ETVXM worldly level process model to be used as guide in writing a plan for software to display information (a GUI) associated with an aircraft in an air traffic control (ATC) system. Among the tasks in your model, include:
   (a) Minimum and maximum values of selected software quality attributes such as maintainability (this requires constructing a table containing maintainability measurements from similar, completed projects as well as the required maintainability level for the ATC project).
   (b) Resource projections.
   (c) Software development schedule.
   (d) Breakdown of software production into suggested increments.
   (e) Allocation of functions to these increments.
   (f) Determination of the relationships between the suggested increments.
   (g) Risk analysis.
   (h) Stakeholders network

2. Using the model in no. 1, construct the following table with a separate row of the table for each task in preparing a plan for displaying information for an ATC system.

Task	Entry	Task	Verify	Exit	Measure
Assign_quality_levels					
Resources					
Schedule					
Increment 1					
Increment 2					
Increment 3					
Risk					
Stakeholders					

3. Create a graphical representation of an ETVXM atomic-level process model for the following tasks described in no. 3 for the GUI for an ATC system:
   (a) Assign_quality_levels task (all necessary details).
   (b) Risk analysis task (the atomic process model for this task will probably have many subtasks to be specified in detail).

4. Devise an atomic process model for measuring the risk that the delivery of a web-based program for the GUI for the ATC system will be late. Hint: assume that this model receives an estimate of project duration (from cleanroom planners).

5. Use the Taguchi measure to measure loss arising from lateness (computed in no. 4), and do the following:
   (a) Assume k = 1 and m = 12 weeks (target duration of software project) in the Taguchi loss formula. Produce a lateness loss plot and identify the point in the plot representing the result from no. 2 using your favorite plotting software.
   (b) Produce loss plots for k = 0.1, 0.25, 0.5, 0.75.

6. Define a worldly level model for evaluating project risks limited to lack of support (r5), development time (r7), which are put into a sequence with the task of measuring whether the release of the tATC will be late. You should provide an ETVXM model for each task in the worldly process model, and include the feedback (in and out) for each task as well as an indication of the inputs (work products, data) and outputs for each task.

7. Define an atomic process model for each task in no. 6.

8. Using the results from problems 4, 5, 6, and 7, write a program that automates the process of estimating the risk that the release of the tATC will be late (will take more time than the cleanroom planning team estimated).

9. Do the following:
   (a) Construct a directed graph for all possible state sequences in a usage model for the tATC.
   (b) Assign probabilities to transitions in the graph in part (a).
   (c) Devise test cases relative to usage scenarios revealed by (a) and (b).
   (d) Identify scenarios where the probability is high that a transition leads to failure.

10. Consider a software product that you regularly use, and:
    (a) Construct two usage models for this software,
    (b) Repeat steps 9(a) through 9(d).

11. Devise an atomic ETVXM process model that gives a detailed view of the inputs, outputs, entry, exit, verification, and measurement features in developing software usage models for the graphical user interface for a air traffic control training program. Your model should identify all of the major task sequences leading to an ATC GUI.

12. The task is to manage a software process tailored to the needs of a team that will develop a training program for air traffic controllers. Do the following:
    (a) In planning what must be done to manage the tATC software process, construct the following table:

Capability Maturity Model KPA	Details of How KPA is Tailored to Developing a tATC

    (b) Devise a means of measuring team performance relative to each KPA in part (a).

13. Give:
    (a) Steps in atomic process model to plan the display of weather information for the training program to stimulate air traffic control.
    (b) Examples of prototype weather information displays.
    (c) Method for verifying the results of parts (a) and (b).
    (d) Exit condition for the weather atomic process model.
    (e) Method for measuring the results produced by the weather atomic process model.

14. Give:
    (a) Steps in atomic process model to plan the display of airport information for the training program to simulate air traffic control.
    (b) Examples of prototype airport information displays.
    (c) Method for verifying the results of parts (a) and (b).
    (d) Exit condition for the airport atomic process model.
    (e) Method for measuring the results produced by the airport atomic process model.

15. Give:
    (a) Steps in atomic process model to plan the display of scoring information resulting from an air traffic control training session.
    (b) Examples of prototype scoring information displays.
    (c) Method for verifying the results of parts (a) and (b).
    (d) Exit condition for the scoring atomic process model.
    (e) Method for measuring the results produced by the scoring atomic process model.

16. Give a complete plan for the development of a tATC.

4.7 REFERENCES

Boehm, B., Egyed, A., Kwan, J., et al. Using the WinWin spiral model: A case study. *IEEE Computer,* **31**(7):33–45, 1998.

Cormier, S., Dack, N., Kaikhosrawkiani, F., Orenstein, O. *ATC Trainer Prototype.* Report, Department of Electrical and Computer Engineering, University of Manitoba, November 1997.

Harel, D. Biting the silver bullet: Toward a brighter future for system development. *IEEE Computer,* **25**(1):8–24, 1992.

Humphrey, W.S. *Managing the Software Process.* Addison-Wesley, Reading, MA, 1989.

IEEE Std. 1058.1-1987. IEEE Standard for Software Project Management Plans. In *IEEE Standards Collection Software Engineering,* IEEE, Piscataway, NJ, 1997.

Ip, S., Lao, N., Thang, P., et al. *Simulation of Interacting Aircraft.* Report, Department of Electrical and Computer Engineering, University of Manitoba, 1998.

Peters, J.F., Agatep, R., Cormier, S., et al. Air traffic control trainer software development: Multi-agent architecture and Java prototype. *Proceeding of the IEEE Canadian Conference on Electrical and Computer Engineering,* Waterloo, Ontario, May 1998.

CHAPTER 5
Requirements Engineering

It is impossible to retrofit quality, maintainability, and reliability.
—A.M. Davis, 1993

Aims

- Identify the basic activities of requirements engineering
- Identify approaches to problem analysis
- Survey approaches to constructing software requirements
- Consider the nonbehavioral features of software requirements
- Measure the quality of software requirements

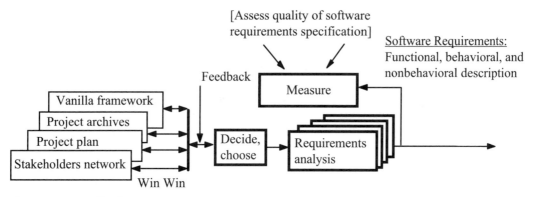

Figure 5.1 Feedback system model of the requirements process.

5.1 INTRODUCTION

In a software process, requirements engineering is the first major activity following the completion of a statement of need resulting from the predevelopment process. Requirements engineering is defined in terms of its major activities: understanding problems (described in a statement of need), solution determination, *and* specification of a solution that is testable, understandable, maintainable, and that satisfies project quality guidelines. The focus of this chapter is on approaches to problem analysis and development of a Software Requirements Specification (SRS) document.

Software Requirement

A software requirement is a description of the principal features of a software product, its information flow, its behavior, its attributes. In sum, a software requirement provides a blueprint for the development of a software product. The degree of understandability, accuracy, and rigor of the description provided by a software requirement document tends to be directly proportional to the degree of quality of the derived product.

The main focus of requirements engineering is on defining and describing *what* a software system should do to satisfy the informal requirements provided by a statement of need. The thinking in requirements analysis is principally in terms of the problem, *not* its solution (Davis, 1993). Requirements analysis is the principal effector process in a feedback system that produces descriptions of the behavioral and nonbehavioral features of software. A universal-level model of the requirements process is shown in Figure. 5.1.

The feedback system model of the requirements process in Figure 5.1 combines the Harel vanilla framework, Boehm Win Win stateholder paradigm, and Humphrey ETVXM architecture. The availability of a completed software development plan and software engineering guide produced by the project planning process triggers requirements analysis. The next step in the requirements process is an assessment of the quality of the requirement specifications. The measurements of the requirements provide feedback to a decider process, which initiate changes in the requirements process to improve its performance and its output. The main results of requirements analysis are as follows:

- *Functional (main actions)*. A functional description identifies system activities.
- *Behavioral (control activities)*. A behavioral description describes the sequencing and possible overlapping of system functions in a hierarchy of control activities. Such activities are likened to a central nervous system, which senses and controls system functions at various levels (Harel, 1992).
- *Nonbehavioral (attributes)*. A nonbehavioral software description of the software includes human engineering and quality assurance planning.

The principal products of a satisfactory requirements process are as follows:

- **Complete Software Requirements Specification** (SRS). A description of a system (its functions, behavior, performance, internal and external interfaces, and its quality attributes).

- **Quality assurance plan.** An indication of the portability, efficiency, reliability, validation and verification criteria, cost, and acceptance criteria to be followed by project teams.

Feedback in the requirements life-cycle stems from prototyping, risk analysis, simulation, modeling, and validation. Requirements specification really is the most challenging part of the software process because it is largely abstract. A requirements engineer lives in a world *before* something is built. Feedback during the requirements life-cycle causes the SRS to evolve into a practical means of designing software. The description of software provided by the SRS provides the basis for the design process in the software life-cycle. Requirement engineering begins with problem analysis.

5.2 PROBLEM ANALYSIS

Problem analysis (also termed requirements analysis) defines the product space of a software process (Davis, 1993). In effect, problem analysis defines the context for possible software solutions to a problem, which has the components shown in Figure 5.2. In other words, problem analysis results in the identification of the environment (people affected by a software product, machines used or affected by the software, services performed, and other items such as traffic flow or communication time), items produced, principal functions performed by people and machines to produce a desired product, methods needed, and scheduling of operations. Three underlying principles of structuring during problem analysis have been identified: partitioning, abstraction, and projection (Yeh & Zave, 1980).

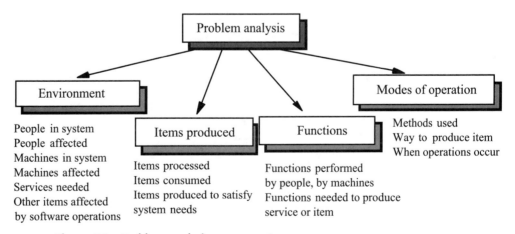

Figure 5.2 Problem analysis components.

- *Partitioning* aggregates the structural relations among objects, functions, and states, and simplifies (compartmentalizes) the structures to be analyzed.
- *Abstraction* identifies the "generic/specific" structural relationships among objects, functions, and states.
- *Projection* provides a "view of" structural relationships among objects, functions, or states. The organizational perspectives of objects, functions, and states are very helpful in developing an understanding of a problem and its solution.

Problem analysis provides a necessary stepping stone leading to development of a software requirements specification. Requirements specification is principally concerned with describing the objects, functions, and states related to a problem.

5.3 SOFTWARE REQUIREMENTS SPECIFICATION

A Software Requirements Specification (SRS) is a description of a particular software product, program or set of programs that performs a set of functions in a target environment (IEEE Std. 830-1993). The SRS emerges from the components of problem analysis. The first drafts of the sections of an SRS will often be written during the decomposition process resulting from problem analysis. During the writing of an SRS, a requirements engineer deals with the five basic issues described in Figure 5.3.

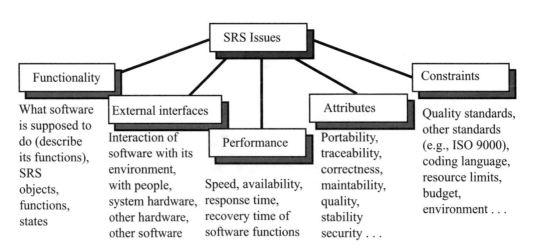

Figure 5.3 Basic issues in writing an SRS.

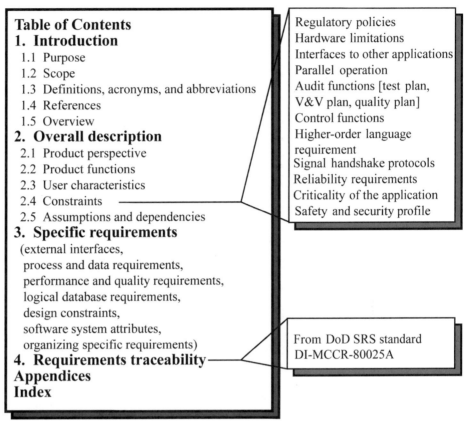

Table of Contents
1. Introduction
  1.1 Purpose
  1.2 Scope
  1.3 Definitions, acronyms, and abbreviations
  1.4 References
  1.5 Overview
2. Overall description
  2.1 Product perspective
  2.2 Product functions
  2.3 User characteristics
  2.4 Constraints
  2.5 Assumptions and dependencies
3. Specific requirements
  (external interfaces,
   process and data requirements,
   performance and quality requirements,
   logical database requirements,
   design constraints,
   software system attributes,
   organizing specific requirements)
4. Requirements traceability
Appendices
Index

Regulatory policies
Hardware limitations
Interfaces to other applications
Parallel operation
Audit functions [test plan,
V&V plan, quality plan]
Control functions
Higher-order language
requirement
Signal handshake protocols
Reliability requirements
Criticality of the application
Safety and security profile

From DoD SRS standard
DI-MCCR-80025A

Figure 5.4 Parts of SRS.

5.3.1 Structure of an SRS

There are many approaches to writing an SRS—see, for example, IEEE, (1993), Dorfman (1997), Dorfman and Thayer (1990), Thayer and Dorfman (1997), DoD (1988). In this section, the description of the parts of the SRS is derived from IEEE Std. 830-1993, with the addition of requirements traceability taken from the U.S. Department of Defense standard [DI-MCCR-80025A]. The structure of the SRS is given in Figure 5.4.

5.3.2 SRS Introduction

The Introduction of an SRS identifies the purpose, scope, definitions, acronyms, abbreviations, references, and overview of the requirements document. The purpose and scope should be linked with the statement of need from the predevelopment process, and will provide refinements derived from problem analysis.

The purpose specifies the intentions and intended audience of the SRS. The scope of the SRS identifies (names) the software products to be produced (e.g., Navigation Manager, Netscape, Object Editor). The capabilities, application, relevant benefits, objectives, and system requirements will also be described in the Scope Section. All terms, acronyms (e.g., OORA), abbreviations (e.g., Std. for Standard), and symbols (e.g., Euler constant $e = 2.718$ or $\exp(x) = e^x$) should be explained so that the SRS can be interpreted. This information can be included in a glossary, symbol table, or appendix, or reference can be made to other documents. The Reference Section of the Introduction provides a complete (possibly annotated) list of all documents referenced in the SRS. Finally, the Overview Section provides a roadmap for the SRS. It describes what the rest of SRS contains, and how the SRS is organized.

5.3.3   Overall Description of the SRS

The Overall Description section of the SRS indicates the general factors influencing the product (outcome of the software process) and its requirements. A summary of the items covered in this part of the SRS is given in Table 5.1. In the case where the software being developed is part of a larger system, the Product Perspective section describes in general terms how the product relates to a larger system. It describes the functionality of and interfaces (system, user, hardware, software, communication) to the larger system, memory constraints,

TABLE 5.1   Parts of Overall Description

Section	Topic	Content
2.1	Product perspective	States if product is self-contained, independent, or if product is part of a larger system
2.2	Product functions	Describes major functions software will perform
2.3	User characteristics	Indicates intended users of product and education level, experience, technical expertise required by users
2.4	Constraints	General description of any items that will limit a developer's options in producing software
2.5	Assumptions, dependencies	Factors (e.g., changes) that can affect the SRS, and assumptions about software
2.6	Apportioning requirements	Identifies requirements that are delayed until future versions of the system

operations, and site adaptation requirements. For example, the software for the motion controller of a mobile robot must interface with the planner (software that constructs models of the environment based on input from various sensors). In that case, the motion controller depends on input from the planner for robot navigation. Product functions should be organized so that they are understandable to the client or anyone else reading the SRS for the first time. Graphical methods can be used to do this. Constraints include regulatory policies, hardware limitations (e.g., product runs only on a Pentium MMX), interfaces to other applications, parallel operation, audit and control functions, high-level language requirements (e.g., C++ must be used), signal handshake protocols (e.g., XON-XOFF), reliability, criticality, and safety and security requirements. Assumptions indicate how changes to the SRS can affect particular SRS sections (e.g., indicating which data flow diagrams are affected by changing existing functions or by adding or deleting functions). Assumptions can also cover risks—costs, legal issues, weakening—if particular requirements are delayed until future versions of the system. Dependencies should also be considered (e.g., product requires Windows 95 or Mac OS).

5.3.4 Specific Requirements

The Specific Requirements section of the SRS provides a description of the observable behavior of a software system. It also includes a description of the nonbehavioral features of the software (performance, design constraints, and software attributes). Observable behavior is described in terms of all inputs into and outputs generated by the specific software functions. The relationships between the inputs and outputs are given. All interfaces between the software and its environment are also specified.

> A *minimum* requirement is that the SRS provide a description of every input (stimulus) into the system, every output (response), and all functions performed by the system either in response to input or in support of an input (IEEE Std 830-1993).

There are a variety of possible technologies that can be used to specify behavioral requirements, which are summarized in Figure 5.5. Here the term *technology* is used in this context to mean the science of practical application of engineering skills. The approaches to specifying software systems are called technologies to emphasize the science (systematic formulated knowledge) that they represent. These approaches have also been characterized as techniques (Davis, 1993). However, the term *technique* emphasizes method (some means of achieving one's purpose skillfully). The translation and application of the acronyms in Figure 5.5 are given in Table 5.2.

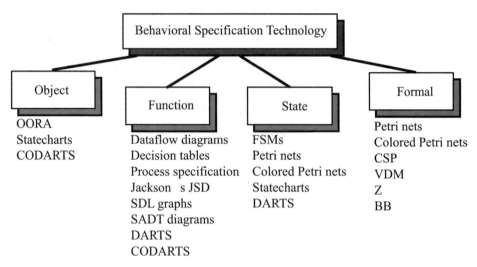

Figure 5.5 Behavioral specification technologies.

TABLE 5.2   Behavior Specification Acronyms

Acronym	Translation	Application
JSD	Jackson System Development	Systems with time dimension
DARTS	Design Approach for Real-Time Systems	State-transition and data flow diagramming real-time systems
CODARTS	COncurrent Design Approach for Real-Time Systems	Large-scale, industrial real-time systems
SDL	Specification Description Language	Communication systems
SADT	Structured Analysis and Design Technique	Control flow in data flow diagrams
FSM	Finite State Machine (found in Statecharts, Petri nets, DARTS, CODARTS, SDL)	Behavior represented with state transition diagrams and state transition tables
CSP	Communicating Sequential Process	Model-oriented specification of concurrent processes
VDM	Vienna Development Method	Model-oriented specification of systems
Z	Z	Combined use of set theory and logic to specify the behavior of a system
BB	Black Box (Cleanroom Engineering Requirements Specification)	Rule-based specification of a software function

5.4 EXAMPLE: VEHICLE NAVIGATION SYSTEM

To begin the process leading to a requirements specification, assume that the problem is to develop a vehicle navigation system. A sketch of a vehicle navigation system similar to one being developed by Toyota (Morita & Mikawa, 1996) is shown in Figure 5.6. The Toyota navigation system is called VICS (Vehicle Information Control System), which supplies real-time (as it happens) information about accidents, traffic jams, and road construction to drivers by means of radio and infrared beacons as well as FM multiplex broadcasting. In the hypothetical navigation system in Figure 5.6, each vehicle is equipped with its own navigation manager (computer, software, interfaces to sensors, and FM multiplexing and infrared beacon receivers as well as a central navigation manager in a Traffic Control Center [TCF]). Expressways are equipped with Radio Beacon Towers (RBTs), FM multiplexing, and Infrared Beacon Towers (IRBTs). The combination of RBTs and FM multiplexing provide selected transmission of traffic flow data at regular intervals (every 5 minutes in the Yokohama system in Japan) to receivers in the broadcast service area. IRBTs are placed at regular intervals on roadways, and perform two-way communication with vehicle terminals. An RBT can perform selected transmission of information on recommended direction of travel with the current location of a vehicle as the origin (beginning coordinate).

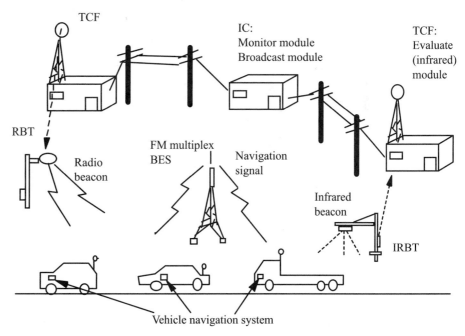

Figure 5.6 Hypothetical vehicle navigation system.

5.4.1   Sample Partitioning and Abstraction

The navigation subsystem in a VICS can be conceptualized in terms of a navigation object, commander function, and commander state (see Figure 5.7). The navigation object is partitioned into four main sub-objects: navigation manager, communication, sensor, and vehicle. Partitioning provides a natural means of organizing views of a problem without making any commitment about particular solutions to the problem. Each of the sub-objects can themselves be partitioned to form a hierachy expressing dependencies among objects. The VICS subobject called navigation manager is decomposed into five subproblems to be analyzed, namely, subfunctions command, plan, scan, change, and actuate. An object can also be decomposed relative to possible states it is in. For example, the vehicle object can assume a number states: navigating, malfunctioning, displaying, correcting, and responding.

5.4.2   Sample Projection

Abstraction identifies instances of objects, functions, and states. Partitioning and abstraction can be combined. For example, instances of a navigation object are automobile, truck, and bus. Similarly, the commanding function can be

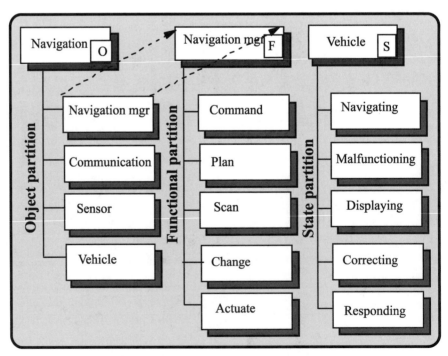

Figure 5.7   Sample Object (O), Function (F), State (s) partitions.

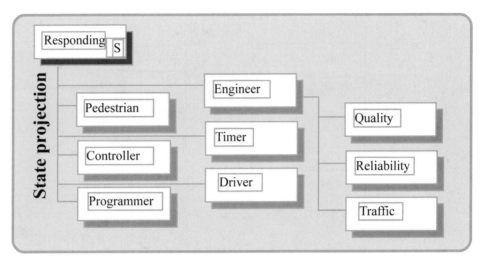

Figure 5.8 Sample state projection.

instantiated in terms of types of command (e.g., emergency, update, location, speed). Projections provide views of (perspectives on) structural relationships among objects, functions, and states. An example of views of the responding state of the commanding process named responding are shown in Figure 5.8. Notice that subprojections are possible. In Figure 5.8, an engineer's view of the responding state in a VICS navigation system has its own projection relative to three engineering perspectives: quality, reliability, and traffic.

5.5 OBJECT-ORIENTED REQUIREMENTS ANALYSIS

The object-oriented approach to specifying a software system is characterized by hierarchies of objects. These hierarchies begin by representing a problem with a context-level object, which can be decomposed into objects representing "explanations" of the problem in terms of subproblems. The basis idea underlying object orientation is an incremental approach to understanding a problem, to hide unnecessary details and make it easier to capture the essential features of a complex system. The standard for requirements specification provided by IEEE includes a template for an OO specification, which is represented as follows.

Object-Oriented Requirements Analysis (OORA) begins by defining objects identified in a partition (Figure 5.9). Five activities are common in an OO approach to problem analysis: specifying objects, attributes, structures, services, and subjects (Booch, 1994; Coad & Yourdon, 1991; Davis, 1993). In the first step

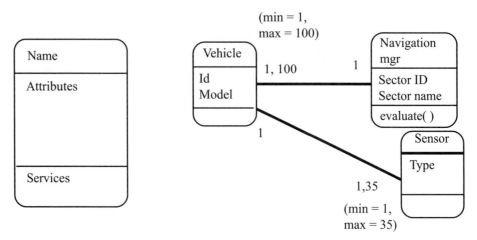

Figure 5.9   Coad object notation.

in OORA, the characteristics of each object in a partition are identified. Names, possible attributes (stores), and services are chosen for each object. Objects are symbolized with rounded-corner rectangles with three horizonal regions: name, attributes list, services list (Coad & Yourdon, 1991). *Attributes* specify storage requirements for all instances of an object (e.g., ID, manufacturer, model, year, capacity for a vehicle object or sector name and sector id for the navigation manager in Figure 5.9). Relationships between objects are specified with what are known as *instance connections* enumerated with either a single integer or a range such as 1, n specifying a minimum = 1, maximum = n. An instance connection specifies the cardinality of a relationship one object has to another. For example, in Figure 5.9, the navigation manager manages between 1 and 100 vehicles, but a vehicle never has more than one navigation manager. Each navigation manager is associated with a sector containing traffic patterns of interest (its attributes sector ID and sector name specify a particular traffic sector). The navigation manager provides an evaluation service. The precise form of this evaluation is still an open question. Each vehicle has a minimum of 1 sensor and a maximum of 35 sensors. A *service* is some operation associated with an object. For instance, the navigation manager object in Figure 5.9 provides an evaluate( ) service (e.g., it evaluates traffic conditions, availability of parking, and so on). Finally, in Object-Oriented Requirements Analysis (OORA), two types of structures are identified: gen-spec and whole-part.

5.5.1   Generic Specification

The notation gen-spec is a shorthand for "generic specification." In the case of a gen-spec structure, a class of objects is identified so that objects that are in-

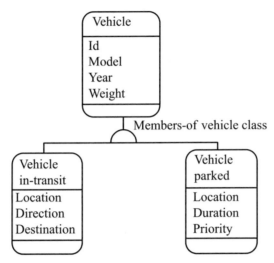

Figure 5.10 Gen-spec diagram.

stances of that class inherit attributes and services provided by members of that class. An example of a gen-spec diagram is given in Figure 5.10. This gen-spec diagram specifies that vehicles that are in-transit or parked both inherit the attributes of the vehicle class: id, model, year, and weight. To capture an organization of objects where some objects are components (part of) of an object, whole-part structures are introduced. Figure 5.11 provides an illustration of a whole-part diagram, where planner, scanner, and changer are parts of the navigation

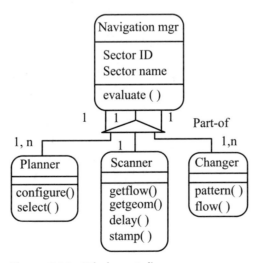

Figure 5.11 Whole-part diagram.

manager. Every navigation manager has between one and many (n) planner and changer objects, and only one scanner object. How the gen-spec or part-whole relationship is realized is not at issue, but rather the focus is on the kind of relationships objects have to each other.

5.5.2 Example: Navigation System OO Analysis

The next OORA stage is to map objects to an object diagram (Figure 5.12). The object diagram for the navigation system in a VICS in Figure 5.13 specifies instance connections for the objects, and a whole-part relationship for the navigation manager, plan, scan, and change objects. The commander and scanner are subobjects of the actuator, which provides the protocol for startup and shutdown of commanding and scanning. The instance connections in Figure 5.13 are summarized in Table 5.3. An instance connection table provides a means of verifying the design for a software system. That is, this type of table can be used to verify that the connections between objects in a design correspond to those specified in the OORA.

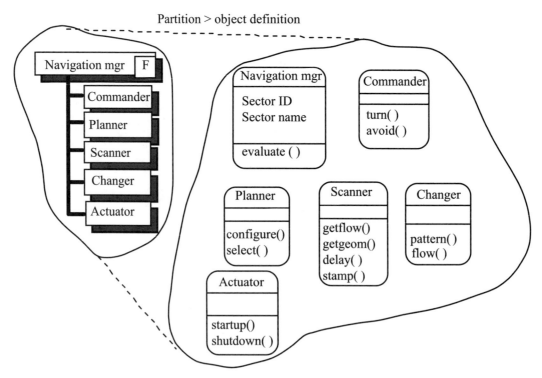

Figure 5.12 Object diagram for navigation system.

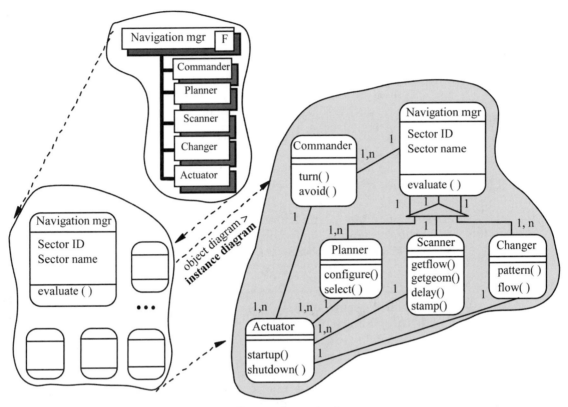

Figure 5.13 Distance diagram for navigation system.

TABLE 5.3 Sample Instance Connections

Object	Connected to	No.	Explanation
Navigation manager	Commander	1, n	1 to n commanders
	Planner	1, n	1 to n planners
	Scanner	1	1 scanner
	Changer	1, n	1 to n changers
Commander	Navigation manager	1	1 navigation manager
	Actuator	1, n	1 to n actuators
Actuator	Commander	1	1 commander
	Planner	1	1 planner
	Scanner	1	1 scanner
	Changer	1	1 changer
Planner	Navigation manager	1	1 navigation manager
	Actuator	1, n	1 to n actuators
Scanner	Navigation manager	1	1 navigation manager
	Actuator	1, n	1 to n actuators
Changer	Navigation manager	1	1 navigation manager
	Actuator	1	1 actuator

5.6 FUNCTION-ORIENTED ANALYSIS

The functional approach to behavioral specification is most commonly represented by the combination of data flow diagrams, data constructs, decision tables, and data dictionaries, which are part of the IEEE Std. 830-1993 for specifying a functional hierarchy. The basics of this approach are given in Section 3.2. The template for organizing a specification using a functional hierarchy is given in Figure 5.14.

5.6.1 Data Flow Diagrams

A combination of what are known as data flow diagrams, data dictionaries, and process descriptions is commonly used in this form of problem analysis (IEEE, 1993). A diagram that specifies the processes (also referred to as bubbles, trans-

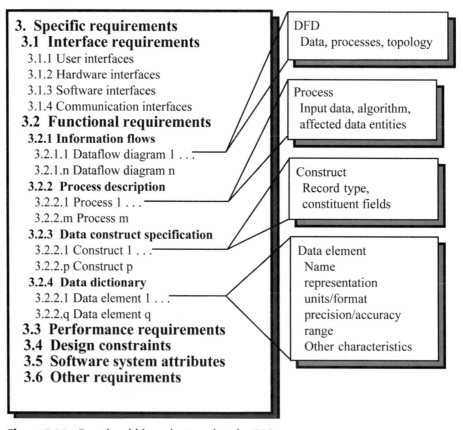

Figure 5.14   Functional hierarchy template for SRS.

TABLE 5.4 DFD Symbols

DFD Symbol	Meaning
(name)	Identifies a transformation (activity) used to process input data and acquire output data
⎯⎯⎯ name ⎯→	Specifies direction of flow of named data
[name]	Identifies a terminator for data (source or destination for data)
⎯⎯⎯⎯ file name ⎯⎯⎯⎯	Identifies a permanent location (file, database, or repository) for data

forms, transactions, activities, operations) and flow of data between them is called a Data Flow Diagram (DFD). A DFD exhibits possible forms of information flow in a system, storage locations for data, and transformations of data as it flows through a system. DFDs provide one of the oldest technologies for problem analysis introduced by DeMarco (1978) as well as by Gane and Sarson (1979). DFDs are easy to use, and very helpful in bridging the gap between the informal descriptions of a system in a statement of need and the development of descriptions of how information flows though a system. The notation for DFDs is summarized in Table 5.4. Bubbles (circles with names) symbolize transformations. Names should be unique. An arrow specifies the direction of data flow. Arrow labels identifies data. Arrows represent a path for flowing data, but do not specify an ordering of events. Rectangles (also called terminators) indicates sources and destinations of data. Finally, parallel lines indicate files, databases, permanent stores for data. The underlying philosophy in constructing DFDs is to discover necessary flows of data between activities associated with objects in a partition. The highest, most abstract level of a DFD consists of one bubble, and is called the *context level*.

Initially, a DFD is usually high-level (omitting all but essential details) consisting of a single bubble. The context-level DFD is then decomposed into a child-DFD. This technique is called leveling. In that case, the context-level DFD is called a parent-DFD. A level 1 DFD decomposition for a traffic scanner is shown in Figure 5.15. The DFD is the beginning of a diagram that models the data flow resulting from the services provided by the scan function (get_flow, get_geom). The get_flow operation uses beacon flow data to determine traffic speed, while get_geom uses the same data to determine the spacing between vehicles that have recently traveled beneath the infrared beacon. The child-DFD clarifies the mechanisms and data needed to achieve a better understanding of the scanning process. The decomposition can be repeated for bubbles inside the child-DFD until dataflow for a software process is understood. In addition, it is helpful to develop a child-DFD incrementally, adding functionally as needed

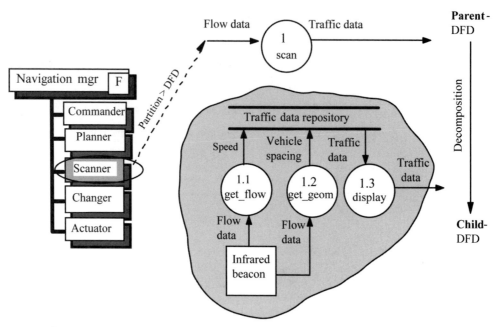

Figure 5.15 Level 1 decomposition of scanner.

to complete the description of a process. For example, notice that the get-geom operation can be decomposed into get_delay and get_stamp operations. This decomposition is shown in Figure 5.16. The get_stamp operation adds a time-stamp to each flow data sample. Instead of continuous sampling of infrared beacon waves, the delay function introduces periodic sampling of traffic data. During the decomposition process, consistency between levels must be maintained. This means that all net flows into and out of a higher level process must match the net inflows and outflows of lower level processes.

5.6.2 Data Dictionaries

A data dictionary stores information about data items found in a DFD (Davis, 1993). A summary of typical information used to construct a data dictionary is given in Table 5.5. A data dictionary supplies information such as data typing, required accuracy of data useful to designers and implementers. *Name, alias, type,* and *description* indicate how to identify, possible other names, type of data, and what and how the data are used, respectively. *Duration, accuracy,* and *range of values* specify life span, required precision in measurements, and all possible values of data items, respectively. *Data flows* specify processes that generate or receive the data. This provides another useful tool in validating a design (making sure that the requirements for a data item are satisfied by a design, and by code).

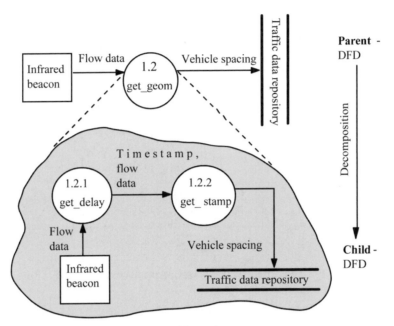

Figure 5.16 Level 2 decomposition of get_geom.

In the case where data are derived from a real-time system, data items can have timing constraints specifying the length of time before the data become out-of-date. For example, traffic flow changes continuously, depending on conditions. So traffic flow data indicating current and near-time flows need to refreshed, replacing old with new data. A sample data dictionary for traffic data in a VICS is given in Table 5.6. A data dictionary can be used to check the completeness and consistency of DFDs. Whenever all bubbles, arrows, and databases (reposi-

TABLE 5.5 Data Dictionary Features

Information Stored	Explanation
Name	Identifies data item
Alias	Identifies other names, abbreviations used to identify a data item
Data structure (type)	Type of data (e.g., integer, char)
Description	Indicates how (why) a data item is used
Duration (begins)	Life span of data (when created)
Accuracy	High, medium, low accuracy
Range of values	Allowable values of data item
Data flows	Identifies process that generate/receive data

TABLE 5.6 Sample Data Dictionary

Name	Type	About	Range	Accuracy	Data Flows
Speed	Real	Average vehicle speed	$0 \leq speed \leq 60$ mph	±0.01	get_flow
Vehicle spacing	Real	Average vehicle spacing	$0 \leq space \leq 1000$ ft	±0.01	get_geom
Flow data location	String	Traffic location	$10 \leq location \leq 30$	Not specified	get_flow get_geom
Flow data volume	Integer	Current traffic volume	$0 \leq volume \leq 4000$ per hr	Not specified	get_flow get_geom
Time stamp	String	Date and time	20 characters	Y2K certified	get_timestamp

tory) have labels and all arrows have sources and destinations, a DFD is considered complete.

5.7 PROCESS SPECIFICATION

A process description can be written in natural language, and have a "comfortable" pseudocode form that is understandable to designers. An approach to process description using natural language is given by Gane and Sarson (1979), and is part of the discussion of Structured Analysis and System Specification (SASS) in Davis (1993). In a DFD, inputs, necessary data, and action(s) are expressed as a single procedure represented by a circle with input and output connections. Another approach to process description is given by Jackson (1983). Jackson uses a process text (a form of pseudocode with Pascal-like keywords and control structures) to describe the affect of action(s) on either the state of a model or on possible system outputs. Because of its conciseness, the form of pseudocode used in this section borrows syntax from C++ to specify control structures in an informal description of a process. For example, the "then" token in a conditional control structure found in Gane and Sarson as well as in Jackson has been dropped. Semicolons separate constructs and the brackets {and} are used to specify the beginning and end of a sequence, respectively. Since a process description is not intended to be a computer program (or even to represent one), words like "input," "retrieve," "for each," "repeat," and "until" are used in an informal way to convey an understanding and description of how input data are transformed by particular actions. The purpose of a process description is to describe procedures (processes represented by dataflow diagrams. A sample process description for a scan operation for a traffic navigation system is given in Figure 5.17.

Scan Process Description

input: m   // measurement based on radiation detected by infrared sensor
 repeat
   periodically estimate speed of traffic based on m;   // get_flow operation
   periodically estimate spacing between vehicles based on m;   // get_geom operation
   save speed, spacing estimates;
 forever
end scan operation

Figure 5.17   Sample process description.

5.8 JACKSON SYSTEM DEVELOPMENT METHOD

The Jackson System Development (JSD) method originated in the mid-1970s (Jackson, 1975) and was refined in 1983 (Jackson, 1983), and is used to model the behavior of real-world entities over time. The JSD uses the following procedure:

- *Action step.* Identify system entities and tasks (actions) symbolized with labeled boxes.
- *Entity structure step.* Order tasks by time.
- *Model step.* Construct entity-relationship diagram (lines connecting boxes).
- *Function step.* Specify functions in text form.
- *Timing step.* Schedule function outputs.
- *Implementation step.* Determine hardware, software needed to implement system.

An example of a JSD diagram for the scanning task in a navigation system for vehicles is given in Figure 5.18. Actions to be selected are specified with boxes inscribed with circles. The scan operation selects either the timer or the forward operation. Repeated actions are specified with boxes inscribed with asterisks. In Figure 5.18, scan, get_flow, and get_geom are iterated.

In JSD, a function specification resembles Pascal procedures with a heading, variable declaration, and procedure body. JSD has a token for selection (**sel**), conditional selection (**alt**), unconditional iteration (**itr**), conditional iteration (**while**), and termination (**end**). Tokens are written in boldface. JSD notation is summarized in Figure 5.19.

Let BEGIN, STGM be variables storing beginning time and starting time grain marker (e.g., millisecond time grain), respectively. The specification of a timer is given in Figure 5.20.

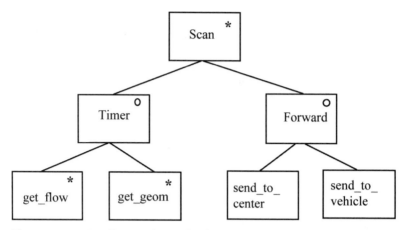

Figure 5.18   JSD diagram for navigation system.

Task Structure	Single Command	Command Sequence	CASE Construct	Unconditional Iteration	Conditional Iteration	If Command
P <cmd> <I/O cmds> PBODY <cmd> <cmds> P **end**	Task x;	A **seq** task x; task y; A **end**	A **sel** (cond B) task x; A **alt** (cond C) task y; A **end**	A **itr** task x; A **end**	A **itr while** (cond B) task x; A **end**	A **alt** (cond B) task x; A **end**

Figure 5.19   JSD syntax.

```
TIMER itr
 read BEGIN & STGM;
 count := 0;
 TIMER-BODY itr while (count > 0)
  count := count - 1;
 TIMER-BODY end
TIMER end
```

Figure 5.20   JSD function specification for timer.

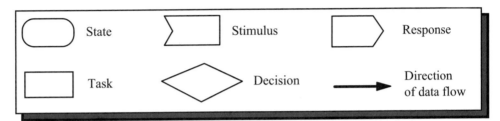

Figure 5.21   SDL graph symbols.

5.9 SDL

The Specification and Description Language (SDL) method is used to specify concurrent, real-time systems (Rockstrom & Saracco, 1982). In software engineering, SDL is widely accepted for use in developing protocol software for the telecommunication industry. An SDL symbols chart is given in Figure 5.21. Let ICC stand for Information Control Center for a vehicle navigation system. Assume that the navigation system software has a communication module used to monitor incoming traffic data from traffic scanners. Incoming traffic data are analyzed to determine if traffic conditions are normal or require correction of detected problems (collision, highway obstruction, and so forth). Under normal driving conditions, vehicles are instructed to continue. In case of a detected problem, the ICC is asked to initiate recovery procedures. An SDL specification of a simple protocol for the communication module is given in Figure 5.22.

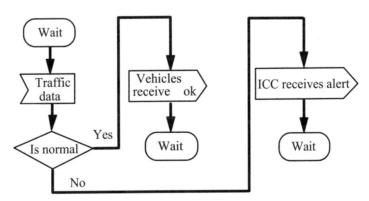

Figure 5.22   Sample SDL protocol for vehicle communication.

5.10 SADT

The Structured Analysis and Design Technique (SADT) provides a graphical description language, which resulted from the inclusion of control flows in data flow diagrams (Marca & McGowan, 1988). The basic approach to understanding a software task in SADT is top-down. To develop an understanding of a system, begin at the top (context level). Then evolve a detailed understanding of a problem by repeated decompositions unfolding from the context level description of a system.

SADT diagrams consist of boxes interconnected by arrows. Boxes are named with action words (e.g., scan, locate, send) representing functions. Arrows represent control data flow (Figure 5.23a). Arrows entering a box on the left provide input, and arrows representing output exit only on the right side of a box. Arrows entering the top of a box specify constraints on the processing performed by a function. Arrows entering the bottom of a box specify how a function is to be performed (resources needed). A single box specifies the context level of a process (the most abstract level), and is labeled with a zero. Context-level boxes can be successively decomposed. The numbers in the right-hand corners of boxes represent dominance levels, zero being the most dominant. A sample SADT diagram relative to requirements analysis is given in Figure 5.23b. The analyze function in Figure 5.23b must ignore the cost of a requirements document, and it must apply the specified quality measures in evaluating a requirement. The resources needed to perform the recover operation specified in Figure 5.23b are indicated with the labels on the arrows entering the bottom of the box.

The recovery process in a traffic navigation system must be performed by an ICC emergency response team using two Silicon Graphics workstations. A sample SADT diagram for the context-level description of traffic navigation recovery process is given in Figure 5.24a. A sample decomposition of the context level for the recovery process is shown in Figure 5.24b. A hierarchy of three tasks in Figure 5.24b is employed as part of a recovery process whenever a traffic problem occurs. The initiate change task is governed by condition C1 (system

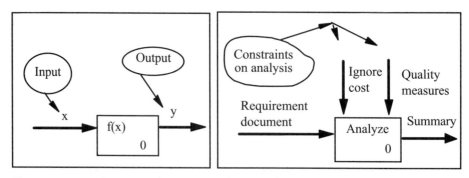

Figure 5.23   A. SADT notation. **B.** Sample SADT diagram.

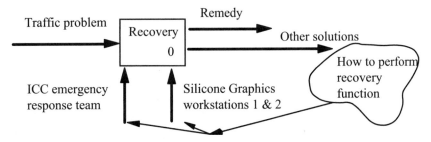

Figure 5.24   A. Sample SADT diagram for traffic navigation system.

goals). Task 2 (determine possible solutions) becomes active whenever it receives a change request. Task 2 requires input about alternate routes and traffic flow (received from hidden sources), and is governed by condition C2 (system rules) as well as the request from task 1 in selecting a solution to the traffic problem. Finally, task 3 (administer new traffic configuration) is constrained by the solution from task 2 and rules governing command sequences. Task 3 also requires two inputs to carry out its work, namely, locations of vehicles affected by change, and status of vehicles affected by change.

Notice that the high-level tasks in Figure 5.24b can also be decomposed. The decomposition is continued until the recovery process is understood. SADT is commonly used in modeling processes in computer integrated manufacturing and military applications. Another application of SADT in modeling reusable software engineering was given by Neighbors (1980).

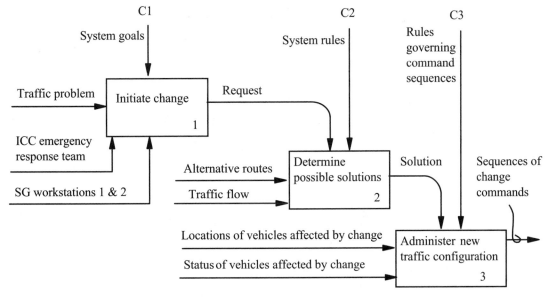

Figure 5.24   B. SADT diagram decomposition for recovery process.

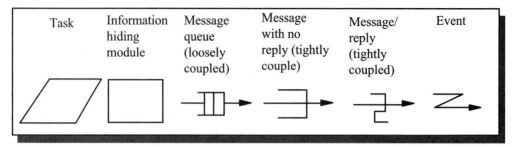

Figure 5.25   DARTS diagram notation.

5.11   DARTS

The Design Approach for Real-Time Systems (DARTS) was introduced by Gomaa (1984). A *real-time system* consists of one or more time-critical tasks, and the enforcement of real-time scheduling of tasks. A time-critical task is a task that must meet a hard (enforced) deadline. The DARTS method decomposes a context-level task into concurrent tasks and defining interfaces between the tasks. DARTS diagram notation is summarized in Figure 5.25.

A message is *loosely coupled* whenever a server sends a message to a client process and the server does need a reply or has other functions to perform after the message is sent. A message is *tighly coupled* if a server sends a message to a client and immediately waits for a response. Examples of the two types of message sending processes are given in Figure 5.26.

An information hiding module is used to encapsulate (hide the contents and internal representation) of data. There are three types of events:

- *External.* Stimulus from external source (usually an interrupt).
- *Internal.* Internal synchronization between source and destination task.
- *Timer.* Periodic activation of a task (activation in regular time intervals).

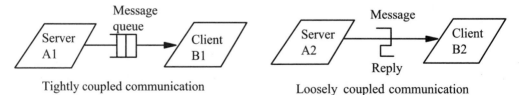

Figure 5.26   Communicating processes.

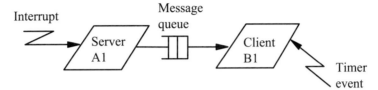

Figure 5.27 DARTS diagram with event-driven tasks.

Sample external and timer events are shown in Figure 5.27. In the process specified in the DARTS diagram in Figure 5.27, each time an interrupt occurs, server A1 sends a message to client B1. Periodically, client B1 processes one of the messages sent by server A1. A DARTS specification for a timer-driven communication protocol for a vehicle navigation system is given in Figure 5.28.

In Figure 5.28, the evaluate data task is activitated periodically to monitor traffic flow data. This task adds a message queue for a sender task that supervises normal traffic conditions, if the traffic flow is normal. In the case where a traffic flow problem is detected by the data evaluation task, a message is sent to the sender task that initiates a recovery procedure. In both cases, the evaluation task does not wait for a reply, since it must be ready to evaluate new traffic conditions the next time it is activated by a hidden timer. The send "ok" task sends a message to affected vehicles and does not wait for a reply. By contrast, the send "alert" task waits for a reply after it sends a message to the recovery task (in some ICC handling traffic problems). The protocol in this DARTS diagram contains several refinements of the communication protocol specified in SDL in Figure 5.22. Communication is now periodic (governed by a timer process) and three types of message sending are specified. These refinements provide very precise information about required synchronization between processes.

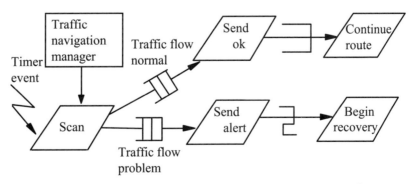

Figure 5.28 DARTS diagram for a vehicle communication protocol.

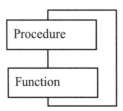

Figure 5.29   Notation for information-hiding module.

5.12 CODARTS

The Concurrent Design Approach for Real-Time Systems (CODARTS) is a refinement of DARTS and an Ada-based form of DARTS named ADARTS (Gomaa, 1993). In CODARTS, a distinction is made between information-hiding modules and tasks. The notation for an information-hiding module is given in Figure 5.29. This gives CODARTS an object orientation, and gives CODARTS a provision for specifying parts of a software system that can be shared, reused, and adapted. Instead of modifying an entire software module, the code in an information-hiding module can be modified to adapt software for a new purpose. These modules also represent code that can be shared between tasks.

For example, in a navigation system for controlling vehicular traffic flow, a variety of tasks can share code to compute desired vehicle speed, as shown in Figure 5.30. The scan and change tasks in Figure 5.30 share the same hidden information module. Periodically, the navigation manager sends a message to the scan task to capture current traffic flow conditions (scan does by executing the get_flow procedure). Also periodically, the on-board vehicle navigation system checks for change speed messages sent by the change task. Each time the change task selects a new vehicle speed, this task also performs a housekeeping operation and clears buffers being used by the hidden module to store traffic flow data.

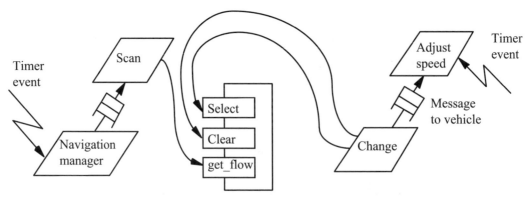

Figure 5.30   CODARTS diagram for vehicle navigation manager.

5.13 STATE-ORIENTED APPROACH TO BEHAVIORAL SPECIFICATION

In a state-oriented approach to specifying the observable behavior of software, an entity is modeled as a state machine. The behavior of an entity is described in terms of the passage of the entity through different states. The state of a software system is defined in terms of the value of the available information about the system at a particular instant in time. State-oriented specifications include variables that change value each time a state change occurs. A classical approach to this form of specification is the finite-state machine.

5.13.1   Finite State Machines

At its lowest level, observable behavior of a system can be described with Finite-State Machines (FSMs), which are special cases of automata (abstract machines) introduced by Alan Turing in 1936 and used by McCulloch and Pitts (1943) to model neurological activity of the brain as neural nets. A state of a system is an internal configuration of the system. The state of a system can be determined by checking the value of one or more state variables. For example, a system might have state variables $q1$, $q2$, $q3$, $q4$ with values from the set {waiting, reading, writing, searching}. A possible state sequence for this hypothetical system might be:

$$\text{waiting} \rightarrow \text{reading} \rightarrow \text{searching} \rightarrow \text{writing} \rightarrow \text{waiting}$$
$$(\text{state q1}) \quad (\text{q2}) \qquad (\text{q3}) \qquad (\text{q4}) \qquad (\text{q1})$$

The arrow symbol specifies a transition from one state to another. In other words, at some instant in time, the system is waiting (to be activated) in state $q1$. When this imaginary system changes to state $q2$ because of some stimulus, its response is to begin reading (data from some store). In the next state, it is searching (presumably through the data it has read), and so on until it returns to $q1$, its waiting state. A finite-state machine M is defined by a five-tuple (Q, F, q_0, S, δ) where

- Q is a finite set of states {q0, q1, q2, . . . , qn}
- F is a subset of final (accepting) states of Q
- q_0 is a single start state in Q
- Σ is an input/output alphabet (all allowable input readable or produceable by M)
- δ: Q $\times$ S $\rightarrow$ Q maps the current input and current state into the next state

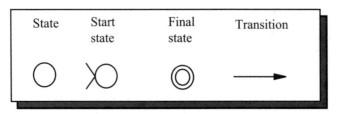

Figure 5.31   Notation FSM diagrams.

Input to an FSM is in the form of strings. For example, let the alphabet for an FSM M1 consist of {a}. Then acceptable input to M1 is always of the form a, aa, aaa, and so on. An example of an unacceptable input string is aaaab, since b is not in the alphabet of M1. An FSM enters a final (accepting) state if it accepts an input. An FSM can be in only one state at any given instant in time. A start state can also be a final state. State machines are represented graphically by state diagrams with the notation shown in Figure 5.31. Each is labeled to indicate an input (stimulus). In the simplest form of FSM, a machine responds to a stimulus by changing state, and nothing else.

Examples of finite state machines are given in Figure 5.32. Machine (a) in Figure 5.32 accepts input with any number of a's. Machine (b) accepts either input containing a single b or strings of the form a, aa, aaa, and so on. This machine cannot respond to more than one stimulus at a time. It either makes a transition from state q1 to state q2 in response to input 'a' or it makes a transition from state q1 to state q3 in response to a stimulus 'b'. Machine (c) can accept input beginning with an even number (0, 2, 4, . . .) of b's followed by 1 or more a's. Let ø represent a non-accepting state of an FSM. Notice that the string ba causes machine (c) make a transition to state q3 and then to reject the input letter a (to enter rejection state ø). Finally, machine (d) accepts any input beginning with 1 b followed by a, or ba followed by ba, and so on. The

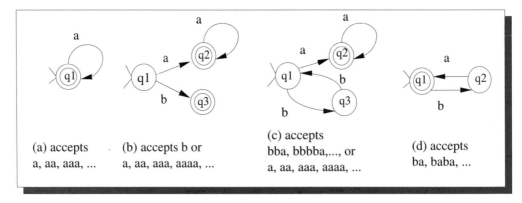

Figure 5.32   Sample finite-state machines.

Input State	a	b
q1	q2	q3
q2	q2	ø
q3	ø	ø

Figure 5.33   State table.

behaviors of FSMs can be represented in table form. For example, a complete representation of the behavior of machine (b) is given in Figure 5.33.

5.13.2 Petri Nets

A Petri net is a form of finite state machine useful in modeling concurrency and asynchronous communication, and was introduced by Karl Petri in 1962. Petri nets are used to describe and analyze the structure and information flow in systems. A Petri net consists of a set of places P, set of transitions T, an input function I, and output function O. Places represent storage for input or for output. Transitions represent activities (transformations) that transform input into output. An input mapping I maps a transition to its input places. An output mapping O maps a transitions to its output places. Petri nets have graphical representation using the notation given in Figure 5.34. Whenever the activity represented by a transition t occurs, this activity is hidden from view. Whenever a transition completes the transformation of its inputs, an event occurs. The transition is said to fire, and its output is deposited in its output places. A token represents a piece of information either to be processed by one or more transitions or information resulting from the firing of one or more transitions. The placement of tokens in a Petri net is called a marking. Petri nets are governed by transition firing rules:

- A transition is enabled if each of its input places has the required number of tokens, one for each arc leading from a place to a transition.
- A transition can only fire if it is enabled.
- Whenever a transition t fires, each of the tokens that enabled t is removed, and transition t places one or more tokens in each of its output places, one for each arc leading from t to an output place.

The significance of the first firing rule is that more than one transition can be enabled at the same time (concurrent processing is possible). An example of concurrency is shown in Figure 5.35. In the second configuration (after transition t1 fires), transitions t2 and t3 are both enabled (the activities represented by these transitions overlap in time). The behaviors represented by the changing

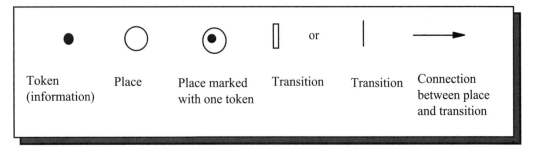

Figure 5.34   Notation for Petri net graphs.

Petri net in Figure 5.35 result from successive firings of transitions which can be explained by writing out some of the applications of the input I and output O mappings:

- Configuration (a): I(t1) = {p1}, with t1 enabled
- Configuration (b): O(t1) = {p2, p3}, I(t2) = {p2}, I(t3) = {p3}, t2 and t3 enabled
- Configuration (c): O(t2) = O(t3) = {p4}

5.13.3   Colored Petri Nets

Colored Petri nets were introduced by Jensen in 1988 to model computation as well as data flows (Jensen, 1996). A colored Petri net (CPN) provides data typing (color sets) and values for tokens, replaces weights with token names, and provides guards (enabling conditions) on transitions. A guard is a boolean expression on a transition t which must be satisfied before t can fire. A sample CPN is given in Figure 5.36, where place p_1 supplies input x of type real to

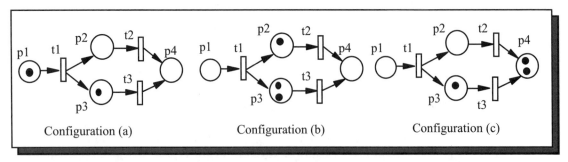

Figure 5.35   Changed Petri net configuration.

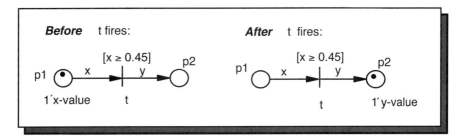

Figure 5.36 Colored Petri net.

transition t, which outputs y to place p_2 whenever the token x in place p_1 satisfies the guard [$x \geq 0.45$]. The notation $1'$x-value specifies what is known as a multiset (also called a bag). The prefix 1 indicates the number of tokens in the multiset (in this case, one token in place p_1), and the suffix indicates that x has been assigned an x-value. Whenever transition t fires, it assigns a value to y (specified by $1'$y-value), which is the name of the token in place p_2.

To simplify Petri net models of complex, large-scale systems, hierarchical Petri Nets (hPNs) were introduced (Huber et al., 1986). In general, an hPN is a CPN with one or more transitions representing subnets (complete processing units) which are Petri nets (Figure 5.37). A Petri net with a single hierarchical transition models the context level of a process. For example, the context level for a manufacturing system robot is shown in Figure 5.38. This Petri net comes from Peters and Baumela (1996). The robot transition in Figure 5.38 monitors the quality of parts moving past it on a conveyer belt, and discards substandard parts. A part is represented by a tuple (size, weight). Place p1 in Figure 5.38 represents the production lane where a sample of three parts is ready to be transported. These parts weigh 1.5, 1.7, and 1.1 gm and have size of 7.0, 7.5, and 5.5 cm, respectively. Places p10 and p11 model a consumption lane and discard bin for unacceptable parts.

The action performed by the classifier robot is modeled by the hierarchical transition labeled Robot, which decomposes to the subnet shown in Figure 5.39. Notice the Goodness transition in Figure 5.39 can also be decomposed into a subnet. The decomposition continues until the problem is understood, and

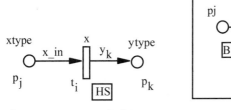

Figure 5.37 Sample hPN.

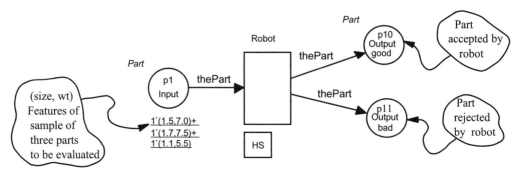

Figure 5.38   Petri net model for a robot.

provides a complete definition of the software for designers. Hierarchical Petri nets simplify the specification of complex systems and lead to object orientation. The robot Petri net in Figure 5.38 and each of its transitions have been modeled with the Design/CPN (Peters & Baumela, 1996). Design/CPN is an industrial-strength toolset for modeling and simulating system behavior. This toolset can be obtained from the web site (Jensen, 1996).

5.13.4 Statecharts

Statecharts were developed by David Harel in 1983 as a visual formalism for describing "raw reactive behavior" (Harel, 1987a, 1987b, 1988; Harel & Grey, 1997; Harel & Naamad, 1996). Statecharts are an extension of finite-state machines to include decomposition and to model the concurrent operation of real-

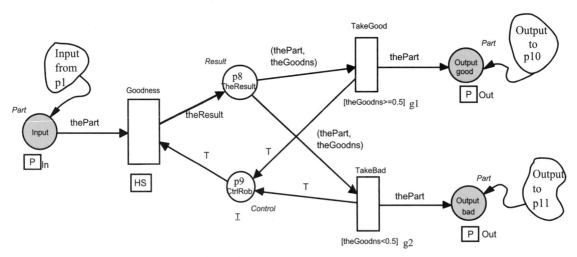

Figure 5.39   Robot subnet.

time systems. A statechart amalgamates a variety of technologies represented by the following formula:

state diagrams + depth + orthogonality + broadcast communication = state-chart

A statechart provides a diagrammatic layout for a software process and makes it possible to model scenarios, Glinz (1995). The notation for a statechart diagram is summarized in Figure 5.40. Boxes with round corners represent states. Arrows represent transitions, and arrow labels specify a triggering action that causes a state transition. States can be decomposed. The result of a decomposition (a statechart within a state) is called a superstate. The process of decomposing a state into subordinate states is called an *or* decomposition. A decomposition of a state leading to concurrent statecharts is called an *and* decomposition. Concurrent statecharts are said to be *orthogonal* to each other to call attention to the independence of the state machines inside the superstate. This feature of statecharts is extremely powerful, since it permits object orientation as well as modeling of concurrent processing inside independent machines. It is this independence that makes statecharts more advanced than hierarchical Petri nets. Although hierarchical Petri nets have a form of object orientation (information-hiding modules), the decomposition of hierarchical transitions may lead to a subnet with concurrent transitions that are themselves hierarchical. However, such a decomposition does not lead to subnets representing independent processes. To preserve this independence, state transitions between orthogonal machines is not allowed. Concurrent machines exchange information using events. An event is initiated whenever there is a change in a condition associated with an event. States are connected by arcs annotated with labels of the form shown in Figure 5.41.

Statecharts permits broadcast communication. This means that all events and the values of any data items can be referenced anywhere in a system (Day, 1993). An example of an and-decomposition of a statechart for a traffic light control system is shown in Figure 5.42. Part (a) of Figure 5.42 contains a high-level statechart for a traffic light controller. The box labeled waiting represents

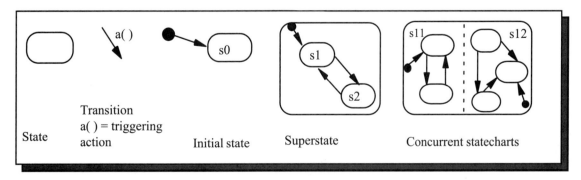

Figure 5.40 Statechart diagram notation.

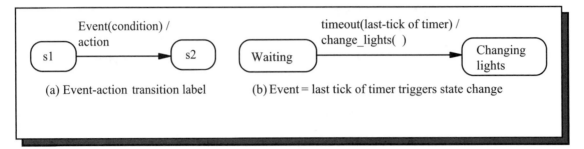

Figure 5.41   Event (condition)/action labeling of transition.

the state of a timer, and is the initial state of the control system. A change( ) action is triggered by the event timeout( ), which causes the system to enter its changing-lights state. The light-change( ) event triggers a clock( ) action causing a transition to the waiting state (the timer begins ticking again until a timeout occurs to delay a light-change). Both waiting and changing lights states can be decomposed. An and-decomposition of changing lights into two independent-state machines (E-W and N-S) is shown in Figure 5.42. The N-S and E-W state machines function concurrently. The N-S statechart, for example, manages the lights regulating traffic in the north-south direction. The initial state of the N-S is red (to allow time to clear the intersection). A similar operation is modeled by the E-W statechart. Statecharts have been implemented with STATEMATE Magnum and Rhapsody. These are COTS products from Ilogix that make it possible to specify a system from three points of view:

- *Functional view.* Data flow diagrams.
- *Behavioral view.* Statecharts.
- *Structural view.* Designs of systems and all environmental components.

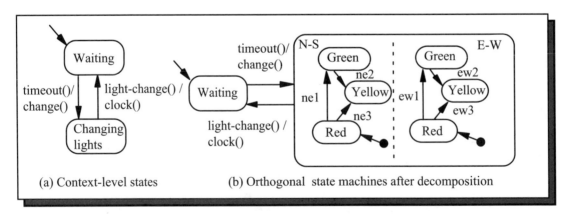

Figure 5.42   And-decomposition of traffic light controller.

STATEMATE makes it possible to simulate the capabilities of a system, since it permits stimulations during simulation, Harel (1990). As a result, the behavior of a system can be tracked in "real-time." In addition, STATEMATE/C and STATEMATE/Ada provide graphical system design capture using the STATE-MATE language, static and dynamic analysis of a system model, user interface mockup and prototyping as well as code generation capabilities for either C- or Ada-based systems (see *http://www.ilogix.com*).

5.14 FORMAL METHODS APPROACH TO SPECIFICATION

A proof represents a logical process which has come to a definite conclusion in a finite number of stages.
—N. WIENER, 1948

The formal methods approach to specifying software requirements is characterized by mathematical descriptions of behavior. A *formal method* consists of a set of techniques and notations that can be expressed mathematically and that are supported mechanically. The motivation for using formal methods is to achieve a rigorous basis for software development, one characterized by reasoning that results from the application of rules of mathematics. A significant benefit of the formal methods approach to specifying software is that it makes it easier to write proofs of conditions that software must satisfy. This approach works well in developing safety-critical systems where system failures can result in the loss of lives or property or environmental catastrophes. Underlying current vigorous and widespread use of formal methods in software development is the need to satisfy ISO 9000 quality certification of software products (ISO, 1991).

5.14.1 Petri Net Properties

Perhaps the earliest example of the formal methods approach comes from Petri nets, which make it possible to describe hardware as well as software structures in terms of input/output mappings and to analyze the operational behavior of a system. Petri nets can be analyzed in terms of liveness, safety, boundedness, and reachability properties. The liveness of a transition is a measure of the number of times the transition can fire. Deadlock is possible if one or more transitions in a Petri net never fire. How a system is initialized is crucial. For example, given the initial markings shown in Figure 5.43, transition t1 either fires infinitely often in net (a) or it never fires (deadlock occurs) in net (b).

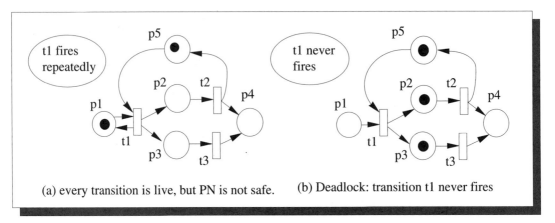

(a) every transition is live, but PN is not safe.   (b) Deadlock: transition t1 never fires

Figure 5.43   Deadlock example.

A Petri net is considered safe if the number of tokens in any place at any given time is never greater than one. The net in part (a) in Figure 5.43 is not safe, but the one in part (b) is safe. Each time transitions t2 and t3 fire in part (a), a token is added to place p4, which will eventually have an infinite number of tokens. If place p4 models a buffer or bin for tokens, buffer overflow will occur. The safety property is a special case of the more general boundedness property of places in a Petri net. In the case where the number of tokens in a place has some upper bound k, the place is k-bounded. In the net in Figure 5.43 (a), each time transitions t2 and t3 fire concurrently, places p1, p2 and p5 are 1-bounded, but place p4 is unbounded. By contrast, place p1 is 0-bounded, and place p4 is 2-bounded in (b) in the case where transitions t2 and t3 fire just once and each transition contributes a token to place p4.

The reachability property of Petri nets is defined in terms of the set of possible of markings that can be reached from an initial markings. A reachability tree is a graph that describes sequences of markings resulting from the firing of transitions after an initial marking. The reachability tree for the net in Figure 5.43(a) is shown in Figure 5.44. This tree represents all possible sequences of firings of transitions. The firing sequence t1, t3 or t1, t2, t1, t3 and so on always has t3 as a leaf node, whereas the firing sequence t1, t2, t1, t2, t1, t2, . . . continues forever with *no* leaf node. A complete study of properties of classical Petri nets can be found in Peterson (1981) as well as in Murata (1989). Reachability analysis of colored Petri nets is presented by Jensen (1996), and has been automated with Design/CPN. Petri net tools have been combined with SADT information modeling in Hilt and others (1994).

5.14.2   Vienna Development Method

The Vienna Development Method originated in the IBM Vienna Laboratory in response to the need for precise specifications of industrial-based systems

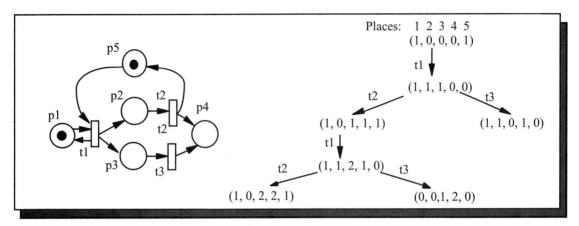

Figure 5.44   Sample reachability tree.

(Bjorner & Jones, 1978; Jones, 1989). A VDM specification employs mathematical notation to achieve precision and brevity. A template for a VDM specification is shown in Figure 5.45. The heading for the specification of a function consists of a name followed by a signature (domain → range for function). The principal goal of VDM is to write specifications that lead to what are known as proof obligations. A *proof obligation* is a condition that must be satisfied for specified states of a system. Proof obligations are written in terms of preconditions and postconditions for a system component. A *precondition* is an assumption about arguments for a function or procedure. A *postcondition* is a requirement about the results computed for the values of arguments described in a precondition. In effect, preconditions and postconditions are boolean-valued functions. For a given proof obligation, it is necessary to show that for all arguments of the type

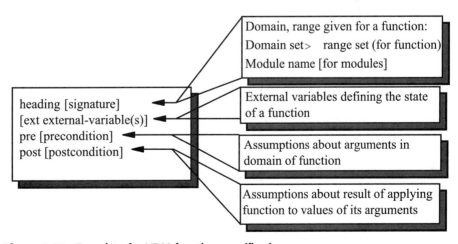

Figure 5.45   Template for VDM function specification.

specified by the precondition, the results produced by a function satisfy the constraints expressed in the postcondition. Let Tp, Tr be the type of an argument in a precondition and the type of the result expressed in the postcondition, respectively. Let pre-f, post-f, Proof-f stand for precondition, postcondition, and proof obligation. Then precondition and postconditions as well as proof obligation can be written as boolean-valued functions with names and signatures as follows:

- pre-f: Tp → bool [precondition truth valued function]
- post-f: Tp × Tr → bool [postcondition truth valued function]
- Proof-f: Tp → Tr [proof obligation truth valued function]

The VDM notation for specifying functions, logic, sets, and proofs is given in Figure 5.46. The notation in Figure 5.46 can be used to write VDM specifications (requirements for software processes). For example, the VDM specification for a timer is given in Figure 5.47. This specification gives the signature for a timer and the data type of its arguments sum and limit (integer). In the precondition, it is assumed that before the timer starts ticking (measuring some duration), its time limit will be greater than zero. Finally, in the postcondition there is the requirement that in every state of the time, the value of the variable sum is always less than or equal to the time limit.

notation	explanation	notation	explanation
f (arg: Type) result: Type	Function	x ∈ A	Membership
		t ∉ A	Not a member
ext rd variable-name: Type	Read-only	{ }	Empty set
wr variable-name: Type	Write/read	¬A	Not A
		B ⊂ A	B subset of A
f: D1 x D2 > Range	Signature	B ⊆ A	Strict set member
f(D)		A ∩ B	Intersection
	And	A ∪ B	Union
∧	Or	A - B	Difference
∨		card A	Size of A
⇒	Implies		
⇔	Equivalent	∀ x ∈ A . property(x)	All x in a *such that* property(x) is true
∀	All	∃ x ∈ A . property(x)	Exists x in a *such that* property(x) is true
∃	Exists		
⊢	Derives	hypothesis ¢ conclusion	Sequent (hypothesis *derives* conclusion)

(left margin: Specification, Logic) *(right margin: Set, Proof)*

Figure 5.46   VDM notation.

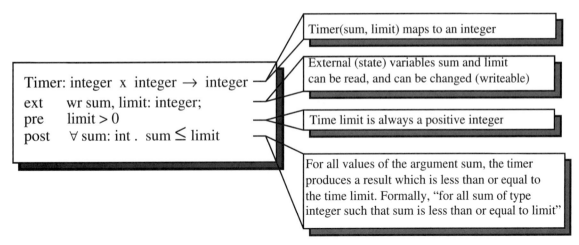

Figure 5.47 VDM specification for a timer.

The VDM notation in Figure 5.46 also makes it possible to give a more precise description of a proof obligaiton. Let d, r be values in the domain D and range R for a function, respectively. Also recall that pre-f and post-f are boolean valued functions (assertions about the preconditions and postconditions in a specification). We write pre-f(d) to mean that the truth value of the precondition depends on the value of the argument d in the domain of a function. Similarly, we write post-f(d, r) to mean that the truth value of the postcondition depends on the values of the argument d and the result computed by a function. Informally, we can explain a proof in the language of logic and sets as follows:

For all d in D such that pre-f(d) holds, we can infer that there exists r in R such that post(d, r) also is true.

Formally, a proof obligation is written in terms of the preconditions and postconditions for the specification for a software construct as follows:

Proof Obligation

$$\forall d \in D \bullet pre - f(d) \Rightarrow \exists r \in R \bullet post - f(d,r)$$

Proof obligations provide hooks (precise means of validating products) for designers and implementers in later stages of software development. Notice that for a specific function or module, the form of pre-f and post-f changes. In the case of the timer in Figure 5.47, for example, pre-f(d) and post-f(d, r) become pre-timer(sum) and post-timer(sum, limit). The proof obligation for the timer specification in Figure 5.47 is written as follows:

Timer Proof Obligation

given
pre - timer(limit) = (limit > 0),
post - timer(sum, limit) = (sum ≤ limit), then
∀ sum ∈ integer • pre - timer(limit) ⇒
∃ limit ∈ integer • post - timer(sum, limit)

The timer proof obligation says that for every state of the timer, the timer generates a value of sum (of ticks) that is always less than or equal to the time limit. It remains to be seen whether a particular design or implementation of the timer specification satisfies the proof obligation. In most cases, it is easy to check "visually" whether the proof obligation is satisfied by comparing the conditions of the obligation against the architecture in a design or the code in an implementation. For example, suppose that the following Pascal code implements the timer specification:

```
function timer: integer;
var limit, sum: integer;
begin
  read(limit);                {get value of limit}
  sum := 0;                   {initialize sum = 0}
  while sum < limit do        {exit from loop if sum ≥ limit}
    sum := sum + 1;           {increment sum by 1}
  timer := sum;               {return the value of sum}
end;
```

A check of the pre-condition of the timer specification reveals that this code is flawed, since the requirement that limit > 0 is not enforced (a zero or negative value could be read). The pre-condition is not satisfied by this implementation. Then we could modify the code as follows:

```
function timer: integer;
var limit, sum: integer;
begin
  read(limit);
  if limit > 0 then begin     {check for valid limit}
    sum := 0;                 {initialize sum = 0}
    while sum < limit do      {exit from loop if sum ≥ limit}
      sum := sum + 1;         {increment sum by 1}
    timer := sum;             {return the value of sum}
  end;                        {while}
  else timer := 0;
end;                          {timer}
```

It is easy to see that the postcondition for the timer is satisfied, since an exit is made from the while loop whenever the value of sum is not less than limit. To demonstrate that a proof obligation is satisfied by a software product, it is necessary to derive the conclusion of the obligation from what we know (knowledge of the workings of the function and the assumptions in the precondition). This derivation is expressed formally as a sequent as follows:

> **sequent** (what is to be derived from hypothesis contained in precondition)
> pre-f(d) ⊢ ∃r ∈ R • post-f(d, r)

The advantage to writing out a sequent is that it provides a recipe for demonstrating that a software product satisfies its requirement. The derivation that needs to be performed to demonstrate that the proof obligation for the timer is satisfied is as follows:

> **sequent** (what is to be derived from hypothesis contained in precondition)
> limit > 0 ⊢ ∃ sum ∈ integer • sum ≤ limit

This sequent is obviously true from what we know about the proposed implementation, and the requirements of the specification. For the sake of completeness, we give a sketch of the proof. To do this, we use a rule from elementary logic called "exists introduction," which says that if a required value of a variable (say x) can be produced, then we can assert that the value exists. The application of the "exists introduction" rule is signified by writing ∃ − I. The steps for a sample proof for the timer to show that the proof obligation for the timer specification is satisfied by the sample code are given in Figure 5.48. Since we have considered all of the cases computed by the timer function and in each case we have been able to derive the conclusion of the sequent, we have proved that the code

Proof:

1	read(limit)	Assumed
2	limit > 0	Assumed
3	limit > 0	From 1, 2
4	sum := 0	Assumed
5	sum < limit	From 3, 4
6	sum := sum + 1	Assumed
7.0	¬ (sum > limit)	Assumed, while condition satisfied
7.1	case 1: sum < limit)	From 7.0
7.2	case 2: sum = limit	From 7.0
8	∃ sum ε integer • sum ≤ limit	From 7.1, 7.2 and ∃ - I
9	sum = limit	Assumed, while condition not satisfied
10	∃ sum ε integer • sum ≤ limit	From 9 and ∃ - I

Figure 5.48   Sample derivation.

satisfies the specification for the timer. It is possible to automate proofs using tools like Gypsy (Good, 1985), m-EVES (Environment for Verifying and Evaluating Software), and HOL (Wing, 1994).

5.14.3 Specifying with Z

Z is a notation for describing the behavior of sequential processes. The Z notation is based on elementary set theory and logic, and was introduced in the early 1980s as part of a project sponsored by the IBM United Kingdom Laboratories. Z stemmed from the work of J.-R. Abrial (Hammond, 1994). A Z description of the functionality of a software system consists of a collection of structures called schemas. A *schema* describes the static (states, invariant relationships) and dynamic (operations, relationships between input and output, state changes that can happen) features of a system. With Z, the description of the behavior of software occurs in measured steps. A schema has the form shown in Figure 5.49. A schema declaration has syntax given in Figure 5.50. The steps in specifying the behavior of software with Z are given next.

Steps in Constructing a Z Specification

Step 1. Decide on the basic sets, operations, and invariant relationships needed to describe the behavior of software to be developed.

Step 2. Introduce a schema to define the state space for the software.

Step 3. Decide what operations are needed to induce state changes.

Step 4. Identify inputs to and ouputs from the system.

Step 5. Introduce schema to induce state changes.

Step 6. For each schema in step 5, give the necessary conditions (pre- and postconditions) that must be satisfied.

The VDM logic notation and ($\wedge$), or ($\vee$), all ($\forall$), exists ($\exists$) as well as the set notation for "member of" ($\in$), "subset of" ($\subseteq$), intersection ($\cap$), union ($\cup$) carries over into Z in writing preconditions and postconditions for a schema. The symbol $\varnothing$ denotes an empty set.

Schema Identifier

Declaration-Part
{status} State space identifier
Variable declaration
Function declaration

Optional pre-condition
Optional post-condition

Figure 5.49   Structure of a Z schema.

SchemaDeclaration ::=
  {status} Identifier   --Status indicates if state space is changed or not
  Identifier: set_type | --Variable declaration
  Identifier : domain $\rightarrow$ range | --Function declaration
  Identifier {? | !}: set_type   --Input operation (?) or output operation (!)
Status ::= Δ |Ξ -- Δ (schema describes state change)
                                --Ξ (state space does not change after operation)

Figure 5.50 Syntax for a Z schema declaration.

5.14.4   Example: Z Specification for tATC

In this section, Z is used to specify a record-keeping system for airspace configurations for a training program of air traffic controllers (the tATC system). Let Display be a set of displays (each showing a different air traffic controller's view of an airspace). Each display is associated with its own name and icons (graphics of an airspace display). Let *known* be a set of recorded airspace displays, and let *airspace* be the name of a function that maps a known airspace to a display. The following schema defines the state space of the tATC display-handling utility.

```
┌─── AirspaceConfig ──────────────────────────
known: ℙ Name × Icon
airspace: Name × Icon → Display
├──────────────────────────
known = dom airspace
└──────────────────────────────────────────────
```

The domain (dom) of the airspace operation is denoted *dom airspace*. The idea behind this schema is to give a concise description of available airspace configurations, and how to establish an indexing system for these configurations. Now we can begin defining "methods" for initializing, changing the set of airspace configurations, drag-and-drop as well as click-and-see operations in an interactive tATC training program. This will require the introduction of schema with preconditions and postconditions on schema operations. The following schema describes the initial state of the tATC system.

```
┌─── initAirspaceConfig ──────────────────────
AirspaceConfig
├──────────────────────────
known = ∅
└──────────────────────────────────────────────
```

In addition, the symbols ? (input) and ! (output) carry over from CSP in specifying input/output operations in Z. The operation to add a new configuration is specified with the AddAirspaceConfig schema.

```
┌─── AddAirspaceConfig ──────────────────────────────────
│ Δ AirspaceConfig
│ config?: Name × Icon
│ display?: Display
│ ─────────────────────────────
│ known ∩ {config? → display} = ∅
│ airspace' = airspace ∪ {config? → display?}
└──────────────────────────────────────────────────────────
```

The declaration Δ AirspaceConfig indicates that the AddAirspaceConfig schema induces a state change. This schema uses the variables known, airspace', and airspace. By convention, unprimed variables denote a state *before* an operation has been performed while primed variables denote the state of a system *after* an operation has been formed (Wing, 1994). The notation config? and display? specifies input operations. The variable *known* is used in the observation (before state change) that the received display does not already belong to the set of "known" configurations. The remaining two variables (airspace' and airspace) make it possible to observe what has happened after a state change. The input of a new configuration (config?) results in the replacement of the set named airspace with a new set of known airspace configurations named known'. This result can be expressed succinctly by asserting

$$known' = known \cup \{config?\}$$

Thanks to the formal use of set and logic notation by Z, this assertion can be proved in a straightforward fashion as follows:

```
┌──────────────────────────────────────────────────────────────────────────┐
│ Proof                                                                      │
│ known' = dom airspace'                              —invariant after operation │
│       = dom(airspace ∪ {config? → display?})        —from schema definition │
│       = dom(airspace) ∪ dom({config? → display?})   —dom, set algebra fact  │
│       = dom(airspace) ∪ {config?}                   —dom of mapping         │
│       = known ∪ {config?}                           —invariant before operation │
└──────────────────────────────────────────────────────────────────────────┘
```

This proof results from rewriting the set description of known', which results from the addition operation. That is, we rely on the fact that known' is the new domain of the airspace operation defined in the first schema that sets up the state space for the airspace-handling software for the tATC. We also use the fact that in the case where the domain of a function is the union of two sets, we can rewrite the second line of the proof relative to the union of the domains. Again, notice the definition of the domain of a function helps us rewrite the third line of the proof. After that, we complete the proof by recalling the invariant given in the AirspaceConfig schema, namely, the set dom(airspace) equals the set called known.

For simplicity, it is assumed that there are two types of icons in an airspace display: buttons to control the display, and graphics representing airspace features. To specify a click-and-see operation, the following schema can be used.

```
┌──── clickAndseeAirspace ──────────────────────────────────┐
│ Δ AirspaceConfig                                          │
│ config?: Name × Icon                                      │
│ button?: Icon                                             │
│ click: Name × Icon × Icon → Name × Icon                  │
├──────────────────────────────────────                    │
│ known ∩ {config?} ≠ ∅ ∧                                  │
│ {button?} ≠ ∅ ∧                                          │
│ click(config?, button?) ∈ airspace                       │
└──────────────────────────────────────────────────────────┘
```

In other words, the inputs to the clickAndseeAirspace schema are some configuration and button. The click operation maps these inputs to a new airspace. It is assumed that some of the graphics in a display can be moved (repositioned) by an air traffic control trainee. This makes it possible for a trainee to customize or tailor a display. For example, it might be useful to be able to change the configuration of a displayed runway by repositioning runway borders (widening, narrowing). We can introduce a schema to describe a drag-and-drop operation.

```
┌──── dragAnddropAirspace ──────────────────────────────────┐
│ Δ AirspaceConfig                                          │
│ config?: Name × Icon                                      │
│ drag: Name × Icon → Name × Icon                          │
│ drop: Name × Icon → Display                              │
├──────────────────────────────────────                    │
│ known ∩ {config?} ≠ ∅ ∧                                  │
│ known ∩ {drag(config?)} ≠ ∅ ∧                           │
│ known ∩ {drop(config?)} ≠ ∅ ∧                           │
│ {drag(config?)} ≠ ∅ ∧                                    │
│ airspace' = airspace − {drag(config?)} ∧                 │
│ airspace" = airspace' ∪ {drop(config?) → Display}        │
└──────────────────────────────────────────────────────────┘
```

Recall that a drag-and-drop operation starts by moving the cursor so that it points to a piece of text or graphic that can be moved. Then press the mouse, and drag the selected item to another area of the display. Release the mouse, and the display has been changed. Drag-and-drop operations can be done, for example, in a Microsoft Word document. The assumption here is that the display of an airspace designed to train air traffic controllers has been designed so that displayed text as well as graphics can be repositioned. The dragAnddropAirspace schema says the drag and drop operations result in a state change, provided that the value of input by config? is known and the drag operation is non-empty. These are the preconditions for a state change. Performing a drag operation results in the deletion of an old configuration of the airspace (the new set of configurations is named airspace'). The new configuration of the airspace resulting from the drop is added to known' (the new set of configurations is named airspace"). A description of the tATC display-handling facility can include an operation to save a copy of display to a file. This is done with the SaveAirspaceConfig schema.

```
┌──── SaveAirspaceConfig ──────────────────────────────
│
│  Ξ AirspaceConfig
│  config?: Name × Icon
│  copy!: Name × Icon
│  ─────────────────────────────
│  config? ∈ known
│  copy! = airspace(config?)
└──────────────────────────────────────────────────────
```

The declaration ΞAirspaceConfig indicates that the copy operation in the SaveAirspaceConfig schema does not cause a state change. The notation copy! specifies an output operation. By continuing this piecewise buildup of the description of the behavior of software, a complete specification can be written in Z.

Z is widely used in the specification of commercial computer systems. Inmos Ltd. has used Z to specify the IEEE. Std 754 Floating Point Arithmetic, which was part of the development of the T800 transputer chip (Hammond, 1994; Shepherd & Wilson, 1989). Evidence of the growing use of Z in industry comes from the CICS project at IBM (Houston & King, 1991). A good description of Z can be found in Spivey (1988, 1992).

5.14.5 Cleanroom Black Box Specification

Specification is the key to a manageable, predictable, and repeatable software process.
—M. DECK, 1996

The cleanroom engineering approach to software development has four primary activities: formal specification of software increments, design, implementation, and team review. Cleanroom specification provides a black box view of an object. A black box specification describes software relative to externally observable behavior and is independent of any design or implementation decisions (Deck, 1996a, 1996b, 1996c). Computer programs are viewed as rules. A program is an effector process that maps inputs (stimuli) to outputs (responses) provided constraining conditions on the inputs are satisfied. Each response to stimuli is accompanied by an update of the state variables associated with the system. Tabular notation is commonly used to specify the parts of a program rule (Dyer, 1992). The structure of a black box specification is given in Table 5.7.

TABLE 5.7   Structure of a Black Box Specification

Stimulus	Condition	Response	Effector Process Update of Model
Input data needed to perform an operation	**Premise** of a rule, which imposes constraints on stimuli before an effector process begins computing	**Output** (conclusion of a rule)	**Assign** new values to state variables

5.14.6   Example: Black Box Specification

To illustrate this idea, consider black box specification of a fault protection monitoring system for the Cassini spacecraft. A monitor program periodically checks for system-level spacecraft malfunctions and invokes fault recovery software whenever a fault is detected (NASA, 1997). Cassini has 18 fault-protection monitors. These monitors are designed to detect loss of commandability (uplink), loss of telemetry (downlink), heartbeat loss (loss of communication between onboard computers), overpressure, undervoltage and over-temperature.

A high-level, black box view of a temperature fault-protection monitoring system is shown in Figure 5.51. Assume that sensor$_1$ . . . sensor$_n$ record tempera-

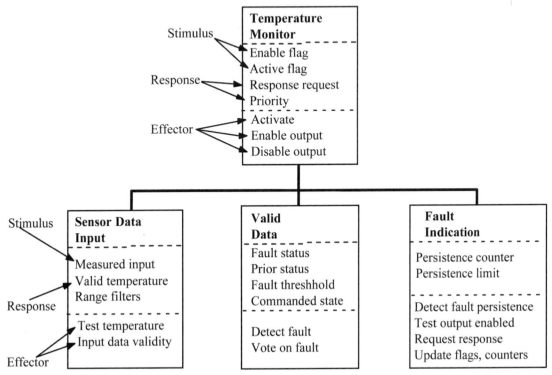

Figure 5.51   Black box view of temperature fault-protection system.

tures of a spacecraft structure. The temperature monitor in Figure 5.51 receives input temperature sensors (its measured state). Periodically, the monitor process executes command sequences stored in memory (its commanded state). Command sequences are uploaded by ground control. In addition, the monitor relies on updates (e.g., prior status in Figure 5.51) to the system resulting from previous monitor updates. From this description of the monitor system requirements, we can begin formulating black box descriptions of the monitoring functions. To begin a black box specification of the system, we can write function rules with the following form:

Monitoring Function Rules

If sensor$_i$ input is read, then test for valid data (measured output).
If sensor$_i$ input is valid (measured input), then test for fault.
If test of sensor$_i$ input data reveals fault, then wait for next sensor reading.
If test of sensor$_i$ input data reveals fault, then declare indication of fault.
If fault indicated by analysis of one or more sensors, then vote on presence of fault.
If fault persists (passes test), then request response.

To achieve a crisper, less wordy description of the function description of the monitor, it is helpful to organize the black box specification as a table. This is illustrated in Table 5.8. The tabular representation of a black box specification makes it easier to validate the specification (ensure that the specification meets client needs). By continuing the black box specification, we eventually arrive at a complete description of the observable behavior of the software. This form of behavioral description gives designers a clear-cut guide to the inputs and conditions needed to stimulate a system to produced required responses. The specification is later elaborated, giving the details concerning the data (ranges and type of data in stimuli and responses).

TABLE 5.8   Tabular Black Box Specification

Stimulus	Condition	Response	Effector Process Update of Model
Temperature sensor$_1$	Measured temperature is in valid range	Valid temperature output	New temperature added to monitor log
Valid temperature input	Valid temperature indicates fault	Declaration of fault	Result of test added to monitor log
Valid temperature input	Valid temperature does not indicate fault	Wait	Nil
Temperature fault	Voting indicates agreement on presence of fault	Declare fault persisting	Increment fault persistence counter
Declaration of persisting fault	Fault persistence counter is greater than 0	Request fault response	Response request added to log

5.15 NONBEHAVIORAL FEATURES OF SRS

The nonbehavioral portion in an SRS identifies *and* specifies each of the required attributes of the software. These attributes include reliability, reusability, availability, portability, maintainability, security, and standards compliance. The level of detail for a nonbehavioral specification must be sufficient to enable designers and implementers to develop the components of a system that satisfy the requirements, and to validate products of the development process.

Reliability is a high-level indicator of the operational readiness of a system (IEEE Std. 982. 1-1988). The key to software reliability improvement is the construction of an accurate history of the errors, faults, and defects associated with software failures. Errors, defects, faults, and failures have a cause–effect relationship to each other. Recall that a *defect* is a product anomaly (e.g., omissions or imperfections found during a software development). An *error* is a human action that results in a software fault. A *fault* is an accidental condition that causes a functional unit not to perform its required operation (e.g., a menu bar button does not respond to a mouse click) or a manifestation of an error in developing the software.

A *failure* is a halt in the ability of functional unit to perform a required operation (e.g., a display locks up, refuses to respond to any mouse click). A principal goal of an effective software process is to track the causes of failures. Examples of measures of reliable software are fault density and defect density given in IEEE Std. 982.2-1988. At the requirements level, a standard (target-values) for maximum fault and defect densities can be established for a software project. For example, required ceilings on these densities might be 4 faults per 1000 lines of source code and 5 defects per 1000 lines of design code. The purpose in doing this is to establish a standard that design teams can use for comparisons of actual densities with required densities. Measures for computing these densities are given in Table 5.9.

To guide the software engineering effort, target values for nonbehavioral software quality requirements can be given. We illustrate this in terms of the reusability requirement for a software project. Recall that reusability is computed relative at least four criteria: self-descriptiveness (SD), modularity (M), portability (P), and platform independence (PI). Then reusability can be estimated with a weighted sum as follows:

$$\text{reusability} = w_1(\text{SD}) + w_2(\text{M}) + w_3(\text{P}) + w_4(\text{PI})$$

A standard for reusability for a software project can be established by giving a "blank" Kiviat diagram specifying the minimum and maximum values for each software attribute to be measured. The Kiviat diagram provides a convient means of comparing actual reusability estimates during the design phase with the project standard. A sample min–max Kiviat diagram to be used in measuring reusability is given in Figure 5.52.

TABLE 5.9   Measures of Fault and Defect Density

Fault Density F_d	F_d Parameters	Defect Density (DD)	DD Parameters
$F_d = \dfrac{F}{KSLOC}$ Example: F = 29 KSLOC = 6 F_d = 29/6 = 4.8 faults/KSLOC	F = total number of unique faults found in a given time interval resulting in failures of a specified severity level KSLOC = number of source lines of executable code and non-executable declarations in 1000s	$DD = \dfrac{\sum\limits_{i=1}^{I} D_i}{KSLOD}$ Example: I = 2 KSLOD = 8 D_1 = 37 D_2 = 15 DD = 52/8 = 6.5 defects/KSLOD	D_i = total number of defects during ith design or code inspection process I = total number of inspections to date KSLOD = number of source lines of design statements in 1000s

An *availability* software requirement specifies the criteria required to guarantee an acceptable availability level for a system. These criteria include checkpoint, recovery, and restart. A *checkpoint* is a point in a computer program at which the program state, status, or computed results are checked or recorded. During development, checkpoints are established by instrumenting a program (inserting write statements to observe what a program is doing at a particular stage during a computation). *Recovery* is concerned with the restoration of a system, program, database, or other system resource to a state in which the system can perform its required functions. A software *portability* requirement stipulates the following items:

- Percentage of system components with host-dependent code.
- Percentage of code that is host dependent.

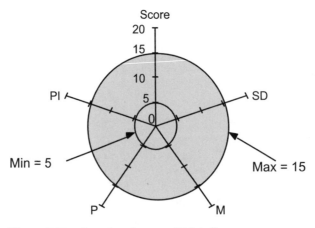

Figure 5.52   Sample min–max Kiviat diagram.

- Use of a proven portable language.
- Use of a particular compiler (e.g., Ada or C++) or language subset.
- Use of a particular operating system (e.g., Sun Solaris).

The *maintainability* of a software system is measured relative to the average values of consistency (c), comment count (cc), complexity (com), modularity (mo), size (s), and degree of parallelism (dop) criteria. Consistency c for a single software module (e.g., C++ or Java class) is measured by counting the number of conflicts with requirements (inconsistencies) and computing

$$c = 1 - \frac{(\text{\# of conflicts with requirements in module})}{(\text{\# of lines of code in module})}$$

[consistency in single module]

For a collection of n modules, the average consistency is the sum of the individual module consistency measurements divided by n.

$$c = \frac{\displaystyle\sum_{i=1}^{n\,\text{modules}}\left[1 - \frac{(\text{\# of conflicts with requirements in module}_i)}{(\text{\# of lines of code in module}_i)}\right]}{n}$$

[average consistency]

For a single module, the complexity (com) of the module is measured by counting the number of decision points and adding 1. The value of com indicates the number of independent paths in a module. This is called the cyclomatic complexity measure (McCabe, 1976), and is covered in more detail in Chapter 9. Modularity (mo) is computed either by comparing the number of modules in a system to the total number of variables or the number of modules compared to the total number of procedures (methods). In what follows, modularity is measured with the ratio

$$mo = \frac{\text{\# of modules}}{\text{Total \# of variables}}$$

The degree of parallelism (dop) of a single software module is a count of the number of processors used (either potentially or actually) to obtain a result. In Pascal, C, or C++ programs, dop $=1$. Notice that in a Java program with n threads (each potentially running on a separate processor), dop $= n$. The maintainability of a software system with one or more modules can be measured with the following weighted sum:

$$m = w_1 c + w_2 cc + (-w_3)com + w_4 mo + (-w_5)s + (-w_6)dop$$

[maintainability measure]

The weights in the maintainability formula will vary and are part of specification of the nonbehavioral requirements of a software product. Increasing values of com (complexity), s (size), and dop (degree of parallelism) tend to diminish

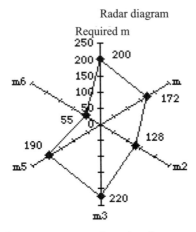

Figure 5.53   Sample radar diagram.

maintainability. Hence, the weights on com, size, and dop are negative. By contrast, increasing values of c (consistency), cc (comment count), and mo (modularity) tend to increase software maintainability. For this reason, c, cc and mo have positive weights. Each maintainability measurement should be compared with some "yardstick" (e.g., ranges of maintainability measurements of known projects as well as the minimum maintainability requirement for a project). For example, assume that project planners have set the minimum maintainability m to be 200, and that no maximum has been specified. Also assume the maintainability measurements labeled m_2, m_3, m_5, and m_6 from four similar software development projects are 128, 220, 190, and 55, respectively. To make comparisons easier, these measurements can be put into a radar diagram and bar graph like those shown in Figures 5.53 and 5.54. These diagrams show

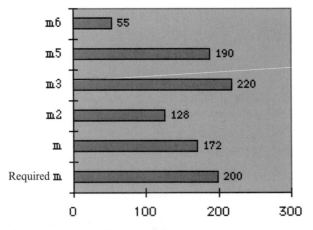

Figure 5.54   Sample bar graph.

how the *actual* measurement m compares with other measurements of maintainability and project requirement (*required* m). Notice that the comparison of m with the project require level of maintainability (m = 200) indicates the need to change the existing modules to raise the maintainability level of the software. The sample value of 172 for the maintainability index m in Figure 5.54 was computed relative to measurements from four software modules in a traffic navigation system. The measurements are summarized in Figure 5.55.

The next step is to measure the degree that the sample software system possesses the criteria used to measure maintainability. A summary of criteria, suggested weights, and criteria measurements is given in Table 5.10.

Maintainability of the fragment of four modules of the traffic navigation system shown in Figure 5.55 is computed as follows:

$$
\begin{aligned}
m = & -0.6 \, (c) + \sin(0.25cc)(cc) - 0.8(com) \\
& + \ln(0.25m)(m) - \ln(0.001s)(s) - 0.1(dop) \\
= & (-0.6)(0.9988) + (0.0997)(0.2283) + (-0.8)(12) \\
& + (-3.5)(0.12) + (0.23)(793) + (-0.1)(2) \\
= & 171.593
\end{aligned}
$$

The weights used in computing the experimental (actual) value of m in Table 5.10 represent the perceived strength of the contribution of each of the maintainability criteria. With the exception of the weight on the comment count, the remaining weights do not change sign in each maintainability measurement. The values of the weights can be made part of the standard established during the requirements phase. The contribution of average comment count to maintainability tends to oscillate (too many comments can sometimes have a negative effect). This is an insight in the Oman maintainability index (Oman, 1997). A

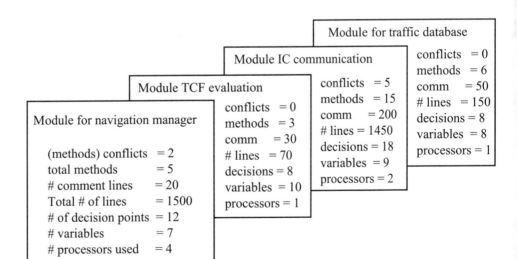

Figure 5.55 Sample measurements.

TABLE 5.10   **Sample Software Criteria Measurements**

Criteria Weights	Measurement
Consistency $w_1 = 0.6$	$c = \dfrac{\left(1 - \dfrac{2}{1500}\right) + \left(1 - \dfrac{0}{70}\right) + \left(1 - \dfrac{5}{1450}\right) + \left(1 - \dfrac{0}{150}\right)}{4} = 0.9988$
Comment count $w_2 = 0.0997$	$cc = \dfrac{\dfrac{20}{1500} + \dfrac{30}{70} + \dfrac{200}{1450} + \dfrac{50}{150}}{4} = 0.2283$
Complexity $w_3 = 0.8$	$com = \dfrac{(12 + 1) + (8 + 1) + (18 + 1) + (8 + 1)}{4} = 12$
Modularity $w_4 = 3.5$	$m = \dfrac{4}{7 + 10 + 9 + 8} = \dfrac{4}{34} = 0.12$
Size $w_5 = -0.23$	$s = \dfrac{1500 + 70 + 1450 + 150}{4} = \dfrac{3170}{4} = 793$
Degree of parallelism $w_6 = -0.1$	$dop = \dfrac{4 + 1 + 2 + 1}{4} = 2$

suggested method for computing the value of the comment count weight w_2 is given in Figure 5.56.

Security of a system is concerned with the required factors to use to protect the software from accidental or malicious access, use, modification, destruction, or disclosure. Requirements can be formulated in terms of the need to utilize specified cryptographic techniques, maintaining history data sets, communication restrictions (presence of firewalls), and integrity checking of critical vari-

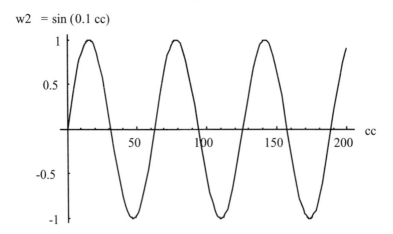

Figure 5.56 Varying weight on module comment count.

ables. Standards for requirements are absolutely essential in regulating software development. For example, a standards requirement might be that the SRS follow the IEEE 830 for object orientation in specifying the observable behavior of a system, or ISO 9000 in preparation for certification of the quality of the software.

5.16 MEASURING THE QUALITY OF THE REQUIREMENTS

The feedback system model of the requirements process includes a measurement step. The quality of the results of requirements analysis are checked. Sample measures of quality of a requirements specifications are given in Table 5.11.

The primary goal of the requirements process is to obtain a good requirements specification. Feedback from the requirements measurement process provides the basis for discussions between a client and the specifier about the goodness of the requirements. The quality of a requirements specification can be assessed relative to its effectiveness, serviceability, and prediction. The *effectiveness* of a specification is identified with the degree that the specification solves the right problem. Effectiveness can be measured by checking the readability, lack of ambiguity, consistency, and completeness of the specification. A specification is

TABLE 5.11 Sample Measures of Good Requirements Specifications

Requirements Quality Factor	Quality Criteria	Measure
Correctness	Completeness	Checklist
	Logical consistency	$1 - \dfrac{\text{\# specified features in conflict with plan}}{\textit{Total} \text{ \# of specified requirements}}$
	Unambiguous	Only 1 interpretation for each requirement
Maintainability	Traceability-to-plan	$\dfrac{\text{\# of planned features met by requirements}}{\textit{Total} \text{ \# of planned features}}$
Understandability	Conformance to standards	Checklist
	Readability	$FOG = 0.4 \left(\dfrac{\text{\# of words}}{\text{\# of sentences}} + \dfrac{\text{\# words with more than 3 syllables}}{\text{\# of words}} \right)$
Requirement maturity	Stability	Frequency of change
Testability	Existence of test strategy	Checklist

serviceable to the extent that it provides a clear-cut basis for software design. Serviceability can be measured relative to the correctness and understandability of the specification. The *prediction* content of a requirements specification provides a set of measures that can be used to predict the final quality of a software product.

It has been observed that it is possible to make relatively accurate predictions if proper measurements are made beforehand (Fenton & Melton, 1996). The trick to this is to prescribe measurements of key attributes (e.g., maintainability, portability, reliability) as part of the requirements. Later measurements of completed projects provide a basis for accurate resource predictions for future projects (Kitchenham & de Neumann, 1990). A checklist gives a list of desired features of a requirements specification, and provides a straightforward method of comparing planned features against specified features of a software product. Checklists are used in cases where there is no adequate measure of the goodness of a requirements specification (Farbey, 1993). The measure of readability in Table 5.11 is called the FOG index (Gunning, 1968).

5.17 TWO-WAY TRACEABILITY REQUIREMENT

An SRS is considered *traceable* if it is written to facilitate referencing individual requirements (Davis, 1993). In addition to traceability of requirements to planned software features, it is also necessary for requirements to facilitate tracing connections between design components and software specification. In other words, an SRS is traceable if the essential flow up and flow down paths between a feature of a design and a corresponding requirement can be identified. Careful and complete numbering of the sections of an SRS provides the basis for tracing upwards and downwards during the software process. Numbering provides a first step in organizing the requirements process. Traceable is an attribute of a good SRS included in the IEEE 830 standard. An SRS is *traced* if a flow up path can be identified between a requirement in the SRS and system level requirements (e.g., in a statement of need). Work has also been done to facilitate making a document traceable with the use of the webware and web-based tools providing a multimedia environment in preparing and searching through documents with hypertext links (Kaiser & Dossick, 1997).

There is a distinction made between a traceable SRS and a traceability requirement. A *traceability requirement* is a quality metric, which provides a thread of origin from a requirement specification to a statement-of-need section (flow up), or from a design or implementation structure to a specific requirement (flow up), or allocation path (flow down) of requirements down to a realization of the requirement. The traceability requirement is carried out in validating a software system. Traceability is computed in terms of R1 (number of requirements satisfied by an architecture or implementation) and R2 (number of original requirements). Let TM be a design-traceability measure. By counting the number of requirements that have been satisfied at particular stage in the software process and also counting the total number of original requirements, we can compute TM as follows:

$$TM = \frac{R1}{R2}$$

5.18 SUMMARY

The prospect of getting the true facts—straight, as it were, from the horse.
—P.G. WODEHOUSE, 1928

A good software requirements document provides a sound, understandable basis for product design and test generation. It tells what must be designed. Being specific about requirements means telling designers and quality engineers what they need to know to build and assess the results of the software process. In specifying software requirements, the guiding principles underlying a good SRS are expressed as rules in Table 5.12.

There are many ways to specify requirements. The acid tests in judging a requirements specification are (1) readability and understandability, (2) correctness and to what extent a specification lends itself to verification, (3) blueprint quality of a specification (designer's view of a specification), and (4) quality of the specification (how good is a requirements specification).

TABLE 5.12   Rules for an SRS

Rule	
1. SRS has all strength attributes	Correct, unambiguous, complete, consistent, ranked (importance, stability, necessity), verifiable, modifiable, traceable
2. SRS is cross-referenced	Create tables cross-referencing parts of SRS, and statement of need
3. All requirements are uniquely identifiable	Number SRS sections, use hypertext links for all components of SRS
4. Organize SRS to maximize readability	Classify features, give indices for names, functions, key terms, symbols

5.19 PROBLEMS

I get you not, friend. Supply a few footnotes.
—P.G. WODEHOUSE, 1918

1. The context-level SADT diagram for modeling a software engineering task is given in Figure 5.57.
   (a) Give table of names of high-level tasks, inputs, and outputs for each task; constraints (if any) on each task; required resources (if any); and comment on acitivity performed by each task used to decompose the task in Figure 5.57. These tasks would be used in carrying out the specification of some software task and providing information useful in the future in determining the reusability of the specification.
   (b) Give an SADT diagram in terms of the task specified in the table in part (a).

2. In terms of requirements for software for a vehicle navigation system like that shown in Figure 5.6, do the following:
   (a) Construct an environment assessment table with the structure shown below:

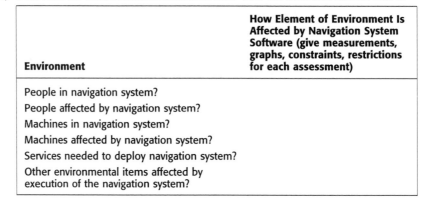

Environment	How Element of Environment Is Affected by Navigation System Software (give measurements, graphs, constraints, restrictions for each assessment)
People in navigation system?	
People affected by navigation system?	
Machines in navigation system?	
Machines affected by navigation system?	
Services needed to deploy navigation system?	
Other environmental items affected by execution of the navigation system?	

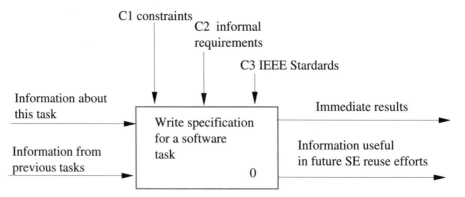

Figure 5.57   SADT diagram.

(b) Construct an output assessment table with the structure shown below:

Output	Explanation of Processing Performed by Navigation System Software
Items processed by navigation system? Items consumed by navigation system? Items produced to satisfy navigation system needs?	

(c) Construct a functions assessment table with the structure shown below:

Input, Function, Output	Explanation of Actions Performed by Navigation System Software
Functions performed by navigation system software? (in, op-1, output): . . . (in, op-n, output): Functions performed by navigation system person(s)? (in, op-1, output): . . . (in, op-n, output): Functions performed by navigation system machines? (in, op-1, output): . . . (in, op-n, output):	

(d) Construct a mode-of-operation assessment table with the structure shown below:

Mode	Explanation of Processing Modes Performed by Navigation System Software
Methods used by navigation system machines? method-1: . . . method-n When operations performed by navigation system machines occur? op-1time: . . .	

op-n time:
States of navigation system:
state-1:
.
.
.
state-n:

3. Do the following:
   (a) Give a function partition diagram for the sensor function of the navigation system from no. 2 (see Figure 5.7).
   (b) Give an informal description (and explanation) of each function from part (a).
   (c) Give a function partition diagram for one of the subfunctions from part (a).
   (d) Give an informal description (and explanation) of each function from part (c).

4. Do the following:
   (a) Give a state partition diagram for the correcting state shown in Figure 5.7.
   (b) Give an informal description (and explanation) of each state from part (a).
   (c) Give a function partition diagram for one of the substate from part (a).
   (d) Give an informal description (and explanation) of each state from part (c).

5. Do the following:
   (a) Give a state projection for responding-engineer-reliability shown in Figure 5.8.
   (b) Explain each state in the project in part (a).

6. Assume that a vehicle running navigation system software is equipped with sensors used to detect obstructions, and that the navigation system has obstacle avoidance capability. Assume that sensing includes obstacle detection, traffic signal light detectors, pedestrian detection, traffic pattern detection, and road surface assessment. Do the following:
   (a) Give an object diagram for the sensor object shown in Figure 5.7 for the navigation system. Hint: Use the information in no. 3, and construct an object diagram starting with the context level for sensing.
   (b) Specify the attributes associated with each object in the sensing subsystem of the navigation system.
   (c) Specify the services (methods, functions) associated with each object in the sensing subsystem of the navigation system.

7. In terms of the sensing subsystem of the navigation system, do the following:
   (a) Create a data flow diagram for obstacle detection sensing, which is part of the sensing subsystem.
   (b) Create a data flow diagram for road surface sensing, which is part of the sensing subsystem.
   (c) Create a data flow diagram for traffic pattern detection, which is part of the sensing subsystem.

8. Refine the data flow diagrams in no. 7 as follows:
   (a) Expand each DFD to include a timing function (sensing performed periodically).
   (b) Give a separate DFD for a timer (its inputs, functions, outputs).

9. Do the following:
   (a) Give a data dictionary for the traffic navigation system for a vehicle.
   (b) Use the data dictionary in part (a) to check the completeness and consistency of the data flow diagram from nos. 7 and 8 for the sensing( ) function of the navigation system.

10. Give process descriptions for each of the major activities of the traffic navigation system for a vehicle.

11. Give:
   (a) A complete SRS for the traffic navigation system for a vehicle.
   (b) The behavioral specification of the navigation system using statecharts.

12. Give:
   (a) Colored Petri net specification of the processes in the vehicle navigation system.
   (b) State table derived from part (a) like that shown in Figure 5.33.

13. Give:
   (a) JSD diagrams to model the behavior of the subsystems of the vehicle navigation system.
   (b) JSD function specification for vehicle navigation system sensing( ) function.

14. Do the following:
   (a) Give a SDL diagram to model communication between the vehicle navigation system and a central traffic monitoring station that communicates with vehicles with shortwave transmissions.
   (b) Give a JSD diagram to model communication between the vehicle navigation system and a central traffic monitoring station that communicates with vehicles with shortwave transmissions.
   (c) Compare the diagrams in parts (a) and (b). Which is better? Why?

15. Do the following:
   (a) Give a high-level SADT diagram (major functions only) for the vehicle navigation system.
   (b) Decompose each of the boxes representing actions in part (a) into separate, more detailed SADT diagrams.

16. Do the following:
   (a) Give a DARTS diagram to model communication between the vehicle navigation system and a central traffic monitoring station that communicates with vehicles with shortwave transmissions.
   (b) Compare and contrast the DARTS diagram with the SDL and JSD diagrams in no. 14.

17. Do the following:
   (a) Give a CODARTS diagram to model communication between the vehicle navigation system and a central traffic monitoring station which communicates with vehicles with shortwave transmissions.
   (b) Compare and contrast the CODARTS diagram with the DARTS diagram in no. 16.

18. Do the following:
   (a) Give a VDM specification for each of the proesses in a vehicle navigation system. Hint: derive the VDM specification from the process descriptions in no. 10.
   (b) Write a proof obligation for each of the VDM specifications in part (a).
   (c) Write a correctness proof for each specification in part (a).

19. How does the description of the behavior of a system with statecharts differ from a data flow diagram approach to describing system behavior?

20. Complexity has been identified as an essential difficulty of software. Comment on how requirements engineering helps solve this problem.

21. How does a vanilla framework help in specifying the conceptual constructs of complex systems?

22. The requirements analysis block in Figure 5.1 is a high-level representation of the beginning of a requirements engineering effort. Decompose this block into connected blocks having an ETVXM architecture. Give the details for each block.

23. Indicate what role stakeholders have in an iterative and interactive development of a requirements description of a system.

5.20   REFERENCES

Bjorner, D., Jones, C.B. The Vienna development method: The meta-language. LCNS, Vol. 61. Springer-Verlag, New York, 1978.

Booch, G. *Object-Oriented Analysis and Design,* 2nd ed. Benjamin/Cummings, Redwood City, CA, 1994.

Coad, P. Yourdon, E. *OOA—Object-Oriented Analysis.* Prentice-Hall, Englewood Cliffs, NJ, 1991.

Davis, A.M. *Software Requirements: Objects, Functions, and States.* Prentice-Hall, Englewood Cliffs, NJ, 1993.

Day, N. An example of linking formal methods with CASE tools (a model checker for statecharts). *Proceedings of CASCON,* Vol. 1, Center for Advanced Studies Conference pp. 97–107, 1993.

Deck, M. *Cleanroom Practice: A Theme and Variations.* Report, Cleanroom Software Engineering, Inc., 1996. Available from *http://www.csn.net/~deckm.*

Deck, M. *Cleanroom and Object-Oriented Software Engineering: A Unique Survey.* Report, Cleanroom Software Engineering, Inc., 1996. Available from http://www.csn.net/~deckm.

Deck, M. *Data Abstraction in the Box Structures Approach.* Report, Cleanroom Software Engineering, Inc., 1996. Available from *http://www.csn.net/~deckm.*

DeMarco, T. *Structured Analysis and System Specification.* Yourdon Press, New York, 1978.

DOD-STD-2167A. *Military Standard: Defense System Software Development.* U.S. Dept. of Defense, Washington, D.C., Feb. 1988.

Dorfman, M. Requirements engineering. In *Software Requirements Engineering*, R.H. Thayer, M. Dorfman, Eds. IEEE Computer Society Press, Los Alimtos, CA, pp. 7–22, 1997.

Dorfman, M., Thayer, R.H. *Standards, Guidelines, and Examples on System and Software Requirements Engineering*. IEEE Computer Society Press, Los Alimtos, CA, 1990.

Dyer, M. *The Cleanroom Approach to Quality Software Development*. Wiley, New York, 1992.

Farbey, B. Software quality metrics: Considerations about requirements and requirements specifications. In *Software Engineering: A European Perspective*, R.H. Thayer, A.D. McGettrick. IEEE Computer Society Press Tutorial, Los Alamitos, CA, pp. 138–142, 1993.

Fenton, N., Melton, A. Measurement theory and software measurement. In *Software Measurement*, A. Melton, Ed. International Thomson Computer Press, London, pp. 27–38, 1996.

Gane, C., Sarson, T. *Structured System Analysis: Tools and Techniques*. Prentice Hall, Englewood Cliffs, NJ, 1979.

Glinz, M. An integrated formal model of scenarios based on statecharts. *Proceedings of the European Software Engineering Conference*, Sept. 1995, pp. 254–271.

Gomaa, H. *Software Design Methods for Concurrent and Real-Time Systems*. Addison-Wesley, Reading, MA, 1993.

Gomaa, H. A software design method for real-time systems. *Communications of the ACM*, **27,** 938–969, 1984.

Good, D.L. *Verification Assessment Study Final Report,* Vol. II: *The Gypsy System*. Report, University of California at Santa Barbara, 1985.

Gunning, R. *The Technique of Clear Writing*. McGraw-Hill, New York, 1968.

Hammond, J.Z. In *Encyclopedia of Software Engineering*, J.J. Marciniak, Ed. Wiley, New York, 1994.

Harel, D. Statecharts: A visual formalism for complex systems. *Science of Computer Programming*, **8:**231–274, 1987.

Harel, D. The ADCAD methodology and STATEMATE1 working environment. *Proceedings of the Conference on Methodologies and Tools for Real-Time Systems*, 1987, pp. I-1, I-10.

Harel, D. On visual formalism. *Communications of the ACM*, May 1988, pp. 514–530.

Harel, D., et al. STATEMATE: A working environment for the development of complex reactive systems. *IEEE Transactions on Software Engineering*, April 1990, pp. 403–414.

Harel, D., Biting the silver bullet: Toward a brighter future for software development, IEEE Computer, vol. 25, no, 1 1992, 8–24.

Harel, D., Grey, E. Executable object modeling with statecharts. *IEEE Computer,* **30**(7):31–42, 1997.

Harel, D., Naamad, A. The STATEMATE semantics of statecharts. *ACM Transactions on Software Engineering Methodology,* Oct. 1996, pp. 293–333.

Hilt, B., El Mhamedi, A., Noaghiu, C. Modeling of information flow approach using SADT and Petri nets. *Proceedings of the Fourth International Conference on Factory 2000— Advanced Factory Automation*, 1994, pp. 326–331.

Houston I., King, S., CICS Project report: Experiences and results from the use of Z in IBM. Proc. of VDM 91. In *Lecture Notes in Computer Science,* S. Prehn, W.J. Toetenel, Eds. No. 551. Springer-Verlag, New York, pp. 588–596, 1991.

Huber, P., Jensen P.K., Shapiro, R.M. Hierarchies in coloured Petri nets. Proc. Int. Conf. Science on Application and Theory of Petri Nets. In Rozenberg, G., Ed. *Lecture Notes in Computer Science,* **483:**261–292, 1986.

IEEE Std. 830-1993. Software Requirements Specification. In *IEEE Standards Collection Software Engineering.* IEEE, NJ, 1997.

IEEE Std. 982.1-1988. IEEE Standard Dictionary of Measures to Produce Reliable Software. In *IEEE Standards Collection Software Engineering.* Piscataway IEEE, NJ, 1997.

IEEE Std. 982.2-1988. IEEE Guide for the Use of Standard Dictionary of Measures to Produce Reliable Software. In *IEEE Standards Collection Software Engineering.* IEEE, NJ, 1997.

International Standards Organization. ISO 9000-3. Quality Management and Quality Assurance Standards—Part 3: Guidelines for the Application of ISO 9001 to the Development, Supply and Maintenance of Software. Geneva, 1991.

Jackson, M. *System Development.* Prentice Hall, Englewood Cliffs, NJ, 1983.

Jackson, M. *Principles of Program Design.* Academic Press, New York, 1975.

Jensen, K. *Coloured Petri Nets: Basic Concepts, Analysis Methods and Practical Use,* Vol. 1, 2nd ed. Springer-Verlag, New York, 1996. See also, Vol. 2, *Analysis Methods,* 1995, and Vol. 3, *Practical Use,* 1997. There is also an excellent web page for colored Petri nets: *http://www.daimi.aau.dk/~kjensen/.*

Jones, C.B. *Systematic Software Development using VDM.* Prentice Hall, Englewood Cliffs, NJ, 1989.

Kaiser, G.E., Dossick, S.E. An architecture for WWW-based hypercode environments. *Proceedings of the 19th International Conference on Software Engineering,* Boston, May 1997, pp. 3–13.

Kitchenham, B.A., de Neumann, B. Cost modeling and estimation. In *Software Reliability Handbook,* P. Rook, Ed. Elsevier Applied Science, Amsterdam, pp. 333–376, 1990.

Marca, D., McGowan, C. *SADT: Structured Analysis and Design Technique.* McGraw-Hill, New York, 1988.

McCabe, T.J. A complexity measure, *IEEE Transactions on Software Engineering,* **2**(4): 308–320, 1976.

McCulloch W.W., Pitts, W. A logical calculus of the ideas immanent in nervous activity. *Bulletin of Mathematical Biophysics,* **9**(1): 39–47, 1943.

Morita, H., Mikawa, T. Development of VICS on-vehicle equipment. *Toyota Technical Review,* **46**(1):33–37, 1996.

Murata, T. Petri nets: Properties, analysis and applications. *Proceedings of the IEEE,* **77**(4):541–580, 1989.

NASA-GB-001-97, Release 1.0. *Formal Methods Specification and Analysis Guidebook for the Verification of Software and Computer Systems.* Available from *http://eis.jpl.nasa.gov/quality/Formal_Methods/.*

Neighbors, J. *Software Construction Using Software Components.* Ph.D. dissertation, Dept. Inform. Comput. Sci., University of California, Irvine, 1980.

Oman, P.W. Using automated software quality models in industry. *Proceedings of the Annual Oregon Workshop on Software Metrics,* Coeur d'Alene, Idaho, May 1997, pp. 1–23.

Peters, J.F., Baumela, L. Modeling the behavior of an assembly-line robot with Design/CPN. Report, Department of Electrical and Computer Engineering, University of Manitoba, 1996.

Peterson, J.L. *Petri Net Theory and the Modeling of Systems.* Prentice Hall, Englewood Cliffs, NJ, 1981.

Petri, C.A., Communication with Automata. NY, Griffiss Air Force Base, 1962.

Rockstrom, A., Saracco, R. SDL—CCITT specification and description language. *IEEE Transactions on Communications,* **30**(6):1310–1318, 1982.

Shepherd, D., Wilson, G. Making chips that work. *New Scientist* Vol. 1664, pp. 61–64, 1989.

Spivey, J.M. *The Z Notation: A Reference Manual,* 2nd ed. Prentice Hall International, London, 1992.

Spivey, J.M. *Understand Z: A Specification Language and Its Formal Semantics.* Cambridge University Press, Cambridge, England, 1988.

Thayer, R.H., Dorfman, M., Eds. *Software Requirements Engineering.* IEEE Computer Society Press, Los Alimtos, CA, 1997.

Wing, J. Formal methods. In *Encyclopedia of Software Engineering,* J.J. Marciniak, Ed. Wiley, New York, 1994.

Yeh, R., Zave, P. Specifying software requirements. *Proceedings of the IEEE,* **68**(9):1077–1085, 1980.

CHAPTER 6
Software Project: Requirements

Architecture in general is frozen music.
—VON SCHELLING, 1916

Aims

- **Select project-specific requirements process model**
- **Apply requirements description techniques**

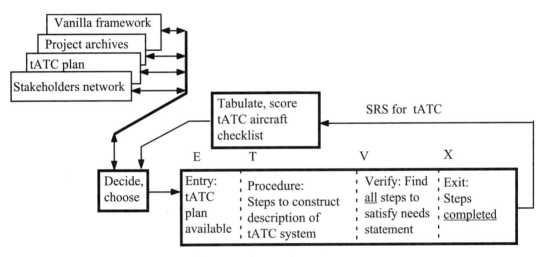

Figure 6.1 Project-specific, feedback system for requirements.

6.1 INTRODUCTION

In developing a requirements specification for a project, it is necessary to do the work within some framework. A project-specific feedback system model of requirements building for a training program for an Air Traffic Control (tATC) system is given in Figure 6.1. The model includes a Humphrey ETVXM architecture to ensure an orderly transition from one task to another in developing an SRS. The availability of a tATC plan is an entry condition that must be satisfied to start the requirements for the system. It is assumed that this plan is the result of interaction with project stakeholders. This interaction continues during the development of system requirements. The procedure block in Figure 6.1 will be fleshed-out by following the IEEE standard for developing a Software Requirements Specification (SRS). The organization of the parts of an SRS described in the IEEE Std. 830-1993 are shown in Table 6.1.

TABLE 6.1 Parts of SRS

SRS Part	Brief Explanation

Table of Contents
1. Introduction
  1.1 Purpose
  1.2 Scope
  1.3 Definitions, acronyms, abbreviations
  1.4 References
  1.5 Overview
	• Comments about intent of SRS
	• Purpose, intended audience of SRS
	• Specify product, function, benefits, goals
	• Terms needed to interpret SRS
	• Documents referenced in SRS
	• What SRS contains, organization of SRS

2. Overall Description
  2.1 Product perspective
  2.2 Product functions
  2.3 User characteristics
  2.4 Constraints
  2.5 Assumptions and dependencies
  2.6 Apportioning of requirements
	• Describe factors affecting product
	• Context (related products) for product
	• Major functions software performs
	• Intended users of product
	• Items limiting development options
	• Any changes affecting requirements
	• Items delayed until future versions of SW

3. Specific Requirements
  3.1 Interface requirements
  3.2 Functional requirements
  3.3 Performance requirements
  3.4 Logical database requirements
  3.5 Design constraints
  3.6 Software system attributes
  3.7 Organizing the specific requirements
	Give sufficient detail to enable designers to design system that satisfies requirements:
	• User, hardware, software, communication
	• Identify basic processing actions of system
	• Static, dynamic numeric reqs on HW/SW
	• Specify any information placed in database
	• Constraints imposed by standards
	• Software attributes serving as requirements
	• How to organize specific requirements

4. Supporting Information
  4.1 Table of contents and index
  4.2 Appendices
	Supply roadmaps for readers of SRS:
	• Identify locations of SRS items
	• Supply sample I/O formats, description of cost analysis studies, results of user surveys, supporting or background data to help readers understand the SRS, packaging instructions for code to meet security, export, initial loading, and other requirements

6.2   CASE STUDY: SRS FOR AIR TRAFFIC CONTROL ASSISTANT

Each of the parts of an SRS for a tATC are given next. The comments in the introduction reflect the perceptions of developers in organizing the SRS.

SRS.1   INTRODUCTION

The development of a Air Traffic Control (ATC) Assistant system is based on discussions with air traffic controllers at a local airport serving a city with a population of 750,000 people. Air traffic control is chiefly concerned with managing aircraft in the neighborhood of an airport. An air traffic controller decides on the movement of aircraft within designated zones, and tracks movements and status of aircraft. Every effort has been made to do requirements engineering in response to a needs statement and tATC plan, which this introduction briefly gives. The ATC Assistant provides several functions:

- Training (tATC) for air traffic controllers through ATC simulation.
- Display subsystem (dATC) used by airport tower controllers.
- Drive plan view display system (pATC) used by controllers in en route centers, which handle aircraft flying between airports at higher altitudes

All forms of the ATC are in response to a need to provide an organized scratchpad used by controllers. This scratchpad makes it possible to track the location of aircraft on the ground or in the air, and to keep track of who is controlling the aircraft. The tATC will provide a tool for training air traffic controllers. The dATC will be incorporated into a data entry and display subsystem (DEDS). It should be noted that current DEDS used in U.S. air traffic control are 1960s-designed displays. Evidence of the need of a new form of DEDS for an dATC can be found in Perry (1997). The pATC is to be used by controllers in en route centers, which handle aircraft flying between airports at higher altitudes. Coverage of the human factors in air traffic control is given in Wickens and others (1997), and at *http://www.nap.edu/*. Plans by the U.S. FAA for modernization of air traffic control and data concerning system capacity can be found at the FAA web site *http://www.faa.gov/*.

SRS.1.1   Purpose

The purpose of this project is to develop a tATC for a metropolitan airport. The tATC will assist air traffic controllers in making decisions in managing air traffic. The current version of the tATC is intended to provide a tool for training air traffic controllers. The goal of the tATC is to provide an interactive environment representing traditional as well as state-of-the-art ATC technologies. The benefit of the tATC is that it will stimulate real-time ATC problems, and enable controllers to become accustomed to handling problem as well as routine aircraft control.

SRS. 1.2 Scope

This document is limited to a description of tATC, a training facility that supports decisions of air traffic controllers in managing air traffic, and is intended to be a tool for training air traffic controllers and not for inclusion in a DEDS. The tATC will simulate actual air traffic control data, conditions, and problems, and require trainees to make decisions in controlling aircraft in designated zones. The tATC is limited to management of air traffic in the neighborhood of an airport tower.

SRS.1.3 Definitions, Acronyms, and Abbreviations

Air Traffic Controller (ATC). Human responsible for airport tower functions.
ATC *Assistant* (tATC). Advisory display subsystem belonging to DEDS.
Airport tower. Monitors aircraft on the ground, giving take-off and landing clearances.
Automated radar terminal system (ARTS). Computer system used by ATCs.
Terminal radar approach control (TRACON). Handles aircraft ascending from and descending to airports.
En route centers. Handles aircraft flying between airports at higher altitudes.
Data entry and display subsystems (DEDS). Displays for data entry and display subsystems.

SRS.1.4 References

IEEE Std. 830-1993, IEEE Recommended Practice for Software Requirements Specifications.

SRS Introduction. Needs statement for the tATC project.

Perry, T.S. In search of the future of air traffic control. *IEEE Spectrum,* **34**(8):18–35, 1997.

SRS.1.5 Overview

The tATC provides an interactive display system runnable with a web browser and a display of a range of choices to be made by an air traffic controller during actual airport tower operations.

SRS.2 OVERALL DESCRIPTION

The main functions associated with this product are described in this section of the SRS. The characteristics of a user of this product are indicated. The assumptions, constraints, and dependencies described in this section result from interaction with project stakeholders.

SRS.2.1 Product Perspective

The tATC system is an interactive tool for training air traffic controllers. It is intended to be used by air traffic controllers in learning to manage the activities of aircraft that come within designated zones of an airport tower.

SRS.2.2 Product Functions

The tATC provides a decision support system for tracking and altering the states of aircraft in designated air traffic zones. A display of weather information from weather sensors is also provided.

Aircraft are identified whenever they enter a controlled air space either through a TRACON or from the identification of aircraft preparing to take off. Aircraft leaving the control space are assigned to an en route center and removed from the list of tATC aircraft. The tATC maintains the following data:

- ATC responsible, identification, type, runway, state, emergency status.
- Temperature, wind (speed, direction), precipitation (type, amount), humidity, visibility, pressure, windsheer, altitude, cloud ceiling. The tATC warns an ATC of significant changes in weather which may affect air traffic flow.
- Identification (direction of runway), aircraft using runway queue, condition (snow, water, dry, rough), surface (gravel, cement, pavement), length, strength. Changes to runway conditions are updated by the ATC and/or ground crews. The tATC will warn ATCs about changes in runway conditions to be used by aircraft.

SRS.2.3 User Characteristics

The user of the tATC should either be an ATC or an ATC trainee under supervision of an ATC. The user will need training to understand and use the system effectively, and will require familiarity with drag-and-drop as well as click-and-see techniques for navigating a document with web browser.

SRS.2.4   Constraints

- The tATC system must allow quick and easy retrieval and input of air traffic control data through the graphical user interface provided by the system.
- The tATC will be user-friendly and easy-to-use by novices as well as professionals.
- The tATC enforces a What-You-See-Is-What-You-Get (WYSIWYG) display (no information is hidden).
- The tATC provides mobile computing capability, and is runnable by any number of ATCs having access to web browsers.
- The tATC maintains a knowledge base about all aircraft in the airspace for an airport tower, runways, and weather.
- The tATC controls the flow of information in the ATC system.

SRS.2.5   Assumptions and Dependencies

The tATC simulates operation of either a dATC or pATC in real-time, and provides continuous update of air traffic flow information. The tATC system is dependent on the operation of a browser on a host computer system. It optionally simulates the use of sensors such as radar, meterological instruments, and information gathered from pilots and ground crews.

SRS.2.6   Apportioning of Requirements

More advanced versions of the ATC called dATC and pATC (not part of this project) will be incorporated into the data entry and display subsystems (DEDS) of the automated radar terminal system (ARTS) and display system for en route centers, respectively.

SRS.3   SPECIFIC REQUIREMENTS

Many choices for this section of the SRS are possible. Because of its simplicity and ease of use, a functional requirements specification template will be followed as described in Figure 6.2.

SRS.3.1   Interface Requirements

The interface for the tATC system requires a combination of interactive, mobile computing software and Java-capable web browsers as well as the availability of workstations connected to the internet to facilitate widescale distribution and easy access to the training tool.

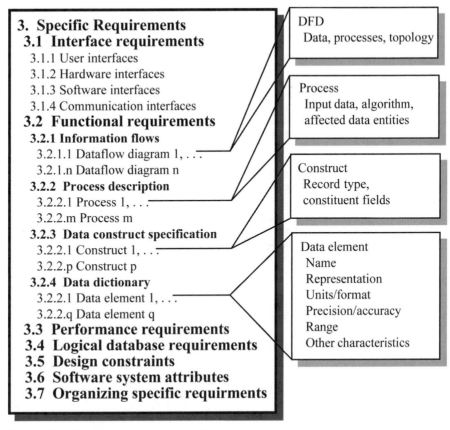

Figure 6.2 Functional requirements template.

SRS.3.1.1 *User Interfaces*

The user interface will be a Java-capable web browser.

SRS.3.1.2 *Hardware Interface*

A work station connected to the internet plus mouse and mousepad.

SRS.3.1.3 *Software Interface*

Java-capable web browser with access to the internet, the Java Development Kit (JDK) from Sun Microsystems or Integrated Development Environment (IDE), and a text editor for preparing HTML files.

SRS.3.1.4 *Communication Interfaces*

Internet access.

TABLE 6.2   Change State of an Aircraft to a New State

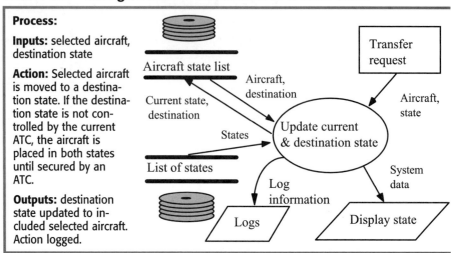

Process:

Inputs: selected aircraft, destination state

Action: Selected aircraft is moved to a destination state. If the destination state is not controlled by the current ATC, the aircraft is placed in both states until secured by an ATC.

Outputs: destination state updated to included selected aircraft. Action logged.

SRS.3.2   Functional Requirements

SRS.3.2.1   *Information Flows*

Data flow diagrams are provided to describe change of state of an aircraft to a new state, secure a plane in multiple states, change plane position within a state, add a plane, and update weather. These data flow diagrams are given in Tables 6.2 to 6.6.

TABLE 6.3   Secure an Aircraft in Multiple States

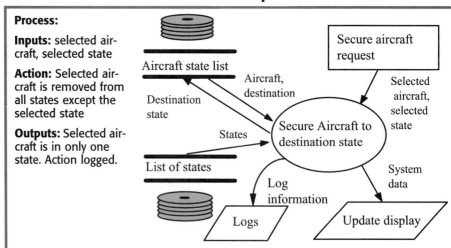

Process:

Inputs: selected aircraft, selected state

Action: Selected aircraft is removed from all states except the selected state

Outputs: Selected aircraft is in only one state. Action logged.

TABLE 6.4 Change Order of Aircraft

Process:

Inputs: Selected aircraft, destination state, position in queue.

Action: Aircraft information is stored. Destination state of aircraft is updated with new position in queue within its current state.

Outputs: Update aircraft entry, updated destination state. Action logged.

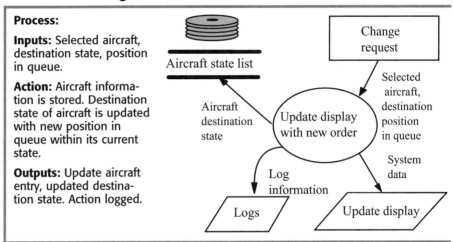

SRS.3.2.2 *Process Description*

A sample process description based on the process information (input, action, output) in Table 6.2 is given in Figure 6.3.

SRS.3.2.3 *Data Construct Specification*

Data constructs are prepared for each piece of data referenced in the data flow diagrams and process descriptions. In IEEE Std. 830-1993, a data construct

TABLE 6.5 Add New Aircraft

Process:

Inputs: New aircraft, destination state

Action: Destination state of aircraft is updated with new aircraft added at end of queue.

Outputs: Updated aircraft entry, updated destination state. Action logged.

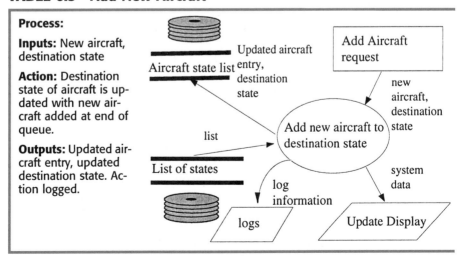

TABLE 6.6   Update Weather Information

Process:

Inputs: Temperature, wind direction/speed, precipitation, type/amount, humidity, visibility, barometric pressure, wind sheer, altimeter reading, cloud height.

Action: Store weather information. Check for major changes in weather state.

Outputs: Update weather information. Alert pilots, ground crews, ATCs of significant changes. Action logged.

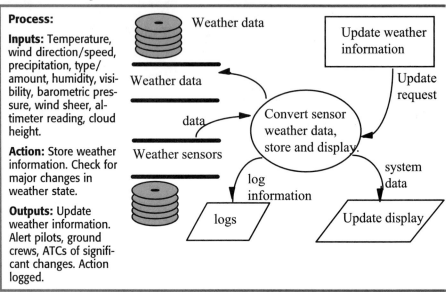

prescribes a data item name and its type. If the type of a data item is a record, its constituent fields are given. If a data construct describes a state, it is expressed in terms of its partition into the parts of the state of a system. In the context of aircraft in an air traffic control system, each aircraft state is partitioned to capture the idea of aggregation/part structural relation among states pertinent to the understanding of a particular state. This approach to specifying states, objects, and functions in problem analysis was introduced by Yeh and Zave (1980). Each state is represented by a record structure consisting of air traffic controller,

Process Name: *Transfer to aircraft to a new state*
For each <u>transfer request</u>
  Input Transfer request for selected aircraft, origin state, destination state;
  Retrieve Aircraft, state from file;
  if selected aircraft is controlled by current ATC {
   move selected aircraft to destination state;
   remove selected aircraft from its origin state
   }
  else if selected aircraft is not controlled by current ATC {
   move selected aircraft to destination state;
   repeat
    aircraft remains in origin state and destination state
   until aircraft is secured by an ATC;
   }

Figure 6.3   Sample process description.

specific aircraft, and other relevant state information needed to define and explain an aircraft state. An aircraft state is represented as a set of possible states of an aircraft. Individual aircraft states are given in record format to specify the aggregative character (composition) of each aircraft state.

changeState = {descending, ascending, landing, taking-off, assigned,
    unassigned, . . .}
descending = {ATC5 (controller 5), TWA 242, descend, flight level 350''
    (35,000 ft)}
ascending = { ATC3 (controller 3), NW 7021, ascend, flight level 230''
    (23,000 ft)}
landing = { ATC1 (controller 1), AC 892, 3 (third in line), 13R (runway 13
    right)}
takingOff = { ATC5 (controller 5), AI977, 5, 2R}
assigned = { ATC3 (controller 1), TWA 242, 5, 13R }
unassigned = { { }, TWA 242, approaching designed zone }

The sample record for the descending state for TWA 242 assigned to ATC5 represents the partition of the state as an aggregate of information as shown in Figure 6.4.

Notice that partitions of data objects of the tATC system can be expressed with record constructs that prescribe the "parts" in an aggregation making up a data object. Examples of data constructs for data objects for the tATC are as follows:

Aircraft = {name, id, flightNo, currentState}
currentState = {inFlight, inLandingQueue, inTakeoffQueue,
    scheduledToArrive}

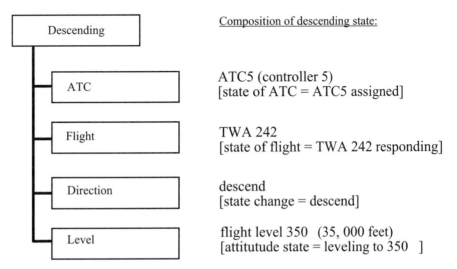

Figure 6.4 Partition of descending state.

inFlight = {name, id, GPS location, aircraft state}
inLandingQueue = {name, id, GPS location, aircraft state, queuePosition}
inTakeoffQueue = {name, id, runway, aircraft state, queuePosition, ETD}
scheduledToArrive = {name, id, runway, aircraft state, ETA}
Aircraft-landing-queue = FIFO list = (Aircraft[i], . . . Aircraft[1])
Runway-queue = FIFO list = (Aircraft[i], . . . Aircraft[1])
weather = {Temperature, wind direction/speed, precipitation, type/amount,
    humidity, visibility, barometric pressure, wind sheer, altimeter reading,
    cloud height}
conflict-prediction = {conflictPair, time, nearMiss, problemAnalysis}
ConflictPair = {Aircraft, Aircraft}
nearMiss: real
problemAnalysis = {[0, 1], N/A}
runway = {integer, string}
gate = {airlineName, integer}

SRS.3.2.4 *Data Dictionary*

Recall that a data dictionary supplies information such as data type, how the data is used, required accuracy, life span of data (optional), and data flows. A partial data dictionary for the tATC system is given in Table 6.7.

SRS.3.3 Performance Requirements

The static as well as dynamic numerical requirements placed on the software or on human interaction with the tATC are described in this section. Examples of performance requirements are as follows:

- *Static.* Number of simultaneous users of tATC is 20 in a training facility with 20 workstations connected to the internet, and running a Java-capable web browser.
- *Static.* Each controller workstation has a high-resolution 2048 × 2048-pixel Sony 20-inch color monitor.
- *Dynamic.* All drag-and-drop operations are accomplished within 100 milli-seconds during tATC interaction sessions.

SRS.3.4 Logical Database Requirements

All tATC transactions are archived ("logged") in a relational database.

SRS.3.5 Design Constraints

The tATC will enforce standards imposed by national and international standards for air traffic control. For example, the version of the tATC to be used in

TABLE 6.7 Partial tATC Data Dictionary

Name	Type	About	Life Span	Accuracy	Data Flows
GPS coords	Tuple	(x,y) coords	30 sec.	TBD	Update, secure, change, add
GPS altitude	Real	Aircraft altitude	30 sec.	±0.01	Update, secure, change, add
GPS time	String	Time of observation	30 sec.	±1 ms	Update, secure, change, add
nearMiss	Real	Estimate possible near miss	10 sec.	±0.01	Update, secure, change, add
conflictPair	Tuple	Current traffic conditions for (flight, flight)	k min.	Not specified	Update, secure, change, add

training controllers of aircraft in U.S. airspace must enforce U.S. Federal Aviation Administration (FAA) standards.

SRS.3.6 Software System Attributes

The tATC software attributes governing system design are given in Table 6.8.

TABLE 6.8 Required Software Attributes

Software Attribute	Explanation
Reliability: The mean time to failure must be 100,000 hours.	The average interfail time (time between failures of the software) must be 100,000 hours.
Security: Preventive measures built into the ATC to prevent accidental or malicious access to the ATC software.	Restrict interaction with software to authorized users. The software is to have a monitoring function to detect and deter unauthorized users.
Maintainability: The system will be designed as an open system (new methods can be added easily). The software will have complete, commented documentation. The Oman maintainability index ≥ 0.85 for the tATC.	$MI = 171 - 5.2*\ln(V) - 0.23*CC - 16.2*\ln(LOC) + 50*\sin(\sqrt{2.4*perCM})$ V = average Halstead volume CC = av. McCabe's cyclomatic complexity LOC = av. lines of code per module $perCM$ = av. % lines of comments/module
Portability: Gilb portability value ≥ 0.9.	Gilb portability = $1 - (ET/ER)$ ET = resources needed to move system to target environment ER = resources needed to create system for resident environment Assumption: $ET \leq ER$

SRS.3.7 Organizing the Specific Requirements

Each major function of the tATC will have a data flow diagram.

SRS.4 SUPPORTING INFORMATION

A keyword index is included in the SRS for the tATC. In addition, the complete SRS for the tATC is encoded in hypertext form so that it can be rendered with a web browser. All key words in the SRS are "hot" (clickable) to link with a related part of the SRS. The motivation for the hypertext form of SRS is to make it easier to trace design components back to specific requirements and vice versa. A fragment of a keyword index for the tATC is given in this section.

SRS.4.1 Keyword Index for tATC

A fragment of a keyword index for the tATC is given in this section.

Keyword Index	*SRS Section*
ATC	1.3
dATC	1.3
pATC	1.3
tATC	1.3
Aircraft state	3.2.3
DEDS	1.3
HTML	3.1.3
Interactive tool	2.1
Java-capable	3.1.3
Real-time simulation	1.2
TRACON	1.3
Training	1.1

SRS.4.2 Appendices

Appropriate appendices to be included in this section are:

- Appendix A. U.S. FAA Air Traffic Requirements Standard.
- Appendix B. Description of Traffic Alert and Collision Avoidance System (TCAS).
- Appendix C. Description of Center-TRACON Automation System (CTAS).

- Appendix D. Description of Wide-Area Augmentation System (WAAS), a network of Global Position Satellite reference stations.

6.3 SRS-3 STATE-BASED VERSION

Executable object models are also called statecharts. A statechart specifies system behavior, how objects communicate and collaborate to accomplish some goal. States describe abstract situations in an object's life-cycle. It is fairly easy to "read" code from a statechart because its arcs are labeled with trigger conditions and lists of actions. A *trigger* is either an event (e.g., mode = stop) or request for an action (e.g., change(term)). An *action* is a sequence of event-generating expressions, or operation calls, or C++ statements. Using the Statemate MAG-NUM toolset, statecharts can be executed, and provide a means of rapid prototyping. Using statecharts, the description of a system can be created in a modular fashion using information hiding. The details of the design of each module are hidden in a layering of statecharts. The states in the top-level description of a module such as an tATC scanner can be decomposed into more detailed statecharts. Lower-level statecharts reveal details that explain the mechanisms underlying a top-level statechart. The visual formalism provided by statecharts aids understanding and facilitates clean, simple descriptions of hierarchies in the operational structure of a system.

This section presents Section 3 of the SRS for the tATC organized by statecharts. To make it easier to read, the skeletal structure of Section 3 is given entirely. Notice that Sections 3.1, 3.3, 3.4, 3.5, and 3.6 are the same as those given in the sample SRS in the previous section, so the details are not repeated. A high-level description of the tATC system is given in Figure 6.5.

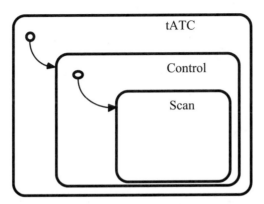

Figure 6.5 Top-level statechart for the tATC.

Section 3 of SRS: A Statechart Approach

SRS 3 Specific Requirements
3.1 External interface requirements
3.1.1 User interfaces
3.1.2 Hardware interfaces
3.1.3 Software interfaces
3.1.4 Communication interfaces
3.2 Statecharts
3.2.1 Statechart 1

SRS.3.2.2 Decomposition of Scan State

A decomposition of the scan state in Figure 6.5 is given in Figure 6.6.

SRS.3.2.3 Decomposition of Aircraft State

A detailed view of the aircraft portion of the user interface for an air traffic control system is given in Figure 6.7. The assumption made in the statechart in Figure 6.7 is that the system relies on input from pilots as well as its sensors (radar) to locate an aircraft in a sector of an airspace in the neighborhood of an airport tower. A controller relies on a user interface to track and guide an identified aircraft.

SRS.3.2.4 Decomposition of Locate State

The locate state in Figure 6.7 decomposes into the statechart in Figure 6.8.

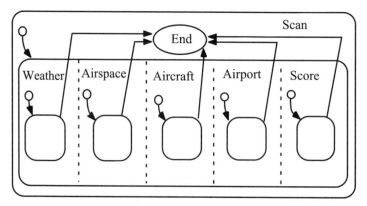

Figure 6.6 Decomposition of tATC scan state.

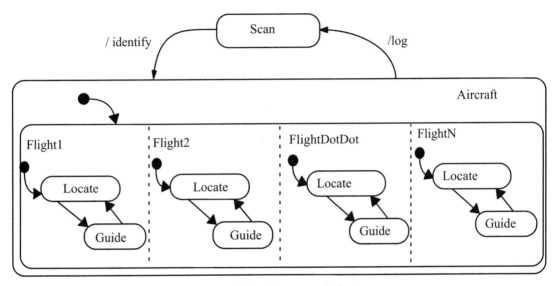

Figure 6.7 Description of aircraft scanner behavior.

SRS.3.2.5 Decomposition of Guide State

Locate and guide functions are associated with each aircraft. Guiding an aircraft requires some form of user interface that makes it possible for a controller to interact with a display. A decomposition of the guide state is given in Figure 6.9. This is a partial description of guide activities, which function independently of each other. The assumption made in this description is that a controller uses mouse clicks to change states in a number of ways:

- Transfer of an aircraft from airport tower to en route center control.
- Enclosing an area of a display with a map indicating a part of the airspace that has been restricted due to some emergency.
- Restriction imposed on aircraft being controlled.
- Talking with pilots and giving instructions.

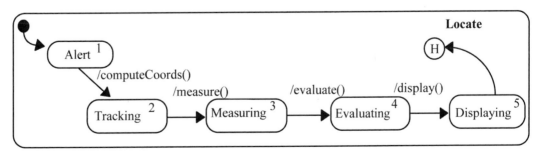

Figure 6.8 Locating an aircraft.

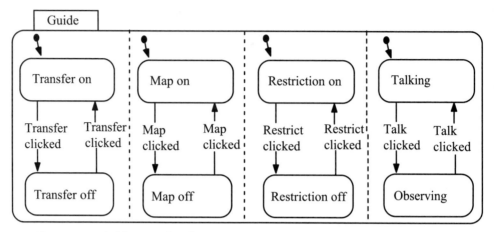

Figure 6.9 Guiding an aircraft.

Notice that each of the states in Figure 6.9 are part of a hierarchy. To see more of this hierarchy, these states must decompose into other statecharts. The decomposition of the states in the guide statechart in Figure 6.9 as well as the remaining parts of Section 3 of the SRS are part of the problem set for this chapter.

Remaining Parts of Section 3 of SRS

3.2.6 Decomposition of weather
3.2.7 Decomposition of airspace
3.2.8 Decomposition of airport
3.2.9 Decomposition of score
3.3 Performance requirements
3.4 Design constraints
3.5 Software system constraints
3.6 Other requirements

6.4 SUMMARY

Thanks to the availability of standards for a software requirements specification, a workable structure for an SRS is known. The contents of an SRS will be guided by a project plan and interaction with project stakeholders. An SRS provides a concise description of an application. The objectives, constraints, and alternatives in developing requirements are garnered from communication with stakeholders. Requirements are developed iteratively based on feedback about baseline documents and evaluation of system prototypes. Systems such as Rhapsody from i-logix can be used to generate code from statechart descriptions. This makes it possible to study the behavior of some part of a system during the execution of a prototype. If code generation facilities are not available, it is still quite easy to code selected increments of a system described in an SRS. This can be done rather quickly, if it is understood that a prototype is very focused, and makes proof-of-concept possible from some part of a system. Rapid prototyping is aided by incremental development of requirements. The design of a hand-coded proto-type should reflect the description of an increment. Finally, notice that it helps to use a top-down approach. Start by staking out your claims about the top-level framework for a system. A top-level state in a statechart, for example, can be decomposed into lower-level, more detailed statecharts. Lower-level descriptions are hidden from view in a top-level statechart. This promotes understanding of the main features and functions of a system. Lower-level statecharts serve as explanations of the main functions of a system.

6.5 PROBLEMS

1. Complete SRS.3.2.2 of the requirements specification for a tATC by giving:
   (a) Process description for each of the tATC processes.
   (b) Decomposition of the move-selected-aircraft-to-destination-state action into a separate process description.

2. Complete SRS.3.2.4 of the requirements specification for a tATC by:
   (a) Completing the data dictionary for this system.
   (b) Verifying the correctness and consistency of the data flow diagrams in SRS.3.2.1.

3. Do the following:
   (a) Give a black box description of the transfer of aircraft to a new state (see SRS.3.2.1).
   (b) Measure the quality of the requirements specification given in part (a).

4. Do the following:
   (a) Rewrite Section SRS.3.2 using Z to describe the basic operations of the air traffic control system (ATC).
   (b) Measure the quality of the requirements specification given in part (a).

5. Do the following:
   (a) Give target maximum values for fault density and defect density.
   (b) Give a Kiviat diagram for the target minimum and maximum reusability measurements for the software modules of the ATCA.

6. Rewrite SRS.3.2 using statecharts instead of data flow diagrams to describe the behavior of the air traffic control system. Hint: The behavior of transfer of aircraft, secure aircraft, change order of aircraft, update display of aircraft, and update weather

information (described with data flow diagrams) can be described relative to orthogonal states in a statechart called ATC.

7. Create an executable prototype of the guide module for an tATC. This is a user interface with a panel of buttons for a controller to use in guiding an aircraft. Your prototype should also make it possible to click a displayed blip representing an aircraft to turn on or turn off the display of a circle surrounding an aircraft being transferred to another controller.

8. Do the following:
   (a) Give a statechart description of a tATC weather module.
   (b) Decompose the statechart in 8(a) to show hidden details.
   (c) Decompose selected states in 8(b) to show more detail.
   (d) Prototype the weather module.

9. Do the following:
   (a) Give a statechart description of a tATC airspace module.
   (b) Decompose the statechart in 8(a) to show hidden details.
   (c) Decompose selected states in 8(b) to show more detail.
   (d) Prototype the airspace module.

10. Do the following:
   (a) Give a statechart description of a tATC airport module.
   (b) Decompose the statechart in 8(a) to show hidden details.
   (c) Decompose selected states in 8(b) to show more detail.
   (d) Prototype the airport module.

11. Do the following:
   (a) Give a statechart description of a tATC score module.
   (b) Decompose the statechart in 8(a) to show hidden details.
   (c) Decompose selected states in 8(b) to show more detail.
   (d) Prototype the score module.

6.6 REFERENCES

Perry, T.S. In search of the future of air traffic control. *IEEE Spectrum,* **34**(8):18–35, August 1997.

Wickens, C.D., et al., Eds. *Flight to the Future: Human Factors in Air Traffic Control.* National Academy Press, 1997. See *http://www.nap.edu/.*

Yeh, R., Zave, P. Specifying software requirements. *Proceedings of the IEEE,* **68**(9):1077–1085, 1980.

CHAPTER 7
Software Design: Architectures

Design and programming are human activities; forget that and all is lost.
—B. Stroustrup, 1991

Aims

- Characterize software architectures
- Identify the kinds of architectural elements
- Consider the application of architectural styles

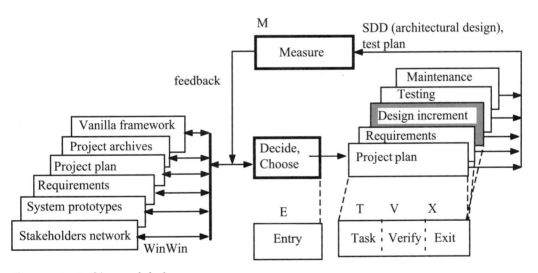

Figure 7.1 Architectural design process.

7.1 INTRODUCTION

Software design immediately follows the requirements engineering phase in a software process. A Software Requirements Specification (SRS) tells us *what* a

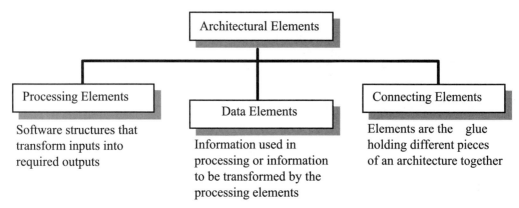

Figure 7.2   Basic kinds of architectural elements.

system does, and becomes input to the design process, which tells us *how* a software system works. Designing software systems means determining how requirements are realized as software structures. The result of the software design process is a Software Design Document (SDD). A high-level feedback system model of the architectural design process is given in Figure 7.1. This is the beginning of software design. This part of software design focuses on identifying the architectural elements of software modules described in the SRS (Figure 7.2).

The availability of a project plan and an SRS constitutes an entry condition for beginning the architectural design of a system. Ideally, architectural design is carried out relative to software increments. The design process "lives" in a vanilla framework, which supports the production of prototypes of system modules. The knowledge gained from prototypes makes it easier to identify the elements of an architecture for an increment. In the case where a visual formalism has been used to describe the functionality and behavior of system components, the design of software architectures is more straightforward. The software design process consists of the following main tasks:

Principal Software Design Tasks Leading to an SDD

- Requirements-to-design: Transforming requirements into architectural elements.
- Verifying and validating designs.
- Performing risk analysis relative to designs.
- Selecting software interfaces (module interconnections, user interfaces).
- Algorithmic explanation of architectures (how they work, steps performed).
- Detailed design (consider alternative architectures, incremental improvements of selected architecture, and complete the software design).

It has become common practice to use the term *architecture* to characterize the internal structure of a software system (IEEE, 1987; IEEE, 1993; IEEE, 1995;

IEEE *Transactions on Software Engineering*, 1995; Shaw & Garlan, 1996; Shumate, 1994; Stroustrup, 1991). A software architecture prescribes *how* software functions, how it is to be implemented. Changes, improvements, and enhancements leading to new software design releases cause software architectures to evolve. Evolution of software designs results from feedback (results of prototyping and simulation, experimentation, validation, and risk analyses). In effect, the software design process is part of a feedback loop as shown in Figure 7.1. Continuation of the iteration in this feedback loop is the result of interaction with project stakeholders.

The main aim of the design process is to provide a clean, relatively simple internal structure for software, which is flexible, extensible, portable, and reusable (Stroustrup, 1991).

- A *flexible* software structure is one that facilitates refinement (changes to accommodate new needs). Changes in the structure (e.g., addition of new input or output interfaces, changes to timing constraints) should be straightforward. Design usually means redesigning existing structures to accommodate new requirements.

- An *extensible* software structure is essentially open, and easily revised to satisfy increased demands or additional devices. In the case of a controller for a collection of transmitters and receivers in a deep space antenna system, for example, there is usually an ongoing problem of adding new devices to be controlled. The controller software is made extensible by making it table-driven (adding a device then reduces to adding an entry in the table referenced by the controller).

- A software architecture is *portable* if it can be made to execute on different platforms as a result of reasonable effort. A well-known example of portable software is the UCSD Pascal system, which translates programs into p-code for a small, hypothetical machine. It then becomes a straightforward task to translate p-code to a particular target machine by writing a p-interpreter in the machine language of the new machine.

- A *reusable* software structure is one that can be extracted from one application and inserted into a new application with reasonable effort. Software reuse is simplified in cases where software systems are constructed using standard architecture models. Two well-known examples of standard architectures are the IBM System Network Architecture and the International Standards Organization open-systems interconnect, seven-layer model for communication systems. Object orientation, interface standardization, and application of standard architecture models pave the way to software reuse.

The object-oriented approach to design encourages building software architectures out of invariant objects (data structures and operations grouped together in a single package). A software structure is defined by its interfaces (its input/

output "ports"). Software interfaces provide a guide for the reuse of a structure in a new application.

7.2 SOFTWARE ARCHITECTURES

We have found that understanding software architecture is the key to developing many important software solutions.
—B. Stroustrup, 1991

A model for describing software architectures was introduced by Perry and Wolf in 1992. A description of a software architecture consists of three basic elements: processing, data, and connecting elements (Figure 7.2).

- A *processing element* is a software structure that transforms its inputs into required outputs.
- A *data element* consists of information needed for processing or information to be processed by a processing element.
- *Connecting elements* are the "glue" that holds different pieces of an architecture together.

For example, a single URL (Uniform Resource Locator) is an Internet command line used to specify an object on the Internet such as a file or newsgroup (Ross, 1996). A URL provides a concise example of architectural elements. Try typing, for example, the URL to find out about new servers and web-related tools in Figure 7.3. Other examples of architectural elements are given in Table 7.1.

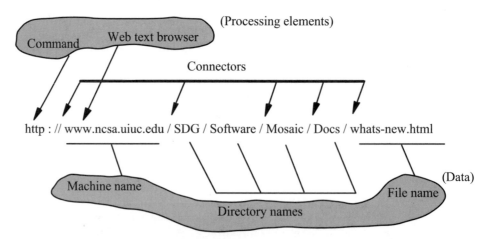

Figure 7.3   Sample architectural elements.

TABLE 7.1 Sample Software Architectures

Architecture	Examples of Architectures		
Elements	Internet Uniform Resource Locator (URL)	Application package: Microsoft Word	Graphical toolset: Mathematica
Processing component(s)	Access method: ftp (file transfer program) file (same as ftp) http (identifies web site) telnet (connect to m/c)	Spelling, grammar, thesaurus, customize, word count	Plot [2D plot] AxesLabel GridLines PlotRange GraphicsArray
Data	Machine name Directory name File name	File name	Expression(s) Example: Sin[x^2]
Connector(s)	://(precedes m/c name) /(precedes directory or filename)	Pull-down menu item button	$\rightarrow$ PlotRange $\rightarrow$ {0, 3.5}

7.3 ARCHITECTURAL STYLES

In developing a software system, it is helpful to organize architectures into families and associate families with typical applications. The benefit of doing this is that it cuts down the time required to select appropriate architectures satisfying requirements in an SRS. A pattern of structural organization in an architecture defines what is known as an *architectural style* (Shaw & Garlan, 1996). An architectural style is characterized as follows:

- *Types of components.* Processing elements used to transform data (e.g., formatting routines in text formatting packages).
- *Types of connectors.* Control and data paths between components.
- *Constraints.* Restrictions on processing, data, and allowable ways to "wire" components together.

Each architectural style has the appearance of a toolbox containing "tools" (architectures) useful in constructing different kinds of software modules. Data flow, virtual machine, domain-specific, call-and-return, independent-process, and repository systems represent examples of various families of software architectures. Architectures having these patterns of organization are shown in Figure 7.4. The discussion of these architectural styles follows the dial in Figure 7.4 in a clockwise direction.

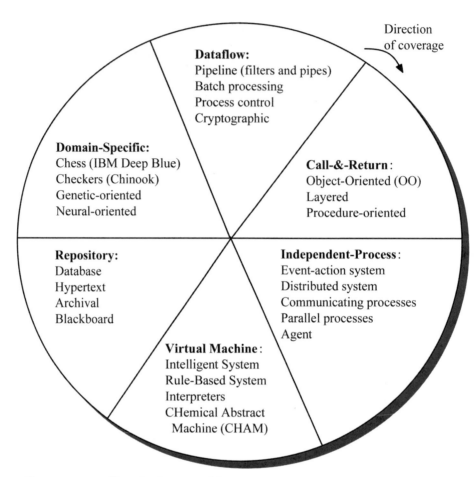

Figure 7.4   Families of software architectures.

7.4 DATA FLOW ARCHITECTURES

A data flow architecture is found in the design of software used to process data streams. Pipelining, batch processing, process control, and cryptographic systems have architectures that fit this pattern (each contains processes that manage streams of data in some fashion). Batch processing is perhaps the oldest example of this architecture, where a data stream consists of jobs that are executed in sequential fashion (a batch job is executed to completion based on initial inputs and processing is not altered until a job is completed). Cryptographic systems are used in communication systems in a secret mapping of each character in a text (input stream) to some other character. The result of encryption is called a cipher text. The remaining two types of data flow architectures (pipelining and process control) are considered in the next two sections.

7.4.1 Pipelines

Pipeline architectures are modeled after assembly lines in manufacturing plants. A product (e.g., automobile, electronic device) is constructed in stages at various stations. Whenever the first station completes its operation on its input, the results are passed to the next station in the pipeline, while the first can begin work on another input. The resulting process exhibits what is known as temporal parallelism (more than one product being produced at the same time). A *pipeline architecture* (in software) consists of processing elements called filters, which are connected together. A filter transforms its inputs and its results become input to the pipe connected to the next filter. The data element in a pipeline is usually called a stream, and the connecting elements between filters are called pipes. An example of pipelining comes from Unix shell programming. Let cat, sort, tail -n, grep pattern be Unix commands to output the contents of a file, sort its input into alphabetical order line by line, output last n lines of a file, and search for lines that match a pattern, respectively. Each of these commands normally sends its output to what is known as standard output (e.g., workstation display). These commands can be used as filters in a pipeline. The Unix symbol 'l' represents a pipe that connects filters together. Let a file named enzyme contain the following lines (displayed with the cat command), derived from the structure of a small hypothetical fragment of DNA described by Crichton (1990) in *Jurassic Park:*

```
%      catenzyme

121  GC  GTTGCTGG  CG  TTT  TTCCA
181  GG  TGGCGAAA  CC  CGA  CAGGA
 61  TG  TTCCGACC  CT  GCC  GCTTA
241  CC  GTTCAGCC  CG  ACC  GCTGC
  1  GC  GTTGCTGG  CG  TTT  TTTCCA
```

The enzyme file provides a stream of data for the Unix pipeline in Figure 7.5. In this pipeline, the input stream is sorted, and then the last two lines of the sorted stream are selected for the grep command, which searches for the pattern ACC of the remaining stream.

7.4.2 Process Control

A *control system* contains interconnected components forming a system that computes a desired response to a stimulus. The basic terminology used in describing control architectures is given in Table 7.2. A cause–effect relationship exists between the components of a control system. A system that maintains a precise relationship between the output and a reference input by comparing them and using the difference as the basis for control is called a *feedback control system.* As an example, consider a programmable thermostatic furnace control system where

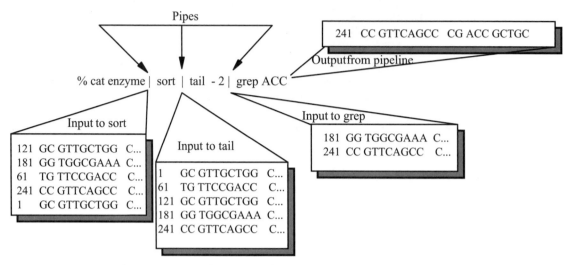

Figure 7.5 Sample Unix pipeline.

TABLE 7.2 Process Control Terminology

Term	Meaning	Model (Example)
Controlled process	Any operation or device to be controlled	(Cause) Input → Process → (Effect) Output
Controlled variable	Quantity or condition that is measured and controlled	[Control variable: v = % valve is open] Flow control valve, Fluid inflow, Outflow
Set point	Desired value for controlled variable	Example: v = 0.25 (valve 25% open)
Summing point	Arithmetic step symbolized by a circle with a cross (+ {−}) at arrow head, which indicates signal is to be added {subtracted}	a → ⊗(+ −) → a - b → Process → u. Summing Point, b ← Sensor

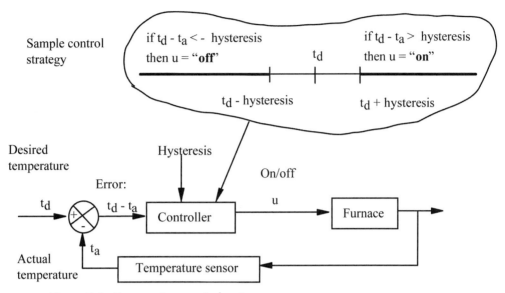

Figure 7.6   Temperature control system.

the set point is the desired room temperature, and switching the furnace on or off is determined by a hysteresis variable. The preset value of the hysteresis variable determines how many degrees the room temperature must rise above or below the set point to switch the furnace off or on. A typical value of hysteresis is 2°C. A block diagram for a simple feedback control process for a furnace is shown in Figure 7.6. A control process implements a control strategy to achieve the desired result. Let the values of the controller response u for the temperature control system in Figure 7.6 belong to the set {on, off, nil}, where u = nil whenever the furnace does not need to change state. Assuming that hysteresis = 2 and desired temperature = 20°C, the control process in Figure 7.6 would have a behavior like the one shown in Table 7.3.

The structure of a feedback control process provides a paradigm for a software architecture, where the components of the process are mechanisms for manipulating process variables relative to one or more set points. The software

TABLE 7.3   Sample Control Process Behavior

Set Point (desired temperature t_d)	Sensed Value (actual temperature t_a)	$t_d - t_a$	Furnace State (control response u) When Hysteresis = 2
20°C	17	2	On
20°C	21	1	Nil
20°C	23	−3	Off

equivalent of a controller is an algorithm like the control strategy in Figure 7.6. The data elements of a control process are represented by process variables (sensed value, set point, manipulated variables) and constraints. The constraints on a control process govern the occurrence of changes in the state of the process being controlled. Constraints are introduced by a designer as a result of the performance requirements of a system. For example, hysteresis is a constraint governing when the state of a furnace should be changed. If the value of hysteresis is too small, the temperature controller is more likely to induce changes in the state of the furnace too often. The control process will be oversensitive to small temperature changes above or below the set point. Cruise controls (for vehicles), navigation systems (for vehicles and ships), guidance systems (for rockets), and robotic controllers are examples of systems that usually contain control processes that are combinations of hardware and software.

7.5 CALL AND RETURN ARCHITECTURES

A *call and return architecture* contains components in master-slave arrangements. This form of software architecture usually has some form of layering or hierarchy (e.g., function call and return in a Java applet included in a web page, main program block and procedures in Pascal, main program and functions in C, or main program and classes in C++).

7.5.1 Object-Oriented Architectures

In object-oriented architectures, objects are instances of classes and interact with each other through function invocations. Each class models some aspect of reality. A real-world entity is represented by an object (instantiation of a class). Classes are specified in terms of their dependencies on other classes. The key dependencies are inheritance and use relationships (Stroustrup, 1991). Interfaces for classes are specified. Classes are designed in hierarchies, as shown in the example of an object-oriented approach to the design of software for a system of robots for a nuclear power plant in Figure 7.7. The C++ code in the figure models the fact that the special-purpose inspector, emergency, and transportation classes are derived from the robot class (at the top of the hierarchy). The strength of the OO paradigm is the modeling of logically separate views of system components (e.g., user-level concepts such as inspector and transportation classes, generalization of user-level concepts embodied in the robot class, hardware resources represented by the IR_{sensor} class). The OO approach facilitates analysis of the relationships between components in the design of a software system.

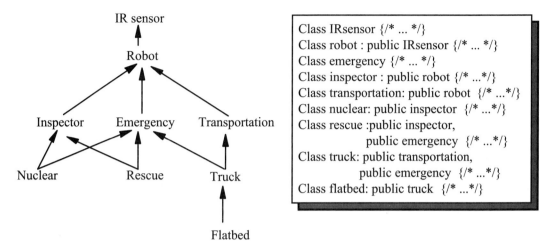

Figure 7.7 OO class hierarchy for robotic system.

Notice that in an OO system interactions between object A and object B require that object A "knows" the identity of object B. This contrasts with components in a data flow architecture. Except for its immediate successor in a pipeline, for instance, a filter does not need to know about other filters in the system.

7.5.2 Layered Architectures

A layered architecture is designed as a hierarchy of client–server processes that minimizes interaction between layers. Each layer acts as a client for the module above it and acts as a server for the module below it in a layered architecture. Layered architectures have been used in database systems, operating systems, computer-to-computer communication systems, and layered control systems for robots. The Digital VAX Virtual Memory System (VMS) architecture in Figure 7.8 is an example (Peters & Holmay, 1990). The user layer of VMS is the only layer visible to a system user. It provides the tools, editors, compilers, and application packages needed by users. The supervisor layer provides the Command Language Interpreter (CLI), which provides an interface between users and inner layers of the operating system. Command lines are typed after the system prompt '$' as in

```
$ show time               {displays current date and time}
20-May-2001 00:05:21
```

The supervisor layer provides system services and a record management system. The kernel layer takes care of memory management, input/output, process and

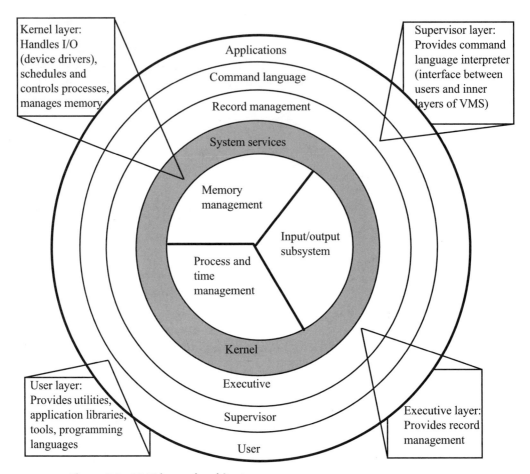

Figure 7.8   VMS layered architecture.

time management. This form of layering is very restrictive to prevent users from tampering with kernel and other system functions. It is a security-minded form of layering.

Other, less restrictive forms of layering are possible, and have been introduced. A recent, and successful alternative to the VMS form of layered architecture has been developed by Brooks in organizing control systems for intelligent autonomous mobile robots (Brooks, 1986). A robot will have the following features:

- *Multiple goals.* Controller must be responsive to high-priority (e.g., avoiding danger like falling) as well as low-priority goals (e.g., analyzing a rock sample).

- *Multiple sensors.* IR, TV, impact, acoustic, GPS.

- *Robustness.* Robot should continue to function if sensors fail.
- *Extensibility.* Ability to add more sensors, capabilities to robot.

Robot actions are grouped together in terms of desired classes of behaviors called competences. A *competence* is a sensor-driven process. Competences are represented by tuples (S, T, A), where S specifies sensory input from one or more sensors, and T performs transformations on inputs and generates output to one or more actuators in the set A. The execution of a competence triggers some form of response to stimuli. The behaviors of a mobile robot are identified with the execution of competence modules (software that implements a particular competence) (Gomi, 1997). A *level of competence* is a desired class of behaviors over all environments that a robot will encounter resulting from the execution of competence modules. The requirements for the control system are expressed informally as follows:

```
Req0:      Robot controller will consist of a small set of
           independent processors that send messages to each other.
Req1:      Each processor implements a competence module.
Req2:      Competences are hierarchical (with different levels of
           abstraction). Here is a list of competences (one per
           processor):
Abstraction Levels
(Lowest)   Level 0: Avoid contact with other objects.
           Level 1: Wander aimlessly without hitting things.
           Level 2: Explore, seeing places in the distance that look
                    reachable, heading for them.
           Level 3: Build map of environment, plan routes from one
                    place to another.
           Level 4: Monitor changes in static environment.
           Level 5: Identify objects.
           Level 6: Plan changes to the world.
(Highest)  Level 7: Reason about behavior of objects.
Req3:      Processes send messages to each other over connecting
           wires (no handshaking or acknowledgement of messages is
           required). Processors run completely asynchronously
           (monitoring input wires, sending messages over output
           wires).
```

A partial representation of the robot control satisfying the informal requirements (only levels 0 to 4 are represented) can be given in the form of statecharts shown in Figure 7.9. The competences are represented by orthogonal statecharts in Figure 7.10 to satisfy the requirement that each competence is carried out by a separate processor that runs asynchronously (there is no form of communication between processors, no shared global memory, no central control). These requirements can be satisfied by separating task-achieving behaviors into layers,

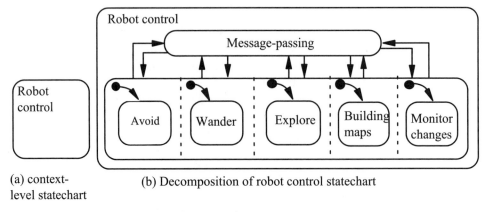

(a) context-
level statechart

(b) Decomposition of robot control statechart

Figure 7.9 Statechart for robot control system.

each with different tasks to perform relative to inputs from sensors, by viewing control in terms of layers of competence (see Figure 7.10).

In the Brooks control system, higher-level layers can subsume the roles of lower level layers whenever they wish to take control. All layers have access to inputs from sensors. The layers below a particular layer (e.g., level 3) form a complete operational control system (levels 2, 1, and 0 control movements of

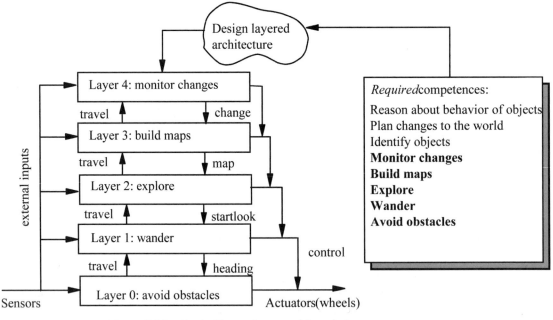

Figure 7.10 Control layers for a mobile robot.

the robot). Each layer is run by its own processor, and processors send messages asynchronously to each other. All processors are created equal (there is no central control within a layer). The Brooks architecture is also an example of the combination of three architectural paradigms: process control, layered, and virtual machine.

The layered form of software architecture has a number of advantages. Layered architectures provide an incremental approach to designing a complex system. This simplifies the development of a system. Layered systems facilitate enhancement (services are added to a layer when needed). Layering works well whenever system requirements call for independent tasks organized hierarchically.

7.6 INDEPENDENT-PROCESS ARCHITECTURES

Independent-process software architectures are characterized by collections of independent, possibly communicating processes. In the case of distributed or parallel processing systems, separate processors are used, and problems are solved cooperatively by communicating machines. The communicating process model was pioneered by Hoare (1978, 1985) and Milner (1980, 1989).

7.6.1 Communicating Processes

A communicating process is an object with input and output ports. A *port* is an identifiable means of "wiring" processes together. Ports are connected by input or output channels. A *channel* provides a means of communication in one direction between two processes. A process with only two channels (one input channel called "left," one output channel called "right") is called a pipe (Figure 7.11). Pipes are connected together to form a pipeline.

Processes can be connected together to form mesh, tree, or any other configuration of concurrent, communicating processes. A sample mesh architecture is shown in Figure 7.12. In the hypothetical mesh architecture, an incoming message contains routing information as well as other information (e.g., steps

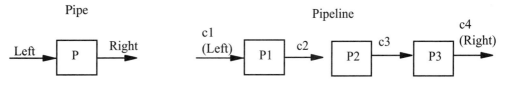

Figure 7.11 Pipe and pipeline.

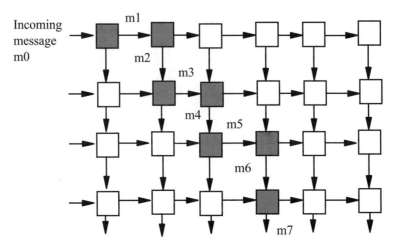

Figure 7.12   Sample mesh architecture.

to be performed in achieving a result). Imagine that the shaded processes each perform some task relative to the message received, and that as the processing continues the sequences of messages m0 to m7 is formed. The final message m7 completes the computational sequence.

A principal advantage to the communicating processes form of architecture is that it leads to extensible structures (ones that can evolve concurrently). Architectures can be extended by adding new channels and concurrent processes. The evolving mesh in Figure 7.13 is an example.

The specification language CSP (Communicating Sequential Processes) was

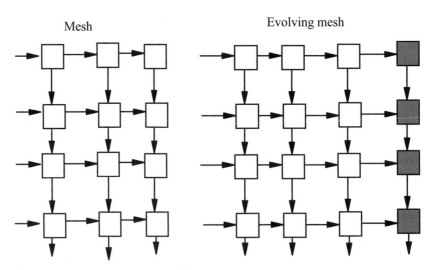

Figure 7.13   Evolving mesh architecture.

TABLE 7.4 CSP Notation

Notation	Meaning	Notation	Meaning
a → P	Event a then process P	(a → P | b → Q)	Choose a → P or b → Q, depending on evaluation of a, b (assume a ≠ b)
P ‖ Q	P in parallel with Q	*P	Iterate P
P ; Q	P (successfully) followed by Q	VM = P	Process P named VM
b * P	While b repeat P	x := e	Assign value e to x
b ! e	Output value of message e on channel b	b ? e	Input message x from channel b

introduced by Hoare (1978, 1985), which is the basis for the programming language Occam. CSP is used as an example of an architectural description language (Inverardi & Wolf, 1995). CSP offers a concise means of creating architectural descriptions of systems of communicating processes. Let P and Q be names of processes and let a and b be names of events. An *event* is an instantaneous, observable occurrence. Specifying a process means describing the behavior pattern of an object. A subset of the notation used by CSP is given in Table 7.4. Let ::= and | be syntactic symbols meaning "is rewritten as" and "or," respectively. These symbols are used to define the syntax for a language. They are known as Bachus Naur Form (BNF) grammar symbols. The syntax for CSP architectural descriptions is given in Figure 7.14.

```
    ::= a → P                        {event a, then process P}
    | cond → Y                       {cond true, then Y where Y = event or Y = process P}
    | P; Q                           {P before process Q}
    | P ‖ Q                          {P in parallel with process Q}
    | *P                             {repeat P indefinitely long}
    | if cond then P else Q          {choose P if cond holds, otherwise choose process Q}
    | x := const                     {assign value of const (constant) to x}
    | STOP                           {process which never engages in any action}
    | SKIP                           {process which does nothing but terminate successfully}
    | wait t                         {delay t ticks of clock}
    | wait t; P                      {delay t before P}
Q ::= P                              {some process P}
a :: =| ch ? msg                     {input message msg on channel ch}
    | ch ! msg                       {output message msg on channel ch}
    | op                             {observable result produced by operation}
    | op(params)                     { observable result produced by operation op with
                                            parameters params}
cond ::= expr                        {condition cond is a boolean expression expr}
params ::= in-list; out-list         {in-list = input parameters, out-list = computed results}
```

Figure 7.14 Syntax for a subset of CSP language.

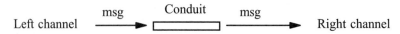

Figure 7.15   Architecture of a pipe.

Receiving a message and sending a message are examples of events. Let left and right be the names of channels for a process named pipe, and let msg be the name of a message passed through the pipe that serves as conduit for a message (Figure 7.15). Now the pipe in Figure 7.15 is described as a process with a message-passing behavior, which repeats itself forever as follows:

$$\text{pipe} = (\text{left}\,?\,\text{msg} \to (\text{right}\,!\,\text{msg} \to \text{pipe}))$$

In other words, in the pipe process, a message named msg is received by the left channel, output by the right channel, and then the process reverts back to pipe (waiting for the next message). To make the pipe process more than a mere conduit for a message, we can endow the pipe with processing capability. Let P be the name of a process that supplies input to a pipe, and let Display be a process that displays the output from a pipe. In addition, let F1, F2, and F3 be filter processes (each transforming its input from a pipe, and supplying output to a pipe). A graphical representation of one form of the architecture of a pipeline running internally on a single workstation is shown in Figure 7.16. Notice that P, F1, F2, F3, and Out could be processes running on various combinations of separate computers connected together in a network. The architecture of this pipeline can be described concisely in CSP as follows:

$$\text{pipeline} = *(\text{P; pipe0; F1; pipe1; F2; pipe2; F3; pipe3; Out})$$

Each one of the pipes in Figure 7.16 is "wired" relative to a specific source of input and output. For the sake of clarity, we use the process name supplying input to a pipe also as the name of the channel on the left side of a pipe. Similarly, the channel for the right side of a pipe is given the same as the process

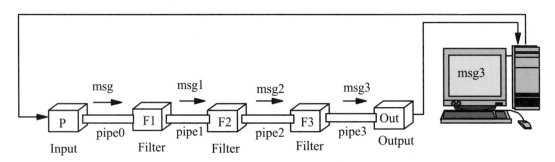

Figure 7.16   Sample pipeline process.

receiving the output of a pipe. These pipes have the following architectural descriptions in CSP:

pipe0 = (P ? msg → (F1 ! msg → pipe0))   {input from P sent to filter F1}
pipe1 = (F1 ? msg → (F2 ! msg → pipe1))   {input from F1 sent to filter F2}
pipe2 = (F2 ? msg → (F3 ! msg → pipe2))   {input from F2 sent to filter F3}
pipe3 = (F3 ? msg → (Out ! msg → pipe3))   {input from F3 sent to Out}

The architecture of each of the filters F1, F2, and F3 can also be described succinctly in CSP. The pipeline architecture can be improved by building into the design a provision for letting filter F1 begin processing the next input to the pipeline without waiting for the rest of the pipeline to complete its processing of the input sent by F1. In other words, the improved architecture would resemble an assembly line in a manufacturing system (e.g., assembly of an automobile). Each time a stage Si in an assembly line completes its work on some feature of a product P1 and forwards it to the stage Si+1, work on the next input Si can be immediately processes produce P2 without waiting for the rest of assembly line to complete its work on P1. This form of a pipeline architecture can also be described in CSP with multiple uses of the parallel ''‖'' operator.

Notice that the output of a filter in a pipeline can be ''wired'' to more than one pipe in add-on pipelines. In other words, parallel pipeline processing is possible. This is shown graphically in Figure 7.17. The advantage to a parallel pipeline is that it provides more than one way to process the input to a pipeline. In the sample pipeline in Figure 7.17, filter F1 serves a preprocessor for two pipelines that are connected by the T-pipe to the output of F1. This form of

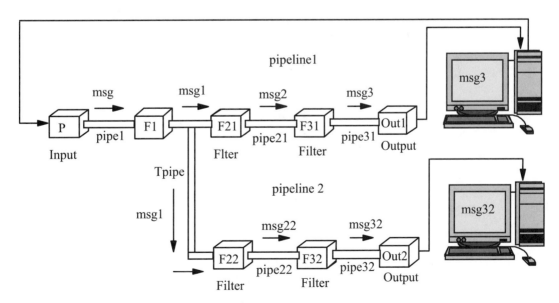

Figure 7.17 Pipelining with a T-pipe.

pipelining could be used to develop multiple views of the same input (e.g., the heading computed by an obstacle avoid module in a multilayered robot control system could be simultaneously processed by wander and explore modules representing parts of separate pipelines). Let pipeline1 and pipeline2 be pipelines. The architecture of these parallel pipelines in Figure 7.17 can be described in CSP as follows:

$$\text{ParallelPipeline} = (\text{pipeline1} \parallel \text{pipeline2})$$

The architecture of the individual pipelines in Figure 7.17 is described in CSP as follows:

$$\text{pipeline1} = *(\text{P}; \text{pipe1}; \text{F1}; \text{Tpipe}; \text{F21}; \text{pipe21}; \text{F31}; \text{pipe31}; \text{Out1})$$
$$\text{pipeline2} = *(\text{P}; \text{pipe1}; \text{F1}; \text{Tpipe}; \text{F22}; \text{pipe22}; \text{F32}; \text{pipe32}; \text{Out2})$$

The architecture of the Tpipe in Figure 7.17 has the following description in CSP:

$$\text{Tpipe} = (\text{F1 ? msg1} \rightarrow ((\text{F21 ! msg1} \rightarrow \text{Tpipe}) \parallel$$
$$(\text{F22 ! msg1} \rightarrow \text{Tpipe})$$
$$)$$

In other words, the Tpipe is configured so that it receives input msg1 from filter F1, and then it concurrently sends message msg1 both to filter F21 and to filter F22. After sending the same message to two filters, the Tpipe waits for the next message from filter F1. Notice that other forms of Tpipes are possible. For example, a Tpipe could be designed that passes its input simultaneously to several, separate pipelines. It is also possible to design a Upipe that takes input from two filters in parallel pipelines and sends the input to a third pipeline. A graphical representation of parallel pipelines with a U pipe is shown in Figure 7.18. The outputs of filters F11 and F12 in the Figure are msg11 and msg12, respectively. These outputs are sent through the Upipe to filter F22, which transforms the combined inputs (msg11, msg12) to produce message m22. The architectural description of a parallel pipeline with a U-shaped pipe can be described succinctly in CSP, and needs to be described separately in CSP.

7.6.2   Agent Architecture

An *agent* is a complete, independent information processing system with its own input/output ports, memory, and internal processing capability. An agent cyclically processes its inputs, updates its own state, and may produce output or change its interest in input event classes. More simply, an agent is a triple (I, Processing, O), with a set of I from a network of channels connected to other

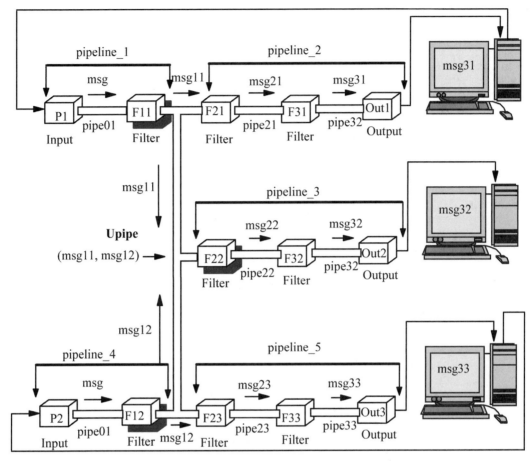

Figure 7.18 Pipelining with a U-pipe.

agents and the environment, transformation capabilities embodied in a Processor, and set of outputs O. An agent that does nothing but "forward" its inputs to other agents is an example of a pipe with the following form:

$$(I, \{\ \}, O) \qquad \text{\{pipe agent\}}$$

The architecture of an agent is determined by selecting its sensors, the structure of its Processor (its capabilities), and its output channels to the outside world (to actuators). Agents in an interactive system that communicate directly with a user are called interactors (Coutaz, 1994) or intelligent agents (O'Leary, 1997). Intelligent agents perform tasks in the background while a user performs other tasks. Agents can function by themselves or cooperatively in a network. Agents can also be incorporated into a real-time system, where the tasks performed by each agent are time constrained (i.e., tasks must be performed before some preset deadline). For example, assume that the requirements for a system are specified as follows:

> ### *Example Requirements for an Agent*
>
> Req1: Construct a system of agents that cooperate to accomplish the system mission.
> Req2: Each agent is designed to work on a designated task.
> Req3: Agents communicate over a network (of channels).
> Req4: Each agent is time constrained (the duration allowed for each task is limited).
> Req5: Agents periodically report the status of their work.
> Req6: Work performed must satisfy a set of quality-of-product standards.
> Req7: Agents have the capability to run Java applets

These requirements can be satisfied by constructing a network of agents managed by a coordinator agent (Peters & Sohi, 1996). These requirements can be partially represented with Petri net description for a sample, time-constrained agent as shown in Figure 7.19. The agent in Figure 7.19 receives a message (task, limit),

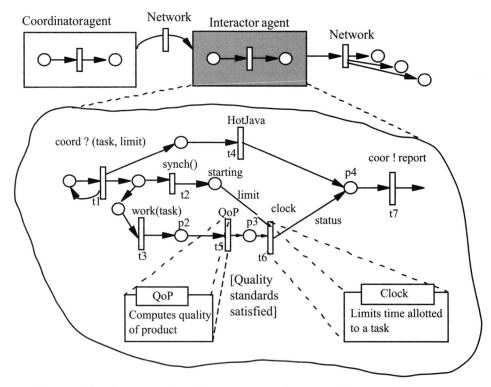

Figure 7.19   Time-constrained interactor agent in a network.

which specifies a task to perform and a limit on the duration allocated to perform the task. The message comes over a channel connected to a coordinator process. The work performed by the interactor agent is constrained by a set of quality-of-product standards represented by the QoP transition and a timer represented by the clock transition. The QoP transition fires whenever the quality standards for a product have been satisfied by the work transition. The work, QoP, and clock transitions are hierarchical, and need to be decomposed to get a better understanding of how the agent functions. Notice also that transition t7 sends progress reports to the coordinator. This transition fires whenever it receives input from the clock transition. The architecture of the subnet for the clock transition can be designed so that reports are sent to the coordinator periodically (say, every 30 seconds) rather than continuously.

A layer in the Brooks control system for intelligent mobile robots is an example of an agent. The required processing components of the Toyota navigation system (information center, individual vehicle navigation systems, communication center) for controlling vehicular traffic is a form of multiagent system. In a multiagent system, the agent model is a realization of the more general notion of distributed artificial intelligence (dAI). A dAI is a collection of cooperating agents with varying degrees of competence. In a dAI, agents can either be cognitive (capable of inference and decision-making as in higher levels of the Brooks control system) or reactive (limited computation ability to process stimuli or input from sensors). Multiagent system models are extremely powerful. Such systems are engineered in terms of a distributed organization of cooperating agents (each with its own particular processing capabilities). It is easy to add agents to such a system, which means that multiagent systems are extensible. The capabilities of an agent can be modified, which means that the agent model is flexible. Internally, the structure of an agent can be built out of interconnected objects so that an object-oriented approach can be taken in the design of agents. Agents in a multiagent system are orthogonal to each other (each performs its tasks independent of other agents in the system), which means that statecharts provide a natural means of specifying the requirements for a multiagent system. Notice, also, that orthogonal statecharts suggests a straightforward *transition from requirements to the design* of a multiagent system. Multiagent systems are modular (a group of agents can be partitioned into subgroups), which suggests that the reusability of agent architectures. In summary, multiagent models support modularity, parallelism, distribution of tasks, flexibility, extensibility, and reuse.

7.7 VIRTUAL MACHINE ARCHITECTURES

A virtual machine is a software architecture endowed with the capabilities of an actual machine. The idea is to design a software architecture with behavior patterns that mimic a physical system when the architecture is implemented and executed. One well-known example is an idealized distributed computer system that runs on a collection of networked machines but has the appearance of ("acts" like) a uniprocessor to users of the system. In this sense, this idealized distributed system is a virtual uniprocessor (Tanenbaum, 1995). Virtual machines are usually layers of software built atop an actual machine, which is not visible to a user. It is the software interface for a virtual machine which a user "sees," not the actual machine. Rule-based systems (e.g., expert systems like Mycin), interpreters (e.g., UCSD Pascal or LISP), quasi-intelligent systems (e.g., planner in Brooks' control system), and Chemical Abstract Machines or CHAMs (e.g., stages of compilers and interpreters viewed as molecular structures interacting with each other) are examples of virtual machines.

7.7.1   Intelligent System Architectures

The software architecture of an intelligent system is a collection of structures making it possible to fetch data (from sensors), process the data, and act on (possibly store) the results of processing. Fetching, processing, and acting can be realized in a variety of ways in intelligent systems:

- ({sensor}, perception, {actuator})
- ({sensor}, dead-reckoning method using metric knowledge, {actuator})
- ({sensor}, plan route, control sequence)
- ({sensor}, monitor execution, physical actions)
- ({sensor}, plan destination sequence, control sequence)
- ({sensor}, go to (competence))

In the context of robotic systems, intelligent systems are adaptive (making adjustments in movements of wheels or legs or belts or arms based on evaluation of inputs from sensors, immediate route-plan, and long-range goals). An Adaptive Intelligent System (AIS) perceives, reasons, acts to achieve multiple goals in dynamic, uncertain, complex environments (Hayes-Roth et al., 1995). The informal requirements for an AIS are as follows:

Req0: An AIS consists of two modules: physical and cognition.

Req1: The physical module implements perception and action in an external environment.

Req2: The cognition module carries out reasoning activities (situation assessment, planning, problem-solving).

Req3: Information flow between modules is bidirectional.

Req4: Each module acts as a filter, where one module transforms the input from another module.

> Req5: Each module contains a world model, set of behaviors, current plan, meta-controller, selected behavior being executed.
>
> Req6: A *meta-controller* follows a system's current control plan by executing the most appropriate enabled behavior.
>
> Req7: A *behavior* contains a potential application of methods to accomplish some task (e.g., reactive control to navigate along a path, reacting to perceived obstacles by changing direction).

An AIS can be represented more formally as a context-level statechart, which is decomposed into orthogonal statecharts representing competences (physical and cognitive). The two statecharts are given in Figure 7.20. A transition from the statechart in part (b) of Figure 7.20 must be made to a software architecture for the AIS, which combines three architectural styles: layering, pipelining and virtual machines. Since each competence in the AIS acts as a filter, it is natural to introduce a bidirectional pipeline architecture to handle information flow between the physical and cognitive competence modules. Since the individual competences are orthogonal to each other and yet represent varying degrees of abstraction (the cognitive competence is more abstract than the physical competence module), an AIS can organize as two layers: a cognitive level and a physical level connected by a pipe. In addition, the competence modules themselves constitute a virtual reasoning system (cognition level) and perception–action virtual machine (physical level). That is, the actions of each competence module mimics an actual machine. The cognitive module mimics a thinking ("human") machine, and the physical module mimics a sensing and reacting

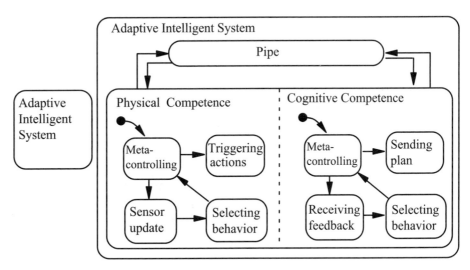

(a) Context-level AIS

(b) Decomposition of AIS into competences

Figure 7.20 Statechart representation of AIS.

(stimulus–response) machine. A CSP architectural description of an AIS is given initially very simply as two high-level communicating processes:

$$AIS = (\text{cognition-process} \parallel \text{physical-process} \parallel \text{pipe})$$

Then the architecture of the individual processes are described in more detail as follows:

$$cognition = (\text{meta-controlling} \rightarrow$$
$$(\text{pipe ? (perceptions, action-feedback)} \rightarrow$$
$$(\text{selecting-behavior} \rightarrow$$
$$(\text{pipe ! (physical actions)} \rightarrow \text{cognition}))))$$

$$physical = (\text{meta-controlling} \rightarrow$$
$$(\text{pipe ? (physical-actions)} \rightarrow$$
$$(\text{sensor-ch ? (sensor-inputs)} \rightarrow$$
$$(\text{select-behavior} \rightarrow$$
$$(\text{pipe ! (world-model)} \rightarrow$$
$$(\text{environment-ch ! (physical-actions)} \rightarrow$$
$$\text{physical}))))))$$

$$pipe = (\text{if cognition-receiving then physical-ch ? (perceptions, action-feedback)}$$
$$\text{else if cognition-sending then physical-ch ! (physical actions)}$$
$$\text{else if physical-receiving then cognition-ch ? (physical-actions)}$$
$$\text{else if physical-sending then cognition-ch ! (world-model)}$$
$$\text{else no-communication then pipe)}$$

Each CSP description identifies a behavior pattern of the competences in an AIS. For example, the behavior pattern for cognition repeats itself infinitely often. The architecture of cognition process is elaborated in CSP as follows.

$$cognition = (\text{meta-controlling} \rightarrow \text{pipe ? (perceptions, action-feedback)} \rightarrow$$
$$\text{selecting-behavior} \rightarrow \text{pipe ! (physical actions)} \rightarrow$$
$$(\text{meta-controlling} \rightarrow \text{pipe ? (perceptions, action-feedback)} \rightarrow$$
$$\text{selecting-behavior} \rightarrow \text{pipe ! (physical actions)} \rightarrow \text{cognition})$$

A more complete description of the AIS architecture can be achieved after the statecharts in Figure 7.20 are made more detailed. That is, condition–action labels need to be added to the statecharts to specify the events leading to each change of state in the two competences. In addition, the orthogonality of the statecharts for the two competences in Figure 7.20 is represented by parallel processes in the CSP description of an AIS. The layering in an AIS is quite different from the one in Brooks' subsumption architecture. Unlike the Brooks control structure, modules in an AIS communicate directly with each other over a pipeline. AIS competences are synchronized.

7.7.2 Chemical Abstract Machine Architecture

A CHemical Abstract Machine (CHAM) software architecture was introduced to describe parallel computation where there is no hint of sequential behavior. The notion of a CHAM was introduced by Bouldol in 1992, and the suitability of CHAMs for software architectural description and analysis has been explored by Inverardi and Wolf (1995). A CHAM takes inspiration from the smallest portion to which a substance can be reduced by subdivision without losing its chemical identity, namely, a molecule. A CHAM is an abstract machine constructed with structures resembling chemical solutions and behaviors modeled after chemical reactions. In a CHAM architecture, processing elements called molecules "live" together in clustering software structures called solutions. Molecules interact with each other according to a set of reaction rules.

A CHAM is constructed by defining molecules m1, m2, . . . , collections of molecules called solutions S, S', . . . , and transformation rules T, T', ... Let S and A be a sensor and actuator, respectively. Both sensors and actuators are represented in software by data structures like records, stacks, queues, and files. Let i(S) and o(A) specify input from a sensor and output to an actuator, respectively. Notice that i(S) and o(A) serve as connectors between molecules. The output of one molecule represented by o(A) can become the input of another molecule, namely, i(o(A)). In addition, let P be a processing element (means of transformation of input to output) in a molecule. In its simplest form, a molecule is built with the elements contained in the set {I, P, O}, where I is a set of inputs, P is a processing element, and O is a set of outputs. The elements I, P, O are the atoms of a molecule. Let $\diamond$ be an infix operator used to bind the atoms of a molecule together.

To see how a CHAM might be used to specify the architecture of a behavior belonging to a competence for a robot, for example, let I, P, O be represented by sensor-signal, operation plan-changes, and output plan. Then the software structure for a competence is represented by the molecules in Table 7.5. This may appear to be just a cosmetic difference between the layered architectural representation of competence levels in Figure 7.10 and molecules in Table 7.5. A layered architecture has the advantage of suggesting increasing levels of

TABLE 7.5 Molecular Descriptions of Competences

Competence level	I	P	O	Molecule
Reasoning	Behavior	Reason	Plan	i(behavior) $\diamond$ reason $\diamond$ o(plan)
Change world	Plan	Formulate	World	i(plan) $\diamond$ formulate $\diamond$ o(state of world)
Notice changes	Scene	Notice	Feature	i(scene) $\diamond$ notice $\diamond$ o(feature of environment)

abstraction in a hierarchy of competences. However, layering tends to hide the intended independence of the processors that implement each level of competence. A layered architecture also hides the evolution (emergent behavior) of competences. There is no suggestion in a layered architecture that a new set of behaviors can emerge from an existing set of behaviors in a competence. A molecular architecture satisfies the requirement that competences be independent of each other. The molecules in Table 7.5 do their processing in parallel. Instead of layers to describe competence levels, molecules describing competence modules are collected together in solutions. Each competence level is realized in a CHAM as a solution. The evolution of a robot control system can be realized by the application of reaction laws so that one solution can be transformed into new solution. Solutions can evolve independently of other solutions. The emergence of new behaviors (ones not built into a competence but resulting from transformations performed by a molecule) can be realized in a CHAM architecture with reaction, extraction, and absorption operations. A molecule can be added to {extracted from} a solution with an absorption {extraction} operation.

Reactions between molecules and solutions of molecules are governed by laws. Let $\rightarrow$ specify a replacement ("rewrite") operation. The notation m $\rightarrow$ m' means that molecule m is replaced by molecule m'. In chemical terms, a reaction occurs. A new molecule emerges as a result of the reaction. Let m1, m2, . . . mk be molecules. The architecture of a solution is represented by molecules separated by commas. Let S, S', S1, S2, . . . Sn be solutions. Let ©, ® represent absorption ("combining") and extraction ("removing") operations, respectively. These operations can be used to combine molecules with solutions *and* to combine one solution with another one. The notation m©S means molecule m is added to solution S. Similarly, the notation m®S means molecule m is extracted (removed from) solution S. The basic CHAM laws are as follows:

> **Reaction laws:** m1, m2, . . . , mk $\rightarrow$ m1, m2, . . . , mk
> **Chemical law:** S $\rightarrow$ S' implies S©S'' $\rightarrow$ S'©S''
> **Absorption law:** m©S $\rightarrow$ S'
> **Extraction law:** m®S $\rightarrow$ S'

Putting these ideas together, we formulate an architectural description language based on the CHAM model. Let P, D, C, M represent processing elements p1, p2, . . . , data elements d1, d2, . . . , communication constructs for input i(D) and output o(D), and molecule M. Borrowing from CSP, the parallelism of molecules m and m' in a solution is represented by writing m $\parallel$ m'. These symbols can be used to describe a sample architectural description language, which is given in Figure 7.21. In other words, a solution can consist of one or more molecules. Notice that solutions can be contained inside solutions. A subsolution is called a membrane. The advantage to the membrane construct

$$S ::= M \mid M \circledR S \mid M \copyright S \mid S \copyright S \qquad \{solution\}$$
$$m ::= C \Diamond P \Diamond C \mid C \Diamond C \mid m \parallel m \qquad \{molecule\}$$
$$P ::= p1 \mid p2 \mid \ldots \mid pk \qquad \{processing\ elements\}$$
$$D ::= d1 \mid d2 \mid \ldots \mid dn \qquad \{data\ elements\}$$
$$C ::= i(D) \mid o(D) \qquad \{input, output\}$$

Figure 7.21 Grammar for CHAM architectural description language.

is that the effects of a transformation can be localized within a membrane. Membranes can evolve independently of other solutions (in particular, other subsolutions in a solution). To illustrate this idea, we use the description language in Figure 7.21 to describe a Brooks robot controller as a molecular structure (Figure 7.22). Notice that a molecule of the form i(data) $\Diamond$ o(data) is a pipe. A pipeline can be designed by combining a pipe with two processing molecules:

$$pipeline = (i(x) \Diamond op1 \Diamond o(x')) \copyright (i(x') \Diamond o(x')) \copyright (i(x') \Diamond op2 \Diamond o(x''))$$

D (data)	P (processing)	Robot Controller Architecture as a Molecular Structure
IR signal	avoid	control = (i(IR signal) $\Diamond$ avoid $\Diamond$ o(move) $\parallel$
object	wander	i(scene) $\Diamond$ wander $\Diamond$ o(move) $\parallel$
scene	explore	i(scene) $\Diamond$ explore $\Diamond$ o(move) $\parallel$
behavior	build map	i(world model) $\Diamond$ build map $\Diamond$ o(map) $\parallel$
task	notice	i(scene) $\Diamond$ notice $\Diamond$ o(change-list)) '
map	reason about world	
plan	perform tasks	(i(object) $\Diamond$ reason about world $\Diamond$ o(task) $\parallel$
world model	formulate plans	i(task) $\Diamond$ perform tasks $\Diamond$ o(action)) '
move	execute plans	
change-list	reason about behavior	(i(world model) $\Diamond$ formulate plans $\Diamond$ o(plan) $\parallel$
	modify plans	i(plan) $\Diamond$ execute plan $\Diamond$ o(action)) $\copyright$
		(i(objects) $\Diamond$ reason about behavior $\Diamond$ o(change-list) $\parallel$
		i (change-list) $\Diamond$ modify plans $\Diamond$ o(plan))
		)

Figure 7.22 CHAM architecture for a robot controller.

To model the evolution of the subsolution representing the highest level of abstraction in a robot controller, the following transformation rules can be defined:

$$E1 = i(objects) \diamond \text{reason about behavior} \diamond o(change\text{-}list) \text{ ©}$$
$$(i(new\ objects) \diamond \text{reason about behavior} \diamond o(change\text{-}list)) \rightarrow$$
$$(i(objects) \diamond \text{reason about behavior} \diamond o(change\text{-}list)) \text{ ©}$$
$$(i(new\ objects) \diamond \text{reason about behavior} \diamond o(new\ change\text{-}list))$$

$$E2 = i(change\text{-}list) \diamond \text{modify plans} \diamond o(plan) \text{ ©}$$
$$(i(new\ change\text{-}list) \diamond \text{modify plans} \diamond o(plan)) \rightarrow$$
$$(i(change\text{-}list) \diamond \text{modify plans} \diamond o(plan)) \text{ ©}$$
$$(i(new\ change\text{-}list) \diamond \text{modify plans} \diamond o(new\ plan))$$

Rules E1 and E2 are examples of reactions. Rule E1 says that repeated observations about changes in the behavior of objects can lead to observations about new behavioral changes. Rule E2 says that repeated reasoning about change-lists can lead to modified plans (combined with "old" plans). Many other transformation rules are possible.

7.8 REPOSITORY ARCHITECTURES

A repository architecture is used to design various forms of information management systems. This form of software architecture is characterized by a central data structure representing the current state, and independent components that operate on a central data store. For example, a reuse library system is a repository used in software factories (Merritt, 1994). A reuse library stores artifacts for later reuse in software development projects, and has led to an order of magnitude increase in software productivity in Japan. Other examples of repositories are database systems, web hypertext environment, archival systems (e.g., city historical record systems), and knowledge-based systems called blackboards.

7.8.1 Reuse Library Systems

A reuse library system includes a central store for artifacts and operations use to manage and evaluate a collection. The artifacts include software system plan, software requirements specification, prototype, program source code, designs, architectures, test plan, test suites, maintenance plan, and documentation. A reuse library has the following requirements:

```
Req0: Storage for artifacts
Req1: Classify artifacts according to keywords
```

```
Req2: Catalogue (alphabetical list with descriptive
      information about) artifacts
Req3: Install artifacts in library
Req4: Evaluate quality of reusable assets in
      inventory
Req5: Estimate value of instances of reuse of
      artifacts
Req6: Retrieve artifacts
Req7: Identify possible artifacts
```

Classifying, cataloguing, and installing function together. Evaluating, estimating, retrieving, and identifying operations represent system structures independent of each other. These observations lead to the statechart in Figure 7.23. Notice that each of these structures filter (transform) the information they receive from each other. Hence, a pipeline architecture would appear to be a good choice to handle communication between these structures. These structures could also be organized in layers or in a multiagent system. Since these structures are nonhierarchical, layering is inappropriate. The orthogonality of these structures represented by the statechart in Figure 7.23 suggests that using a multiagent system architecture for the reuse system is more appropriate. Since agents normally rely on message passing over a network to communicate with each other, the choice of an agent-oriented architecture would be mean connecting agents together over a network instead of a pipeline.

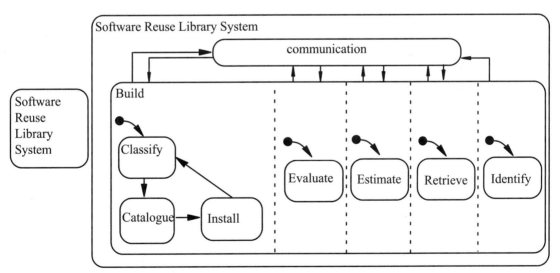

(a) Context-level reuse library

(b) Decomposition of Reuse Library System

Figure 7.23 Statecharts for a software reuse library system.

7.8.2   Blackboard Architecture

A blackboard architecture is a knowledge-based form of repository appropriate in applications requiring cooperative problem solving by virtual minds, human minds, or both (Hayes-Roth, 1985). A typical blackboard system has a structure like the one shown in Figure 7.24. A blackboard has three basic components:

- *Knowledge sources.* Independent processes whose actions are triggered by satisfaction of particular conditions.
- *Blackboard.* Repository of problem-solving state data, organized in an application-dependent hierarchy: level n (highest) to level 1 (lowest).
- *Control.* Monitors information in the blackboard, maintains permissible combinations of knowledge source activations, schedules pending knowledge-source activations (KSAs), evaluates local problem-solving goals, and executes scheduled KSAs to solve some problem specific to the blackboard.

The activity of a knowledge source is event driven. Each change in the blackboard is an event that can satisfy the condition of one or more knowledge sources. Whenever the condition in a knowledge source is satisfied, this adds a Knowledge Source Activation Record (KSAR) to a queue, and eventually triggers an action by the knowledge source. The steps in setting up a control plan for a blackboard are shown in the statechart in Figure 7.25. The *strategy* state develops a sequential plan (action sequences) for solving a problem. Completion of a strategy session is followed by a change of state to Evaluation. In the *evaluation* state, local problem-solving goals are determined. Next the *scheduling* state determines scheduling criteria and sets of pending KSAs are arranged hierarchically (soonest KSA,

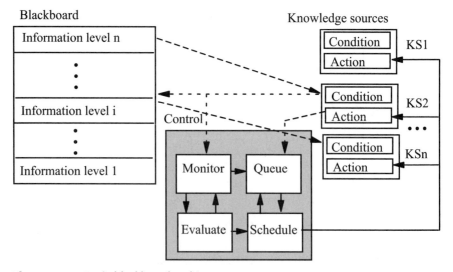

Figure 7.24   Basic blackboard architecture.

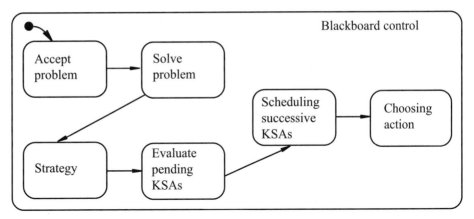

Figure 7.25 Blackboard control.

followed by next soonest KSA, and so on). The chosen knowledge source action is the highest one in the trigger list of KSAs determined by the scheduler.

An application of the blackboard of interest in software development is the Design Evolution Blackboard (DEB), which provides global workspace used in the engineering design of a product (Londono et al., 1989). The requirements for a DEB are as follows:

Example Requirements for a Design Evolution Blackboard

Req0: Designers interact and reach a consensus about pieces of a design before they incorporated into a solution in a Product Process Organization (PPO).

Req1: A repository system supports communication and cooperation between designers.

Req2: Designs, intentions, and actions are stored as assertions on the blackboard, and become conditions for actions by one or more KSA.

Req3: A virtual designer (condition, design-action) is a knowledge source.

Req3: The blackboard helps a Process Leader (PL) coordinate design activities.

Req4: Established mechanisms (scheduling suggestions) that a PL can use to develop, assign, and keep track of tasks.

Req5: The blackboard helps a PL detect conflicts and guides evolution of PPO by identifying constraints (timing, resource) and dependencies.

Req6: The blackboard schedules final sign-off, assisting PL in keeping track of task completion, assuring acceptance of assertions of quality.

Req7: The blackboard maintains a quality product structure tree.

Req8: Blackboard communication is over a network.

A blackboard architecture works well for a DEB for several reasons. First, the work done by one designer affects what is done by other designers. A blackboard provides a natural partition of different parts of a design problem among groups of designers. The blackboard provides a conduit for information to designers who are affected by particular dependencies (how their actions affect other designers). Dependency tables are published on the blackboard. The completion of one action by a designer (triggered by a knowledge source) moves the design process forward, causing the next knowledge-source actions to be carried out.

7.9 DOMAIN-SPECIFIC ARCHITECTURES

A domain-specific software architecture is tailored to the needs of a particular application domain. For example, software for the IBM Deep Blue chess-playing system and Chinook checkers-playing system consists of processing elements designed to carry out strategies to win a game (Schaeffer, 1997). Neural-based software architectures are designed with a repetition of processing elements called neurons. The neural computing paradigm takes its inspiration from neurological activity of the brain. Genetic-based software architectures are designed with processing elements (mutation, selection, reproduction, crossover, fitness) inspired by evolution in nature. This form of domain-specific software has its realization in genetic programming (Koza, 1993).

7.9.1 Genetic-based Architectures

> **The genetic programming paradigm parallels nature in that it is a never-ending process.**
> —(J.R. KOZA, 1993)

Software architectures representing the genetic programming paradigm are designed to track the evolution of a population of computer programs. The overall aim of genetic programming is to arrive at a population judged to be most fit to solve a particular problem. The basic building blocks of genetic programs are functions and terminals. A non-exhaustive list of examples of functions and terminals is given in Table 7.6. The combination of functions and terminals in an architecture will depend on some intended language such as Pascal, LISP, or C.

7.9.2 Example: Behavior of an Ant

For example, to describe the software architecture intended to simulate the behavior of an ant, let {if-food-ahead, eat, find, prog1, prog2, prog3} and {(left),

TABLE 7.6 Functions and Terminals

Functions	Terminals
• Operations +, −, *, /, . . . • Functions sin, cos, exp, log, . . . • Connectors or, and, not • Conditionals if . . . then . . . else . . . • iteration do . . . until • Recursion	• Atoms representing inputs, sensors, detectors, state variables • Atoms representing functions with no specific arguments (e.g., left, right, move) • Constants (e.g., 3, nil)

(right), (move)} be the function and terminal sets, respectively. Assume that the move operation causes an ant to go forward an unspecified distance. Also assume that the operation left {right} cause ant to change its direction of movement and turn left {right}. A sequence (move) (left) specifies that an ant moves ahead and then turns left. The sample genetic program for a wandering ant is given in Figure 7.26.

```
(prog1 (left)                        {turn left}
   (prog2 (move) (right))            {move ahead, then turn right}
      (prog3 (move) (move) (move) (left)))) {move ahead 3 cells, then turn left}
```

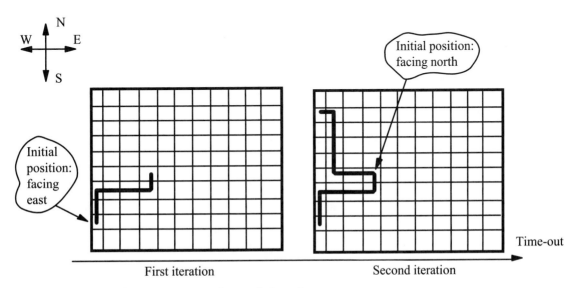

Figure 7.26 Sample wandering of an ant.

The equivalent of this LISP program in Pascal is

```
procedure move; begin {locomotion instructions} end;
procedure right; begin {locomotion instructions} end;
procedure left; begin {locomotion instructions} end;
begin
  left;
  move; right;
  move; move; move; left;
end;
```

This program repeats itself for a fixed length of time, and then times out. During one iteration, an ant traverses 9 cells in its world. The behavior repeats itself until a time-out occurs (Figure 7.27). A description of an ant finding food is given as follows:

```
(if-food-ahead (move)                           {move ahead}
  (if-food-ahead (move) (find) (eat) (right))   {move ahead, find food, eat, move right}
```

This time an ant moves ahead if it sees food. It finds food, it eats it, and then moves right. It continues search until it cannot see food or stops as a result of a timeout or bumping into a wall. Assume that an ant can see the contents of cells up to two cells ahead of itself. A sample search with two iterations is shown in Figure. 7.27, where food is represented by boxes. Even if a time-out does not occur, the ant in Figure 7.27 makes no further moves (it sees no food after the second iteration).

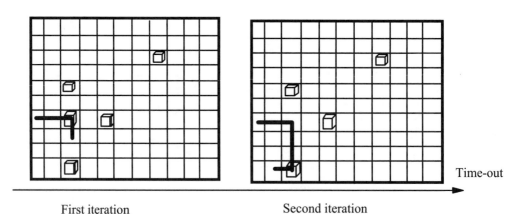

First iteration   Second iteration

Figure 7.27   Sample search for food.

7.9.3 Measuring Fitness

In the natural world, it appears that only the fittest survive. The parallel of biological fitness is found in the genetic programming paradigm in terms of measurements of performance of members of a population of programs. Assuming we have a population of tiny programs, the performance of a population can be measured with what is known as a fitness function. The simplest form of fitness function is known as raw fitness, which is a count of the number of successes achieved by members of a population. In the case of assessing the fitness of ant, raw fitness would be equal to the total number of pieces of food found by an ant during its life span. Raw fitness can be compared with some ideal value in what is known as a standardized fitness function. Let r(i, t) be the raw fitness of a population member i at any generational time t. Let rmax be the highest possible raw fitness value. Then standardized fitness s(i, t) of a population member at time t is given by

$$s(i, t) = r_{max} - r(i, t) \qquad \text{\{standardized fitness\}}$$

The *smaller* the value of s(i, t), the more optimum is the behavior of the population member. In the case of an ant searching for food, the goal is to pick the best of a generation of ants using raw fitness and standardized fitness. For example, if we let two ants, ant1 and ant2, make up a population representing the 30th generation. Then assume that these ants wander during some time interval t (Figure 7.28). Sample fitness values given in Table 7.7 show that ant2 is the best of its generation.

7.9.4 Genetic Processing Operations

The genetic processing operations reproduction, crossover, and mutation are applied to population members to create the population for a new generation, and achieve improved overall fitness in succeeding generations (Figure 7.29).

7.9.5 Application of Genetic Operations

In the sample population of ants in Figure 7.28, Ant 2 is the best of its generation, and is selected for reproduction (Ant 1 does not survive) after two iterations of

TABLE 7.7 Sample Fitness Values

Ant1, r_{max} = 150	Ant$_{2,r_{max}}$ = 150
r(30, t) = 30	r(30, t) = 90
s(30, t) = 150 − 30 = 120	s(30, t) = 150 − 90 = 60

Ant 1

if-food-ahead (move)
 (if-food-ahead (move) (eat))

rnax = 8
r(1, t) = 2
s(1, t) = 8 - 2 = 6

Ant 2

if-food-ahead (move) (eat)
 (if-food-ahead (move) (eat) (right))

rnax = 8
r(2, t) = 4
s(2, t) = 8 - 4 = 4

Apply **select** operation:
s(2, t) < s(1, t), so select s(2, t)

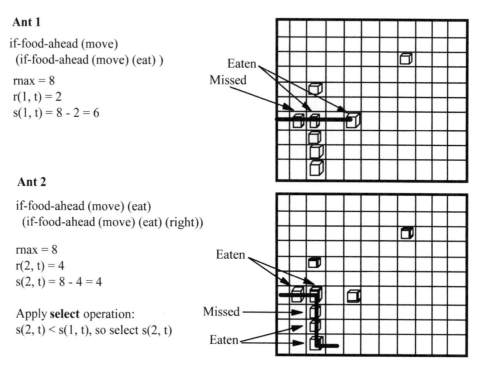

Figure 7.28   Selection of best ant.

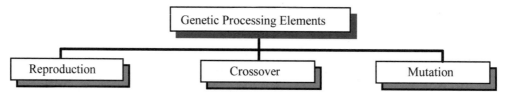

This is the basic engine of Darwinian natural selection and survival of the fittest.
Method:
(1) **Select** member of current population based on some
selection method based on a fitness measure.
(2) **Copy** without alteration selected individual from current population in the new population (next generation)

This is the equivalent of sexual recombination (new offspring consist of parts taken from each parent).
Method:
(1) **Select two parents** from a population, each with the same fitness, using the same selection method used for reproduction.
(2) **Independently select** random crossover fragment in each parent.
(3) **Replace** crossover fragment in one parent with the crossover fragment in the other parent.

Introduce random changes in structures of a population member.
Method:
(1) **Randomly select** point to be mutated (e.g., terminal in a program),
(2) **Replace** selected structure with new structure (e.g., old terminal (left) with (move))

Figure 7.29   Genetic processing operations.

its program. That is, to improve the performance of the population in the next generation, Ant 2 would be reproduced (the new population would consist of two copies of Ant 2). To illustrate how the crossover operation works, we will introduce a third ant. Let if-food-here be the name of a boolean-valued function that causes an ant to check if there is food in its current location (if-food-here returns true in the case where food is found). Assume we have an Ant 3 represented by the following code:

```
Ant 3:
if-food-ahead (move) (eat) (move)
  (if-food-here (eat) (right))
```

After two iterations, Ant 3 has eaten four pieces of food. So Ant 3 has the same fitness as Ant 2 in Figure 7.28. To perform a crossover operation, select Ants 2 and 3 based on the fact that they have the same "high-achieving" fitness. Then randomly select crossover points in each ant. For example, select the terminals (eat) (move) in line 1 of Ant 3 and terminals (eat) (right) in line 2 of Ant 2 as the crossover fragments. Then swap the fragments, and study the performance of these ants in the next generation. As an example of mutation, randomly select a fragment to be mutated in one of the ants. Assume (move) in line 1 of Ant 1 is the selection point, and replace (move) with (right), chosen randomly from among all of choices of combinations of terminals that could be plugged into the mutation point. Then study the performance of this ant in the next generation. This becomes more interesting in the case where the genetic processing operations are applied to larger populations (hundreds of ants, for example).

From a software design point-of-view, the challenge is to see how this form of software architecture might be applied. This is not as difficult as it might first seem. We might, for example, take an evolutionary approach in the contexts shown in Table 7.8. In each case in Table 7.8, a particular genetic processing architecture would be set up. Population members would be identified and represented in some convenient fashion (e.g., tasks 1, 2, 3 of several agents as

TABLE 7.8 Sample Applications of Genetic Programming Paradigm

Architecture	Population	Raw Fitness
Multiagent system	Agents	Number of times an agent completes its task before a time-out
Reuse library	Artifacts	Number of times artifact is reused
Brooks controller	(S, T, A) behaviors in a competence level	Number of times the application of a behavior leads to a goal
Blackboard	Knowledge sources	Number of times the action of a KS is triggered in solving a problem

binary strings 001, 010, and 110). The population would then evolve as a result of repeated application of the genetic processing operations.

7.10 Summary

> The term *architecture* is used here to describe the attributes of a system as seen by the programmer, i.e., the conceptual structure and functional behavior, as distinct from the organization of the data flow and controls, the logical design, and the physical implementation.
> —*IBM Systems Journal,* 1964

Software architectures are considered at the beginning of a software design process. This part of the design process begins with the selection of architectures and architectural elements. Selection of architectures is done in the context of software requirements given in an SRS. Processing, data, and connecting elements make up the fabric of a software architecture. It is often the case that a particular software architecture will represent a mixture of architectural styles: repository, data flow, call and return, independent-process, virtual machine, and domain-specific. The Adaptive Intelligent System (AIS) architecture, for example, combines layered and pipeline architectures. The challenge in selecting appropriate architectures for software is to make selections based on insight gained from the study of a project blueprint (description in a software requirements document), experience with architectural elements in similar systems and good taste.

7.11 PROBLEMS

1. (**Case Study**: Architecture of tATC)
    Figure 7.30 contains a top-level statechart for a training program for air traffic controllers (call it tATC). The decomposition of the Scan state in Figure 7.30 into orthogonal states is given in Figure 7.31.
    (a) Give a software architecture that could be used to design a training program for air traffic controllers based on the description of Scan in Figure 7.31. Assume that training is required for an air traffic control system for commercial aircraft for a major metropolitan airport.
    (b) Decompose the airspace and weather states in Figure 7.31. Hint: Refer to the summary of the tATC needs statement given in Chapter 2 to fill in the details

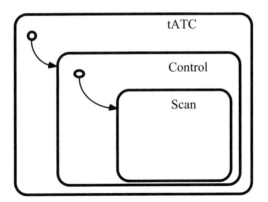

Figure 7.30 Top-level statechart for the tATC.

in describing the functionality of the tATC in moving from state to state contained in the decomposition of airspace and aircraft. Be sure to give a condition-action label for each arc connecting states in the decomposition.
  (c) Identify the processing elements, data, and connectors for the architecture selected in part (b).

2. Given the temperature control system in Figure 7.6, give:
  (a) Flowchart (all inputs, decisions made) for the controller.
  (b) Pseudocode for the control algorithm.

3. Create an example of a six-level class hierarchy in C++ OR Java.

4. Does Unix have a layered architecture? If so, identify the layers.

5. Does Windows95 have a layered architecture? If so, identify the layers.

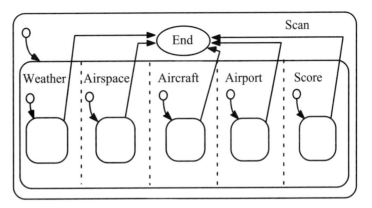

Figure 7.31 Decomposition of tATC scan state.

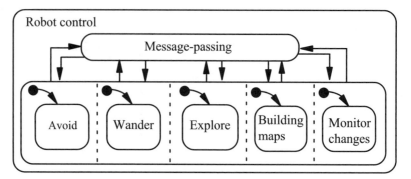

Figure 7.32 Statechart for robot control system.

6. What are the highest and lowest levels of abstraction in the ISO Open System Interconnection data communication model?

7. The statechart in Figure 7.32 is incomplete.
   (a) Extend the statechart in Figure 7.32 to include the remaining competence modules in the Brooks system.
   (b) Expand the layered architecture in Figure 7.30 in terms of the architecture in problem 7(a).

8. A sample mesh architecture is given in Figure 7.33.
   (a) Give: an architectural description of the mesh architecture in Figure 7.33 in CSP. Hint: Assume that all processors in each row in the mesh are parallel processing elements. Also assume that a processor in the first row can forward a message to another processor in the same row or to one in the next row. Information flow follows the indicated arrows.
   (b) Refine the architectural description in (a) so that processor p1 can begin processing a new data item while another sequence of computations is being performed by one or more of the other processors in the mesh.
   (c) Give an algorithm that gives the steps required so that processor p1 transforms its input, and then the message is forwarded to processor p10.

9. Give an architectural description of filters F1, F21, and F22 in the pipeline in Figure 7.34.

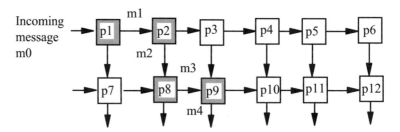

Figure 7.33 Sample mesh architecture.

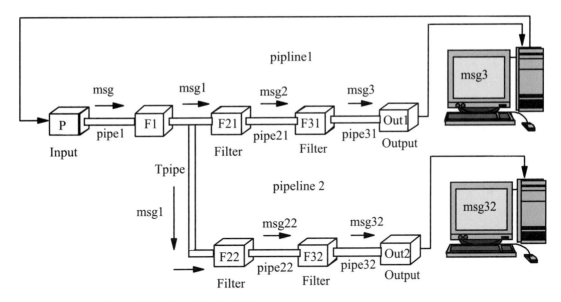

Figure 7.34 Parallel pipelining.

10. Give:
    (a) Verbal description of a U-shaped pipe in a pipeline architecture in Figure 7.35.
    (b) An architectural description of the Upipe in Figure 7.35 in CSP.
    (c) An architectural description of filters F11, F21, F22, F12, and F23 in Figure 7.35 in CSP.

11. Give the statechart equivalent of the software architecture of an agent described with a Petri net in Figure 7.19.

12. Give an architectural description (in CSP) of the agent where the functional specification has been given with the statechart in problem 11.

13. Give an architectural description (in CSP) of a multiagent system as an extension of problem 12.

14. Give a CHAM architectural description of the interaction of the processing elements risk analysis module for a risk engineering assistant.

15. A statechart for a software reuse library system is given in Figure 7.36. Give:
    (a) Blackboard (BB) architecture for the build module. In doing this, specify the form of the knowledge sources, and specific conditions that will trigger actions by the control unit of the blackboard.
    (b) Describe each of the processing elements to be used in the BB architecture.

16. Give the architecture for a software system used to simulate an ant that will find and eat all the food in its environment represented by a grid 3 m × 3 m with grid cell size of 10 cm × 10 cm.

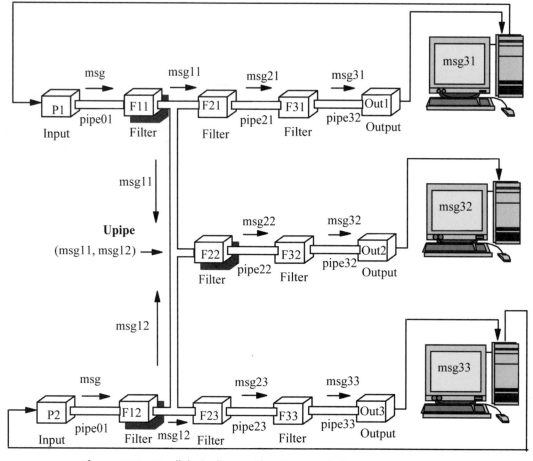

Figure 7.35 Parallel pipelines with a U-shaped pipe.

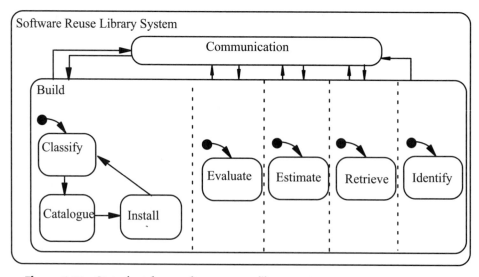

Figure 7.36 Statechart for a software reuse library system.

17. Give the following:
    (a) Architecture for a software system to simulate a population of k food-finding, food-eating ants.
    (b) Fitness function used to select fittest ants.
    (c) Architectural elements which facilitate the simulation of the evolution of the population of ants.
    (d) Simulation of prototype of newly designed system.

18. Give the following:
    (a) A genetic architecture for the build module of the software reuse library system. That is, identify the population members and the basis for measuring raw fitness. Notice that the population might be reuse strategies of the form ⟨condition, action⟩ or they might be software objects.
    (b) Simulation of evolution of population based on natural selection (reproduction of the fittest members appearing in succeeding generations) over 10 generations.
    (c) Average fitness in each generation.

19. Do the following:
    (a) Give a description of the requirements for an office surveillance robot.
    (b) Give a set of statecharts to specify the surveillance robot controller.
    (c) Identify one or more architectures suitable for designing the surveillance system.
    (d) Prototype each architecture in part (c).

20. Design a blackboard architecture for the surveillance system described in problem 19(a) and 19(b).

21. Do the following
    (a) Give architectural design of the surveillance system described in problem 19(a) and 19(b) using the chemical abstract machine approach.
    (b) Compare the CHAM architecture in (a) with the blackboard architecture in problem 20.

7.12 REFERENCES

Boudol, G. The chemical abstract machine. *Theoretical Computer Science,* **96**:217–248, 1992.

Brooks, R. A. A robust layered control system for a mobile robot. IEEE Journal of Robotics and Automation **RA-2**(1):14–23, 1986.

Coutaz, J. Architectural design of user interfaces. *Encyclopedia of Software Engineering.* Wiley, New York, 1994.

Crichton, M. *Jurassic Park.* Ballantine Books, New York, 1990.

Gomi, T. *Evolutionary Robotics.* AAI Books, Kanata, Ontario, 1997.

Hayes-Roth, B. A blackboard architecture for control. *Artificial Intelligence,* **26**:251–321, 1985.

Hayes-Roth, B., Pfleger, K., Lalanda, P., et al. A domain-specific software architecture for adaptive intelligent systems, *IEEE Transactions on Software Engineering*, **21**(4):288–301, 1995.

Hoare, C.A.R. *Communicating Sequential Processes*. Prentice-Hall, Englewood Cliffs, NJ, 1985.

Hoare, C.A.R. Communicating sequential processes, *Communications of the ACM*, **21**(8):666–677, 1978.

IEEE Std. 1074-1995. IEEE Standard for Developing Software Life Cycle Processes. In *IEEE Standards Collection Software Engineering*. IEEE, Piscataway, NJ, 1997.

IEEE Std. 1016.1-1993. IEEE Guide to Software Design Descriptions, in *IEEE Standards Collection Software Engineering*. Piscataway, NJ, IEEE, Inc., 1997.

IEEE Std. 1016-1987. IEEE Recommended Practice for Software Design Descriptions. In *IEEE Standards Collection Software Engineering*. Piscataway, NJ, IEEE, Inc., 1997.

IEEE Transactions on Software Engineering, **21**(4), 1995. Special issue on software architecture.

Inverardi, P., Wolf, A.L. Formal specification and analysis of software architectures using the chemical abstract machine. *IEEE Transactions on Software Engineering*, **21**(4):373–386, 1995.

Kepner, C.H., Tregoe, B.B. *The Rational Manager*. McGraw-Hill, New York, 1965.

Koza, J.R. *Genetic Programming: On the Programming of Computers by Means of Natural Selection*. MIT Press, Cambridge, 1993.

Londono, F., Cleetus, K.J., Reddy, Y.V. A blackboard scheme for cooperative problem-solving by human experts. Report CERC-TR-TM-89-001, Concurrent Engineering Research Center, West Virginia University, 1989.

Marciniak, J.J. Reviews and audits. In *Software Engineering*, M. Dorfman, R.H. Thayer, Eds. IEEE Computer Society Press, Los Alimitos, CA, pp. 256–276, 1997.

Merritt, S. Software reuse. *Encyclopedia of Software Engineering*. Wiley, New York, 1994.

Milner, R. *Communication and Concurrency*. Prentice-Hall, Englewood Cliffs, NJ, 1989.

Milner, R. *A Calculus of Communicating Processes*. Lecture Notes in Computer Science (LNCS) 92. Springer-Verlag, New York, 1980.

O'Leary, D.E. The internet, intranets, and the AI renaissance. *IEEE Computer*, **30**(1):71–79, 1997.

Perry, D.E., Wolf, A.L. Foundations for the study of software architecture. *ACM SIGSOFT Software Engineering Notes*, **17**(4):40–52, 1992.

Peters, J.F., Holmay, P. *The VMS User's Guide*. Digital Press, Bedford, MA, 1990.

Peters, J.F., Sohi, N. Coordination of multiagent systems with fuzzy clocks. *Concurrent Engineering: Research and Applications*, Vol. 4, no. 1 **4**(1):73–88, 1996.

Ross, P.W., Ed. *The Handbook of Software for Engineers and Scientists*. CRC Press, Boca Raton, 1996.

Schaeffer, J. *One Jump Ahead: Challenging Human Supremacy in Checkers*. Toronto, Ontario *Globe and Mail*, 1997.

Shaw, M., Garlan, D. *Software Architecture: Perspectives on an Emerging Discipline*. Prentice-Hall, Englewood Cliffs, NJ, 1996.

Shumate, K. Design. *Encyclopedia of Software Engineering*. Wiley, New York, 1994.

Stroustrup, B. *The C++ Programming Language.* Prentice-Hall, Englewood Cliffs, NJ, 1991.

Tanenbaum, A.S. *Distributed Operating Systems.* Prentice-Hall, Englewood Cliffs, NJ, 1995.

Thayer, R.H., Royce, W.W. *Software System Engineering.* IEEE Computer Society Press, Los Alimitos, CA, 1990.

CHAPTER 8
Design Elaboration

Science is an elaboration.

—Dove, 1856

There are two ways of constructing a software design: one way is to make it so simple that there are obviously no deficiencies; the other way is to make it so complicated that there are no obvious deficiencies.

—C. A. R. Hoare, 1985

Aims

- Make the transition from design to code
- Identify programming paradigms
- Verify the functional correctness of each software increment

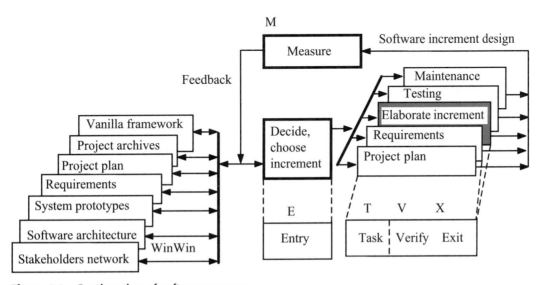

Figure 8.1 Continuation of software process.

8.1   INTRODUCTION

At this point in the software process, the architectural design of a software increment has been completed. Its structure has been identified. In keeping with the ETVXM architecture of a feedback model of the software process in Figure 8.1, the entry conditions must be satisfied before the next design activity can begin. Commitment to the architectural design by project stakeholders, a stable architectural design, the availability of project plan, and requirements are needed to begin design elaboration. The vanilla framework in Figure 8.1 represents an object-oriented design approach. The design process continues with the iterative development of selected software increments with agreed-upon architecture.

Elaborating a design means to work out in detail and complete the software being built. The steps in elaborating a design comprise what is known as an implementation process in IEEE Std. 1077-1995 (Software Life Cycle Processes) and ISO 9000-3-1992. The creation of test data for an implementation is a direct result of a test plan, which usually accompanies a design document. The intent behind a test plan is to gain assurance that a computer program functions according to plan. To gain confidence in a design elaboration, a completed elaboration is subjected to a correctness proof relative to design requirements incorporated as a comment in the code. A straightforward application of the cleanroom method comes next in the elaboration process. Design elaboration is done in reasonable increments to make it easier to verify design requirements, and to test program features in a stepwise fashion. At each stage in the design elaboration process, attention is given to the correlation between completed code and corresponding design components. It should be obvious where a design component is realized in an elaboration.

Design elaboration is part of what is commonly known as the implementation process. Implementation occurs at the tail end of software design process. The implementation process has four principal tasks: selecting test data relative to a test plan, design elaboration (developing source code), verifying and validating the design (V & V), and integration. The implementation process mirrors the recommendations of the IEEE Std. 1077-1995 (Software Life Cycle Processes) and ISO 9000 (Part 3.1 1992, Section 5.6.3) on implementation (ISO, 1992). This process has four main tasks:

Principal Software Implementation Tasks

- Selection of test data
- Design elaboration: Incremental development (coding)
- Verifying functional correctness and validating source code
- Integration of software modules

The focus in this chapter is on an approach to design elaboration based on what is known as the cleanroom method introduced by Mills (1975) and elaborated in Mills, and others (1987), Mills (1994), and Selby and others (1987).

Depending on how programs are viewed, alternative approaches to software development are possible. The methods of two such approaches (traditional and cleanroom) are shown in the flowchart in Figure 8.2. In the case where software is developed informally and intuitively, verifying software reduces to following a test plan and an experimentation process. Testing and coding changes continue until testing occurs without failures and the software product is certified. In the case where designs are treated as strict rules for mathematical functions, then a cleanroom method for software development is possible as explained in Mills (1994) and Dyer (1992). In developing program code, the cleanroom method begins with a design elaboration step. This step is followed by the definition of test data and the formulation of a rule used to verify the correctness of the elaboration step. At the highest level (occurring at the beginning of design elaboration), data definition and decision logic for a program are identified. The decision logic is in the form of rules (checkpoints that are assertions about the elaborated design) that must be satisfied by the software. A design elaboration step is verified by making sure that the code satisfies the rules at each of the checkpoints.

The cleanroom method relies on incremental, well-formed specifications, designs, and coding instead of testing to obtain zero-defect software. The proof of the method is in using it without finding any failures in the developed software. There are a number of instances demonstrating the success of the method. The

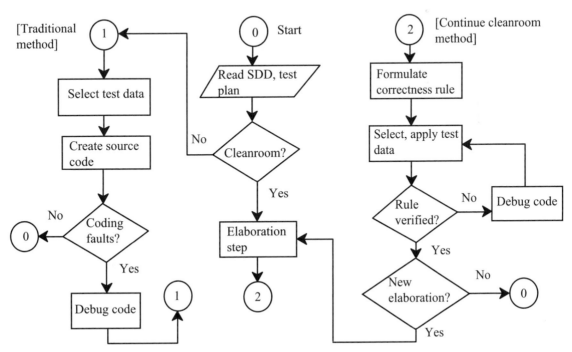

Figure 8.2 Two approaches to software development.

cleanroom method was used in 1980 to develop a 25 KLOC program for a network of 20 miniprocessors for the U.S. Census, and operated for 10 months without failures. In 1984, the method was used to develop a 65 KLOC program for IBM wheelwriter typewriter products controlled by three microprocessors, and ran with no failures. A third example of the application of the cleanroom method is the 500 KLOC program used in 1984 to control five computers for the U.S. space shuttle. This program had one failure in attempting to synchronize the five computers for liftoff in the first flight, and had no failures in flight. The traditional and cleanroom approaches to software development are aided by box structured views of software.

8.2 INCREMENTAL APPROACH TO DESIGN ELABORATION

> **The basic strategy adopted for the task of verification is that the designer should use formal "proofs" at each step in refinement, keeping these as simple as possible.**
> —D. Budgen, 1994

An incremental software process provides an organization of the life-cycle that focuses on incremental development of a product. Instead of treating product design, testing, and implementation as sequential elements in a life-cycle, an incremental software process consists of a pipelining of certified executable product increments (Currit et al., 1986). In effect, incremental software development of software products can be viewed as a form of pipelining as shown in Figure 8.3. The process in Figure 8.3 begins with a description of features

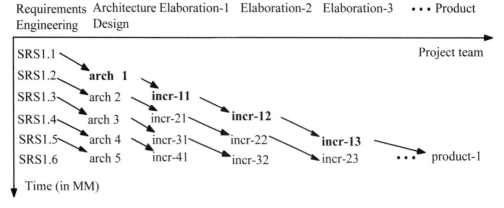

Figure 8.3 Pipelining during incremental software process.

represented in a requirements document (SRS1.1). The completion of the requirements for the first increment releases the requirements team to begin working on the requirements for the next increment (SR1.2). At the same time, another project team begins work on the design of the architecture for the first increment (arch1). The completion of arch1 initiates the beginning of the activities of the software increment elaboration team in Figure 8.3 in producing the first increment (incr11). Once the elaboration of incr11 has been certified, elaboration of incr12 begins while elaboration of incr21 begins. In other words, the incremental design process exhibits a form of temporal parallelism. Eventually, project teams work in parallel. In effect, parallel development of multiple increments of a software system can be carried out over time.

During incremental software development, early increments (increments 11, 12, 13, . . . , leading to product-1, version 1 of a product) are more mature and better tested, and more is known about a product than with later increments leading to a new version of the product. Ideally, each increment is subjected to rigorous development, so that later increments will evolve in the same way as earlier increments during design elaboration. It has been found that an average fractional improvement of the Mean Time To Failure (MTTF) of a product results from an incremental approach to software development. The evidence indicating a gradual lengthening of the interfail time interval for software increments comes from a 1980 study of nine large IBM software products as well as in studies of more recent software products (Adams, 1980; Currit et al., 1986; Dyer, 1992). The MTTF tends to decrease after certifying each engineering change as a result of elaboration leading to a new software increment. For example, in certifying a project with increments averaging 10,000 lines of code, the following interfail times for functions in increments with cumulative defects were found:

- Increment 1: Interfail time of 24,000.00 seconds
- Increment 2: Interfail time of 100,000.00 seconds
- Increment 3: Interfail time of 160,000.00 seconds

A graph reported in Currit and others (1986) exhibiting increasing interfail times relative to three increments during design elaboration is shown in Figure 8.4.

The main thing to notice about an incremental approach to software development is that the bridge to the next increment in the pipeline hinges on the certification of the current increment. Rather than wait until the completion of an implementation to carry out certification, it is easier to certify the code in a software increment. The completed product output by the pipeline process will consist of a collection of certified increments. Notice that in the case where different objects are developed incrementally, the integration of the objects into a single system is made easier. After the objects themselves have been certified, the focus of certifying shifts to the integration of the objects and to the correct behavior of the interfaced objects.

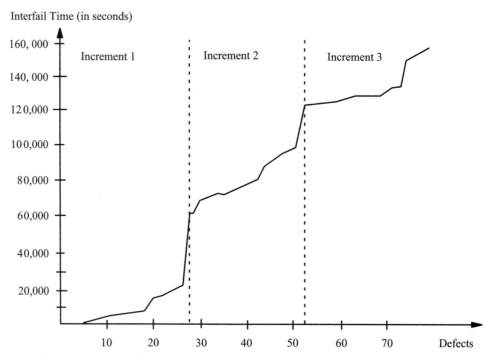

Figure 8.4 Interfail times for design elaboration increments.

8.2.1 Choices in an Incremental Approach

Design elaboration hinges on a number of choices in an incremental approach to software development:

- Box structure
- Programming style
- Test data and features to be tested

First, it is necessary to decide how fine-grained the elaboration will be. This choice amounts to selecting some form of box structure (e.g., black box vs. clear box), which is a granular description during elaboration of the design. Second, it is necessary to choose a programming style in the transition from design to code. Finally, a design elaboration takes into account a test plan (items and features to be tested) provided in each set of design documents. This means that it is necessary to select test data (e.g., boundary values) and specific features to be used in verifying an executable software product.

8.2.2 Box Structures

Box structured views of software are based on the Parnas usage hierarchy of modules (Mills, 1994; Parnas, 1972). A box structure provides a standard, fine-grained subdescription for software modules. Box structures provide convenient entry points in developing and analyzing software. A description of four types of boxes is given in Figure 8.5. Box structures form an abstraction hierarchy. Black, state, and clear box structures are part of a modular view of programming. A software module is an information-hiding construct introduced by Parnas (1972). Ideally, a software module that provides a definition of data, constants, and operations to be performed on the data encapsulates what is known as an abstract data type. The least abstract form of box structure is the clear box. In a *clear box* approach, the internal control structures of a program module are developed and analyzed. In a *black box* approach to software design, a software module is defined in terms of a mathematical function, its stimuli and responses. In a more abstract view of software, state box structures are introduced. A *state box* structure describes software relative to sequences of states, each with its own stimuli and responses. The state box approach is ideally suited for software design based on finite state machines or on statecharts.

An *object box* describes an instance of a class together with an assertion about its required structure, its connections to other classes, and its responses to stimuli. The use of input and output ports in ''wiring'' connections between object boxes is inspired by Milner (1989). An object box is viewed as a structure with ''wires'' connecting it to other classes, input ports (entry points for stimuli), and output ports (exit points for responses to stimuli). A sample object box structure and its refinement are shown in Figure 8.6. Initially in describing an object box structure, the connections of the box to other box structures, input and output

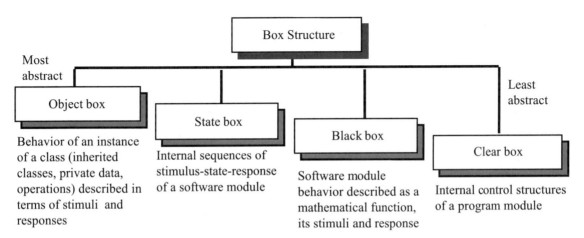

Figure 8.5 Types of boxes.

ports are specified (Figure 8.6a). The object box is annotated with an assertion, which must be satisfied by the box structure. Next, the box structure is elaborated (given more detail) with a new assertion, and how the inherited operation op() in object c1 is used by box b to compute the value of response y (Figure 8.6b). Notice that in both cases, the assertions are easily verified (the correctness of the box structure is assured).

In a stepwise elaboration of software design leading to analyzable code, object box structures provide a crisp and higher level of abstraction. Object boxes also provide another form of information hiding in software development. By contrast with a software module, an object is an instance of class (or type) that "lives" within a hierarchy of classes and can inherit features of classes in the hierarchy.

Verifying design elaborations is aided by the selection of one of more box structures. In an object-oriented approach to design elaboration, all three forms of box structures are useful. A flowchart showing the application of box structures in software development is given in Figure 8.7. The flowchart represents an object-oriented approach to the decomposition of the design elaboration step in software development. In effect, selection of a box structure provides an approach to stepwise decomposition of software design leading to code.

In the transition from requirements to design, state box structured views assist in verifying designs. In the transition from design to program code, the remaining three forms of box structures are useful in a stepwise decomposition of a design. Design decomposition begins at the highest level with object box views of software. Object boxes define both the position of an object in a hierarchy of objects (inherited structures from other objects in the hierarchy) and its internal data and operations. This is the scaffolding level of object-oriented programming. The scaffolding (hierarchy of objects) must be correct, and satisfy

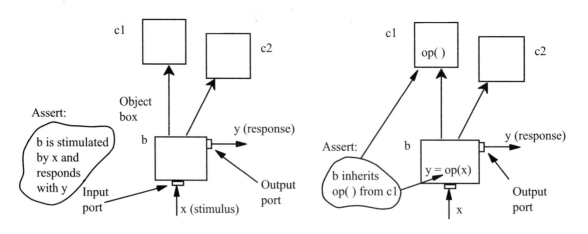

(a) Object box structure   (b) Elaboration of object box

Figure 8.6   Object box structure.

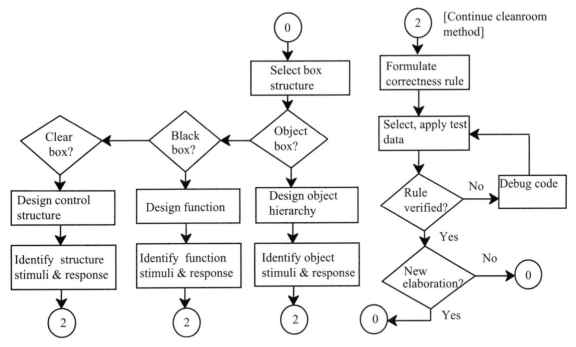

Figure 8.7 Design elaboration with box structures.

design criteria. The black box view of an object assists in defining individual operations of an object. Each operation is defined in terms of a mathematical function, its stimuli and required response. Each operation must also satisfy design criteria (usually expressed concisely as rules). An *operational rule* is an assertion identifying a required response by an operation to stimuli. Finally, a clear box view of an object is defined stepwise. Each elaboration of a clear box structure adds to the control structures needed to implement an operation of an object. The stepwise elaboration of a clear box continues until an object completely implements a design and has been certified to be correct.

8.2.3 Programming Styles

In implementing a software system, the creation of source code depends on the choice of an appropriate programming style. A selection of possible program-ming styles is given in Figure 8.8. C++, Objective C, Eiffel, J++, Java, Ada, and Smalltalk are examples of object-oriented programming languages. C++ was designed by Stroustrup (1991) and provides a concise, convenient vehicle for representing and analyzing object box structures. Features of C++ are extensions of C, Simula, and other languages. C++ belongs to the family of programming languages shown in Figure 8.9.

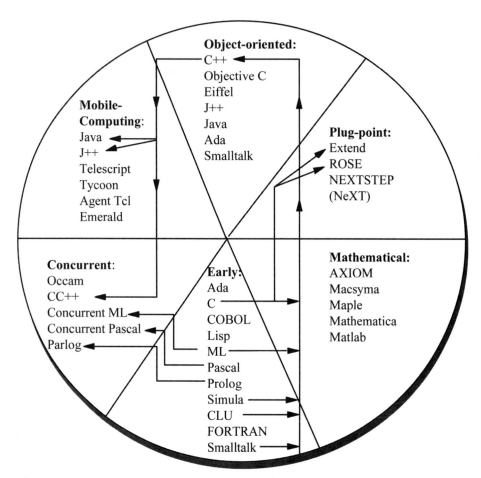

Figure 8.8 Programming styles.

An OO programming style is characterized by information hiding, data abstraction, modularity of construction, standardization of components, and inheritance. Central to this approach to coding is design elaboration with inheritance where the common behavior of objects form a grouping of object types (classes) in a hierarchy. This feature of OO programming is referred to as "abstracting out" common behavior with the identification of a base or superclass (Rumbaugh et al., 1991). C++, Objective C, and Java provide syntactic and semantic extensions of C and Simula. The class construct used in C++ comes from Simula. C++ is discussed in detail later in this section. Objective C is an extension of C developed by Brad Cox at the Stepstone Corporation (Cox, 1991). Eiffel is a language for object-oriented software engineering in which every value is an object, reference to an object, or void (a reference that is not currently tied to an object). As in Java, code in Eiffel must be expressed within a class

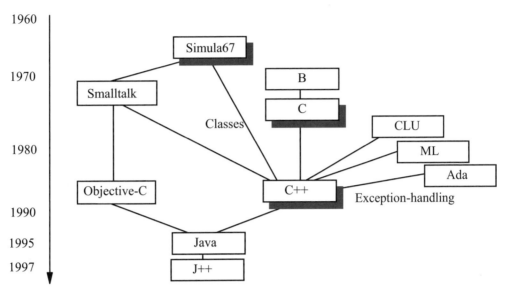

Figure 8.9 Development of C++.

(Howard, 1996). Ada supports a structured approach to program construction with what are known as packages and tasks. Ada achieves a weak form of object orientation with information hiding, data abstraction, and modularity, but has no inheritance. In Ada, specification and implementation units are separately compiled. Interaction between program units is limited to what is allowed in a specification. Smalltalk is a pure object-oriented language developed by a group lead by Alan Kay at the Xerox Palo Alto Research Center in the 1970s (Lalond & Pugh, 1991).

Java, J++, Telescript, Tycoon, Agent Tcl, and Emerald are recent additions to a family of mobile code languages (MCLs), which also support object-oriented programming. An MCL makes it possible to move execution units (EUS) to different sites. Java from Sun Microsystems (Sun, 1995), Telescript from General Magic (Magic, 1995), and J++ from Microsoft are examples of what are known as weak MCLs. With a *weak MCL,* an EU dynamically links code downloaded from a site. In the case of Java and J++, a downloaded Java applet is compiled locally to create an EU for a local web presentation. These are examples of weak MCLs. Tycoon (Mathiske et al., 1994), Agent Tcl (Gray, 1995), and Emerald (Black et al., 1988) are examples of strong MCLs. With a *strong MCL,* both code as well as execution state are moved to a different site. That is, with a strong MCL, an EU is suspended, transmitted to a destination site, and resumed at the new site (Carzaniga et al., 1997). The Object Management Group (OMG) defines an Object Management Architecture (OMA) for MCL development environments. At the heart of the OMA is the Object Request Broker (ORB), which provides capabilities that allow objects to interact and work. The structure of an

ORB-based component is defined by the Common Object Request Architecture (CORBA), which hides the location of components from a programmer (OMG, 1995). In a CORBA framework, no distinction is made between interaction among components on the same host system and the interaction of components on different hosts of a computer network. Examples of design elaboration with Java as the target code are given later in this section.

Occam, Concurrent C++ (CC++), Concurrent ML, Concurrent Pascal, and Parlog (an extension of Prolog that supports logic programming) provide facilities for concurrent programming. Occam was developed by Inmos as an implementation of the Communicating Sequential Processes (CSP) language for transputers. Occam programs rely on indentation and control tokens instead of semicolons and {, } (as in C, C++) to identify the parts of a control block. The result is readable, concisely written code. Concurrent C++ was developed by Gehani at Bell Labs during the late 1980s and early 1990s as an extension of C++. Concurrent ML is an extension of Milner's ML programming language. Both languages are called applicative or functional languages because problems are solved by applying a function rather than with variables and the assignment statement.

Extend, Real-time Object-oriented Software Environment (ROSE), and NEXTSTEP provide a drag-and-drop environment for software development. Extend and ROSE are similar. Each provides libraries of boxlike icons with ports or plug-points. Software development is carried out by dragging appropriate icons onto the workspace and wiring them together by a control drag of the cursor from the plug-point of one object to a plug-point of another object. Extend provides a variety of plotters to display output in graphical as well as table form. The web page *http://www.next.com* provides a good introduction to NEXTSTEP, which is a multi-user operating system from NeXT Computer (1993). NEXTSTEP provides a Project Builder that controls the construction of a project, and an Interface Builder that makes it possible to build a user interface by dragging objects from palettes and dropping them into windows. Objects can be connected to each other by a control drag from one object to another one.

AXIOM, Macsyma, Maple, Mathematica, and Matlab are examples of systems that provide facilities for implementing and graphing mathematical formulas, numeric and symbolic computation and various forms of plotting. Each of these systems provide extraordinarily powerful, easy-to-use development environments. AXIOM was developed by the Mathematical Sciences Department of the Research Division at IBM (Sutor, 1996). Graphing in AXIOM is usually done with built-in draw function. The AXIOM system provides a compiler used to create libraries of categories, domains, and packages. It also has a browser that uses a display engine called HyperDoc. Additional information about AXIOM is available at *http://www.nag.co.uk*. Macsyma is a symbolic-numerical-graphics program resulting from a research project at MIT in 1968 (Macsyma, 1995). In a comparison of AXIOM 1.2, Macsyma 419, Maple V.3, and Mathematica 2.2 conducted by Michael Webster at the University of New Mexico in 1994, 131 problems were

TABLE 8.1   Webster Scoring of Performance of Symbolic Computation Systems

AXIOM 1.2	Macsyma 419	Maple V.3	Mathematica 2.2
59	108	91	87.5

solved by each system, and Macsyma scored highest (Table 8.1). Mathematica has two main features:

- An integrated system that includes numeric computing, graphics, symbolic, and algebraic manipulation, and interprocess communication. The system also supports conversion of graphical output to .eps, .tiff, .gif, and other formats to facilitate making graphs available for browsing on the web.
- A high-level programming language, which supports an object-oriented approach (including inheritance) (Maeder, 1994, 1996).

In Mathematica, a problem is solved by defining one or more functions. This contrasts with Maple, Matlab, and Macsyma programming. Maple programming is procedural (functions, procedures, parameter, and variable declarations are possible), and resembles Pascal. Matlab stands for MATrix LABoratory and is a product from The MathWorks. The syntax for Matlab programs resembles C. Macsyma programming is also procedural, and contains most common control constructs. The syntax for Macsyma programs resembles FORTRAN.

8.3   DESIGN ELABORATION WITH OBJECT STRUCTURES

The OO style of software elaboration is illustrated with two examples of C++ programs. Each of these examples illustrate incremental development of a software design in terms of the application of object, black, and clear box structures and a cleanroom approach to the elaboration of source code. A main feature of the cleanroom approach is the verification of the functional correctness of a design elaboration. The functional correctness of the code for a software increment is verified as follows.

- *Function.* Assert what is expected when program is executed.
- *Design.* Code to implement software increment.
- *Proof.* Identify lines of code that satisfy the assertion(s).

More than one assertion is possible in setting up a functional correctness check. The idea is to assert in plain language what functions an increment is expected to perform during execution. It helps to number of lines of code in an increment for easy reference. Finally, in the proof step, work through each of the assertions for an increment. In each case, indicate which lines of code satisfy an assertion. Failure to verify an assertion leads to further elaboration of the code until it is possible to satisfy an assertion.

8.3.1   OO Example: Computing Complements

To illustrate the box structured approach, we begin with the requirements and design for computing the complement of values of an exponential function (Table 8.2). The elaboration of design D-6 begins with the object box structure shown in Figure 8.10.

8.3.2   Representation of Object Boxes in C++

Every C++ program has the structure shown in Figure 8.11. The C++ program in Figure 8.11 compiles and runs but does nothing. Every C++ program must contain the function main(), which provides stimuli for other functions in the

TABLE 8.2   Sample Software Requirements and Design

Software Requirements	Software Design
Req-1: Compute values of an exponential function.	D-1: Let m = modal point, s = spread, and Compute $f(x) = \exp[-((x - m)/s)]$, with values restricted to [0, 1].
Req-2: Restrict computed values to [0, 1].	D-2: Restrict min $<$ x $<$ max, s $>$ 0.
Req-3: The response of each input is the complement of f, namely, 1 − f.	D-3: Compute complement = 1 − f.
Req-4: Program must recover (not fail).	D-4: Exception condition if input x $\leq$ m.
	D-5: Respond either with f(x) or exception condition flag.
	D-6: Use a layered architecture with layers named Base and Derived.
	D-7: Computation handled by Base layer, responding handled by Derived layer.
	D-8: Environment provides stimulus.
	Test plan: • Test item: Input x. • Features to be tested: Values of x outside required range do not cause failure.

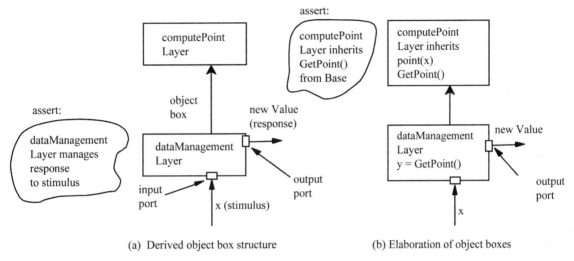

(a) Derived object box structure   (b) Elaboration of object boxes

Figure 8.10 Object box structure and elaboration.

program. Single-line comments begin with // (the end-of-line marks the end of the comment). Single-line as well as multi-line comments are bracketed with /* and */. In C++, a class is a type (data + operations). The syntax for a class is given in Table 8.3. A class can belong to a hierarchy of classes and inherit features from other classes ("parent" classes) in the hierarchy. A class that inherits from a parent class is called a subclass or derived class. A parent class is also called a base class. A subclass inherits public methods and variables from a parent class. A method is another name for a function. The declaration "public Base" in the Derived class example in Table 8.3 indicates that this class inherits the Base class. The hierarchy in Table 8.3 represents the object box structure in Figure 8.6a. In addition, access to a class member (data or method) can be public, protected, or private:

- *Public* member. Usable by any function.
- *Protected* member. Usable by member functions of a class and friends of the class in which it is declared or by friends of classes derived from this class.
- *Private* member. Usable by member functions of class and friends of the class in which it is declared.

```
// declaration of "included" libraries
// declaration of classes:
main() { }
```

Figure 8.11 Complete, skeletal C++ program.

TABLE 8.3   Structure of a Class

Structure of a Class	Example Classes
class name {/* *data member declarations *method declarations */ };	class Base {/* ... */}; //Derived manages response to stimulus. class Derived: public Base {/* *data declaration for response; *declaration data-handling functions*/};

A friend of a class is a class that can access private members of another class. The syntax for declaring methods and variables with private and public members as well as the elaboration of the object box structure in Figure 8.10 is shown in Table 8.4. C++ will be used in the object box elaboration of design components D-6 and D-7:

D-6: Use a layered architecture with layers named computePointLayer and dataManagementLayer (Figure 8.12).

D-7: Data management performed by Base layer, computation handled by Derived layer.

The transition to C++ begins with a complete program that compiles and runs but contains only stubs (empty program structures) that do nothing. This program will provide the scaffolding for design elaboration, and the transition to code that fulfills design requirements.

TABLE 8.4   Declaring Members of a Class

Class Syntax	Example (Skeletal Form)

class Base {
 private:
  //private data member
 public:
  //public methods
  type op1();
  type op2();
  //other methods: ...
};
 	
//Definition of op1() method:
type Base :: op1() {/* ... */}
 	
//Definition of op2() method:
type Base :: op2() {/* ... */}
	class computePointLayer {
	 private:
	  float pt; //response
	 public:
	  void point(short baseValue);
	  float GetPoint();
	};
	
	//define point function:
	void computePointLayer::point(short baseValue) {/*
	assign computed value to pt */}
	
	//define GetPoint function:
	float computePointLayer::GetPoint() {/*
	  returns value of pt */}

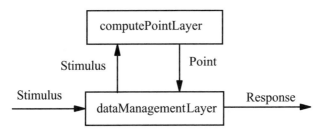

Figure 8.12 Layered architecture.

Proposed Design

```
1 /*  assert: separate computation into two layers where (a) one layer
  *(named computePointLayer) provides point-finding service, (b) another
  *layer provides a data management service, responding to a stimulus with
  *the display of a value found by the computePointLayer, and
  *(c) provide source of stimulus.
  */
2 #include <iostream.h>              //library of input/output functions
3 #include <math.h>                  //library of mathematical functions

4 class computePointLayer {/*
5  private:
6    float pt;                       //response
7  public:
8    void point(short baseValue);    //assigns point-value to pt
9     float GetPoint(); ...*/};      //returns value of pt

10class dataManagementLayer : public computePointLayer {/*
11 private:
12   float newValue;                 //stores returned value
13 public;
14   void SetMembers(float stimulus); /* uses point-finding service
                                          provided
                                       * by computePointLayer */
15   void PrintDataMembers();...*/};  //displays response to stimulus
16 main() { }                        //stimulutes data mgmt layer
```

Correctness Proof

```
1(a) one layer provides point-finding service (satisfied by lines 4 to 9), and
1(b) another layer provides data management (satisfied by lines 10 to 15), and
1(c) provide source of stimulus (satisfied by line 16).
```

Included in the proposed program design are the libraries of functions that will be used: iostream.h (library of input/output functions) and math.h (library of mathematical functions). The functions in <iostream.h> are used for converting objects such as type int and float to sequences of characters and vice versa. Included in this library are cout (pronounced "see out") for standard output used to direct output to a user's terminal. The output operator ≪ is used to direct values to standard output. Either an endl or '/n' can be used to insert a newline into the output stream. Also included in <iostream.h> is cin (standard input) used with the ≫ (input operator). Here are some sample output commands:

```
cout < endl;                                                //newline
cout < '\n';                                                //newline
cout << "Hello, world!" << '\n';                            //print string
cout << "arithmetic expression = "<< (2001*5 + 1) << '\n';  //print string & value
cout << "Enter value of stimulus";                          //prompt for value
cin >> stimulus;                                            //assign input to stimulus
```

A complete description of <stream.h> is given by Stroustrup (1991). A complete description of the functions in <math.h> is given by Kernighan and Ritchie (1988). These libraries are included in the scaffolding for the program being designed to make it easier to see the complete picture.

The elaboration of the design will be done stepwise, one layer at a time. First, the elaboration of each of the layers of layered design is carried out as an object box structure represented in C++, where the class called computePoint-Layer serves as the topmost layer in a layered architecture.

Design Elaboration

```
1 //assert: computePointLayer (a) computes value and (b) returns computed value.

2 class computePointLayer {
3 private:
4  float pt;                                   //for computed value
5 public:
6  void point(short baseValue);
7  float GetPoint();
8 };

9 //define point function:
10 void computePointLayer::point(short baseValue, int flag) {/* compute values */}
11 //define GetPoint function:

12 float computePointLayer::GetPoint();
13 {/* return pt; */}                          //returns computed value
```

Correctness Proof

```
1(a) computes value (satisfied by line 10), and
1(b) returns computed value (satisfied by lines 12 and 13)
```

The actions performed by point() and GetPoint() in lines 9 and 11 are comments so that the code compiles with functions as stubs. The elaboration of the design continues with a C++ class called Derived, which serves as a sublayer in a layered architecture.

Design Elaboration

```
1 //assert: dataManagementLayer (a) manages data and (b) displays response to stimulus.
2 class dataManagementLayer: public computePointLayer{
3 private:
4  float new Value;                        //to store returned value
5 public:
6  void SetMembers(float stimulus);
7  void PrintDataMembers();
8 };

9 //define SetMembers function:
10 void dataManagementLayer::point(float stimulus){
11  point(stimulus);                       //Base layer function computes value
12  newValue = GetPoint(); }               //new Value stores returned value

13 //define PrintMembers function:
14 float dataManagementLayer::PrintDataMembers(){/*
15  cout << newValue;                      //display response (=newValue)
16 */}
```

Correctness Proof

```
1(a) manages data (satisfied by lines 10 to 12), and
1(b) displays response to stimulus (satisfied by
lines 13 to 15).
```

The SetMembers function relies on the point function in computePointLayer to calculate a response to each stimulus. The value computed by point() is returned to SetMembers and assigned to the variable newValue. The PrintMembers function displays the response to a stimulus by sending the value of newValue to standard output. The elaboration of the main() function in the proposed design responds to the design component labeled D-8 (environment design component).

D-8: Environment provides stimulus.

Design Elaboration

```
1 {*assert:
  *(a) stimulus from environment,
  *(b) stimulate layer,
  *(c) elicit response.
  *}

2 main () {
3   dataManagementLayer box;              //box is type dataManagementLayer
4   float x;                              //standard input is assigned to x

5   cout << "Enter value between 75 & 100:"; //prompt for stimulus
6   cin >> x;                            //input from environment
7   box.SetMembers(x);                   //stimulate object box
8   box.PrintDataMembers();              //stimulate response
9 }
```

Correctness Proof

```
1(a) stimulus from environment (satisfied by line 6), and
1(b) stimulate layer (satisfied by line 7), and
1(c) elicit response (satisfied by line 8).
```

To arrive at a more realistic rendition of the layer, the design is elaborated using black box and clear box structures.

8.3.3   Design Elaboration of a Black Box Structure

The only task of the point() function in the Base class is to compute the complement of an exponential function. The elaboration of point() is done in terms of the following design specification:

D-1: Let m = modal point, s = spread, and   {parameters to be used}
Compute $f(x) = \exp[-((x - m)/s)]$ {Gaussian distribution}
with values of $f(x)$ restricted to $[0, 1]$ {from software requirement}
D-3: Compute complement $= 1 - f(x)$

The aim of this stage of the design process is to define a mathematical function that computes a value (named level) in a Gaussian distribution and its complement (Figure 8.13).

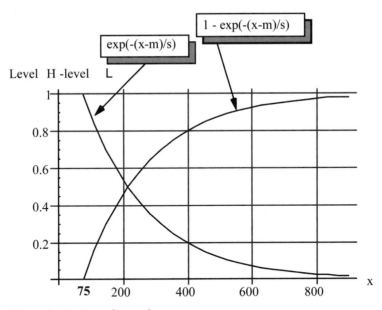

Figure 8.13 Sample graphs.

Proposed Design

```
1 //assert: point function (a) computes value and (b) stores complement of
  //value.

2 void computePointLayer::point(short baseValue){
3 private:
4    float pt;                                    //for computed value
5    float s;                                     //spread variable
6    float m;                                     //modal point variable
7    float level;                                 //variable for intermediate value

8 public:
9 void point(short baseValue) {
10    s = 500;                                     //sample spread
11    m = 75;                                      //sample modal point

12    level = exp(-((baseValue - m)/s));           //computes point in distribution
13    pt = (1 - level); }                          //complement of level
14 }
```

Correctness Proof

1(a) computes value (satisfied by line 12), *and*
1(b) returns computed value (satisfied by line 13)

The exp() function comes from the <math.h> library. The computation in line 12 can be rewritten as follows:

$$\exp(-((baseValue - m)/s)) = e^{-\left(\frac{baseValue - m}{s}\right)}$$

In a normal Gaussian distribution, the (baseValue − m) and s terms are squared, but have been left unsquared to simplify the initial design of the point() function. It is also easy to verify that all values of baseValue are greater than m and that the values of level in the point() function are in [0, 1]. For values of baseValue less than m, the values of level will be greater than 1, which violates the design requirement. Notice that the effect of square of the terms of the formula in point() is to produce a symmetrical graph about the modal point (m = 75 in the design). Both graphs are shown in Figure 8.14. To experiment with these functions, try out the following Mathematica program:

```
pt[x_,m_,s_]=Exp[-((x - m)/s)];       (*define non-squared function *)
y1 = Plot[pt]stimulus,75,500],        (*plot function *)
  {stimulus,-100,900]]                (*stimulus in [-100, 900] *)
Gauss [x_,m_,s_]=Exp[-((x - m)/\2/s/2)];  (*define squared function *)
y2 = Plot[Gauss[stimulus,75,500],     (*plot function *)
  {stimulus,-100,900}]                (*stimulus in [-100, 900] *)
y2=Show[y1, y2,                       (*combine the graphs *)
  GridLines -> Automatic,             (*show grid lines *)
  AxesLabel-> {"stimulus", "response"}]  (*label the axes *)
```

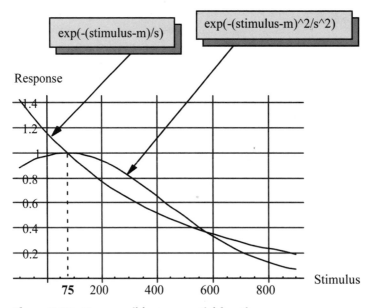

Figure 8.14   Two possible exponential functions.

The design of the point() function can be made more general by replacing fixed values of m and s with values supplied by the dataManagementLayer. Further generalization is possible by adding a second function to computePointLayer (call it Gauss()), which would compute values in the squared form of the exponential formula (see Figure 8.14). Then the dataManagementLayer would choose one either point() or Gauss() to respond to stimuli. The choice of one of these functions can be governed by input from main().

To check that values of level are within the required range, the point function can be instrumented. That is, an *instrumented function* contains lines of code to make it possible to observe computed values.

Design Elaboration

```
1 //assert: (a) display computed value and (b) display complement of computed value.

2 void computePointLayer::point(short baseValue) {
3 private:
4    float pt;                                      //for computed value
5    float s;                                       //spread variable
6    float m;                                       //modal point varibale
7    float level;                                   //variable for intermediate value

8 public:
9 void point(short baseValue) {
10   s = 500;                                        //sample spread
11   m = 75;                                         //sample modal point

12   level=exp(-((baseValue - m)/s));                //computes point in distribution
13   cout<< "level="<<level<<endl                    //display computed value
14   pt=(1 - level);                                 //complement of level
15   cout<< "complement of level="<<pt<< endl}       //display complement
16 }
```

Correctness Proof

> 1(a) computes value (satisfied by line 13), *and*
> 1(b) returns computed value (satisfied by line 15)

The design requirement in D-1 (restrict computed values to [0, 1] is carried out by the data management functions. A clear box structured approach to the dataManagementLayer is taken because the attention is on individual control structures needed to complete the design.

8.3.4   Design Elaboration with Clear Box Structures

The clear box approach is appropriate for the elaboration of the control structures needed for the data management functions. The elaboration is carried out incrementally ("small" steps) and continues until all of the necessary control structures are in place. It is necessary that the data management function Set-Members() satisfy design component D-4, and that PrintDataMembers satisfies D-5.

D-4: Exception condition if input x ≤ m.
D-5: Respond either with f(x) or exception condition flag.

These design requirements will be handled separately. An exceptionCondition variable, flag parameter and if-else control structure is added to the SetMembers function to satisfy component D-4 of the design.

Design Elaboration

```
1 /*assert: SetMembers
  * (a) includes data member to handle exceptions,
  * (b) performs computation for values of stimulus in acceptable range,
  * (c) unacceptable values lead to an exception condition.
  */

2 class dataManagementLayer: public computePointLayer {
3 private:
4   float newValue;                    //to store returned value
5   float exceptionCondition;          //stores exception flag

6 public:
7   void SetMembers(float stimulus,    //stimulus from environment
8                   float flag);       //used for exception condition
9 //void PrintDataMembers();           //not included in elaboration
10 };

11 //define SetMembers function:
12 void dataManagementLayer::point(float stimulus){
13   exceptionCondition=flag;           //assign user-defined flag

14   if((stimulus > 75.0) && (stimulus <//stimulus range?
        1000.0)) {
15       point (stimulus);              //compute response
16   newValue = GetPoint();}            //get response
17   else                               //get response
18   newValue = exceptionCondition,     //set up exception condition
19 }
```

Correctness Proof

> 1(a) includes data member to handle exceptions
> (satisfied by line 5 and line 8), *and*
> 1(b) performs computation for acceptable stimuli
> (satisfied by lines 14 to 16), *and*
> 1(c) unacceptable values lead to an exception
> condition (satisfied by lines 17 to 18).

Notice that this design elaboration affects the design of the main() function, since the SetMembers() function now has a second flag parameter. Hence, the design of main() must be further elaborated so that it is in agreement with SetMembers(). For simplicity, the flag parameter will be set equal to −1, since the values computed by the point() function will always be greater than zero. This feature of main() can be made more general in further design elaborations.

Design Elaboration

```
1 //assert: value of exception flag include in SetMembers() parameter list.
  //warning: this version of main replaces the one in Section 6.2.2

2 main() {
3   dataManagementLayer box;        //box is type dataManagementLayer
4   float x;                        //standard input is assigned to x

5   cout << "Enter value between    //prompt for stimulus
          75 & 100:";
6   cin >> x;                       //input from environment
7   box.SetMembers(x, -1);          //stimulate object box, give flag
8   box.PrintDataMembers();         //stimulate response
9 }
```

Correctness Proof

> (1) value of exception flag include in SetMembers()
> parameter list (satisfied by line 7).

To complete the design, the control structure of the PrintDataMembers() function will be given.

Design Elaboration

```
1 /*assert: SetMembers
  * (a) prints computed value when no exception occurs,
  * (b) announces occurrence of exception condition
  */

2  //define PrintDataMembers function:

3  void         Derived::PrintDataMembers() {
4  if (newValue != exceptionCondition)
5      cout << "no exception condition raised, and computed value ="
6          << newValue << '\n' << '\n';
7  else
8  cout << "exception condition flag ="
9      << exceptionCondition << '\n'<<'\'n;
10 }
```

Correctness Proof

1(a)prints computed value when no exception occurs (satisfied by lines 4 to line 6), *and*
1(b) announces occurrence of exception condition (satisfied by lines 7 to 9).

8.3.5 Checking the Test Plan

The test plan for the program designed in this section has two features, shown in Figure 8.15. To make it easier to input different input values, the design of the main() function can be elaborated to include an iteration control structure (infinite loop with the while construct from C).

Test plan:
- **Test item**: input x.
- **Feature to be tested**: Values of x outside required range do not cause failure.

Figure 8.15   Test plan.

Design Elaboration

```
1 //assert: test item value can be entered more than once.
  //warning: this version of main replaces the one in Section 6.2.4

2 main () {
3   dataManagementLayer box;       //box is type dataManagementLayer
4   float x;                       //standard input is assigned to x

5     while (1) {                  //begin infinite loop
6     cout << "Enter value between 75 //prompt for stimulus
      & 100:";
7     cin >> x;                    //input from environment
8     box.SetMembers(x, -1);       //stimulate object box, give flag
9     box.PrintDataMembers();      //stimulate response
10  }
11 }
```

Correctness Proof

(1) test item value can be entered more than once
(satisfied by lines 5 to 10).

A sample run of the program with the new form of main() is shown in Figure 8.16.

```
Enter a value between 75 and 1000: 76
level = 0.998002
complemented level = 0.00199801
no exception condition raised, and computed value = 0.00199801

Enter a value between 75 and 1000: 0
exception condition flag = -1

Enter a value between 75 and 1000:
```

Figure 8.16 Sample run of C++ program.

8.4 EXAMPLE: ROBOT CONTROL SYSTEM

The sample program designed in the previous section suggests how to make the transition from architectural design to code for a layered control system for a mobile robot. The requirements and the design components for a program to simulate a controller are summarized in Table 8.5. Recall that a competence is a sensor-driven process, which performs transformations of its inputs and generates output to one or more actuators. The results of a computation by a competence are also shared with other competences. A level of competences is a desired class of behaviors over all environments that a mobile robot will encounter. The layered architecture called for in component D-1 of the design can be realized with a hierarchy of C++ classes.

TABLE 8.5   Requirements and Design of Robot Controller

Software Requirements	Software Design
Req-1: Robot controller will consist of a collection of processors that send messages to each other.	D-1: Competences are organized in a layered architecture.
Req-2: Each processor runs a competence module.	D-2: Avoid layer responds to inputs from sensors and interacts with robot motors to avoid objects.
Req-3: Competences are hierarchical.	D-3: Wander controls the wheel motors to control movements of robot in spaces where no obstacles are detected (robot wanders freely).
Req-4: Each competence receives input from sensors (inputs from environment).	
Req-5: Some competence can subsume (take over) the control functions of competences below it in the hierarchy.	D-4: Explore "looks" for reachable places, and can interrupt wandering.

Req-6: The competences include
    level 0: Avoid
    level 1: Wander
    level 2: Explore
    level 3: Plan
    level 4: Monitor changes
	D-5: Plan devises routes for robot to follow.
	D-6: Monitor looks for changes in environment.
	D-7: Wander can assume the control functions of the Avoid layer.

Req-7: A competence receives input from the competence above it and below it in the hierarchy.	D-8: Explore can assume the control functions of Wander and Avoid layers.
Req-8: A competence (either indirectly or directly sends control signals to actuators such as motors to turn wheels).	**Test plan**: T-1: Test item is stimulus. T-2: Features to be tested:
Req-9: A robot should continue to function if one or more of its sensors fail.	• Wandering, if no obstacles detected. • Avoidance, if obstacles detected.

Proposed Design

```
1 /* controller design will
   * (a) provide layering of competences,
   * (b) each layer has access to sensors,
   * (c) Wander can subsume Avoid,
   * (d) Explore can subsume Avoid and Wander,
   * (e) Plan can subsume Explore,
   * (f) Monitor can subsume Plan,
   /*
2 #include <iostream.h>              // use cout, cin and other i/o
                                     functions
3 #include <math.h>                  // use math functions for simulation
4 class Layer {                      // begin layered architecture
5 public:
6     int sensing(float seed); };    // all layers inherit sensing
                                     capability
7 int Layer::sensing(float seed)     // provides input from sensors
  {/*... */}
8 class Avoid: public Layer {/* ... */};   // Avoid competence
9 class Wander: public Layer,        // Wander inherits sensing
10    public Avoid {/* ... */};      // Wander can subsume Avoid
11 class Explore: public Layer,      // Explore inherits sensing
12    public Avoid,                  // Explore can subsume Avoid
13    public Wander {/*... */};      // Explore can subsume Wander
14 class Plan: public Layer,         // Plan inherits sensing
15    public Explore {/* ... */};    // Plan can subsume Explore
16 class Monitor: public Layer,      // Monitor inherits sensing
17    public Plan {/* ... */};       // Monitor can subsume Plan
18  main() {/* input from environment */}   // stimulates competences
```

Correctness Proof

1(a) provide layering of competences (satisfied by lines 4 to 17), and
1(b) each layer has access to sensors (satisfied by lines, 8, 9, 11, 14, 16), and
1(c) Wander can subsume Avoid (satisfied by line 10), and
1(d) Explore can subsume Avoid and Wander (satisfied by lines 12, 13), and
1(e) Plan can subsume Explore (satisfied by line 15), and
1(f) Monitor can subsume Plan (satisfied by line 17).

To make it possible to experiment with the completed design, sensing will be simulated by computing a value representing input from an infrared sensor. This will be done with a black box structure (definition of a mathematical function).

8.4.1 Design Elaboration of Sensing Function

The only task of the sensing() function in the Layer class is to compute a pseudo-random number representing input from an infrared sensor. Numbers in a sequence of numbers are random if each member of the sequence is equally likely to occur. Psuedo-random numbers belong to periodic number sequences with members that appear to be random. Techniques for computing pseudo-random numbers are given in Knuth (1981).

Design Elaboration

```
1/* (a)sensing() computes a pseudo-random number,
 * (b) computed values are in {0, 1, 2, 3}.
 */

2   //define sensing() function:
3   class Layer {                        //base class
4     private:
5       int trunk;                       //used to truncate away fraction part
6     public:
7       int sensing(float seed); };      //sensing function inherited by all
                                         //layers

8   int Layer::sensing(float seed) {     //definition of sensing
9     seed = log(seed);                  //compute natural log of number
10    trunk = seed;                      //trick: assign integer part of seed to
                                         //trunk
11    seed = seed - trunk;               //subtract away integer part of seed
12    seed = 4 * seed;                   //seed now in 0 to 3.99999 range
13    trunk = seed;                      //trick: assign integer part of seed to
                                         //trunk
14    return(trunk);                     //return pseudo-random number
15 }
```

Correctness Proof

1(a) sensing()computes a pseudo-random number (satisfied by lines 9 to line 13), and
1(b) computed values are in {0, 1, 2, 3} (satisfied by lines 12, 13).

Sensing (seed)

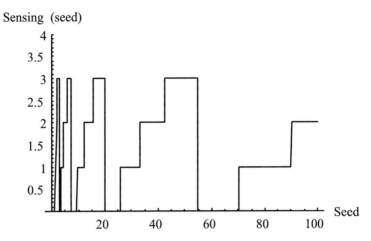

Figure 8.17 Distribution of pseudo-random numbers.

A plot of the pseudo-random numbers computed by the sensing() function with the value of seed incremented by 1 in the range [1, 100] is shown in Figure 8.17. The gaps along the x-axis represent zero values, and each step exhibits clusters of values (e.g., 1's between 26 and 37). The pseudo-random numbers produced by sensing() will result in zigzag movements of the robot, which is sometimes wandering (no obstacles detected when sensing() outputs a zero) and avoiding obstacles (obstacles detected whenever sensing() outputs a nonzero value). The random values produced by the sensing() function will stimulate the robot to go on a random walk (moving in different directions randomly and traveling along paths of random length) similar to the one shown in Figure 8.18. To track the computations performed by the sensing() function, it is helpful to instrument it.

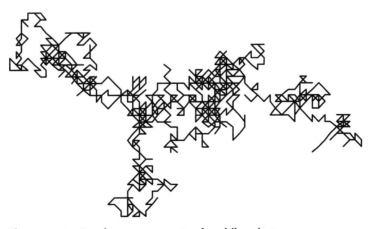

Figure 8.18 Random movements of mobile robot.

Design Elaboration

```
1 //sensing() instrumented to observe compution steps

2   //define sensing() function:
3   class Layer {                    //base class
4     private:
5       int trunk;                   //used to truncate away fraction part
6     public:
7       int sensing(float seed); }; //sensing function inherited by all
                                     //layers

8   int Layer::sensing(float seed)  //definition of sensing
{
9     cout << "seed = "<< seed << endl;
10    seed = log(seed);             //compute natural log of number
11    cout << "log(seed) = " << seed << endl;
12    trunk = seed;                 //trick: assign integer part of seed to
                                    //trunk
13    cout << "truncated part = " << seed << endl;
14    seed = seed - trunk;          //subtract away integer part of seed
15    cout << "fraction = " << seed << endl;
16    seed = 4 * seed;              //seed now in 0 to 3.99999 range
17    cout << "fraction = " << seed << endl;
18  trunk = seed;                   //trick: assign integer part of seed to
                                    //trunk
19  cout << "random number = " << seed << endl;
20  return (trunk);                 //return pseudo-random number
21 }
```

Correctness Proof

(1) The function sensing() is instrumented to observe computation steps (satisfied by lines 9, 11, 13, 15, 17, 19).

A clear box structured approach works well in elaborating the design of a move() function for the Avoid class.

8.4.2 Design Elaboration of Avoid Layer

The elaboration of the Avoid competence module is governed by D-2 of the software design:

D-2: Avoid layer responds to inputs from sensors and interacts with robot motors to avoid objects.

This is accomplished by elaborating the move() function of the Avoid class. The move() function relies on input from the sensing() function to control the movements of the robot in avoiding obstacles.

Design Elaboration

```
1/* (a) Avoid() provides obstacle-avoidance for robot motions,
 * (b) Sensing something on left and right causes robot to move left,
 * (c) Sensing something on left causes robot to move right,
 * (d) Sensing something on right causes robot to move left,
 * (e) Sensing no obstacles causes robot to do nothing,
 */
2 class Avoid: public Layer {                //derived class representing Avoid
                                             //layer

3   private:
4     int val;                               //used to truncate away fraction
                                             //part

5     string direction;
6   public:
7     string move(float thisSeed);           //sensing function inherited by
                                             //all layers

8 };
9 string Avoid::move(float thisSeed){        //definition of sensing
10    val = sensing(thisSeed);               //compute floating point number

11    if (val == 3)                          //left and right IR see something
12    direction = "leftRobot.motor[0]        //turn left
            = 10";
13    else if (val == 2)                     //left IR sees something
14    direction ="rightRobot.motor[0] = -10";//turn right
15    else if (val == 1)                     //right Ir sees something
16    direction = "leftRobot.motor[0] = 10"; //turn left
17    else                                   //no obstacles detected
18    direction = "Null";                    //do nothing
19 return direction;                         //return state of robot
20 }
```

Correctness Proof

1(a) Avoid() provides obstacle-avoidance (satisfied by lines 11 to line 18), and
1(b) something on left and right causes robot to move left (satisfied by line 11, 12), and
1(c) something on left causes robot to move right (satisfied by line 13, 14), and
1(d) something on right causes robot to move left (satisfied by line 15, 16), and
1(e) Sensing no obstacles causes robot to do nothing (satisfied by line 17, 18).

This form of the Avoid competence module merely suggests the basic operation of avoidance of obstacles would have separate functions for turning, forward motion, determining how long each motor should operate, and speed of motor operation. The Avoid module works in conjunction with the Wander module. The elaboration of the Avoid module is governed by part D-3 of the software design.

D-3: Wander controls the wheel motors to control movements of robot in spaces where no obstacles are detected (robot wanders freely).

In the first elaboration, the focus is on designing the monitor function of the Wander module so that it captures the state of the robot (engaged in obstacle avoidance or idling).

Design Elaboration

```
1 /* Wander(),
   * (a) monitors state of Avoid competence module, and
   * (b) captures current state, and
   * (c) displays current state, and
   * (d) responds to stimulus from environment
   */
2   class Wander: public Layer, public   //begin Wander layer inherits
    Avoid
3   {                                      //Layer, and Avoid features
4      private:
5         string state;                    //used to store Avoid state
6      public:
7         void monitor(float startup);    //used to track Avoid state
8   };
9   void Wander::monitor(float startup) //definition of monitor function
{
10     state = move(startup);            //initialize
11     cout << "state of Avoid = "       //display state of Avoid competence
          <<state<<endl;
12  }
```

Correctness Proof

1(a) monitors state of Avoid competence module (satisfied by lines 9 to line 12), and
1(b) captures current state (satisfied by lines 5, 10), and
1(c) displays current state (satisfied by line 11), and

1(d) responds to stimulus from environment (satisfied by lines 9 to 12).

This preliminary version of Wander captures the state of the Avoid competence module (whether the robot is avoiding an obstacle or not), but has no provision for taking advantage of the situation in the case where the robot "sees" nothing to avoid. This observation leads to the next elaboration of the design. For the sake of completeness, and to make it easier to install completed classes into the scaffolding for the robot control system, the entire class (not just the monitor operation) is given next.

Design Elaboration

```
1  /* Wander(),
    * (a) responds to stimulus from environment,
    * (b) repeatedly captures current state of robot,
    * (c) displays current state,
    * (d) simulates wandering while robot is not avoiding obstacles
    */

2   class Wander: public Layer, public      //begin Wander layer inherits
      Avoid                                 //Layer, and Avoid features
3     {
4   private:
5     string state;                         //used to store Avoid state
6   public:
7     void monitor(float startup);          //used to track Avoid state
8   };
9   void Wander::monitor(float             //definition of monitor function
      startup) {
10  state = "Null";                         //initialize state
11  while (state == "Null") {               //begin iteration with possible
                                            //wandering
12    state = move(startup);                //capture current state of robot
                                            //motors
13    cout << "state of Avoid = "           //display state of robot
           << state << endl;
14    if (state == "Null" )                 //see if robot is avoiding
                                            //osbtacle
15       cout << "I'm wandering..."         //simulate wandering
         << endl;
16    ++startup;                            //startup = startup + 1
17  }                                       //end while
18 }                                        //end monitor
```

Correctness Proof

> 1(a) responds to stimulus from environment (satisfied by lines 9 to 18), *and*
> 1(b) repeatedly captures current state of robot (satisfied by lines 11 to 17), *and*
> 1(c) displays current state (satisfied by line 13), *and*
> 1(d) simulates wandering while robot is not avoiding obstacles (satisfied by line 14, 15).

Further elaboration of the Wander module would separate the monitoring function from the act of wandering. To simulate wandering, wanderTurn(), wanderRight(), wanderLeft(), and wanderForward() functions would be introduced. If we assume that the robot has just two motors (one for each wheel like those on a Khepera robot), the discovery that the robot is in its "Null" state (not avoiding obstacles, motors idle) would cause the Wander module to randomly select wanderForward (to actuate both robot motors for forward motion) or wanderTurn. The wanderTurn operation randomly selects either wanderRight() to turn on the motor for the left wheel, or wanderLeft() to turn on the motor for the right wheel. In addition, the remaining competences (Explore, Plan, Monitor) require design elaboration. To obtain a complete preliminary version of the robot control system, it is necessary to elaborate the design of main(), which supplies stimuli for wandering and avoiding.

8.4.3 Design Elaboration of main( )

The design of main should be carried out stepwise to facilitate observation of the behavior of the robot control system simulation at different stages in its development. The main() function serves as driver for the system, supplying stimuli to trigger wandering and obstacle avoidance.

Design Elaboration

```
1 /* (a) introduce object of type Wander,
   * (b) provision for stimulus test item,
   * (c) test item value from user stimulates monitoring.
   * warning: this version of main() replaces main() in Section 6.3
   */
2 main () {
3   Wander box;                          // box is type Wander
4   float stimulus;                      // provision for test item

5     cout << "Enter startup (floating   // prompt for stimulus
      point) value:";
6     cin>>stimulus;                     // input from environment
7     box.monitor(stimulus);             // stimulate wandering, avoiding
8 }
```

Correctness Proof

```
1(a) introduce object of type Wander (satisfied by line
3), and
1(b) provision for stimulus test item (satisfied by line
4), and
1(c) test item value from user stimulates monitoring
(satisfied by lines 5 to 7).
```

Combining this version of main() with the Avoid and Wander class designs in the scaffolding in Section 6.3 makes it possible to simulate the interaction of two of the layers of the control system on a very primitive level. The main() function can be elaborated to provide repeated stimulation of the monitoring function.

Design Elaboration

```
1/* (a)introduce object of type Wander,
 *  (b) provision for stimulus test item,
 *  (c) repeatedly stimulate monitoring operation
 *  (d) limit the number of iterations.
 *  warning: this version of main() replaces main() in Section 6.3
 */

2 main () {
3   Wander box;                      //box is type Wander
4   float stimulus;                  //provision for test item

5     stimulus = 0.1;                //initialize stimulus
6     while (stimulus < 100) {       //begin iteration
7       box.monitor(stimulus);       //stimulate wandering, avoiding
8       stimulus = stimulus + 5;     //increment stimulus by 5
9     }
10 }
```

Correctness Proof

```
1(a) introduce object to type Wander (satisfied by line
3), and
1(b) provision for stimulus test item (satisfied by line
4), and
1(c) repeatedly stimulate monitoring operation
(satisfied by lines 5 to 8), and
1(d) limit the number of iterations (satisfied by lines 5
and 7).
```

The robot control system has been implemented in C++ using the Metrowerks CodeWarrior IDE (Integrated Development Environment), which runs in Win32, Mac OS, MIPS, Motorola 680x0, and PowerPC. A snapshot of a sample run of the control system is given in Figure 8.19.

```
seed = 1
log(seed) = 0
truncated value = 0
fraction = 0
4 * seed = 0
random number = 0
direction robot moves = Null

I'm wandering...
seed = 2
log(seed) = 0.693147
truncated value = 0
fraction = 0.693147
4 * seed = 2.77259
random number = 2
direction robot moves = rightRobot.motor()

seed = 6
log(seed) = 1.79176
truncated value = 1
fraction = 0.791759
4 * seed = 3.16704
random number = 3
direction robot moves = leftRobot.motor()

seed = 11
log(seed) = 2.3979
truncated value = 2
fraction = 0.397895
4 * seed = 1.59158
random number = 1
direction robot moves = lef Robot.motor()

seed = 16
log(seed) = 2.77259
truncated value = 2
fraction = 0.772589
4 * seed = 3.09035
random number = 3
direction robot moves = leftRobot.motor()
```

Figure 8.19   Sample run of robot control system.

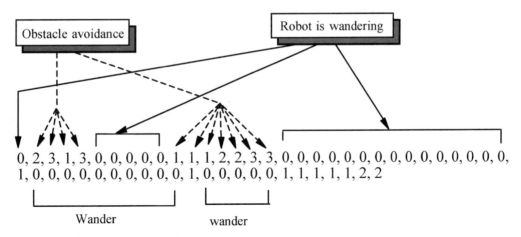

Figure 8.20 Robot behaviors.

8.4.4 Test Plan for Control System

The sample run of the robot control system program satisfies the requirements of the design test plan. To see this, notice that varying the leading digit of the fraction part of log(seed) in the sensing() function gives rise to a sequence of pseudo-random numbers. For example, in the complete sample run, the following sequence was created: 0,2,3,1,3,0,0,0,0,0,1,1,1,2,2,3,3,0,0,0,0,0,0,0,0,0,0,0,0,0,0, 0,0,1,0,0,0,0,0,0,0,0,0,0,1,0,0,0,0,0,0,1,1,1,1,1,2,2. In the context of robot control, this sequence of random numbers is associated with the robot behaviors shown in Figure 8.20.

The behaviors shown in Figure 8.20 satisfy the requirements of the test plan in Figure 8.21. The two versions of main() have stimulated the control system repeatedly (this satisfies T-1 of the test plan). The behaviors in Figure 8.20 show that the robot wanders whenever no obstacles are detected. Otherwise, in the case where obstacles are detected, the behavior in Figure 8.20 indicates that the robot takes avoiding action. These two behaviors satisfy T-2 of the test plan.

The selection of hundreds of sequences of random numbers can be accomplished by initializing the stimulus variable in main() using the time functions available in the <time.h> library. The stimulus variable could be initialized, for example, with the time in seconds returned by the clock() function. The design of the main() function can be improved by letting the user determine the number

---

Test plan:
T-1: Test item is stimulus.
T-2: Features to be tested:
• Wandering, if no obstacles detected.
• Avoidance, if obstacles detected.

Figure 8.21 Test plan.

of iterations, the initial value of the stimulus, and the size of increment of the stimulus. To make it easier to insert a variety of test items, the while loop should provide an option that makes it possible for the user to enter a particular stimulus or to step through the loop without intervention.

8.5 SUMMARY

> As surprising as it may seem, it requires less human effort to produce zero defect software with new methods.
> —Harlan Mills, 1994

An overview of the design elaboration process has been given in this chapter. The design of a software increment brings many results of the software process together. From the beginning of the process, there has been iterative interaction with project stakeholders. This interaction started with project planning, which results in a very detailed perspective concerning the expectations of stakeholders concerning the software products produced by the process. This is the Win Win part of a spiral process. The process continues with problem analysis, and a description of the activities, control functions, data, data flow, objectives, constraints, dependencies, and performance and quality requirements for software to be developed. The plan and requirements description initiate the work of a project team which designs the architecture of selected software increments. The availability of a plan, requirements, and architecture begins the elaboration of a software increment. Over time, the activities of project teams will overlap and will be performed in parallel. The software process then takes on the appearance of a pipeline in a manufacturing system.

Design elaboration leads to the production of source code for a software increment. The source code step given in IEEE Std. 1077-1995 requires a choice of a programming style. The object-oriented programming style has been illustrated in the context of C++. The C++ programming language incorporates the good features of several other languages (mainly C and Simula), and is easy to use. A cleanroom approach to the elaboration of source code is illustrated in this chapter.

8.6 PROBLEMS

> Little things are elaborated with an infinity of pains.
> —Jowette Plato, 1875

1. A log() function is used in line 9 of the robot sensing() function in Figure 8.22. Elaborate the design of this function in terms of:

   (a) An exp(), an exponential function and compare with the log() function.
   (b) A function of your choice so that the sensed values have a random distribution.
   (c) Plot the values obtained from line 10 with log().
   (d) Plot the values obtained from (b).
   (e) Plot the values obtained from (c).
   (f) Give a combined plot from (c), (d), and (e), and comment on the plots.

```
1 /* (a) sensing() computes a pseudo-random number,
 *  (b) computed values are in {0, 1, 2, 3}.
 */

2    // define sensing() function:
3    class Layer {                        // base class
4      private:
5        int trunk;                        // used to truncate away fraction part
6      public:
7        int sensing(float seed); };       // sensing function inherited by all layers

8    int Layer::sensing(float seed) {      // definition of sensing
9      seed = log(seed);                   // compute natural log of number
10     trunk = seed;                       // trick: assign integer part of seed to trunk
11     seed = seed - trunk;                // subtract away integer part of seed
12     seed = 4 * seed;                    // seed now in 0 to 3.99999 range
13     trunk = seed;                       // trick: assign integer part of seed to trunk
14     return(trunk);                      // return pseudo-random number
15   }
```

Figure 8.22 Sensing function for a robot.

2. Elaborate the design of the sensing() function in problem 1 based on the following information:

   • Random number representing ambient radiation detected by an IR sensor after a fixed time interval (IR receiver off, then IR receiver on) whenever an object is detected. Detector range: 0 to 880 nanometers (nm) wavelength.

   • Random number represented detected radiation (after a fixed time) after an infrared light has been emitted by one or more IR sensors. Emitter range: 0 to 880 nm wavelength.

   • Get detected value.

   • Change the state of a sensor every 600 ms.

   Assume that detector outputs a low value (= 0) if it detects nothing and a high value (= 1) if an obstacle is detected. The C code for this type of operation is given in Figure 8.23. In other words, change the sensing function so that it closer to an operational version for a simple emitter, detector system.

```
int ir_status = 0;
void ir_detector() {
    bit_set(portD, 0b00000100);
    sleep(0.000600);
    val_on = peek(portE);
    bit_clear(portD, 0b00000100);
    sleep(0.000600);
    val_off = peek(portE);
    if ((val_off & ~val_on & 0b00000100) == 0b00000100)
        ir_status = 1;
    else
        ir_status = 0;
}
```

Figure 8.23   Sample C code for sensing.

3. Elaborate the design of the sensing() function in problem 2 so that it determines the distance between a robot and a detected object. Distances are represented by random numbers in the range from 0 to 100 cm.

4. Do the following:
   (a) Create a test plan for the Explore function of the mobile robot controller.
   (b) Elaborate the design of an Explore function of the mobile robot controller. Note: this should be done incrementally (in small steps). Use the cleanroom method to guarantee the correctness of each stage of the elaboration.

5. Incorporate the Explore function into the robot control system, and:
   (a) Instrument Explore to observe its behavior.
   (b) Give a sample run with the operation of the new layer of the control system.

6. Do the following:
   (a) Devise a test plan for the planning layer of the mobile robot control system.
   (b) Incrementally design the Planning layer of the mobile robot control system. This is D-5 in Table 8.5: Plan devises routes for robot to follow.
   (c) Verify the correctness of the proposed design.
   (d) Trace design components back to specific requirements.
   (e) Assume that a robot plans a route based on the selection of paths containing objects furthest away (as estimated with sensors). Give a simulation of the new control program and verify results in terms of the test plan in (a).

7. Do the following:
   (a) Devise a test plan for the monitor layer of the mobile robot control system.
   (b) Incrementally design the Planning layer of the mobile robot control system. This is D-6 in Table 8.5: Monitor looks for changes in environment.
   (c) Verify the correctness of the proposed design.
   (d) Trace design components back to specific requirements.
   (e) Assume that a robot detects changes in positions of detected objects based on the selection of paths containing objects furthest away (as estimated with sensors).

Give a simulation of the new control program and verify results in terms of the test plan in (a).

8. Do the following:
   (a) Devise a test plan for the Wander layer to subsume the control function of the avoid layer of the mobile robot control system.
   (b) Elaborate the design the Wander layer of the mobile robot control system. This is D-7 in Table 8.5: Wander can assume the control functions of the Avoid layer.
   (c) Verify the correctness of the proposed design.
   (d) Trace design components back to specific requirements.
   (e) Assume that wander subsumes the avoid layer control function whenever it detects least two clear paths (no obstacles in two directions). Give a simulation of the new control program and verify results in terms of the test plan in (a).

9. Do the following:
   (a) Devise a test plan for the Explore layer to subsume the control function of the Avoid and Wander layers of the mobile robot control system.
   (b) Elaborate the design the Explore layer of the mobile robot control system. This is D-8 in Table 8.5: Explore can assume the control functions of Wander and Avoid layers.
   (c) Verify the correctness of the proposed design.
   (d) Trace design components back to specific requirements.
   (e) Assume that Explore subsumes the control functions of Wander and Avoid layers whenever it detects one clear path (no obstacles in some direction). Also assume that control reverts back to the Wander layer whenever more than one clear path is detected by the Explore layer. Give a simulation of the new control program and verify results in terms of the test plan in (a).

Note: The next several problems reference the requirements for a traffic light controller shown in Figure 8.24. The requirements and design of this controller are also given in Table 8.6.

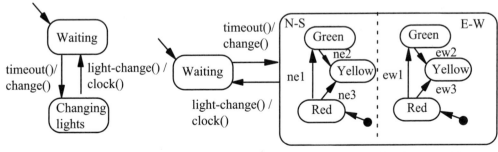

(a) Context-level states   (b) Orthoganal state machines after decomposition

Figure 8.24 Statechart describing a traffic light control system.

10. Use an object box structured approach to elaborate:
    (a) D-1 design element in Table 8.6 using an object-oriented approach.
    (b) Prove the correctness of your elaboration.

TABLE 8.6   Requirements and Design for a Traffic Light Control System

Software Requirements	Software Design
Req-1: A traffic light controller regulates the lights for a traffic intersection. Req-2: Light changes occur at timed intervals. Req-3: The traffic light control system has the following methods: • Clock. • Change. Req-4: The traffic light control system has the following states: • N-S (regulate north-south lights). • E-W (regulate east-west lights). • Waiting. Req-5: All lights are reset to red for a fixed time interval before the lights in a new direction are changed.	D-1: Architecture: control structure D-2: Each set of lights changes every 120 seconds. D-3: Controller performs the following operations: • Start clock. • Reset clock. • Reset lights. • Change_lights. D-4: Time interval can be changed. **Test plan**: Test items: Time interval Features to be tested: • Changing lights. • Reset clock. • Reset lights.

11. Use a clear box structured approach to elaborate:
    (a) D-3 design element in Table 8.6 using an object-oriented approach.
    (b) Prove the correctness of your elaboration.

12. Elaborate the design from problem 11 in terms of:
    (a) D-2 design component in Table 8.6.
    (b) Prove the correctness of your elaboration.

13. Elaborate the design from problem 12 in terms of:
    (a) D-4 Time interval can be changed.
    (b) Prove the correctness of your elaboration.

14. Complete the implementation of the traffic light controller so that:
    (a) The change method is instrumented.
    (b) Obtain a sample of the output when the completed program is run.

15. Instrument the program from problem 14 as follows:
    (a) The reset clock method.
    (b) The reset lights method.
    (c) Obtain a sample of the output when the completed program is run.

16. Verify the program from problem 15 by following the test plan in Table 8.6.

Note: The template for an object-oriented requirements specification is given in Figure 8.25.

17. Give the requirements and design for card index system for a rendition of the IEEE 630 template in Figure 8.25 in a C++ environment. That is:
    (a) Create a table given the specific requirements and design components for the index system.
    (b) Create a test plan (test items and features to be tested) for the card index system.

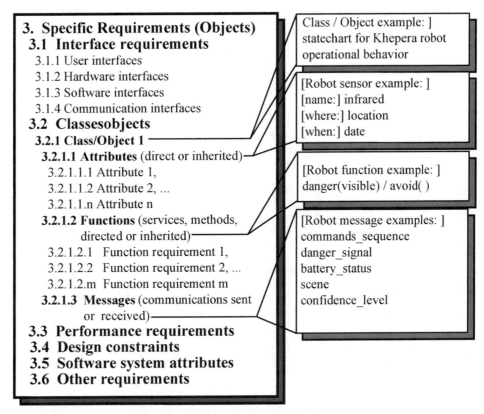

3. Specific Requirements (Objects)
3.1 Interface requirements
  3.1.1 User interfaces
  3.1.2 Hardware interfaces
  3.1.3 Software interfaces
  3.1.4 Communication interfaces
3.2 Classesobjects
  3.2.1 Class/Object 1
    3.2.1.1 Attributes (direct or inherited)
    3.2.1.1.1 Attribute 1,
    3.2.1.1.2 Attribute 2, ...
    3.2.1.1.n Attribute n
    3.2.1.2 Functions (services, methods,
       directed or inherited)
    3.2.1.2.1 Function requirement 1,
    3.2.1.2.2 Function requirement 2, ...
    3.2.1.2.m Function requirement m
    3.2.1.3 Messages (communications sent
       or received)
3.3 Performance requirements
3.4 Design constraints
3.5 Software system attributes
3.6 Other requirements

Class / Object example:]
statechart for Khepera robot
operational behavior

[Robot sensor example:]
[name:] infrared
[where:] location
[when:] date

[Robot function example:]
danger(visible) / avoid( )

[Robot message examples:]
commands_sequence
danger_signal
battery_status
scene
confidence_level

Figure 8.25   IEEE 630 template for object specification.

Note: Req-1 is that there is a separate button for 3.1, 3.2, 3.3, 3.4, 3.5, and 3.6 of Figure 8.25. This requirement is to be included in the requirements given in problem 13(a).

18. Do the following:
  (a) Design an object box structured view of the index system in problem 17.
  (b) Incrementally elaborate the design of (a) first with the object box method in creating an object-oriented program.
  (c) Specify all inputs and outputs to the object box for the program.
  (d) Specify all major methods belonging to the box structure(s) you design.
  (e) Verify the correctness of each elaboration.

19. Incrementally elaborate the design from problem 18 using the clear box view of each method, and:
  (a) Elaborate and verify each method separately.
  (b) Indicate which of the design elements are reflected in the elaboration.
  (c) Verify the correctness of each elaboration.
  (d) Check each elaboration with a web browser or applet viewer.
  (e) Give a screen print showing the result of running your elaboration.

20. Create an .html file which implements the applet class created in problem 19, and:
  (a) Run the new index system.
  (b) Give a screen print for each state displayed in your program.

21. Use the program in problems 15 and 16 to verify that the competed product satisfies the components of the test plan created in problem 17(b).

Note: An object diagram for a traffic navigation manager is given in Figure 8.26.

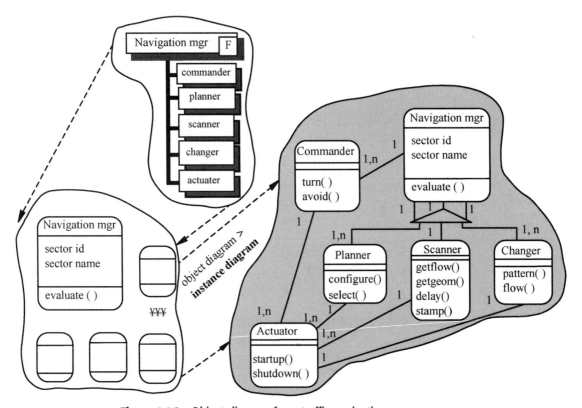

Figure 8.26 Object diagram for a traffic navigation manager.

22. Give the requirements and design for a traffic navigation manager based on the object diagram in Figure 8.26. That is:
    (a) Create a table given the specific requirments and design components for the navigation system.
    (b) Create a test plan (test items and features to be tested) for the navigation system.

Note: Here is a partial list of requirements and design components:
Req-1: There is a method for navigation mgr, command, plan, scan, change, actuate.
Req-2: The navigation system is interactive.
Req-3: The navigation system can be simulated.
Req-4: The entire navigation system is platform independent.
D-1: The traffic navigation system has a front panel displayed by a web browser.
D-2: Each navigation system method is represented by its own pulldown menu.
These requirements and design components are included in the requirements given in (a).

23. Incrementally elaborate the design of the traffic navigation manager in problem 22 first with the object box method in creating an object-oriented program.

(a) Specify all relevant libraries needed for the navigation program.
(b) Specify all inputs and outputs to the object box for the program.
(c) Specify all methods associated with the final version of the object box for the navigation program.
(d) Verify the correctness of each of your elaborations.

24. Incrementally elaborate the design from problem 23 using the clear box view of each method, and:
(a) Elaborate and verify each method separately.
(b) Indicate which of the design elements are reflected in the elaboration.
(c) Verify the correctness of each elaboration.
(d) Each elaboration is to be checked with sample runs of your program.
(e) Give a screen print showing the result of running of each of your elaborations.

25. Use the program in problem 24 to verify that the competed product satisfies the components of the test plan created in 22(b).

26. A data flow diagram for the scanner in a navigation system is given in Figure 8.27 and its decomposition in Figure 8.28. Do the following:
(a) Elaborate the scanner method from problem 24 to include a timer operation. That is, a scan should be performed periodically (after each timeout of a timer).
(b) Verify the correctness of your design.
(c) Add to the requirements and design components from problem 18 to reflect this change in the design.
(d) Modify the test plan from problem 18 to take into account this new feature of the scanner.

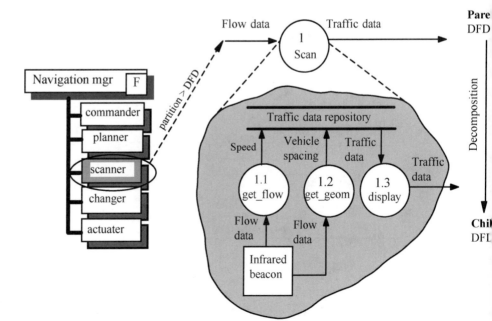

Figure 8.27 Scanner method for navigation system.

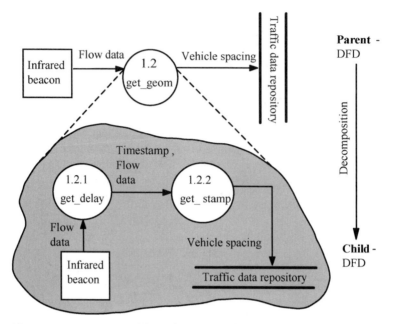

Figure 8.28   Decomposition of get_geom for navigation system.

27. Implement the scan operation from problem 26, and:
   (a) Give a sample run.
   (b) Give screen prints showing different states resulting from the operation of the timed scanner.

Note: An SADT diagram for the change operation in a traffic navigation system is shown in Figure 8.29.

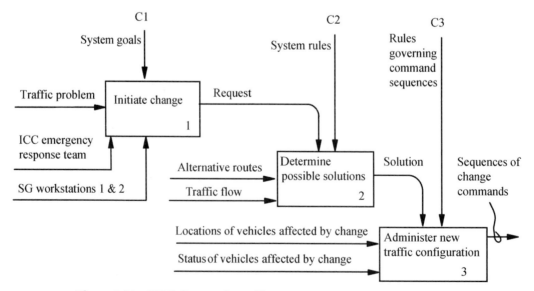

Figure 8.29   SADT diagram for traffic management.

28. Do the following:
    (a) Elaborate the change method from problem 24 in terms of the change operation in Figure 8.29. That is, the new version of the change operation should respond to traffic problems (stimulus from environment about a traffic problem that causes the navigation system to respond). The change operation then initiates changes (instructions sent to a problem solver, which determines alternative routes, and status of affected vehicles). The problem solver then transmits the solutions(s) to affected vehicles.
    (b) Verify the correctness of your design.
    (c) Add to the requirements and design components from problem 8. No. 16 to reflect this change in the design.
    (d) Modify the test plan from problem 18 to take into account this feature of the scanner.

29. Implement the change operation from problem 28, and:
    (a) Give a sample run.
    (b) Give screen prints showing different states resulting from the operation of the change method.

8.7 REFERENCES

Adams, E.N. *Minimizing Cost Impact of Software Defects.* IBM Research Division Report RC8228 (35669), April 11, 1980.

Black, A., Hutchinson, N., Jul, E., Levy, H. Exploiting code mobility in decentralized and flexible network management. *ACM Transactions on Computer Systems,* **6**(1), 1988.

Carzaniga, A., Picco, G.P., Vigna, G. Designing distributed applications with mobile code paradigms. *Proceedings of the 19th International Conference on Software Engineering,* Boston, May 1997, pp. 22–33.

Cox, B. *Object Oriented Programming: An Evolutionary Approach.* Addison-Wesley, Reading, MA, 1991. See also an OO short course and Objective C programming at *http://www.cs.indiana.edu/classes/c304/oop-intro.html.*

Currit, P.A., Dyer, M., Mills, H.D. Certifying the reliability of software. *Transactions on Software Engineering,* **SE-12** (1):3–11, 1986.

Dyer, M. *The Cleanroom Approach to Quality Software Development.* Wiley, NY, 1992.

Gray, R.S. Agent Tcl: A transportable agent system. *Proceedings of the CIKM'95 Workshop on Intelligent Information Agents,* 1995.

Howard, R. Eiffel: A language for object-oriented software engineering. In *The Handbook of Software for Engineers and Scientists,* P.W. Ross, Ed. CRC Press, Boca Raton, pp. 315–339, 1996.

ISO 9000-3. Guidelines for the application of ISO 9000 to the development, supply and maintenance of software. In ISO 9000, *Quality Management and Quality Assurance Standards,* part 3. International Standards Organization, Geneva, Switzerland, 1992.

Kernighan, B.W., Ritchie, D.M. *The C Programming Language.* Prentice-Hall, Englewood Cliffs, NJ, 1988.

Knuth, D.E. *The Art of Computer Programming.* Addison-Wesley, Reading, MA, 1981.

Lalond, W., Pugh, J. *Inside Smalltalk*. Prentice-Hall, Englewood Cliffs, NJ, 1991.

Macsyma Mathematics and System Reference Manual, 15th ed. Cambridge, MA, Macsyma Inc., 1995.

Maeder, R.E. *The Mathematica Programmer II*. Academic Press, New York, 1996. Note: This book includes a CD ROM with notebooks and HTML documents.

Maeder, R.E. *The Mathematica Programmer*. Academic Press, New York, 1994.

Magic, G. *Telescript Language Reference,* October 1995.

Mathiske, B., Matthes, F., Schmidt, J. On migrating threads Technical Report, Fachbereich Informatik Universitat, Hamburg, 1994.

Milner, R. *Communication and Concurrency*. Prentice-Hall, Englewood Cliffs, NJ, 1989.

Mills, H. Cleanroom testing. In Encyclopedia of Software Engineering, J.J. Marciniak, Ed. Wiley, New York, 1994.

Mills, H.D. How to write correct programs and know it. *International Conference on Reliable Software,* Los Angeles, pp. 363–370, 1975.

Mills, H.D., Dyer, M., Linger, R.C. Cleanroom software engineering. *IEEE Software,* Sept. 1987, pp. 19–25.

NeXT Computer, Inc. *Object Oriented Programming and Objective C Language*. Addison-Wesley, Reading, MA, 1993.

Object Management Group (OMG). *CORBA: Architecture and Specification,* August 1995.

Parnas, D.L. On the criteria to be used in decomposing systems into modules. *Communications of the ACM,* **15,** Dec. 1972, pp. 1053–1058.

Rumbaugh, J., Blaha, M., Premerlani, W., et al. *Object-Oriented Modeling and Design*. Prentice Hall, Englewood Cliffs, NJ, 1991.

Selby, W., Basili, V.R., Baker, T. Cleanroom software development: An empirical evaluation. *IEEE Transactions on Software Engineering,* **13**(9):1027–1037, 1987.

Stroustrup, B. *The C++ Programming Language*. Addison-Wesley Reading, MA, 1991.

Sun Microsystems. *The Java Language Specification*. Palo Alto, CA, October 1995.

Sutor, R. AXIOM. In *The Handbook of Software for Engineers and Scientists,* P.W. Ross, Ed., CRC Press, Boca Raton, FL, pp. 794–820, 1996.

CHAPTER 9

Design Elaboration: Mobile Computing

The network, by and large, starts to behave like a sea of computation on which you go rafting.

—JAMES GOSLING, 1997

Aims

- Make the transition from design to mobile computing code
- Identify essential elements of mobile computing applications
- Consider approach to developing zero-defect mobile computing software

---

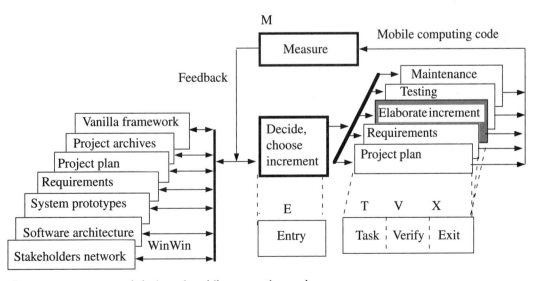

Figure 9.1 Incremental design of mobile computing code.

9.1   INTRODUCTION

The software process in Figure 9.1 has been specialized to produce code for mobile computing applications. In mobile computing, the aim is to develop a program that compiles into code accessible by web browsers. The feedback system model in Figure 9.1 retains the Win Win Stakeholders element and the Humphrey ETVXM architecture to ensure an orderly progression through the activities to produce software products. The decision to implement a design in mobile computing code comes from project planners at the beginning of a project. The design of a mobile computing application will reflect stakeholders' priorities concerning commercial products. It has been observed that priorities concerning commercial software have changed since the early 1990s (Gosling, 1997). A comparison of these differing priorities is given in Table 9.1. The priorities are arranged in descending order with the highest priority given first. In the early 90s, compatibility was uppermost in the minds of software developers. For example, files created in Microsoft Excel 4.0 or earlier can be converted to the new format in Excel 5.0 or Excel 98. By contrast, the consumer electronics industry

TABLE 9.1   Differing Priorities in Descending Order (Early 1990s)

Commercial Software	Consumer Electronics
Compatibility: The ability of two or more software components to perform requires their functions while sharing the same hardware or software environment.	Security
Performance: The degree to which a software component accomplishes its designated functions within given constraints such as speed, accuracy, and memory usage.	Networking
Portability: The ease with which a software component can be transferred from one hardware or software environment to another.	Portability
Reliability: The ability of a software component to perform its required functions under stated conditions for a specified period of time.	Reliability
Networking: A provision for connecting computers over a network so that an application is continuously running on a remote machine while waiting for (and interacting with) network traffic.	Performance
Multithreading: The ability of one program to do more than one thing concurrently (e.g., printing while receiving a fax).	Multithreading
Security: Virus-free, tamper-free software.	Compatibility

considered secure networking and portability more important than compatibility. Over recent years, there has been a noticeable shift in priorities in the software industry. Mainstream software consumer electronics priorities have become more important in software development. This is partly explained by the dramatic increase in the demand for software in the home.

Networking nowadays is a dominant feature of consumer electronics as well as in computer and software industries. VCRs are connected to TVs. Laptops now have built-in modems so that a laptop can be directly connected to a phoneline. Networking has a much higher priority in the software industry now than it did in the early 90s. E-mail and web addresses inserted into PowerPC Microsoft Word 98 documents, for example, become live links to the Internet and to web pages. Web pages have become commercial windows for companies. Software supporting virtual classrooms and virtual malls is also of interest. Architecture neutrality has become an important issue in the software industry. There is interest in developing software that is platform neutral.

Architecture neutrality is realized in the context of mobile computing. To gauge the strength of mobile computing software, consider the case of multithreading and portability. A multithreaded program is an extension of multitasking (more than one program appearing to run at the same time), where individual programs have the ability to run multiple computations concurrently. In a mobile computing environment such as Java, there is a provision for multiple threads of execution (e.g., listening to an audio clip while scrolling down a page and running an application in the background), having the capacity to take advantage of multiprocessor systems provided the base operating system is designed for multiprocessing.

Portability is a key feature of mobile computing programs, which can be shipped across the Internet and run with a local web browser. As a result, mobile computing software provides the basis for a global village, a context for sharing computation, and providing a framework for mobile computing applications (Black et al., 1988; Carzaniga et al., 1997; Munson & Dewan, 1997; Wood et al., 1997). As a result, concurrent software development is made easier. The focus of this chapter is on the application of the design elaboration process in developing zero-defect mobile computing software.

9.2 DESIGN ELABORATION: MOBILE COMPUTING

Two examples of design elaboration of mobile computing programs are given in this section. The coding for both examples is in terms of Java applets. An applet is a mini-application that runs Java code inside a web browser (Arnold & Gosling, 1998).

9.2.1   Basic Features of Java

Java is an object-oriented programming language. The syntax for Java programs borrows from C (control structures) as well as C++ (terminology and declaration of classes). In Java, a class is a type (collection of data and methods that operate on the data). An object is an instance of a class. A Java program consists of one or more classes. Each class has exactly one superclass or parent, but a class can have many subclasses arranged in a hierarchy. An applet is a Java class that is loaded and run by a running Java application or by a web browser or applet viewer. A flowchart for a typical Java development is shown in Figure 9.2. Integrated Development Environments (IDEs) provide an editor (for preparing ./java and ./html source code), compiler, debugger, profiler, pretty printer, and applet viewer to develop programs. A variety of IDEs are available:

- Roaster from Natural Intelligence (target: PowerMac),
  http://www.roaster.com.
- CodeWarrior Java IDE from Metrowerks with compilers for C, C++, Pascal, and Java (targets: PowerMac, PC), *http://www.Metrowerks.com.*
- Jfactory from Rogue Wave (target: PC), *http://www.roguewave.com.*
- Cafe for 95/NT from Symantec (target PC), *http://cafe.symantec.com.*

The Java Developer's Kit (JDK) is also downloadable from Sun Microsystems web site: *http://java.sun.com/java.sun.com/products/JDK.* The JDK includes a compiler,

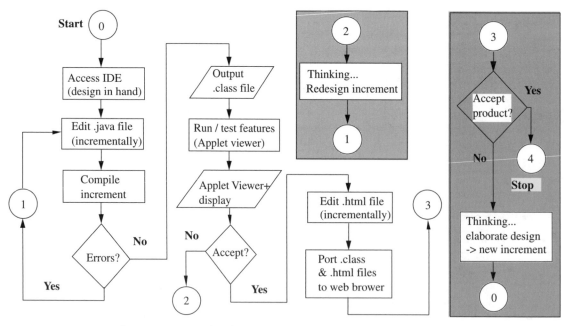

Figure 9.2   Java development environment.

```
imports java.applet.Applet;                    // superclass Applet
// declaration of other imported Java classes
public class thisScaffolding extends java.applet.Applet { /*
  // declarations of variables
  // methods */}
```

Figure 9.3 Scaffolding for a Java applet.

debugger, and applet viewer. JDK 1.2 (now called JDK 2) is now available. See also the description of Java in *The Java Language Specification* (Sun, 1995).

As in C++, a // marks the beginning of a single-line comment and /* */ bracket multi-line comments. In Java, every class is subclass of the base or superclass named Applet. Every applet has the form shown in Figure 9.3. A file containing the text for an applet is given a .java extension. The thisStub.java applet can be compiled and run, but will do nothing. A java development environment has an abstract windowing toolkit (awt), which provides a collection of classes for building a Graphical User Interface (GUI). With awt, it is possible to create windows; draw geometric shapes and strings (with colors); manipulate images; introduce buttons, dialogue boxes, scroll bars, and pulldown menus; and control layouts of components with container objects. A complete description of awt is given by Flanagan (1997). A Graphics class is contained in awt that provides methods for selecting colors, drawing strings in specified areas of a display, and rendering images and shapes. For example, the Graphics class has methods named setColor and drawString, which will be used to construct an elementary applet. An invocation of the setColor( ) method has the form

```
setColor(Color.c);   /*Note:  c can be replaced by
                      *black,  blue,  cyan,  darkGray,  gray,  green,  pink,
                      *LightGray,  magenta,  orange,  red,  white,  yellow*/
```

If we invoke this method with setColor(Color.green), whatever is drawn will have a bright, springtime green color. An invocation of the drawString method has the form

```
drawString(String str, int x, int y);   //e.g. drawString("treetop", 80, 50)
```

The width and height are integers specifying the number of pixels of the display enclosing the string that is drawn.

Let seTest.java be the name of a file containing an applet. The empty methods section and name of the thisScaffolding class in Figure 9.3 can be replaced with a new name (seTest) and a paint( ) method with a paint object name g as shown in Figure 9.4. The result of compiling seTest.java is a file named seTest.class,

```
imports java.applet.Applet;                    // Applet superclass
imports java.awt.*                             // abs. windowing toolkit

public class seTest extends java.applet.Applet {   // your applet is public
  public void paint( Graphics g ) {            // painting method
    g.setColor(Color.green);
    g.drawString("RE -> Design -> Incr1 ->... -> Incrn -> product", 100, 50)
    }                                          // end of painting method
}                                              // end of new applet
```

Figure 9.4   Applet named seGraphics.java.

which is runnable with a web browser. Running this applet with an applet viewer produces the window shown in Figure 9.5.

To see the result of running this new applet class with a web browser, do the following:

- Put the seTest.class file (result of compiling seTest.java) in an Internet directory (it is easiest if this file is in the same directory as your home page HTML file).
- Put the seTest.java file in the same internet directory as the one containing seTest.class (this will make it possible for you to provide a hypertext link to this file, if you want to check the syntax of seTest.java).
- Create an HTML with an <applet> tag like that shown in Figure 9.6.

Now try launching this HTML file with a web browser, which will now have a display like the one shown in Figure 9.7.

The appearance of a text displayed by a running applet (its font, attributes such as bold or italics, and font size) can be controlled by importing the java.awt.-

Figure 9.5   Display produced by applet.

```
<html>
<title>seTest</title>
<body>
<hr>
<applet code="seTest.class" width=200 height=50>
</applet>
<hr>
<a href="seTest.java">The source.</a>
</body>
</html>
```

Figure 9.6 HTML file with applet tag.

Font class. The fonts supported by Java 1.0 are TimesRoman, Helvetica, Courier, Dialog, and DialogInput. A variable of f of type Font is invoked as follows:

```
Font f = new Font(String name, int style, int size);
```

The style may be PLAIN, BOLD, ITALIC or the sum BOLD+ITALIC. The size parameter specifies the font size. The new keyword is used to create an object

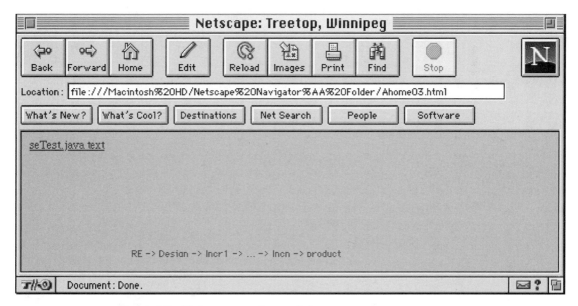

Figure 9.7 Netscape running applet.

```
/*
  applet displays colorful string in TimesRoman, style boldface, size 36
*/

import java.applet.Applet;
import java.awt.*;
import java.awt.Font;

public class seElab extends java.applet.Applet {

Font f = new Font("TimesRoman", Font.BOLD, 36);

public void paint(Graphics g) {
  g.setFont(f);
  g.setColor(Color.red);
  g.drawString("RE->Design->Incr1->...->incrn-> product", 200, 130);
  }
}
```

Figure 9.8   Elaborated applet design.

of the specified type. To see this, try elaborating seTest.java and create a new applet named seElab.java as shown in Figure 9.8.

After modifying the html file in Figure 9.6, a web browser will run the applet class to produce the display shown in Figure 9.9. Notice that only part of the

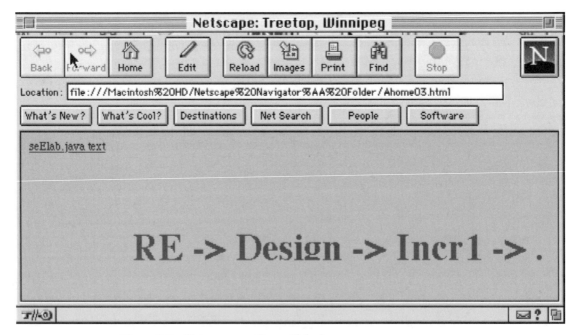

Figure 9.9   Netscape running seElab.class.

string "RE–>Design–>Incr1–>. . .–>Incrn–>product" is displayed. The width and height parameters must be adjusted to capture the entire string.

9.2.2 Init( ) Method for Applets

The method init( ) is the Java equivalent main( ) in C++. The purpose of init( ) is to initialize variables, and provide stimuli for other methods included in an applet. However, unlike C++, init( ) does not have to be included in applet in the case where there are no variables to initialize. To do this, the getParameter( ) method defined in the Applet class itself is used. This method looks up and returns the value of a named parameter specified for an applet in an HTML file. First try setting up a new applet named seExp.java, which is an elaboration of seElab.java. Initially, it is helpful to maintain a collection of tiny applets which exhibit a progression of ideas and applet constructs. For this reason, each design elaboration leads to a new applet. This is a matter of personal preference, not a requirement.

```
/*
   applet displays colorful string provided by HTML param
*/
import java.applet.Applet;
import java.awt.*;
import java.awt.Font;

public class seExp extends java.applet.Applet {

  Font f = new Font("TimesRoman", Font.BOLD, 18);
  int xDist = 100;
  int yDist = 95;
  String toScreen;

public void init( ) {
  toScreen = getParameter("htmlString");
  }

public void paint(Graphics g) {
  g.setFont(f);
  g.setColor(Color.magenta);
  g.drawString(toScreen, xDist, yDist);
  }
}
```

After compiling seExp.java, a copy of the seExp.class and seExp.java files must be downloaded to an Internet directory accessible by your home page. Then an HTML file must be set up to reference an applet with a string parameter as in Figure 9.10. The result of running the seExp applet class is shown in Figure 9.11.

```
<html>
<title>Runs seExp applet with indicated string parameter</title>
<body>
<hr>
<applet code="seExp.class" width=200 height=50>
<param name = "htmlString" value="Design incr-i">
</applet>
<hr>
<a href="seExp.java">The source.</a>
</body>
</html>
```

Figure 9.10   HTML file with applet tag.

By introducing an array of colors, and putting calls to the Graphics methods, it is possible to begin animating a display. An array declaration has the form

```
type arrayName[] = {x1, x2, x3, ..., xn}
```

where x1, x2, x3, . . . xn have the declared type. For example, an array of elements of type Color is declared as follows:

```
Color color[] = {Color.green, Color.magenta,
                 Color.yellow }
```

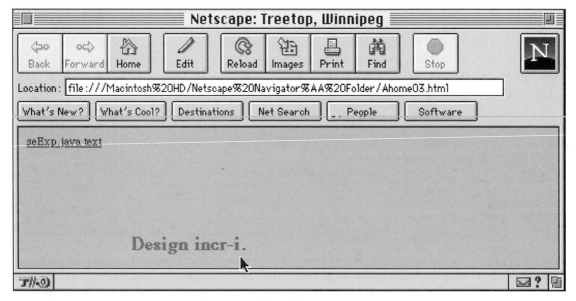

Figure 9.11   Netscape running seExp.class.

where color[0] = Color.green, color[1] = Color.magenta, and so on. A for loop in Java has the same syntax as in C++ or C. The Graphics class has a fillOval( ) method, which draws an oval with a filled-in color. The syntax for this method is

```
fillOval(int x, int y, int width, int height);
```

By calling setColor(color[i]) with the value of I changing inside a for-loop and varying the values of the parameters of fillOval( ), it is possible to create an applet that constructs a succession of ovals with the appearance of a rainbow. A sample run of an applet called seFuzzy is shown in Figure 9.12. The source text for seFuzzy.java is shown in Figure 9.13. In the sample run of the applet in Figure 9.13, notice that the ovals drawn by seFuzzy are lopped off. By adjusting the values of the parameters used in calling fillOval, more *or* less of the rainbow can be displayed. To see the effect the init( ) method has on the running of this applet, try out the alternative version of the seFuzzy applet shown in Figure 9.14.

9.2.3 Java Classes: Inheritance

The Applet superclass is the first parent (root of a tree) of Java applets. A Java class can extend any other class. For example, assume we have the classes shown in Table 9.2. The Applet class is the parent (superclass or base class) of the airCraft class. This is the beginning of a hierarchy of classes where autoPilot has the airCraft class as its parent. The rudderControl and followPath classes have autoPilot as their parent. Each of these classes is developed as a separate applet,

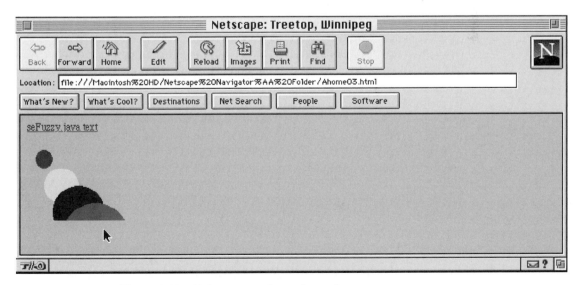

Figure 9.12 Netscape running seFuzzy.class.

```
/*
   applet displays rainbow of expanding ovals.
*/
import java.applet.Applet;
import java.awt.*;
import java.awt.Graphics;
import java.awt.Color;

public class seFuzzy extends java.applet.Applet {
 int x, y, w, h;
 Color color[] = {Color.green, Color.red, Color.yellow,Color.blue,
           Color.magenta, Color.green, Color.red, Color.yellow};

 public void init() {
  int x = 115;
  int y = 55;
  int w = 80;
  int h = 80;
  }

 public void paint(Graphics g) {
  for (int i=1; i<10; ++i) {
   g.setColor(color[i]);
   g.fillOval(x+10*i,y+20*i,w+20*i,h+20*i);
   }
  }
 }
```

Figure 9.13 Text for seFuzzy.java.

and the .class files which result from compiling these applets must be made accessible to the other classes in the hierarchy. The hierarchy is shown graphically in Figure 9.15.

One or more Java classes can be structured so that each one implements the same parent class called an interface, inheriting the methods of the parent as well as adding new methods appropriate for the needs of a particular implementor class. An interface is a list of methods that *must be* implemented by a class. A principal advantage to this approach to constructing applets is that an applet can both extend another class as well as implement *one or more* interfaces. For example, we can define an interface class that the plotPosition and followPath classes in Figure 9.15 both implement while at the same time extending the autoPilot class. The structure of an interface and its implementation is shown in Table 9.3.

A class that implements an interface provides an implementation of one or more methods in the interface. The plotPosition class both extends the autoPilot

```
/*
   applet displays rainbow of expanding ovals.
*/
import java.applet.Applet;
import java.awt.*;
import java.awt.Graphics;
import java.awt.Color;

public class seFuzzy extends java.applet.Applet {

Color color[] = {Color.green, Color.red, Color.yellow,Color.blue,
             Color.magenta, Color.green, Color.red, Color.yellow};

public void paint(Graphics g) {
  int x = 115;
  int y = 55;
  int w = 80;
  int h = 80;

  for (int i=1; i<10; ++i) {
   g.setColor(color[i]);
   g.fillOval(x+10*i,y+20*i,w+20*i,h+20*i);
   }
  }
}
```

Figure 9.14 Alternative version of seFuzzy.java.

TABLE 9.2 Hierarchy of Classes

Applet → airCraft	airCraft → autoPilot autoPilot → rudderControl autoPilot → followPath

import java.applet.Applet;
import java.awt.*;
public class airCraft extends Applet {
 float airspeed;
 float height;
 public int sensing( ) {/*...*/}
}
	class autoPilot extends airCraft {
	 String status[ ] = {...}; //status array
	 // inherits airspeed, height
	 void stability( ) {/*
	 // inherits sensing( ) */}}
	class plotPosition extends autoPilot {
	 // inherits status[ ]
	 // inherits stability( )}
	class followPath extends Autopilot {
	 // inherits status[ ]
	 // inherits stability( )}

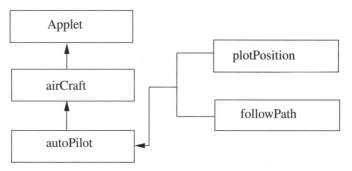

Figure 9.15 Sample applet hierarchy.

class and implements aircraftData methods (not necessarily all of them). The followPath class extends the autoPilot class and implements methods from two interfaces, namely, processCommand and courseData. The result is a very rich composition of classes, as shown in Figure 9.16.

Introducing an interface makes it possible for more than one class to implement the methods in the same interface. Packages of classes and arrays of classes are also possible, but are not covered here. A presentation of packages is given by Lemay and others (1996) and Cornell and Horstmann (1997). Arrays in a class hierarchy are covered by Niemeyer and Peck (1996). An excellent introduction to classes as well as Java itself is given by Flanagan (1997) as well as by Cornell and Horstmann (1997).

TABLE 9.3 Hierarchy of Classes

Interface	airCraft → autoPilot autoPilot → plotPosition aircraftData → plotPosition autoPilot → followPath aircraftData → followPath

public interface aircraftData {
 public float airSpeed( );
 public float currentHeight( );
 public float windSpeed( );
 public String currentHeading( );
 public String currentOutsideTemp( ); }
public interface processCommand {
 public String actOnCommand(String cmd);
 public int verifyCommand( );
 public String changeHeading( );
 public float adjustHeading( ); }
	class autoPilot extends airCraft {
	 // inherits airCraft methods}
	
	class plotPosition extends autoPilot
	 implements courseData
	{
	 // inherits autoPilot methods
	 // implements courseData methods }
	
	class followPath extends Autopilot
	 implements courseData, processCommand
	{
	 // inherits autoPilot methods
	 // implements courseData methods
	 // implements processCommand methods}

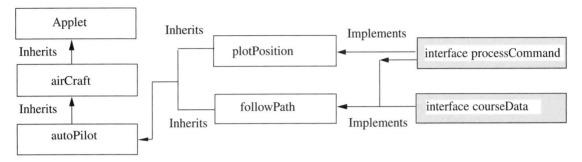

Figure 9.16 Interfaces and implementations.

9.3 EXAMPLE: DESIGN ELABORATION IN JAVA

The design elaboration method used in developing object-oriented programs is applicable in developing mobile computing programs in Java. We illustrate the approach with an application of the object box structure for the layout of an applet and clear box structure to deal with necessary control structures for methods for an interactive index card system. In the discussion of a clear box view of methods for the index card system, additional information about Java (creation of buttons, application of the if-else statement) will be given. The requirements and design for the card system are given in Table 9.4.

9.3.1 Design Elaboration with an Object Box

At this stage in the design elaboration process, we will be principally occupied with the following design components in setting up a Java program:

D-1: Card index system is hierarchical.
D-5: Cards (with labels) are set up and continuously displayed.
D-6: Clicking a card causes the index associated with data associated with clicked button to be displayed.

A single applet class called seCard will be represented with the object box structure shown in Figure 9.17. The java.applet.Applet class is the superclass for the index card system, which also utilizes methods belonging to the abstract windowing toolkit (awt) package of classes. The java seCard class is designed to output the panels of two buttons and to respond to a mouse click on a button by displaying the information associated with the "clicked" button. The structure of the java program containing seCard is shown next.

TABLE 9.4   Requirements and Design for an Index Card System

Requirements	Design
Req-1: Interactive system for index cards.	D-1: Card index system is hierarchical.
Req-2: Each card has a title.	D-2: Architecture processing element for each card is a one-element pipeline: mouseClick → processClick → display
Req-3: Each card hides information.	D-3: Architecture for card system: concurrent pipelines.
Req-4: All cards are visible.	D-4: Each pipeline is represented by a displayed button.
Req-5: (I, Action, O) triples: • (title, button_panen.add, card) • (color, setBackground, display) • (color, setForeground, display) • (info, card_panel.add, { }) • (mouseClick, card_layout.show, display)	D-5: Cards (with labels) are set up and continuously displayed. D-6: Clicking a card causes the index associated with data associated with clicked button to be displayed. D-7: Displays include background and foreground colors for buttons, and background color for cards.
Req-6: Displays are colorful.	D-8: Cards can be added. D-9: Card information is changeable. D-10: A card title is changeable. *Test plan*: Test item: mouseClick Features to test: • Flip through index cards. • Changing card title. • Changing card content. • Adding index cards.

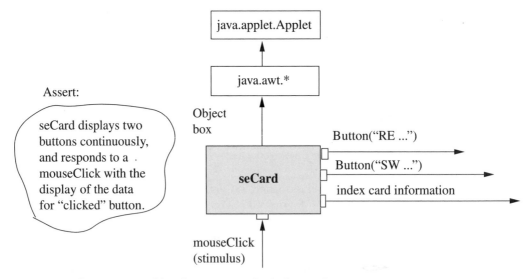

Figure 9.17   Object box structure for index card system.

```
1  /* assert:
   * (a) seCard is a subclass of java.applet.Applet.
     (b) classes in java.awt.* are available for use by seCard.
     (c) seClass is derived from java.applet.Applet.
     (d) provision for continuous display of two buttons
     (e) displays information associated with index card
     (f) Design D-1: Java program is hierarchical.
   */

2  import java.applet.Applet;    // make classes in Applet available
3  import java.awt.*;            // make classes in java.awt.*
                                    available

4  public class seCard extends java.applet.Applet { // seCard
                                                    // subclass
                                                    // of Applet

5  // declarations using Panel( )
6  // init() method (show buttons)
7  // card_panel method to set up index cards
8  // action method to respond to mouse click
9  }
```

Correctness Proof

```
1(a) seCard is a subclass of java.applet.Applet
(satisfied by line 2), and
1(b) classes in java.awt.* are available for use by
seCard (satisfied by line 3), and
1(c) seClass is derived from java.applet.Applet
(satisfied by line 4), and
1(d) provision for continuous display of two buttons
(implicitly satisfied by line 6), and
1(e) displays information associated with index card
(implicitly satisfied by line 7), and
1(f) Design D-1:Java program is hierarchical
(satisfied by lines 1 to 4).
```

The object box needs to be refined further before elaborating seCard with a clear box structure approach. The elaboration of seCard in graphical form is shown in Figure 9.18. The elaboration of seCard in Figure 9.18 is more definite about what must be done to set up the index card system (initialized buttons with init( ) and response to stimulus from the environment by action( )). With a small Java program, the elaborations shown in Figures 9.17 and 9.18 could be done in a single step. The elaboration steps have separated to clarify the design process leading to Java code. The Java program containing seCard (call it seCard.java) now has more detail.

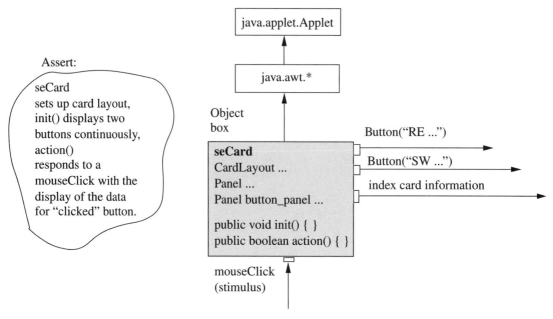

Figure 9.18   Elaboration of seCard box structure.

```
1    /*assert:
     * (a) set up new index card information
       (b) set up new button panel
       (b) provision for continuous display of two buttons
       (c) displays information associated with index card
       (d) Design D-5 Cards continously displayed.
       (e) Design D-6 Clicking a card displays card data

2    import java.applet.Applet;    // make classes in Applet available
3    import java.awt.*;            // make classes in java.awt.* available

4    public class seCard extends java.applet.Applet {    // seCard a
                                                          // subclass of
                                                          // Applet
5      CardLayout card_layout = new CardLayout();         // type CardLayout
                                                          // from java.awt.*
6      Panel card_panel = new Panel();                    // type Panel from
                                                          // java.awt.*
7      Panel button_panel = new Panel();                  // type Panel from
                                                          // java.awt.*

8    public void init() {                                 // initialize index
                                                          // card display
```

```
9      // set up continuous display of two buttons
10     }

11     public boolean action (Event evt, Object arg) {      /* sets up two
                                                            * pipeline:
                                                            * mouse Click ->
                                                            * react -> display
                                                            */
12     // set up response to mouse click
13     }

14 }
```

Correctness Proof

1(a) set up new index card information (satisfied by lines 5 and 6), *and*
1(b) set up new button panel (satisfied by line 7), *and*
1(c) provision for continuous display of two buttons (satisfied by lines 8 to 10), *and*
1(d) displays information associated with index card (satisfied by lines 11 to 13), *and*.
1(e) Design D-5:Cards continuously displayed (same as 1(c)), *and*
1(f) Design D-6:Clicking a card displays card data (same as 1(d)).

For the sake of clarity and at the risk of being slightly verbose, the design components D-5 and D-6 are stated in their original formulation and in a slightly different fashion in the context of lines of code in the seCard class. Notice that inclusion of the declarations for card_panel and button_panel stretches the idea of an object box, which is supposed to exhibit the structure but not the content of the object. Normally these declarations would appear in the ''look-inside'' clear box structure during design elaboration of a method or a class. The declarations have been included here to make it clearer what ammunition is needed to set up the init( ) and action( ) methods inside the seCard class. CardLayout is a class in java.awt.* used to present different screen arrangements to a user (the screen arrangements are called cards).

9.3.2   Design Elaboration with a Clear Box

At this stage in the design elaboration of the seCard class, we take a clear box approach and look inside at lines of code needed to implement the methods of this class. The concern now is with satisfying the following design components:

D-2: Architecture processing element for each card is a one element pipeline:

mouseClick -> processClick -> display

D-3: Architecture for card system: concurrent pipelines.
D-4: Each pipeline is represented by a displayed button.
D-5: Cards (with labels) are set up and continuously displayed.
D-6: Clicking a card causes the index associated with data associated with clicked button to be displayed.

We first tackle the issue of setting up the displayed buttons using the init( ) method. Before continuing the elaboration of the design of the seCard class, you might want to try experimenting with displaying buttons but not as part of a panel. To see this, try creating the simple Java program called seButton to display two labeled buttons given next.

```
import java.applet.Applet;                        // superclass
import java.awt.*;                                 // windowing
                                                   // toolkit

public class seButton extends java.applet.Applet { // seButton a
                                                   // subclass of Applet
  Button button1 = new Button ("Req Engineering"); // set up first
                                                   // button
  Button button2 = new Button ("SW Architecture"); // set up second
                                                   // button

public void init() {
  add(button1);                                    // adds labeled
                                                   // button1 to
                                                   // display
  add(button2);                                    // adds labeled
                                                   // button2 to
                                                   // display

 }
}
```

After compiling seButton.java, setting up an .html file with the <applet> tag for seButton.class, and porting seButton class and html file to the Internet for browsing, the result of running this applet is shown in Figure 9.19.

Next the code to display buttons that are part of a panel is introduced in the elaboration of the seCard Java program. The clear box structure rendering design component D-5 is given next.

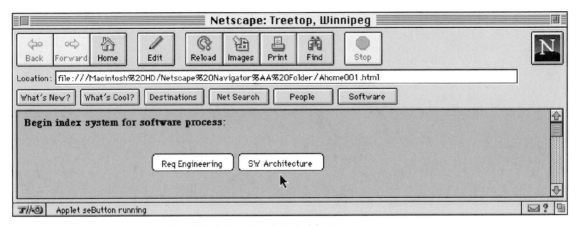

Figure 9.19 Displaying two labeled buttons.

```
1    /* assert:
     * (a) set up new index card information
     * (b) set up new button panel
     * (c) Design D-5 Cards are set up and continuously displayed.
*/
2    import java.applet.Applet;          // Java classes in Applet
                                         // available
3    import java.awt.*;                  // Java classes in java.awt.*
                                         // available

4    public class seCard extends        // seCard a subclass of Applet
        java.applet.Applet {
5    CardLayout card_layout = new       // type CardLayout from
     CardLayout();                      // java.awt.*
6    Panel card_panel = new Panel();    // type Panel from java.awt.*
7    Panel button_panel = new           // type Panel from java.awt.*
     Panel();

8    public void init() {               // initialize index card display
9     setLayout(new                     // setLayout method from
      BorderLayout());                  // java.awt.*
10    button_panel.add(new              // add is a Panel method
      Button("Req..."));
11    button_panel.add(new              // add invoked for second button
      Button("SW..."));
12    add("North", button_panel);
13    card_panel.add("RE", new          // defines card panel named "RE"
      Label("What ..."));
```

```
14   card_panel.add("SW", new Label    // defines card panel named "SW"
     ("How..."));
15   add("Center, card_panel);         // display centered
16 }

17 public boolean action (Event        /* sets up two pipeline:
      evt, Object arg) {               *mouseClick -> react -> display
                                       */
18 // set up response to mouse
   // click
19   }
20 }
```

Correctness Proof

> 1(a) set up new index card information (satisfied by
> lines 13 and 15), *and*
> 1(b) set up new button panel (satisfied by lines 9 to
> 12), *and*
> 1(c) provision for continuous display Design D-5:
> *Cards are set up and continuously displayed*
> (satisfied by lines 8 to 16).

You can run a check on the claim in Part 1(c) of the correctness proof by compiling the seCard.java program just the way it is now (with no action( ) method). The result of running the seCard.class with the Netscape web browser is shown in Figure 9.20. Notice that the information associated with the button

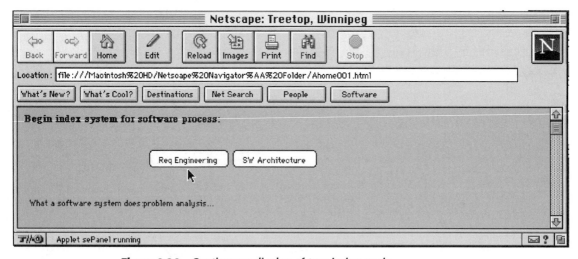

Figure 9.20   Continuous display of two index cards.

labeled "Req Engineering" is displayed. Also, notice that you can click on either of these buttons (a blinking occurs when this is done, but nothing else). Now the elaboration of the design of the seCard class continues with the code needed to make the index card system responsive to mouse clicks. This part of the elaboration responds to design component D-6 (Clicking a card causes the index associated with data associated with clicked button to be displayed). Setting up the pipelines that respond to mouse clicks is handled in the action( ) method of the seCard class. This is yet another application of the clear box view of a method during design elaboration.

```
1   /* assert:
    * (a) set up pipeline for "Req Engineering" button
    * (b) set up pipeline for "SW Architecture" button

    * (d) D-6 (Clicking a card causes the index associated with data
    associated with * clicked button to be displayed).
*/

2   imports java.applet.Applet;              // Java classes in Applet
                                             // available
3   import java.awt.*;                        // Java classes in java.awt.*
                                             // available
4   public class seColor extends             // seColor a subclass of
        java.applet.Applet {                 // Applet
5     CardLayout card_layout = new           // type CardLayout from
        CardLayout();                        // java.awt.*
6     Panel card_panel = new Panel();        // type Panel from java.awt.*
7     Panel button_panel = new Panel ();     // type Panel from java.awt.*

8     public void init() {                   // initialize index card
                                             // display
9       setLayout(new BorderLayout());       // setLayout method from
                                             // java.awt.*
10      button_panel.add(new Button("Req...")); // add is a Panel method
11      button_panel.add(new Button("SW...")); // add invoked for second
                                             // button
12      add("North", button_panel);
13      card_panel.add("RE", new Label                  // defines card
        ("What..."));                                    // panel named "RE"
14      card_panel.add ("SW", new Label      // defines card panel named
        ("How..."));                         // "SW"
15      add("Center", card_panel);           // display centered
16    }

17    public boolean action (Event evt,      /* sets up two pipelines:
        Object arg) {                        * mouseClick -> react -> *
                                             * display
                                             */
```

```
18    if(evt.target instanceof Button) {        // mouse click ->
19     if (arg.equals("Req Engineering"))        // button "Req ..." (react ->
20       card_layout.show(card_panel, "RE");     // display card_panel labeled
                                                  // "RE"

21    if (arg.equals("SW Architecture"))         // button "SW ..." (react) ->
22       card_layout.show (card_panel, "SW");    // display card_panel labeled
                                                  // "SW"
23    return true;                               // ends pipeline process
24    }
25    return false;                              // neither button was clicked
26    }
27  }
```

Correctness Proof

```
1(a) set up pipeline for "Req Engineering" button
(satisfied by lines 18 to 20), and
1(b) set up pipeline for ''SW Architecture'' button
(satisfied by lines 18, 21 to 22), and
1(c) D-6: Clicking a card causes the index associated
with data associated with clicked button to be
displayed (satisfied by lines 17 to 26).
```

You can verify the claim in 1(c) of the correctness proof by compiling seCard.java and running the seCard.class with a browser. The result is a display like the one shown in Figure 9.21. Notice that now if you click on either button, a "pipeline"

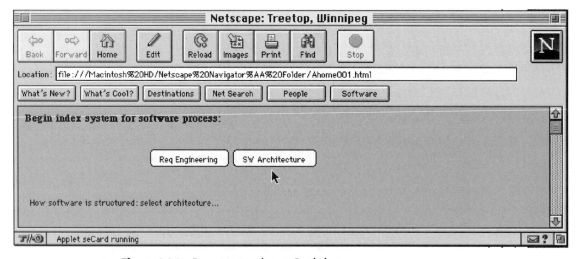

Figure 9.21   Browser running seCard.class.

How software is structured: Select architecture . . .

Figure 9.22 Information on "SW Architecture" index card.

process is activated and the information corresponding to the clicked button will be displayed. In the sample run in Figure 9.21, the result of clicking on the button labeled "SW Architecture" produced the display shown in Figure 9.22. The design requirement

D-7: Displays include background and foreground colors for buttons, and background color for cards

can be realized in another elaboration of the seCard.java given next.

```
1   /* assert:
    * (a) set up background color for buttons
    * (b) set up foreground color for buttons
    * (b) set up background color for card panel
    * (d) D-7 Displays include background and foreground colors for
    buttons, and    * background color for cards
*/

2   import java.applet.Applet;      // Java classes in Applet
                                    // available
3   import java.awt.*;              // Java classes in java.awt.*
                                    // available

4   public class seCard extends    // seCard a subclass of Applet
       java.applet.Applet {
5     CardLayout card_layout = new // type CardLayout from java.awt.*
        CardLayout();
6     Panel card_panel = new       // type Panel from java.awt.*
        Panel();
7     Panel button_panel = new Panel // type Panel from java.awt.*
        ();

8     public void init() {         // initialize index card display
9       setLayout(new             // setLayout method from
          BorderLayout());        // java.awt.*
10      button_panel.add(new      // add is a Panel method
          Button("Req..."));
```

```
11    button_panel.add(new            // add invoked for second button
         Button("SW..."));
12    button_panel.setBackground      // Panel setBackground method used
         (Color.green);
13    button_panel.setForeGround      // Panel setForeGround method used
         (Color.red);
14    add("North", button_panel);
15    card_panel.add ("RE, new        // defines card panel named "RE"
         Label("What..."));
16    card_panel.add("SW", new        // defines card panel named "SW"
         Label("How..."));
17    card_panel.setBackground        // Panel setBackground method used
         (Color.yellow);
18    add ("Center", card_panel);     // display centered
19 }

20 public boolean action (Event       /* sets up two pipelines;
      evt, Object arg) {                *mouseClick -> react -> display
                                        */
21 if (evt.target instanceof          // mouse click ->
      Button) {
22  if (arg.equals("Req              // button "Req ..."(react)->
      Engineering"))
23     card_layout.show(card_         // display card_panel labeled "RE"
         panel, "RE");

24  if (arg.equals("SW               // button "SW ..." (react) ->
         Architecture"))
25     card_layout.show(card_         // display card_panel labeled "SW"
         panel, "SW");
26  return true;                      // ends pipeline process
27  }
28  return false;                     // neither button was clicked
29 }
30 }
```

Correctness Proof

1(a) set up background color for buttons (satisfied by line 12), *and*
1(b) set up background color for card panel (satisfied by line 13), *and*
1(c) D-7: Displays include background and foreground colors for buttons, and background color for cards (satisfied by lines 8 to 19).

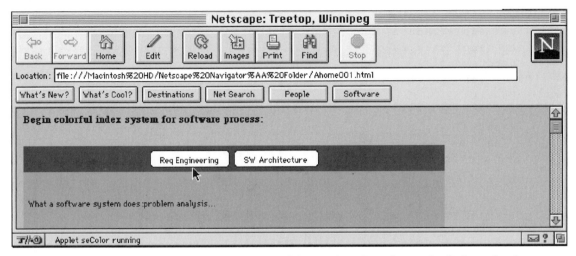

Figure 9.23 Browser running elaborated version of seCard called seColor.class.

To separate this new version of the index card system from the earlier (noncolored) version, seCard.java has been renamed seColor.java. A sample run of the seColor.class is shown in Figure 9.23.

There are still outstanding design components to be elaborated. For example, some thought should be given to how one might add new index cards, change the titles, and change the information displayed each time one of the buttons is clicked. To start this new round of design elaborations, it is possible to make changes in button names using the PARAM NAME option for applets in HTML, and adding lines of code to the java program to cause the browser to see if an alternative to the name given in the program can be found in the .html file. To see this, try the elaboration of the D-10 design component:

D-10: A card title is changeable.

```
1   /* assert:
    * (a) set up possibility of
    * button name change
    * (b) D-10 A card title is
    changeable
    */

2   imports java.applet.Applet;      // Java classes in Applet
                                     // available
3   import java.awt.*;               // Java classes in java.awt.*
                                     // available
```

```
4    public class seColor extends        // seColor a subclass of Applet
        java.applet.Applet {
5    CardLayout card_layout = new         // type CardLayout from java.awt.*
        CardLayout();
6    Panel card_panel = new              // type Panel from java.awt.*
        Panel();
7    Panel button_panel = new            // type Panel from java.awt.*
        Panel();
8    String name;                        // name of type String

9    public void init() {                // initialize index card display
10    this.name = getParameter           // try to get this.name from .html
        ("name");                        // file
11    if (this.name == null)             // did .html file give a name?
12    this.name = "Req                   // if not, use default this.name
        Engineering";                    // value

13   setLayout(new BorderLayout());      // setLayout method from
                                         // java.awt.*
14   button_panel.add(new                // add is a Panel method
        Button(this.name));
15   button_panel.add(new Button("SW     // add invoked for second button
        ..."));
16   button_panel.setBackground          // Panel setBackground method used
        (Color.green);
17   button_panel.setForeground          // Panel setForeground method used
        (Color.red);
18   add("North", button_panel);
19   card_panel.add ("RE", new Label     // defines card panel named "RE"
        ("What ..."));
20   card_panel.add("SW", new Label      // defines card panel named "SW"
        ("How..."));
21   card_panel.setBackground            // Panel setBackground method used
        (Color.yellow);
22   add("Center", card_panel);          // display centered
23   }

24   public boolean action (Event        /* sets up two pipelines:
        evt, Object arg) {               * mouseClick -> react -> display
                                         */
25   if (evt.target instanceof           // mouse click ->
        Button) {
26   if (arg.equals(this.name))          // button "Req ..." (react) ->
27      card_layout.show(card_           // display card_panel labeled "RE"
        panel, "RE");
```

```
28   if (arg.equals("SW             // button "SW ..." (react) ->
       Architecture"))
29      card_layout.show(card_       // display card_panel labeled "SW"
          panel, "SW");
30   return true;                   // ends pipeline process
31   }
32   return false;                  // neither button was clicked
33   }
34 }
```

Correctness Proof

```
1(a) set up possibility of button name change
(satisfied by lines 8, 10-12), and
1(b) D-10: A card title is changeable (satisfied by
lines 8 to 23).
```

In this case, it is necessary to set up a more sophisticated .html file, if you want to change the default button name given by the applet class. Try setting up the following .html file:

```
<HTML>
<HEAD>
<TITLE> Treetop, Winnipeg </TITLE>
</HEAD>
<BODY>
<P><b>Begin colorful index system for software process:
</b></P><BR>
<applet code="seColor.class" width=500 height=100>
<PARAM NAME = name VALUE = "Design Elaboration">
</applet>
</BODY>
</HTML>
```

After compiling the new version of the index card system (call it seChange. java), running this applet class with a browser produces the result shown in Figure 9.24. The name of the left button in Figure 9.24 has now been changed from the default ''Req Engineering'' to ''Design Elaboration''. Notice that the technique used to change the name of one button can be used again to change the name of the other button. In this case, it is necessary to introduce a second variable name2 of type String, and to incorporate name2 in the init( ) and action( ) methods. The changes in the index card system ap-

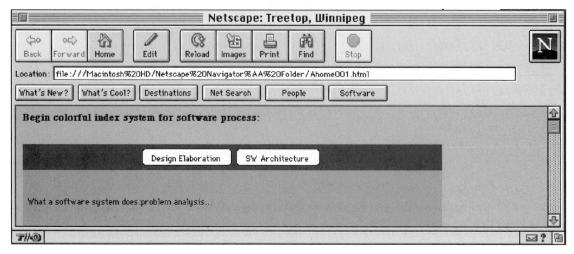

Figure 9.24   Browser running seChange.class.

plet are shown in boldface in a new applet named seParam.java in Figure 9.25.

Now it is necessary to modify the .html file and add two parameters called name 1 and name2, which the applet in Figure 9.25 will use to change the names of the two buttons. The new .html file (with changes in boldface) is given in Figure 9.26. The result of running the .html file in Figure 9.26 is shown in Figure 9.27.

The design elaboration for the index card system is not complete. First, there is still the problem of being able to change the information associated with each index card. Second, design elaboration (a white box view of the Java applet) should introduce lines of code to make it possible to add index cards to the system. This is left of future work.

In addition, now that a preliminary version of the index card system is running, it is appropriate to consider a more elaborate web page. It would be appropriate to display a clip showing the implementation process (this could be displayed in the upper righthand corner of the page which displays the buttons for the index card system). From an aesthetics point of view, it would also help to display other "eye-catching" information (e.g., a photo of "Java's best friend"). Let designElaboration.gif be a file containing a graph of the implementation process. Also, let lab.jpg be a file containing a photo of Java's best friend. In addition, use the alignment options for images to align the display of design-Elaboration.gif on the righthand side of the page (use align = "right"). An .html file to carry out these suggestions is given in Figure 9.28. A new sample run of the seColor.class using the .html file shown in Figure 9.28 is given in Figure 9.29.

```
import java.applet.Applet;
import java.awt.*;

public class seParam extends java.applet.Applet {
 CardLayout card_layout = new CardLayout();
 Panel card_panel = new Panel();
 Panel button_panel = new Panel();
 String name1;
 String name2;

 public void init() {
   this.name1 = getParameter("name1");
   this.name2 = getParameter("name2");
   if (this.name1 == null)
    this.name1 = "Req Engineering";
   if (this.name2 == null)
    this.name2 = "SW Architecture";

  setLayout(new BorderLayout());
  button_panel.add(new Button(this.name1));
  button_panel.add(new Button(this.name2));
  button_panel.setBackground(Color.green);
  button_panel.setForeground(Color.red);
  add("North", button_panel);

  card_panel.setLayout(card_layout);
  card_panel.add("RE", new Label(" Transition from architectures to code..."));
  card_panel.add("SW", new Label(" How software is structured: select architecture..."));
  card_panel.setBackground(Color.yellow);
  add("Center", card_panel);
  }

 public boolean action(Event evt, Object arg) {
  if (evt.target instanceof Button) {
   if (arg.equals(this.name1))
    card_layout.show(card_panel, "RE");
   else if (arg.equals(this.name2))
    card_layout.show(card_panel, "SW");
   return true;
   }
  return false;
  }
}
```

Figure 9.25 The Param applet with two possible name changes.

```
HTML>
<HEAD>
<TITLE> Treetop, Winnipeg </TITLE>
</HEAD>
<BODY>
<a href="seParam.java">seParam.java source file</a>
<br>
<P><b>Begin colorful index system for software process: </b></P><BR>
<applet code="seParam.class" width=500 height=100>
<PARAM NAME = name1 VALUE = "Design Elaboration">
<PARAM  NAME = name2 VALUE = "Cleanroom  Method">
</applet>
</BODY>
</HTML>
```

Figure 9.26   The .html file with two parameters.

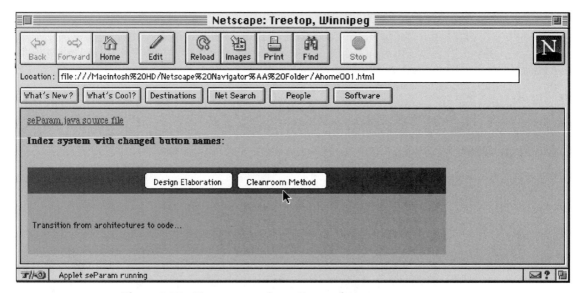

Figure 9.27   Netscape running seParam.class.

```
<HTML>
<HEAD>
<TITLE> Treetop, Winnipeg </TITLE>
</HEAD>
<BODY>
<b>Design elaboration process: </b"><BR>
<img src="designElaboration.gif" align="right">
<BR>
Java's best friend:
<br>
<IMG SRC="lab.jpg"  HEIGHT=125 WIDTH=100>
<BR>
<P><b>Explore the software process: </b></P><BR>
<applet code="seColor.class" width=500 height=100>
</applet>
</BODY>
</HTML>
```

Figure 9.28   Sample .html file.

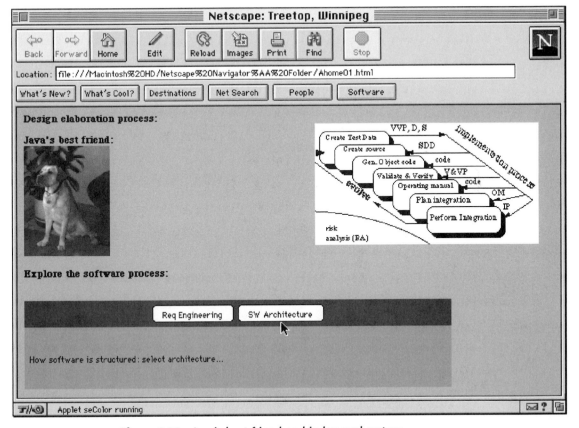

Figure 9.29   Java's best friend and index card system.

9.4 SUMMARY

> **Later on, to wake you up a bit . . . , we'll give**
> **you a nice cup of Java, strong and hot.**
> **—J. MILLAR, 1945**

A number of examples of design elaborations leading to Java programs have been given in this chapter. Design elaboration using box structured views of software increments facilitates correctness checking, and the development of zero-defect code. Box structured views of software in the context of mobile computing works well, and provides a convenient framework for developing large-scale applications. The creation-of-source-code step given in IEEE Std. 1077-1995 requires a choice of a programming style. The object-oriented programming style has been illustrated in this chapter in terms of mobile computing with Java. Mobile computing has the appearance of a paradigm shift in computer programming. The appearance of a paradigm shift in mobile computing stems from the accessible, dynamic environment that it makes possible.

9.5 PROBLEMS

> **Much of a bean's behavior is simplified if you**
> **follow expected design patterns.**
> **—JAMES GOSLING, 1998**

1. The requirements for a mobile robot control system are given in Table 9.5. A statechart representation of the functional requirements of the control system is also given in Figure 9.30. The choice of a layered architecture for the mobile robot control system is shown in Figure 9.31. Do the following:
   (a) Develop a detailed test plan for assessing the design elaboration of the first three layers shown in Figure 9.31.
   (b) Elaborate the design in Figure 9.31 using an object box structured view of the complete architecture in the context of mobile computing in keeping with design component D-1:

   D-1: Competences are organized in a layered architecture.

   Note: The aim of the design elaboration is to produce a *mobile computing* program that can be run by a web browser to simulate the behavior of a "moving" mobile robot.

   (c) Give a black box specification for each of the functions in each of the first three layers in Figure 9.31.
   (d) Verify the correctness of the proposed design.

TABLE 9.5 Requirements and Design for a Mobile Robot Control System

Software Requirements	Software Design
Req-1: Robot controller will consist of a collection of processors that send messages to each other.	D-1: Competences are organized in a layered architecture (see Fig. 9.3).
Req-2: Each processor runs a competence module.	D-2: Avoid layer responds to inputs from sensors and interacts with robot motors to avoid objects.
Req-3: Competences are hierarchical.	D-3: Wander controls the wheel motors to control movements of robot in spaces where no obstacles are detected (robot wanders freely).
Req-4: Each competence receives input from sensors (inputs from environment).	
Req-5: Some competence can subsume (take over) the control functions of competences below it in the hierarchy.	D-4: Explore "looks" for reachable places, and can interrupt wandering.

Req-6: The competences include
    level 0: Avoid
    level 1: Wander
    level 2: Explore
    level 3: Plan
    level 4: Monitor changes
	D-5: Plan devises routes for robot to follow.
	
	D-6: Monitor looks for changes in environment.
	
	D-7: Wander can assume the control functions of the Avoid layer.

Req-7: A competence receives input from the competence above it and below it in the hierarchy.	D-8: Explore can assume the control functions of Wander and Avoid layers. *Test plan*:
Req-8: A competence (either indirectly or directly sends control signals to actuators such as motors to turn wheels).	T-1: Test item is stimulus. T-2: Features to be tested: • Wandering, if no obstacles detected. • Avoidance, if obstacles detected.
Req-9: A robot should continue to function if one or more of its sensors fail.	

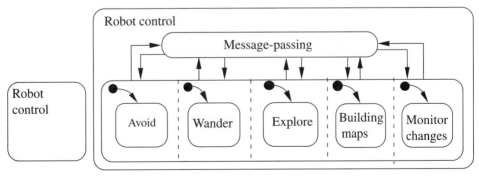

(a) context-level statechart   (b) Decomposition of robot control statechart

Figure 9.30 Requirements for a mobile robot control system.

2. Do the following:
   (a) Give a clear box design for each of the functions specified in problem 1(c) for the avoid layer in Figure 9.31.

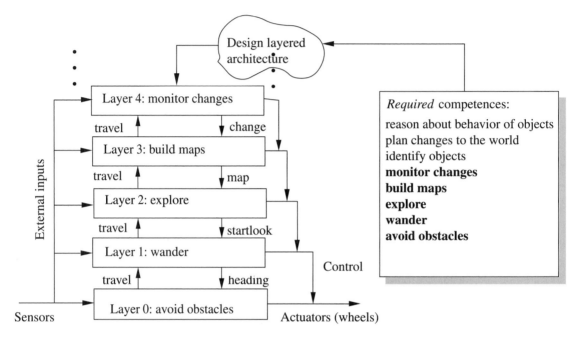

Figure 9.31   Control layers for a mobile robot.

   (b) Elaborate the design of the avoid layer from (a) as a mobile computing program in keeping with design component D-2:

D-2: Avoid layer responds to inputs from sensors and interacts with robot motors to avoid objects.

Note: Include a high-level view of a sensing method in the design of the avoid layer.

   (c) Verify the correctness of the proposed design.

3. Do the following:
   (a) Give a clear box view of the sensing method from the requirements specified in problem 1(c) to develop the Java equivalent of the C++ sensing function given in Figure 9.32.
   (b) Elaborate the design in (a). Verify the correctness of each elaboration of the proposed design.
   (c) Use System.out.println( ) to instrument the sensing method, and display on a standard console the succession of computations it performs.
   (d) Give a sample run of the program with either an applet viewer or web browser.

```
1 /* (a) sensing() computes a pseudo-random number,
 *  (b) computed values are in {0, 1, 2, 3}.
 */

2   // define sensing() function:
3   class Layer {                          // base class
4      private:
5        int trunk;                         // used to truncate away fraction part
6      public:
7        int sensing(float seed); };        // sensing function inherited by all layers

8   int Layer::sensing(float seed) {        // definition of sensing
9     seed = log(seed);                     // compute natural log of number
10    trunk = seed;                         // trick: assign integer part of seed to trunk
11    seed = seed - trunk;                  // subtract away integer part of seed
12    seed = 4 * seed;                      // seed now in 0 to 3.99999 range
13    trunk = seed;                         // trick: assign integer part of seed to trunk
14    return(trunk);                        // return pseudo-random number
15  }
```

Figure 9.32 Sensing function for a robot.

4. Do the following:
   (a) Elaborate the design of the sensing method from problem 3(a) in terms of an exp( ), an exponential function and compare with the log( ) function. *Hint*: the exp( ) function is available in java.lang.Math.
   (b) Elaborate the design of the sensing method from 3(a) in terms of a function of your choice so that the sensed values have a random distribution.
   (c) Plot the values obtained sensing( ) with log( ).
   (d) Plot the values obtained from (a).
   (e) Plot the values obtained from (b).
   (f) Give a combined plot from (c), (d), and (e), and comment on the plots.

5. Elaborate the design of the sensing( ) method in problem 3 based on the following information:

   - Random number representing ambient radiation detected by an IR sensor after a fixed time interval (IR receiver off, then IR receiver on) whenever an object is detected. Detector range: 0 to 880 nanometers (nm) wavelength.
   - Random number represented detected radiation (after a fixed time) after an infrared light has been emitted by one or more IR sensors. Emitter range: 0 to 880 nm wavelength.
   - Get detected value.
   - Change the state of a sensor every 600 ms.

Assume that detector outputs a low value (=0) if it detects nothing and a high value (=1) if an obstacle is detected. The C code for this type of operation is given in Figure 9.33. In other words, change the sensing function so that it is closer to an operational version for a simple emitter, detector system.

```
int ir_status = 0;
void ir_detector() {
   bit_set(portD, 0b00000100);
   sleep(0.000600);
   val_on = peek(portE);
   bit_clear(portD, 0b00000100);
   sleep(0.000600);
   val_off = peek(portE);
   if ((val_off & ~val_on & 0b00000100) == 0b00000100)
      ir_status = 1;
   else
      ir_status = 0;
}
```

Figure 9.33   C code for sensing( ).

6. Elaborate the design of the sensing( ) method in problem 4 so that it determines the distance between a robot and a detected object. Distances are represented by random numbers in the range from 0 to 100 cm.

7. Do the following:
   (a) Based on the requirements specified in problem 1(c), give a clear box design of each of the functions in the wander layer of the robot control system.
   (b) Elaborate the design of each of the functions of the Wander layer of the mobile robot control system that *runs as a simulation in a mobile computing environment.* Do this in keeping with design component D-3:

   D-3: Wander controls the wheel motors to control movements of robot in spaces where no obstacles are detected (robot wanders freely).

   (c) Verify the correctness of the proposed design.

8. Do the following:
   (a) Devise a test plan for the Wander layer to subsume the control function of the avoid layer of the mobile robot control system.
   (b) Elaborate the design of the new version of the Wander layer of the mobile robot control system which *runs in as a simulation in a mobile computing environment.* This new version of Wander should satisfy design component D-7 in Table 5:

   D-7: Wander can assume the control functions of the Avoid layer.

   (c) Verify the correctness of the proposed design.
   (d) Trace design components back to specific requirements.
   (e) Assume that wander subsumes the avoid layer control function whenever it detects least two clear paths (no obstacles in two directions). Give a simulation of the new control program and verify results in terms of the test plan in (a).

9. Do the following:
   (a) Create a test plan for the Explore function of the mobile robot controller.
   (b) Give a black box specification of each of the functions of the Explore layer in Figure 9.31.
   (c) Give a clear box design for each of the functions specified in (b).
   (d) Elaborate the design of an Explore layer of the mobile robot controller in keeping design component D-4 in Table 9.5:

   D-4: Explore "looks" for reachable places, and can interrupt wandering.

   Note: The design elaboration of Explore should be done incrementally (in small steps). In addition, the design elaboration should lead to a new version of the mobile computing program from problem 1, which can be run with a web browser.

   (e) Use the cleanroom method to guarantee the correctness of each stage of the elaboration.
   (f) Give screen prints that display the behavior of the robot during a simulation.

10. Do the following:
    (a) Instrument Explore design from problem 9 to observe its behavior.
    (b) Give a sample run with the operation of the new layer of the control system.

11. Do the following:
    (a) Devise a test plan for the planning layer of the mobile robot control system.
    (b) Give a black box specification of each of the functions of the planning layer in Figure 9.31.
    (c) Incrementally design the planning layer of the mobile robot control system, which runs as a simulation with a web browser. This is D-5 in Table 9.5:

    D-5: The Planning layer devises routes for a robot to follow.

    (d) Verify the correctness of the proposed design.
    (e) Trace design components back to specific requirements.
    (f) Assume that a robot plans a route based on the selection of paths containing objects furthest away (as estimated with sensors). Give a simulation of the new control program and verify results in terms of the test plan in (a).

12. Do the following:
    (a) Devise a test plan for the monitor layer of the mobile robot control system.
    (b) Give a black box specification of each of the functions of the monitor layer in Figure 9.31.
    (c) Incrementally design the Monitor layer of the mobile robot control system, which runs as a simulation with a web browser. This is D-6 in Table 9.5:

    D-6: Monitor looks for changes in environment.

    (d) Verify the correctness of the proposed design.
    (e) Trace design components back to specific requirements.
    (f) Assume that a robot detects changes in positions of detected objects based on

the selection of paths containing objects furthest away (as estimated with sensors). Give a simulation of the new control program and verify results in terms of the test plan in (a).

13. Do the following:
   (a) Devise a test plan for the Wander layer to subsume the control function of the avoid layer of the mobile robot control system.
   (b) Elaborate the design of the Wander layer of the mobile robot control system, which runs as a simulation with a web browser. This is D-7 in Table 9.5:

   D-7: Wander can assume the control functions of the Avoid layer.

   (c) Verify the correctness of the proposed design.
   (d) Trace design components back to specific requirements.
   (e) Assume that Wander subsumes the avoid layer control function whenever it detects least two clear paths (no obstacles in two directions). Give a simulation of the new control program and verify results in terms of the test plan in (a).

14. Do the following:
   (a) Devise a test plan for the Explore layer to subsume the control function of the Avoid and Wander layers of the mobile robot control system.
   (b) Elaborate the design of the Explore layer of the mobile robot control system. This is D-8 in Table 9.5:

   D-8 Explore can assume the control functions of Wander and Avoid layers.

   (c) Verify the correctness of the proposed design.
   (d) Trace design components back to specific requirements.
   (e) Assume that Explore subsumes the control functions of Wander and Avoid layers whenever it detects one clear path (no obstacles in some direction). Also assume that control reverts back to the Wander layer whenever more than one clear path is detected by the Explore layer. Give a simulation of the new control program and verify results in terms of the test plan in (a).

Note: The next several problems reference the requirements for a traffic light controller shown in Figure 9.34. The requirements and design of this controller are also given in Table 9.6.

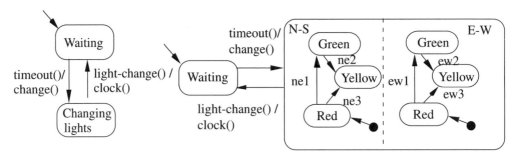

(a) Context-level states   (b) Orthogonal state machines after decomposition

Figure 9.34 Statechart describing a traffic light control system.

TABLE 9.6 Requirements and Design for a Traffic Light Control System

Software Requirements	Software Design
Req-1: A traffic light controller regulates the lights for a traffic intersection. Req-2: Light changes occur at timed intervals. Req-3: The traffic light control system has the following methods: • Clock. • Change. Req-4: The traffic light control system has the following states: • N-S (regulate north-south lights). • E-W (regulate east-west lights). • Waiting. Req-5: All lights are reset to red for a fixed time interval before the lights in a new direction are changed. Req-6: Simulate the traffic light controller in a mobile computing environment.	D-1: Architecture: control structure. D-2: Each set of lights changes every 120 seconds. D-3: Controller performs the following operations: • start clock • reset clock • reset lights • change_lights D-4: Time interval can be changed. *Test plan*: Test items: time interval. Features to be tested: • Changing lights. • Reset clock. • Reset lights.

15. Do the following:
    (a) Use an object box structured approach to elaborate D-1 design element in Table 9.6 using an object-oriented approach with *the aim of developing a mobile computing application program that simulates the operation of the traffic light control system.*
    (b) Prove the correctness of your elaboration.

16. Do the following:
    (a) Use a clear box structured approach to elaborate D-3 design element in Table 9.6 using an object-oriented approach with *the aim of developing a mobile computing application program.*

    D-3: Controller performs the following operations:
    - start clock
    - reset clock
    - reset lights
    - change_lights

    (b) Prove the correctness of your elaboration.

17. Do the following:
    (a) Elaborate the design from problem 16 in terms of D-2:

    D-2: Each set of lights changes every 120 seconds.

    (b) Prove the correctness of your elaboration.

18. Do the following:
(a) Elaborate the design from problem 17 in terms of D-4:

D-4: Time interval can be changed.

(b) Prove the correctness of your elaboration.

19. Do the following:
(a) Complete the implementation of the traffic light controller so that the change method is instrumented,
(b) Obtain a sample of the output when the completed program is run.

20. Instrument the program from problem 19 as follows:
(a) The reset clock method.
(b) The reset lights method.
(c) Obtain a sample of the output when the completed program is run.

10 Verify the program from problem 19 by following the Test Plan in Table 9.6.

Note: The template for an object-oriented requirements specification is given in Figure 9.35.

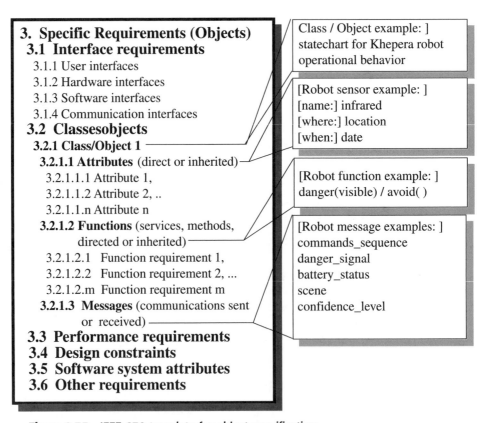

Figure 9.35   IEEE 630 template for object specification.

21. Give the requirements and design for card index system for a rendition of the IEEE 630 template in Figure 9.35 *in a mobile computing environment*. That is:
    (a) Create a table given the specific requirements and design components for the index system.
    (b) Create a test plan (test items and features to be tested) for the card index system.

Note: Req-1 is that there is a separate button for 3.1, 3.2, 3.3, 3.4, 3.5, and 3.6 of Figure 9.35. This requirement is to be included in the requirements given in (a).

22. Incrementally elaborate the design of the index system in problem 21 first with the object box method in creating a Java program.
    (a) Specify all relevant Java packages of classes needed for the Java program.
    (b) Specify all inputs and outputs to the object box for the Java program.
    (c) Verify the correctness of your elaboration.

23. Incrementally elaborate the design from problem 22 using the clear box view of each method, and:
    (a) Elaborate and verify each method separately.
    (b) Indicate which of the design elements are reflected in the elaboration.
    (c) Verify the correctness of each elaboration.
    (d) Each elaboration is to be checked with a web browser or applet viewer.
    (e) Give a screen print showing the result of running your elaboration.

24. Create an .html file that implements the applet class created in problem 23, and:
    (a) Run the new index system.
    (b) Give a screen print for each state displayed by the web browser as a result of each mouse click.

25. Use the program in problem 24 to verify that the completed product satisfies the components of the test plan created in 21(b).

Note: An object diagram for a traffic navigation manager is given in Figure 9.36.

26. The aim of this project is to develop a *mobile computing application program that simulates a traffic navigation manager and is executed by a web browser*. Do the following:
    (a) Give the requirements and design for a traffic navigation manager based on the object diagram in Figure 9.36. That is, create a table given the specific requirements and design components for the navigation system.
    (b) Create a test plan (test items and features to be tested) for the card index system.

Note: Here is a partial list of requirements and design components:
Req-1: There is a method for navigation mgr, command, plan, scan, change, actuate.
Req-2: The navigation system is interactive.
Req-3: The navigation system can be simulated.
Req-4: The entire navigation system is platform independent.

D-1: The traffic navigation system has a front panel displayed by a web browser.
D-2: Each navigation system method is represented by its own pulldown menu.

These requirements and design components are included in the requirements given in (a).

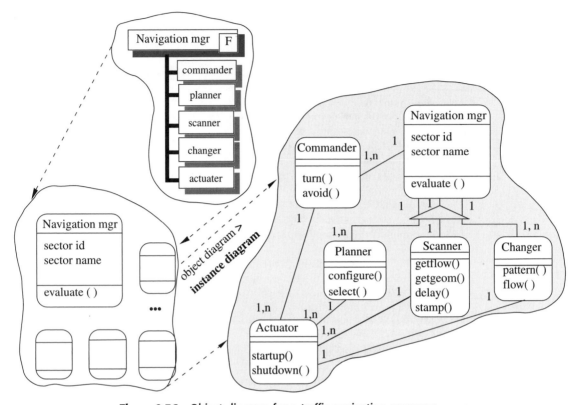

Figure 9.36 Object diagram for a traffic navigation manager.

27. Incrementally elaborate the design of the traffic navigation manager in problem 26 first with the object box method in creating a Java program:
    (a) Specify all relevant Java packages of classes needed for the Java program.
    (b) Specify all inputs and outputs to the object box for the Java program.
    (c) Verify the correctness of your elaboration.

28. Incrementally elaborate the design from problem 27 using the clear box view of each method, and:
    (a) Elaborate and verify each method separately.

Note: include the elaboration of scanner and change operations in the development of the navigation system. The scanner operation should be governed by random numbers representing each of the following: number of vehicles per time interval, average speed, road condition(s), and weather. The change operation initiates changes in traffic patterns based on evaluation of scanner output.

    (b) Indicate which of the design elements are reflected in the elaboration.
    (c) Verify the correctness of each elaboration.

(d) Check each elaboration with a web browser or applet viewer.

(e) Give a screen print showing the result of running your elaboration.

29. Create an .html file that implements the applet class created in problem 28, and:
    (a) Run the new traffic navigation manager system.
    (b) Give a screen print for each state displayed by the web browser as a result of each mouse click.
    (c) Give a listing of the .html file used.

30. Use the program in problems 28 and 29 to verify that the completed product satisfies the components of the test plan created in 26(b).

31. Data flow diagrams for the scanner in a traffic navigation system and the decomposition of the get_geom operation are given in Figure 9.37.

    Do the following:
    (a) Elaborate the scanner method from problem 28 to include a timer operation. That is, a scan should be performed periodically (after each timeout of a timer).
    (b) Verify the correctness of your design.
    (c) Add to the requirements and design components from problem 26 to reflect this change in the design.
    (d) Modify the test plan from problem 26 to take into account this feature of the scanner.

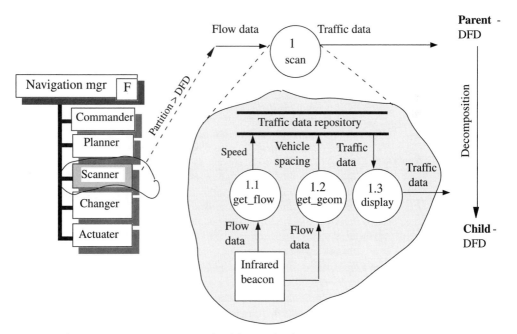

Figure 9.37 A. Scanner method for navigation system.

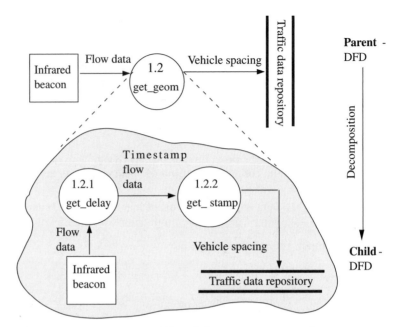

Figure 9.37 B. Decomposition of the get_geom operation.

32. Implement the scan operation from problem 31, and:
   (a) Give a sample run.
   (b) Give screen prints showing different states resulting from the operation of the timed scanner.

Note: An SADT diagram for the change operation in a traffic navigation system is shown in Figure 9.38.

   Do the following:
   (a) Elaborate the change method from problem 28 in terms of the change operation in Figure 9.38. That is, the new version of the change operation should respond to traffic problems (stimulus from environment about a traffic problem reported by scanner( ), which causes the navigation system to respond). The change operation then initiates changes (instructions sent to a problem solver, which determines alternative routes, and status of affected vehicles). The problem solver then transmits the solution(s) to affected vehicles.
   (b) Verify the correctness of your design.
   (c) Add to the requirements and design components from problem 26 to reflect this change in the design.
   (d) Modify the test plan from problem 26 to take into account this feature of the scanner.

33. Implement the change operation from problem 32, and:
   (a) Give a sample run.
   (b) Give screen prints showing different states resulting from the operation of the change method.

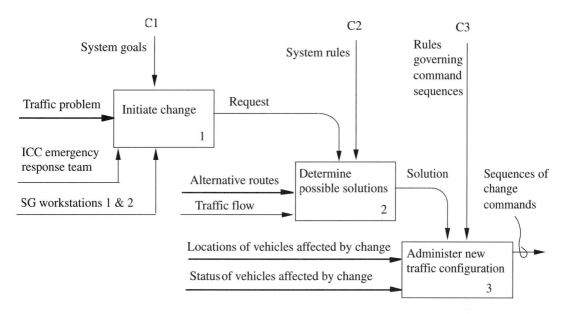

Figure 9.38 SADT diagram for traffic management.

9.6 REFERENCES

Arnold, K., Gosling, J. *The Java Programming Language.* Addison-Wesley, Reading, MA, 1998.

Black, A., Hutchinson, N., Jul, E., Levy, H. Exploiting code mobility in decentralized and flexible network management. *ACM Transactions on Computer Systems,* **6,** (1), 1988.

Carzaniga, A., Picco, G.P., Vigna, G. Designing distributed applications with mobile code paradigms. *Proceedings of the 19th International Conference on Software Engineering,* Boston, May 1997, pp. 22–33.

Cornell, G., Horstmann, C.S. *Core Java.* SunSoft Press, Mountainview, CA, 1997.

Flanagan, D. *Java in a Nutshell: A Desktop Quick Reference,* 2nd ed. O'Reilly & Associates, Sebastopol, CA, 1997.

Gosling, J. The feel of Java. *IEEE Computer* **30,** (6):53–58, 1997.

Lemay, L., Perkins, C.L., Webster, T. *Teach Yourself Java for MacIntosh in 21 Days.* Hayden Books, New York, 1996.

Munson, J.P., Dewan, P. Sync: a Java framework for mobile collaborative applications. *IEEE Computer,* **30** (6):59–66, 1997.

Niemeyer, P., Peck, J. *Exploring Java.* O'Reilly & Associates, Sebastopol, CA, 1996.

Sun Microsystems. *The Java Language Specification,* Palo Alto, CA, October 1995.

Wood, K.R., Richardson, T., Bennett, F., et al. Global teleporting with Java: Toward ubiquitous personalized computing. *IEEE Computer* **30** (2):53–60, 1997.

CHAPTER 10
Software Project: Design

Take care of your sense, and the sounds will take care of themselves.
—LEWIS CARROLL, 1865

Aims

- Consider details of air traffic control displays and tracking
- Consider how to choose a software architecture
- Incrementally develop tATC design
- Correlate design with requirements
- Validate each software design
- Verify functional correctness of each software design
- Instrument a design

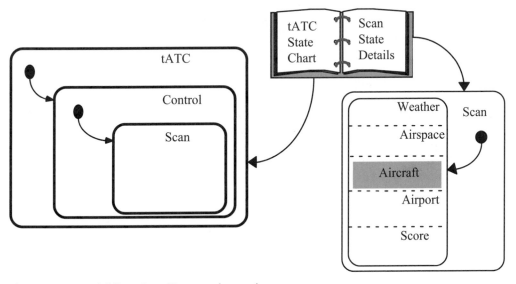

Figure 10.1 Unfolding air traffic control statechart.

10.1 INTRODUCTION

The design of a training program for air traffic controllers (tATC) grows out of a number of documents derived from the software process. The aim of this chapter is to suggest how one might elaborate the design of the components of the scan state of the tATC shown in Figure 10.1. The focus of this chapter is on the incremental development of the aircraft component of the air traffic control scanner. The display and tracking of aircraft is central to the operation of an tATC system. Java has been selected in the design of the scanner because it lends itself to the display of the dynamics of aircraft moving through an airspace. The choice of Java also makes it possible to produce one of the required products mentioned in the mission statement for this project. A required product for this project is a user-interface for the tATC that runs on the web.

10.2 GETTING STARTED

Starting a software design process is analogous to selecting a path in hiking downward to the banks of a river flowing through a canyon surrounded with steep walls. From the rim of a deep canyon, a river flowing through the canyon has the appearance of a ribbon of blue silk. The details of the canyon floor and the white water of its flowing river are hidden. The shape but not the details of things can be seen from the top of a deep canyon. Following a trail guide, a walk far enough down into a canyon like the Grand Canyon makes it possible to see the details of the canyon. The use of a trail guide is analogous to following requirements and architecture descriptions to get closer to the code for a software system.

The knowledge gained by traversing the upper trails of a canyon tends to make it easier to choose a good route to reach the next place along the trail. In the case of software design, the documents, knowledge, and experience gained from earlier phases of a software process make the steps in the design process easier to identify. This means taking a look at the details in the description of the atomic process for a software project. The entry, verification, and exit conditions detailed in an atomic-level design process model provide a guide to starting, producing, and completing required products. Beginning the design of a particular software product starts after the entry conditions have been satisfied. In the case of starting the design of the components for the tATC scanner, the details concerning the application, steps in an atomic-level design process, and requirements as well as architectural-description of an aircraft scanner must be available.

10.2.1 Application: Air Traffic Display

> **A program can be viewed as executable knowledge.**
> —WATTS HUMPHREY, 1989

A key entry condition in beginning a design process is an acquisition of the details of an application. Knowledge of these details is needed so that designers do not work in a vacuum. Design choices are tied to application restrictions and needs. A typical air traffic control system is organized around three facilities:

- Airport tower, which monitors aircraft on the ground, issuing landing and take-off clearances.
- Terminal radar approach control (Tracon), which manages aircraft ascending from and descending to an airport.
- Enroute center, which handles aircraft flying between airports.

In this chapter, the focus will be on simulating a partial Tracon display based on information available from the U.S. Federal Aviation Administration (FAA) and NASA Ames Research Center web sites (NASA, 1999). A sample air traffic display is shown in Figure 10.2. Details about the Center Tracon Automation

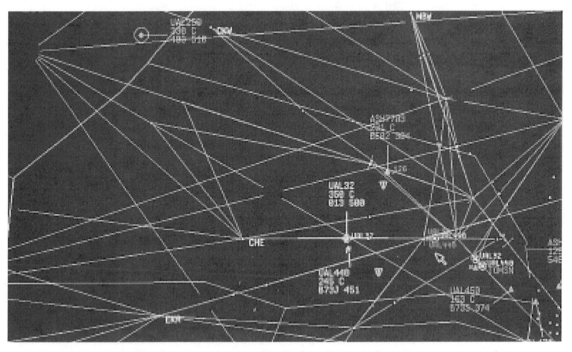

Figure 10.2 Sample air traffic display. Photo credit: NASA Ames Research Center.

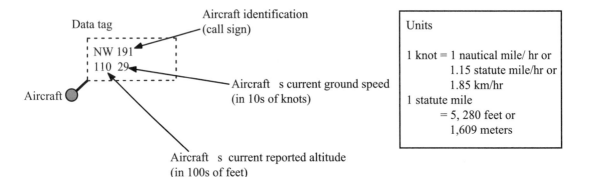

Figure 10.3   Display of aircraft with its data tag.

System can found at *http://www.arc.nasa.gov*. A description of the jobs of controllers working in airport towers, Tracons, and enroute centers as prepared by the U.S. National Air Traffic Controllers Association. This information can be found at *http://www.newc.com/natca/*. A report concerning the human factors in air traffic control can be purchased through the National Academy Press web site *http://www.nap.edu/*.

Each aircraft being tracked is represented with an icon (e.g., a small disk). Each aircraft also has a flight data tag associated with it. A sample data tag for flight NW 191 is given in Figure 10.3. The data tag for flight NW 191 follows the moving aircraft icon. A minimal data tag for flight NW 191 is shown in Figure 10.3. The first line of the data tag gives the aircraft call sign (its identification used by a controller). The second line of the tag has two fields. The first field (numeral 110 in line 2 of the tag in Figure 10.3) gives the current reported altitude in hundreds of feet. The second data field in line two of the tag gives an aircraft's current ground speed of 29 in tens of knots. A knot equals one nautical mile per hour, which is approximately 1.85 kilometers (1.15 statute miles) per hour. A statute mile (also called a land mile) equals 5,280 feet or 1,609 meters. In the sample display in Figure 10.3, NW flight 191 has an altitude of 11,000 feet and a ground speed of 290 knots or 333.5 statute miles per hour.

In the periodic scan of air traffic, conflict alerts will be displayed in cases where there is a separation violation. Such a violation occurs whenever the distance of one aircraft ahead or behind another aircraft violates the required separation distance between aircraft. A conflict alert occurs in the case where a conflict between aircraft trajectories is predicted by a tracking system such as the Final Approach Spacing Tool (Davis et al., 1991, 1994). A simplified version of the separation problem will be considered in the design of an aircraft scanner (Figure 10.4). In the figure, aircraft NW 191 and JAL 207 are at points A and B. NW 191 has coordinates (x1, y1) while JAL 207 has (x2, y2). The separation distance between these aircraft is computed using the following formula:

$$\text{aircraft\_separation} = \sqrt{(x_2 - x_1)^2 - (y_2 - y_1)^2}$$

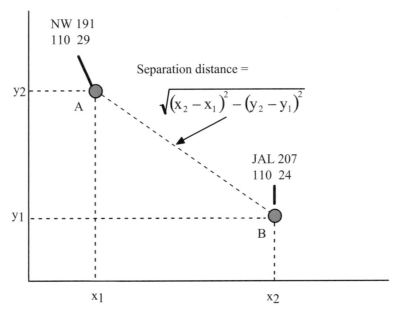

Figure 10.4 Separation distance between two aircraft.

Measuring separation distance between aircraft makes it possible to determine when potential conflicts and possible dangerous situations exist. In such cases, some form of warning should be displayed by the tATC system to warn controllers. Two problems will be considered in this chapter: (1) simulation of air traffic displays (aircraft icon plus data tags), and (2) tracking of separation distance between aircraft (warnings accompany violations).

10.2.2 Atomic-Level Design Process

A key entry condition in beginning a design process is the availability of atomic-level task sequences in designing a software product. The atomic-level design process model provides a framework for getting started. The steps in an atomic design process model are tied to project planning decisions, and a knowledge of the needs of an application. Indications of intended design increments will be included in the steps. The sequencing of the steps at the atomic level defines a design methodology.

An overview of the atomic-level design process for the tATC scanner is shown in Figure 10.5. The notation (A) in Figure 10.5 identifies an atomic-level design process. The atomic-level processes identified correspond to the weather, airspace, aircraft, airport, and score scanners of the air traffic control program. Each of these atomic-level processes provides a roadmap in starting the design of a tATC module. In each case, the entry condition in starting a design process

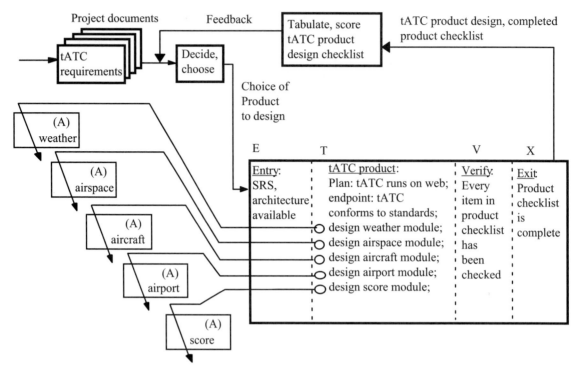

Figure 10.5 Atomic-level design process.

is the availability of a number of documents. Chief among these documents are the Software Requirements Specification (SRS) and Software Architecture (SA). The SA is derived from the SRS during the design process. The SRS and SA provide a detailed description of the requirements and architectural description of the software to be developed. The SRS will provide a detailed description of the principal features of the software, its information flow, its behavior, and its attributes. The availability of an architectural description of the software is another key entry condition for a design process. The SA describes the structure of the software. The major processing elements, data, and connecting elements are described in the SA. The project plan, software engineering guide, standards collection, resource libraries, and tools as well as the SRS and SA for the current and previous projects will guide the decision-making of a design team.

We will look more closely at the details provided by the (A) aircraft in Figure 10.5 before we consider the requirements and architecture for the aircraft component of the tATC scanner. An overview of the sequence of states in a feedback model of an atomic-level design process in designing an aircraft display is given in Figure 10.6. The atomic process begins in the choice (C) state, where a project team decides on the next unit of work for a design team. The atomic design process in Figure 10.6 has four principal states: entry (E), task (T), verify (V), and exit (X). The entry state (E) marks the beginning of the design process.

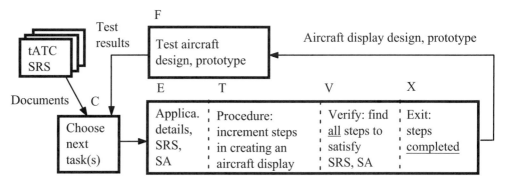

Figure 10.6 Atomic-level process to design aircraft scanner.

Details concerning the restrictions and needs for an aircraft display, a requirements description and architectural structure of an aircraft display system must be available to start the design process. The task state (T) of the design process is identified with the details steps of a procedure for designing an aircraft display. At the completion of a design increment, a design team enters the verify (V) state. In this state, a design team ensures that a software increment satisfies the SRS and SA. Next, the design team enters an exit state (X). To exit the design process, the design team makes sure that all of the required steps for the current increment have been completed. Based on the results produced by the design team, the project team enters the feedback (F) state. Feedback for a design project is derived from testing a software increment.

The atomic-level model in Figure 10.6 gives the steps in a procedure to use in designing an aircraft display.

Steps in Designing Aircraft Display

Step 1. (E) Check details of the application (e.g., FAA, NASA web sites, local airport).

Step 2. (E) Check description of requirements for an aircraft display.

Step 3. (E) Check architectural description of aircraft display software.

Step 4. (T) Choose color and icon for aircraft display. Next do12.

Step 5. (T) Increment 1: Prototype successive views of moving aircraft. Next do12.

Step 6. (T) Increment 2: Prototype display with aircraft coordinates (no data tag). Next do12.

Step 7. (T) Increment 3: Prototype moving aircraft with data tag. Next do12.

Step 8. (T) Increment 4: Prototype delay between radar scans. Next do12.

Step 9. (T) Increment 5: Architectural design to handle coordinates and periodic redisplay. Next do12.

Step 10. (T) Increment 6: Elaborate architectural design with measure and evaluate methods. Track single aircraft relative to a fixed position. Display warning if aircraft is too close to the fixed position. Next do12.

Step 11. (T) Increment 7: Elaborate measure and evaluate design relative to two moving aircraft. Next do12.

Step 12. (V) Validation: Validate design relative to SRS and SA.

Step 13. (X) Check that all steps have been completed. Document design.

Step 14. (F) Functional correctness: Verify code carries out specified function.

Steps 5 through 11 in the atomic process in Figure 10.6 specify software increments to be designed. For example, the first software increment tracks a moving aircraft icon. Once this increment is completed, then the increment is validated. The design is "synchronized" with the requirements. Next in step 13 the exit conditions are checked (required steps must be completed). After that, functional correctness verification is carried out in step 14. A check on functional correctness of code can be carried out using the Harlan Mills schema (Mills, 1975).

- *Function.* Assertion(s) about the functional behavior of the code.
- *Design.* Code to implement specified function.
- *Proof.* Demonstrate that code satisfies the assertions about required behavior.

The functional correctness step provides needed feedback in making decisions about the next steps in the design process. Notice that the focus of the increments in steps 5 through 7 is on coding that satisfies the requirements. Focus on the structure of the software (its architecture) becomes the focus in the design increments in steps 9 through 11. The movement in steps 9 through 11 is toward greater modularization of the code in an effort to make the code easier to maintain. This effort is in keeping with the classical idea of information hiding (Parnas, 1972, 1986).

10.2.3   Requirements for Aircraft Scanner

To carry the design process further, the requirements for an aircraft must be considered. The availability of a requirements description is an entry condition for every atomic-level design process model. For simplicity, only the requirements for a module to simulate an air traffic control display of the location, data tag, and status of each displayed aircraft will be considered. A partial summary of the requirements for such a module is given in Table 10.1. A description of the functional requirements for an aircraft display is given in terms of statecharts in this section. Statecharts provide a rich and expressive notation for describing

TABLE 10.1 Requirements for Locate Module

Software Requirements	Comments
Req-1: A colored icon represents an aircraft.	Small disk for aircraft icon. Green color.
Req-2: Display data tag for each aircraft.	Minimum data tag gives flight call sign, altitude, and ground speed in FAA format.
Req-3: Color-coded data tag for each aircraft.	Cyan (greenish blue) for planes being handled controller. Green for planes handled by other controllers. White for transfers of responsibility. Red for emergency.
Req-4: Data tag shadows aircraft icon.	Coordinates of tag close to icon coordinates.
Req-5: Determine coordinates of each aircraft.	Vary the position of aircraft randomly.
Req-6: Measure separation distance.	6.1: Measure relative to a fixed position. 6.2: Measure distance between aircraft.
Req-7: Evaluate separation distance.	Distinguish long, short, too short distances.
Req-8: Display distance status.	"Far"(long), "close"(short), "too close".
Req-9: Periodically update display.	Insert delay between scans.

the behavior of complex systems at different levels of abstraction. In the design of user interfaces, statecharts are also appealing for a number of reasons pointed out by Horrocks (1999):

- Minor details of a user interface can be hidden.
- Object-oriented approach in describing system behavior.
- The objects in a user interface have default behavior defined by classes of objects.

A high-level statechart for an aircraft portion of the user interface for an air traffic control system is given in Figure 10.7. Each time an aircraft has been identified for monitoring and control, the user interface for a tATC moves from its scan to a flight observation state. The basic behavior associated with each flight observation state is locating and guiding aircraft in an airspace sector. The details of the behavior associated with locating and guiding aircraft are hidden in the locate and guide states of Figure 10.7. The concurrency expressed by the orthogonal states provides a means of separating the details of different flights. In this section, the focus is on learning more about the behavior (detailed conditions and actions) associated with the locate state.

The locate state decomposes into the statechart in Figure 10.8. A controller is first alerted about the need to track a particular aircraft. This is state 1 in Figure 10.8. The action of determining the coordinates of an identified aircraft causes a controller to enter state 2 (tracking). The tracking system will measure separation distances between aircraft (enter state 3). The evaluation of separation

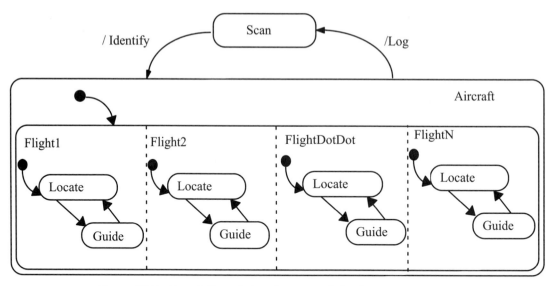

Figure 10.7 Description of aircraft scanner behavior.

distances between aircraft leads to state 4. The results of the previous actions are displayed (state 5). Next there is a transition to what is known as a history state (H). The history mechanism provides a basis for remembering the last state the statechart was in. In the case of the statechart in Figure 10.8, arrows marking the transition to the guide state as well as out of the aircraft state to scan state are hidden by (H). The history mechanism was proposed by Harel (1987) to reduce clutter in a description. In the case of the statechart in Figure 10.8, a delay is also associated with the history state (remembering to guide an identified aircraft and scan the airspace relative to other aircraft, weather, airport, and possible emergencies). This delay arises naturally in the periodic inspection of a radar display and other elements of the environment by an air traffic controller.

It has been observed that user interface software is event-driven (Horrocks, 1999). For each observable occurrence that satisfies a condition for a transition from the current state to the next state, a sequence of actions is executed in

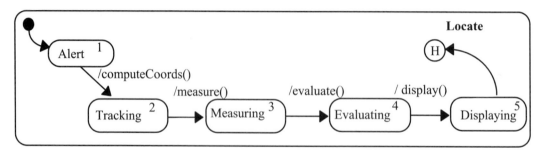

Figure 10.8 Locating an aircraft.

TABLE 10.2   Event–Action Sequence for Aircraft Statechart

Current State	Event	Action	Next State
1 (alert)	Call from pilot	Compute coordinates	2
2	Pause	Measure separation distance	3
3	Click evaluate button	Evaluate measurements	4
4	Pause	Set color of display; Draw oval to pinpoint aircraft	(H)

response to the event. An observable occurrence can be some event like a mouse click or result of a computation such as the measurement of separation distance between aircraft. The software then waits for the next condition for a new sequence of actions to be satisfied. This event-action paradigm can be applied to the study of statecharts. An event-action view of the statechart in Figure 10.8 is given in Table 10.2. An event-action table is useful because it provides details about every state transition in a statechart. Hence, event-action details aid in the understanding of a description. The details of each of the states in Table 10.2 still need to be considered. This is done in connection with each of the increments in the atomic-level design process. This will make it easier to check each increment against the requirements. At this point, it also helps to hide some of the details of the description in considering the architecture of the software.

10.2.4   Selection of Architecture of Aircraft Scanner

The architecture of software can be gleaned from its requirements description. In choosing the architecture of the software for the scanner, we can look at the configuration of states in the statechart for the locate module. The configuration of the locate states suggest dependencies and ways of structuring the code. The details about the processing elements, data, data flow, and connections between processing elements can be found in an event-action table for a statechart. Architecture selection can be made with the help of checklists which serve as aids in matching descriptions with candidate architectures. The statechart in Figure 10.9 describes a sequence of states without some of the details given earlier. The selection of an architecture for the locate module can be done in two steps. First, candidate architectures are identified. This is done in Table

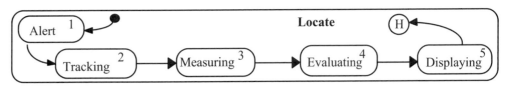

Figure 10.9   Simplified statechart for locate module.

TABLE 10.3   Search for Candidate Architectures

Candidate Architecture	Consider/Reject	Reason
Virtual machine	Reject	Locate software does not create the appearance that something exists which, in fact, does not exist (e.g., intelligence).
Independent process	Reject	Locate not an orthogonal state.
Call-and-return	Consider	Locate statechart describes interaction between processes.
Repository	Reject	Locate does not archive data.
Data flow	Consider	Sequence of processes in locate statechart.
Domain specific	Reject	Reusability of locate module in applications such as traffic navigation. No attempt to tailor locate to a specific domain.

10.3. Two possible architectures fall out of Table 10.3: call-and-return and data flow. Specifically, layered and pipeline architectures have features matching the description in the locate statechart in Figure 10.9. To narrow the design down to a single architecture, a detailed checklist is completed based on the features of the candidate architectures compared with the statechart description. Each feature is scored. The total scores for each architecture are then compared. This is done in Table 10.4.

The scoring in Table 10.4 points to pipelining as an appropriate architecture for the locate module. Notice, also, that the transition between states in the locate statechart is one way, from "left to right." This suggests the need for one-

TABLE 10.4   Scoring Candidate Architectures for Locate Module

Architecture	Comparison Between Architectural Feature and Statechart			
	Sequence of States	Transform Input into Output	Client/Server Hierarchy	Score
Pipeline:	1	1	0	2
Layered: Server / Client	1	0	0	1

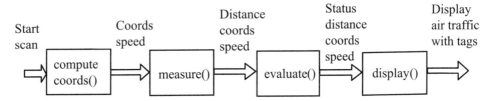

Figure 10.10 Pipeline architecture of locate module.

way communication in software used to implement the locate statechart. For example, a computeCoords() method determines the coordinates of an aircraft, and passes the coordinates to a measure() method. The computeCoords() method should be designed to begin computing new coordinates after it communicates with measure(). It "ignores" what measure() does. In other words, computeCoords() does not play the role of a client in relation to measure(). This rules out a layered architecture, which has a client–server structure. In a layered architecture, adjacent layers have a client–server relationship requiring two-way communication. In Table 10.4, a score equal to 1 indicates that the candidate architecture possesses a particular feature. A zero score indicates that the candidate architecture lacks a particular feature.

To complete the architectural description of the locate module, each action associated with a state transition in the statechart in Figure 10.9 is matched with a filter in a pipeline. Recall that a pipeline filter transforms its input, and communicates the result to the next filter in the pipeline. There are four principal actions in the locate statechart: computeCoords(), measure(), evaluate(), and display(). A pipeline is designed with four filters as shown in Figure 10.10.

10.3 INCREMENTAL DESIGN OF AIRCRAFT SCANNER

There is a danger in creating cluttered displays.
—BEN SHNEIDERMAN, 1998

At this point, the entry conditions for the atomic-level design process model for the aircraft scanner have been satisfied.

Step 1. (E) Check details of the application (e.g., FAA, NASA web sites, local airport).

Step 2. (E) Check description of requirements for an aircraft display.

Step 3. (E) Check architectural description of aircraft display software.

These three entry conditions for the design process have been satisfied relative to the locate module for the aircraft scanner. First, two principal features (aircraft data tags and separation distance) of scanning aircraft in an air traffic control display have been checked. This is step 1 in the atomic model. Second, a statechart description of the scanner module has been given. This is step 2 in the design process. Third, the availability of an architectural description (pipelining) of the locate module satisfies the third entry condition of the design process.

10.4 PROTOTYPING AIRCRAFT DISPLAYS

In designing a display of aircraft that are part of the airspace being scanned by an air traffic controller, the human factors in getting and holding attention should be taken into account (Harwood, 1993). Basically, this means that the aircraft scanner should provide a simple, easy-to-view, well-organized, and carefully labeled display to guide controller actions. It has been pointed out that a principal danger in designing a display is clutter (Shneiderman, 1998). Attention-getting techniques such as overuse of color, different size and types of fonts, and blinking should be used conservatively in the design of the display. Design of different forms of air traffic displays are considered in this section. This will take care of steps 4 and 5 in the atomic-level design process.

Step 4. (T) Choose color and icon for aircraft display.

Step 5. (T) Increment 1: Prototype successive views of moving aircraft.

As a first increment in developing an tATC display, just the display of a single moving aircraft is considered. The aircraft will be represented by a disk having a green color. These design choices are in agreement with Req-1 of the locate module requirements. A statechart giving a more detailed description of the tATC display state is given in Figure 10.11 inside Table 10.5. The x, y coordinates provide input to the statechart in the figure. This input comes from another part of the system that determines the coordinates of an aircraft. The x, y coordinates make it possible to position an aircraft icon. The details of the statechart in Figure 10.11 are given in the event-action table (Table 10.5). The selection of an icon color (state 5.1) results in a transition to a color state (5.2). Next, the dimensions and location of an icon are established. The icon is drawn in color (5.3), which completes the display. The statechart is a partial description of the display function of the program. The events and actions are expressed in a form of pseudocode (a bit of plain language with some programming notation). The ':=' represents an assignment and a ';' (semicolon) identifies the end of an element in a sequence. The numerical values in the assignments in Table

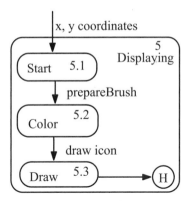

Figure 10.11   Statechart.

10.5 are intended to be suggestive (they can be changed, especially after you have a chance to experiment with executable code). Notice also that the separate actions in an event-action table serve as a behavioral description, not code. For example, the four actions in the transition from state 5.2 to 5.3 can be coded in one Java statement.

```
g.fillOval(x,y,9,9); //assign x, y coords, length,
                     //width, and draw disk
                     //centered at x, y
```

TABLE 10.5   Statechart/Event–action Table for Aircraft Display

Display Statechart	Current State	Event	Action	Next State
	5	Start	x := prev_x − (r mod 36); y := prev_y − (r mod 36);	5.1
	5.1	Color_selected	color := green; preparePaintBrush;	5.2

	5.2	Pause	assignCoords(x, y);
			width := 9;
			length := 9;
			drawIcon;
				5.3

	5.3	Icon_drawn	remember	(H)

Figure 10.11   Statechart.

To carry out the design of the first increment in the design process, a Java program is written to simulate snapshots of moving aircraft displayed on an tATC screen (Figure 10.12). A sample display taken from an applet viewer resulting from the execution of the program in Figure 10.12 is shown in Figure 10.13. A single aircraft is tracked moving erratically across the screen. The next task is to check the functional behavior of the program against its requirements. Notice that this first increment in the design process satisfies Req-1 (disk icon in color), Req-3 (color coding), and Req-5 (vary the position of the displayed aircraft randomly). This means the code is validated with respect to these requirements. However, the code in Figure 10.12 does not satisfy the remaining requirements for the locate module. The functional correctness of the design in Figure 10.12 is judged relative to the assertion in line 1. This assertion is satisfied by lines 17 to 25 of the code.

10.4.1   Displaying Aircraft Data Tag

The next increment of the locate module design displays an aircraft data tag. The goal in designing this increment is to satisfy several more of the requirements given in Table 10.6. To support the design process, the display statechart in Figure 10.11 needs to be elaborated. This is done in the statechart in Figure 10.14. The event-action sequence corresponding to the statechart is given in Table 10.7. This elaboration is needed to give a more detailed view of the functional behavior of the display function.

The coordinates of the aircraft icon can be used to position the data tag so that it follows the aircraft icon as it moves across the screen (Figure 10.15). For example, flight JAL 207 is shown slowing its ground speed. In the actions in the transition from state 5.3 to 5.4, notice that the x-coordinate is adjusted to move the first line of text of the data to right of the aircraft icon. For the second line of the data tag, the y-coordinate is adjusted so that the lines move down in the display. Again it should be observed that the numerical values in an event-action table are advisory. These values will need to be changed later to make room for a line pointing from the data tag to an aircraft icon. The line connecting the icon to its data tag is helpful whenever a display becomes cluttered with many aircraft icons. To demonstrate how the tag follows the movement of an aircraft icon, the screen is not refreshed (screen cleared) after each display of the icon. The principal code segment of the locate module is given in Figure 10.16. Not shown in the code is a declaration of a spd variable. This variable is used to keep track of the varying ground speed of an aircraft.

A sample applet viewer screen produced by the elaborated display module is given in Figure 10.15. A comparison between the software design in Figure 10.16 and its requirements needs to be considered next. The software design in Figure 10.16 satisfies Req-1 (disk icon in color), Req-2 (display data tag), Req-4 (tag shadows aircraft icon), and Req-5 (vary the position of the displayed aircraft

```
1    //  Assert: aircraft icon (green in color) randomly moves across display
2    import java.awt.*;       //abstract window toolkit
3    import java.applet.Applet;
4    import java.util.*;
5    import java.lang.Math;

6    public class aircraft000 extends Applet {
6    Graphics        g;
7    int             x = 100;              // starting x coord.
8    int             y = 100;              // starting y coord.
9    int             view = 0;             // zero views
10   Random          r = new Random();     // randomly vary coords.

11   public void init() {
12     g=getGraphics();                    // start graphics
13   } //init

14   public void update (Graphics g){      // control view
15     int prev_x, prev_y;                 // store old coords.

16     while (view <12) {                  // up to 12 views
17     view++;                             // increment counter
18     prev_x=x;                           // store old x coord.
19     prev_y=y;                           // store old y coord.
20     x=prev_x - (r.nextInt()%36);        // vary x randomly
21     y=prev_y - (r.nextInt()%36);        // vary y randomly
22     g.setColor(Color.green);            // color of aircraft icon
23     g.fillOval(x,y,9,9);                // view aircraft position
24     } // while
25   } //update

26   public void paint(Graphics g){
27     g.setPaintMode();                   // prepare for display
28     update(g);                          //  attempt new scan
29     } // paint
30     } //aircraft000
```

Figure 10.12 Program to display randomly moving aircraft.

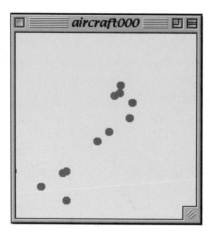

Figure 10.13 Successive views of aircraft.

TABLE 10.6 Requirements for the New Software Increment

Software Requirements	Comment
Req-2: Display data tag for each aircraft.	Minimum data tag gives flight call sign, altitude, and ground speed in FAA format.
Req-3: Color-coded data tag for each aircraft.	Cyan (greenish blue) for planes being handled by a controller. Green for planes handled by other controllers. White for transfers of responsibility. Red for emergency.
Req-4: Data tag shadows aircraft icon.	Coordinates of tag close to icon coordinates.

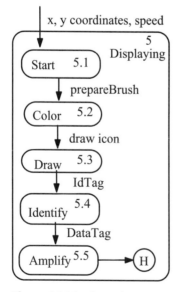

Figure 10.14 Statechart.

TABLE 10.7   Statechart/Event–Action Table for Aircraft Display Increment

Display Statechart	Current State	Event	Action	Next State
	5	Start	x := prev_x − (r mod 36); y := prev_y − (r mod 36);	5.1
	5.1	Color_selected	color := green; preparePaintBrush;	5.2

	5.2	Pause	assignCoords(x, y);
			width := 9;
			length := 9;
			drawIcon;
				5.3

	5.3	Icon drawn and pause	color := cyan;
			x := x + 14;
			drawLineOne(id, x, y);
				5.4

	5.4	Line 1 of tag drawn	y := y + 14; drawLineOne(alt, speed, x, y);	5.5
	5.5	Line 2 of tag drawn	remember	(H)

Within the Display Statechart column:

x, y coordinates, speed

5 displaying

- start 5.1
- prepareBrush
- color 5.2
- draw icon
- draw 5.3
- IdTag
- Identify 5.4
- DataTag
- Amplify 5.5 → (H)

Figure 10.14   Statechart.

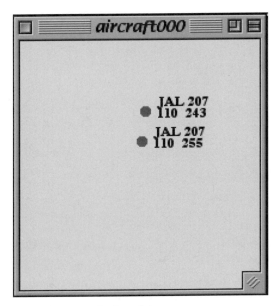

Figure 10.15   Display of data tag.

```
1.  //  Assert: Color-coded data tag is displayed
2.  public void update (Graphics g){          // control view
3.  int prev_x, prev_y;                        // store old coords.
4.  int prev_spd;                              // store old speed

5.  while (view < 2) {                         // up to 2 views
6.      view++;                                // increment counter
7.      prev_x=x+2;                            // store old x coord.
8.      prev_y=y+2;                            // store old y coord.
9.      prev_spd = spd;                        // store old speed
10.     x=prev_x - (r.nextInt()%36);          // vary x randomly
11.     y=prev_y - (r.nextInt()%36);          // vary y randomly
12.     spd = prev_spd - (r.nextInt()%20);    // vary speed randomly
13.     g.setColor(Color.green);              // color of aircraft icon
14.     g.fillOval(x,y,9,9);                  // view aircraft position
15.     g.setColor(Color.cyan);              // color of data tag
16.     g.drawString("JAL 207",x+14,y);      // line 1 of sample data tag
17.     g.drawString("110 "+ spd,x+14,y+10); // line 2 of sample data tag
18. } // while
19. } //update
```

Figure 10.16 Code to display data tag.

randomly). The code is validated with respect to these requirements. The line of code

```
g.setColor(Color.cyan);     //color of data tag
```

paints the data tag greenish blue. This satisfies the color coding scheme for Req-3. This requirements is made clear in the assignment in the event-action Table 10.7:

```
color:=cyan;
```

Verification of the functional correctness of the code in Figure 10.16 is straightforward.

- *Function.* Assert: Color-coded data tag is displayed.
- *Design.* Code to implement specified function is given in Figure 10.16.
- *Proof.* Line 15 satisfies the color-coding requirement for the data tag; *and* Line 16 displays the aircraft call sign, *and* Line 17 displays the altitude and ground speed of aircraft (this satisfies line 1 assert).

```
1   // Assert:  An aircraft icon is displayed periodically
2   public class aircraft003 extends Applet implements Runnable {
3   Graphics        g;                          // introduce graphics
4   Thread          my_thread = null;           // introduce thread
5   Int             x = 100;                     // starting x coord.
6   Int             y = 100;                     // starting y coord.
7   Random          r = new Random();            // randomly vary coords.

8   public void init() {                         // same as in Fig. 16 // }

9   public void start() {
10  if (my_thread==null) {
11  my_thread = new Thread(this);                // creates thread
12  my_thread.start();                           // starts thread of control
12.1   } //if
13  } //start

14  public void stop() {
15  my_thread = null;                            // to nullify thread
16  } //stop

17  public void run() {
18    while (my_thread != null) {
19      repaint();                               // applet to be redrawn
20      try {                                    // exception thrown
21        Thread.sleep(1500);                    // sleep thread 1500 milliseconds
22      } // try
23      catch (InterruptedException e) {}        // catch exception
24    } // while
25    my_thread = null;                          // initialize thread
26  } //run

27  public void update (Graphics g){             // this method changes // }

36. public void paint(){                        // same as in Fig. 16 // }

37  } //aircraft003
```

Figure 10.17 Periodic display of airspace.

10.4.2   Periodic Displays with a Thread

Until now, a while loop has been used to display different views of a moving aircraft icon. There is still the requirement that the tATC display simulate periodic rather than a continuous scan of an airspace. This is requirement Req-9. To simulate periodic update of tATC displays in a dynamically changing environment, a thread is introduced into the software design. A thread is a sequence of steps executed one at a time (Oaks and Wong, 1997). A thread object named ping, for example, can be created in a Java program by declaring

```
Thread ping = new Thread();
```

This declaration creates an object of type Thread called ping. Threads have their own life-cycle defined by three methods named start, run, and stop. A start method is introduced to spawn a new thread of control based on the data in a thread object. A thread becomes active or inactive by invoking it or putting it to sleep with a run method. A thread can be forcibly stopped by invoking a stop method.

In the case of the air traffic control display, a single thread can be used to control the execution sequence in creating an aircraft display. Simulation of periodic behavior is achieved by repeated activation of a thread of control of an execution sequence to update an airspace display. After the execution of the last step in a sequence controlled by a thread, the run() method puts the thread to sleep. Sleep intervals are measured in milliseconds. A new increment of the locate module with a thread is given in Figure 10.17. The declaration ''implement Runnable'' in Figure 10.17 specifies that the class contains a run() method. For simplicity, only a moving tagless aircraft icon is displayed.

The thread in Figure 10.17 is put to sleep every 1500 milliseconds, which puts a delay between outputs in the display. The update method has been simplified (Figure 10.18). A while loop is no longer needed to create a display

```
public void update (Graphics g){
  int prev_x, prev_y;                    // use to store old x-,y- values

  prev_x=x;                              // store old x-value
  prev_y=y;                              // store old y-value
  x=prev_x - (r.nextInt()%36);           // new x-value
  y=prev_y - (r.nextInt()%36);           // new y-value
  g.setColor(Color.green);               // color of aircraft icon
  g.fillOval(x,y,9,9);                   // display aircraft icon
} // update
```

Figure 10.18   Revised code update method.

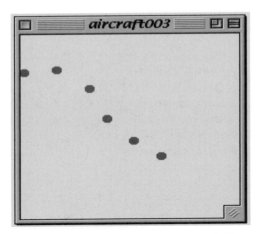

Figure 10.19   Perodic display of aircraft icon.

that follows the changing positions of an aircraft icon. Now, each time a thread reawakens, the sequence of steps governed by the thread updates the display with the new position of a moving aircraft.

A sample applet viewer display produced by the program in Figure 10.17 is given in Figure 10.19. The software design in Figure 10.17 satisfies Req-1 (disk icon in color), Req-5 (vary the position of the displayed aircraft randomly), and Req-9 (periodically update display). Hence, the code is validated with respect to these requirements. The functional correctness of the code is verified as follows.

- *Function.* Assert: An aircraft icon is displayed periodically.
- *Design.* Code to implement specified function is given in Figure 10.17.
- *Proof.* Line 21 causes delay in between displays (this satisfies the assertion).

10.5 IMPLEMENTING ARCHITECTURAL DESIGNS

The next task in the design process is to implement the architecture of the locate module for an aircraft traffic display. This is done in three steps.

Step 9.   (T) Increment 5: Architectural design to handle coordinates and display. Next validate and verify the design.

Step 10.   (T) Increment 6: Elaborate architectural design with measure and evaluate methods. Track single aircraft relative to a fixed position.

Display warning if aircraft is too close to the fixed position. Next validate and verify the design.

Step 11. (T) Increment 7: Elaborate measure and evaluate design relative to two moving aircraft. Next validate and verify the design.

These steps are taken from the atomic-level design process model given earlier. Steps 9 and 10 are carried out in this section. Step 11 is left for future work in the problem set for the chapter. The design process now turns its attention to implementing a pipeline architecture for the tATC locate module.

10.6 DESIGNING WITH MAINTENANCE IN MIND

It helps to design with maintenance in mind. The underlying motivation for selecting a software architecture is to make the software easier to understand and to maintain. In the case of the architectural choice for the locate module for air traffic control, changes to the functional behavior of the software can be made relative to filters in the pipeline. New filters are easily added to the pipeline. Existing filters in the pipeline can be modified. In effect, the selection of a software architecture facilitates a process called chunking in comprehending a software design. A *chunk* conceptually binds together items with similar or related attributes to form a unique item. In the case of the tATC software, chunking occurs when a "locate pipeline" is identified with locating an aircraft. The items in this chunk are the pipeline filters used to locate and display an aircraft. The understanding of the individual filters (how they function) dominates the design process. This understanding is reflected in the code and its documentation, and serves to make the code more maintainable. From a maintainer's point-of-view, a match must be made between the idea of a locate pipeline and code segments. In the software increment prescribed by step 9, a pipeline is used to determine the current position of an aircraft and to update an air traffic display.

10.7 INCREMENT WITH PARTIAL PIPELINE ARCHITECTURE

A pipeline like the one in Figure 10.20 guides the design of the next software increment for the tATC project. In the new software increment for the locate module, each processing element in the pipeline in Figure 10.20 is represented

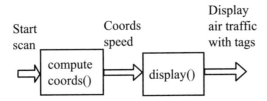

Figure 10.20 Reduced pipeline architecture.

by a method in the code. This increment is also designed relative to the following software requirements.

```
Req-1:  A colored icon represents an aircraft.
Req-2:  Display data tag for each aircraft.
Req-3:  Color-coded data tag for each aircraft.
Req-4:  Data tag shadows aircraft icon.
Req-5:  Determine coordinates of each aircraft.
Req-9:  Periodically update display.
```

Two methods named computeCoords() and display() are designed to form a pipeline. The behavior of computeCoords() is described by the statechart in Figure 10.21. The corresponding event-action sequence is given in Table 10.8. The execution of the pipeline begins by activating computeCoords. The actions of computeCoords are described in detail in Table 10.8. Basically, computeCoords transforms its inputs (current x, y aircraft coordinates and current aircraft ground speed), and computes new coordinates and speed using a random number generator. The output of computeCoords flows to the next filter in pipeline,

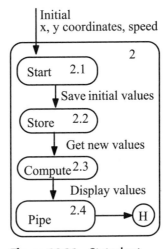

Figure 10.21 Statechart.

TABLE 10.8   Statechart/Event–Action Sequence for computeCoords Method

ComputeCoords Statechart	Current State	Event	Action	Next State

	2.1	Start	prev_x := x;
			prev_y := y;
			prev_spd := spd;
				2.2

	2.2	Pause	x := prev_x − (r mod 36); y := prev_y − (r mod 36); spd := prev_spd − (r mod 20);	2.3
	2.3	Computing coordinates completed	Pipe values to next filter in the pipeline	2.4
	2.4	Output values	Remember next transitions	(H)

Figure 10.21   Statechart.

display. The skeleton for a Java program to implement the pipeline is given in Figure 10.22.

The init(), start(), run(), and stop() methods in Figure 10.22 are the same as those given earlier. The update method in Figure 10.22 now starts processing in the pipeline by calling computeCoords(). The display() method uses the input it receives from computeCoords() to display the new position of an aircraft and its data tag. Three iterations of this pipeline are shown in the sample output in Figure 10.23. Next, the design in Figure 10.22 needs to be validated relative to the project requirements and the architectural description. Starting with the requirements, the sample pipeline output in Figure 10.23 shows a colored icon representing an aircraft being displayed (Req-1). Each appearance of the aircraft icon is accompanied by a data tag (Req-2). The data tag is colored coded with cyan. This color is bluish green. This identifies the aircraft by a controller at a workstation. This is part of the color-coding scheme used in the High Desert Tracon, a civilian air traffic facility developed by the BDM Corporation and installed at Edwards Air Force Base in 1993 (Perry, 1997). Hence, the design satisfies the color-coding requirement for data tags (Req-3). In the display in Figure 10.23, the data tag shadows its aircraft icon. This satisfies the fourth requirement (Req-4). The computeCoords() method in the program satisfies the fifth requirement (Req-5). Finally, the presence of the sleep feature provides the basis for periodic display of the relative position and tag of an aircraft (Req-9). This means that except for Req-3, the design satisfies the requirements for this increment.

The design of the current increment also satisfies the pipeline architectural requirement. The update() method starts the execution of the pipeline by calling

// Assert: A colored-coded aircraft icon with data tag is displayed periodically
// import packages needed for thread with pipeline

```
public class aircraft004 extends Applet implements Runnable {
// declarations
public void init() { /* set up graphics, font used in display */ }
public void start() { /* start thread to control pipeline */}
public void stop() { /* method to stop thread */ }
public void run() { /* method to put thread to sleep periodically */}

public void update (Graphics g){              // start pipeline process
 g.setPaintMode();
 computeCoords();
 } //update

public void computeCoords(){                  // begins pipeline
  int prev_x, prev_y;                         // store old coords.
  int prev_spd;                               // store old speed

  prev_x=x;                                   // store old x coord.
  prev_y=y;                                   // store old y coord.
  prev_spd=spd;                               // store old speed
  x=prev_x - (r.nextInt()%36);                // vary x randomly
  y=prev_y - (r.nextInt()%36);                // vary y randomly
  spd=prev_spd - (r.nextInt()%20);            // vary speed randomly
  display(x, y, spd, g);                      // output to pipeline
  } //computeCoords

public void display(int x, int y, int spd, Graphics g) {
  g.setColor(Color.green);                    // color of aircraft icon
  g.fillOval(x,y,9,9);                        // view aircraft position
  g.setColor(Color.cyan);                     // color of tag
  g.drawString("JAL 207",x+14,y);             // first line of data tag
  g.drawString("110"+ spd,x+14,y+10);         // second line of data tag
  } // display

public void paint(Graphics g){
  update(g);                                  // restart pipeline
  } // paint                                  // thread goes to sleep here
 } //aircraft004
```

Figure 10.22 Preliminary design of pipeline.

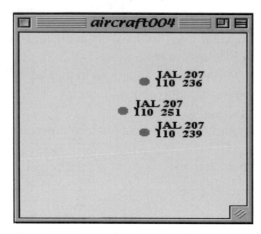

Figure 10.23   Pipeline output.

computeCoords(). The computeCoords() and display() methods in Figure 10.22 serve as filters in a pipeline. The "pipe" connection between these two methods comes from the underlying parameter-passing mechanism provided by Java. All parameters to Java methods are "pass by value" (Arnold & Gosling, 1998). This means, for example, that the values of parameters in the display() method in Figure 10.22 are copies of values of the arguments used by computeCoords() in the call

```
display(x,y, spd,g);    //output to pipeline
```

An iteration of the pipeline is completed when the display() method uses the values it receives from computeCoords() to show the new position of an aircraft being monitored.

Verifying the functional correctness of the code in Figure 10.22 will require matching the actions performed by particular lines of the code against the parts of the assertion in the beginning comment for the code. Verifying the functional correctness of the code in Figure 10.22 is part of the problem set for this chapter.

10.7.1   Elaboration of Pipeline Design

The elaboration of the design of software to display air traffic is guided by the architectural description of the pipeline in Figure 10.24. The shaded boxes

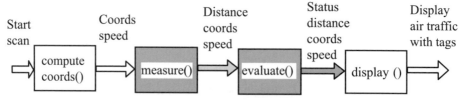

Figure 10.24   Expanded pipeline architecture.

TABLE 10.9   Requirements Guiding Design of Software Increment

Software Requirements	Comments
Req-6: Measure separation distance.	6.1: Relative to a fixed position 6.2: Between aircraft.
Req-7: Evaluate separation distance. Req-8: Display distance status.	Distinguish long, short, very short distances. "far"(long), "close"(short), "too close"

represent new filters added to the pipeline from the previous section. The coordinates and speed of an aircraft provide input to the measure filter in the pipeline. The measure filter adds a separation distance to the information it puts in the pipe connecting it to the evaluation filter. The elaboration of the architectural design is also guided by the software requirements given in Table 10.9. The new software increment will measure separation distances. This part of the design begins with measure the distance between an aircraft and a fixed position. This fixed position can represent some location (e.g., runway or airport tower) of interest to air traffic controllers.

The separation distance is evaluated. There are three evaluation criteria in the requirements. The software should distinguish between long, short, and very short distances. These categories need to be clarified. A clearer view of the measurement and evaluation processes can be derived from the statecharts and event-action descriptions of the software. A statechart for the measure filter of the locate module pipeline is given in Figure 10.25. In addition, an event-action description of the measure filter is given in Table 10.10. The separation distance is computed by the measure filter relative to an aircraft at coordinates (x, y) and a fixed position (k_x, k_y). The values of k_x and k_y are suggested as a place to start testing the software. The measure filter outputs the separation distance as well as the coordinates and speed. At this point, the measure filter is in its pipe state (3.3). Its output is transmitted over some form of "pipe" to the next filter in a pipeline.

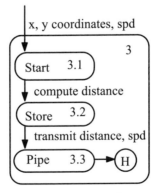

Figure 10.25 Statechart.

TABLE 10.10 **Statechart/Event–Action Table for Measure Method**

Measure Statechart	Current State	Event	Action	Next State
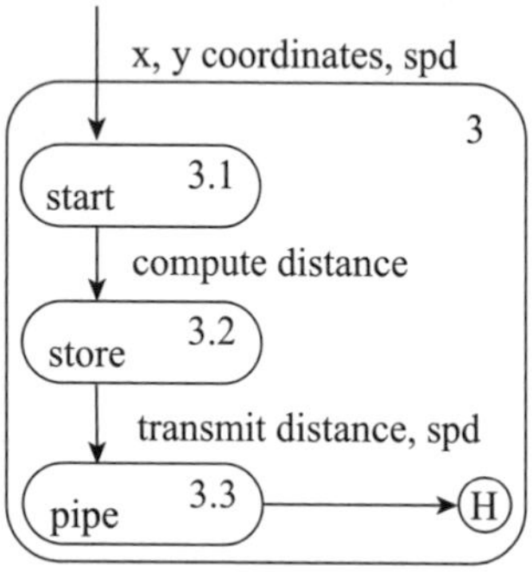	3.1	Start	$k_x := 30;$ $k_y := 30;$ Distance $:= \sqrt{(x - k_x)^2 + (y - k_y)^2}$	3.2
	3.2	Pause	Output x, y, spd, d	3.3
	3.3	Transmit	Remember	(H)

(Figure within table:)

x, y coordinates, spd

3

start 3.1

compute distance

store 3.2

transmit distance, spd

pipe 3.3 → (H)

Figure 10.25 Statechart.

There is a transition from the measure state in Table 10.10 to a hidden evaluate state. A statechart description of the evaluate state is given in Figure 10.26. The input to this statechart comes from the output of the measure filter in the pipeline. This input contains the coordinates and speed of an aircraft as well as the separation distance (denoted sd) of an aircraft from a fixed point. Recall that in statecharts, the notation © denotes the beginning of alternatives in an if-then-else action. In the case where sd is less than some minimum, the status variable has the value zero. There are two other cases to consider. If sd is less than some limit, then status has the value 1. Otherwise, status has the value 2.

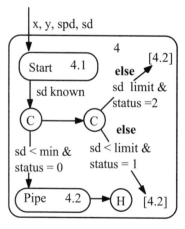

Figure 10.26 Statechart.

TABLE 10.11 Statechart/Event–Action Table for Evaluate Method

Evaluate Statechart	Current State	Event	Action	Next State

	4.1	Start	min := 25;
			limit := 50;
			(sd < min) & (status := 0);
			(sd < limit) & (status := 1);
			(sd ≥ limit) & (status := 2);
				4.2

	4.2	Transmit	Output x, y, spd, status	(H)

Figure 10.26 Statechart.

The evaluate module enters its pipe state after it has evaluated the separation distance. The suggested minimum separation distance in Table 10.11 is measured in hundreds of feet. A value of 25 for min represents 2500 feet. Similarly, a value of 50 for limit in Table 10.11 represents 5000 feet.

The basic features of the design of the next software increment are given in Figure 10.27. With one major exception, the methods referenced in the comments in Figure 10.27 are the same as in the increment in the previous section. The exception is the display method, which now handles the display of the current location of an aircraft and its data tag as well as its status. The program in Figure 10.27 draws a line between a fixed point and the current location of an aircraft. Instead of clearing the screen after each display, each new display includes the output of the previous displays. In the sample output from the execution of the Java program in Figure 10.27 given in Figure 10.28, the ground speed of flight JAL 207 is decreasing. A sample Java console display produced by the same program is given in Figure 10.29.

10.7.2 Instrumenting Software

The sample code in Figure 10.27 provides an example of what is known as instrumented software. Software is instrumented by inserting code at key probe points to make it possible to measure execution characteristics of interest. In the case of the locate module, System.out.print statements have been inserted to follow the execution of the pipeline filters. The sample Java console in Figure 10.29 shows the results of executing the System.out.print statements. This tech-

```
//  Assert-1: software measures separation distance.
//  Assert-2: software evaluates each separation distance.
//  Assert-3: software displays separation distance status.

public class aircraft004 extends Applet implements Runnable {
// declarations of variables as well as init, start, run, stop methods

public void computeCoords(){                                    // begin pipeline
// determine new coordinates of aircraft
  System.out.println("->track->");                             // begin pipeline trace
  measure(x,y,spd);                                            // transmit x, y, speed
  } //computeCoords

public void measure(int x, int y, int spd) {                   //  continue pipeline
double sd;                                                      //  stores sd

sd = (Math.sqrt((x - 30) * (x - 30) + (y - 30) * (y - 30)));   // distance from (30, 30)
System.out.print("measure->" + space + "->eval->");            // add to pipeline trace
evaluate(sd,x,y,spd);                                          // transmit sd, x, y, speed
}

public void evaluate(double distance, int x, int y, int spd) { // continue pipeline
  int status;                                                  // stores status

  g.clearRect(0,0,350,20);                                     // clear display
  if (distance < 25){ status = 0;                              // distance < min
  } // if
  else if (distance < 50) { status = 1;                        // distance < limit
  } // else
  else { status = 2;                                           // distance >= limit
  }; // else
  display(x, y, spd, status, g);                               // transmit x, y, spd, status, g
  System.out.println("display ->");                            // add to pipeline trace
  } // evaluate

public void display(int x, int y, int spd, int status, Graphics g) {
  g.setColor(Color.green);                                     // color of aircraft icon
  g.fillOval(x,y,9,9);                                         // view aircraft position
  g.fillOval(30,30,9,9);                                       // view fixed position
  g.drawLine(x,y,30,30);                                       // connect the two points
  g.setColor(Color.cyan);                                      // color of data tag
  g.drawString("JAL 207",x+14,y);                              // aircraft call sign
  g.drawString("110  "+ spd,x+14,y+10);                        // tag altitude, speed
  if (status == 0){                                            // sd below minimum
  g.drawString("Status: Warning! Very Close",10,10);           // display warning
  } // if
  else if (status == 1) {                                      // sd below limit
  g.drawString("Status:Close",10,10);                          // display "close"
  } // else
  else {                                                       // sd above limit
  g.drawString("Status: Far",10,10);                           // display "far"
  }; // else
  } // display

public void paint(Graphics g){                                 /* restart pipeline */ }
  } //aircraft004
```

Figure 10.27 Design with expanded pipeline.

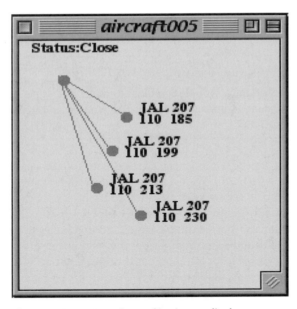

Figure 10.28   Sample applet viewer display.

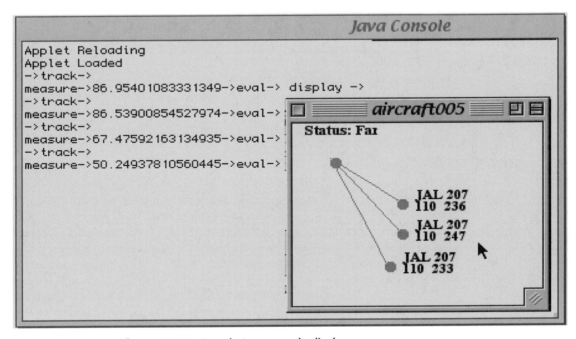

Figure 10.29   Sample Java console display.

nique comes from performance engineering that is guided by an instrumenting heuristic (Smith, 1994).

Instrumenting Heuristic

• Instrument systems as you design them to make it possible to measure and analyze workload scenarios, resource requirements, and performance goal achievements.

Instrumenting a program injects a data-collection mechanism into a design. For example, the System.out.print statements make it possible to collect two kinds of data: pipeline actions and measurements of separation distances. The sequences of pipeline actions tell us that the pipeline is functioning correctly (data flows from filter to filter in the pipeline, and matches the flows of data implied by the architectural design. In addition, the measurements printed out in Figure 10.29 make it possible to compare separation distances with displayed aircraft status. It is easier to understand this second point by comparing each new Java console output with each new applet viewer display during the execution of the program. The idea for instrumenting software comes from what is known as the second law of process control engineering.

Second Law of Process Control

• You must understand a process before you can control it (Luyben, 1997).

The application of this law to software design is fairly obvious. Control of a software design (knowing when to refine it, to correct it) depends on a knowledge of how the program behaves during its execution.

10.7.3   Build Sizes

The development of software in builds offers an approach to controlling the design process. A *build* is a set of functionally related modules of a software system. The use of builds is one of the most common adjustments to the waterfall software process model. This means that software is developed incrementally. There is a general rule in estimating a build size for small software increments relative to the number of steps in a correctness proof that a build satisfies its specification. The number of steps in verifying a build tends to increase logarithmically with the number of lines in a build. Table 10.12 illustrates this with examples drawn from a collection of 25 small-scale software projects written in Java. The build sizes in column 1 of Table 10.12 represent average Java class sizes. For example, three Java classes had an average of 24 lines with corresponding proofs of specification with average length of 4. In other words, small builds tend to lead to small proofs. This is not as surprising as it may seem, since a

TABLE 10.12   Size of Build versus Size of Proof of Build

Size of Build Increment (lines of code)	Size of Proof (lines of proof)	log₂ (Size of Build), Size ≤ 1000
{three classes with size 24,	{av. no. of lines = 4,	{4.58496,
two classes with size 50,	av. no. of lines = 6,	5.64386,
five classes with size 75,	av. no. of lines = 6,	6.22882,
ten classes with size 100,	av. no. of lines = 7,	6.64386,
two classes with size 250,	av. no. of lines = 8,	7.96578,
one class with size 500,	av. no. of lines = 9,	8.96578,
two classes with size 1000}	av. no. of lines = 10}	9.96578}

single step in a correctness proof often refers to more than one line in an increment. In addition, it is often the case that only selected lines of an increment need to be referenced in verifying a correctness condition. This general rule needs to be checked against application modules written in other programming languages as well as other Java classes. There is also the issue of what form the rule might have for large-scale projects with increments in higher ranges such as the 5000 or 10,000-line range.

10.8 SUMMARY

Besides controllers themselves, pilots, human factors researchers, commercial and military airlines, and national, international, and local air traffic regulatory agencies are among the stakeholders in developing a training program for air traffic controllers. A sampling of these stakeholders should be consulted in developing a prototype for a tATC system. A knowledge of this application can be gleaned from discussions with stakeholders, available publications, and numerous web pages on air traffic control. An orderly transition through the software design process is a fringe benefit of incorporating the Humphrey ETXVM architecture in the software process model used in structuring project activities. By taking time to move through the hierarchy from a high-level description of the software process to project-specific and task-specific models of the process, a project team can gauge its understanding of a project. It takes considerable time to formulate procedures to be carried out at the project level, and then to identify the sequence of steps as well as the details of the steps themselves at the atomic (task) level. Project stakeholders help out in penetrating the inner workings of a software process by establishing entry conditions that must be satisfied before beginning a project procedure. Stakeholders can also help in formulating exit conditions to determine when a project team has completed its work on a baseline document. Entry and exit conditions will flow out of a knowledge of project objectives, constraints, and dependencies gleaned from interactions with stakeholders.

For a complex system, the availability of a technology that supports the vanilla framework paradigm is important. Such a technology aids in specifying, designing, and testing the conceptual constructs of software being built. The assumption is that the description notation and semantics support the design of a complex system hierarchically and modularly. At each level in the hierarchical description of a system, only those details needed to understand the functionality and behavior of the level are visible. The remaining system details are hidden from view, but are accessible by decomposing the states of a particular level of the hierarchy into a network of states at a lower level. After the requirements for a system have been established, the design process begins with the selection of an increment to be developed. This selection is aided by experience with the operation of prototypes during the planning and requirements phases of a project as well as interaction with project stakeholders. For each selected increment, the architecture of the increment is designed. The availability of a plan, requirements, and software architecture triggers the elaboration of software increments.

10.9 PROBLEMS

1. Refine the display method in the Java aircraft program so that a line is drawn between the data tag and the corresponding aircraft icon in an tATC display. See Figures 10.3 and 10.4 for examples.

2. Modify the display method so that an aircraft icon turn red whenever the separation distance between two aircraft is violated.

3. Modify the display method so that the data tag for an aircraft has a third line with two data fields. The first field at the beginning of the third tag line specifies a runway (e.g., 18R or 3L). The second data field of the third tag line gives either an airspeed advisory shown in tens of knots (e.g., 10 indicating an advisory airspeed of 100 knots) or an advised heading in tens of degrees (magnetic north) preceded by an "H" for heading.

4. Write a program that does the following:
   (a) Displays a randomly moving aircraft.
   (b) Displays the (x, y) coordinates of each appearance of an aircraft icon. The display should resemble the one in Figure 10.30.

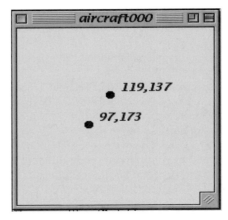

Figure 10.30 The (x, y) coordinates of aircraft.

5. Consider the first instant when two aircraft begin approaching the same endpoint (e.g., a runway). The distance of each aircraft to an endpoint C is measured. Let distance A be the distance of aircraft A from an endpoint C, and let distance B be the distance of aircraft B from C. Further, let separation D be the required separation distance that must be maintained between aircraft. The normalized separation distance NSD is computed as follows.

$$NSD = \frac{|distanceA - distanceB|}{separationDistance}$$

6. Do the following:
   (a) Introduce a Java method called NSD, which computes the normalized separation distance between aircraft A and B relative to a fixed point C.
   (b) Introduce a Java method called conflictAlarm, which evaluates each NSD value and displays a conflict alarm message whenever NSD < 0.5.
   (c) Introduce a Java method called divert, which simulates the delay (slowing down) of an aircraft in conflict with another aircraft. Consider diverting the aircraft to avoid conflict.
   (d) Give a sample run of the aircraft display with the NSD feature.

7. Do the following:
   (a) Incorporate each of the features in problems 1 through 3 into the aircraft display program.
   (b) Modify the design of the aircraft display program so that up to 10 aircraft can be displayed.
   (c) Let the initial number of aircraft in a display vary randomly.
   (d) Give a sample run.

8. Modify the display method in problem 4 so that a speed advisory in aircraft tag is displayed in orange.

9. Modify the display method in problem 5 so that a speed advisory reverts to its normal color (e.g., blue) when an aircraft executes or passes the advisory.

10. A partial description of the guide operation of the aircraft module is given in Figure 10.31. Do the following:
    (a) Check *http://www.arc.nasa.gov* for details about Tracon displays. Also check with local airport tower controllers concerning the details of what is done in transferring an aircraft from local control to the control of enroute center as well as Tracon display options.
    (b) Prepare an atomic-level design process description of the steps in creating a control panel used by controllers to select different tATC operations.
    (c) Decompose the transfer state in Figure 10.31 and give more detail about the transfer operation whenever a controller clicks the transfer control button on the tATC display.
    (d) Design the architecture of a software module to handle aircraft transfers.
    (e) Elaborate the design of the transfer module in (d).
    (f) Create a button panel with a transfer aircraft option that activates the transfer module whenever it is clicked by a controller.

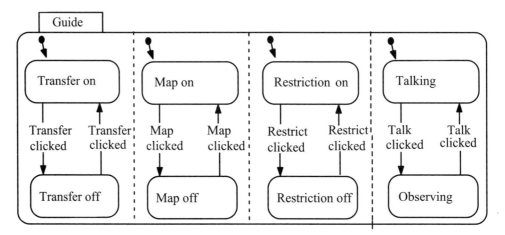

Figure 10.31 Guide statechart.

11. Repeat 10(b) to (f) in designing a module to support the map operation in Figure 10.31. The map software module should have the following features:
    (a) Selecting a map from a map repository for display by a controller.
    (b) Provision of pen that makes it possible for a controller to draw a map within an airspace being displayed.
    (c) Erase a displayed map.
    (d) Edit a displayed map.
    (e) Annotate a displayed map.

12. Repeat 10(b) to (f) in designing a module to support the restriction operation in Figure 10.31. The restriction software module should have the following features:
    (a) Restricting access to a mapped region being displayed by a controller.
    (b) Canceling a restriction.

13. Repeat 10(b) to (f) in designing a module to support the talk operation in Figure 10.31. The talk software module should have the following features:

(a) Selecting talk opens a window in the display that records controller instructions and pilot responses.

(b) Exchanges between a controller and pilot should be time and date stamped.

14. Add a line to Table 10.13 for each of the functional correctness checks you perform for the problems in this chapter. What can you conclude?

TABLE 10.13 Size of Build versus Size of Proof of Build

Size of Build Increment (lines of code)	Size of Proof (lines of proof)	$\log_2$ (Size of Build), Size $\leq$ 1000

10.10 REFERENCES

Arnold, K., Gosling, J. *The Java Programming Language,* 2nd ed. Addison-Wesley, Reading, MA, 1998.

Davis, T.J., Erzberger, H., Green, S.M., Nedell, W. Design and evaluation of an air traffic control final approach spacing tool. *Journal of Guidance Control and Dynamics,* **14** (4):848–854, 1991.

Davis, T.J., Krzechzowski, K.J., Bergh, C. The final approach spacing tool. *Proceedings of the 13th IFAC Symposium on Automatic Control in Aerospace,* Palo Alto, 1994.

Harel, D. "Statecharts: A visual formalism for complex systems," *Science of Computer Programming,* vol. 8, pp. 231–274, 1987.

Harwood, K. Defining human-centered system issues for verifying and validating air traffic control systems. In *Verification and Validation of Complex and Integrated Human Machine Systems,* J. Wise, V.D. Hopkin, P. Stager, Eds. Springer-Verlag, Berlin, 1993.

Horrocks, I. *Constructing the User Interface with Statecharts.* Addison-Wesley, Reading, MA, 1999.

Luyben, M.L., Luyben, W.L. *Essentials of Process Control.* McGraw-Hill, New York, 1997.

Mills, H. The new math of computer programming. *Communications of the ACM,* **18**(1), 1975.

National Aeronautics and Space Administration, 1999. See *http://www.ctas.arc.nasa.gov.*

Oaks, S., Wong, H. *Java Threads.* O'Reilly & Associates, Sebastopol, CA, 1997.

Parnas, D.L. A technique for software module specification with examples. *Communications of the ACM,* **15**(2):330–336, 1972.

Parnas, D.L., Clements, P.C. A rational design process: How and why to fake it. *IEEE Transactions on Software Engineering,* **12**(2):251–257, 1986.

Perry, T.S. In search of the future of air traffic control. *IEEE Spectrum,* **34**(8):18–35, 1997.

Schneiderman, B. Designing the Use Interface: Strategies for Effective Human-Computer Interaction, third edition. Reading, MA, Addison-Wesley, 1998.

Smith, C.U. Performance engineering. In *Encyclopedia of Software Engineering,* J.J. Marciniak, Ed. Wiley, New York, 1994.

CHAPTER 11
Software Design: Validation and Risk Analysis

Our brains have been built by natural selection to assess probability and risk, just as our eyes have been built to assess electromagnetic wavelength.

—R. DAWKINS, 1986

Aims

- Examine approaches to validating software designs
- Examine approaches to risk analysis
- Develop algorithm for risk analysis
- Incrementally improve software designs

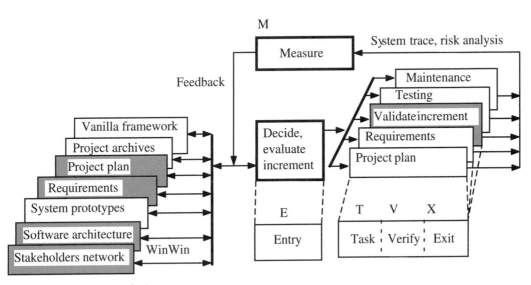

Figure 11.1 Software design process.

11.1 INTRODUCTION

The design of a software increment is considered complete after it has been checked against requirements (validation), its functional correctness has been checked and its features have been tested (verification), and the risk associated with it has been determined (risk analysis). These activities depend on interaction with project stakeholders. The shaded inputs to the decider process in Figure 11.1 each play a role in validating, verifying, and risk analysis. During the validation of an increment, the required features described in the project plan, requirements and architecture are checked against the design of the increment. A simple trace connecting features in the design back to uniquely identified items in project baseline documents begins the validation process. This chapter focuses on validating software designs and performing risk analysis relative to a design.

11.2 VALIDATING SOFTWARE DESIGN

> *Verification:* **Are we building the product right?**
> *Validation:* **Are we building the right product?**
> **—B. BOEHM, 1988**

There are five parts in validating and verifying a software design described in the IEEE Std. 1012-1986 on software verification and validation. Design V&V is summarized in Figure 11.2. In this section, the main features of traceability analysis are presented.

11.2.1 Tracing Designs to Requirements

During the design process there is a flow down from requirements to designs as shown in Figure 11.3A. An algorithm for establishing a trace process using hypertext documents is shown in Figure 11.3B. The basic idea in Figure 11.3B is to establish a web-based presentation of all software requirement and design documents that facilitates cooperative software development. All documents are linked to each other.

A sample trace is shown in Figure 11.4. Requirements engineers and software designers corroborate design artifacts and track changes more easily. The selection and development of software architectures and other design artifacts constructed during the design process is carried out with requirements in mind. The underlying, crucial assumption in Figure 11.4 is that specific requirements

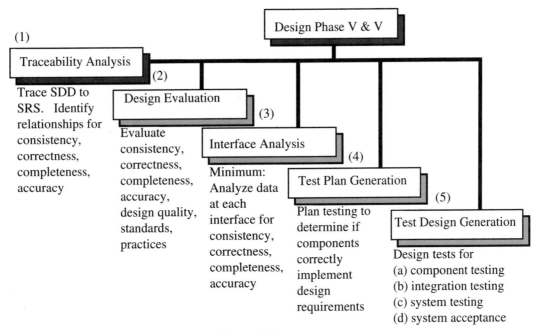

Figure 11.2 Summary of design V&V.

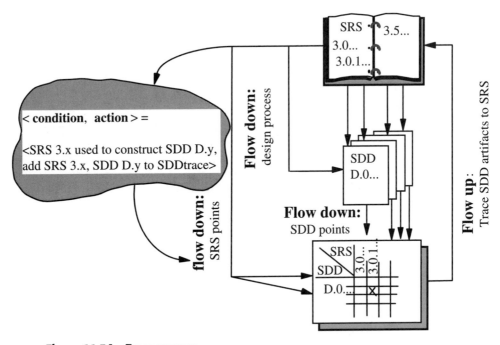

Figure 11.3A Trace process.

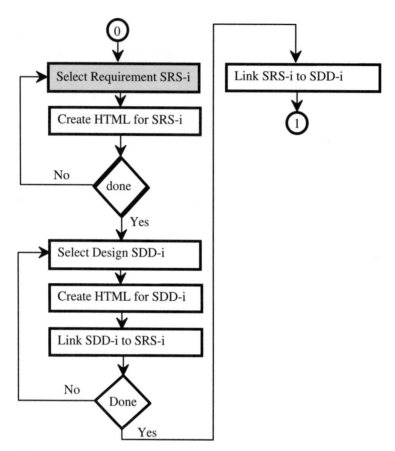

Figure 11.3B Hypertext approach to tracing designs.

have unique numbers, which makes it possible to trace design components back to a specific requirement. For example, the choice of a layered architecture for a mobile robot control system in D.0.1 of the SDD can be traced back to requirement 3.2.1 (separate processing elements represented by orthogonal statecharts) in the SRS. The CSP description of how the avoidance module works in D.0.2.1 is traced to the statechart in requirements 3.2.1.1 (Avoid obstacles module). The provision for separate processors, one for each layer, is traced back to the process descriptions in section 3.2.2 of the SRS; and so on.

Traceability analysis requires tracing each component of an SDD back to the SRS. Periodically, it should be possible to trace (flow up from) a specific design component to a specific requirement. Traceability analysis is made easier by having a repository structure (call it SDDtrace) in place during the design process. The SDDtrace repository will have the appearance of a blackboard, which operates concurrently with the construction of the SDD. Each

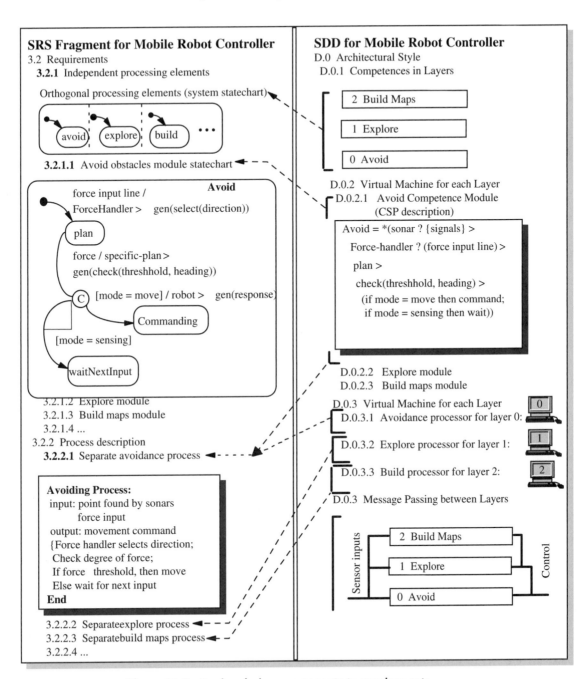

Figure 11.4 Tracing design components to requirements.

point in the SRS can be associated with a condition-action pair of the following form:

> Satisfy(condition) → (action)
> <SRS 3.x used to construct SDD D.y, add SRS 3.x, SDD D.y to SDDtrace>

The initial problem solved by the SDDtrace is the construction of some form of a trace table. This can be done by constructing a Requirements Traceability Matrix (RTM) or creating a web hypertext for design artifacts with links to requirements. An RTM is a table that correlates design components with specific requirements (Davis, 1993; Dorfman & Thayer, 1990). The structure of an RTM is shown in Figure 11.5. Two entry system styles are represented in the figure:

- X-entry system (an X indicates a match between a design artifact and requirement).
- Numeric-entry system (entry indicates degree design artifact satisfies requirement).

The simplest style is an X-entry system. In each case where no X entry appears in a row, this indicates that a design artifact helps satisfy a requirement (Davis, 1993). In the case where no Xs appear in a row, this indicates an extraneous design component. The X-entry system is a form of boolean estimation, where

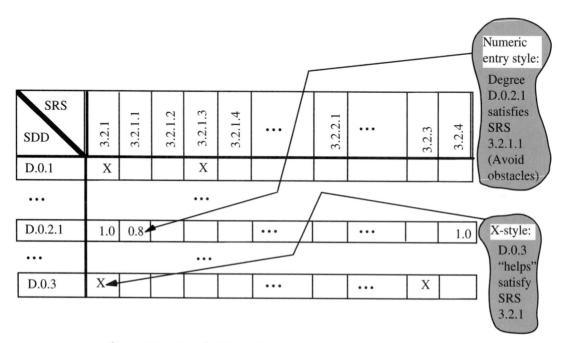

Figure 11.5 Sample RTM with two forms of entry systems.

placement of an X is equivalent to a 1 ("true"), and absence of an X is equivalent to a 0 ("false"). The numeric entry system is based on estimates of the degree to which a design artifact helps satisfy a requirement (the estimate is made by a human). Numeric estimates belong to interval [0, 1]. The advantage to the numeric entry system is that it makes it possible to estimate the degree of satisfaction of design components. Let $e_{i1}, e_{i2}, \ldots e_{ij}$ be entries in a row for a design artifact D. Then a measure of the degree that D satisfies the requirements is obtained from the average of the entries $e_{i1}, e_{i2}, \ldots e_{ij}$ in row i of an RTM as follows:

$$\overline{deg\text{-}of\text{-}satisfaction} = \frac{\sum\limits_{j}^{n} e_{ij}}{n}$$

{average design trace requirement}

Notice now that degree of satisfiability in a row of the RTM can now be instrumented relative to a threshold (e.g., average degree of satisfaction ≥ 0.75). Then the traceability measure becomes

$$\overline{deg\text{-}of\text{-}satisfaction} = \frac{\sum\limits_{j}^{n} e_{ij}}{n} \geq threshold$$

{design trace threshold requirement}

All requirements may not have equal importance. In that case, weights $w_{i1}, w_{i2}, \ldots w_{ij}$ can be associated with corresponding requirements in each column of the RTM. Then the weighted traceability measure becomes

$$\overline{deg\text{-}of\text{-}satisfaction} = \frac{\sum\limits_{j}^{n} w_{ij} e_{ij}}{\sum\limits_{j}^{n} w_{ij}} \geq threshold$$

{weighted design trace requirement}

Both forms of design traces have advantages. The average design trace measure with a threshold makes it possible to detect design attributes with weak links to requirements (ones where the sum of the row entries is greater than zero, but less than some preset threshold). This is an improvement over the traditional RTM, where satisfiability is either zero (no X entries) or not (one or more X entries). The weighted design trace requirement makes it possible for software system managers (and clients) to express preferences. Each weight represents some degree of importance of a requirement, and serves as a red flag for design engineers. Requirements with higher weights would receive more attention. This approach will affect cost estimates, and budgeting. That is, requirements with higher-valued weights would represent minimum requirements for a project. A correlation between the set of minimum requirements and their cost to arrive at a minimum project budget.

11.2.2 Hypertext Design Tracing

An automated approach to requirements tracing through hypertext linking has been suggested recently by Palmer (1997). Hypertexts are documents designed for delivery over the internet, or for display *locally* on a workstation running World Wide Web (WWW or, simply, web) browsers such as Netscape Navigator or Microsoft Internet Explorer (Graham, 1996; Musciano & Kennedy, 1997). The HyperText Markup Language (HTML) provides a means of describing what a text means by using instructions embedded in a document which specify the appearance of a document to be delivered electronically by means of a web tool. Sections of an HTML text are identified with markup tags. The heading of an HTML document begins with

```
<!--begin hypertext document-->
<HTML>
<HEAD>
<TITLE>Software Design Document (SDD) artifact</TITLE>
</HEAD>
```

Comments consists of any characters inside <! comments >, and are not displayed by a browser. Comments are surrounded by --, and can be empty. <! > is a legal comment. The notation </ is used to mark the beginning of a section (e.g., </HEAD> marks the end of the heading). The body of an HTML document begins with <BODY> and ends with </BODY>. Each section of an HTML body begins with <Hk> and ends with </Hk>, where k is a positive integer. Image files are stored in graphics interchange format (gif) files, and have a .gif extension. Let robot.gif be an image file. The HTML line

```
<IMG SRC="robot.gif">
```

specifies that robot.gif is an image element, and SRC indicates that "robot.gif" is the name of the image file that follows. Line breaks (at the ends of lines) are hardcoded with a <BR> to indicate that the text that follows begins on the next line. Multiple blank lines are inserted with a repetition of
 (e.g.,

 for two blank lines). Emphasis {strong emphasis} strings begin with <EM> {<STRONG>} and end with </EM> {</STRONG>}. Paragraphs begin with <P> and end with </P>. Unordered lists (lists where each item is indented and begins with a bullet) begin with <UL> and end with </UL>. A list item begins with <LI> and ends with an optional </LI>. Table 11.1 shows a sample HTML document and what is displayed by a web browser. The result of running the HTML file in Table 11.1 is shown in Figure 11.6.

TABLE 11.1   Sample HTML Document and What Web Browser Displays

HTML Document (file name is "sample.html")	Displayed by Web Browser (Use browser open file to display page)
\<HTML\>	Software Design Process
\<H1\> Software Design Process \</H1\>	
\<BODY\>	
\<BR\>	
\<UL\>	
\<P\> Steps: \</P\>\<BR\>	Steps:
\<LI\> Consult SRS \<EM\> repeatedly \</EM\>	• Consult SRS *repeatedly*
\<LI\> Design software architectures	• Design software architectures
\<LI\> Trace SDD artifact back to SRS	• Trace SDD artifact back to SRS
\</UL\>	
\<BR\>	
\<!--draw horizontal line--\>	
\<HR\>	
\</BODY\>	
\</HTML\>	

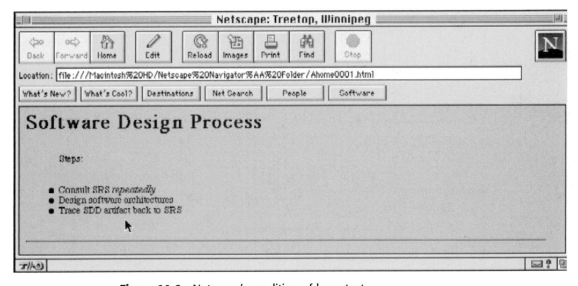

Figure 11.6   Netscape's rendition of hypertext.

Hypertexts can have "hot" words {phrases} signifying links to other HTML documents. A link begins with an anchor <A> and ends with </A>. The link itself begins with HREF=, standing for Hypertext REFerence. Let SDD321.html be the name of an HTML file in your current directory. The following HTML line inserts a hot phrase into your document:

```
<!--insert hot phrase "SDD artifact 3.2.1" into HTML text.-->
<A HREF="SDD321.html">SDD artifact 3.2.1</A>
```

The target of a hypertext link is indicated by HREF=, which is assigned the Universal Resource Locator (URL) of the target document or resource. For example, the URL could be another web site such as the Department of Electrical and Computer Engineering home page, as in

```
<!--insert hot phrase which targets the URL for another website:-->
<A HREF = "http://www.ee.umanitoba.ca">ECE home page</A>
```

TABLE 11.2 Hypertext Software Design Artifact With Link to SRS Requirement

SDD HTML Document (file name is "SDD021.html")	Image File Targeted by SDD (SDD021arch.gif targeted by SDD021.html)
<HTML>	
<H1> Software Design artifact </H1>	
<BODY>	Avoid = *(sonar ? {signals} →
<P> Avoidance Module: </P> 	Force-handler ? (force input line) →
<IMG SRC="SDD021arch.gif">	plan →
 	check(threshhold, heading) →
<!--hot phrase is "SRS statechart . . ."-->	(if mode=move then command;
<!--use link to trace artifact to SRS-->	if mode=sensing then wait))
<A HREF="SRS3211.html">SRS statechart for avoid obstacles module </A>	
<!--draw horizontal line-->	
<HR>	
</BODY>	
</HTML>	

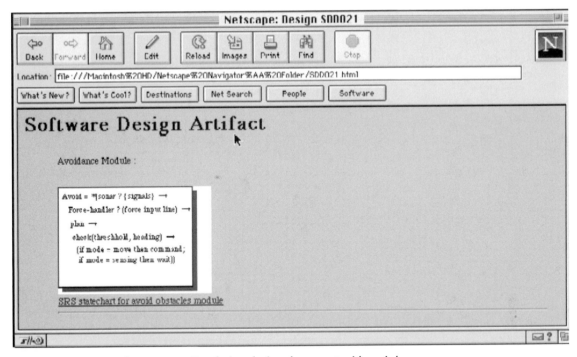

Figure 11.7   Rendering design document with web browser.

It is now possible to create elementary hypertext documents for the parts of an SRS and artifacts in an SDD. Let SRSavoid.gif be an image file containing the statechart for section 3.2.1 in an SRS for the a robot controller. Also let SDD021arch.gif be an image file showing a software architecture (described with CSP) for an avoid competence module. The HTML file SDD021.html, with link to the SRS3211.html file and pointer to the SDD03arch.gif image file, is shown in Table 11.2. The result of rendering the SDD021.html file with Netscape is shown in Figure 11.7.

The HTML file SRS321.html with link to file D03.html and pointer to the SRSavoid.gif image file are shown in Table 11.3, which completes the hypertext trace of a software design artifact to an SRS requirement. The result of rendering the SRS hypertext document in Table 11.3 is shown in Figure 11.8. The hypertext approach to tracing software process documents has many advantages. First, tracing flow down and flow up between the SRS and SDD is automated with forward and reverse HREF links as shown in Tables 11.2 and 11.3. Second, HREF links are unique, and continue throughout the life span of a software system. This facilitates maintenance of the software later when there are questions about which parts of an SDD and SRS are affected by changes. In other words, HREF links facilitate evolution of a software system. Finally, and perhaps most importantly, hypertext versions of part or all of the SRS and SDD documents facilitate communication between software engineers.

TABLE 11.3 Hypertext SRS Requirement With Link to SDD Artifact

SRS HTML Document (file name is "SRS321.html")	Image File by SRS (SRSavoid.gif targeted by SRS321.html)
`<HTML>` `<H1> Software Requirement </H1>` `<BODY>` ` ` `<P> Statechart: </P> ` `<IMG SRC="SRSavoid.gif">` ` ` ` ` `<!--hot phrase is "SDD software . . ."-->` `<!--use link to trace artifact to SRS-->` `<A HREF="SDD021.html">SDD software` `  architecture for avoid module</A>` ` ` `<!--draw horizontal line-->` `<HR>` `</BODY>` `</HTML>`	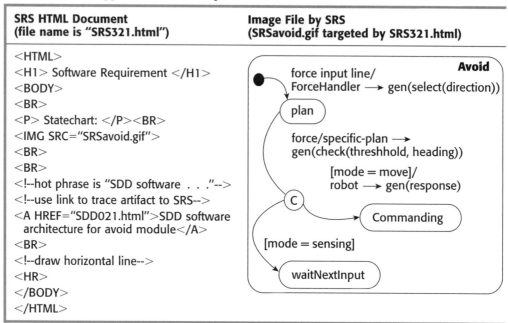

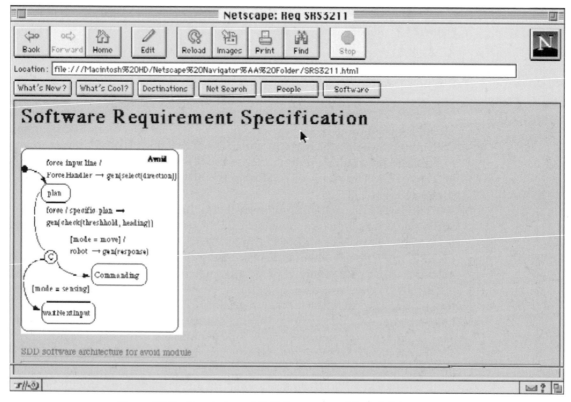

Figure 11.8 Rendering of SRS document with web browser.

11.3 BASIS FOR SDD EVALUATION

Sensing + Selecting + Perceiving = Seeing.
—A. HUXLEY, 1943

The second part of tracing SDD artifacts back to requirements in the SRS leads to a basis for evaluating the following attributes of software design:

- *Consistency.* Degree of uniformity, standardization, and freedom from contradiction among software documents.
- *Correctness.* Degree to which each SDD artifact meets SRS requirements.
- *Completeness.* (1) SDD artifact represents everything in corresponding SRS requirement(s), (2) all responses of software architecture to realizable classes of input data in all realizable situations are represented, (3) all SDD artifacts are uniquely identified (numbered).
- *Accuracy.* (1) Qualitative assessment of SDD artifact being free from error, and (2) quantitative assessment of degree to which SDD artifact contains error.

Evaluation of consistency of a software design is subtle. Estimating consistency or the degree to which a design meets standards requirement can be determined by running a check on how closely a design process follows a prescribed standard such as IEEE Std. 1016-1987, *Recommend Practice for Software Design Descriptions* and IEEE Std. 1061.1-1993, *Guide to Design Descriptions.* This is not as easy it may seem, since what used to be called design descriptions (e.g., data flow diagrams, JSD diagrams, SADT diagrams, statecharts, Petri nets, VDM formal specifications) are now called requirements specifications as evidenced in Davis (Davis, 1993), *and* the IEEE Std. 830-1993 on software requirements specifications. The focus on architectures as the first step in the software design process is a more recent and fruitful development and described in detail in IEEE Std. 1074-1995. Assessment of the degree to which software design artifacts are free from contradiction is another subtle matter. Freedom from contradiction in a design can be gauged by checking corresponding requirements in the SRS to make sure that the opposite of what was required has been built into a design. For example, in section 3.2.1.1, the condition [mode = sensing] leads to the waitNextInput state in the statechart in Figure 11.8. This would be contradicted, for example, if the corresponding architectural description were of the form

if mode = sensing then command

{action should be ''wait''}

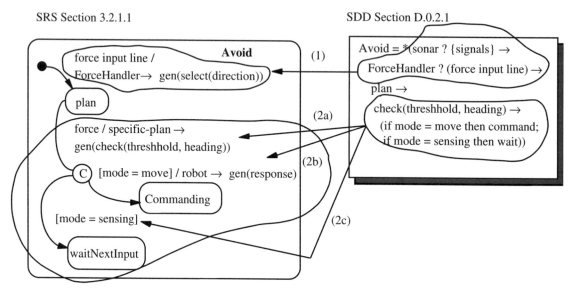

Figure 11.9   Traced design incomplete component.

Correctness or estimating the degree to which a software artifact satisfies SRS requirements can be accomplished by using the numerical-entry approach to filling in a Requirements Traceability Matrix (RTM). By inserting numerical entries in the RTM, the groundwork has been laid for evaluation of the completeness of an SDD.

The *completeness* of an SDD requires a check be made to ensure that an SDD artifact represents everything in the SRS requirements. Notice, for example, that design of the Avoid Competence Module (part D0.2.1 in the SDD in Table 11.3) is found to be incomplete when checked against the statechart in the hypertext form of section 3.2.1.1 of the SRS in Table 11.2. That is, the if-then processes in D.0.2.1 do not exactly correspond to the conditional branch labeled C in the statechart in 3.2.1.1 in the SRS (Figure 11.9). It is immediately apparent from the trace in Figure 11.9 that the design artifact needs to be improved so that it is more complete. Part (1) of the trace reveals that design of the Avoid module in Table 11.3 is incomplete. That is, reception of the "force input line" from the ForceHandler in the Avoid module is reflected in the CSP description:

ForceHandler? (force input line)
{receive force input line from ForceHandler}

However, in the SRS statechart, "force input line" is a condition for the Force-Handler to trigger the select() operation in the Avoid module. The select()

operation in the statechart is missing in the design. Parts (2a), (2b) and (2c) of the trace reveal that the design is both inconsistent and incomplete. First, the state names "command" and "waitNextInput" in the statechart do not match the process names "command" and "wait" in the CSP description (this is a blatant inconsistency), unless one wants to argue that process names should resemble but not be the same as names of states. Since state names suggest underlying, hidden activities ongoing until a state change occurs, it would seem better to let process names in the CSP description match state names in the statechart. Second, all three condition-action labelings of the arcs in the statechart are not reflected in the CSP description. Hence, the CSP description is judged trebly incomplete. The CSP description needs to be revised so that it will be more complete. Finally, notice that the CSP description reveals that the SRS itself is incomplete, since part (1) of the trace manifests an apparent inconsistency between a provision for input from sonar units, and the SRS module does not mention input from sonar needed by the ForceHandler object to invoke the select object. That is, sonar input is needed to compute the force input line. Otherwise, the select object cannot determine the direction the robot should travel. This indicates the SRS also needs to be revised. The revision of the Avoid module is given in section 11 as part of the discussion of software interfaces.

Accuracy assessments of an SDD are both qualitative and quantitative. Words like "zero," "low," "medium," and "high" can be used to annotate the entries in an RTM, when comparing an SDD artifact with SRS requirements. All of assessments of SDS artifacts should be "zero" to achieve a worthy design. The extent of allowable or possible error in a design is built into a software quality plan for the system. The quantitative assessments of freedom from error can be inferred from low "degree of satisfaction" values in the numerical entry system for filling in an RTM. The lower the "degree of satisfaction" in comparing a design with requirements, the greater the likelihood of error in the design. Another means of checking accuracy quantitatively is to tally up the omissions of conditions for actions in a design. The higher the tally, the greater the chance of error. The CSP architectural description of the Avoid Competence Module in Table 11.3 gets a "low" qualitative assessment and a quantitative score of 2, since the first two of the condition/event $\rightarrow$ gen(action) are ignored in the design.

To complete the basis for evaluation of a design, lists of checkpoints in the design-to-SRS trace need to be created. These checks will include verifying that all parts of an SDD have been numbered, and that all SDD artifacts satisfy one or more requirements. If the numerical entry system is used for in filling in an RTM, then threshold values and degrees of satisfaction need to be added for each design artifact. This information is put in an evaluation plan. In addition, indications of measures to be used in computing consistency, correctness, and quantitative forms accuracy need to be built into an evaluation plan.

11.4 RISK ENGINEERING: MANAGEMENT AND ANALYSIS

> **Software safety failure is any software system behavior that involves risk to human life, risk of injury, or risk of equipment damage.**
> —J.D. MUSA, A. IANNINO, K. OKUMOTO, 1990

The beginnings of risk engineering in the software process can be traced back to the spiral software process model introduced by Boehm (1988) and described in considerable detail by Boehm (1989a, 1989b) and Carr and others (1993), Charette (1994), and Gluch (1995). Risk engineering occupies a prominent part of the IEEE Std. 1074-1995 software life-cycle. *Risk* is some potential loss that exists among one or more choices available for selection. A taxonomy of risk engineering is given in Figure 11.10.

11.4.1 Risk Management

Risk Management has five principal activities: planning, control, monitoring, directing, and staffing. *Planning* requires a determination of which risk analysis recommendations (to be given to the risk analysis group) are feasible, reassigning resources to accomplish risk analysis. *Controlling* is chiefly concerned with averting identified risks with greatest importance. *Monitoring* activities are explained in

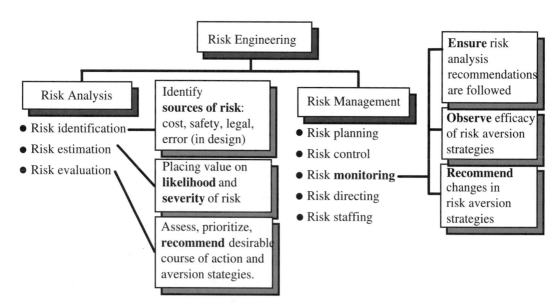

Figure 11.10 Taxonomy of risk engineering.

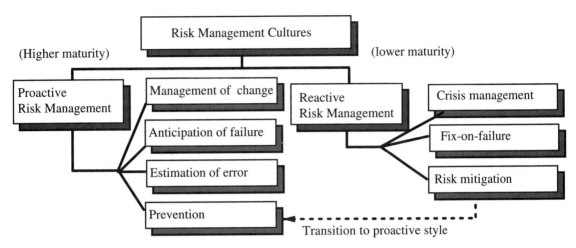

Figure 11.11 Risk management cultures.

Figure 11.10. *Directing* is concerned with guiding the risk management effort, integrating it into the overall software life-cycle, and determining when to conduct additional risk analysis. Finally, *staffing* is concerned with selecting personnel to implement risk aversion recommendations (from risk analysis group). The capability maturity of a software development group can be judged in terms of risk management culture engaged in by the project organization. There are basically two forms of risk management cultures, shown in Figure 11.11.

Risk analysis has three principal activities: identifying, estimating, and evaluating risks. The sources of risk to be identified include cost (possible discrepancies between budgeted and estimated costs); possible liability (legal) risks due to product failure or economic losses; safety and security considerations, which might endanger human life or the environment, or compromise the integrity of the system; and implementation, testability, and maintainability concerns. Each identified source of risk must be subjected to likelihood and severity of risk analysis. Let $pr(risk_i)$, C_i be the probability of $risk_i$ occurring and measure of severity of $risk_i$ occurring (e.g., severity computed as a consequence of failures due to technical factors, changes in cost and in scheduling), respectively. Then risk is computed as a probabilistic sum as follows:

$$Risk = pr(risk_i) + C_i - pr(risk_i)C_i$$

{Quantification of risk}

The severity of risk can be assessed qualitatively or quantitatively. For example, quantitative assessments of severity can be given with words like "zero," "very low," "low," "medium," "high," or "very high" by an experienced risk engineer. Quantitative assessments are given in the range from 0 to 1. In IEEE Std. 1044.1-1995 on software anomalies, project risks is explained in terms of an appraisal of risk relative to software defects and enhancements. There is some degree of risk every time a software system is enhanced (changed) because of the ripple effect changes have on the statement of need, SRS, SDD, coding, testing, and maintainability of a system.

11.4.2 Project Risk

Project risk can be estimated qualitatively as shown in Table 11.4. The principal goal of risk analysis is to develop a set of risk aversion strategies. In the context of the design process, a risk aversion strategy is to perform detailed design to build fault-tolerance features into the software architecture or to enhance the design to achieve a more desirable system behavior which will improve safety, security, testability, and maintainability of the system. Recommendations concerning risk aversion strategies are communicated to the risk management group. Risk engineering continues through the software life-cycle. There is constant give and take between risk analysis and risk management processes. This give and take usually is in the form of message passing between the two processes (composition of humans, computers, tools, webware).

The requirements of risk engineering as a potential software product is represented as a superstate in the statechart in Figure 11.12. Using the information already given about the activities in risk analysis and risk management, it is possible to decompose the statechart in Figure 11.12. This will mean putting in condition/action labels on the arcs and decomposing individual states to achieve a better understanding of the risk management process. The required inputs, outputs, and exception conditions of each activity should also be given to assist in software design. Notice that the orthogonality of the statechart in Figure 11.12 suggests that either a multiagent system or layered architecture could be used, with agents or layers connected to a message-passing network. Also notice that a blackboard architecture could be incorporated into the risk management process. Recall that each knowledge source is represented by a condition-action pair. An action is triggered and scheduled for execution whenever the knowledge

TABLE 11.4   Project Risk

IEEE 1044.1-1995 Risk Classification Scheme	Description
High	Fixing anomaly or implementing enhancement has a high risk of negative impact on the project
Medium	Fixing anomaly or implementing enhancement has a medium risk of negative impact on the project
Low	Fixing anomaly or implementing enhancement has little risk of negative impact on the project
Zero	Fixing anomaly or implementing enhancement has a negligible ("zero") risk

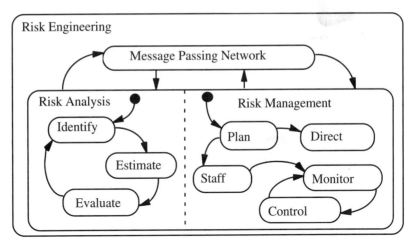

Figure 11.12 Risk engineering statechart.

source condition is satisfied. In a blackboard form of proactive risk management, a knowledge source could have one of the following forms:

<condition>		**<action>**
(risk analysis need)	→	(risk analysis request)
(identify possible source of failure)	→	(risk analysis request)
(anticipated failure)	→	(risk analysis request)
(risk aversion strategy received)	→	(initiate implementation of risk aversion strategy)

It should then be possible to design a risk engineering assistant tool, which could be used by risk engineers to help automate risk analysis and management.

11.5 DESCRIBING SOFTWARE INTERFACES

Specifying a software interface for an architectural component of a software design (i.e., operation, function, or procedure) means identifying the name and type of input and output data as well as exception conditions (constraints) on processing performed by the component. Software interfaces for both internal (intramodular information flow) and external interaction (intermodular communication) must be specified. The specification of software interfaces is illustrated in terms of an obstacle avoidance module for a mobile robot. First, a block diagram of the avoid module is given with minimum detail to give an overview of the basic requirements (Figure 11.13). The sonar module makes it

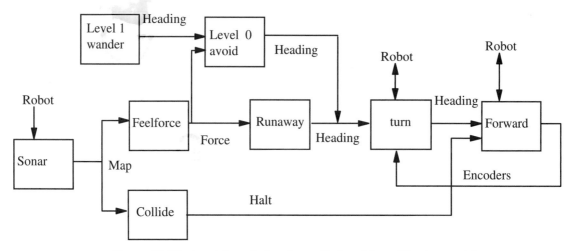

Figure 11.13   Level 0 control system with input from Wander module.

possible for the robot to map its surroundings, detect objects moving toward it, and detect obstacles. The word sonar is a contraction of the words *so*und *na*viga-tion *r*anging. A sonar sensor transmits an ultrasonic pulse and detects the re-flected pulse. The time it takes for a pulse to travel to an object and bounce back gives an indication of the depth of the object. The sonar module on a robot produces a robot-centered map giving the coordinates of obstacles in the path of the robot. The feelforce module sums the results of considering each detected object as a repulsive force and generates a resulting force to be used in changing the position of the robot.

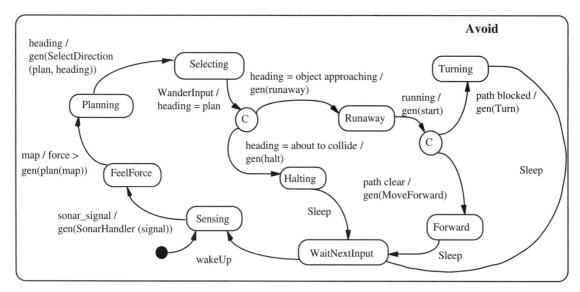

Figure 11.14   Refined statechart for Avoid module.

Whenever something approaches, the robot runs away from it. It is timid. To avoid colliding with a stationary object, it halts and gets its bearings (maps its next move). The wander module computes headings that the robot uses to determine what to do next. The runaway module monitors the ''force'' produced by sonar-detected objects and sends commands to the turn module if the force is above some threshold. The turn and forward modules communicate directly with the robot.

The requirements implicit in the block diagram for the Avoid module in Figure 11.13 can be represented more precisely in a statechart (Figure 11.14). In constructing the statechart, a SonarHandler operation is included to produce a sonar-map (coordinates of objects in the path of the robot) from sonar inputs. The action of SonarHandler causes the Avoid module to enter its FeelForce state. This map produced by the SonarHandler makes it possible for the Avoid module to begin planning, and enter its Planning state. A heading received from the Wander module of the robot (see Figure 11.14) makes it possible to select a direction of travel (the Avoid module enters its Selecting state). Evaluation of the heading (and other information) allows the robot to choose either to run away from an approaching object or halt to avoid a collision.

Based on the statechart in Figure 11.14, an architectural description of the Avoid module can be given concisely in CSP. This will lead to a specification of the interfaces for the Avoid module. The architecture is described in Figure 11.15.

```
Avoid = *(sonar ? {signal} →          /* input from sonar */
  SonarHandler ! (signal) →            /* sonar signal sent to SonarHandler */
  SonarHandler ? map →                 /* sonar map received from SonarHandler */
  plan ! map →                         /* use map to beginning planning next move */
  plan ? force →                       /* estimate of force received from plan */
   Wander ? heading →                  /* receive heading from Wander module */
   SelectDirection ! (force, heading) → /* send force, heading to SelectDirection module */
   SelectDirection ? heading →         /* receive new heading fron SelectDirection */
   (if (heading = object approaching   /* run away if object is approaching */
      and force ≥ threshhold)          /* significant force required */
   then  (runaway(force);
          start(force);                /* start runaway process */
          if path blocked
          then
            turn(heading); wait t
          else if path clear
          then
            MoveForward(heading); wait t
      else if heading = about to collide /* halt if a collision is about to happen */
      halt; wait t))
```

Figure 11.15 Avoid module for robot.

TABLE 11.5   **Sample Software Interfaces**

Routine	Input	Output	Exception Condition
SonarHandler	map: signal	map: (x-coord, y-coord)	none
plan	map: (x-coord, y-coord)	force: real	map $\neq$ empty
Wander	status: record	heading: (x-coord, y-coord)	none
SelectDirection	force: real, heading: (x-coord, y-coord)	force: real	force > 0
runaway	force: real		force $\geq$ threshold
turn	heading: (x-coord, y-coord)	control signal to robot motor	none
wait t	t: int	none	$t > 0$
MoveForward	heading: (x-coord, y-coord)	control signal to robot motor	none
halt	none	control signal to robot motor	none

The Avoid module is a revision of the same module given earlier in Table 11.3. In the new version of the Avoid module, input and output to a number of processes (hidden software routines) are represented: SonarHandler, plan, Wander (a module in the next layer above the Avoid module), SelectDirection, runaway, turn, wait, MoveForward, and halt. The specification of interfaces for these routines is given in Table 11.5.

11.6 ALGORITHMS

For each processing element of a selected software architecture, it is necessary to give an algorithm that explains how the processing element functions. An *algorithm* is a complete, effective, finite, step-by-step procedure for performing a task. A *complete* algorithm is one where all of the necessary steps are given. An *effective* procedure is one that always produces a result in a finite number of steps. A common method for representing algorithms is to create a control flow diagram called a flowchart, which describe sequences of operations on data. A flowchart specifies the operations, data (input and output) needed to compute a result. The basic flowchart symbols are given in Figure 11.16. Start, stop, and control points are represented with a circle. A control point is a circle labeled with a numeral, and is used to simplify flowcharts. Instead of numerous drawing arcs back to the same control point, each arc is connected to a circle with the

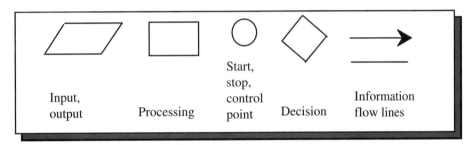

Figure 11.16 Basic flowcharting symbols.

same label. We illustrate this idea in terms of a flowchart for a high-level algorithm for risk analysis (Figure 11.17). Since risk analysis continues indefinitely long, the wait process in the figure represents a timer that periodically wakes up the risk analysis process and triggers an inspection of a message queue. If the message queue is empty, the process goes back to sleep. Otherwise, risk analysis begins by identifying the sources of a particular risk identified in a message received from the risk management process. After a risk average strategy has been output, the risk analysis process goes back to sleep. Notice that by inserting a control point (a circle labeled with a 2) just before the read-message-queue trapezoid, it is possible to exit from the risk average strategy process box and see if another message has arrived before sleeping.

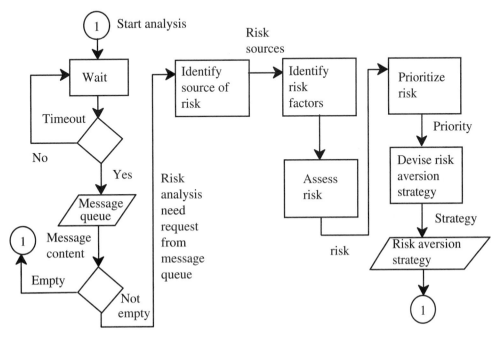

Figure 11.17 Flowchart for risk analysis method.

To achieve a better understanding of an algorithm in flowchart form, the boxes representing processing can be decomposed into separate flowcharts giving the detailed processing steps. In other words, algorithms are developed incrementally by repeated refinements of processing elements represented in a flowchart. For example, the risk assessment box in the flowchart in Figure 11.17 can be decomposed to reveal how to measure risk. Risks are measured in terms of the combined effect of the likelihood of a source of risk occurring and the magnitude of the severity of a failure due to technical, cost, and scheduling factors for a project. Likelihood of risk occurring is measured in terms of the magnitude of likelihood of failure factors (maturity, complexity, and dependency) concerning hardware and software used in a development project. Let P_f be the probability of failure of the hardware and software calculated in terms of the likelihood factors. Let C_f be a measure of the severity of the failure due to changes in the severity factors (technical, cost, scheduling) for a project. Then risk is computed as a probabilistic sum as follows:

$$\text{risk} = P_f + C_f - P_f * C_f$$

$$\{\text{Risk assessment as probabilistic sum}\}$$

The terms of the risk assessment formula are computed using the probabilities and weights given in Table 11.6.

Let C_{tech}, C_{cost}, and C_{sched} represent the severity of risk of failure due technical, cost, and scheduling factors, respectively. In addition, let w_{tech}, w_{cost}, and w_{sched} be the weights (degrees of importance) for C_{tech}, C_{cost}, and C_{sched}, respectively. Notice that the sum of the weights for severity levels must also equal 1. Then P_f (likelihood of risk) and C_f (severity of risk) are computed with the following formulas:

$$P_f = w_1 P_{M_{hw}} + w_2 P_{M_{sw}} + w_3 P_{C_{hw}} + w_4 P_{C_{sw}} + w_5 P_D$$

$$C_f = w_{tech} C_{tech} + w_{cost} C_{cost} + w_{sched} C_{sched}$$

TABLE 11.6   Probabilities and Weights Needed to Compute Risk

Probabilities to Compute	Explanation
P_{Mhw}	Probability of failure due to degree of hardware maturity
P_{Msw}	Probability of failure due to degree of software maturity
P_{Chw}	Probability of failure due to degree of hardware complexity
P_{Csw}	Probability of failure due to degree of software maturity
P_D	Probability of failure due to dependency on other items (existing system, contractors, scheduling, performance)
w_1, w_2, w_3, w_4, w_5	Weights (degrees of importance) Note: $$\sum_{i=1}^{5} w_i = 1$$

TABLE 11.7   Template for Computing Likelihood Values

Maturity (Hardware) P_{Mhw}	Maturity (Software) P_{Msw}	Complexity (Hardware) P_{Chw}	Complexity (Software) P_{Csw}	Dependency Factors P_D
(0.1) Existing	(0.1) Existing	(0.1) Simple design	(0.1) Simple design	(0.1) Existing system
(0.3) Minor redesign	(0.3) Minor redesign	(0.3) Minor increase	(0.3) Minor increase	(0.3) Scheduling
(0.5) Major change	(0.5) Major change	(0.5) Moderate increases	(0.5) Moderate increases	(0.5) Performance
(0.7) New, similar hardware	(0.7) New, similar software	(0.7) Significant increases	(0.7) Significant increases	(0.7) Scheduling with new system
(0.9) State-of-the-art hardware	(0.9) State-of-the-art software	(0.9) Externally complex	(0.9) Externally complex	(0.9) Performance depends on new system

A straightforward way to organize the information needed to compute the likelihood and severity values is to set up a table for each one. New tables would be constructed for each project. Computations of likelihood values would be made with the template with *suggested* magnitudes shown in Table 11.7. The magnitudes are suggested by Thayer and Royce (1990), and are unlikely to fit each project. Each of the entries could be computed in terms of some reasonable distribution of the values relative to domain knowledge concerning each of the factors. For example, maturity levels could be computed in terms of the length of time that either hardware or software has been in use in an organization with the assumption that an organization always starts with the most recent version. Let t be the number of months of usage, and the likelihood of failure due to the maturity of the hardware and software be computed using $\exp(-t/k)$. We already know that probability of failure decreases as the number of months that hardware and software are in use increases. Assuming that an organization maintains the hardware and software from 1 to 36 months, a graph of maturity levels is given in Figure 11.18 with $k = 20$. The value of k should be adjusted and will depend on how fast a group can adjust to changes in hardware and software. A more mature organization would use smaller values of k to estimate the likelihood of failure for the maturity risk factor. For example, for $k = 5$, the maturity levels graph is given in Figure 11.19.

Magnitudes of the likelihood of failure due to complexity and dependencies can be estimated in the same way. An approach to computing the severity levels for the technical, cost and scheduling factors for a project is shown in Table 11.8. Again, notice that the severity estimates are subjective, and should be computed more carefully in relative to a particular organization and project. The same approach suggested for computing likelihood values can also be used

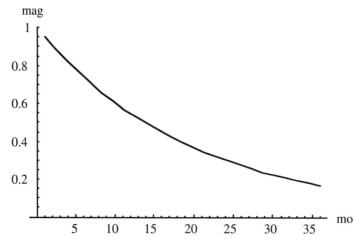

Figure 11.18 Likelihood of failure relative to slow increase in maturity levels.

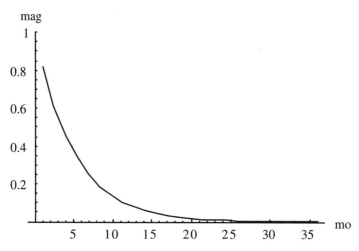

Figure 11.19 Likelihood of failure relative to faster increase in maturity levels.

TABLE 11.8 Estimating Magnitudes of Severity Factors

Magnitude of Severity	Technical Factor C_{tech}	Cost Factor C_{cost}	Scheduling Factor C_{sched}
0.1 (Low)	Unimportant	Within budget, minimal changes	Scheduling changes have little impact
0.3 (Minor)	Minor reductions in performance	Budget exceeded 1 to 5%	Minor scheduling slippages (<1 mo)
0.5 (Moderate)	Moderate reduction in performance	Budget increases 5 to 20%	Schedule slippages (<3 mo)
0.7 (Significant)	Significant decrease in performance	Budget increases 20 to 50%	Schedule slippages (<6 mo)
0.9 (High)	Technical goals can not be achieved	Budget increases over 50%	Schedule slippages over 6 mo

TABLE 11.9 Sample Likelihood and Severity Estimates

Likelihood Estimates	$P_{M_{hw}}$	$P_{M_{sw}}$	$P_{C_{hw}}$	$P_{C_{sw}}$	P_D
	0.1	0.45	0.2	0.5	0.7
Weights	0.1	0.2	0.1	0.2	0.4

Severity Estimates	C_{tech}	C_{cost}	C_{sched}
	0.2	0.7	0.4
Weights	0.1	0.6	0.3

to estimating severity levels. Putting all of this together, sample estimates of likelihood and severity are given in Table 11.9. For simplicity but unrealistically, it is assumed that all factors are equally important and have a weight of 1. Then risk for the sample values in Table 11.9 are computed as follows:

$$P_f = w_1 P_{M_{hw}} + w_2 P_{M_{sw}} + w_3 P_{C_{hw}} + w_4 P_{C_{sw}} + w_5 P_D$$
$$= 0.1(0.1) + 0.2(0.45) + 0.1(0.2) + 0.2(0.5) + 0.4(0.7)$$
$$= 0.5$$
$$C_f = w_{tech} C_{tech} + w_{cost} C_{cost} + w_{sched} C_{sched}$$
$$= 0.1(0.2) + 0.6(0.7) + 0.3(0.4)$$
$$= .56$$
$$risk = P_f + C_f - P_f C_f$$
$$= 0.5 + 0.56 - (0.5)(0.56)$$
$$= 0.78$$

With this information, we can now construct a flowchart representing a decomposition of the risk assessment block in the flowchart in Figure 11.17. The decomposition flowchart is given in Figure 11.20.

Algorithms can also be specified in some form of pseudocode, which easily translates into executable code. The basic syntax for a pseudocode form of algorithm is given in Figure 11.21. Sample pseudocode for risk analysis (derived from the flowchart in Figure 11.20) is given in Figure 11.22. The usual if-then-else (conditional) and while, repeat (iteration) control structures are used in the processing part of the pseudocode. A function heading has the form identifier(input-list; output-list). Borrowing from Occam, the PAR and PAR End constructs are used to specify concurrent operations. Constraints are an optional part of an algorithm and flow naturally from the exception conditions specified for software design interfaces. Constraints are written in VDM style

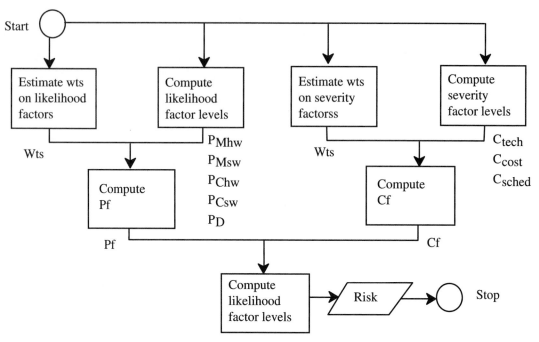

Figure 11.20   Algorithm for risk assessment.

using a combination of mathematics and logic to verify the correctness of the algorithm.

Notice that since the value of timeout is never changed (its value is always true in Figure 11.22, the waiting continues for another t ticks of the hidden timer after each derivation of a risk aversion strategy. No check is made to see if the queue has messages until the wait process finishes its next round of ticks. This suggests that the pseudocode could be refined to make it possible to check the message queue after a strategy has been found and before waiting resumes.

Input list	/* name: data type */
Output list	/* name: data type */
Constraints (pre- and post-conditions}	/* boolean conditions on inputs and outputs */
{	
operation$_1$; ... ; operation$_n$;	/* transformation of inputs to produce outputs */
}	

Figure 11.21   Pseudocode syntax.

```
input:    message_queue: list of messages;
          message: (date, time, item_to_be_evaluated);
output:  risk_aversion_strategy: (source_of_risk, likelihood, severity, list_of_steps)
post: risk_aversion_strategy    ≠ ( )                    /*strategy is not an empty list */
{
   timeout, empty, queue_status: bool;
   empty := true;
   timeout := true;
   repeat                                                /* begin infinite loop */
     if not timeout then wait(t);                        /* wait t ticks of clock */
     read(message_queue; queue_status,message);          /* check message queue */
     if queue_status = empty then {   }                  /* continue waiting if queue empty */

     else if queue_status    ≠ empty                     /* begin processing need request */
         then {
           Identity_source_of_risk(message; risk);       /* output risk */
           Identify_risk_factors;                        /* likelihood and severity */
           Assess_risk;                                  /* Compute risk */
           Prioritize(risk, likelihood, severity; priority); /* output priority */
           Devise_strategy(risk, likelihood, severity,
                      priority; risk_aversion_strategy);  /* output risk aversion strategy */
         }
   forever;
}
```

Figure 11.22 Pseudocode for risk analysis.

11.7 DETAILED SOFTWARE DESIGN

Detailed software design (also called design elaboration) culminates the design process. IEEE Std. 610.12-1990 describes detailed design as a process of refining and expanding preliminary design of a system or component to the extent that the design is sufficiently complete to be implemented. Detailed design results in a complete, verified description of the software architectures, key algorithms, interfaces, and assumptions about each component of the design. Detailed design begins with an assessment of the chosen software architecture and possible alternative architectures to ensure that the most satisfactory architecture is subjected to refinement.

Necessary Features		Candidate Architecture 1			Candidate Architecture 2		
Optional Features	wt		score	wt x score		score	wt x score
Performance total =							

Figure 11.23   Structure of Kepner-Tregoe table.

11.7.1 Evaluating Alternative Architectures

The selection of the "right" architecture to use in a software design is demanding. Notice that in many cases, a particular architecture represents a mixture of architectural styles. Examples of this have already been seen with the Brooks' robot control system, Hayes-Roth Adaptive Intelligent System, and Risk Engineering Assistant. A reasonable approach to solving the problem of selecting an architecture is to devise a scoring system so that architectures can be compared. A version of the Kepner-Tregoe Evaluation Table can be used to do this (Kepner & Tregoe, 1965). The structure of this table is given in Figure 11.23. To set up a Kepner-Tregoe Evaluation Table for a particular project, it is necessary to itemize the necessary (must have) and optional (wanted) features that architectures should possess. It is also necessary to assign weights to the optional features. Architectures failing to satisfy the necessary requirements are immediately eliminated. Then the choice of the best among the remaining architectures is guided by the scoring system in Figure 11.23. We illustrate this approach to choosing an architecture in terms of developing a Risk Engineering Assistant (Table 11.10).

11.7.2 Incremental Improvement of Selected Architectures

The incremental improvement of a selected software architecture can be achieved by refining the preliminary architectural description. How this is done will vary depending on the system being developed. This incremental development of the architectural description should continue until the architecture is under-

TABLE 11.10 Risk Engineering Assistant Architecture Evaluation

Necessary Features	Agent Architecture			Layered Architecture			CHAM Architecture	
• Easy to implement	Yes			Yes			No	
• Message passing	Yes			Yes			Yes	
• Familiarity	Yes			Yes			No	(Reject)

Optional Features	Wt	Score	Wt × Score	Score	Wt × Score		Wt × Score	
• Parallel computing	0.2	Yes 45	9	Yes 20	4			
• Genetic	0.5	No 0	0	No 0	0			
• Short design time	0.9	Yes 30	27	Yes 70	63			
• Extensible	0.7	Yes 90	63	Yes 95	85.5			
• Flexible	0.9	Yes 95	85.5	Yes 95	85.5			
Performance total =			184.5	(Select)	219			

stood, and the description provides a straightforward bridge to implementation. An example of incremental development of an architecture has already been given in terms of the architectural description of the Avoid competence module for a mobile robot. By way of a second, and simpler illustration of incremental improvement of an architecture, a preliminary and refined description of the risk analysis module for a risk engneering assistant will be given. Recall from the statechart for a risk engineering assistant that risk analysis and risk management are represented by orthogonal statecharts connected by a message passing network. The statechart representation can be realized in a layered architecture like the one shown in Figure 11.24. The beauty of a layered architecture is that it represents not only the possibility of parallel computation but also increasing levels of abstraction. Layer 0 (risk management) might be described as the source of actions in a software development environment. Its decisions will cause changes in resource allocation, budgeting, and software and hardware acquisition and utilization. Layer 1 (risk analysis) is once removed, and is concerned with mathematical models and risk aversion strategies, not with actions. The architecture

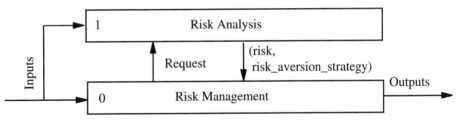

Figure 11.24 Layered architecture for risk engineering assistant.

risk_analysis = *(risk_management ? (request) →   /* risk analysis request received */
    identify(request; sources_of_risk) →   /* send request to identify module */
    estimate(sources_of_risk; risk) →   /* estimate module computes risk */
    evaluate(risk, sources_of_risk;
    risk_aversion_strategy) →   /* determine strategy */
    risk_management ! risk_aversion_strategy → SKIP)

Figure 11.25   Description of risk analysis module.

of the complete risk engineering assistant can be described concisely in CSP as follows:

```
RiskEngineeringAssistant = (message_passing_network ‖
                            risk_analysis ‖
                            risk_management)
```

Each of the processing components of the architecture can be decomposed to achieve a better understanding of the software. Recall that the statechart for risk analysis has three basic components: identify, estimate, and evaluate. The risk analysis module can be described in Figure 11.25. The notation op(in-list; out-list) is used in the description in Figure 11.25. The result computed by an operation is an event. For example, the result computed operation estimate(sources_of_risk; risk) is an estimate of the risk associated with the identified sources of risk. The operation SKIP is used to terminate a computation in an orderly fashion. The *-notation indicates that risk analysis is repeated an indefinite number of times, which is realistic. Only a preliminary view of the architecture of the risk analysis module is given in Figure 11.25. The next step is to refine this description. We illustrate this in terms of a decomposition of the estimate operation.

```
estimate(sources_of_risk; risk) = (identify? likelihood_factors, severity_factors →
(estimate_likelihood_wts(likelihood_factors; Lwts) → SKIP ‖
estimate_likelihood_levels(likelihood_factors; Pmhw, Pmsw, Pchw, Pcsw, Pd) → SKIP ‖
estimate_severity_wts(severity_factors, Swts) → SKIP ‖
estimate_severity_levels(severity_factors, Ctech, Ccost, Csched) → SKIP);
(compute_likelihood(Pmhw, Pmsw, Pchw, Pcsw, Pd, Lwts; Pf) → SKIP ‖
compute_severity(Ctech, Ccost, Csched, Swts; Cf → SKIP);
compute_risk(Pf, Cf; risk)
)
```

The description of risk analysis reflects fact that concurrent processing is possible. For example, estimates of the both kinds of weights as well as estimates of the levels can be done in parallel. Each of the processing elements in the architectural

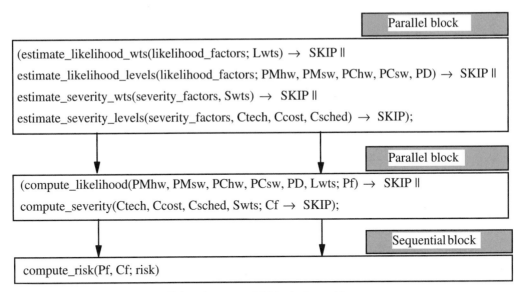

Figure 11.26 Parallel and sequential blocks in architecture.

description will lead to algorithms giving the steps needed to obtain results. The architectural description shows the structure of the software while hiding the details that will be needed to implement the architecture. The SKIP operation is put into the description both to indicate that a processing element has completed its work and to maintain the syntactical requirements of the language. That is, it is necessary that every process have the form

$$event \rightarrow process$$

Also, notice that the architecture for risk analysis contains a mixture of concurrent and sequential processing summarized in the blocks in Figure 11.26. Refinements and improvements of the architectures are followed by validation, added risk analysis, a complete description of the interfaces, and incremental improvements of required algorithms.

11.7.3 Incremental Improvement of Algorithms

Incremental improvement of algorithms is a necessary part of detailed design. This is accomplished by decomposing the parts of an algorithm until an algorithm is completely understood. This effort complements the refinements of the architectural descriptions of a system. For example, the parts of the algorithm represented in the flowchart for risk analysis given earlier can be refined further. A sample refinement of this algorithm written in pseudocode is given in Figure 11.27.

```
input:   source_of_risk, likelihood_factors, severity_factors;
output:  risk
post:    0 ≤ risk ≤ 1                                    /* risk belongs to [0, 1] */
{
  read(source_of_risk, likelihood_factors, severity_factors);
  PAR
   estimate_likelihood_wts(likelihood_factors; w1, w2, w3, w4, w5);
   estimate_likelihood_levels(likelihood_factors; P_Mhw, P_Msw, P_Chw, P_Csw, P_D);
   estimate_severity_wts(severity_factors, wtech, wcost, wsched);
   estimate_severity_levels(severity_factors, C_tech, C_cost, C_sched);
  PAR End;
  PAR
   Pf := w1P_mhw + w2P_msw + w3P_chw + w4P_csw + w5P_D;
   Cf := wtechC_tech + wcostC_cost + wschedC_sche ;
  PAR End;
  risk := Pf + Cf - PfCf;
}
```

Figure 11.27 Refinement of risk analysis algorithm.

11.8 SUMMARY

Approaches to validating software designs and performing risk analysis are studied in this chapter. Validation of a software design is made easier by setting up a hypertext document with links between key parts of a design in a design document and corresponding parts of the requirements. There are a number of advantages to setting up a hypertext document. First, team members can cross-check design components with requirements with a web browser. Second, the hypertext documents have a desirable side effect: collaboration between software engineering team members is made easier. Third, it is fairly easy to add missing links that are discovered during the trace of a design.

11.9 PROBLEMS

> **Nothing has really happened until it has been recorded.**
>
> —Virginia Woolf

1. (Case Study: Validation and Risk Assessment for tATC). A statechart for the behavior of the airspace module in a training program for air traffic control (tACT) is given in Figure 11.28 (Agatep et al., 1997).
   (a) Give a complete architectural description for the airspace module described in Figure 11.28.

(b) Validate the architectural description in (a).

(c) Give a risk assessment of the airspace module described in (a).

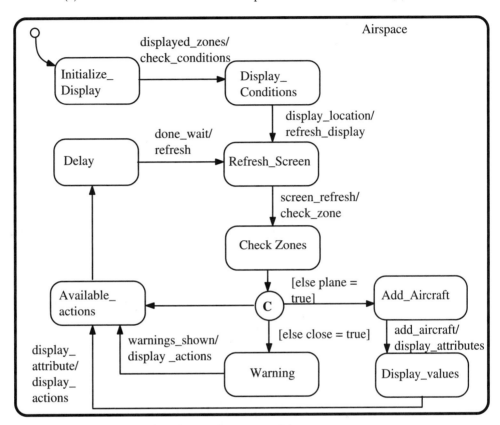

Figure 11.28 Statechart for an airspace module.

2. A temperature control system is described in Figure 11.29.
   (a) Give a statechart description of the temperature control system in Figure 11.29. The arcs in your statechart should have condition-action labels.
   (b) Using CSP, give an architectural description of the control system described in (a).
   (c) Validate the architectural design in (b).
   (d) Give a risk assessment of the control system described in (a) and (b).

3. Give a risk assessment of C++ programs.

4. Give a risk assessment of the Unix operating system.

5. Give a risk assessment of the Windows95 operating system.

6. Give a risk assessment of the Windows NT operating system.

7. A layered architecture for a robot control system is given in Figure 11.30.
   (a) Give a collection of statecharts to describe in detail the behavior of the system in Figure 11.30.

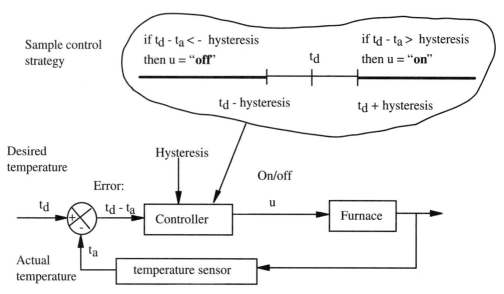

Figure 11.29   Description of a temperature control system.

(b) Using CSP, give a complete architectural description of the system described in (a).
(c) Validate the architecture in (b).
(d) Give a risk assessment of the system described in (a) and (b).

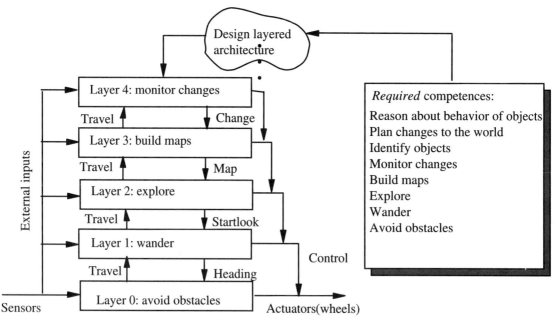

Figure 11.30   Statechart for robot control system.

8. A sample mesh architecture is given in Figure 11.31. Give:
   (a) A risk assessment message-passing in the mesh architecture described in Figure 11.31.
   (b) A risk response strategy based on the risk assessment in (a).

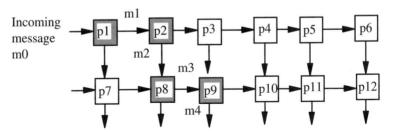

Figure 11.31 Sample mesh architecture.

9. Give a risk assessment of the Kepner-Tregoe scoring system whenever it is used to evaluate hardware and/or software.

10. An evolving mesh architecture is shown in Figure 11.32.
    (a) Give a statechart description of the evolving mesh.
    (b) Give a CSP description of the architecture of the evolving mesh described in (a).
    (c) Validate the architectural description in (b).
    (d) Give a risk assessment of evolving mesh architectures.

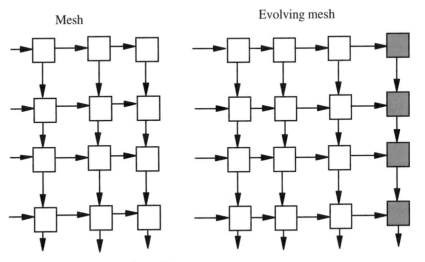

Figure 11.32 Evolving mesh architecture.

11. A pipeline process is described in Figure 11.33.
    (a) Give a statechart description of the pipeline process in Figure 11.33.
    (b) Give a CSP description of the architecture of the pipeline process described in (a).
    (c) Validate the architectural description in (b).
    (d) Give a risk assessment of pipeline processes.

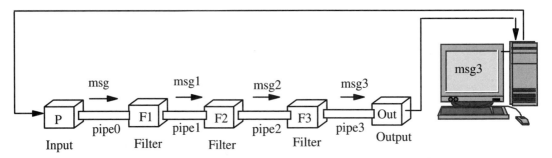

Figure 11.33   Pipeline process.

12. A parallel pipeline process is described in Figure 11.34.
  (a) Give a statechart description of the parallel pipeline process in Figure 11.34.
  (b) Give a CSP description of the architecture of the parallel pipeline process described in (a).
  (c) Validate the architectural description in (b).
  (d) Give a risk assessment of parallel pipeline processes.

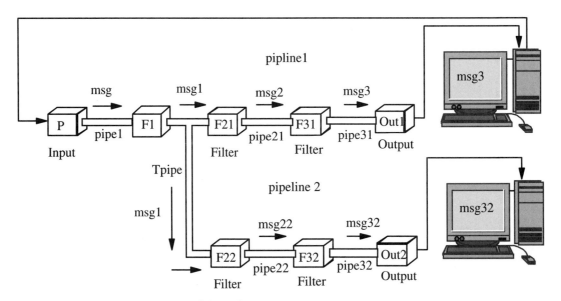

Figure 11.34   Parallel pipeline process.

13. A statechart describing an adaptive intelligent system is given in Figure 11.35.
  (a) Give a decomposition of the statechart description in Figure 11.35.
  (b) Give a CSP description of the architecture of the adaptive intelligent system described in (a).
  (c) Validate the architectural description in (b).
  (d) Give a risk assessment of adaptive intelligent systems.

14. A statechart for a software reuse library system is given in Figure 11.36.

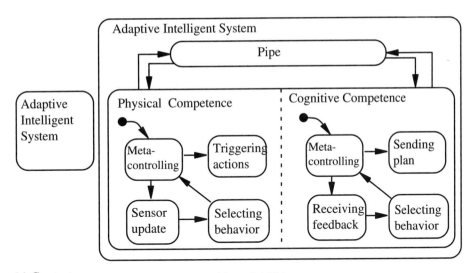

(a) Context-level AIS

(b) Decomposition of AIS into competences

Figure 11.35 Statechart for an adaptive intelligent system.

(a) Give a decomposition of the statechart description in Figure 11.36.
(b) Give a CSP description of the architecture of the software reuse library system described in (a).
(c) Validate the architectural description in (b).
(d) Perform risk analysis on the software reuse library system as described in (a) and (b). To do this, compute all necessary weights, likelihood and severity levels, and derive a final estimate.

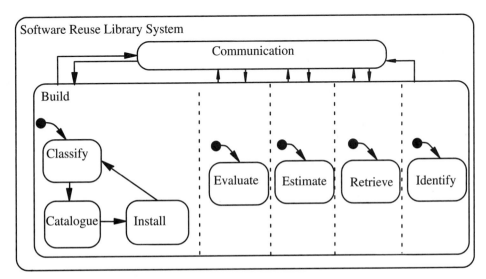

Figure 11.36 Statechart for a software reuse library system.

15. Construct a Kepner-Tregoe evaluation table in terms of the architectures identified in problem 14.

16. Give an objective method of computing the weights for the Kepner-Tregoe table in problem 16. Hint: pick an appropriate distribution function to compute weights between 0 and 1 and which match your intuition of how the weights should be selected.

17. Construct a Kepner-Tregoe evaluation table in terms of competing architectures for the communication module of the software reuse library system (pipeline, message-passing network). Identify "must have" and "wish list" criteria to be used in the table, and compute the weights to complete the table, and select the best choice.

18. (Tracing a design with links between window frames). It is possible to organize a web page display of software engineering documents with separate windows called frames. This description of how this is done is based on a study by Cormier and others (1998). Three HTML tags are used by Netscape and Internet Explorer to create a frame document: <frameset>, <frame>, and <noframes> (Musciano & Kennedy, 1997). A sample HTML text needed to create a multi-window display is given in Figure 11.37. The individual window frames are defined by separate source files. In this case, there are three source files: mainmenu.html, submenu.html, and body.html. Each source file is an HTML file that organizes a separate window frame. Since we are interested in organizing software development documents, a display is split into windows relative to software development documents in Figure 11.38. The mainmenu file controlling the display in Figure 11.38 is given in Figure 11.39.

The submenu of the mainmenu in Figure 11.37 is defined by

```
<html>
 <head>
  <title>
  SRS blank form
  </title>
 </head>
</HTML>
```

The body of the mainmenu in Figure 11.37 is defined by

```
<html>
 <head>
  <title>
  SRS blank form
  </title>
 </head>
</HTML>
```

```
<html>
<head><title>SRS and Design</title></head>
<frameset cols="200,*">
<frame src=mainmenu.html name="menu"
scrolling="auto" marginheight=5 marginwidth=5>
<frameset rows="150,*">
<frame src=submenu.html name="submenu"
scrolling="auto" marginheight=0 marginwidth=0>
<frame src=body.html name="body" >
</frameset>
</frameset>
</html>
```

Figure 11.37 Setup for a multiwindow frame display for tracing documents.

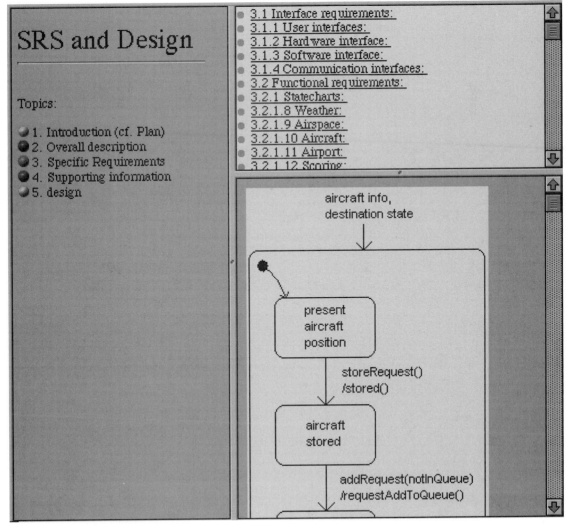

Figure 11.38 Multiple window frames in organizing documents.

```
<html>
<head>
<title>Main menu for the side </title></head>
<body background="newback2.gif ">
<base TARGET=submenu>
<br><font size=+3> SRS and Design </font><hr><br>
<a> Topics:</a><br><br>
<A HREF="submenu1.html">
<IMG SRC="yellow_ball.gif "border=0 HEIGHT=10 WIDTH=10></a>
1. Introduction (cf. Plan) <br>
<A HREF="submenu2.html">
<IMG SRC="red_ball.gif " border=0 HEIGHT=10 WIDTH=10><b
target="body"></b></a>
href="submenu2.html"
2. Overall description <br>
<A HREF="submenu3.html">
<IMG SRC="orange_ball.gif " border=0 HEIGHT=10 WIDTH=10></a>
3. Specific Requirements <br>
<A HREF="submenu4.html">
<IMG SRC="purple_ball.gif " border=0 HEIGHT=10 WIDTH=10></a>
4. Supporting information <br>
<a href="design.html">
<img src="yellow_ball.gif " border=0 HEIGHT=10 WIDTH=10></a>
5. design <br>
<br><br><br><br>
</body></base>
</html>
```

Figure 11.39   The mainmenu.html for a window frame.

Do the following relative to requirements documents for a training program for air traffic controllers:

(a) submenu1.html (1. Introduction) referenced in Figure 11.39 is defined as follows:

```
<HTML>
<BODY text="00ffff" bgcolor="ffffff"
<UL>
<base target = "body">
<LI><A HREF=b1.html#1>1 Introduction: </A>
<LI><A HREF=b1.html#0>1.01 Needs Statements: </A>
<LI><A HREF=b1.html#0>1.02 Plan: </A>
<LI><A HREF=b1.html#0>1.03 Software Engineering Guide: </A)
<LI><A HREF=b1.html#1.1>1.1 Purpose: </A>
<LI><A HREF=b1.html#1.2>1.2 Scope: </A>
<LI><A HREF=b1.html#1.3>1.3 Definitions, acronyms, and abbreviations: </A>
<LI><A HREF=b1.html#1.4>1.4 References: </A>
<LI><A HREF=b1.html#1.5>1.5 Overview: </A>
</UL>
</base>
</HTML>
```

Define the components of submenu1.html. Your Introduction should have links to corresponding parts of the Needs Statement, Plan, and Software Engineering Guide.

(b) Define b1.html (1.01 Needs Statements) referenced in (a).

(c) Define b1.html (1.02 Plan) referenced in (a).

(d) Define b1.html (1.03 Software Engineering Guide) referenced in (a).

(e) Define submenu2.html (2. Overall description) referenced in Figure 11.39 relative to:

2.1 Product Perspective

2.2 Product Functions

2.3 User Characteristics

2.4 Constraints

2.5 Assumptions and Dependencies

2.6 Apportioning of Requirements

(f) Define each of the components of submenu2.html in (e). Your submenu2.html document should be linked to the Needs Statement, Plan, and Software Engineering Guide. Be sure to include drawings, charts, tables linked to needs, plan, and guide to make it easier to do traces of the requirements.

(g) Define submenu3.html (3. Specific Requirements) in Figure 11.39:

3.1 Interface Requirements

  3.1.1 User interface

  3.1.2 Hardware interface

  3.1.3 Software interface

  3.1.4 Communication interfaces

3.2 Functional Requirements

  3.2.1 Statecharts

    3.2.1.8 Weather

    3.2.1.9 Airspace

    3.2.1.10 Aircraft

    3.2.1.11 Airport

    3.2.1.12 Score

  3.2.2 Process description

  3.2.3 Data construct specification

  3.2.4 Data dictionary

3.3 Performance requirements (includes Kiviat diagrams)

3.4 Logical database requirements

3.5 Design constraints

3.6 Software system attributes (includes Kiviat diagrams)

3.7 Organizing the specific requirements

(h) Define each of the components of submenu3.html in (g). Your submenu3.html document should be linked to the Needs Statement, Plan, and Software Engineering Guide. Be sure to include drawings, charts, tables linked to needs, plan, and guide to make it easier to do traces of the requirements.

(i) Define submenu4.html (4. Supporting information) in Figure 11.39:

4.1 Keyword Index for t-ATCA

4.2 Appendices

(j) Define each of the components of submenu4.html in (i). Your submenu4.html document should be linked to the Needs Statement, Plan, and Software Engineering Guide. Be sure to include drawings, charts, tables linked to needs, plan, and guide to make it easier to do traces of the requirements.

19. (Tracing a design with links between window frames). Do the following:
    (a) Define submenu5.html (5. Design) in Figure 11.39:

    5.1 Architectures Chosen
    5.1.1 Architecture of weather system
    5.1.2 Architecture of airspace system
    5.1.3 Architecture of aircraft system
    5.1.4 Architecture of airport system
    5.1.5 Architecture of score system
    5.2 Detailed Architectural Descriptions
    5.2.1 Detailed architecture of weather system
    5.2.2 Detailed architecture of airspace system
    5.2.3 Detailed architecture of aircraft system
    5.2.4 Detailed architecture of airport system
    5.2.5 Detailed architecture of score system
    5.3 Validation of Design
    5.4 Risk Analysis

    (b) Define each of the components of submenu5.html in (a). Your submenu5.html document should be linked to the Requirements, Plan, and Software Engineering Guide. Be sure to include drawings, charts, tables linked to requirements, plan, and guide to make it easier to do traces of the requirements.

20. There are a number of risks related to air traffic control. Do the following:
    (a) Give a taxonomy of air traffic control risks. The taxonomy should be organized relative to risk classes (weather, airspace, aircraft, airport), risk elements (e.g., cloud ceiling, humidity, number of aircraft, airspace zones), and attributes (e.g., scale, stability, aircraft control, air space display, schedule, delays, emergencies, communication, and so on).
    (b) Give a statechart for a risk management module for the training program for air traffic controllers.
    (c) Select the architectures in the design of risk management software for the tATC described with statecharts in (b).

21. Design a hypertext document to cross-reference the architectures and requirements described in 1(b) and (c).

11.10   REFERENCES

Agatep, R., Evans, D., Inthalansy, S., et al. *t-ATCA*. Report, Department of Electrical and Computer Engineering, University of Manitoba, 1997.

Boehm, B.W., Ed. *Software Risk Management*. IEEE Computer Society Press, Los Alamitos, CA 1989a. p. 434.

Boehm, B.W. *Tutorial: Software Risk Management*. IEEE Computer Society Press, Washington, D.C., 1989b.

Boehm, B.W. A spiral model of development and enhancement. *IEEE Computer,* **21:** 21–72, 1988.

Carr, M.J., Konda, S.L., Monarch, I., et al. *Taxonomy-Based Risk Identification.* Technical report CMU/SEI-93-TR-6, Carnegie Mellon University Software Engineering Institute, 1993. Available from *http://www.rai.com.*

Charette, R.N. Risk management. *Encyclopedia of Software Engineering.* Wiley, New York, 1994.

Cormier, S., Dack, N., Orenstein, O., Kaikhosrawkiani, F. *ATC Trainer Prototype.* Report, Department of Electrical and Computer Engineering, University of Manitoba, 1998.

Davis, A.M. *Software Requirements: Objects, Functions, and States.* Prentice-Hall, NJ, 1993.

Dorfman, M., Thayer, R.H. *Standards, Guidelines, and Examples on System and Software Requirements Engineering.* IEEE Computer Society Press, Los Alamitos, CA, 1990.

Gluch, D.P. *An Experiment in Software Development Risk Information Analysis.* Technical report CMU/SEI-95-TR-014, Carnegie Mellon University Software Engineering Institute, 1995. Available from *http://www.rai.com.*

Graham, I.S. *The HTML Sourcebook: A Complete Guide to HTML 3.0.* Wiley, New York, 1996.

IEEE Std. 1074-1995. IEEE Standard for Developing Software Life Cycle Processes. In *IEEE Standards Collection Software Engineering.* IEEE, Piscataway, NJ, 1997.

IEEE Std. 1016.1-1993. IEEE Guide to Software Design Descriptions. In *IEEE Standards Collection Software Engineering.* IEEE, Piscataway, NJ, 1997.

IEEE Std. 1016-1987. IEEE Recommended Practice for Software Design Descriptions. In *IEEE Standards Collection Software Engineering.* IEEE, NJ, 1997.

Kepner C.H., Tregoe, B.B. *The Rational Manager.* McGraw-Hill, New York. 1965.

Marciniak, J.J. Reviews and audits. In *Software Engineering.* M. Dorfman, R. H. Thayer, Eds. IEEE Computer Society Press, Los Alimitos, CA, pp. 256–276, 1997.

Merritt, S. Software reuse. In *Encyclopedia of Software Engineering.* Wiley, New York, 1994.

Musciano, C., Kennedy, B. *HTML: The Definitive Guide.* O'Reilly & Associates, Sebastopol, CA, 1997.

Musa, J.D., Iannino, A., Okumoto, K. Software Reliability. McGraw-Hill Publishing Co., New York, 1990.

Palmer, J.D. Traceability. In *Software Engineering.* M. Dorfman, R. Thayer. IEEE Computer Society Press, Los Alamitos, CA, pp. 266–276, 1997.

Perry, T.S. In search of the future of air traffic control. *IEEE Spectrum,* **34**(8):18–35, 1997.

Shumate, K. Design. In *Encyclopedia of Software Engineering.* Wiley, New York, 1994.

Thayer R.H., Royce, W.W. *Software System Engineering.* IEEE Computer Society Press, Los Alimitos, CA, 1990.

CHAPTER 12
Software Testing

The principal objective of software testing is to
gain confidence in the software.
—P.D. COWARD, 1997

Aims

- Explore dynamic and static testing methods
- Identify and experiment with black and white box testing
- Analyze advantages and limitations of testing methods

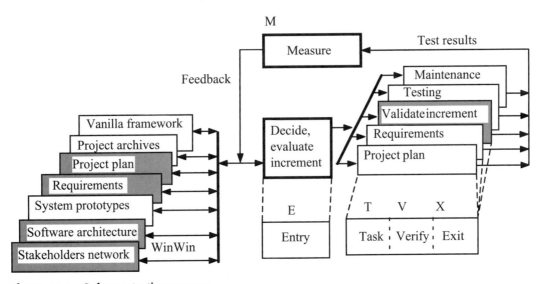

Figure 12.1 Software testing process.

12.1 INTRODUCTION

Software testing determines when a software system can be released and gauges
future performance. The context for testing is shown in the software process
model in Figure 12.1. Testing is a major source of feedback and provides a basis

437

for interaction with project stakeholders. With the growing complexity of software systems, it is not surprising that a substantial percentage of a software development budget (in the range of 30 to 50%) is spent directly on software testing. And, it becomes apparent that a lot of effort has been put into the development of sound models of testing (Rapps & Weyuker, 1985) and the construction of automated tools supporting testing (Horgan et al., 1994).

Software testing encompasses a rich spectrum of testing strategies. These include dynamic versus static testing, and white (glass) box testing versus black box testing. Glass and black box testing are just instances of the fundamental classes of approaches to software testing. Dynamic testing is sometimes called software testing or simply dynamic analysis. *Dynamic analysis* requires that software be executed with test data. It relies on the use of probes inserted into a program. A *probe* is a statement inserted into a program. Probes can either be a simple output statement to track the values of variables during program execution, or a probe can make calls to analysis routines that keep track of the number of times elements of a program are executed. The key objective of dynamic analysis is to experiment with the behavior of the software in order to detect errors. As stated by Myers (1976) ''testing is the process of executing a program with the intent of finding errors.'' As the error detection is a main thrust of software testing, it triggers interest in developing adequate test data sets (test sets) so that they sensitize (activate) errors. Similarly, one has to allocate a certain amount of time (testing time) to complete testing, especially in large software systems, and develop different testing strategies that tend to implement a sound trade-off between coverage of testing and amount of time allocated to testing.

Static testing is also called static analysis. By contrast with dynamic analysis, static testing does not require software to be executed with test data. *Static analysis* encompasses program proving, symbolic execution, anomaly analysis, inspections, and code walkthroughs. Program proving requires specifying preconditions on inputs, and postconditions on outputs. Symbolic execution occurs when symbolic rather than numeric values of program variables are used. Anomaly analysis searches for anomalous program features (e.g., code that is never executed). The intent of the static style of testing is to analyze a software system and deduce its current operation as a logical consequence of the ensuing design decisions. Most importantly, the static mode of testing requires no execution of software (that stands in a sharp contrast with the previously discussed dynamic style of software testing). For instance, any modern compiler can help complete a part of static testing (static analysis of code). There are two main avenues pursued here. One hinges on highly formal methods of logic while the second approach relies on a number of heuristics and gets quite informal. With the growing complexity of software systems, the role of software testing becomes essential. A wealth of experience with software testing has resulted in the accumulation of sound testing practices and useful guidelines. One of these guidelines comes from Myers (1976).

Guidelines for Software Testing
• Determine when to stop testing.
• Assign the responsibility of testing your program to a tester (not yourself).
• Describe the expected results for every test case.
• Avoid nonreproducible or on-the-fly testing.
• Write test cases for invalid as well as valid input conditions.
• Inspect the result of each test thoroughly.
• Assign your most creative programmers to testing

12.2 TAXONOMY OF SOFTWARE TESTING

A taxonomy of software testing is part of a study in Coward (1997). Classifying or putting the various forms of software testing into groups of related test procedures produces such a taxonomy. The two major groupings of software testing are as follows:

- *Black box testing.* This approach focuses on inputs, outputs, and principle function of a software module.
- *Glass box testing.* This approach looks into the structure of code for a software module.

Black box testing is also called functional testing. The starting point of black box testing is either a specification or code. In the case of code, test data stimulate software to check if desired functions are provided. The contents of the box are hidden. Stimulated software should produce desired responses. *Glass box testing* is also called structural testing. This form of testing focuses on the detailed design of software rather than on functions (black boxes). In structural testing, statements, paths (feasible and infeasible), and branches are checked for correct execution. A taxonomy of these forms of testing is given in Table 12.1. One should become aware of inevitable limitations of testing. There are two fundamental sources of the limitations of testing:

- *Intractability.* To test exhaustively even a small program could take years. A simple example is provided in Huang (1975).
- *Undecidability.*

TABLE 12.1   Taxonomy of Forms of Testing

	Black Box (Functional)	Glass Box (Structural)
Dynamic	Random testing Domain testing Cause–effect graphing	Computation testing Domain testing Path-based testing Data generation Mutation analysis
Static	Specification proving	Code walkthroughs Inspections Program proving Symbolic execution Anomaly analysis

Various testing techniques can be classified according to the view they take on the systems. As discussed in Morell and Deimel (1992), these views of software are ordered based on increasing information content. The details are summarized in Table 12.2.

Another interesting taxonomy of software testing embraces the following categories:

- *Specification oriented.* Here test data are developed from documents and understandings intended to specify a system's behavior. The sources used here include actual written specifications and high-level as well as low-level designs. Specification-oriented testing assumes a functional view of the software and is sometimes referred to as *black box* testing.

- *Implementation oriented.* In this class of testing methods, test data are guided by information derived from the implementation (Howden, 1975). Each execution of a program exercises a particular path in a program.

- *Error oriented.* The emergence of this class is motivated by the potential presence of errors in the programming process.

A more detailed classification of these tests is shown in Figures 12.2 to 12.4.

Then there are important nontechnical issues. Who performs testing? Should testing be completed by the programmer previously involved in the coding process? Or should one look at some other alternatives such as independent testing, exchanging code among members of the same programming team, or simply leave testing to an end user? Each of these alternatives has its own pros and cons. There is also a fundamental question about a length of testing activities where two somewhat conflicting points of view have to be taken into consideration. The one is expressed by software designers who strive for fault-free product. The second standpoint is expressed by project managers who may look into timeliness of the project. Before we get into a detailed discussion of various approaches to testing, it is worth underlining the main steps that are omnipresent in any testing scheme, despite its underlying character.

TABLE 12.2   Views of Software

View of Software	Description	Instruments
Textual	Program code treated as a sequence of characters or tokens.	Software measures such as program lengths, frequency of occurrence of identifiers. *Note:* Text editors, line counters, scanners support this view.
Syntactic	Program treated as a hierarchy of syntactic elements determined by the grammar of a programming language. Programs then decompose into subprograms, and subprograms decompose into statement groups, and so on.	Statement counts, function calls, frequency of variable use, and so on. *Note:* Instrumentation entails reports of a program's execution profile (statements and branches executed).
Control flow	Analysis of program execution relative to the execution order of program elements, and identification of control flow relations. *Example:* If B is executed immediately after A, then (A, B) is a control flow relation.	Control flow graphs are directed graphs (a node of a graph corresponds to a program element, an arc represents an ordered pair in a control flow relation. A path through a control flow graph refers to a potentially executable sequence of program elements.
Data flow	Analysis of program execution relative to data access behavior, and identification of data flow relations. *Example:* If element B uses (refers to) a data object that was potentially defined at element A, then (A, B) is in the data flow graph and is a data flow relation.	Data flow graphs are directed, labeled graphs corresponding to a data flow relation. A program can be represented as a flow graph annotated with information about variable definitions and references.
Computation flow	A program is viewed as a collection of computations treated as a trace of data states produced in response to a particular input.	Fault seeding, mutation analysis, and sensitivity analysis.
Functional	A program is viewed as functions that are denoted as a set of ordered pairs (x, y) where y is the output produced by the program that halts on input x.	Symbolic analysis leading to symbolic execution that accepts symbolic input for a program.

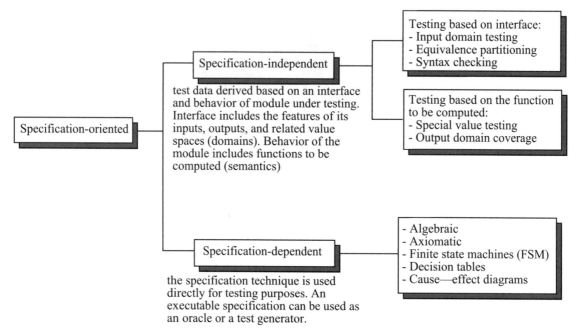

Figure 12.2 Specification-oriented software testing.

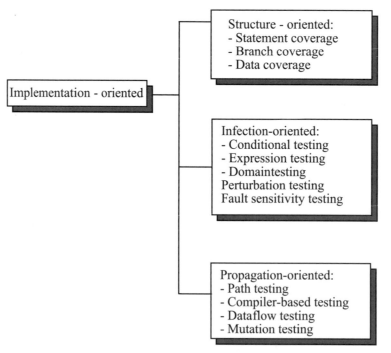

Figure 12.3 Implementation-oriented software testing.

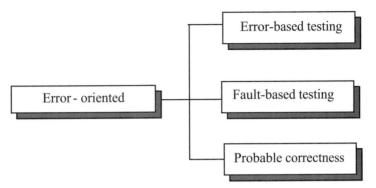

Figure 12.4 Error-oriented software testing.

> ### *Main Steps in a Testing Scheme*
>
> - Select *what* is to be measured (quantified) by the test. Before developing a test, one should identify the goals of the test. Such goals could be different (for example, testing for reliability, testing for completeness of requirements).
> - Decide *how* whatever is being tested is to be tested. Once we know what is to be tested, one has to decide how to carry out a relevant test. This means one has to decide which test is the most suitable and what sort of test items need to be used.
> - Develop the test cases. For already accepted type of testing one has to create a collection of test cases (test situations) to exercise the system under testing.
> - Determine what the expected results of the test should be and form the test oracle. These are predicted results (testing oracles) for a set of tests.
> - Execute the test cases. During this step one uses a specialized type of software called a test harness that helps execute the code and collect the results of the testing.
> - Compare the results of the test to the test oracle.

12.3 LEVELS OF SOFTWARE TESTING

Software testing is carried out at different levels throughout the entire software life-cycle. Testing starts with individual software components. Each component should be checked functionally and structurally. Testing is also necessary during the integration of software components to ensure that each combination of components is satisfactory. System and acceptance testing follow component and

TABLE 12.3   Levels of Software Testing

Testing	Definition	Purpose	Traceability
Component	Verify the implementation of design of a software element (e.g., function, module).	Ensure program logic is complete and correct. Ensure that component works as designed.	Trace each test to detailed design.
Integration	Hardware and software elements are combined and tested until the entire system has been integrated.	Ensures that design objectives are satisfied.	Trace each to test to a high-level design.
System	Test integration of entire hardware and software.	Ensure that software as a complete entity complies with its operational requirements.	Trace test to system requirements.
Acceptance	Determine if test results satisfy acceptance criteria of project stakeholders.	Ensure that objectives of stakeholders are satisfied (Win Win requirement).	Trace each test to stakeholder requirements.

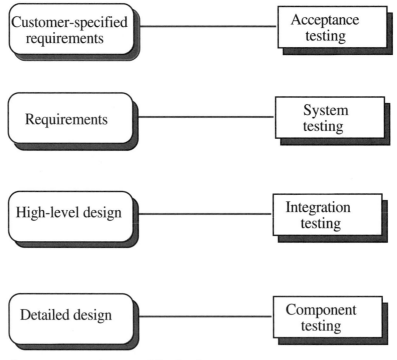

Figure 12.5   Testing traceability levels.

integration testing. The IEEE standard on software verification and validation (IEEE Std. 1059-1993) identifies four levels of testing. An explanation of the levels of testing is given in Table 12.3. The span of each level of testing (testing traceability) throughout the system's life-cycle is illustrated in Figure 12.5.

12.4 TEST ACTIVITIES

In software testing we encounter a number of key activities:

- Test plans
- Test design
- Test cases
- Test procedure
- Test execution
- Test report

A *test plan* indicates the scope, approach, resources, and the schedule of testing activity. At this stage, one indicates what is to be or not to be tested and which tasks to perform. In addition, it is necessary to identify the sources and levels of risk in testing. Software testers are also identified. Test planning may begin as soon as the requirements are completed. The key features in a test plan are given in Table 12.4.

It is difficult to determine when to stop testing or when a reasonable number of faults have been detected. For these reasons, criteria should be provided as a guideline for test completion. *Test designs* refine the approach in a test plan.

TABLE 12.4 Key Features of Software Test Plan

Test Plan Feature	Explanation
Transitioning	Give a transition diagram for testing with entry condition for testing activity.
Estimates	Estimate number and duration for each test case.
Completion	Give exit condition for each testing activity.
Risk analysis	Identify risk sources and levels.
Allocation	Allocate resources for planned test activities.

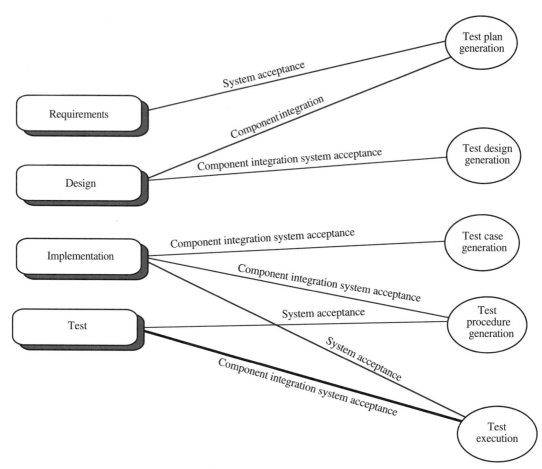

Figure 12.6   Test activities in software life-cycle.

Test designs also identify specific features to be tested by the design, and define the associated test cases. It is strongly suggested that tests should be designed for regression testing (tests previously executed can be repeated at a later point in development and maintenance). The *test cases* and test procedures are constructed in the implementation phase. One should strive for the most compact (smallest) collection of test cases (batteries) that still meet the goal. Good test cases have a high probability of detecting undiscovered errors. A *test procedure* identifies all steps required to operate the system and exercise the specified test cases to implement the already defined test design. *Test execution* is the exercising of the test procedures. Test execution starts from the component level and moves up to the integration, system, and acceptance level. A *test report* summarizes all outcomes of testing and highlights the discrepancies detected. Testing activities are distributed across the entire software life-cycle as shown in Figure 12.6.

12.5 TYPES OF SOFTWARE TESTS

In light of the diversity of existing software testing, it is advantageous to consider the types of tests as they become available to a designer. This will also help identify the scope of a particular test and clarify its main advantages and disadvantages as well as make the developer aware about the limitations of this test.

- *Functional tests* are used to exercise the code with nominal inputs (input values) for which the expected values are available. We also know the boundary conditions for these inputs. For instance, functional testing of matrix multiplication can involve some data (matrices) for which the results are known in advance.

- *Performance tests* are utilized in order to determine the widely defined performance of the software system such as an execution time associated with various parts of the code, response time (in case of embedded systems), and device utilization. The intent of this type of testing is to identify weak points of a software system and quantify its shortcomings, leading to further improvements.

- *Stress tests* are designed to break a software module. This type of testing determines the strengths and limitations of the software.

- *Structure tests* are aimed at exercising the internal logic of a software system.

- *Testing in the small–testing in the large.* The underlying criterion concerns which part of the system is subject to testing. If we are concerned with individual modules, procedures, and functions, this leads to testing in the small. Testing in the large is primarily devoted to integration testing when the system is developed out of some already constructed modules.

- *Black box–white (glass) box testing.* As the name suggests, the criterion leading to this type of discrimination specifies whether the internal (logical) structure of the system is available for testing purposes. If so, we are concerned with white box testing. If the internal structure is not available or exercised when developing the test suite, we confine ourselves to black box testing. Depending which way was selected, the points of view on testing are also radically different. In black box testing we are interested to test *what* the system is *supposed* to do. The testing is worked out from input data perspective; subsequently we see if the outputs (actions) of the software match the expected values. Functional, stress, and performance tests fall under this general category. In white box testing, testing concentrates on *what* the system *does*. Essentially, using detailed knowledge of code, one creates a battery of tests in such a way that they exercise all components of the code (say, statements, branches, paths). Structural testing subsumes white box testing.

12.6 BLACK BOX TESTING

As already discussed, black box testing does not require any code structure in order to set up meaningful tests. In the following, we discuss some representatives of this category of testing: syntax-driven testing, decision-based testing, and the cause–effect graph approach. We discuss the form of these tests and identify categories of software systems that are the most suitable for the specific test.

12.6.1 Syntax-Driven Testing

This class of black box testing is particularly applicable to systems whose specifications are described by a certain grammar. This holds, for instance, in compilers and syntactic pattern classifiers. As formal specifications of such systems are expressed in a standard BNF notation (or, equivalently, production rules), the generation of test cases follows a straightforward guideline.

Generate tests cases such that each production rule is applied (tested) at least once.

As an example, consider a class of simple arithmetic expressions described by the production rules:

```
<expression>::=  <expression>+<term>|
                 <expression>-<term>|
                 <term>
<term>::=  <term> * <factor>|
           <term>/<factor>|
           <factor>
<factor>::=<identifier>|  (<expression>)
<identifier>::=a|b|c|d|e...|z
```

The set of test cases for syntax-driven testing contains expressions that exercise the above rules. Sample expressions along with corresponding production rules being exercised by the expressions are given in Figure 12.7.

12.6.2 Decision Table-Based Testing

This form of testing is of particular interest when the original software requirements have been formulated in the format of "if-then" statements (rules). For instance, a text editor falls under the category of software systems suitable for

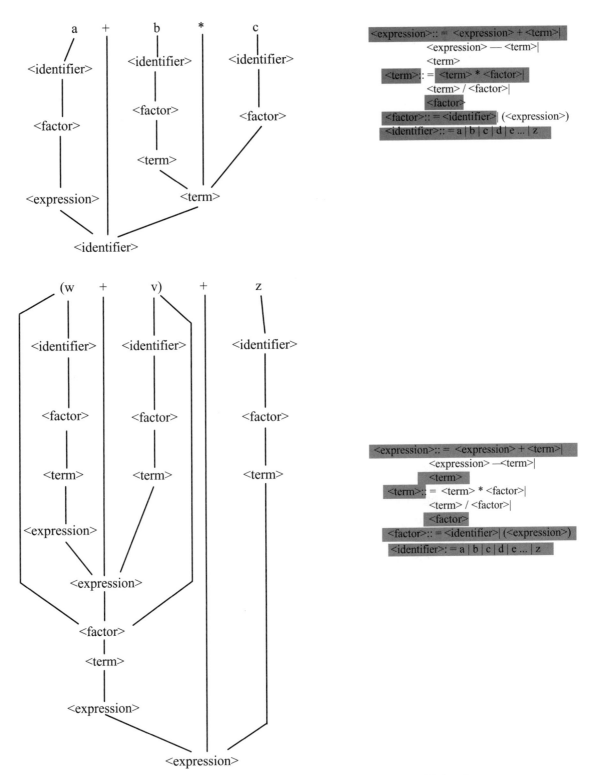

Figure 12.7 Test cases and tested production rules (highlighted).

this type of testing. Similarly, rule-based systems are useful examples of rule-based structures. A rule has the following form:

Form of a Rule

If $cond_1$ and $cond_2$ and $cond_3$ and . . . and $cond_n$ then $action_j$.

A decision table is composed of a number of columns that comprise all test (requirement) situations. The upper part of the column contains conditions that must be satisfied. The lower portion of a decision table specifies the action that results from the satisfaction of conditions in a rule. A sample decision table is given in Figure 12.8.

12.6.3   Example: Toy Text Editor

As an example, consider a toy text editor with a very limited repertoire of actions applied to a selected part of a text. The toy text editor has the following functions: copy, paste, boldface, underline, and select. The conditions in the text editor identify editing actions to be completed. Editing actions are triggered conditions that are satisfied. A decision table for the toy editor is illustrated in Figure 12.9. The number of conditions ($n = 4$) stipulates $2^4 = 16$ columns of the complete decision table. Note that a text needs to be selected prior to any further action taken. As a refinement, one may consider an additional condition in the decision

conditions

condition 1	1
condition 2	1
condition 3	0
condition 4	0
condition 5	1
	0
	..
	0

actions

	0
	0
action j	1
	0

Figure 12.8   Sample decision table.

	1	0	0		
copy function selected	1	0	0		
paste function selected	0	1	0		**conditions**
underline function selected	0	0	1		
....	0	0	0		
copy text	1	0	0		
paste text	0	1	0		**action**
underline text	0	0	1		

Figure 12.9   Toy text editor decision table.

table that deals with the selection of text. Decision tables can also be transposed so that all conditions for a rule are now located in a row while the corresponding actions follow in the same row. A sample transposed decision is given in Figure 12.10.

12.6.4 Example: Liquid Level Control

As another example we study a simple control problem that leads to specifications (and tests) expressed in the language of decision tables. Here we deal with two sensors indicating the level of liquid in a container and two valves used as actuators (Figure 12.11). Sensor 1 detects an upper acceptable level of liquid. Sensor 2 sends a signal if the level is below an acceptable level. Each sensor generates 1 if the level of liquid exceeds the corresponding level. Otherwise, the sensor produces zero. There are two valves; the input valve opens once the level goes below the lower limit (sensor 2 gets active). The output valve opens once too much liquid has been accumulated in the tank (upper acceptable level where sensor 1 is active). The control rules are straightforward:

- If sensor 1 is active (too high a level of liquid), then open output valve.
- If sensor 2 is active (too low a level of liquid), then open input valve.

Conditions (Text Editing Function Selected)				Actions		
Copy	Paste	Underline	Boldface	Copy	Paste	Underline
1	0	0	0	1	0	0
0	1	0	0	0	1	0
0	0	1	0	0	0	1

Figure 12.10 Transposed decision table for toy text editor.

452

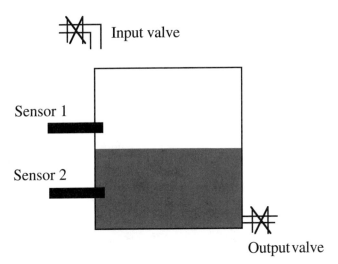

Input valve

Sensor 1

Sensor 2

Output valve

Figure 12.11 Sample liquid level.

Additionally, we include a warning action that occurs when the sensor at the lower level produces erroneous results. Because of the number of the sensors, the complete decision table has $2^2 = 4$ columns (Fig. 12.12). If we are not concerned with fault sensors (just simply ignoring this scenario), we can reduce the size of the decision table as shown in Figure 12.12. In general, for "n" conditions we end up with 2^n combinations, since each column of the table must be exercised at least once. Hence 2^n is the number of test cases. Even for modest values of "n," the resulting decision table could become fairly large. The reason for this combinatorial explosion is self-evident: We do not take into account some constraints between the condition variables that embrace physical or conceptual limitations between the variables. The third column in the decision table in Figure 12.12B can be easily dropped. In the next section, we discuss a method of cause–effect graphs that is aimed at eliminating the shortcoming of combinatorial explosion of rows and columns in a decision table.

12.6.5 Cause–Effect Graphs in Functional Testing

The main disadvantage of the generic method of decision tables is that all inputs are considered separately even though the requirements (and the real-world problem) strongly suggest another way of handling the problem of testing. The independence of inputs is also assumed in boundary value analysis and equivalence class partitioning. Cause–effect graphs capture relationships between specific combinations of inputs (causes) and outputs (effects). These specific cases rather than all possible combinations help avoid combinatorial explosion associated with any standard decision table. Causes and effects are represented as nodes of a cause–effect graph. Such a graph includes a number of intermediate nodes linking

Conditions

S1	0	1	1
S2	0	0	1

Actions

Open output valve	0	0	1
Open input valve	1	0	0
Send faulty message			

Figure 12.12B Reduced decision table.

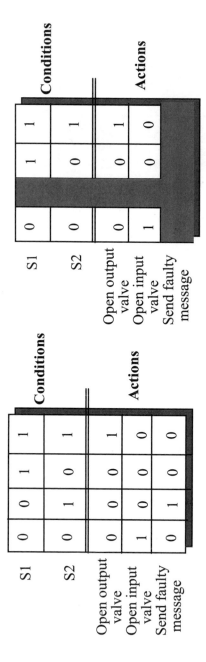

Conditions

S1	0	0	1
S2	0	1	1

Actions

Open output valve	0	0	1
Open input valve	1	0	0
Send faulty message	0	0	0

Figure 12.12A Control decision table.

causes and effects in the formation of a logical expression. Consider, for example, a simple automated teller machine (ATM) banking transaction system. The list of causes and effects for an ATM are as follows.

Causes

C_1: Command is credit
C_2: Command is debit
C_3: Account number is valid
C_4: Transaction amount is valid

Effects

E_1: Print ''invalid command''
E_2: Print ''invalid account number''
E_3: Print ''debit amount not valid''
E_4: Debit account
E_5: Credit account

The cause–effect graph as shown in Figure 12.13 has four input (cause) nodes and five output (effect) nodes. The nodes in between the input layer (that

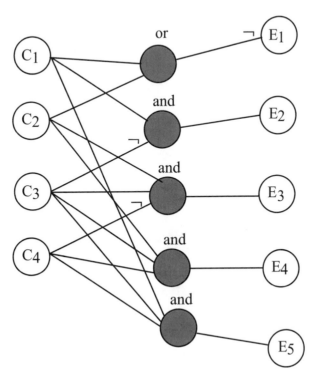

Figure 12.13 Cause–effect graph.

TABLE 12.5 Description of Processing Nodes Used in a Cause–Effect Graph

Type of Processing Node	Description
and	Effect occurs if all inputs are true(1)
or	Effect occurs if at least one input is true(1)
negation ⌐	Effect occurs if input are false(0)

contains causes) and the output layer (representing effects) realize "and" or "or" operators. The negation symbols ($\neg$) placed over some connections states that the effect is true once the associated node is false. Table 12.5 summarizes the meaning of these operators.

The cause–effect graph helps determine the corresponding test cases. These test cases are revealed by tracing back the truth values of the selected causes starting with a graph like the one in Figure 12.14. We are interested in determining the causes for E_3. From the graph one immediately learns that C_2, C_3, and $\neg C_4$ affect E_3 while the remaining causes have no impact on this effect. As such, we can regard them as *don't care* (x) conditions. This observation chiefly reduces a size of the induced decision table. The resulting column in the decision table to be used in the generation of the test cases reads as

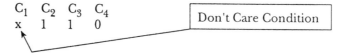

$$\begin{array}{cccc} C_1 & C_2 & C_3 & C_4 \\ x & 1 & 1 & 0 \end{array}$$

Don't Care Condition

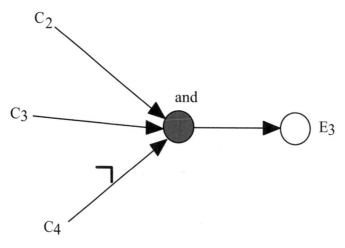

Figure 12.14 Determining causes for effect E_3.

C_1	0	1	x	x	1
C_2	0	x	1	1	x
C_3	x	0	1	1	1
C_4	x	x	0	1	1
E_1	1	0	0	0	0
E_2	0	1	0	0	0
E_3	0	0	1	0	0
E_4	0	0	0	1	0
E_5	0	0	0	0	1

Figure 12.15 ATM cause–effect decision table.

Notice that E_3 does not depend upon C_1, hence the reason for the introduction of a don't care condition. If don't care (x) conditions were not considered, the resulting portion of the decision table will contain $2^1 = 2$ columns involving an enumeration of the values of C_1. In general, if our intent is to generate a reduced form of the decision table, we adopt a backtracking mechanism when traversing the cause–effect graph from effects to causes (Ghezzi et al., 1991):

- In tracing back through an *or* node whose output is *true,* we use only input combinations that have only one true value. This selection is based on an assumption that combining two causes does not alter the effect of each cause. For example, for three causes (a, b, and c) affecting the or node (to be in the true state), we consider only <a=true, b=false, c=false>, <a=false, b=true, c=false>, <a=false, b=false, c=true>.

- In tracing back through an *and* node whose output is false, we use only input combinations that have only a single false value. For the previous example, we admit <a=false, b=true, c=true>, <a=true, b=false, c=true>, <a=true, b=true, c=false>.

The complete decision table for the cause–effect graph of the ATM transaction consists of five columns with a substantial number of don't care conditions (Figure 12.15). If we were to ignore them, it would lead to a table with $2^4 = 16$ columns.

The cause–effect graphs can be augmented by incorporating additional constraints between inputs. Their graphical notation is shown in Figure 12.16. This helps reduce the number of test cases as one envisions constraints between the variables, and some potential combinations of inputs are ruled out from the testing procedure.

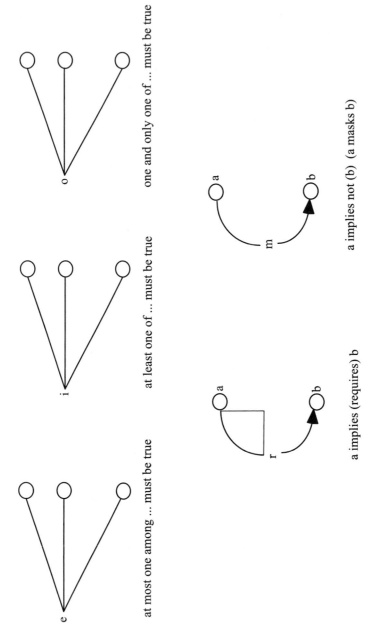

at most one among ... must be true

at least one of ... must be true

one and only one of ... must be true

a implies (requires) b

a implies not (b) (a masks b)

Figure 12.16 Extension of relations in cause–effect technique.

12.7 TESTING BOUNDARY CONDITIONS

Quite often, glass box testing (as relying on the structure of the code) does not test cases that are not explicitly visible or emphasized enough. Consider the following conditional statement:

$$\text{if } (x > y) \text{ then } S_1 \text{ else } S_2$$

This form of a conditional statement is quite generic and is encountered in many problems. For example, we may think of two sensors whose readings (x and y) are used to make some decision, namely S_1 or S_2. The relational condition, $x > y$, determines two equivalence classes:

- Ω_1 An equivalence class for values of x and y such that $x > y$.
- Ω_2 An equivalence class for values of x and y such that $x \leq y$.

The equivalence classes Ω_2 and Ω_2 consist of pairs of readings (x, y) that make the associated relational condition true or false. The branch coverage criterion (that requires testing all branches in the program) selects two combinations of inputs: one coming from Ω_1 and the second from Ω_2 as shown in Figure 12.17.

The branches $x > y$ and $x < y$ are tested. However, the case $x = y$ has never been tested. More precisely, the case $x = y$ is a part of Ω_2. This case occurs with zero probability. Hence, this case will not be selected for testing. Even so, testing

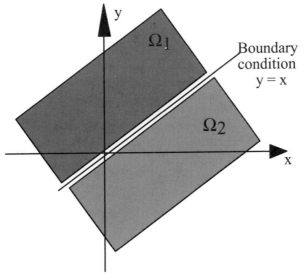

Figure 12.17 Testing boundary condition $y = x$.

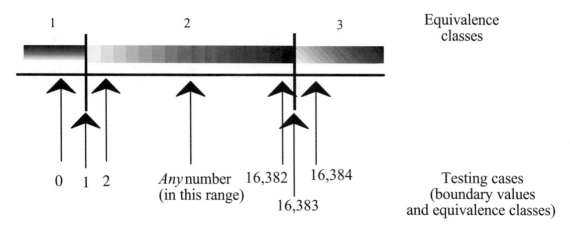

Figure 12.18   Equivalence class and boundary value test cases.

the boundary condition $\{(x, y)|\ y=x\}$ is, nevertheless, of genuine interest. By doing that one could eventually comprehend a way in which the equality $x = y$ is realized and modify the condition part of the original statement, if the program realization does not meet requirements or it happens that there are some implementation concerns. An interesting example of boundary testing originates in the case of a certain array of data (vectors) used to store a series of readings. Suppose the specifications for this data structure state that it should be able to handle any number of vectors (data) ranging from 1 to 16,383 (that is $2^{14} - 1$). Equivalence class testing leads to the following equivalence classes:

- $Class_1$: array including less than one data vector
- $Class_2$: any number of data vectors situated in the range from 1 to 16,383
- $Class_3$: more than 16,383 data vectors

In view of the above specifications, any test case from the second equivalence class should be handled correctly. For the first and third equivalence class one should get an error message. Boundary value analysis leads to new test cases relative to values adjacent to the boundaries. This idea is illustrated in Figure 12.18. In total, this produces 7 test cases. The selection of such additional (boundary) cases is supported by practice that suggests that these test cases increase the probability of detecting a fault.

12.8 EXHAUSTIVE TESTING

Exhaustive testing falls under the category of black box testing. While completely impractical, it gives us a better insight into the complexity of testing and quantifies limits of practical usefulness of any brute-force approach to testing. In a nutshell, an exhaustive test must show that the code is correct for all *possible* inputs. We need more clarification regarding the input—the ensuing discussion is very much oriented toward hardware aspects of realization of the code. Consider a simple quadratic equation $ax^2 + bx + c = 0$ to be solved with respect to x. Here a, b, and c are the parameters of the equation. From a functional point, the corresponding procedure transforms a three-dimensional space of parameters (a, b, c) into the two-variable space of solutions (roots) (r_1, r_2). The exhaustive testing starts with an internal representation of the parameters. Assume that the resolution is based on 16-bit number representation. Thus each input produces 2^{16} different values, which in turn implies 2^{16} test cases. On the whole, we end up with $2^{16} * 2^{16} * 2^{16} = 2^{48}$ test cases that need to be exercised, and this is probably not feasible.

12.9   STRUCTURAL TESTING

In structural testing, we are interested in the development of test cases based upon the structure (internal logic) of the code under testing. There are several classes of testing depending on how thorough and time demanding the process of testing has to be. We proceed with some basic categories such as statement, branch, and path coverage tests.

12.9.1   Statement Coverage

Statement coverage, the weakest form of testing, requires that every statement in the code has been executed at least once. Consider the following part of the code that is supposed to compute the absolute value (abs) of y:

```
begin
if (y ≥ 0) then y = 0 - y;
abs = y;
end;
```

The test case $y = 0$ is enough to execute all statements as shown in Figure 12.19. Nevertheless, this form of testing is not sufficient to detect an evident fault occurring in this code. That is, the code in Figure 12.19 makes abs negative for positive values of y and negative values of y remain negative, which is incorrect. In addition, the test $y = 0$ does not tell that the absolute value is not being computed by this program.

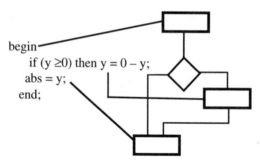

Figure 12.19   Statement coverage testing.

12.9.2   Branch Coverage

The branch coverage form of structural testing focuses on testing branches in code. Test cases are selected in such a way that each branch in the code is executed at least once. This requires that each decision box is evaluated to true and false at least once. Returning to the previous example, the two test cases $y = 0$ and $y = -5$ are sufficient to execute both branches of the decision box. For y=0, we get abs =0. For y=−5, we get abs =−5, which indicates an existence of fault. Indisputably, these test cases help detect the fault. As this type of testing focuses on exercising branches of the decision box, it is also referred to as a decision coverage criterion.

12.9.3   Condition/Branch Coverage

In the condition/branch coverage form of structural testing, every branch must be invoked at least once and all possible combinations of conditions in decisions must be exercised. While the branch coverage is stronger than statement coverage, it is still not capable of capturing faults associated with decisions carried out in presence of multiple conditions. Consider, for instance, the following statement:

```
if ((x < level_2) && (y > level_1) {
    z = compute (x,y); else z = compute_altern(x,y);
    }
```

Now consider the following test cases:

```
x = -4, y = 10
x = -6, y = 12
```

In the first case, the decision box returns false and only one branch of the code is executed. In the second case, the decision box evaluates to true and leads to

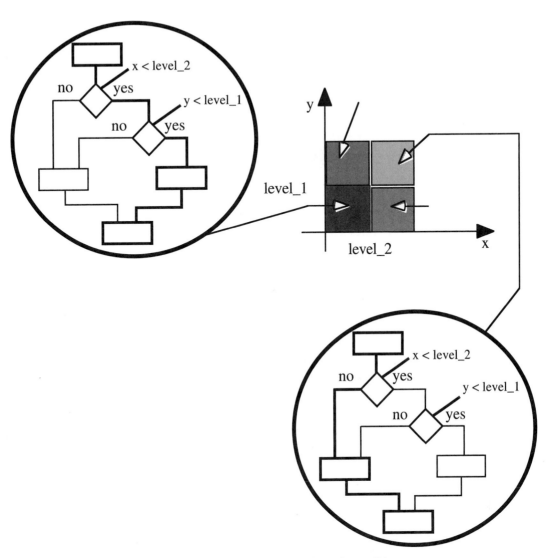

Figure 12.20 Testing cases for complete branch conditions.

the execution of the remaining branch of the code. This interesting situation is illustrated in Figure 12.20. Notice, however, that if the fault has been associated with the compound condition of the decision box, it becomes undetected. Thus the decision testing should be augmented by the requirement of exercising all subconditions occurring in the decision box. Returning to the previous example, since the decision box involves two subconditions, one can envision two additional pairs to be exercises (true, false) and (false, true). One of them (true, false) is shown in Figure 12.21.

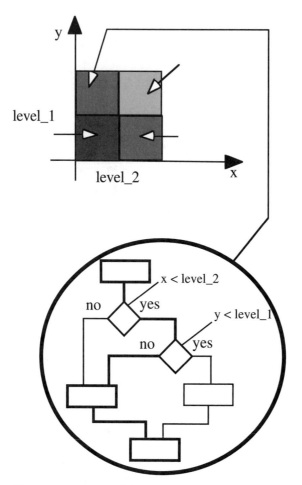

Figure 12.21   True–false test case.

The four test cases in this example meet the requirements of condition/ branch coverage. Observe, however, that multiple condition coverage may be quite challenging. If each subcondition is viewed as a single input, then this multiple input condition coverage testing is analogous to exhaustive testing. As usual, "n" subconditions require 2^n test cases. This may not be feasible if "n" gets relatively high. Hopefully, in many domains, the value of "n" is still small and the conditions/branch testing remains feasible. Figure 12.22 summarizes the results coming from the literature (Chilenski & Miller, 1994) elaborating on the distribution of "n" for several types of software modules.

Noticeably, in avionics (and other real-time embedded systems), one may encounter expressions with many subconditions. Then it becomes impractical to generate test cases meeting the condition/branch coverage criteria. To alleviate these difficulties one may illustrate some modifications to the condition/

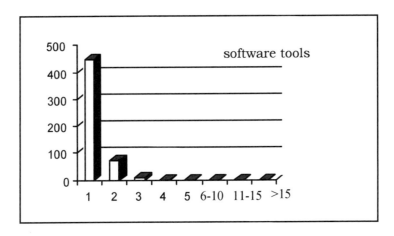

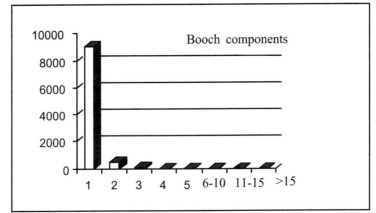

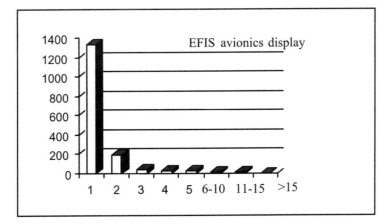

Figure 12.22   Number of branches in complex system modules.

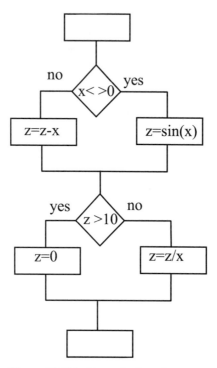

Figure 12.23 Example flowchart.

branch coverage criterion in order to reduce the number of required tests; the reader may refer to Foster (1984) and Tai and Su (1987) for pertinent details.

12.9.4 Path Coverage

The path coverage criterion considers all possible logical paths in a program and leads to test cases aimed at exercising a program along each path. This leads us to the concept of the path coverage criterion. In many cases, this criterion can be too impractical, especially when it comes to loops in the program that may easily lead to a very high number of paths. Nevertheless, the use of the path coverage criterion may help detect faults easily omitted by the branch coverage criterion. The weakness in attempting to test each decision box in a flow diagram is illustrated in Figure 12.23.

The test cases that support branch coverage criterion-selected values of x and z are the following:

```
{x  =  2,  z  =  6}
{x  =  0,  z  =  12}
```

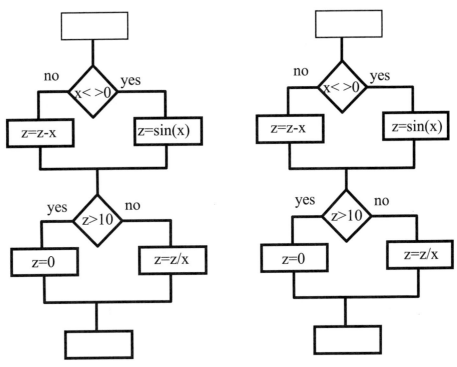

Figure 12.24 Enumeration of branch coverage testing.

An execution of these two test cases does not guarantee that the software is error free. Consider a situation where at some point of computation x assumes the value of zero. Then the division z/x indicated in one of the statement boxes in the flowchart produces a failure. This scenario is not taken into account when designing the above test cases. As a result, the test case set for the flowchart in Figure 12.23 must be augmented. Suggested additional test cases are as follows:

```
{x = 1, z = 5}
{x = 2, z = 15}
{x = 0, z = 7}
{x = 0, z = 13}
```

Figures 12.24 and 12.25 underline a difference between branch and path coverage testing criteria. Interestingly, even in this simple situation the number of paths to be covered is higher than the number of branches.

12.9.5 Example: Testing tATC System

The Java code in this section contain a Change method for the class Plane in the tATC system. The Change method is responsible for changing the altitude,

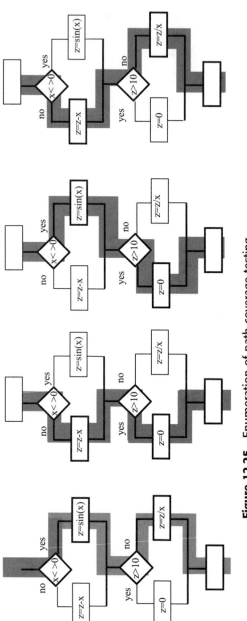

Figure 12.25 Enumeration of path coverage testing.

velocity, or heading of an aircraft. This Java code has been derived from a prototype of a training program for air traffic controllers (Agatep et al., 1997). More specifically, the Change method alters the status of an aircraft relative to its altitude and velocity. Depending on the current values of the altitude and velocity, specialized functions are invoked, namely, increase_alt_1 and increase_alt_2, as well as decrease_alt_1 and decrease_alt_2 (the choice depends on the current altitude value) and increase_vel_1, increase_val_2, decrease_vel_1, and decrease_vel_2. Notice also that m_plane is an object in class Plane, where m_plane.z_pos and m_plane.vel deal with its altitude and velocity, respectively.

```java
public void Change (int m_plane, int plane_alt, int plane_vel, int plane_head){


// altitude changes; 1: increase altitude, 2: decrease altitude,
// 0: no changes
// velocity changes; 1: increase velocity, 2 - decrease velocity
// 0: no changes


if ((m_plane.crashed == false) && (m_plane.landed == false)){
//altitude change
      if (plane_alt == 1){
                  if (m_plane.z_pos < 6000){
                               m_plane.z_pos = m_plane.z_pos
                                 +increase_alt_1 (m_plane.z_pos);
                                       }
                        else m_plane.z_pos = m_plane.z_pos
                                       +increase_alt_2(m_plane.z_pos);
                  }
else
  if (plane_alt == 2){
                if (m_plane.z_pos>500) {
                                   m_plane.z_pos = m_plane.z_pos +
                                   decrease_alt_1(m_plane.z_pos);
                                       }
                        else m_plane.z_pos = m_plane.z_pos
                                       +decrease_alt_2(m_plane.z_pos);


                  }
//velocity changes
    if (plane_vel == 1){
                    if (m_plane.vel < 800){
                                       m_plane.vel = m_plane.vel +
                                       increase_vel_1(m_plane.vel);
                                           }
                        else m_plane.vel = m_plane.vel +
                                increase _vel_2(m_plane.vel);
                  }
```

```
else
  if (plane_vel == 2){
              if (m_plane.vel>200){
                              m_plane.vel = m_plane.vel
                              +decrease_vel(m_plane.vel);
                                   }
                    else m_plane.vel = m_plane.vel +
                                   decrease_vel_2(m_plane.vel);
                 }
} //Change
```

For testing purposes, we concentrate on the altitude path of the method. To exercise different coverage criteria, the following test cases are considered.

```
                          Test Cases
• Statement coverage
{plane_crashed = false, plane_landed = false, plane_alt =1, m_plane.z_pos = 7000}
{plane_crashed = false, plane_landed = false, plane_alt =1, m_plane.z_pos = 5000}
{ plane_crashed = false, plane_landed = false, plane_alt =2, m_plane.z_pos =400}
{ plane_crashed = false, plane_landed = false, plane_alt =2, m_plane.z_pos =700}

• Branch coverage
{plane_crashed = false, plane_landed = false, plane_alt =1, m_plane.z_pos = 7000}
{plane_crashed = false, plane_landed = false, plane_alt =1, m_plane.z_pos = 5000}
{ plane_crashed = false, plane_landed = false, plane_alt =2, m_plane.z_pos =400}
{ plane_crashed = false, plane_landed = false, plane_alt =2, m_plane.z_pos =700}
{ plane_crashed = false, plane_landed = false, plane_alt =3}

• Path coverage
The path coverage criterion produces the same collection of testing cases as in
branch coverage.
```

A partial flowchart of the Change method of the tATC system is given in Figure 12.26.

12.9.6 Complexity of Path Coverage Testing

Due to the complexity of path coverage, it is essential to count and enumerate the number of paths in a program. Let us start with a graph representing the flow of control that does not include loops. In this case the number of paths is determined by the number of decision nodes and their distribution. Two extreme cases that determine the bounds on the number of paths in a graph are envisioned in Shooman (1983). These extreme cases are illustrated in Figure 12.27. In a flowchart with branch merging the decision boxes are "stacked" on each other. This is the case in Figure 12.27a. Branch merging leads to 2^n possible paths.

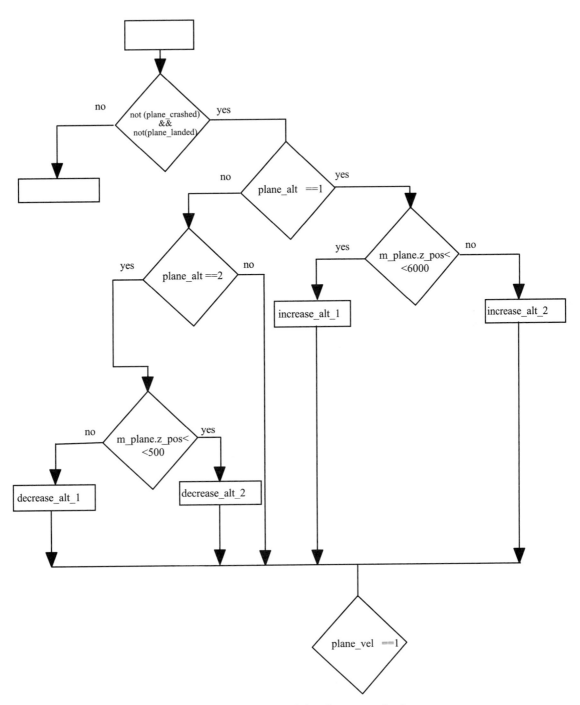

Figure 12.26 Partial flowchart of the change method.

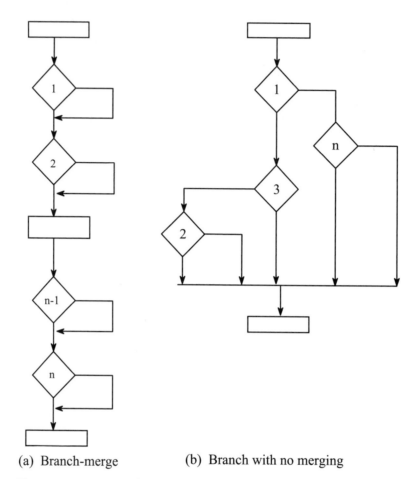

(a) Branch-merge   (b) Branch with no merging

Figure 12.27   Two path coverage cases. **A** Branch merge. **B** Branch with no merging.

This constitutes an upper bound of the number of paths in the graph. In a flowchart with multiple branches and no merging, decisions are not stacked. In a flowchart with n decisions with no merging, there are $n+1$ possible paths. This is a lower bound of the paths in code containing branches with no merging. Notice that these two bounds are very different, even for moderate values of "n." Hence, the "true" number of paths existing in a program becomes bounded in the following way.

> Bounds on the Number of True Paths
> lower bound $\leq$ number of paths $\leq$ upper bound
> Specifically,
> $n+1 \leq$ number of paths $\leq 2^n$

To make these bounds meaningful, one can dissect the original graph into several parts and determine the bounds separately. Consider, for instance, a graph containing 6 decision nodes. This produces the bounds equal to 7 and 64. Now, it is possible to dissect the graph into three subgraphs so that each of them includes only 2 decision nodes. For each subgraph, the bounds are very close to each other:

$$3 \leq \text{number of paths in a sub-graph} \leq 4$$

Because we have broken the original graph into three subgraphs, the number of paths that need to be tested in the resulting graph is as follows:

$$27(=3*3*3) \leq \text{number of paths in graph} \leq 64(=4*4*4)$$

12.9.7 Path Testing in Graphs with Loops

In a looping graph, it is necessary to define a path first. Path coverage for loops will be restricted to loops that are traversed only once. Using this approach, it is possible to transform any graph with a loop to its loopless equivalent. The idea is to split any node, say A, which is terminal of a feedback path into A and A'. The new split portion of the node with feedback edge is connected to the end node or any other node below. The following code uses a for loop to add the elements of matrix a until a matrix element is found which equals a target value:

```
for (int i=0; i <n; i++) {
if (a[i] == target) break continue_comput;
s=s+a[i];
}
continue_comput: System.out.println(sum_is +s);
```

The matrix addition code can be rewritten with a while construct:

```
i=0;
while (a[i]!=target) {
i++; s+= a[i]
}
```

Similarly, the matrix addition code can be rewritten with a repeat loop as follows:

```
i=0;
do { a[i]; i++; s=s+a[i]}
while (a[i]!= target);
```

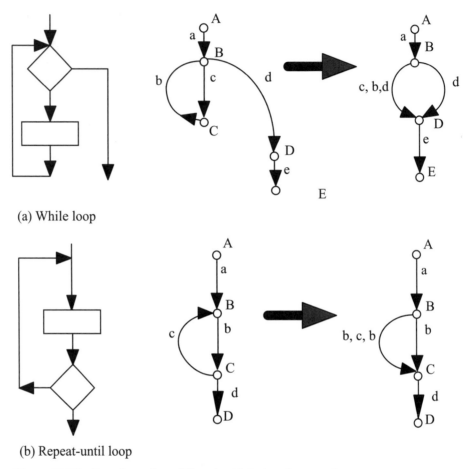

(a) While loop

(b) Repeat-until loop

Figure 12.28   Transformation of flowchart into loopless graphs.

The basic constructs of structural programming can be easily transformed into loopless graphs (Figure 12.28). The enumeration of the paths comes in the form of sums of products of the edges of the loopless graph. As an example, let us focus on the graph in Figure 12.29. We start with the edges that evidently become parts of all paths. These are a and h. Then

$$PGF = aPGF_\alpha h$$

where

PGF = path-generating function
α = path generating function for the subgraph from B and E

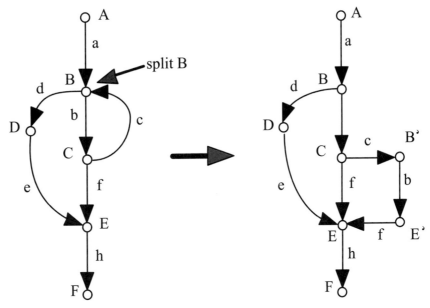

Figure 12.29 Conversion of a graph into its loopless equivalent.

In the sequel, we build up path generating functions for α, PGF_α. From the graph we read

$$PGF_\alpha = de + b\,PGF_\beta$$

where the plus sign stands for the *or* operation. The final level of nesting concerns the most nested part of the subgraph

$$PGF_\beta = f + cbf$$

Returning to the original expression and expanding it in steps, we obtain

$$PGF = aPGF_\alpha h = a(de + b\,PGF_\beta)\,h = a(de + b(f + cbf))h$$
$$= adef + abfh + abcbfh$$

As becomes quite apparent, the number of paths could be enormously high, especially for large chunks of code with a significant flow of control. This limits the applicability of this testing approach. One can show that there are many situations when path testing is not practically feasible. A simple example coming from Meyers (1976) is an excellent illustration of this infeasibility. The flowchart

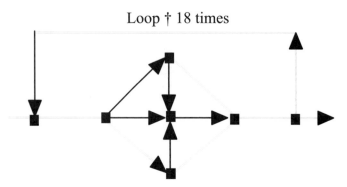

Figure 12.30   Computing a number of paths in a simple flowchart.

in Figure 12.30 is straightforward and simple but the number of paths associated with it is enormously high. To start with, note that there are 5 possible paths through the diamond in the center. As the looping is less than 19, we get the number of paths by summing up consecutive looping through the flowchart, that is

$$5^1 + 5^2 + \ldots + 5^{18} = 4.77{*}10^{12}$$

These calculations indicate that path testing should be treated with caution. Moreover, one should be aware that even the path converge criterion may not be able to eliminate all faults. The reason behind that is quite straightforward. Path testing exercises program logic (data and flow of control) assuming that the transformation from the software specification to the detailed design and coding is complete (that all the requirements have been taken care of). Any missing elements are quite difficult, if not impossible, to test. Similarly, implementation issues such as dimensionality of structures, either static or dynamic, as well as pointers inherent in the language of implementation are not tackled by this form of testing.

12.10 TEST COVERAGE CRITERIA BASED ON DATA FLOW MECHANISMS

The types of testing coverage discussed so far are the most commonly encountered in the literature. There are some other, more comprehensive taxonomies introducing additional coverage criteria that lead to more detailed description of data flow characteristics (Horgan et al., 1994). The data flow orientation in testing relies on an observation that data structures and their usage are essential components of any code and these need to be taken into consideration when looking into an overall issue of software testing.

12.10.1 Main Categories of Data Flow Coverage Criteria

The main categories of data flow-oriented test coverage are as follows:

```
basic block
all-use
c-use
p-use
du-path
```

To illustrate these forms of test coverage, the following Java code fragment is introduced:

```
sum = 0;
prod = 0;
i = 1;
while (i <= n)
    {
        sum+ = i;
        prod* = i;
        i++
    }
if (k == 0) print_results1;
if (k == 1) compute;
```

This code can be viewed as a sequence of basic *blocks* that are consecutive parts of code that execute together without any branching. An example of the basic block in the above code is as follows.

```
sum+ = i;
prod* = i;
i++
```

C-use, p-use, and all-use are all more specialized categories of data flow coverage criteria with an emphasis on a *definition-use* pair and a distribution of this pair across the code. A *definition* concerns a statement at which a variable is assigned an initial value. For instance, the following statements are examples of definitions:

```
i = 1;
sum = 0;
prod = 1;
```

An occurrence of this specific variable is its *use*. So the uses of the first variable come in the form:

```
i++;
prod* = i;
```

The use of sum occurs in the statement

```
sum+ = i;
```

If the use appears in a computational expression, the pair is a c-use. If the use occurs inside a predicate, then the resulting pair is a p-use. A du-path is a path from a variable definition to its use that contains no redefinition of the variable. An example of a du-path is an execution of a sequence that starts at i=1, loops once in the body of the while statement, and then continues. Paths with two or more loops from i=1 to sum+ = i are not du-paths, as the statement i++ redefines the value of I. These coverage cases are summarized as follows. Either a c-use or a p-use is called all-uses, as shown in Figure 12.31. A summary of the coverage categories is given in Table 12.6.

12.10.2   Data Flow Testing Based on Data

Data flow testing can be accomplished by analyzing changes to data and data structures. There are three possible actions on data (Beizer, 1990):

- Defined (d). The data structure is defined, created, or initialized when it is given a valid state.

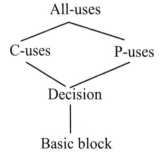

Figure 12.31   Hierarchy of different data flow coverage criteria.

TABLE 12.6   Coverage Categories

Coverage	Explanation	Examples
basic block	A part of code that executes without any branching.	```sum = 0; prod = 0; i = 1; while (i <= n) { sum+ = i; prod* = i; i++ } if (k == 0) print_results1; if (k == 1) compute;```
all-use	A path starts from a definition of the variable and ends at a statement in which it becomes used.	```sum = 0; prod = 0; i = 1; while (i <= n) { sum+ = i; prod* = i; i++ } if (k == 0) print_results1; if (k == 1) compute;```
c-use	A path starts from a definition of the variable and ends at a statement in which it is involved in computing.	```sum = 0; prod = 0; i = 1; while (i <= n) { sum+ = i; prod* = i; i++ } if (k == 0) print_results1; if (k == 1) compute;```
p-use	A path starts from a definition of the variable and ends in a statement in which it appears inside a certain predicate.	```sum = 0; prod = 0; i = 1; while (i <= n) { sum+ = i; prod* = i; i++ } if (k == 0) print_results1; if (k == 1) compute;```
du-path	A path starts from a definition of the variable and ends in a statement in which it becomes used. The variable is not redefined in terms of its value.	```sum = 0; prod = 0; i = 1; while (i <= n) { sum+ = i; prod* = i; i++ } if (k == 0) print_results1; if (k == 1) compute;```

TABLE 12.7   Anomalies

Category of Anomaly	Description
dd	The data structure is defined twice without an intervening use; probably harmless, but suspicious
dk	The data structure is defined and killed without ever using it; probably a fault
du	The data structure is defined and killed; a normal use
kk	The data structure is killed twice; either vindictive or a fault
kd	The data structure is killed and then redefined; a normal use
ku	An attempt to use the data structure after it has been killed; clearly a fault
ud	The data structure is defined after a use; a normal situation
uk	The data structure is killed after a use; a normal situation
-k	Killing a data structure that has been neither defined nor used; possibly a fault
-d	The first definition in the path; normal
-u	The first use in the path; there is no evidence of definition; possibly a fault
-k	The data structure killed; normal
-d	The last thing done to the data structure in the path was to define it; possible fault
-u	The last thing done to the data structure in the path was to use it; normal

- Killed (k). The data are killed, undefined, or released when the data cease to have a state (e.g., a loop variable is undefined when a loop is exited). Note that d and k are complementary operations

- Used (u). The data are used either for computing (c) or in a predicate (p). These actions correspond to the notion of c-uses and p-uses discussed in the previous section.

There are a number of anomalies associated with these actions. Each anomaly is denoted by a two-letter pair or a letter and a dash. A list of anomalies is given in Table 12.7.

12.11 GUIDELINES IN APPLYING COVERAGE TECHNIQUES

There are some practical guidelines for using coverage techniques (Miller et al., 1994).

Guidelines for Using Coverage Testing Techniques

- Statement coverage can be accepted as the minimum testing requirement (note that paths, not statements alone transform input into output, and this implies that statement coverage needs to be regarded as a weak coverage measure). It can be used at the module level with less than 5000 lines of code. To make this testing effective, 100% coverage is necessary. Statement coverage is only about 50% as effective as branch coverage.
- Branch coverage is most effective for control flow coverage testing completed at the module level. The required level of coverage is 85%.
- Completing a set of path tests can take 8 to 10 times as much as it takes to get branch coverage. This style of testing applies to critical modules and is limited to a few functions with life criticality features (medical systems, real-time controllers).

12.12 REGRESSION TESTING

The intent of regression testing is to rerun automatically some tests for a software whenever a slight change to the product has been made. There are two main activities (phases) of regression testing.

Steps in Regression Testing

- Capturing a test (or a battery of tests) for replay. The rule is that one goes for a suite of strong tests (namely those with a high coverage level).
- Comparing new outputs (responses) with old ones (baselines) to make sure that there are no unwanted changes.

The two steps in regression testing are run automatically in the background. For effective regression testing, some auxiliary arrangement of the test suite must be accomplished. Furthermore, an extra sophistication is required if the user wants tests with some unwanted differences to pass through—this comes in the form of programmable differencing engines. Here the exceptions to be ignored are programmed in by a user-supplied control script. The effectiveness of regression testing is expressed in terms of two conditions: (1) how hard it is to construct and maintain a suite of respective tests and (2) how reliable the system of regression testing is. Notice that it could be fairly tedious to program the test oracles differencing system to produce the right effect.

12.13 STATIC SOFTWARE TESTING

Unlike dynamic forms of testing, static software testing is not concerned with the execution of code. There are two classes of static testing techniques:

- *Informal.* Informal testing includes code walk-throughs and inspections.
- *Formal.* Formal testing includes correctness proofs and symbolic execution.

12.13.1 Informal Techniques

Informal testing techniques are usually identified with code inspection and walkthroughts. Both of these testing techniques were introduced in the late 1970s. These techniques are similar inasmuch as both are informal. Yet there is still an essential difference between these techniques. Software inspections are feedback oriented whereas walkthroughs promote interaction between testers, project team members and stakeholders.

12.13.2 Inspections

Inspections are activities carried out by a team of individuals (experts) reviewing a document (design or code) with an intent of finding faults. Inspections were first proposed in 1976 by Fagan with the aim of testing designs and code. The method was developed within IBM. An inspection comprises five formal steps:

- *Overview.* The overview session concentrates on an overview of the documents to be inspected
- *Preparation.* The participants try to understand the document in detail. Here lists of fault types and their frequency found in recent inspections are usually very helpful aids as they help concentrate on the areas that are highly error prone
- *Inspection.* At the beginning, one participant walks through the code in the document with the inspection team, ensuring that every item is covered, and every branch is taken at least once. Each participant proceeds

with his or her own activities presenting their checklists. The purpose of inspection is to find and document faults, not to remove them. The leader of the inspection team (moderator) is in charge of preparing a written report of the inspection, to ensure appropriate follow-up.

- *Rework.* At this stage the faults and problems noted in the written report are resolved
- *Follow-up.* The moderator ensures that all issues raised have been resolved. All fixes must be checked to ensure that no new faults have been introduced. If more than 5% of the material inspected has been reworked, then the team reconvenes for a 100% reinspection.

The team responsible for inspections consists of 3 to 6 individuals. For instance, in the case of design inspection, the team includes a moderator, designer, implementer, and tester. Any inspection should use a checklist of potential faults (e.g., for design inspection one may have items regarding items of the specification document, correspondence between actual and formal arguments in interfaces, compatibility of software design with the existing hardware, and so forth). The product of the inspection is a record of fault statistics. Faults must be recorded by severity level, from major to minor, and by fault type. The experimental results of inspections are reported by Fagan (1976, 1986), Jones (1978), and Bush (1990). An important part of any inspection concerns feedback, as shown in Figure 12.32. To make inspections successful, one may consider them to be of an iterative character. Code inspections are restricted to the code itself. Therefore the activities are aimed at the discovery of commonly made errors or errors coming from specific classes. The following are common errors detected during inspection.

Common Errors Detected by Code Inspections

- Uninitialized variables
- Jumps into loops
- Nonterminating loops
- Array indexes out of bounds
- Actual–formal parameter mismatches

12.13.3 Structured Walkthroughs

Structured walkthroughs (Yourdon, 1979) deal with organized events whose role is to scrutinize a particular software product, namely a design, a code module, a chapter of a user's guide, a test plan, and so forth. The participants of this meeting look at the artifact from different points of view with an intent of finding as many errors as they can. The action is guided by a presenter who presents the product and walks them through it. Any errors are recorded by a coordinator.

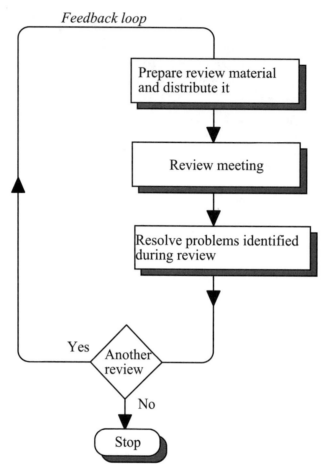

Figure 12.32   General scheme for software inspections.

The group concentrates on error detection, not error correction. The team is composed of the following individuals:

- *Presenter.* Usually this is a person who produced the item to be reviewed.
- *Coordinator.* The responsibility of this person is to chair the walkthrough.
- *Secretary.* The person assures that the relevant material is prepared beforehand, and that records are taken and given to the presenter.
- *Maintenance oracle.* This individual represents the people who will be responsible for maintaining the product.
- *Standards bearer.* This person is responsible for item for adherence to the local standards that apply to the reviewed item.
- *User representative.* This individual represents the views of the users.

The successful walkthrough relies on a prior preparation of the relevant material. The presenter chooses other participants and nominates a coordinator. The item to be reviewed should be manageable so that it could be reviewed in a matter of two hours. The item to be reviewed should be considered complete by the producer.

12.14 FORMAL TECHNIQUES

Formal techniques concern correctness proofs and symbolic execution. Correctness proofs hinge on an observation that any code (program) is a formal object while any program specification can be realized as a formal method. This means that one concentrates on an equivalence between the program and its specification. The equivalence can be shown in a form of a formal mathematical proof. The technique is based on proving this equivalence. Symbolic execution uses symbols instead of simple numerical values (as done during computer execution) and hence exploits classes of data. To illustrate the essence of this idea, we use a piece of code as follows:

```
x = y*7;
if (x >a) then a = a+x-3
        else y = sin(x+2);
```

In Figure 12.33, capital letters such as X and Y denote symbolic values (these correspond to the variables originally used in the code). Assume at the beginning of the symbolic execution that $x = X$ and $a = A$. Once executed symbolically, the first statement yields $X = Y*7$. The remaining variables are left unchanged. The decision box can be activated in either way (the comparison $Y*7 > A$ may yield true or false). We select one of the executions as a triple

```
<symbolic variables value, execution path, path condition>
```

Two execution paths are associated with the annotated control flow graph in Figure 12.33.

12.15 TESTING IN THE LARGE

As opposed to testing in the small, testing in the large is concerned with testing of the overall software system composed of modules. The style of testing depends very much on the already assumed strategy of system design. Let us recall briefly

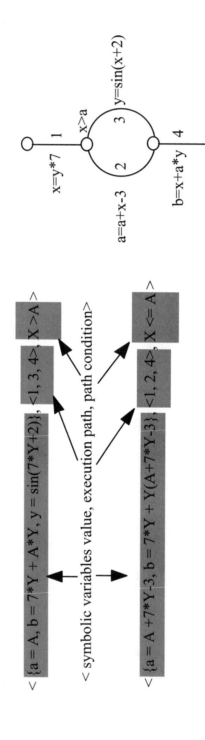

Figure 12.33 Symbolic execution of a program.

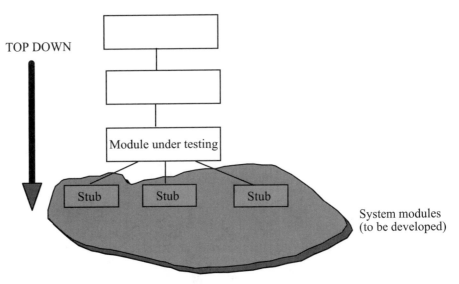

Figure 12.34 Top-down system testing.

that in the assumed top-down design procedure (which comprises a series of successive refinements), we have to equip the module under testing with stubs whose role is to emulate some not-yet developed and more detailed modules of the system shown in Figure 12.34.

In the bottom-up design philosophy, we develop the system starting from detailed modules and implementing more general functions. To test modules, we need drivers that furnish all necessary and not-yet-implemented control activities shown in Figure 12.35. We consider a detailed example of one of the clustering

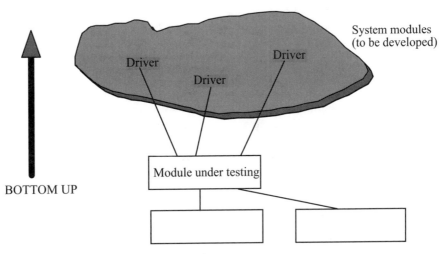

Figure 12.35 Bottom-up system testing.

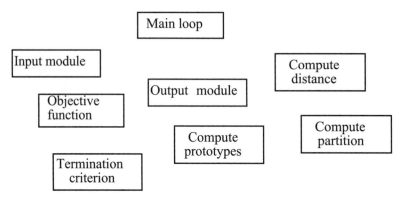

Figure 12.36   Modules of the clustering algorithm.

methods viewed as an optimization procedure. In this clustering (grouping), one splits a data set into a number of groups. This occurs through an iterative optimization of a performance index (objective function). The results of clustering are represented in terms of a partition matrix and a number of prototypes (centers of clusters), one for each cluster. The partition matrix as well as the prototypes are updated throughout iterations so that the objective function becomes minimized. As usual for any iterative solution to an optimization problem, there is a termination criterion. Once it is satisfied, the optimization is completed. Additionally, we have some input-output modules, an initialization module, and a main loop module. More specialized modules deal with computing prototypes, computing partition matrix, expression termination criterion, determining distance function, and so on. These modules are shown in Figure 12.36. The general framework of the clustering algorithm can be summarized as follows:

```
input_data;
initialize;
compute_partition;     //main loop
compute_prototypes;
output_results;
```

Figure 12.37 illustrates the top-down design paradigm applied to a clustering system. We have exemplified some main links between the modules as well as identified the form of stubs being used therein. Similarly, Figure 12.38 shows the bottom-up testing paradigm.

Depending on the assumed general design approach, several generic integration testing methods are pursued, namely

- Bottom-up testing
- Top-down testing
- Big-bang
- Sandwich

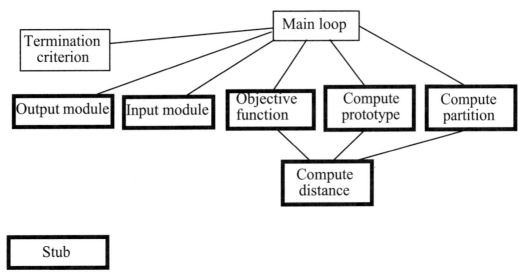

Figure 12.37 Top-down design and testing.

To illustrate these ideas of testing, we use a simple hierarchy of modules as in Figure 12.39. Several classes of integration testing are summarized in Table 12.8. Bottom-up testing (which concurs with bottom-up design) starts with the most specific (detailed) modules (E, F, G) and proceeds up to the higher levels of the hierarchy. Note that some of the modules have not been tested separately (say B, D, or A). The modified version of bottom-up testing takes care of bottom-up testing such modules separately. Top-down testing proceeds with the module (A) situated at the top of the hierarchy. Again, as in bottom-up testing, some modules are not tested separately.

Big bang testing is quite challenging and risky as we integrate all modules in a single step and test the resulting systems. Sandwich testing attempts to

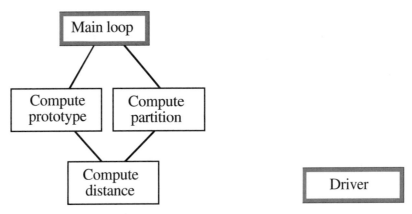

Figure 12.38 Bottom-up design and testing.

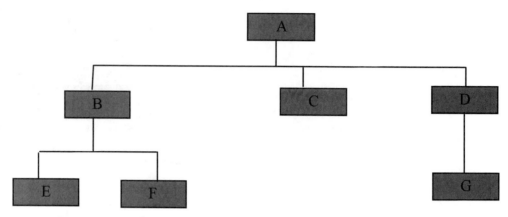

Figure 12.39   A hierarchy of software modules.

combine the ideas of bottom-up and top-down testing by defining a certain target layer somewhere in between the lower and upper layer of the original hierarchy of the modules. Note that in bottom-up testing the target layer was the highest one in the overall hierarchy. Similarly, the focal layer in top-down testing is the lowest layer in the hierarchy.

Each type of integration testing exhibits very different characteristics. Figure 12.40 summarizes the types of integration testing in light of a set of essential

Type of integration testing

	Bottom-up	Top-down	Big-bang	Sandwich
Integration	Early	Early	Late	Early
Time to working system	Late	Early	Late	Early
Drivers needed	Yes	No	Yes	Yes
Stubs needed	No	Yes	Yes	Yes
Ability to test paths	Easy	Hard	Easy	Medium
Ability to plan and control	Easy	Hard	Easy	Hard

Figure 12.40   Integration testing—an overview.

TABLE 12.8 Classes of Integration Testing

Type of Testing	Description	Example
Bottom-up	System developed starting from detailed modules. Testing (concuring with the bottom-up philosophy) starts from the detailed modules and proceeds up to the higher levels of hierarchy. Testing requires drivers. Some modules may not be tested separately.	
Top-down	System developed starting from most general modules. Testing (concuring with the top-down design philosophy) starts from the most general module. Testing requires stubs. Some modules may not be tested separately	
Big bang	All modules integrated in a single step (big bang) and tested as an entire system.	
Sandwich	Testing combines the ideas of bottom-up and top-down testing by defining a certain target layer in the hierarchy of the modules. The modules below this layer are tested following bottom-up approach, whereas those above the target layer are subject to top-down testing.	 Target layer is situated between A and (B, C, D)

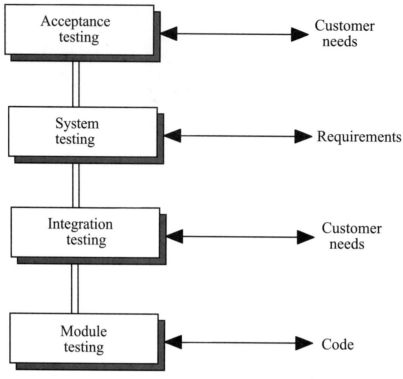

Figure 12.41   Levels of system testing.

criteria such as integration moment and ability to test specific paths. Based on these characteristics, one can make necessary testing decisions. In general, the type of integration testing is heavily affected by the design philosophy followed. An overview of the levels of system testing is given in Figure 41.

12.16 SUMMARY

No issue is meaningful unless it can be put to the test of decisive verification.
—C.S. LEWIS, 1934

The issue of software testing needs to be thoroughly addressed in any software project. In particular, one should become fully aware of the implications of the usage of specific testing methodology (for instance, dynamic versus static), the depth of coverage supported by particular testing method, costs associated with the testing procedure, and a need for a rational tradeoff between all of these

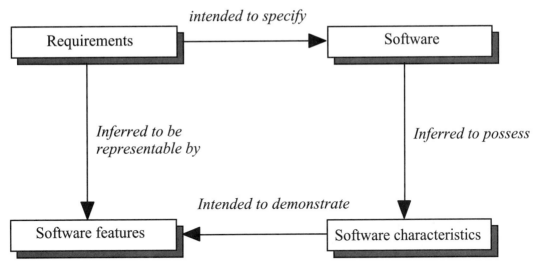

Figure 12.42 Software testing model.

aspects. The point of view highlighted in Morell and Deimel (1992) is worth recalling as it sheds light on the essence of software testing. Testing seeks to determine whether the intended relationship between requirements and software has been achieved. Software cannot be directly measured against requirements. Rather than do that, testing is concerned with a number of software features. Similarly, software possess a number of characteristics. A characteristic is a trait, quality, or property of the software. The characteristics are determined either through static or dynamic analysis. Software characteristics intend to demonstrate existence of assumed software features. The yardstick of software testing activities is software specifications as shown in Figure 12.42. Typically, a software system is "confronted" with a real-world problem that a user's specification has anticipated. Correct responses to stimuli by a software system constitute a "proof of the pudding." One should be aware that a system may pass all software testing activities but still fall short in its responses to stimuli.

12.17 PROBLEMS

> **Testing can show the presence, but never the absence of errors in software.**
> —E. Dijkstra, 1969

1. It is evident that the condition/branch testing coverage may not be feasible for higher values of "n". To figure out the range of required tests, consider several values of "n" (say 5, 10, 20, and so on) and determine the number of tests.

(a) Consider the lower and upper bound expression on the number of paths in a loopless control graph. Calculate these bonds for several values of "n". Elaborate on the practicality of the obtained range of the bounds.

2. A fragment of code below concerns a forward elimination phase of Gaussian elimination; it scans down the column to find the largest element (in rows past the ith one). The row containing this element is exchanged with the ith and, subsequently, this variable is eliminated in the equations i+1 to N:

```
eliminate ()
    {
        int i,j,k,max;
        float t;
        for (i=1; i < = N; i++)
            {
                max = i;
                for (j=i+1; j<=N; j++)
                    if (abs(a[j][i] > abs(a[max][i])max=jj
                    for (k=i; k   = N+1; k++)
                        {t = a[i][k];
                            a[i][k] = a[max][k];
                                a[max][k]=t;}
                for (j=i+1; j <=N; j++)
                    for (k = N+1; k >=i; k---)
                        a[j][k]- = a[i][k] * a[j][i]/a[i][i];
                }
            }
```

(a) Draw a flowchart of this code.
(b) Propose test cases that exercise coverage criteria:

- Statement coverage
- Branch coverage
- Condition/branch coverage
- Path coverage

3. Consider the flowchart shown in Figure 12.43. If you are interested in any number of traversals of the loop that could be within the range from 0 to 100, how many paths can you enumerate?

4. Consider the flowchart in Figure 12.44. How many test cases would you need to exercise branch coverage criterion and path coverage criterion?

5. Build a decision table and propose a collection of test cases in the following control problem. The system is equipped with two sensors, one of which measures a temperature of a medium. The second is used to measure its pressure. Depending upon the conditions (Figure 12.45), some discrete control actions of flow velocity are taken—these are qualified as ZERO, NEGATIVE, and POSITIVE.

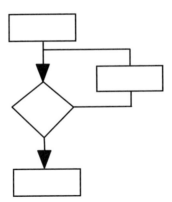

Figure 12.43 A flowchart to be analyzed.

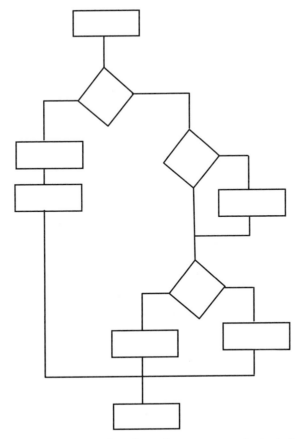

Figure 12.44 A flowchart of a program to be tested.

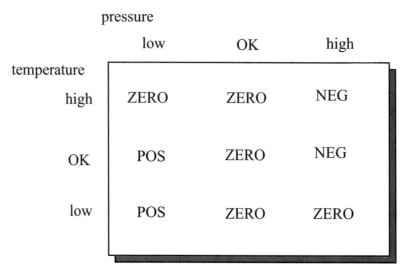

Figure 12.45   Control actions to be taken.

6. Consider the software specification of a transmission system where:

   • The character in column 1 must be an A, B, or C.
   • The character in column 2 must be a digit.
   • The character in column 3 must be a digit greater than 5.

   In this situation, the file update is completed (an update message is issued). If the first character is incorrect, send message M_1. Similarly, in the case of the second character being incorrect, send message M_2. Message M_3 is issued once the third character is incorrect. Design a cause–effect graph and propose a reduced decision table for testing the software.

7. The idea of tracing back an effect depends very much upon the type of aggregation of causes. Elaborate on these scenarios:
   (a) The effect should be tested (x is set true). The combination of causes is either OR-wise or AND-wise.
   (b) The effect should be suppressed (x is set false). The combination of causes is again completed either OR-wise or AND-wise. How should the causes be set up (false or true)? Can you notice any resemblance between these four cases? Is there any recommendation regarding testing procedure?

8. What is the boundary condition for the following conditional statement?

```
if (x < sin(w*y))&& (w==y*0.2) printf(x*x) else pow=exp(-w)
```

Justify your choice.

9. Consider the problem of computing a value of a polynomial of the third order:

$$a_0 + a_1x + a_2x^2 + a_3x^3$$

What is the number of test cases one should develop for exhaustive testing assuming that one uses 32 bits to represent real number coefficients? Assuming that each test case uses up to 7 μsec, how much time is needed to perform this testing?

10. Consider a program that reads two 64-bit integer numbers. How much time would it take to complete exhaustive testing, assuming that an execution of each test case uses up 10^{-9} sec.

11. Consider the code fragment

```
dx=0.1;
N=50;
for {i=0; i<=N; i++}
      {z[i]=sin(x)/ (x-2.5); x=x+dx}
```

There is an evident fault in the code. Which type of the coverage criterion should be exercised to detect it?

12. The classic example of testing comes from Myers (1976): "A small program reads three integer values representing the inputs and prints a message stating whether the triangle is scalene, isosceles, or equilateral." Show a flowchart of the program. Suggest a white-box testing methodology and develop relevant test cases.

13. The code below describes an insertion algorithm. Propose test cases meeting statement and branch coverage criteria. Suggest test cases for the black box style of testing

```
insertion_procedure (int a[], int p[], int N)
{int i, j, k
for (i=0; i<=N; i++) p[i] =i;
for {i=2; i<=N; i++}
      {k = p[i]; j=i;
      while (a[p[j-1]] >a[k]) { p[j]= p[j-1]; j - -}
      p[j]=k;
      }
}
```

14. The test-related reliability model assumes that the probability of failure, P, is computed as a product of two components:

$$P = P_mP_u$$

where P_m is the probability of invoking an error that was overlooked during testing and P_u stands for the probability that this error is invoked by the user. Assuming that "n" out of N possible inputs invoke the fault and "+" tests are applied independently, compute P. Plot P as a function of the ratio $\frac{n}{N}$. Does P exhibit an extremum? What does it mean?

15. Considering the equivalence classes formed in the space of readings of two sensors as in Figure 12.46, suggest test cases for such equivalence classes. What would the test cases for boundary values testing? Assume that the readings of the sensors come as positive integers.

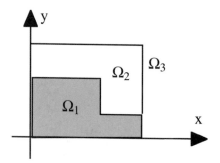

Figure 12.46   Equivalence classes in two-dimensional space of sensor readings.

16. For the hierarchy of software modules in Figure 12.47, propose several types of integration testing (bottom up, top down, sandwich).

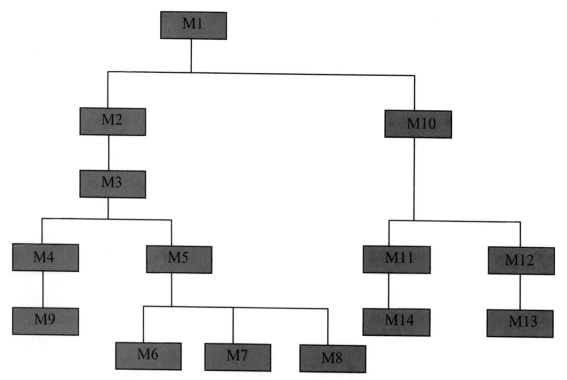

Figure 12.47   Modular software to be tested.

17. Propose several ways of testing software whose specifications are expressed in terms of statecharts. Classify your testing approaches along the line of static–dynamic and black box–glass box testing classification schemes.

18. How does software portability affect ways in which it becomes verified? If necessary, elaborate on specific modifications to the testing methods discussed in this chapter to make it possible. Which category of the testing methods will your proposals fall into?

19. What are the key types of programming languages forming the backbone of Java? In your opinion, what makes Java unique? Why?

20. Considering the identified features of Java, what should be the main thrust of software testing written in Java?

12.18 REFERENCES

Agatep, R., Evans, D., Inthalansy, S., et al. *tATC Project.* Report, Department of Electrical and Computer Engineering, University of Manitoba, Winnipeg, November 1997.

Beizer, B. *Software Testing Techniques,* 2nd ed. Van Nostrand Reinhold, New York, 1990.

Bush, M. Improving software quality: The use of formal inspections at the Jet Propulsion Laboratory. *Proceedings of the 12th International Conference on Software Engineering,* Nice, France, pp. 196–199, 1990.

Chilenski, J.J., Miller, S.P. Applicability of modified condition/decision coverage to software testing. *Software Engineering Journal,* September 1994, 193–200.

Coward, P.D. A review of software testing. In *Software Engineering,* M. Dorfman, R. H. Thayer, IEEE Computer Society Press, Los Alimitos, CA, pp. 277–286, 1997.

Fagan, M.E. Advances in software inspections. *IEEE Transactions on Software Engineering,* SE-**12**(7):744–751, 1986.

Fagan, M.E. Design and code inspections to reduce errors in program development. *IBM Systems Journal,* **15**(3):182–211, 1976.

Foster, K.A. Sensitive test data for logic expressions. *ACM SIGSOFT Software Engineering Notes,* **9**: 120–125, 1984.

Ghezzi, C., Jazayeri, M., Mandrioli, D. *Fundamentals of Software Engineering.* Englewood Cliffs, NJ, Prentice Hall, 1991.

Horgan, J.R., London, S., Lyu, M.R. Achieving software quality with testing coverage measures. *IEEE Computer,* September 1994:60–69.

Howden, W.E. Methodology for the generation of program test data. *IEEE Transactions on Computers,* C-**24**(5):554–560, 1975.

Huang, J.C. An approach to program testing. *ACM Computing Surveys,* **8**(3):113–128, 1975.

IEEE Std. 1059-1993. *IEEE Guide for Software Verification and Validation Plans.* In *IEEE Standards Collection Software Engineering.* IEEE, Piscataway, NJ, 1997.

Jones, T.C. Measuring programming quality and productivity. *IBM Systems Journal,* **17**(1): 39–63, 1978.

Meyers, G.J. *Software Reliability.* Wiley, New York, 1976.

Miller, E., Steiner, D.A., Symons, G.J. Testing tools. In *Encyclopedia of Software Engineering*, Vol. II, J.J. Marciniak, ed. Wiley, New York, pp. 1353–1358, 1994.

Morell, L.J., Deimel, L.E. Unit analysis and testing. Carnegie Mellon University, Software Engineering Institute Report SEI-CM - 9-2.0, 1992.

Myers, J.P. The complexity of software testing. *Software Engineering Journal*, January 1992, 13–24.

Rapps, S., Weyuker, E.J. Selecting software test data using dataflow information. *IEEE Transactions on Software Engineering*, SE-11(4): 367–375, 1985.

Shooman, M. *Software Engineering.* McGraw Hill, New York, 1983.

Tai, K.C., Su, H.K. Test generation for Boolean expressions. *Proceedings of the 11th International Symposium on Computer Software and Applications* COMPSAC'87, Tokyo, October 1987, pp. 278–283.

Von Mayrhauser, A. *Software Engineering.* Academic Press, Boston, 1990.

Yourdon, E. *Structured Walkthroughs.* Yourdon Press, New York, 1979.

CHAPTER 13

Software Measures

Only a goal of measurement determines the appropriateness of [software] measures.
—Victor R. Basili, 1994

In mesure is tresure.
—Skelton, 1529

Aims

- Identify software measures and measurements
- Measure complexity of software systems
- Assess strengths and weaknesses of common software measures
- Consider software measures for object-oriented software systems

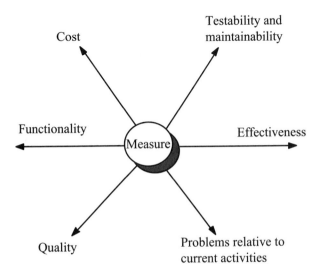

Figure 13.1 Knowledge gained from software measures.

13.1 INTRODUCTION

Software measures are mappings from objects in software entities to numbers or symbols to quantify a software attribute (Conte et al., 1986; Fenton, 1990). As a result, our knowledge of the software amplifies. The knowledge gained from software measurement is portrayed in Figure 13.1, which is summarized as follows.

- *Cost,* which affects relevant planning relative to future projects.
- *Testability and maintainability* of the current processes and products.
- *Effectiveness* of a software product.
- *Problems* to be identified relative to current activities.
- *Quality* of the process-product targeting attributes such as reliability, portability, and maintainability of the delivered software system.
- *Functionality* and user-friendliness of a product from a user's point of view.

For example, quantifying the number of independent paths in a program (termed the complexity level of software) provides us with an indication of its testability and maintainability (McCabe, 1976). Again, for example, it is possible to quantify effort required in the development of a software system. Measures of effort help gauge allocation of resources needed to test, modify, and maintain a system. One of the chief benefits of software measurement is an indication of what might be done to improve the software process (its software engineering mechanisms) as well as the software entities derived from the process. In effect, measurements provide valuable feedback in the evolution of the software process. In software engineering, the term *software metric* is often used. A software metric is a simple quantitative measure derivable from any attribute of the software life cycle (Fenton & Kaposi, 1987). Common uses of the term *metric* in software engineering have been identified in (Fenton, 1991) and are summarized in Table 13.1.

Software metrics make it possible for software engineers to measure and predict software processes, necessary resources for a project, and work products

TABLE 13.1   Forms of Software Metrics

Interpretation of "Software Metric"	Example
Number derived from a software process or product or resource	Lines of Code (LOC) per programmer month
Scale of measurement	Nominal classification of software failures
Identifiable software attribute	Platform independence of a program
Data-driven model (describes a dependent variable which is a function independent variables)	Effort as a function of KDSI (thousands of delivered source instructions) in Boehm's COCOMO model (Boehm, 1981)

relevant for a software development effort. Software metrics quantify properties of existing as well as planned software products (Bieman, 1995). The aim of this chapter is to provide an introduction to software measurement, which serves as a foundation for quantifying software (i.e., for software metrics).

This chapter introduces various approaches to measuring software and explores a number of classes of software measures. We discuss size, data, and logic-based software complexity measures each of which forms a broad category of software measures. Then we discuss a category of software measures developed within the realm of Software Science. Afterwards we familiarize the reader with the measures originating from the notion of entropy. Finally, we elaborate on some software measures useful in object-oriented software systems.

13.2 SOFTWARE MEASURE AND SOFTWARE MEASUREMENT

The flat-roof of any building that hath but one spout for carrying off the water, might be a measurer of the different quantities of the fallen rain.
—T. Harmer, 1764

A software measure provides software engineers with a means of quantifying the assessment of a software product. In addition to the basic definition of a software measure, it is necessary to consider related notions that help place an overall process of software measuring in a broader application perspective. It will then become apparent how results computed with software measures become essential in the assurance of quality of software products.

> A *software measure* is a mapping from a set of objects in the software engineering world into a set of mathematical constructs such as numbers or vectors of numbers (McClure, 1994).

The objects in the software engineering world could have different meaning: We talk about products, processes, and projects. Each of them could be measured. When an outcome of the mapping is a single number, we are concerned with scalar software measures (such as lines of code); if the result is a collection of numbers, we are dealing with a vector type of software measures. The mappings themselves can be developed on different scales (nominal, ordinal, interval, and

TABLE 13.2   Different Scales in Measurement Theory

Scale	Description	Examples
Nominal	Denotes membership in a class (supports equivalence relations)	Labeling, classifying entities (e.g., slow, fast)
Ordinal	Measurement expresses comparative judgment, imposes an ordering of terms (supports equivalence relations, e.g., "≥")	Preference
Interval	Measurement expresses distance between pairs of items (supports equivalence relations and known ratio of intervals)	Time (calendar), temperature (centigrade, fahrenheit)
Ratio	Measurement denotes a degree in relation to standard where a software entity manifests chosen property (supports equivalence relations, known ratio of intervals, and known ratio of any two scalar values)	Time (interval), temperature (absolute), length

ratio). Table 13.2 defines the scales and provides illustrative examples. It is important to realize what capabilities are offered by the scales and what type of calculations are permitted once we confine ourselves to a certain scale.

A software measurement is a technique or method that applies software measures to a class of software engineering objects to achieve a predefined goal. Five characteristics of software measurement can be identified (Basili, 1989; Basili, 1988).

- *Object of measurement* ranging from products (e.g., source code, software designs, software requirements, software test cases) to processes (e.g., architectural design process, coding and unit test processes, system test processes) and projects.

- *Purpose of measurement* such as characterization, assessment, evaluation, prediction.

- *Source of measurement* such as software designers, software testers, and software managers.

- *Measured property* such as cost of software, reliability, maintainability, size, portability.

- *Context of measurement* where software artifacts are measured in different environments (including people, technology, resources available), which are specified in advance before applying some software measures.

13.3 SIZE, DATA, AND LOGIC-BASED SOFTWARE COMPLEXITY MEASURES

There are a significant number of software measures devoted to the measurement of a program's size, related data structures, and logic structure of the code itself. This number is growing and, unfortunately, there is no agreement as to which of such measures are the most meaningful and useful, how to determine the values of the measures, and what these values really mean. To compare "apples with apples," one should use the same measures over a number of codes to compare these codes in a rational way. In many situations, one should pay special attention to time logs of the metrics and make sure that the compared codes pertain to the same or similar time moments or phases of a software process. Since the collection of the existing software measures is quite large, we will cover a selection of them. Our intent is to concentrate on commonly used measures. In the sequel, we discuss key size measures, data structure measures, and logic structure data.

13.3.1 Size Measures

Size measures are perhaps among the most commonly used. In fact, they are the most obvious and conceptually straightforward as capturing the bulk size of the code. In many cases these are synonymous to lines of code metric. To everybody in the software community, both on the designer's as well as user's side, this measure is a good indicator of the magnitude of the software system, implying features such as memory requirements, maintenance effort, and development time. The size measures have several appealing features. They are easy to determine (once the system has been completed) and form one of the most important factors influencing software development, including its productivity.

13.3.2 LOC Measure

The count of the lines of code, LOC—or more practically thousands (K) of lines of code, or KLOC, for short—is the most dominant in the class of size-oriented software measures. In spite of its conceptual simplicity, there is some ambiguity concerning a way of counting these lines. Should comments be included? How are several statements in the same line treated? To resolve such difficulties, we need to agree upon some counting criteria. First, we exclude comments and blank lines. All statements in a single line of code count as a single LOC. All lines containing program headers and declarations contribute to the overall LOC count as well. Consider, for example, the Java code implementing a standard

```
1  public void paint ( Graphics g )
2  {
3  print (g, "Sequence in original order ", a, 25, 25);
4  sort();
5  print(g, "results", a,25, 55);
6  }
7  public void sort()
8  {
9  for (int pass=1; pass <a.length; pass++)
10 for (int i=0; i<a.length; i++)
11 if (a[ i ] > a[ i+1] )
12 { hold = a[i];
13 a[i] = a[i+1];
14 a[1+1]=hold;
15 }
16 }
```

Figure 13.2 Java bubble sort.

bubble sort algorithm in Figure 13.2. Adopting the assumed counting criteria, the discussed code has 16 LOC. Interestingly, one can obtain the equivalent code consisting of 10 LOC. This happens after a slight rearrangement of the code for the bubble sort shown in Figure 13.3.

Although LOC is a very simple and straightforward measure to compute, the Java code in Figures 13.2 and 13.3 points out some drawbacks to the LOC measure. Namely, the LOC measure is very sensitive to layout of the code. Depending on that, one can witness a substantial variation in the produced LOC (in the previous example we got 16 versus 10 LOC). Furthermore, the LOC measure may not fully reflect the complexity of code. Some lines may be more difficult to code (and comprehend) than others. This is, unfortunately, ignored by the LOC measure. As usual, there is a somewhat expected trade-off between simplicity of the measure itself and its discriminatory abilities.

```
1  public void paint ( Graphics g )
2  {
3  print (g, "Sequence in original order ", a, 25, 25); sort(); print(g, "results", a, 25, 55);
4  }
5  public void sort()
6  {
7  for (int pass=1; pass <a.length; pass++)
      8  for (int i=0; i<a.length; I++) if (a[ i ] > a[ i+1] )
9  { hold = a[i]; a[i] = a[i+1]; a[i+1]=hold; }
10 }
```

Figure 13.3 Shortened bubble sort code.

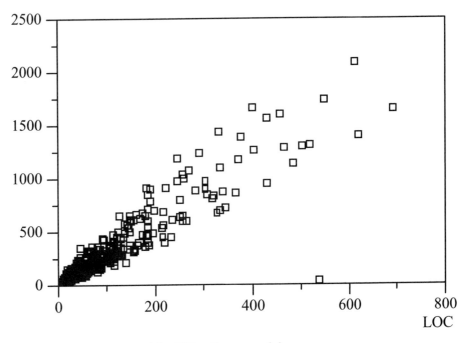

Figure 13.4 N versus LOC for MIS software modules.

We exemplify this claim by considering 390 software modules of a medical image system (MIS) as studied by Munson and others (1996). The program size measure correlates nicely with the LOC measure (Figure 13.4). The data points are nicely centered along a regression line, that is, N = a + b*LOC. The parameters of this function (namely, a and b) are easily derived using any statistical package.

13.4 SOFTWARE SCIENCE MEASURES

The next step in developing a software size measure is to consider the basic units of program syntax. Halstead (1977) proposed a collection of software measures known as Software Science. The position taken in this pursuit is such that one should start considering basic building ''blocks'' of each program and assess complexity based on an interaction and proportions between these basic entities. The building blocks are just entities that imply a certain performance of a program, and these are just operators and operands. As a conceptual environment for a family of software measures, this approach looks attractive, especially for extensive theoretical investigations. The metrics may also shed light on the problem of software complexity from the standpoint of information theory and, subsequently, help reveal more sound links between a general notion of complexity and the particular model of complexity used in this setting.

Software science promotes an interesting point of view of software. Any computer program (code) is a composition of operators and operands (a fairly basic and fixed alphabet of symbols). Design and coding activities lead to a final code mapping our initial software specifications. The complexity of the problem may become reflected in the resulting code—an organized population of operators and operands. Before moving to the series of software measures developed in Software Science, we recall the basic notation. By N_1 and N_2 we denote the total number of operators and operands occurring in the code. The length, N, is taken as a sum of these two

$$N = N_1 + N_2$$

Similarly, as before, by η_1 and η_2 we denote a number of unique operators and operands standing in the code.

13.4.1   Program Length

The first hypothesis of Software Science states that the length of a well-structured code should be a function of η_1 and η_2 only. The resulting length expression is defined as

$$\hat{N} = \eta_1 \log_2 \eta_1 + \eta_2 \log_2 \eta_2$$

A distinction is made between $\hat{N}$ and N. The notation $\hat{N}$ (reads "N hat") denotes an actual value and N denotes an estimated value. If the number of operands and operators are known in advance (prior to coding), we can easily estimate the length of the program. The approximate values of the number of operators can be based upon the characteristics of the programming language used. The estimate of the number of operands could be based upon some prior domain knowledge while dealing with some problems of a similar character. Let us again consider the bubble sort code and determine its length. The detailed calculations of the respective occurrences of the symbols are shown in Table 13.3.

The estimated length of the program is equal to

$$\hat{N} = 12\log_2 12 + 14\log_2 14 = 96.32$$

In fact, this estimate produces a certain bias towards higher values of the length of the program, as its actual value is $31 + 35 = 66$ symbols. Let us now estimate the length of the code used to determine a partition matrix. The breakdown of the occurrences of the symbols is provided as follows.

TABLE 13.3 Bubble Sort Code and its Operators and Operands

```
1   public void paint ( Graphics g )
2   {
3   print (g, "Sequence in original order", a, 25, 25);
4   sort();
5   print(g, "results", a, 25, 55);
6   }
7   public void sort()
8   {
9   for (int pass=1; pass <a.length; pass++)
10  for (int i=0; i<a.length; i++)
11  if (a[i]>a[i+1])
12      {hold=a[i];
13      a[i]=a[i+1];
14      a[i+1]=hold;
15      }
16  }
```

Operators	Occurrences	Operands	Occurrences
public	2	paint	1
void	2	Graphics	1
()	2	sort	1
.	6	25	2
int	3	55	2
++	2	a	5
[]	3	1	4
{}	4	pass	3
for	2	a.length	2
=	2	i	7
+	2	hold	2
>	1	g	2
		o	1
		print	2
$\eta_1 = 12$	$N_1 = 31$	$\eta_2 = 14$	$N_2 = 35$

Operators	Occurrences	Operands	Occurrences
public	2	djk	3
int	2	dik	5
float	5	sum	8
()	24	i	12
{}	6	c	1
<	5	0	5
++	5	k	4
for	5	Nm	1
[]	17	l	6
distance	3	n	1
partition	1	xk	2
void	1	x	1
!=	2	vj	1
double	1	vi	1
java.lang.Math.pow	2	0.0	4
/	4	2	2
-	4	p	2
return	1	1	2
;	3	j	3
=	15	u	2
$\eta_1 = 20$	$N_1 = 108$	a	3
		b	3
		$\eta_2 = 22$	$N_2 = 72$

Finally, the length estimate is given as

$$\hat{N} = 20\log_2 20 + 22\log_2 22$$

The length formula exhibits a strong information theoretic flavor and does not take into consideration the style of programming and a different treatment of symbols (some operands may occur more often—this is not taken into consideration in the basic length equation). The differences between N and $\hat{N}$ are explained through impurities in programs (Halstead, 1977).

13.4.2 Program Volume Measure

The program volume V is another measure proposed by Halstead and expressed as

$$V = N\log_2 \eta$$

It is interpreted as the number of mental comparisons required to write a program of length N. The second factor, that is $\log_2 \eta$, expresses the number of attempts

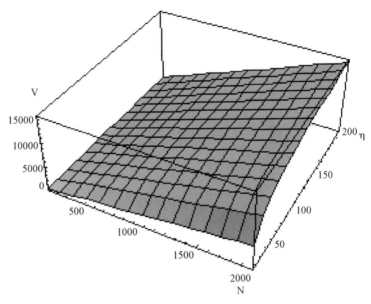

Figure 13.5 V as a function of N and η.

in a binary search applied to a vocabulary of size η. The formula stipulates that in coding activities one follows this particular style of simple search. This is, perhaps, the most questionable assumption made about the model—one may argue that programming is far more sophisticated than selecting a token from a finite repertoire of operators and operands. To illustrate this idea, the relevant plots of V as a function of N and η for some selected values of the arguments are shown in Figure 13.5.

13.4.3 Potential Volume Measure

The potential volume measure is aimed at the determination of the most condensed form of the code: Evidently, the highest level of compactness can be envisioned when we reference the already written procedure (module). For example, we have

```
compute (inputs, outputs)
```

The potential volume of such a procedure, V*, is computed as

$$V^* = (2 + \eta_2^*) \log_2 (2 + \eta_2^*)$$

where η_2^* represents the number of conceptually unique inputs and outputs; here 2 is added to account for the procedure call (say, compute) and a grouping symbol (a pair of parenthesis). For instance, the called procedure

---
```
inversion(a, b, c)
```
---

exhibits the potential volume equal to

$$V^* = (2 + 3) \log_2 (2 + 3) = 5\log_2 5 = 11.61$$

The main difficulty with the use of V* resides with the determination of the number of conceptually unique inputs and outputs. Quite often, especially for larger projects, the estimate of the input-output parameters could be tedious and unreliable.

13.4.4 Program Level

The potential volume can be used as an important yardstick one can use to measure some other implementations of the same algorithm. This comparison is worked out in the form of so-called program level L defined as a ratio

$$L = \frac{V^*}{V}$$

where V is a volume of another implementation originating from the same requirement. If V = V* then L = 1. In general, V < V* and L is below 1. The inverse of L

$$D = \frac{1}{L}$$

is known as a difficulty. For low-level languages (such as assemblers), the resulting volume is high, and so is the difficulty of the implementation. This observation sounds very convincing. Usually understanding any code in assembly language is significantly more difficult than comprehending the equivalent code in any high-level language. In general, the higher level of the programming language used, the lower the level of difficulty of the produced code. As the potential volume metric V* is difficult to determine, another estimate of the program level was proposed (Halstead, 1977):

$$\hat{L} = \frac{2}{\eta_1} \frac{\eta_2}{N_2}$$

The rationale behind this formula is that if the ratio $\eta_1/2$ increases (more operators in the code), this causes the level of difficulty to increase. Moreover, if some operands are used repetitively, this also contributes to the increase of the difficulty level.

13.4.5 Effort and Time Measures

In Software Science a metric was proposed expressing effort (E) to implement the software. It is defined as

$$E = \frac{V}{L}$$

Accepting the estimate of the program level we get

$$E = \frac{V}{\hat{L}}$$

Inserting the previously obtained expressions we derive

$$E = \frac{V^2}{V*} = \frac{(N\log_2 \eta)^2}{V*}$$

and

$$E = \frac{\eta_1 N_2 \log_2 \eta}{2\eta_2}$$

The unit of measurement of E is elementary mental discrimination. There is an interesting aspect on how the effort metric correlates with software modularity. Modularity is commonly emphasized as an important design aspect with many well-understood advantages. The effort of modularity is well reflected in the values of the associated effort. Consider that a code is organized in the form of two modules. It is justifiable to assume that the vocabulary for each module is the same as originally used within the entire code, that is $\eta = \eta(1) = \eta(2)$, where $\eta(1)$ and $\eta(2)$ denote the vocabularies used for the individual modules. Furthermore we have

$$N = N_1 + N_2$$

Similarly, assume that $V* = V*(1) = V*(2)$. Then the effort associated with each module is

$$E(1) = \frac{(N(1)\log_2 \eta)^2}{V*}$$

$$E(2) = \frac{(N(2)\log_2 \eta)^2}{V*}$$

Let us contrast the sum of these two expressions with the overall effort associated with the original code. Here

$$E = \frac{(N(1)\log_2 \eta + N(2)\log_2 \eta)^2}{V*}$$

In other words, $E > E(1) + E(2)$. This is an interesting finding: The effort measure associated with building modular software is lower than that put into constructing systems without any provisions for modularity. If we were given a speed at which the mental discrimination is carried out, we can convert effort E into the programming time

$$T = \frac{E}{\beta}$$

where β is the number of elementary discriminations per second. In fact, some studies in psychology (Stroud, 1967) suggest that the human mind can complete between 5 to 20 elementary discriminations per second (that is $\beta \in [5, 20]$). This allows us to compute values of T. For instance, if a problem requires 2000 discriminations, the programming time is limited by the values.

$$T_{low} = \frac{2000}{20} = 100[sec]$$

$$T_{up} = \frac{2000}{5} = 400[sec]$$

The complexity metrics originating from Software Science exhibit an interesting and sound background with useful insights into the very nature of programming activities and the programming environment. By their nature, they concentrate on the code itself. At the same time the metrics should be able to predict some characteristics of software such as cost, development time, and reliability. There should be a high (or meaningful) correlation between the values of the metric and the predicted software quality. The experimental findings are not consistent, and in some cases the Software Science metrics did not correlate well with the predicted results themselves.

Let us continue with the medical image processing module and plot the relationship between the number of changes made to the modules and some metrics such as LOC, estimated program size, and cyclomatic complexity (Figure 13.6). The number of changes can be regarded as a viable indicator about the effort necessary to develop the module. As seen in Figure 13.6, some of the relationships are evident. Nevertheless none of the measures performs really well. In general, there is no one-to-one correspondence between the values of the metric and the number of modifications of the module. As of today, these measures (and many others) are still controversial. The number of software

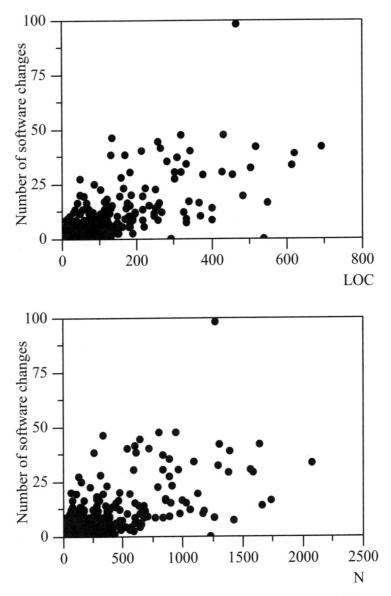

Figure 13.6   Changes for selected software metrics for the set of MIS software modules.

metrics is steadily growing. Several of them rely on Software Science and attempt to improve the original methods. In this sense, Software Science is a fruitful research avenue with significant implications for the practice of software development.

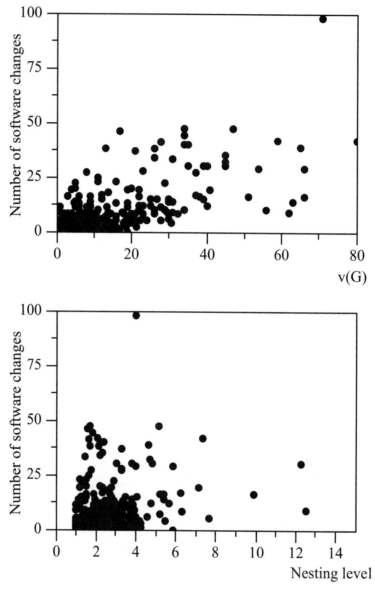

Figure 13.6   *(Continued)*

13.5 SIZE MEASURE BASED ON ZIPF'S LAW

Yet another software size measure concerns a function count. This measure is particularly useful in describing large software systems. If one fixes a size of a module to "m" lines of code, then a prediction of a size of the code gets quite reliable. Otherwise, the quality of the prediction based on function count becomes quite questionable and the ensuing estimates should be treated with caution. The program length measure correlates in an interesting way with a far more general law originating from Zipf's studies on natural languages (Zipf, 1949).

The intent of Zipf's studies was to investigate dependencies between frequencies of some words in a sample of text. In spite of fundamental differences, computer languages can be studied in the same framework. Let us get to the hypothesis (Zipf's law) formulated in natural languages. Given is a sample of "n" tokens (words, symbols, and so forth). We count how often individual words occur in the sample (text). The number of occurrence is denoted by n_r. More precisely, the subscript (r) is used to denote a rank of the token (ranking is performed based on its occurrence frequency). Thus the most frequently occurring type of token is denoted by n_1, the next one by n_2, and so on. If there are "t" types of tokens, we get

$$\sum_{r=1}^{t} n_r = n$$

The relative frequency f_r is expressed as the ratio of n_r and n,

$$f_r = \frac{n_r}{n}$$

The hypothesis formulated by Zipf concerns the frequency of occurrence f_r and the corresponding rank r. Experimental results support an interesting claim that the product of the frequency and a power function of the ranks,

$$f_r r^\alpha = c$$

where "c" is a certain constant. Moreover, as a first approximation α can be set to 1. This produces a so-called Zipf's first law of the form

$$f_r r = c$$

or equivalently

$$n_r = \frac{cn}{r}$$

13.5.1 Sample Application of Zipf's Law

Next, consider a Java code fragment that increments sensor values within predefined boundaries. This code will be used to illustrate all of the necessary computations needed to apply Zipf's law.

```
for (int i=0; i < length; i++){
if ((sensor[i] > lower_bound) && (sensor[i] < upper_bound)) {
   sensor[i]++;
   modif++;
   }
}
```

We identify the tokens in this code and count their number, which are also converted into frequencies of their occurrence:

Token	Number of tokens (n_r)	Frequency f_r
for	1	0.027
sensor	3	0.081
modif	1	0.027
++	3	0.081
int	1	0.027
i	6	0.162
lower_bound	1	0.027
upper_bound	1	0.027
length	1	0.027
{ }	2	0.054
[ ]	3	0.081
=	1	0.027
&&	1	0.027

Zipf's law can be used to derive a length of a document (n) for a given number of classes of tokens. Using the above expression, we start with a summation in (1)

$$\sum_{r-=1}^{t} n_r = cn \sum_{r=1}^{5} \frac{1}{r} \tag{1}$$

The harmonic series is approximated in (2).

$$\sum_{r=1}^{t} \frac{1}{r} = 0.5772 + \ln t + \frac{1}{2t} + \ldots \tag{2}$$

By substituting (2) into (1), the formula in (3) is obtained.

$$n = cn(0.5772 + \ln t) \qquad (3)$$

Then the constant c in (3) is computed as shown in (4).

$$c = \frac{1}{0.5772 + \ln t} \qquad (4)$$

We can use original Zipf's law in a different way by focusing on the ranks of the tokens. A reasonable assumption would be to consider that the rarest type of tokens occurs only once. Thus

$$1 = \frac{cn}{t}$$

and

$$c = \frac{t}{n}$$

Then the size of the document (number of tokens) can be computed by substituting the new value of c into equation (3). The result is given in (5).

$$n = \frac{t}{n} n(0.5772 + \ln t) = t(0.5772 + \ln t) \qquad (5)$$

The parameter t in (5) denotes the number of types of tokens. One should stress that the estimated size of the document could vary in comparison to its actual value. This is not surprising as we considered the model in its simplest format. In particular, the value of the power function (α) may be different from 1 for a certain document under consideration.

13.5.2 Zipf's Law Versus Halstead

At this point, it is worth comparing the length estimate developed by Halstead

$$N = \eta_1 \log_2 \eta_1 + \eta_2 \log_2 \eta_2 \qquad (6)$$

and the one resulting from the Zipf's law

$$N' = t(0.5772 + \ln t) \qquad (7)$$

Parameter "t" is the size of the vocabulary, namely, $\eta_1 + \eta_2$. By substituting $\eta_1 + \eta_2$ into equation (7), we derive the formula in (8).

$$N' = (\eta_1 + \eta_2)(0.5772 + \ln(\eta_1 + \eta_2)) \qquad (8)$$

The comparison can be conveniently summarized by observing a ratio N/N' for different values of η_1 and η_2 (it is symmetrical with respect to both arguments). In some limit cases one can get this ratio in a direct way. For instance, assume that the number of operands η_2 dominates the number of operators, $\eta_2 \gg \eta_1$. This leads to several simplifications

$$N \approx \eta_2 \log_2 \eta_2$$

Moreover

$$N' = \eta_2(0.5772 + \ln \eta_2) \approx \eta_2 \ln \eta_2$$

Hence

$$\frac{N}{N'} = \frac{\log_2 \eta_2}{\ln \eta_2} = 1.4427$$

meaning that Zipf's length is smaller than the length derived by Halstead. In other words, the Zipf's length can be viewed as a lower bound of the results derived using the second approach. Further enhancements of Zipf's law (giving rise to more comprehensive expressions) are discussed in Shooman (1983).

13.6 DATA STRUCTURE MEASURE

Most software processes involve input and output data. Hence, software measurement includes a consideration of data structures of software systems. The most evident measure is to count the number of all variables (VAR) in the code. For instance, the Java code considered earlier contains four variables: a, pass, i, and hold. Using the Halstead measure of the number of operands η_2, VAR is included in the operand count.

$$\eta_2 = VAR + \text{unique constants} + \text{labels}$$

13.7 LOGIC STRUCTURE MEASURE

Logic structure metrics attempt to quantify a feature that is the most profound in any code: its logic structure. It is self-explanatory that the flowchart of a code says a lot about its complexity: the higher the complexity of the code, the more difficult it is to understand the associated flowchart. A measure of the underlying graph properties of the flowchart is needed.

13.7.1 Software Cyclomatic Complexity

A straightforward way to assess the complexity of a method is to count the number of decisions in the flow diagram representation of the method as shown in Figure 13.7. This is known as the cyclomatic complexity measure introduced by McCabe in 1976. The measure proposed by McCabe computes a number (or simply cyclomatic complexity) $v(G)$, where G stands for the associated graph of the flowchart. Essentially, this metric measures the number of linearly independent paths through a program. The form of these paths and their number strongly relate to the anticipated difficulties when testing and maintaining the software. The cyclomatic complexity represents the same property as the cyclomatic number utilized in a directed graph. The accepted definition of such a notion comes in the form

$$v(G) = e - n + 2p$$

where e is the number of edges, n is the number of nodes, and p is the number of connected components in the graph. Usually $p = 1$ so that $v(G)$ reduces to the form

$$v(G) = e - n + 2$$

Let us determine $v(G)$ for some flowcharts. This is helpful in gaining a better insight into the meaning of the complexity measure. In the corresponding graph, one regards statement and decision boxes as nodes of the graphs. The links between them are the edges of the produced graph.

For the flowchart in Figure 13.8 we have $e = 9$, $n = 8$, so that $v(G) = 9 - 8 + 2 = 3$. The lowest cyclomatic complexity results in flowcharts that represent

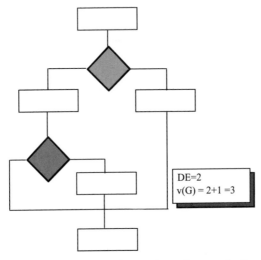

Figure 13.7 Measuring cyclomatic complexity.

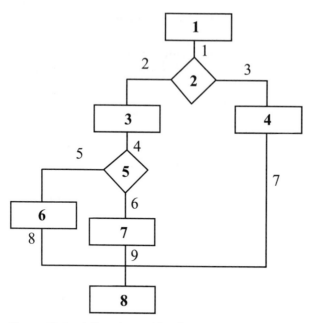

Figure 13.8   A flowchart with edges and nodes identified.

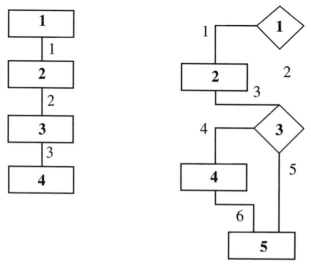

Figure 13.9   Examples of two flowcharts with different v(G) values.

a direct flow of control (like the one exhibited in Figure 13.9), v(G) = 3 − 4 + 2 = 1. Note that the value of v(G) does not depend on the number of statements in the flowchart. For the graph with a substantial number of decision boxes the values of v(G) are higher, refer again to Figure 13.9, e = 6, n = 5, v(G) = 6 − 5 + 2 = 3.

13.7.2 Example: Cyclomatic Complexity of tATC Method

In this section, the cyclomatic complexity of the Change method for the tATC system is measured. Recall that the Change method is responsible for changing the altitude, velocity, or heading of an aircraft. The following Java code has been derived from a prototype of a training program for air traffic controllers (Agatep et al., 1997):

```
public void Change (Plane m_pPlane, int m_nAlt, int m_nVel, int m_nHeading){
//this part of code deals with the altitude; 0 means no change, and
//1-increase altitude by 500 m,
//2-decrease altitude by 500 m

if(m_pPlane.crashed ==false)&&(m_pPlane.landed==false){
 if(m_nAlt ==1){
 if(m_pPlane.m_nZPos<6000){
   m_pPlane.m_nZPos = m_pPlane.m_nZPos +500//increase altitude by 500 m
  }
 }
if(m_nAlt ==2){
 if (m_pPlane.m_nZPos > 0){
   m_pPlane.m_nZPos = m_pPlane.m_nZPos −500 //decrease altitude by 500 m
   }
}}
//this part of the code deals with aircraft velocity
if (m_nVel ==1){
 if (m_pPlane.m_nVelocity <1200){
   m_pPlane.m_nVelocity = m_pPlane.m_nVelocity +200
   }
 }
else if (m_nVel ==2){
 if (m_pPlane.m_nVelocity > 0){
   m_pPlane.m_nVelocity = m_pPlane.m_nVelocity −200
   }
}
//this part of the code deals with aircraft heading
if((m_pPlane.m_nHeading ==m_pPlane.m_nNewHeading)&&(m_nHeading != 8)) {
   M_pPlane.m_nNewHeading = m_nHeading;
   }
} //Change
```

The graph of this class is rather large. It can be shown that the cyclomatic complexity of this code is 12. The higher the value of $v(G)$, the higher the cyclomatic complexity of the flowchart. What is also highly intuitive, the flowchart with high $v(G)$ is more difficult to comprehend. The corresponding code is also difficult to maintain. As suggested by McCabe, a reasonable limit of the cyclomatic complexity measure is 10; beyond this boundary the code ceases to be manageable. A suggested remedy is to split the code into several modules so that the value of $v(G)$ for each module does not exceed 10.

The computations of $v(G)$ relies on the flowchart of the code, which can become quite cluttered. One simplification of this process can be done by associating $v(G)$ with the number of predicates used in decision boxes, or the number of decision boxes. In fact, it was found that $V(G)$ can be computed as follows:

$$v(G) = DE + 1$$

DE stands for the number of decision boxes present in the flowchart. Two approaches to computing $V(G)$ are shown in Figure 13.10. $V(G)$ is computed either by counting the number of nodes and edges (Figure 13.10a) or by counting the number of decisions (Figure 13.10b). Since there are two decision boxes in both cases, $V(G) = 3$. Highlighted code for the Change method is given in Figure 13.11. The number of shaded decision boxes is 11. Notice that a decision box with a composite condition should be treated differently.

13.7.3 Additive Feature of Cyclomatic Complexity

An interesting and useful property of the cyclomatic complexity is that this complexity measure is additive. In other words, the cyclomatic measure of the modular system is equal to the sum of the cyclomatic complexities of the individual modules (Conte et al., 1986),

$$v(G) = v(G_1) = v(G_2) + \ldots + v(G_c)$$

where $v(G_1)$, $v(G_2)$, $\ldots$ $v(G_c)$ are the complexity measures of the individual modules. To elaborate on that, refer to Figure 13.12. It is enough to show that the additivity property holds for any two modules.

In Figure 13.12, notice that the two connecting edges express the interaction between two particular software modules. That is, module "i" and module "j" interact (one calls the other), hence this adds two extra edges between the corresponding graphs. For module "i" one gets $v(G_i) = e_i - n_i + 2$. Similarly, the same applies to the second module, $v(G_j) = e_j - n_j + 2$. In general, for the two modules we get

$$
\begin{aligned}
v(G_i \cup G_j) &= (e_i + e_j + 2) - (n_i + n_j) + 2 \\
&= (e_i - n + 2) + (e_j - n_j + 2) \\
&= v(G) + v(G)
\end{aligned}
$$

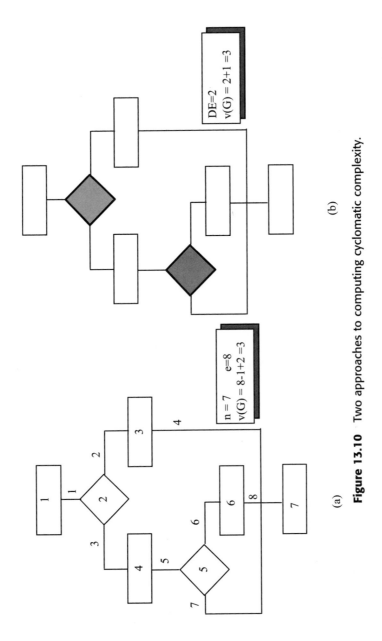

Figure 13.10 Two approaches to computing cyclomatic complexity.

```
public void Change (Plane m_pPlane, int m_nAlt, int m_nVel, int m_nHeading){
// this part of code deals with the altitude; 1 - increase altitude by 500 m; 0 - no change
// 2 - decrease altitude by 500 m
if (m_pPlane.crashed ==false) && (m_pPlane.landed==false){
  if (m_nAlt ==1){
    if (m_pPlane.m_nZPos <6000){
      m_pPlane.m_nZPos = m_pPlane.m_nZPos +500          // increase altitude by 500 m
    }// if
  } // if
  if (m_nAlt ==2){
    if (m_pPlane.m_nZPos > 0){
      m_pPlane.m_nZPos = m_pPlane.m_nZPos -500          // decrease altitude by 500 m
    } // if
  }} // if
// this part of code deals with velocity
  if (m_nVel ==1){
    if (m_pPlane.m_nVelocity <1200) {
      m_pPlane.m_nVelocity = m_pPlane.m_nVelocity +200
    }
  }
    else if (m_nVel ==2){
      if (m_pPlane.m_nVelocity > 0) {
        m_pPlane.m_nVelocity = m_pPlane.m_nVelocity -200
      } // if
    } // else
// this part of code deals with the heading
  if (( m_pPlane.m_nHeading == m_pPlane.m_nNewHeading) && (m_nHeading != 8)) {
    M_pPlane.m_nNewHeading = m_nHeading;
  } // if
} // Change
```

Figure 13.11   Computing cyclomatic complexity using decision boxes.

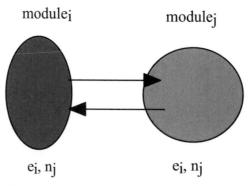

module$_i$ module$_j$

e$_i$, n$_j$ e$_i$, n$_j$

Figure 13.12   Computing V(G) for two software modules.

Consider, for instance, two Java methods where a test_sensor method invokes a method named filter in the event that the reading of an individual sensor exceeds the boundaries:

```
public test_sensor () {
int length,
for (int i=0; i < length; i++){
if (sensor[i] < lower_bound) || (sensor[i] > upper_bound) {
sensor[i]=filter(sensor[i]);
}
}
public double filter (double x) {
double y;
y=0.5*(x +x_old);
return y;
}
```

In this case, test_sensor invokes filter with the current reading of the sensor. The filter returns its filtered value as shown in Figure 13.13. In the case of "c" modules, one obtains (9).

$$v(G) = \sum_{i=1}^{c} v(G_i) \tag{9}$$

where "c" is the number of the software modules of the system. Recall that $V(G)$ is calculated as follows when c equals 1 and is computed using (10).

$$v(G_i) = DE_i + 1 \tag{10}$$

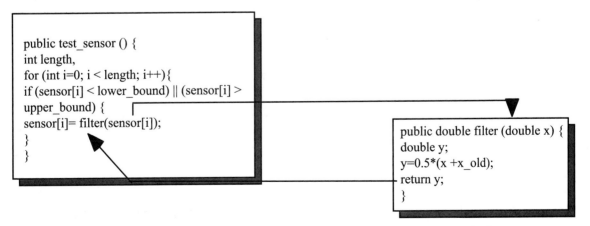

Figure 13.13 Communication between sensor_read and filter methods.

By substituting the equation for V(G) in (10) into equation (9), the new formula for computing V(G) is obtained in (11).

$$v(G) = \sum_{i=1}^{c} DE_i + c \qquad (11)$$

For the code in Figure 13.14, with two methods, the number of the corresponding decision boxes in $DE_1 = 5$ and $DE_2 = 1$, respectively. Hence, the cyclomatic complexity of the entire code is equal $V(G) = 6 + 2 = 8$.

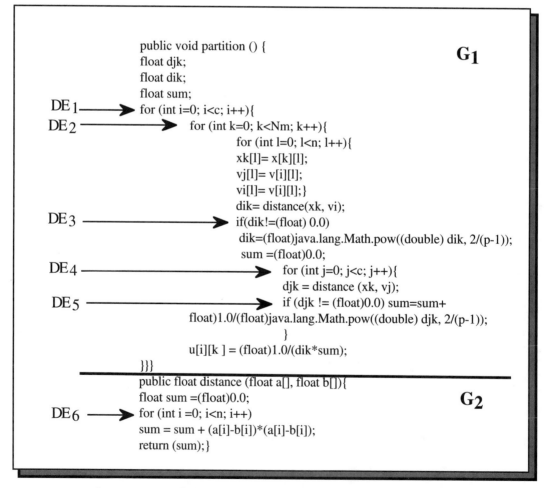

Figure 13.14   Calculations of V(G) for two methods.

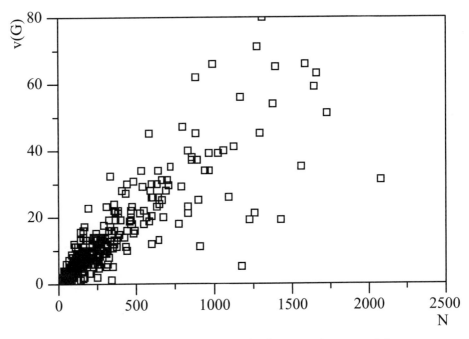

Figure 13.15 Distribution of v(G) versus N for the MIS software modules.

Returning to the software modules of the MIS, the experimental relationships between v(G) and N are shown in Figure 13.15.

13.7.4 Reachability Measures

A Reachability software measure was proposed by Schneidewind and Hoffman (1979). It attempts to characterize the complexity of a flowchart by qualifying a number of unique ways (paths) one can reach from each node of the resulting graph. The higher the Reachability value, the higher the complexity of the flowchart. The notion of Reachability deals with the number of unique ways of reaching each node. As the number of paths could be high (especially in the case of loops in a graph), the paths of interest exclude those with backward loops traversed more than once. The average reachability, $\overline{R}$, is taken as the total number of paths divided by the number of nodes

$$\overline{R} = \frac{\text{total number of paths}}{\text{number of nodes}}$$

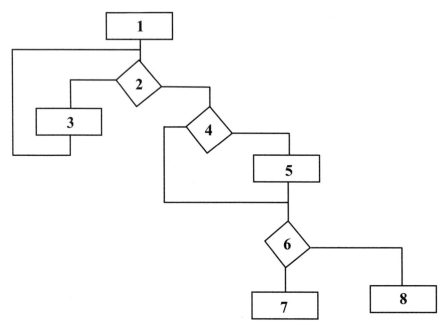

Figure 13.16   Example flowchart.

To discuss the details, let us consider the flowchart in Figure 13.16. The enumeration of all paths is the first step in the calculations of the reachability metric. From Figure 13.16, the following paths can be identified:

```
node 1: {1}
node 2: {1,2,3,2}, {1,2}
node 3: {1,2,3}
node 4: {1,2,3,2,4}, {1,2,4}
node 5: {1,2,4,5}, {1,2,3,2,4,5}
node 6: {1,2,3,2,4,5,6} {1,2,4,5,6}, {1,2,3,2,4,6}, {1,2,4,6}
node 7: {1,2,3,2,4,5,6,7} {1,2,4,5,6,7}, {1,2,3,2,4,6,7}, {1,2,4,6,7}
node 8: {1,2,3,2,4,5,6,8} {1,2,4,5,6,8}, {1,2,3,2,4,6,8}, {1,2,4,6,8}
```

One should stress that for each node we determine all paths that terminate at this particular node. For example, for the second node in Figure 13.17 we have two distinct paths. The first path goes directly to node 2. The second path traverses through nodes 2 and 3 and loops back to 2.

Thus the reachability measure is equal to

$$\overline{R} = \frac{\text{total number of paths}}{\text{number of nodes}} = \frac{1+2+1+2+2+4+4+4}{8} = \frac{20}{8} = 2.5$$

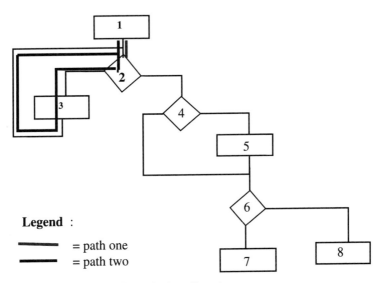

Legend :

────── = path one

────── = path two

Figure 13.17 Sample paths in a flowchart.

The number of paths (N_p) for node 7 is 4. The cyclomatic complexity measure-ment for the flowchart is $3 + 1 = 4$ that is $N_p \geq v(G)$.

13.7.5 Nesting Levels Measure

The nesting levels measure is useful when it comes to expressing the depth of nesting of loops, one inside another. It is natural to expect that higher nesting (depth) levels contribute to more complex codes. The nesting levels measure (Dunsmore and Gannon, 1980) is computed by assigning a level of depth to each executable statement in a code and averaging these values. The assessment of the levels is realized according to the following rules:

- The first executable statement has a nesting level 1.
- If statement "s1" is at level k and statement "s2" follows it sequentially (in terms of its execution), then it assumes the same nesting level (k).
- If statement "s1" is at level k and statement "s2" is in the range of a loop or a conditional transfer controlled by "s1", then the nesting level of s2 is k+1.

Consider, for example, the Java bubble sort code. The nesting levels are computed following the above stated assignment rules; the nesting levels of the individual statements are also indicated in the code:

```
1   public void paint (Graphics g)
    {
    1   print (g, "Sequence in original order ", a, 25, 25);
        1   sort();
            1 print(g, "results", a,25, 55);
    }
                1   public void sort()
            {
                1   for (int pass=1; pass <a.length; pass++)
                2   for (int i=0; i<a.length; I++)
                3   if (a[i] > a[i+1])
                4   { hold = a[i];
                4   a[i] = a[i+1];
                4   a[i+1] = hold;
            }
        }
```

The average nesting level $\overline{NL}$ (that becomes representative for the entire code) is taken as an average

$$\overline{NL} = \frac{\text{sum of all nesting levels}}{\text{number of statements}}$$

These computations can be captured in an equivalent fashion by writing down the nesting level metric as

$$\overline{NL} = \frac{\sum iL(i)}{\text{number of statements}}$$

where $L(i)$ denotes the number of nodes at level i. Commonly, this metric is referred to a program bandwidth (BW). For the above code, a number of observations can be made:

- Sum of all nesting levels is $1 + 1 + 1 + 1 + 1 + 1 + 2 + 3 + 4 + 4 + 4 = 33$.
- Number of statements is 11.
- Resulting nesting level metric equals $33/11 = 3$.

Figure 13.18 summarizes the relationships between the nesting level and the size of the code $(LOC - N)$ and the nesting level and $v(G)$ reported for the MIS modules. First, the bandwidth measure does not correlate well with N; this is expected as these two metrics concentrate on two very different facets of software complexity (structure versus bulk size of the code). Second, the lack of correlation becomes more visible for larger sizes of the modules.

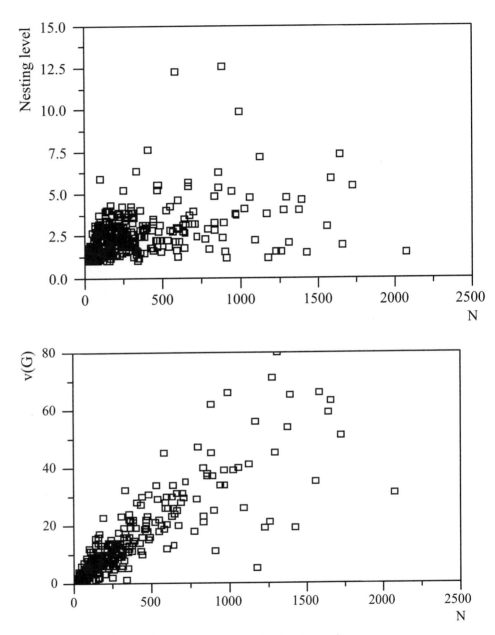

Figure 13.18 Relationships between nesting level, v(G), and N.

13.8 ENTROPY-BASED SOFTWARE MEASURE

The notion of entropy is fundamental to all faculties of information processing. It has been found useful in software engineering (Davis & LeBlanc, 1988; Harrison, 1992). The ways in which entropy can be used are numerous. The use of the entropy measure in the framework of software engineering calls for the attachment of meaning to the basic symbols. This step constitutes the fundamental step in the development of the entropy-based software metrics. What seems to be quite natural is to view the symbols as the operators used in the code and calculate their entropy of these operators. Before proceeding with a detailed analysis, recall the notion of entropy in connection with the information in a message. In this context, entropy is a measure of the average information rate of a message or language.

Consider a finite set of symbols—an alphabet consisting of symbols a_1, a_2, . . . , a_n and strings of symbols with the following form:

$$a_1 a_4 a_n$$
$$a_2 a_4 a_6 a_8 a_{n-1} a_n$$

Strings of symbols are examples of messages. More specifically, algebraic expressions are nothing but strings of symbols. The symbols include variables (a, b, d, f, h, w, x, y, z) and algebraic operations (+, *, **, −, sin). Examples of such expressions are written as follows:

$$a + b*x − d*f*h − w**2$$

or

$$(5*x + y**3 − \sin(z))$$

Furthermore let us assume that each symbol occurs with probability p_1 such that $p_1 + p_2 + . . . p_n = 1$. The amount of information conveyed by symbol p_i is defined as follows:

$$I_i = -\log_2 p_i$$

Note that if $p_i = 0$ or $p_i = 1$, $I_i = 0$ while I_i attains a maximal value for $p_i = \frac{1}{2}$. This accounts for a maximal level of information carried by the one-symbol message. The entropy measure is additive, that is to say for a finite string of symbols $a_1 a_2 . . . a_i . . . a_j$, the entropy of the overall string $H(a_1 a_2 . . . a_i . . . a_j)$ computes as follows:

$$H = -\sum_{i=1}^{j} p_i \log_2 p_i$$

This formula represents the average information rate per symbol. The variable p_i is the probability of occurrence of the ith symbol in a message. More specifically relative to computer program code, the empirical probability of occurrence of the i-th operator p_i is computed as follows:

$$p_i = \frac{n_i}{n}$$

where n_i is a frequency of occurrence of this operator while "n" stands for the number of all occurrences of the operators. Then entropy of a software module is computed as follows:

$$H = -\sum_{i=1}^{j} \frac{n_i}{n} \log_2 \frac{n_i}{n}$$

where j denotes the number of classes of the operators. This entropy-based measure, called the average information content classification (AICC), was introduced by Harrison (1992) and has been used to assess data communications software systems. It was observed that this metric exhibits a good correlation with the error spans.

13.8.1 Entropy Measure Based on Equivalence Classes

The entropy-based software metric discussed by Davis and LeBlanc (1988) exploits the notion of entropy at a higher conceptual level by considering so-called chunks of code. A chunk could be a single statement, a block of code, or a module itself. An important notion is an equivalence class of chunks. The concept of the equivalence class is based on their in-degree and out-degree as they occur in a flowchart (Figure 13.19). Two chunks are equivalent if they are characterized by the same in-degree and out-degree of links with the environment. For instance, A and C fall into the same equivalence class (2 in-degree, 2 out-degree); similarly B and E are the elements of the same equivalence class (1 in-degree, 3 out-degree). In the simplest version, we are concerned with a first-order entropy by making entropy sensitive to the increasing amount of structure by considering

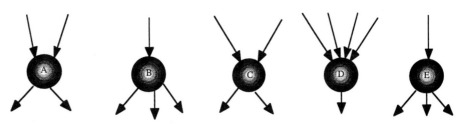

Figure 13.19 Examples of equivalence classes.

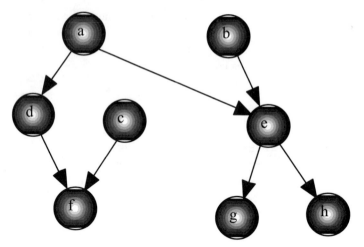

Figure 13.20 An example flowchart with chunks of code.

the chunk neighbors. The entropy is computed with respect to the chunks situated in the same equivalence class. More specifically, we get

$$H = H_1 + H_2 \ldots + H_p$$

where H_k denotes the entropy computed for the i-th group of chunks (equivalence class). A flowchart representing chunks of code is given in Figure 13.20. First, let us identify the chunks as they fall under difference equivalence classes (the same values of in-degree and out-degree):

```
0 in-degree, 1 out-degree: b,c
1 in-degree, 0 out-degree: f,g,h
1 in-degree, 1 out-degree: d
2 in-degree, 2 out-degree: e
0 in-degree, 2 out-degree: a
```

The probabilities associated with the equivalence classes are equal to $\frac{2}{8}, \frac{3}{8}, \frac{1}{8}, \frac{1}{8}, \frac{1}{8}$, respectively (note that we deal with 8 chunks). Subsequently, the entropy equals

$$H = \left[\frac{2}{8} \log_2 \left(\frac{2}{8} \right) + \frac{3}{8} \log_2 \left(\frac{3}{8} \right) + \frac{1}{8} \log_2 \left(\frac{1}{8} \right) + \frac{1}{8} \log_2 \left(\frac{1}{8} \right) + \frac{1}{8} \log_2 \left(\frac{1}{8} \right) \right]$$
$$= 1.09$$

Note that the minimum entropy occurs when all the chunks are situated in the same equivalence class,

$$H = 0$$

The maximum entropy happens when the chunks are placed in separate classes (one chunk per class)

$$H = \log(n)$$

where "n" stands for the number of chunks.

13.8.2 Example: McCabe Versus Entropy Measure

In what follows, we consider two flowcharts shown in Figure 13.21, and determine their McCabe cyclomatic measure as well as the entropy measure. What is of interest to us are the individual statements (of course, these can be viewed as blocks of statements). First, we determine the equivalence classes for the flowcharts. For flowchart G:

```
1 in-degree 1 out-degree: b,c,e,f
2 in-degree 0 out-degree: g
0 in-degree 2 out-degree: a
1 in-degree 2 out-degree: d
```

The equivalence classes are {a}, {b, c, e, f}, {d}, {g}.

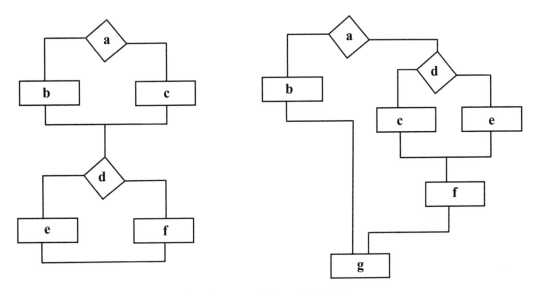

Figure 13.21 Two flowcharts: G (left) and G′ (right).

For flowchart G': {a}, {b, d, e}, {c}, {f}, {g}:

```
1 in-degree 1 out-degree: b, c, e
0 in-degree 2 out-degree: a
1 in-degree 2 out-degree: d
1 in-degree 1 out-degree: f
2 in-degree 0 out-degree: g
```

The equivalence classes are formed as {b, c, e}, {a}, {f}, {g}, {d}. The entropies for G and G' are given next. Entropy for flowchart G:

$$H = -\sum_{\substack{\text{over four} \\ \text{classes}}} P(A_i)\log_2 P(A_i) = -\left[\frac{1}{7}\log_2\frac{1}{7} + \frac{4}{7}\log_2\frac{4}{7} + \frac{1}{7}\log_2\frac{1}{7} + \frac{1}{7}\log_2\frac{1}{7}\right]$$

$$= 1.664$$

Entropy for flowchart G':

$$H = -\sum_{\substack{\text{over five} \\ \text{classes}}} P(A_i)\log_2 P(A_i)$$

$$= -\left[\frac{1}{7}\log_2\frac{1}{7} + \frac{3}{7}\log_2\frac{3}{7} + \frac{1}{7}\log_2\frac{1}{7} + \frac{1}{7}\log_2\frac{1}{7} + \frac{1}{7}\log_2\frac{1}{7}\right] = 2.128$$

The calculations of the cyclomatic complexity measure for flowcharts G and G' produce the following results:

$$v(G) = DE + 1 = 2 + 1 = 3$$
$$v(G') = DE' + 1 = 2 + 1 = 3$$

Thus G and G' are equivalent in terms of the cyclomatic complexity measure. On the other hand, the entropy measure is capable of distinguishing between these two flowcharts. A visual inspection may suggest that the diversity of the structure of G' is higher than the one represented by G; furthermore, the structure of G looks more "regular" than G'.

13.9 INFORMATION FLOW SOFTWARE MEASURE

An information flow metric was introduced by Henry and Kafura (1981). This metric measures the complexity of code structure by concentrating on flow of

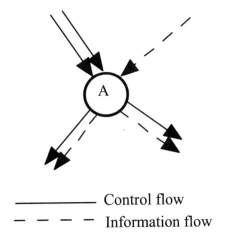

———————— Control flow

— — — — Information flow

Figure 13.22 Fan-in and fan-out of module A.

control and information within the module. The measure aims at expressing both links between modules as well as size. Central to the definition of the Henry and Kafura metric are fan-in and fan-out. The fan-in of module A is the number of local flows into A increased by the number of data structures from which A retrieves information. The fan-out of module A is the number of local flows from module A plus the number of data structures that A updates. For instance, the fan-in of A in Figure 13.22 is 4 (3 local flows and one information flow) and its fan-out is 4 (2 local flows and 2 information flows).

The information flow metric is defined as the product of length, fan-in, and fan-out:

$$\text{Information Flow} = \text{length} * (\text{fan-in} * \text{fan-out})^2$$

Let us analyze this measure in more detail:

- The product fan-in * fan-out describes all possible combinations of an input source to an output source.
- The power is used to reflect a complexity of the connections.
- The size of the module is captured in terms of the standard count of the number of statements.

The study by Henry and Kafura (1981) reported on the experiments on the UNIX procedures; the distribution of complexities is shown as follows:

Ordered information flow complexity	Number of UNIX procedures
1	17
10	38
10^2	41
10^3	27
10^4	26
10^5	12
10^6	3
10^7	1

A high complexity of the information flow of some procedures identify them as eventual bottlenecks and potential troublesome points of the entire system. A high fan-in and fan-out shows a significant number of connections, meaning that a module may perform more than one function. To summarize, the classification of the software metrics focusing on a code itself involves three basic categories (classes) depending on which aspect of the code is taken into consideration.

1. *Lexical content of code.* The metrics in this class rely on counting the occurrence of basic building blocks (operators and operands), branches in a code (McCabe cyclomatic metric), or statements of different type. Evidently, one concentrates on the counting of lexical tokens without any semantics taken into consideration. The measures of this type have been found useful in practice by delivering good performance prediction abilities.

2. *Information theoretic measures.* In one way or another, these measures rely on the fundamental notion of entropy. There is a well-established theoretical ground for these measures however their practical applications is somewhat limited.

3. *Flow-oriented measures.* They concentrate on expressing connectivity in a system by observing the flow of information or control among system components.

One should mention a general approach where several software metrics are combined together forming a synthetic complexity measure in an attempt to capture the genuine sense of the software complexity. An example coming from this class of methods is a Maintainability Index (MI) introduced by Oman (1997). It computes as a nonlinear function of some individual software metrics, that is:

$$MI = 171 - 5.2 \ln(\overline{V}) - 0.23 \, \overline{v(G)} - 16.2 \ln(\overline{LOC}) + 50 \sin(\text{sqrt}(2.4 \, \overline{CM}))$$

where the contributing metrics are averaged over the number of software modules as follows:

- Average Halstead's volume, $\overline{V}$
- Averaged cyclomatic complexity, $\overline{v(G)}$
- Averaged number of lines of code, $\overline{LOC}$
- Average percent of lines of comments, $\overline{CM}$

The main advantage of such composite software measures is that they can reflect different aspects of the notion of complexity and blend their facets in an efficient numerical way; the latter is realized through building some regression models (note that the MI metrics contains a series of them). At the same time, the numerical flexibility is also a certain disadvantage of the model. MI may need calibration before it can be applied to a particular software project.

13.10 SOFTWARE MEASURES FOR OBJECT-ORIENTED SYSTEMS

Object-oriented system with their distinct design objectives and goals, calls for a completely new suite of software measures. As the underlying philosophy is different from the others, the concept of the metric has to be revisited. In a nutshell, the object-oriented (OO) methodology centers around objects. Objects stand in sharp contrast to the function-oriented view of software development and analysis. Recall that classes encapsulate both data and functions (methods) and these two components have to be taken into consideration. The object-oriented approach has made a substantial change in the way in which software systems are designed. In general, we may conveniently regard a class as a blueprint (or prototype) that embraces the variables and methods common to all objects of a certain nature (Figure 13.23). Object-oriented design methods combine elements of three basic design facets encountered in software engineering, namely data design, architectural design, and procedural design:

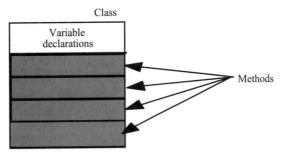

Figure 13.23   Class as blueprint of all objects of a certain category.

- Data abstractions are formed by identifying classes and objects.
- By coupling operations to data, modules become specified and form structures.
- By developing the mechanisms for using the objects, one constructs interfaces.

13.10.1 Example: Family of Robots

We study the concepts of objects and object-oriented design by considering a family of robots. We evolve the robots and keep adding more capabilities that help robots perform better in their environment. A robot moves in a two dimensional world—a grid of integer coordinates. It can move in eight directions: up, down, left, right, up_left, up_right, down_left, down_right. The robot reacts to commands by moving along one of these directions (Figure 13.24).

The robot can be modeled as a class with the following skeletal structure:

```
class Robot {
public int x, y;

method up;
method down;
method left;
method right;
method up_left;
method up_right;
method down_left;
method down_right;
}
```

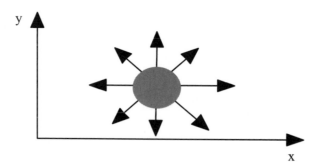

Figure 13.24 All possible moves of a robot in a two-dimensional world.

The methods concerning the possible moves of the robot have not been identified so far—we will get to this in a moment. Evidently, the class of robots encapsulates both data and methods. Now we can declare sample objects as follows.

```
Robot newRobot; simpleRobot; smallRobot;
```

The examples of messages concern the moves of the robot, say

```
SimpleRobot.up(); smallRobot.down_right(); newRobot.up_left();
```

Now consider the methods responsible for moving a robot:

```
public void up(){
y=y+1;
}

public void up_right () {
x=x+1;
y=y+1;
}

public void down_right () {
x=x+1;
y=y-1;
}
```

The Robot class can be written as follows:

```
class Robot {
public int x, y;

    public void up() { y=y+1;}
    public void down () {y=y-1;}
    public void right () {x=x+1;}
    public void left () {x=x-1;}
    public void up_right () {x=x+1; y=y+1;}
    public void down_right () {x=x+1; y=y-1;}
    public void up_left () {x=x-1; y=y+1;}
    public void down_left () {x=x-1; y=y-1;}
}
```

The robot has fairly limited capabilities, as it simply follows commands and moves accordingly. We can make it a bit more sophisticated by adding some sensors so that it can detect obstacles and return information about distance between itself and the obstacles. The resulting robot will inherit all the methods of the previous class Robot and adds an extra one that determines the distance between itself and an obstacle. The obstacle can be viewed as a class Obstacle. It can be accessed by invoking the methods of the class, say Obstacle.x and Obstacle.y, that are used to determine the coordinates of the obstacle.

As before, let us start with the skeleton of the Robot_sense:

```
class Robot_sense extends Robot {
    determine_distance     // here we calculate distance between the robot
    and the obstacle
}
```

The calculations of the distance function use the sum of squared differences between the x and y coordinates of the robot and the obstacle:

```
public double distance (){
double xdiff = x - Target.x;
double ydiff = y - Target.y;
return Math.sqrt(xdiff*xdiff + ydiff*ydiff)
}
```

The Robot_sense class can be written as follows:

```
class Robot_sense extends Robot {
    public double distance () {
    double xdiff = x - Target.x;
    double ydiff = y - Target.y;
    return Math.sqrt(xdiff*xdiff + ydiff*ydiff)
        }
}
```

The next improvement of the robot is not only determining distance but also sending a warning if it gets too close to an obstacle. A warning comes in the form of a condition. If the distance between the robot and the obstacle is less than a threshold value, then a warning is issued. We can treat this new species of robots as a class called Robot_sense_warn, which inherits all the features of the previous class, Robot_sense, augmented by an extra method named warn. The Robot_sense_warn is written as follows:

```
class Robot_sense_warn extends Robot_sense {
    public Boolean warn () {
    double xdiff = x - Target.x;
    double ydiff = y - Target.y;
    return { if (xdiff <a && ydiff <a) warn = True else warn = False}
}
```

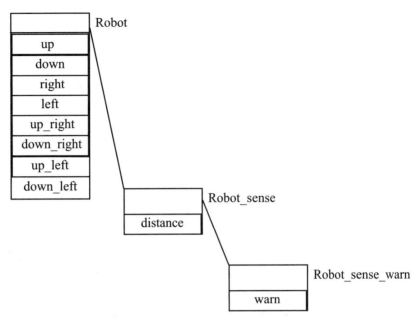

Figure 13.25 A hierarchy of robots.

These objects (robots) form an evident hierarchy as shown in Figure 13.25.

There is a series of approaches to introducing OO-inclined software metrics (Coplien, 1993; Lake & Cook, 1992). In the following discussion, we analyze some of the representative OO-oriented software metrics as studied by Chidamber and Kemerer (1994). Before moving into detailed measures, we would like to stress that object-oriented design places greater emphasis on the design phase of the life-cycle. During the design phase, one decomposes the system into object classes, the building blocks of the object-oriented approach. The object class itself requires a suitable selection of software metrics. The features of the object class, such as number of attributes the class contains, the number of methods called from other classes, the number of methods outside the class that are called, and the placement of the class inheritance, are quite obvious characteristics to look into. Nevertheless, classes themselves should be considered as more than a collection of methods and attributes. This is explained as follows. Classes generate objects by a process of instantiation, and therefore a class cannot be treated in a two-dimensional sense. Several unique features of object-oriented design—such as message passing, inheritance, and polymorphism—call for relevant software measures. By inheritance we mean a relationship among classes where one class shares the structure or methods defined in another class (single inheritance) or in more than one class (multiple inheritance). A graphical representation of inheritance comes in the form of an inheritance graph or inheritance tree. Polymorphism deals with an ability of two or more objects to interpret a message differently at execution, depending upon the superclass of the calling object.

13.10.2 Weighted Methods per Class Measure

We consider a class C with several methods $m_1, m_2, \ldots m_p$. The complexity of each method is expressed with the use of some standard software measures (which is justifiable as these are just parts of code adhering to the standard style of design and coding). The Weighted Methods per Class (WMC) measure is a sum of the complexities of the methods:

$$WMC = C_1 + C_2 + \ldots + C_p$$

where C_i stands for the software complexity metric of the i-th method. The higher the value of WMC, the more complex the class. The WMC metric focuses on methods in a class and does not concentrate at least directly on the interaction between classes. Moreover, the data component of the class is not included. Also, relationships between the classes are not quantified. Let us proceed with the robot example. Figure 13.26 includes the values of the cyclomatic complexity computed for each method for the individual class.

13.10.3 Depth of Inheritance Tree Measure

The role of the next measure is to capture properties originating from the inheritance relation. The depth of inheritance is a length from the node where the class is located to the root of the tree. In the case of multiple inheritance, the Depth of Inheritance Tree (DIT) measure is the maximum length from the node to the root. In the tree in Figure 13.27a (with multiple inheritance), the DIT is equal to 3. For the tree in Figure 13.27b, the DIT is equal to 4. The DIT for the hierarchy of robots is 3. The deeper a class in the hierarchy, the greater the number of methods it is likely to inherit, making it more difficult to predict its behavior. Moreover, deeper trees contribute to higher design complexity.

13.10.4 Number of Children Measure

The Number of Children (NOC) measure quantifies a number of immediate subclasses subordinated to a class in the class hierarchy. The NOC measure relates to the notion of scope of properties. It measures how many subclasses are going to inherit the methods of the parent. The NOC for class B in hierarchy in Figure 13.27a is 2 while the NOC for class C in Figure 13.27b is 1. The NOC for the hierarchy of robots is 1. This measure raises a point of reusability: The greater the number of children, the greater the possibility of reuse.

13.10.5 Lack of Cohesion in Methods Measure

The Lack of Cohesion in Methods (LCOM) measure concentrates on cohesion between the methods used by a class. The LCOM measure is defined as follows:

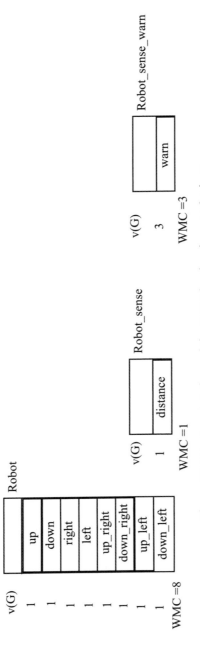

Figure 13.26 Computations of the WMC for the classes of robots.

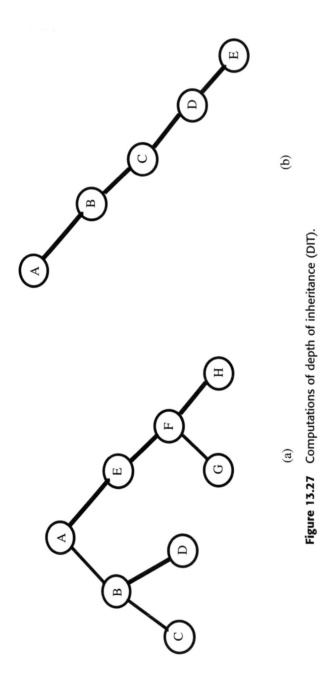

(a)

(b)

Figure 13.27 Computations of depth of inheritance (DIT).

$$LCOM = \begin{cases} \text{card (P)} - \text{card (Q)}, & \text{if card (P)} > \text{card (Q)} \\ 0, & \text{otherwise} \end{cases}$$

Denote by I_j a set of instance variables used by method m_j. Each class contains "n" methods ($m_1, m_2, \ldots m_n$). We form two families of pairs of the methods in the class,

$$P = \{(I_i, I_j) \mid I_i \cap I_j = \varnothing\}$$

and

$$Q = \{(I_i, I_j) \mid I_i \cap I_j \neq \varnothing\}$$

where $\cap$ stands for the operation of intersection of two sets; $\varnothing$ denotes an empty set. If all sets $\{I_1, I_2, \ldots, I_n\}$ are empty, then let $P = \varnothing$. For example, in class with 4 methods with

$$I_1 = \{a, b, c\}$$
$$I_2 = \{a, e, f, w\}$$
$$I_3 = \{x, y, z\}$$
$$I_4 = \{v, u, k\}$$

the calculations proceed as follows. First, we compute all intersections:

$$I_1 \cap I_2 = \{a, b, c\} \cap \{a, e, f, w\} = \{a\}$$
$$I_1 \cap I_3 = \{a, b, c\} \cap \{x, y, z\} = \varnothing$$
$$I_1 \cap I_4 = \{a, b, c\} \cap \{v, u, k\} = \varnothing$$
$$I_2 \cap I_3 = \{a, e, f, w\} \cap \{x, y, z\} = \varnothing$$
$$I_2 \cap I_4 = \{a, e, f, w\} \cap \{v, u, k\} = \varnothing$$
$$I_3 \cap I_4 = \{x, y, z\} \cap \{v, u, k\} = \varnothing$$

Next

$$P = \{(I_1, I_3), (I_1, I_4), (I_2, I_4), (I_3, I_4)\}$$
$$Q = \{I_1, I_2\}$$

and finally

$$LCOM = \text{card}(P) - \text{card}(Q) = 5 - 1 = 4$$

The LCOM measure reveals the disparate nature of methods in the class. The higher the value of LCOM, the lower the similarity between the methods in the class. As usual, a lack of cohesion implies that the class should be split into two or more subclasses. Low values of LCOM point out complexity of the class and signal an increasing likelihood of errors that may occur.

13.10.6   Coupling Between Object Classes Measure

The Coupling Between Object classes (CBO) measure for a class is a count of the number of other classes to which it is coupled. CBO relates to the notion that an object is coupled to another object if one of them acts on the other. Namely, methods of one class use methods or instance variables of another. An improvement of modularity is achieved when interobject class couples is minimized. Evidently, the larger the number of couples, the higher the sensitivity to changes in other parts of the design. As usual the enhanced modularity contributes to higher maintainability and understandability of the code.

13.10.7   Response For a Class Measure

The Response For a Class (RFC) measure is the response set for the class. More formally,

$$RFC = M \cup \bigcup_i R_i$$

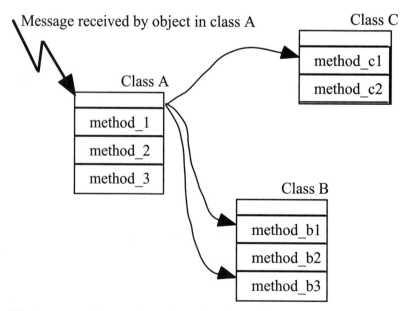

Figure 13.28   Computations of RFC for class A.

where M is a set of all methods in the class, and R_i is a set of methods called by method "i". We can rewrite the above RFC expression assuming that the class encapsulates "p" methods:

$$RFC = M \cup \bigcup_i R_i = M \cup R_1 \cup R_2 \cup \ldots \cup R_p$$

Thus the response set of a class is a family of methods that can be executed in response to a message being received by an object in that class. In the computation shown in Figure 13.28, RFC $= 4 + 2 + 1 = 7$. As RFC includes methods from outside the class, this software metric serves as a measure of potential interaction between the class and other classes. Finally, Table 13.4 summarizes a number of software measures oriented toward measuring essential features of object-based software products (Archer, 1995).

TABLE 13.4 Object-Oriented Software Measures

Features of Object-Oriented Software	Software Measures
System	• System complexity (total length of inheritance chain) • System reuse (% reused "as is" classes) • Object counts (count of object instances in the system) • Program complexity (defined as the sum of the complexity of the main program and the complexity of the class hierarchies in the system)
Coupling and uses	• Operation coupling measure (a count of the number of operations that access other classes, are accessed by other classes, and cooperate with other classes) • Count of uses
Inheritance	• Average inheritance depth • Depth of inheritance tree (DIT) • Number of children (NOC)
Class	• Class complexity (parent count and progeny count) • Class reuse (% of inherited methods that are overloaded) • Response to a class (RFC) • Weighted methods per class (WMC) • Lack of cohesion of methods (LCOM) • Data abstraction coupling (number of abstract data types) • Number of local methods (count of number of methods in a class)
Method	• Software science measures • Cyclomatic complexity • Lines of code

13.11 SOFTWARE QUALITY IMPROVEMENT PARADIGM

The improvement of software quality requires a comprehensive software measurement methodology to be incorporated as a part of the Quality Improvement Paradigm (McClure, 1994). It encompasses six steps:

- Characterize the current project and its environment using measures and models.
- Set a collection of quantifiable goals for successful performance or improvement in the specific project.
- Choose the appropriate process model, and decide upon supportive methods and tools.
- Execute the process, construct the products, collect and validate the measures. Complete their analysis to generate real-time feedback for corrective actions.
- Analyze the measurement data to evaluate current practices, determine problems, record findings, and make recommendations as to the future project improvements. Once more advanced models are considered, one should become cognizant of efficacies of experimental data (e.g., skewed distributions) to be taken care of (Myrvold, 1990).
- Package the experience in the form of updated and refined models.

13.12 SUMMARY

The weakest link of a chain is the measure of its strength.
—C. W. HOSKYNS, 1852

We have studied the fundamental problem of software metrics, identified the key goals to be achieved there, and discussed a number of detailed software measures. This chapter concentrates primarily on software product; the issue of some other software measures dealing with software processes and design are important yet somewhat distinct from those raised here. There are several general points to be made. First, most product measures are still focused on software code. Static code models are geared towards computing software size and software complexity. It is quite evident that Halstead's software science complexity measures, McCabe's cyclomatic complexity measures, and information flow measures (and their variations) are commonly used in measuring properties of software. The experience stemming from the use of these metrics is somewhat mixed.

They work nicely in some cases in correlating with predicted software quality, and perform poorly in some other cases. This suggests a need to use a battery of these metrics rather than relying on a few selected measures. Second, it should be stressed that in many cases, a previous experience with working with some software metrics could have a significant impact on a potential utilization of the software metric itself (both knowledge and a previous exposure to such instruments could vary significantly creating an additional bias towards specific measures). Third, there is a strong consensus about software measures as expressed by Rombach and others (1993):

- The scope of measurement needs to include entire projects, products, and processes.
- The purposes of measurement are understanding, planning and control, and improvement.
- One has to reflect a role people play in software projects (from planners to system developers).
- The properties being measured depend very much on the scope, purpose, and perspective of interest; in fact, there is no fixed set of software measures.
- One should strive for a development of empirically oriented software development models.

Moreover, the models should take into account the changing environment within which all projects are carried out.

The meaning of software complexity could be very different depending which software product we are talking about and which phase of software development we are zooming in. In general, however, we are primarily concerned with what is usually called psychological or cognitive complexity (Curtis et al., 1979; Ory, 1983). As stated by Melton and others (1990): "psychological complexity measures should actually quantify the elusive notions of understandability, maintainability, estimated production costs, etc." It should also be mentioned that the algorithmic complexity one encounters in algorithm analysis is concerned with the nature of the algorithm (method) itself. It may have some unavoidable impact on the resulting cognitive complexity. However, this topic is not studied in this framework.

13.13 PROBLEMS

Dry Measure is different both from Wine and
Ale Measure.
—J. WARD, 1709

1. Consider two ways of constructing a program:

   • As a simple piece of code of size N
   • As a set of "c" modules each of size N_i, $i = 1, 2, \ldots c$

   If you can vary the sizes of the individual modules N_i, when can you anticipate the highest gain in the reduction of the effort measure when comparing development of such modular software with the design of a single piece of code? Are the findings based on this analysis meaningful? Are there any points missing? Hint: Start with only two modules (c = 2). Next try to generalize your findings.

2. Which software complexity metrics would you recommend to deal with recursive functions? Justify your choice.

3. Check whether the general postulates discussed in section 13.8 apply to software effort.

4. For the flowchart in Figure 13.29, determine the following complexity metrics: volume, LOC, cyclomatic complexity, and entropy.

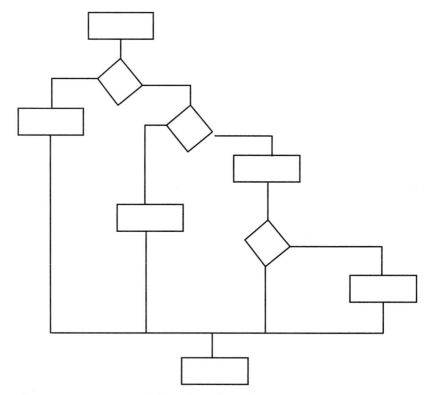

Figure 13.29   An example flowchart of a code.

5. Consider the following fragment of code in Java:

```java
{
xPos=20;
for (int i=0; i<a.length; i++)
{if (i < low || i > high) gg.drawString (" ", xPos, yPos);
else
if (i == mid) gg.drawString(String.valueOf(a[i]) + "*", xPos, yPos);
else gg.drawString(String.valueOf(a [i]), xPos, yPos);
xPos+ = 30;
}
yPos+=20;
}
```

Determine its average reachability index, nesting level, and length.

6. A class concerning a window displayed in the screen is introduced as follows:

```
    class Window
{int identifier;
short x, y;
short width, height;
char visible // 0 - visible, 1 - not visible
string name; // name of window
public:
char*getName ();

void minimize_Window () {width=10; height=20;}

void move_and_enlarge() {x=new_x; y=new_y; width=20; height=30;}

void maximize_height() {width=400;}
```

Determine the LCOM metric for this class.

7. How is the modularization effect quantified by the information flow software metric? Consider the following problem (Figure 13.30). The module of length L is split into two submodules (module_1 and module_2) each of length $L/2$. How many links between the submodules are allowed so that we maintain the value of the information flow metric at the same level as found for the original module?

8. Explain an origin of discrepancies between the program length metric and the original length of the code.

9. Discuss the use of Zipf's law with pseudocode to predict length.

10. In the flowchart in Figure 13.31, identify equivalence classes and calculate entropy. Determine also the information flow software metric; the sizes of the modules are (A) 4 KLOC, (B) 900 LOC, (C) 1KLOC, (D) 3KLOC, (E) 500 LOC.

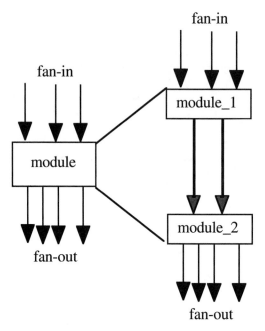

Figure 13.30 Module and submodules with fan-in and fan-out determination.

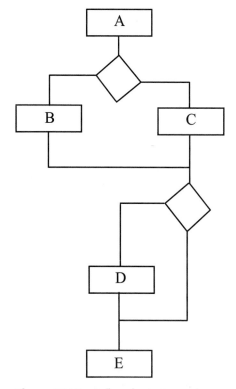

Figure 13.31 A flowchart of a code.

11. Draw four different flowcharts whose cyclomatic complexity is equal to 5. Calculate their entropies and average reachability.

12. What is the maximal program length $\hat{N}$ assuming a fixed size of a vocabulary η?

13. Consider a medium size piece of code in Java or C++. Count the number of tokens and plot their frequencies and ranking. Apply Zipf's law to estimate the size of the code. How does it compare to the real size of the code?
    Repeat the same experiment using a short 1–2 page excerpt from any software manual. Compare the results.

14. Repeat the derivation of the size of the document based on the Zipf's law assuming that the rarest type of token appears "p" times. Plot this size as a function of "p". Interpret the obtained graph.

15. Identify some potential shortcomings of the Henry-Kafura metric. Hint: Could you envision a nontrivial procedure for which this metric assumes zero?

16. The Fogg index is an example of a document-oriented metric and as such can be used to determine complexity of software documents written in a natural language. The metric assesses the readability of text based upon the length of sentences and the number of "hard" words. The measure is computed on the basis of sampling text at the rate of about 100 lines per four pages. The features of this text sample include several characteristics such as the number of sentences, number of words, and number of syllables. The Fog index is computed as:

$$FI = 0.4*(word/sentence + (hard\_words)/100)$$

The word is classified as hard if it has more than three syllables not counting (1) words that are capitalized, (2) combinations of short words such as manhole, and (3) verbs that are made into three syllables by adding "-ed", "-es", and the like. The index is interpreted using the scale:

- FI < 5: fairly easy
- 5 < FI < 8: standard
- 8 < FI < 11: fairly difficult
- 11 < FI < 17: difficult
- FI > 17: very difficult

    (a) Pick up any software manual and calculate the Fog index.
    (b) Compare two software manuals (from two software companies) in terms of their readability. If very different, comment on the origin of these differences.

17. A part of the ATC system in Java dealing with the aircraft is shown below:

```
    // Object aircraft when first used in simulation
Airplane() {
x = 41000;

y = 0;                                                // desired release point
h = 1995 + (int) (Math.random()* 10);                 // start altitude
dis_h = 2000;                                         // desired altitude
if (Math.random() < .5)
random_speed = (int) (Math.random()* 200);            // set speed from 300 to 500
else
random_speed = -1* (int) (Math.random()* 200);        // sets speed from 300 down to 100
air_speed = (SPEED + random_speed);                   //initial speed value equal 300
AirSpeed=new String(Integer.toString(air_speed));     //Send speed value to screen
FlightNo=new String("FY" + Integer.toString((int) (Math.random()*100)));

Alt=new String(Integer.toString(h));                  //Send altitude to screen
direction = SOUTH;                                    //Start status set
status = NORMAL;

random_course = (int) (Math.random()* 2000.0);        // Vary course by random increment
ackStr=new String();
        }
```

Count the number of operators and operands; estimate the length of the code.

18. The power law (Zipf relationship) $y = Cx^a$ can be viewed as the solution to the differential equation

$$\frac{dy}{y} = a\frac{dx}{x}$$

Show that if x changes from x to $x'(x' > x)$ then y is magnified by a factor $(x'/x)^a$.

19. Perform detailed computations for the effort measure to show which of the fundamental software complexity measures have been satisfied.

20. Perform detailed computations for the entropy-based software complexity measure.

21. The complexity of the software module (Card & Glass, 1990) is expressed as a sum of two components:

$$c = f*f + \frac{V}{f+1}$$

where "f" denotes a fanout of the module while V stands for the number of input-output variables. Minimize the complexity. Do the following:
(a) Elaborate on the relationship between f and V resulting from this optimization. Interpret the obtained results.

(b) Generalize the result for the entire system composed of several modules. Note that the measure is additive, meaning that we add up the first and the second component over all the modules.

13.14 REFERENCES

Agatep, R., Evans, D., Inthalansy, S., et al. *t-ATCA Project.* Report, Department of Electrical and Computer Engineering, University of Manitoba, Winnipeg, November 1997.

Archer C. *Measuring Object-Oriented Software Products.* Software Engineering Institute, Carnegie Mellon University, Rep. SEI-CM-28, 1995.

Basili, V.R. Software development: A paradigm for the future. *Proceedings of the 13th Annual International Computer Software and Applications Conference,* Orlando, Sept. 1989.

Basili, V.R. The TAME project: Towards improvement-oriented software environments. *IEEE Transactions on Software Engineering,* SE-**14**:758–773, 1988.

Bieman, J.M. Metric development for object-oriented software. In *Software Measurement,* A. Melton, Ed. International Thomson Computer Press, London, 1996.

Boehm, B.W., Software Engineering Economics. Prentice-Hall, Englewood Cliffs, NJ, 1981.

Card, D.N., Glass, R.L. *Measuring Software Design Quality.* Prentice Hall, Englewood Cliffs, NJ, 1990.

Chidamber, S.R., Kemerer, C.F. A metrics suite for object oriented design. *IEEE Transactions on Software Engineering,* **20**(6):476–493, 1994.

Conte, S.D., Dunsmore, H.E., Shen, V.Y. *Software Engineering Metrics and Models.* Benjamin, Menlo Park, CA, 1986.

Coplien, J. *Looking Over One's Shoulder at a C++ Program.* AT&T Bell Labs. Tech. Memo, January 1993.

Curtis, B., Sheppard, S.B., Milliman, P., et al. Measuring the psychological complexity of software maintenance tasks with the Halstead and McCabe metrics. *IEEE Transactions on Software Engineering,* SE-**5**(2):96–104, 1979.

Davis, J.S., LeBlanc, R.J. A study of the applicability of complexity measures. *IEEE Transactions on Software Engineering,* **14**(9):1366–1372, 1988.

Dunsmore, H.E., Gannon, J.D. Analysis of the effects of programming factors on programming effort. *Journal of Systems and Software,* **1**:141–153, 1980.

Fenton, N.E. *Software Metrics. A Rigorous Approach.* Chapman & Hall, London, 1991.

Fenton, N.E. Software metrics; theory, tools and validation. *Software Engineering Journal,* January 1990, 65–78.

Fenton N.E., Kaposi, A.A. Metrics and software structure. *Journal of Information and Software Technology,* **29**:301–320, 1987.

Halstead, M.H. *Elements of Software Science.* North Holland, New York, 1977.

Harrison, W. An entropy-based measure of software complexity. *IEEE Transactions on Software Engineering,* **18**(11):1025–1029, 1992.

Henry, S., Kafura, D. Software structure metrics based on information flow. *IEEE Transactions on Software Engineering*, SE-**7**(5):510–518, 1981.

Lake, A., Cook, C. *A Software Complexity Metric for C++*. Tech. rep. 92-60-03, Oregon State University, 1992.

Lind, R.K., Vairavan, K. An experimental investigation of software metrics and their relationship to software development effort. *IEEE Transactions on Software Engineering*, **15**(5):649–653, 1989.

McCabe, T.J. A complexity measure. *IEEE Transactions on Software Engineering*, SE-**2**(4):308–320, 1976.

McClure, C. Measurement. In *Encyclopedia of Sofware Engineering*, J.J. Marciniak, Ed., Vol. 1. Wiley, New York, pp. 646–660, 1994.

Melton, A.C., Gustafson, D.A., Bieman, J.M., Baker, A.L. A mathematical perspective for software measures research. *Software Engineering Journal*, May 1990, 246–254.

Munson, J.C., Khoshgoftaar, T.M. Software metrics for reliability assessment. In *Software Reliability Engineering*, M.R. Lyu, Ed. Computer Society Press, Los Alamitos, CA, pp. 493–529, 1996.

Myrvold, A. Data analysis for software metrics. *Journal of Systems Software*, **12**:271–275, 1990.

Oman, P.W. Automated software quality models. *Proceedings of the 8th Workshop on Software Metrics*, AOWSM'97, Coeur d'Alene, Idaho, 1997.

Ory, Z. An integrating common framework for measuring cognitive software complexity. *Software Engineering Journal*, September 1983, 263–272.

Rombach, D., Basili, V.R., Selby R., Eds. Experimental software engineering. *Proceedings of the International Workshop*, Dagstuhl, 1992, Springer-Verlag Lecture Notes Series, Heidelberg, 1993.

Schneidewind, N., Hoffmann, R.H. An experiment in software error data collection and analysis. *IEEE Transactions on Software Engineering*, SE-**5**(3):276–286, 1979.

Shooman, M.L. *Software Engineering*. McGraw-Hill, New York, 1983.

Stroud, J.M. The fine structure of psychological time. *Annals of the New York Academy of Science*, **138**:623–631, 1967.

Zipf, G.K. *Human Behavior and the Principle of Least Effort: An Introduction to Human Ecology*. Addison-Wesley, Reading, MA, 1949.

CHAPTER **14**
Software Cost Estimation

> When using a mathematical model, careful
> attention must be given to the uncertainties in
> the model.
> —R. P. FEYNMAN, 1989

Aims

- Examine some basic concepts of software cost estimation
- Consider difficulties and sources of uncertainty in software cost estimates
- Consider main classes of cost estimation models

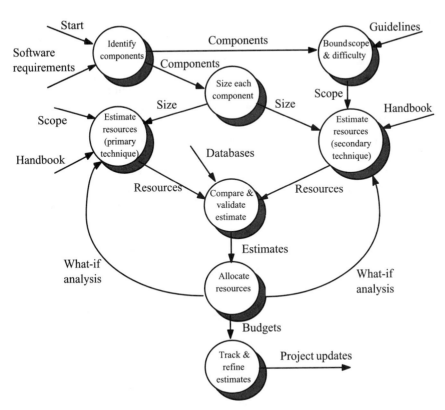

Figure 14.1 An approach to constructing software cost estimates.

14.1   INTRODUCTION

> "Big grey limousine."
> "Expensive?"
> "Looked as if it had cost the earth."
> —P. G. WODEHOUSE, 1924

This chapter is concerned with software cost estimation. A high-level description of the software cost-estimation process is shown in Figure 14.1. The software cost-estimation problem deserves special attention for the following reasons:

- The development of any software product is usually a unique undertaking. There are no two identical systems or projects. Very often software projects are very different from each other and any experience gained in the past needs to be used with caution. Simply, the new circumstances could be very different: we are faced with new specifications, new hardware and software platforms, new development tools and design methodologies. When considered together, it becomes apparent that the resulting uncertainty about the required resources and associated costs is immense and cannot be ignored.

- With the increased size of software projects, any estimation mistakes (that lead either to overestimation or underestimation of the cost) could cost a lot in terms of resources allocated to the project. Too limited resources may delay the project. The use of excessive resources means genuine losses in terms of time and revenue.

- The uncertainty about cost estimates is usually quite high. Put differently, what any cost estimation model can provide is rather a rough estimate. The discussed models deliver a single number but this result should be treated with a big grain of salt. Be very skeptical about it. Instead of confining the estimation to a single number, one is usually better off by considering an interval of potential estimates. In practice, one should take into consideration three numbers: the most likely cost value, its upper bound, and its lower bound. These three numbers, rather than a single estimate, reflect the factor of uncertainty associated with any cost estimation pursuits. The uncertainty becomes an inherent component of any software project. The level of uncertainty may eventually go down over the course of the project (Figure 14.2). This could happen naturally (as we become more and more confident about the details of the project and aware of its progress) or could be controlled through setting up some additional checkpoints.

As summarized by Reifer (1994), the need for cost estimation models is justified for a number of common project requirements:

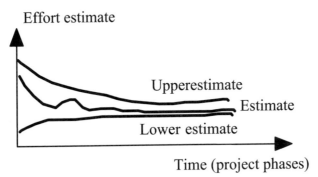

Figure 14.2 Uncertainty reduction over the course of software project.

- Identify, prioritize and justify resource (staff, time, capital) needs.
- Negotiate adequate budgets and establish staffing plans.
- Make cost, productivity, quality, and functionality trade-offs.
- Need to quantify the impact of risk.
- Assess the impact of changes and permit replanning to deal with them.
- Modify budgets to address unexpected events and contingencies.

There are two principal software process cost predictors: expected effort and elapsed time spent on the project. Methods of cost estimation encountered in practice have been identified by Kitchenham (1994) as follows:

1. *Expert opinion.* Expert opinions are essentially estimates or guessing based on some personal experience acquired in the past.

2. *Analogy.* Analogy forms a more formal approach than the previous one. The key point of the method is to exercise some judgment based upon some previous projects, use the estimates obtained from previous projects, and apply them to the current project. The initial estimate is usually adjusted based on the difference between the previous projects and the current one. The term "difference" is used in a general sense as we employ this notion (and eventually quantify it) when making attempts to evaluate how similar (or different) such projects are. The results of the produced estimates hinge quite strongly on the ability to assess and properly quantify a relevant level of similarity existing between the projects. One may also misjudge similarities and differences and this may become a source of some erroneous estimates.

3. *Decomposition.* The decomposition method involves breaking a product up into its smallest components (when we are concerned about the product) or decomposing a project into smaller subtasks. The corresponding estimates made for the individual components are afterwards summarized to produce an overall estimate. The summarization is usually realized via

some sort of averaging effect that may be eventually adjusted (weighted) reflecting the complexity of the individual components.

4. *PERT models.* In this class of models, the required effort is estimated based on worst, best possible, and most likely estimates that are combined using the well-known formula:

$$\text{Effort} = \frac{\text{lower estimate} + 4* \text{most likely estimate} + \text{upper estimate}}{6}$$

The method allows to compensate for risk by developing a weighted estimate. The individual estimates are derived using either the analogy technique or Delphi method.

5. *Mathematical models.* These models come in the form of relationships correlating some input measures with the overall effort. The well-known models are the COCOMO effort model, Rayleigh curve models, and Albrecht's function point models. In some cases these are regression models, meaning that the parameters of the models are determined with the use of standard methods of statistics (by determining regression lines or curves).

Despite the diversity of the existing methods, they fall under a general taxonomy of effort estimation models that emphasize a way in which we carry out these estimation activities. They are essentially bottom-up or top-down estimations. Bottom-up estimations are based on estimating the effort for individual tasks (or subsystems); subsequently the overall effort is taken as a sum of the contributing efforts. The method is straightforward, but it may overlook some system level factors. Similarly, one may question the way in which the overall effort is determined. Top-down estimation is used to provide total project estimates; afterwards the individual tasks (subsystems) are considered to constitute a proportion of the total effort. Eventual conflicts are continuously resolved by determining how to meet requirements in the presence of limited resources. In considering the class of mathematical models, one can distinguish between several main classes (Figure 14.3).

The chapter elaborates on the main cost and effort estimation models that come in the form of some relationships between variables. We start with the function points model and then discuss the COCOMO model. Finally, we introduce a Delphi technique and show its role in the process of cost estimation.

14.2 FUNCTION POINTS MODELS

This class of models usually referred to as Albrecht's function points (Albrecht, 1979; Albrecht & Gaffney, 1983; Garmus & Herron, 1995) is related to requirement specification documents where the functionality of a software system is

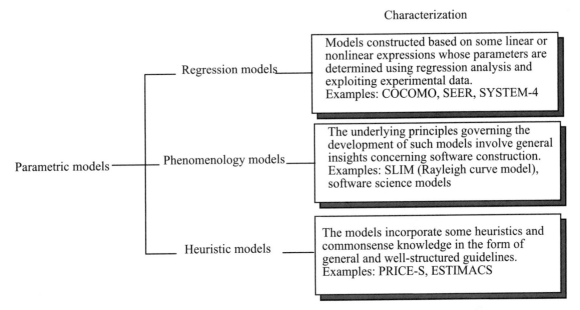

Figure 14.3 Classes of mathematical models used in effort determination.

determined. In essence, such function points models are based on visible features of the system that are weighted accordingly to produce an overall score. The intent is to construct a measure of product size that can be available early in the development process. Furthermore, the method is technology independent. It is based on the notion of function points regarded as a measure of functionality in a system. The starting point of the construction of the model is to determine a number of items occurring in the system (these counts are usually derived from the specification document).

External inputs are the inputs from the user that provide distinct application-oriented data. Examples of such inputs are file names and menu selections.
External outputs are directed to the user; they come in the form of various reports and messages.
User inquiries are interactive inputs requiring a response.
External files deal with all machine-readable interfaces to other systems.
Internal files are the master files in the system.

Even though these software features are defined rather informally, it is not difficult to identify them when working with a specific system. To accommodate various levels of complexity of each subfunction, one adds a subjective complexity rating. The rating includes three levels of complexity: simple, average, or complex. The suggested mapping of these three levels on a numerical scale is shown next.

Item	Simple	Average	Complex
External input	3	4	6
External output	4	5	7
User inquiry	3	4	6
External file	7	10	15
Internal file	5	7	10

Just by comparing the above numbers, we learn that external files carry the most weight. Internal files also make a significant contribution to the complexity of a program. External output, external input, and user inquiry have lower ranking in this scheme. The high ranking of external files and internal files is not surprising. This ranking is a consequence of the high weight associated with the development of integration links within the same system or interfacing with other systems. Subsequently, the *unadjusted function count* (UFC) is determined by counting the number of items falling under these categories and combining them additively using the corresponding weight factors:

$$UFC = \sum item_i \, w_i$$

During the second phase, the function points count is further refined by including a so-called technical complexity factor (TCF) that multiplicatively modifies the original value of the UFC, producing the adjusted function point count FP:

$$FP = UFC * TCF$$

The computations of TCF are completed using the experimentally derived formula

$$TCF = 0.65 + 0.1 \sum_{i=1}^{14} f_i$$

with f_i being detailed factors contributing to the overall notion of complexity. The factors are listed in Table 14.1. Each factor is rated on 0 to 5 scale with 0 being irrelevant and 5 standing for essential.

The calculations of TCF imply a range of its possible values to be confined to the range 0.65 (all factors rated as irrelevant) to 1.35 (all factors being essential). This implies that the modifications of the values of TCF remain within the range of $\pm 35\%$ of the nominal values. As an example, let us consider a simple industrial controller. Its specifications can be briefly outlined as follows:

TABLE 14.1 Factors Contributing to Albrecht's Technical Complexity (TCF)

◆ Reliable backup and recovery	◆ Data communications
◆ Distributed functions	◆ Performance
◆ Heavily used configuration	◆ Online data entry
◆ Operational use	◆ Online update
◆ Complex interface	◆ Complex processing
◆ Reusability	◆ Installation ease
◆ Multiple sites	◆ Facilitate change

0   5

Description of an Industrial Controller

The controller accepts two inputs: discrete (sampled) signals of temperature and volume coming from a system under control. The controller checks these signals against some threshold values. If the sampled signals are within an envelope formed by the thresholds, the controller generates the corresponding control signal. If the signals are outside the bounds formed by the thresholds, an alarm control scenario becomes invoked; the pertinent parameters of the controller are read from a separate file (alarm control file). The same file contains also a number of other optional versions of the controller's parameters so that an appropriate control scenario could be assumed. The readings of the sensors as well as the control actions taken are archived in a file. The user (operator) is continuously updated about the status of the system including the values of the input variables (along with some auxiliary information such as moving averages, and dispersion of the signals) and the control actions taken. Another report is displayed about the alarm cases—these are flagged out separately.

The analysis of the specifications leads us to the outline of the system (Figure 14.4), which portrays all functionalities of the system. The figure helps us count the items that contribute to the function points. We get

A = the number of external inputs = 2 (temperature signal, volume signal)
B = the number of external outputs = 4 (alarm report, status of the system, control signal, readings of the sensor)
C = number of inquiries = 0
D = number of external files = 1 (archive file)
E = number of internal files = 1 (alarm control file)

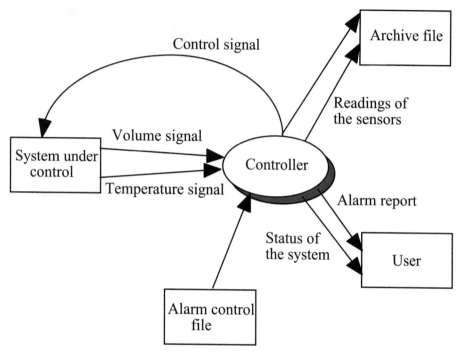

Figure 14.4 Identified functionalities of the control system.

We start with an average complexity for each item. The calculations of the UFC produce

$$UFC = 4A + 5B + 4C + 10D + 7E = 8 + 20 + 0 + 10 + 7 = 45$$

To get a better feeling about the computational bounds we get when changing the values of functions, we treat them as simple and afterwards switch to complex. This leads to the bounds for all functions treated as simple:

$$UFC = 3A + 4B + 3C + 7D + 5E = 6 + 16 + 0 + 7 + 5 = 34$$

Following are the bounds for all functions treated as complex:

$$UFC = 6A + 7B + 6C + 15D + 10E = 12 + 28 + 0 + 15 + 10 = 65$$

If, on average, an FP takes 2 person days of effort to implement, then these bounds convert into the temporal range from 68 to 130 days. For the average complexity we require 90 days to implement. Let us concentrate on a part of

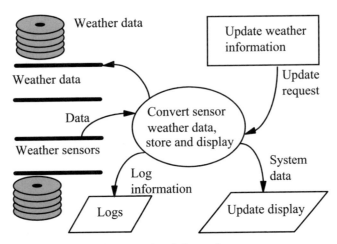

Figure 14.5 Update weather information.

the tATC system dealing with update of weather information (Figure 14.5). Based on that, let us identify the required components to determine points.

```
External inputs: none
External outputs: 1 (update display)
User inquiries: 1 (update request)
External files: 2 (weather sensors, weather data)
Internal files: 1 (logs)
```

Owing to the character of the system, we assume the levels of complexity of all items to be the highest (they are regarded complex on the three-level scale). The UFC is then calculated as follows:

$$UFC = 1*7 + 1*6 + 2*15 + 1*10 = 7 + 6 + 30 + 10 = 53$$

If we consider adjusted point count FP, the range of possible values spreads from 34.45 (0.65*53) to 71.55 (1.35*53).

The overall scheme portraying the use of the function points model is illustrated in Figure 14.6. An important feature of the function points model is that they can be used right at the very beginning of the project. This, however, could act as a two-edged sword: the estimates could be very approximate and imply that the resulting estimates should be treated with caution.

There are some points to be made about the use of the function points models; hopefully they help avoid eventual pitfalls associated with these models.

- They are based on a complete software specification.
- It is very likely that the results produced by these models can underestimate the reality; this phenomenon happens because of the coarser level

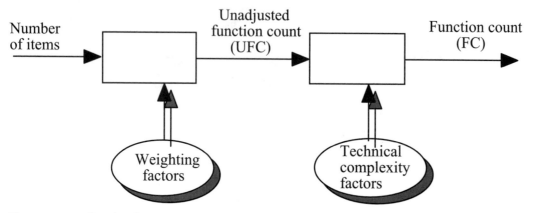

Figure 14.6   Albrecht's function points model—a general scheme.

of details shown in the specification document than the one occurring in the actual implementation.

- Function points are always affected by a certain degree of subjectivity that comes into the estimation process. To reduce this effect, one has to employ detailed counting rules and make sure that they are applied in a consistent and coherent manner.

- The function points approach to software cost estimation ignores effort-reducing technologies such as integrated development environments, CASE tools, executable process descriptions (e.g., statecharts with STATE-MATE), object orientation, and reuse libraries. In addition, the interaction of time-saving technologies as well as the interact of processing complexity factors is ignored. Extensions of Albrecht's method are considered in Peters and Ramanna (1996, 1998a, 1998b). Case studies and function counting practices can be obtained from the International Function Points User's Group (IFPUG), Blendonview Office Park, 5008-28 Pine Creek Drive, Westerville, OH 43081-4899.

14.3 THE COCOMO MODEL

The COCOMO (COnstructive COst MOdel) model is the most complete and thoroughly documented model used in effort estimation. COCOMO is based on Boehm's analysis of a database of 63 software projects (Boehm, 1981). The model provides detailed formulas for determining the development time schedule, overall development effort, effort breakdown by phase and activity, as well as maintenance effort. COCOMO estimates the effort in person-months of direct labor (let us recall that a working month consists of 152 hours of working time).

The primary effort factor is the number of source line of code (SLOC) expressed in thousands of delivered source instructions (KDSI). These instructions include all program instructions, format statements, and job control language statements. They exclude comments and unmodified utility software. The COCOMO model relies on two assumptions. First, it is linked to the classic waterfall model of software development. Second, good management practices with no slack time are assumed. The model is developed in three versions of different level of detail: basic, intermediate, and detailed. We will discuss the first two of them. Furthermore, the overall modeling process takes into account three classes of systems:

1. *Embedded.* This class of systems is characterized by tight constraints, changing environment, and unfamiliar surroundings. Projects of the embedded type are novel to the company, and usually exhibit temporal constraints. Good examples of embedded systems are real-time software systems (say, in avionics, aerospace, medicine).

2. *Organic.* This category encompasses all systems that are small relative to project size and team size, and have a stable environment, familiar surroundings, and relaxed interfaces. These are simple business systems, data processing systems, small software libraries.

3. *Semidetached.* The software systems falling under this category are a mix of those of organic and embedded nature. Some examples of software of this class are operating systems, database management systems, and inventory management systems.

14.3.1 The Basic Form of the COCOMO Model

This basic form of the COCOMO model is based exclusively on program size expressed in KDSI. The underlying formula assumes the form

$$\text{Effort} = a * \text{KDLOC}^b$$

where "a" and "b" are two parameters of the model whose specific values are selected upon the class of the software system. The basic form of the COCOMO model uses the following expressions. For embedded systems:

$$\text{Effort} = 3.6 * \text{KDLOC}^{1.20}$$

For organic systems:

$$\text{Effort} = 2.4 * \text{KDLOC}^{1.05}$$

For semidetached systems:

$$\text{Effort} = 3.0 * \text{KDLOC}^{1.12}$$

One should underline that the form of the above models (power functions) as well as their parameters are results of some curve fitting to the existing experimental data (previous software projects). This means that the COCOMO models attempt to approximate the experimental data and, to some extent, could be biased by the specificity of the projects used to construct the model. It means that the models can have difficulties when coping with software projects that are very different from those used in the design of the COCOMO model. The plots of the effort viewed as a function of KDLOC for the three categories of software are illustrated in Figure 14.7. Note that significant differences occur for higher values of KDLOC. They become even more profound for higher sizes of the software. There is some explanation to this phenomenon: most software projects falling under the distinguished categories are in range of 100 to 200 KDLOC.

The COCOMO model determines the development schedule, M (expressed in months) using the previously calculated effort. We get the following. For embedded systems:

$$M = 2.5 * \text{Effort}^{0.32}$$

For organic systems:

$$M = 2.5 * \text{Effort}^{0.38}$$

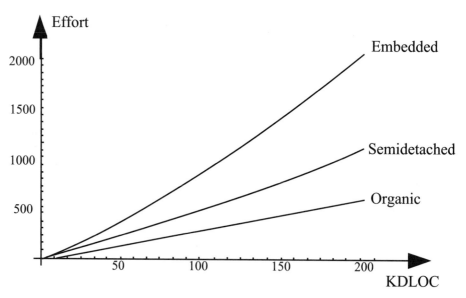

Figure 14.7   Effort as a function of KDLOC for embedded, organic, semidetached software.

For semidetached systems:

$$M = 2.5 * \text{Effort}^{0.35}$$

Again, as before, these models are formed based upon some regression analysis where the nonlinear relationships are formed based upon the experimental data. The same comments as made before hold here. We should be aware of some limitations of the models when the new project for which an estimate needs to be done varies significantly from the projects being used in the design of the COCOMO model. Subsequently, the resulting plots of effort as a function of KDLOC are shown in Figure 14.8.

COCOMO is also used to estimate software maintenance (support effort). The formula is based on the previous effort estimate,

$$\text{Effort}_{\text{maintenance}} = \text{ACT} * \text{Effort}$$

where ACT is annual change traffic that is a fraction of KDLOC undergoing change during the year. The intent of the basic COCOMO model is to produce some estimates of the required effort or development schedule variables. As indicated by Boehm, this model is "within a factor of 2, 60% of the time" on the COCOMO database.

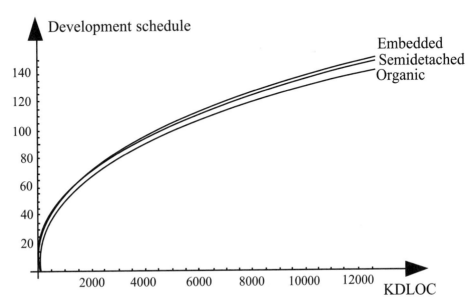

Figure 14.8 Development schedule as a function of KDLOC.

14.3.2 The Intermediate COCOMO Model

This model, the most commonly used, is a refinement of the basic model. The improvement comes in the form of 15 attributes of the product. For each of the attributes, the user of the model has to provide a rating using the following six-point scale.

```
VL (very low)
LO (low)
NM (nominal)
HI (high)
VH (very high)
XH (extra high)
```

The list of attributes is composed of several features of the software and includes product, computer, personnel, and project attributes as follows (Boehm, 1981).

Product attributes:

- Required reliability (RELY). It is used to express an effect of software faults, ranging from slight inconvenience (VL) to loss of life (VH). The nominal value (NM) denotes moderate recoverable losses.
- Data bytes per DSI (DATA). The lower rating comes with lower size of a database.
- Complexity (CPLX). The attribute expresses code complexity, again ranging from straight batch code (VL) to real-time code with multiple resource scheduling (XH).

Computer attributes:

- Execution time (TIME) and memory (STOR) constraints. This attribute identifies the percentage of computer resources (time and memory) used by the system. NM states that less than 50% is used; 95% is indicated by XH.
- Virtual machine volatility (VIRT) is used to indicate the frequency of changes made to the hardware, operating system, and overall software environment. More frequent and significant changes are indicated by higher ratings.
- Development turnaround time (TURN). This is a time from when a job is submitted until output becomes received. LO indicates a highly interactive environment; VH quantifies a situation when this time is longer than 12 hours.

Personnel attributes:

- Analyst capability (ACAP) and programmer capability (PCAP) describe skills of the developing team. The higher the skills, the higher the rating.
- Applications experience (AEXP), language experience (LEXP), and virtual machine experience (VEXP). These are used to quantify the number of experience in each area by the development team; more experience, higher rating.

Project attributes:

- Modern development practices (MODP) deals with the amount of use of modern software practices such as structured programming and object-oriented approach.
- Use of software tools (TOOL) is used to measure a level of sophistication of automated tools used in software development and a degree of integration among the tools being used. Higher rating describes higher levels in both aspects.
- Schedule effects (SCED) concerns the amount of schedule compression (HI or VH), or schedule expansion (LO or VL) of the development schedule in comparison to a nominal (NM) schedule.

The mapping from the categorical values attached to the successive attributes (VL, LO, NM, etc.) into the corresponding numerical rating is included in Table 14.2. Depending upon the product, each attribute is rated and these partial results are multiplied giving rise to the final product multipler (P). Then the effort formula is expressed as

$$\text{Effort} = \text{Effort}_{nom} * P$$

where Effort_{nom} arises in the following form depending on the type of software. For embedded systems:

$$\text{Effort}_{nom} = 2.8 * \text{KDLOC}^{1.20}$$

For organic systems:

$$\text{Effort}_{nom} = 2.8 * \text{KDLOC}^{1.05}$$

For semidetached systems:

$$\text{Effort}_{nom} = 2.8 * \text{KDLOC}^{1.12}$$

TABLE 14.2   Intermediate COCOMO Attributes

	VL	LO	NM	HI	VH	XH
RELY	0.75	0.88	1.00	1.15	1.40	
DATA		0.94	1.00	1.08	1.16	
CPLX	0.70	0.85	1.00	1.15	1.30	1.65
TIME			1.00	1.11	1.30	1.66
STOR			1.00	1.06	1.21	1.56
VIRT		0.87	1.00	1.15	1.30	
TURN		0.87	1.00	1.07	1.15	
ACAP	1.46	1.19	1.00	0.86	0.71	
AEXP	1.29	1.13	1.00	0.91	0.82	
PCAP	1.42	1.17	1.00	0.86	0.70	
LEXP	1.14	1.07	1.00	0.95		
VEXP	1.21	1.10	1.00	0.90		
MODP	1.24	1.10	1.00	0.91	0.82	
TOOL	1.24	1.10	1.00	0.91	0.83	
SCED	1.23	1.08	1.00	1.04	1.10	

Note that these are essentially the same relationships as for the basic model with the changes in only one parameter, a; the other one, b, remains unchanged. The effort model is designed using regression techniques; the values of the parameters in the model reflect the data used in the estimation procedure. If any attribute is rated nominal, then it has no effect on the values of P, and subsequently does not change the values of effort. Note also that some attributes may compensate; namely an increase of the values in one attribute becomes offset by the decrease of some other. The estimates of the development schedule are the same as in the basic model. The support effort is calculated using the following formula.

$$\text{Effort}_{\text{maintenance}} = \text{ACT}* \text{Effort}_{\text{nom}}*P$$

Boehm states that the intermediate COCOMO model produces sound results "within 20%, 68% of the time" (again as tested on the COCOMO database).

14.3.3   Example

As a comprehensive example we consider a software with an estimated size of 300 KDLOC. The software is a part of control system of a smart vehicle initiative. The system collects the readings from various sensors, processes them (this phase includes such activities as filtering and sensor fusion), and develops a schedule of pertinent control actions. Let us complete a detail cost estimation procedure by using the discussed versions of the COCOMO model. As we are apparently dealing with an example of an embedded system, the basic form of the cost estimation model leads to the person-month effort expressed as Effort = $3.6 * 300^{1.20} = 3379$ person-months. Subsequently, the development time amounts to M = $2.5*3379^{0.32} = 33.66$ months. Further refinement using the intermediate COCOMO model requires a specification of the detailed software attributes:

```
RELY   HI   1.15
DATA   HI   1.08
CPLX   NM   1.00
TIME   VH   1.30
STOR   VH   1.21
VIRT   NM   1.00
TURN   LO   0.87
ACAP   HI   0.86
AEXP   HI   0.91
PCAP   NM   1.00
LEXP   NM   1.00
VEXP   NM   1.00
MODP   NM   1.00
TOOL   LO   1.10
SCED   VH   1.10
```

Combined, they give rise to a value of the scaling factor P equal to 1.6095. The nominal effort is equal $2.8*300^{1.20} = 2628$ person-months. This result modified by the correction factor yields 4229 person-months, which is significantly higher than the estimate coming from the basic COCOMO model. The reason behind this increase was a set of attributes exceeding their normal levels.

14.4 DELPHI METHOD OF COST ESTIMATION

As became obvious in the previous analysis, a number of parameters need to be determined based on as expert's (or designer's) estimates. The accuracy of these is crucial to the performance of the model that has to be calibrated to the needs of the specific software organization. One may also expect that a group of experts (designers) can do a better job than a single individual. The Delphi method helps coordinate a process of gaining information and generating reliable estimates. The group estimating procedure governed by the Delphi method comprises a series of the following steps:

- Coordinator presents each expert with a specification of the proposed project and other relevant information.
- Coordinator calls a group meeting where experts discuss the estimates.
- Experts fill out estimation forms indicating their personal estimates of total project effort and total development effort. The estimates are given in an interval format: the expert provides the most likely value along with an upper and lower bound.
- Coordinator prepares and circulates summary report indicating the group estimates and the individual estimates.
- Coordinator calls a meeting during which experts discuss current estimates.

The process is repeated until a consensus is reached. The group estimate is taken as an average of the weighted individual estimates, computed as

$$\text{estimate} = \frac{\text{lower bound of estimate} + 4* \text{most likely estimate} + \text{upper bound of estimate}}{6}$$

The variance of the individual estimate is defined as

$$\text{variance} = \frac{\text{upper bound of estimate} - \text{upper bound of estimate}}{6}$$

The group variance is the average of the variances of the individual estimates. Let us illustrate the Delphi method by a short example. We are interested in a software project whose objective is to develop a new specialized user interface for a smart highway initiative. The required software system has to deliver comprehensive information about the current traffic conditions, display some predictions, and identify spots of potential congestion. There are five experts involved in the process of cost estimation (expressed in months of development). The coordinator provides each of them with the details of this project. In the first round, the experts return their estimates in an interval form as illustrated in Figure 14.9. The coordinator calculates the averages estimates and circulates these findings among the experts. Subsequently, such findings are used during the second meeting. The variance of the individual estimates and group variance are shown in Table 14.3. At the next meeting, the experts discuss the current estimates and proceed with further refinements (Figure 14.10). Again, the variances (both individual and for the entire group) are shown in Table 14.4.

The group variance could serve as an interesting indicator of convergence of the entire estimation process. As a matter of fact, the variance obtained after the second iteration becomes lower. Our hope is that the group variance will be getting lower from iteration to iteration, which could be regarded as a sound indicator of reaching consensus among experts.

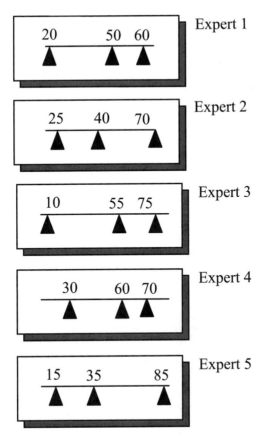

Figure 14.9   The first round of building estimates of development time.

**TABLE 14.3   Computing
Estimates and Variance:
A First Iteration**

Expert No.	Estimate	Variance
1	46.7	6.7
2	42.5	7.5
3	50.8	10.8
4	56.7	6.7
5	40.0	11.7
Average	47.3	8.6

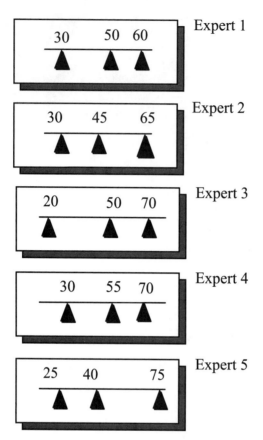

Figure 14.10 Estimation of development time—a second iteration.

TABLE 14.4 Computing Estimates and Variance: A Second Iteration

Expert No.	Estimate	Variance
1	48.3	5.0
2	45.8	5.8
3	48.3	8.3
4	53.3	6.7
5	50.0	8.7
Aversge	49.1	6.8

14.5 SUMMARY

The unit price of hardware is going down . . . .
On the other hand software costs are rising
equally dramatically.
—K. HEGGSTAD, 1977

The cost estimation process is an interesting mix of formal models and experience that are included in this chapter. In this sense, the overall modeling process is not straightforward and requires a significant level of proficiency. To produce meaningful and reliable estimates, the cost estimation process needs to be thoroughly arranged and carefully followed. As discussed by Reifer (1994), it embraces eight essential phases (as shown in Figure 14.1):

- Identification of software components
- Estimation of size of the components
- Estimation of scope and difficulty of the job
- Estimation of resources needed for each component
- Validation of resource estimates
- Allocation of resources to the schedule
- Tracking and refining the estimates

These phases coincide with a project management plan as included in IEEE Standard 1058.1 (1987). We have studied the most commonly encountered software cost estimation models. The reader can also refer to some interesting and promising alternatives exploiting machine learning (Porter & Selby, 1990; Srinivasan & Fisher, 1995), the case-based approach (Vicinanza et al., 1990), and neural networks (Srinivasan & Fisher, 1995).

14.6 PROBLEMS

1. What activities could be overlooked using bottom-up effort estimation? What could be missing in the top-down estimation? Classify the estimation methods: estimation by analogy, expert opinion, cost models, and decomposition as being either bottom-up or top-down approaches.

2. Consider the Rayleigh curve model. Discuss the effect of extending the delivery date by 5, 10, 15 . . . 100%. Repeat the same calculations for the effect of accelerating the project by 5, 10, 15, . . . , 50%. Plot and interpret the obtained results.

3. The estimated size for a military software is 10^6 KDSI. What is the expected effort obtained with the use of the COCOMO model?

4. Complete the following project-cost estimation method matrix by quantifying a level of suitability of the corresponding methods with regard to the type of the project. Quantify the level on a three-point scale: very suitable, suitable, not suitable

	Analogy	Parametric Models	Delphi
Small project			
Risky project			
Large project			

5. Which of the two parameters, a or b in a* $KDLOC^b$, has more evident impact on the values of effort in the basic COCOMO model?

6. Compare and contrast the basic COCOMO model with Albrecht's function points model.

7. In the intermediate COCOMO model, identify several detailed situations when several attributes can offset each other.

8. Carry out a sensitivity analysis for the Albrecht's function points model. Compare the findings with the results of the pertinent analysis completed for the COCOMO model.

9. The cost estimation models are judged using both subjective and objective criteria. Discuss why the objective criteria alone are not enough.

10. Discuss the strengths and weaknesses of the main classes of cost estimation models.

11. Given the experimental data shown in Figure 14.11, which type of regression model would you recommend (that is a form of the effort–size relationship). What could you say about the quality of the model constructed based on these data sets?

12. The objective is to develop an intelligent robot to navigate semi-autonomously in an unknown territory. The robot collects information about the environment through five sensors, processes these readings, and generates control signals that are applied to two stepping motors. Moreover, all readings of the sensors as well as control actions are sent in a wireless mode to a control workstation. When some predefined conditions (stored in a separate file) are satisfied, then control commands coming from the workstation can override the actions of the robot. Identify functionalities of the system and use the function point model to carry out software cost estimation.

13. The Walston-Felix cost estimation model reads as

$$effort = a*size^b$$

where a = 5.2 and b = 0.91 and the size is given in KLOC. Compare the results given by this model with those obtained by the COCOMO model. Where can you envision the most evident differences? Why?

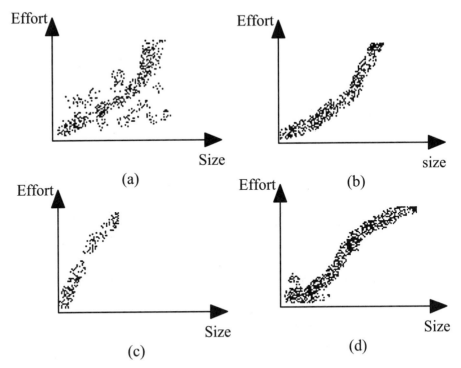

Figure 14.11 Experimental results in the effort–size coordinates.

14. Consider the use of the function points method in measuring the cost of a system described by statecharts. Where can you envision necessary changes? Of what nature?

15. How can the function points method be applied to object-oriented systems? Consider eventual levels of complexity expressed in terms of objects and their interaction with the environment (including other objects).

14.7 REFERENCES

Albrecht, A.J. Measuring application development productivity. *Proceedings of the IBM Application Development Joint SHARE/GUIDE Symposium,* Monterey, CA, 1979, 83–92.

Albrecht, A.J., Gaffney, J. Software function, source lines of code, and development effort prediction: A software science validation. *IEEE Transactions on Software Engineering.* **9:**639–648, 1983.

Boehm, B.W. *Software Engineering Economics.* Prentice Hall, Englewood Cliffs, NJ, 1981.

Conte, S.D., Dunsmore, H.E., Shen, V.Y. *Software Engineering Metrics and Models,* Benjamin/Cummings, Menlo Park, CA, 1986.

Garmus, D., Herron, D. *Measuring the Software Process: A Practical Guide to Functional Measurement.* Prentice Hall, Englewood Cliffs, NJ, 1995.

IEEE Std. 1058-1987, *Software Project Management.* IEEE Press, New York, 1987.

Kitchenham, B. Making process predictions, In *Software Metrics: A Rigorous Approach,* N. E. Fenton. Chapman & Hall, London, 1994.

Park, R.E. Price S: The calculations within and why. *Proceedings of the ISPA 10th Annual Conference,* Brighton, England, July 1988.

Peters J.F., Ramanna, S. Multicriteria decision-making in software cost estimation: Concepts and fuzzy Petri net model. In *Computational Intelligence in Software Engineering,* W. Pedrycz, J.F. Peters, Eds. Singapore, World Scientific, 1988a, 339–370.

Peters J.F., Ramanna, S. Software deployability decision system framework: A rough sets approach. IPMU'98, Paris, June 1998b. 1539–1545.

Peters, J.F., Ramanna, S. Application of Choquet integral in software cost estimation. *IEEE International Conference on Fuzzy Systems,* New Orleans, Sept. 1996, pp. 862–866.

Porter, A., Selby, R. Empirically guided software development using metric-based classification trees. *IEEE Software,* **7**:46–54, 1990.

Reifer, D.J. Cost estimation. In *Encyclopedia of Software Engineering, Vol. I,* J.J. Marciniak, Ed. Wiley, New York, pp. 209–220, 1994.

Srinivasan, K., Fisher, D. Machine learning approaches to estimating software development effort. *IEEE Transactions on Software Engineering,* **21**:126–137, 1995.

Steward, D.V. *Software Engineering with Systems Analysis and Design.* Brooks/Cole, Monterey, CA, 1987.

Vicinanza, S., Pritulla, M.J., Mukhopadhyay, T. Case-based reasoning in software effort estimation. *Proceedings of the 11th International Conference on Information Systems,* 1990, pp. 149–158.

CHAPTER **15**
Software Reliability

Reliability is probably the most important of
the characteristics inherent in the concept
"software quality." Software reliability
concerns itself with how well the software
functions to meet the requirements of the
customer.

—J. MUSA AND OTHERS, 1990

Aims

- Define software reliability and analyze its role in software
  systems
- Study two main types of reliability models: time-dependent and
  time-independent
- Develop reliability characteristics based on experimental data
- Correlate software reliability and software design practices

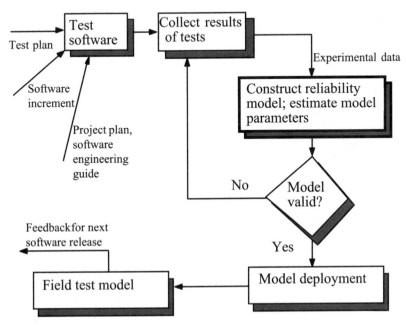

Figure 15.1 Process of reliability estimation.

15.1 INTRODUCTION

This chapter introduces the basic concepts, techniques, and models of software reliability. Roughly speaking, reliability aims at fault-free performance of software systems. Software is considered highly reliable if one can rely on it and use it without any hesitation in critical applications. It is indisputable that with the continuously growing size and complexity of systems being designed, software reliability becomes an important feature of any software system (Lyu, 1996; Musa, 1975, 1979; Musa et al., 1990; Shooman, 1983). The importance of software reliability will grow in the years to come, particularly when we will be targeting more critical areas of applications in the aerospace industry, satellites, and medicine. Software reliability goes hand-in-hand with software verification. Testing techniques are associated with the required reliability characteristics. The overall organization of the process of reliability determination of any software system is shown in Figure 15.1. We witness an inherently iterative character of all computations of software reliability. This general layout of the process helps navigate through the main methodological and algorithmic phases in establishing the reliability of a system. The process starts with software testing and the collection of test results. A reliability model of the system being built uses the input from software testing to assess the validity of the system.

15.2 BASIC IDEAS OF SOFTWARE RELIABILITY

In this section, we establish a vocabulary of some basic terminology of software reliability and underline differences between reliability of software and reliability in general. Despite their similarities, there are some interesting and important differences that predetermine a specificity of the latter. Thus it is of primordial importance to properly define the notion itself and quantify the main notions of reliability. First, let us distinguish between faults and failures. We say that a software system contains a *fault* if for some input data the behavior of the system is incorrect, that is, different from the one included in software specification. For each execution of the software system where its output is incorrect, we talk about software *failure*. Thus the failure is a consequence of a certain fault being left in software, as suggested in the flow diagrams in Figure 15.2. That is, a fault which causes a failure has not been eliminated during the processes of development and testing. This is the case in Figure 15.2b, where selected inputs results in an execution sequence (represented by the shaded path in the flow diagram) where an encountered fault results in software failure. Obviously, the failure could be caused by something other than a software fault, say human error or hardware failure. These situations are generally excluded from our

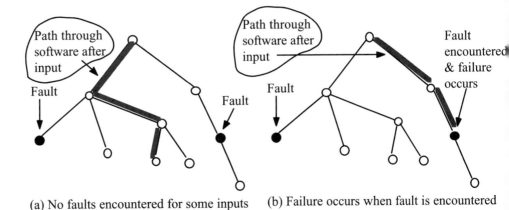

(a) No faults encountered for some inputs (b) Failure occurs when fault is encountered

Figure 15.2 Execution of software modules.

analysis and reliability modeling. Importantly, not every software fault can lead to software failure. It could well be that for some inputs exercised in the system, there will not be any situation activating a module in which the fault has been located. This is the case in Figure 15.2a, where selected inputs results in execution sequence (represented by the shaded path in the flow diagram) where no fault is encountered.

Software reliability contrasts sharply with hardware reliability. Unlike hardware, software does not age (there are no parts to wear out). Improved software reliability results from a vigorous program of fault discovery and removal. This contrasts with increased hardware reliability resulting from the use of better parts (e.g., space-hardened, radiation-resistant instead of ordinary chips for spacecraft computers). We illustrate the issue of faults in software relative to a water tank where a level of water needs to be stabilized within some range. As shown in Figure 15.3, the tank is equipped with three sensors, sens1, sens2, and sens3 that supply information about the current level of water. Depending on the readings of these sensors, some control actions are taken. More precisely, we have the following control actions:

- If the level is lower than the one indicated by sens1 (excessively low level of water), then the system generates an underflow signal.
- If the level is higher than the one indicated by sens1 and lower than signaled by the second sensor, sens2, then the control system opens valve1.
- If the level is higher than the one indicated by sens2 and lower than sens3, then the control system opens valve2.
- If the level is higher than the one indicated by sens2, then the control system generates an overflow signal.

The flowchart of the control algorithm is shown in Figure 15.4. Consider, for example, a fault that has happened at the coding level:

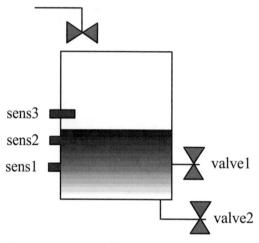

Figure 15.3　Controlling a water tank; indicated are sensors and valves.

```
if ((sens1 == 1) && (sens2 == 0)) then valve1
```

Assume that one of the conditions in this statement has been erroneously coded as follows:

```
if ((sens1 == 1) && (sens2 == 1)) then valve1
```

This fault may result in a failure. It may also be dormant and not lead to any failure. The invocation of some conditions (more precisely, having the second sensor activated) makes the program follow the path along which the failure occurs (Figure 15.5). In the recorded response of the system we identify time slices over which the level of water exceeds some level and activates the second sensor. Intuitively, if the level of the water has never reached high enough to activate the second sensor, then the fault would not be detected. The reliability of the software would have been perceived as being equal to one. The longer the system activates the second sensor, the lower the system's reliability. In light of this, an intuitively appealing expression for resulting reliability can read as the ratio

$$R = 1 - \frac{T'}{T}$$

where T' denotes a cumulative length of time intervals and T denotes a total amount of time over which we record the behavior of the system (Figure 15.6).

The area of reliability occupies a significant role in software engineering. The study of reliability has been vigorously conducted since 1970. Interestingly, the first works on this subject can be found in the 1950s. It embraces a broad

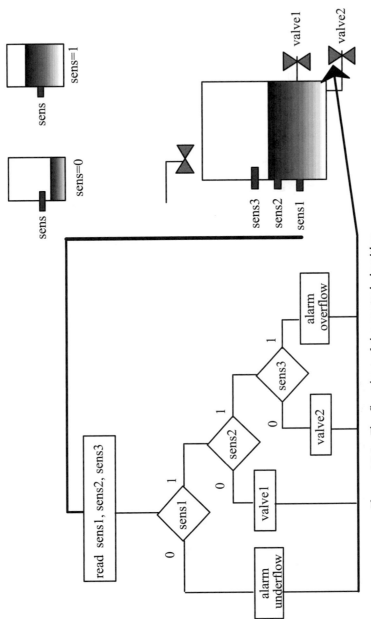

Figure 15.4 The flowchart of the control algorithm.

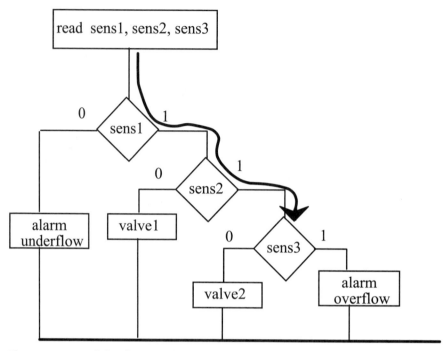

Figure 15.5 Path leading to software failure.

range of software reliability models and incorporates various technologies aimed at the development of reliable software products. The reader may refer to three comprehensive literature sources on this subject (Lyu, 1996; Musa et al., 1990; Xie, 1991).

Reliability must be quantified so that we can compare software systems. The commonly accepted definition of software reliability is anchored in the setting

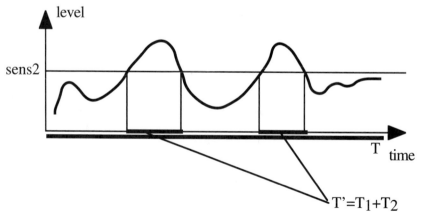

Figure 15.6 Liquid level as a function of time.

of the theory of probability. According to the classic definition, *software reliability* is a probability that the software system will function without failure under a given environment and during a specified period of time. Note that the definition alludes to the environmental conditions and emphasizes a time window over which the functioning of the software should be assured. Furthermore, the statements about reliability are issued in terms of the corresponding probabilities.

Are the mechanisms responsible for software faults probabilistic? The faults may occur at many phases of software development and are primarily caused by some design imperfections rather than imperfections of a physical fabric of the product (as may be encountered in semiconductor devices, aerospace, or other areas). These causes are deterministic, yet difficult to project and quantify. Due to the complexity of the entire phenomenon, probability calculus is one of the commonly endorsed modeling alternatives. In this context, it is worth contrasting software reliability with reliability of hardware (or, more generally, any physical construct):

- Software has no aging property. In this sense, the factor of time is not explicitly involved. Unlike mechanical or electronic components that are subject to wearing out, software constructs are not tangible.
- There are different sources of improving reliability. In software we use intensive testing to obtain systems of higher level of reliability. In hardware we go for better materials and improved design practices as well as exercise fault-tolerant approaches with built-in redundancies.
- Copies of software systems are identical. Thus a standard redundancy method successfully exploited in hardware design (e.g., achieving higher reliability by adding identical elements) does not work in software systems.

In this chapter we will be studying both nonrepairable as well as repairable systems. The first category is characterized by software reliability. Repairable systems are described by software availability.

15.3 COMPUTATION OF SYSTEM RELIABILITY

Knowing the reliability of individual components, one can easily compute the reliability of some architectures commonly encountered in practice. As an example, we analyze series, parallel, and r-out-n configurations (Figure 15.7).

15.3.1 Series Configuration

In a systems topology, the elements are placed in series or in parallel as in Figure 15.7. Consider first the reliability of a series topology. The functioning of the

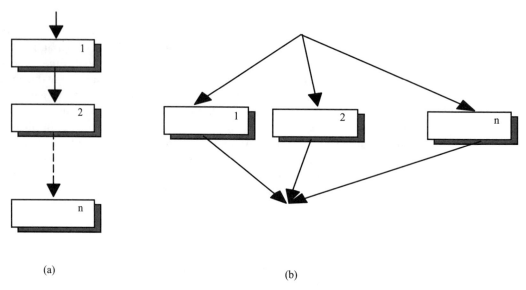

(a)

(b)

Figure 15.7   Series (i) and parallel (ii) organization of subsystems.

system is assured while all elements are functioning properly. An example of the series architecture can be illustrated by considering four subsystems (packages, modules, classes, and so on) aimed at processing sensor data in an air traffic control system:

```
Module 1: reading data
Module 2: cleaning data (elimination of outliers and
filtering noise)
Module 3: processing data
Module 4: printing results
```

A general structure of the tATC system can be portrayed as shown in Figure 15.8 with a series structure. In software engineering, a series configuration pertains to a sequence of software modules within which the flow of data and control occurs in series. The probability P expresses the probability of success of an intersection (&) of events of the following form:

> module 1 is functioning *and* module 2 is functioning *and . . . and* module n is functioning

Assuming that the failures of the modules constitute independent events, this leads to the following expression for the reliability of the whole system given in (1).

$$R(t) = \prod_{i=1}^{n} R_i(t) \qquad (1)$$

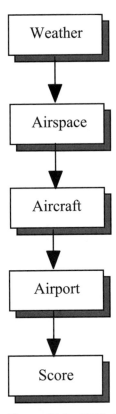

Figure 15.8 tATC structure for reliability computation.

In (1), R_i denotes the reliability of the i-th module. As indicated by (1), the reliability of the system decreases once the number of subsystems increases. It can be seen that quite a dramatic drop in reliability occurs when the number of the modules (subsystems) goes up quickly. To see this, consider the following experiment. For instance, if the individual subsystem has the reliability $R = 0.999$, then 10 of them put in series produce the overall reliability 0.999^{10}, that is, 0.99. Notice that 100 of these reduce the reliability down to 0.9048. Continuing this expansion of a sequential distribution of subsystems, it turns out that 1000 of the same modules lead to the overall reliability of 0.3677.

15.3.2 Parallel Configuration

A parallel configuration occurs in a situation when at least one module is necessary to assure functioning of the entire system (see Figure 15.7b). Here it is easier to compute a probability of a failure rather than that of successful performance of the system. Consider the following events:

module$_1$ is not functioning *and* module$_2$ is not functioning . . . *and* module$_n$ is not functioning

Again, assuming independence of failures of the corresponding modules, one gets (2).

$$R(t) = 1 - \prod_{i=1}^{n} (1 - R_i(t)) \qquad (2)$$

15.3.3 P-out-of-n Configuration

In a p-out-of-n configuration, p-out of-n elements (modules) should be functioning to assure functioning of the system. In a simplified analysis we consider that all the elements are identical and function independently. Then the reliability function reads as in (3).

$$R(t) = \sum_{k=r}^{n} \binom{n}{k} R^k(t) (1 - R(t))^{n-k} \qquad (3)$$

Interestingly, the parallel as well as series configurations are subsumed as the two limit cases of the r-out of n configuration. Let $r = 1$, that is a parallel configuration. This yields

$$R(t) = \sum_{k=1}^{n} \binom{n}{k} R^k(t) (1 - R(t))^{n-k} = 1 - \prod_{i=1}^{n} (1 - R(t))$$

For the series structure, $r = n$, one derives

$$R(t) = \sum_{k=n}^{n} \binom{n}{k} R^k(t) (1 - R(t))^{n-k} = \binom{n}{k} R^n(t) = R^n(t)$$

Assume that the intent is to maintain the reliability of the ATC system over 0.90. More descriptively, in the Kiviat representation of the system we require that the system is located as illustrated in Figure 15.9, where system reliability is required to be in the range (min, max) = (0.9, 1.0).

Let us determine the reliability of two parallel modules inside aircraft module for the tATC system, namely, simulate and button (Figure 15.8). Assume that the reliability of the simulate module is 0.95 and the reliability is 0.99. First, write out the failure model for the two modules put in parallel,

$$1 - R_{modules} = (1 - R_2)*(1 - R_3) = (1 - 0.95)*(1 - 0.99)$$

Then compute the reliability of the two modules

$$R_{modules} = 1 - (0.05)(0.01) = 0.9995$$

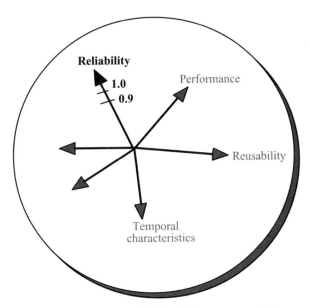

Figure 15.9   System reliability: Kiviat representation.

Let the weather, airspace, and airport modules in the tATC shown in Figure 15.8 have reliabilities of 0.96, 0.92, 0.999, respectively. In the next step determine the reliability of the entire system,

$$R = R_1 * R_{aircraft} * R_4 * R_5 = 0.96*0.9995*0.92*0.999 = 0.8819$$

The calculations reveal that the expected reliability of the tATC system cannot be met.

15.4 CLASSES OF SOFTWARE RELIABILITY MODELS

There are a vast number of methods aimed at computing software reliability. In spite of their diversity, they can be categorized as shown in Figure 15.10. This taxonomy coincides with the classifications commonly encountered in the literature (Shooman, 1983; Xie, 1991). In this hierarchy, there are two essential conceptual levels. The models are either time-*dependent* or time-*independent*. In the sequel, they may concentrate either on time between faults or consider a number of faults for a fixed (specified) time interval. As far as time-independent reliability models are concerned, we distinguish between fault seeding and input-domain based models.

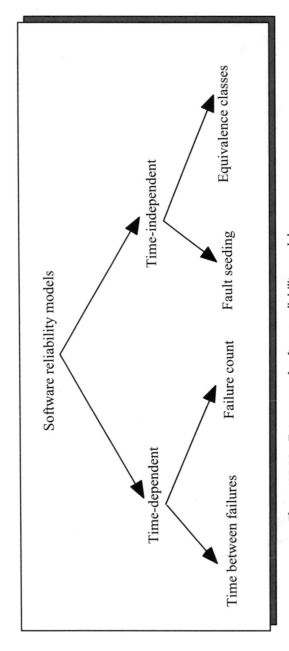

Figure 15.10 Taxonomy of software reliability models.

15.5 TIME-DEPENDENT SOFTWARE RELIABILITY MODELS

The category of time-dependent reliability models is one of the earliest classes studied from the inception of the area. The underlying reliability relationships supported by these models express them as functions of time. This leads to a quantification of time between successive failures or failure counts completed over time.

15.5.1 Time Between Failure Reliability Models

The models falling in this category are the earliest encountered in the literature (Jelinsky & Moranda, 1972). Originally, the model was introduced in the framework of research on Navy projects for McDonnell Douglas and is also called a de-eutrophication reliability model. The underlying idea is to model time between successive failures. This time variable itself is regarded as a random variable characterized by a certain probability density function. The models in this class vary with respect to the assumptions made with regard to the form of the hazard function. We review a number of representative example models. The Jelinsky-Moranda (1972) model, the first in this class, starts with a hazard function expressed in (4).

$$z(t_i) = \Delta[N_0 - (i - 1)] \qquad (4)$$

An illustration of stairlike hazard function is shown Figure 15.11. The failures occur at some discrete time moments. In the model, we are concerned with the

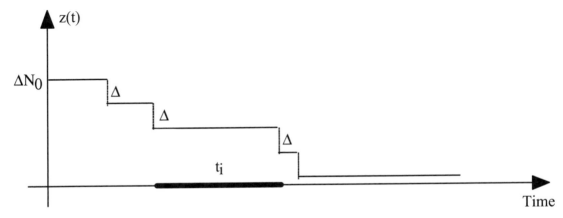

Figure 15.11 A stairwise form of a hazard function.

time intervals between successive failures, t_1, t_2, . . . etc. The model hinges on several assumptions:

- The number of initial faults (N_0) is unknown.
- Detected fault is removed and no new faults are introduced.
- Time intervals between failures (t_i) are independent exponentially distributed random variables as expressed in (5).

$$P(T < t_i) = z(t_i) \exp(-z(t_i)t_i) \tag{5}$$

- All faults contribute to the same extent to failure intensity.

The form of the model (failure rate) is straightforward: $z(t)$ becomes simply a stairlike function with steps of height equal to Δ. These describe the failure intensity contributed by each fault. Finally, the MTTF after "n" faults have been detected is computed as in (6).

$$MTTF = \frac{1}{\Delta(N - n)} \tag{6}$$

To develop the model given some experimental data, one needs to determine two unknown parameters, namely Δ and N_0. The first one, Δ, describes a size of the step (we assume that the size of the steps is time independent, that is, it does not depend on time). N_0 denotes an initial number of faults existing in the system. The standard way of estimating the parameters of the reliability model is to maximize the associated likelihood function. This is, in fact, a standard approach in constructing statistical models. Let us recall that the likelihood function of N_0 and Δ is defined as in (7).

$$L(t_1, t_2, . . . , t_n; N_0, \Delta) = \prod_{i=1}^{n} P(T_i < t_i) = \prod_{i=1}^{n} z(t_i) \exp(-z(t_i)t_i) \tag{7}$$

Now taking advantage of the assumption about the form of respective random variables, the likelihood function is given in (8).

$$L(t_1, t_2, . . . , t_n; N_0, \Delta) = \prod_{i=1}^{n} \Delta[N_0 - (i - 1)] \exp(-\Delta(N_0 - i + 1)t_i)$$

$$= \Delta^n \left[\prod_{i=1}^{n} (N_0 - i + 1) \right] \exp\left(-\Delta \sum_{i=1}^{n} (N_0 - i + 1)t_i \right) \tag{8}$$

The objective of the likelihood method is to maximize L with respect to Δ and N_0 as in (9).

$$\max_{\Delta, N_0} L \tag{9}$$

This can be done using equations (10) and (11).

$$\Delta = \frac{1}{\sum_{i=1}^{n}(N_0 - i + 1)t_i} \tag{10}$$

$$\sum_{i=1}^{n}(N_0 - i + 1)t_i = \frac{n\sum_{i=1}^{n}t_i}{\sum_{i=1}^{n}(N_0 - i + 1)} \tag{11}$$

Equations (10) and (11) are solved numerically with respect to the parameters of the model. Consider, for example, a sample of software reliability data summarizing time moments between failures of a software module $t_1 = 7$, $t_2 = 11$, $t_3 = 8$, $t_4 = 10$, $t_5 = 15$, $t_6 = 22$, $t_7 = 20$, $t_8 = 25$, $t_9 = 28$, $t_{10} = 35$. The plot of this data reflecting a cumulative number of failures over time is shown in Figure 15.12.

Using any method of nonlinear optimization, equations (10) and (11) give rise to the values $\Delta = 0.0096$ and $N_0 = 11.6$. The estimated MTTF computed with the aid of equation (6) leads to the result in (12).

$$MTTF = \frac{1}{0.0096(11.6 - 10)} = 65.1 \tag{12}$$

There are a number of interesting augmentations of these basic reliability models. Especially, the assumption about the faults being of the same size is questioned

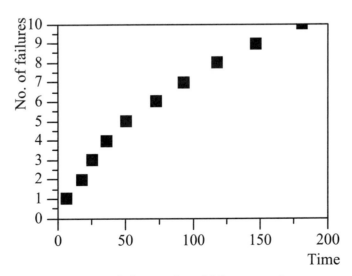

Figure 15.12 Cumulative number of failures over time.

quite often. Figure 15.13 represents software faults of equal and different size. Some of these faults are eventually removed. In Figure 15.13b, the reliability model is augmented for $t_1 > t_0$. It is reasonable to assume that earlier failures are caused by faults having a high probability of detection. Subsequently, it means that large faults are likely to be dealt with earlier in the debugging process. To alleviate the shortcoming about the same size of all faults, several reliability models have been proposed. For instance, Xie and Bergman (1988) introduced $z(t_i)$ to be a power-type function of remaining faults as expressed (13).

$$z(t_i) = \Delta [N_0 - (i - 1)]^\alpha \tag{13}$$

It is assumed that $\alpha > 1$ in (13). Notice that for $\alpha = 1$, we obtain the original Jelinsky-Moranda reliability model. Another form of the reliability model assumes an exponential function given in (14).

$$z(t_i) = \Delta [e^{\beta(N_0 - i + 1)} - 1] \tag{14}$$

It is assumed in (14) that $\beta > 0$, which is an auxiliary parameter of the hazard function. Note that the decrease in the failure intensity at the beginning of the debugging process is much faster than at a later time. Figure 15.14 contrasts the discussed model by showing the intensity rate $z(t_i)$ treated as a function of "i". Figure 15.14 represents selected hazard functions: linear; power, $\alpha = 3$; and exponential, $\beta = 0.01$. For all plots of hazard functions in Figure 15.14, $N_0 = 200$ and $\Delta = 0.02$. To make the reliability model more realistic, we can introduce a notion of imperfect debugging, where it is assumed that each fault is removed with a certain probability p. Then the resulting hazard function is expressed as in (15).

$$z(t_i) = \Delta [N_0 - p(i - 1)] \tag{15}$$

A simple transformation of $z(t_i)$ sheds light on the interpretation of this probability as an essential part of the modified hazard function. We get

$$z(t_i) = \Delta p \left[\frac{N_0}{p} - (i - 1) \right]$$

Put

$$\Delta' = \Delta p \quad N_0' = \frac{N_0}{p}$$

Hence

$$z(t_i) = \Delta' [N_0' - (i - 1)]$$

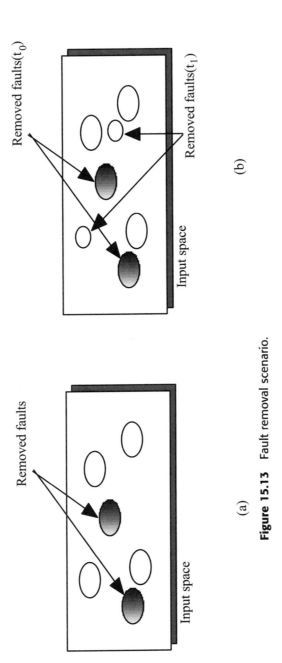

Figure 15.13 Fault removal scenario.

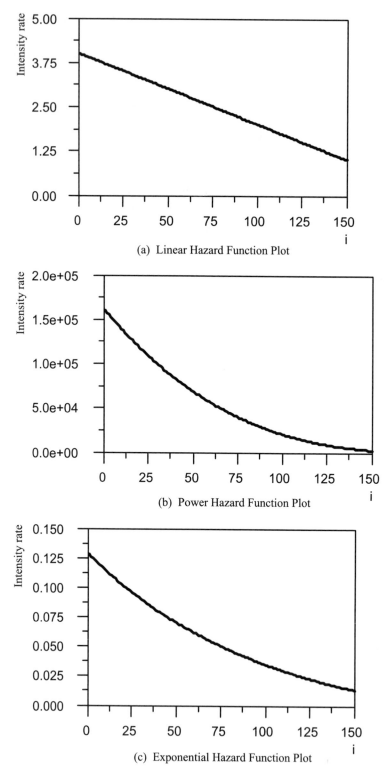

Figure 15.14 Selected hazard functions plots.

In comparison with the original formula, the equivalent number of the initial faults has increased while the intensity of removal Δ' has been reduced correspondingly.

Models were also proposed that deal with time-dependent failure intensity function. Schick and Wolverton (1978) made an assumption that the times between failures are expressed as in (16).

$$z(t_i) = \Delta[N_0 - (i - 1)]t_i \qquad (16)$$

Therefore $z(t_i)$ depends on "i", the number of removed faults and the time t_i since the removal of the last fault. In general, one may consider $z(t_i)$ to be a certain function of time $g(t_i)$,

$$z(t_i) = \Delta[N_0 - (i - 1)]g(t_i)$$

The time dependency of $z(t_i)$ has been questioned as a suitable model of a pure software system; instead one may claim that such reliability models become more relevant when studying software and hardware behavior of the systems.

15.5.2   Fault Counting Reliability Models

In this category of reliability models we are concerned with counting the number of faults detected in a certain time interval (fault counting model). The Goel-Okumoto reliability model (1979) is one of the simplest yet representative, models falling under this category. The pertinent assumptions made about the model are enumerated as follows:

- Cumulative number of faults detected at time "t" follows a Poisson distribution.
- All faults are independent and can be detected at the same rate.
- All detected faults are removed; no more faults are introduced.

Thus, the probability of "k" faults detected in time "t", $P(N(t) = k)$ is equal to (17).

$$P(N(t) = k) = \frac{(m(t))^k}{k!} e^{-m(t)} \qquad (17)$$

This expression describes a so-called nonhomogeneous Poisson process. Moreover, $m(t)$ stands for an expected cumulative number of failures detected in $[0, t]$. In the Goel-Okumoto model we assume that $m(t)$ is modeled as a two parameter function in (18).

$$m(t) = a(1 - e^{-bt}) \qquad (18)$$

where a, b > 0. The following limit conditions hold.

$$m(\infty) = a \quad m(0) = 0$$

The first limit condition is the expected number of faults to be detected, then "a" is the final number of faults while "b" is the failure occurrence rate per fault. The expected number of remaining faults at time "t" is computed as in (19).

$$N(\infty) - N(t)$$

and

$$m(\infty) - m(t) = a - a(1 - e^{-bt}) = ae^{-bt} \tag{19}$$

As becomes obvious from (19), the expected number of faults is an exponential function of time. The failure intensity function, $\mu(t)$, defined as the derivative of m(t)

$$\mu(t) = \frac{dm(t)}{dt}$$

gives rise to

$$\mu(t) = ab\exp(-bt)$$

Practically, it has been observed that the software failure intensity increases slightly at the beginning of any testing and then begins to decrease. To cope with this tendency, Goel (1985) introduced a modified version of m(t) assuming the form shown in (20).

$$m(t) = a(1 - \exp(-bt^c)) \tag{20}$$

with one extra parameter (c). Again, even with this modification, the form of m(t) exhibits an exponential-like shape. Many experimental data reveal that the curve of the cumulative number of faults is often S-shaped (Figure 15.15). Several S-shaped models have been proposed in the literature (Ohba, 1984; Wood, 1996; Yamada et al., 1983). In particular, we write (21)

$$m(t) = a[1 - (1 + bt)e^{-bt}] \tag{21}$$

where b > 0. Here the expected number of remaining faults at time "t" is equal to

$$m(\infty) - m(t) = a(1 + bt)e^{-bt}$$

The execution time reliability model introduced by Musa (1975, 1987) relies on an important observation that all modeling should be based on an execution

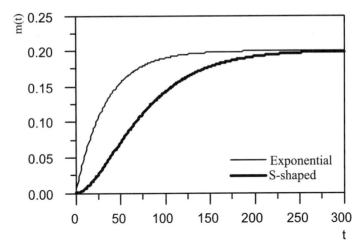

Figure 15.15 S-shaped versus exponential shape of m(t).

time (the time expressed in terms of CPU time) rather than elapsed calendar time (wall-clock time). It is quite noticeable that software testing activities are uniform in execution time rather than calendar time; the first time scale is a more reasonable measure of time for constructing and utilizing reliability models. Denote the execution time by τ in order to distinguish it from the wall-clock time (t). For the Musa's basic execution time model, the cumulative number of failures, $m(\tau)$ is introduced in the form,

$$m(\tau) = \beta_0[1 - \exp(-\beta_1\tau)]$$

where β_0, β_1 are two positive parameters. The failure intensity function equals

$$m(\tau) = \beta_0\beta_1 \exp(-\beta_1\tau)$$

For large values of β_1 the failure intensity function decreases rapidly. The speed of changes is controlled by the values of β_1. There is an interesting rationale behind the form of $m(\tau)$. First, $\mu(\tau)$ is assumed (which sounds like a reasonable assumption) to be proportional to the number of faults remaining in the software system. This reads as

$$\mu(\tau) = a[N_0 - m(\tau)]$$

where N_0 is an initial number of faults in the software. Suppose now that the fault correction rate is proportional to the failure occurrence rate,

$$\frac{dm(\tau)}{d\tau} = b\mu(\tau)$$

Combining these two expressions, we have

$$\frac{dm(\tau)}{d\tau} + abm(\tau) - abN_0 = 0$$

The solution to the differential equation with $m(0) = 0$ yields

$$m(\tau) = N_0(1 - \exp(-ab\tau))$$

15.6 TIME-INDEPENDENT SOFTWARE RELIABILITY MODELS

The software reliability models discussed so far hinged on the factor of time as an essential, if not dominant, component. In contrast, static models of software reliability are not concerned with time in an explicit fashion but rather attempt to reveal relationships between detected and undetected faults as static dependencies. The static models of software reliability embrace two representative models, namely fault injection and input domain models.

15.6.1 Fault Injection Model of Software Reliability

A seeding methods idea proposed by Mills in 1970 and discussed by Schick and Wolverton (1978) and Duran and Wiorkowski (1981), among others, is straightforward and intuitively appealing. Software models include faults. Any testing technique is geared to discover and eliminate them. An interesting and important question is about the number of faults in the system in the case where we know the outcomes of the already detected faults. What originates from statistics and known as capture-recapture sampling can be used in software reliability environments. We insert into a software module a certain number of faults (seeded or artificial faults) and proceed with its testing, counting the number of seeded and inherent (ingenious) faults (Figure 15.16). The number of remaining

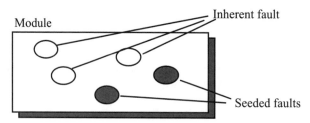

Figure 15.16   Seeding software faults.

faults can be estimated based on the number of both types of faults already detected.

Denote by N and A the number of inherent and seeded faults, respectively. Similarly, "i" and "f" stand for the number of inherent and seeded faults found during the testing. Assuming that the character of the seeded faults is the same as the original ones (so they are not distinguishable by the testing method), the obvious relationship holds:

$$\frac{A}{f} = \frac{N}{i}$$

and, as a consequence, the estimated number of inherent faults comes from the relationship (22).

$$N = \frac{A}{f} i \tag{22}$$

15.6.2 Example: Code with Faults

As an example, let us consider a part of the code given in Figures 15.17 to 15.19 (this code concerns computing a partition matrix and prototypes), which includes a number of faults that are highlighted in the code. The nature of the faults in Figure 15.18 is such that they are not detected by a compiler. The faults include replacement of the variables, changes to relational operators, and so on. Knowing the nature of the faults we can inject a handful of artificial faults ($A = 6$). Artificial faults (marked with small starts) are shown in Figure 15.18. After testing, we end up with $f = 2$ and $i = 3$ inherent and seeded faults found (Figure 15.19). Faults removed in Figure 15.19 are indicated with arrows. From (22), it is determined that the number of inherent faults N is equal to 9. Moreover, one can come up with some confidence levels about the number of faults. If not all artificial faults have been found, then (cf. Gilb, 1977; Myers, 1975):

$$\text{prob(no more than E faults)} = \begin{cases} 0, \text{if } i > E \\ \dfrac{\dbinom{A}{f-1}}{\dbinom{E+1+A}{EW+f}}, \text{if } i \le E \end{cases}$$

If all artificial faults have been found, then:

$$\text{prob(no more than E faults)} = \begin{cases} 0, \text{if } i > E \\ \dfrac{A}{A+E+1}, \text{if } i \le E \end{cases}$$

```
public void main_iteration_loop(){
initialize_partition ();
for(int iter=0; iter<iter_max+20; iter++){          //main iteration loop comprised of
compute_prototype ();                                // updates of prototypes and partition
compute_partition();                                 // matrix
}}

public void initialize_partition (){                //initialize partition matrix to random
for (int i=1 ; i<c; i++){                            //numbers; normalize each column to
        for (int k=0; k<Nm;k++){ // 1
                u[i][k]=(float) java.lang.Math.random();
        }}
        for(int k=1; k<Nm; k++){
        float sum=(float)0.0;
                for (int i=0; i<c; i++){
                sum = sum + u[i] [k];}
                for (int i=0; i<c; i++){
                u[k][k]=u[i][k]/sum;        //normalization to 1
                }
}}

public void compute_prototype (){                   // calculate prototypes
float s1=(float)0.0;
float s2=(float)1.0;
for (int i=0; i<c; i++){                              // cluster loop
for (int j=0; j<n; j++){                              // dimension loop
for (int k=0; k<Nm; k++){                             //summation over data
s1=s1+(float)java.lang.Math.pow((double) u[i][k],m)*x[k] [j];
s2=s2+(float)java.lang.Math.pow((double) u[i][k],m);
}
v [i][j]= s1/s2;}}}

public void compute_partition () {                  //calculate partition matrix
float djk;
float dik;
float sum;
for (int i=0; i<c; i++){
for (int k=0; k<Nm-1 ; k++){
        for (int 1=0; 1<n; 1++){
        xk[1]= x[k][1];
        vj[1]= v[i][1];
        vi[1]= v[i][1];}
        dik= distance(xk, vi);                       //calculate prototype-pattern distance
        if(dik!=(float) 0.0) dik=(float)java.lang.Math.pow((double) dik, 1/(m-1));
        sum =(float)0.0;
                for (int j=0; j<c; j++){
                djk = distance (xk, vi);
                if (djk != (float)0.0) sum=sum+
                (float)1.0/(float)java.lang.Math.pow((double) djk, 2/(m-1));
                }
u[i][k] = (float)1.0/(dik*sum);                       //i,k element of partition matrix
}}}

public float distance (float a[], float b[]){       /Euclidean /distance function
float sum =(float)0.0;
for (int i=0; i<n; i++)
sum = sum + (a[i]−b[i])*(a[i]−b[i]);
return (sum);}
}
```

Figure 15.17 A part of code with faults (highlighted).

```
public void main_iteration_loop(){
initialize_partition ();
for(int iter=1; iter<iter_max+20; iter++){          //main iteration loop comprised of
compute_prototype ();                                // updates of prototypes and partition
compute_partition();                                 // matrix
}}

public void initialize_partition (){                //initialize partition matrix to random
for (int i=1 ; i<c; i++){                             // numbers; normalize each column to
          for (int k=0; k<Nm-1,k++){       // 1
                    u[i][k]=(float) java.lang.Math.random();
                    }}
                    for(int k=1 ; k<Nm; k++){
                    float sum=(float)0.0;
                              for (int i=0; i<c; i++){
                              sum = sum + u[i] [k];}
                              for (int i=0; i<c; i++){
                              u[k][k]=u[i][k]/sum;            //normalization to 1
                              }

}}

public void compute_prototype (){                   // calculate prototypes
float s1=(float)0.0;
float s2=(float)1.0;
for (int i=1; i<c; i++){                             // cluster loop
for (int j=0; j<n; j++){                             // dimension loop
for (int k=0; k<Nm; k++){                            //summation over data
s1=s1+(float)java.lang.Math.pow((double) u[i][k],m)*x[k] [j];
s2=s2+(float)java.lang.Math.pow((double) u[i][k],m);
}
v [i][j]= s1/s2;}}}

public void compute_partition () {                  //calculate partition matrix
float djk;
float dik;
float sum;
for (int i=0; i<c; i++){
for (int k=0; k<Nm-1 ; k++){
          for (int 1=0; 1<n; 1++){
          xk[1]= x[k][1];
          vj[1]= v[i][k];
          vi[1]= v[i][1];}
          dik= distance(xk, vi);                    //calculate prototype-pattern distance
          if(dik!=(float) 0.0) dik=(float)java.lang.Math.pow((double) dik, 1/(m-1));
          sum =(float)0.0;
                    for (int j=0; j<c; j++){
                    djk = distance (xk, vi);
                    if (djk != (float)0.0) sum=sum-
                    (float)1.0/(float)java.lang.Math.pow((double) djk, 2/(m-1));
                    }
u[i][k ] = (float)1.0/(dik*sum);                     //i,k element of partition matrix
}}}

public float distance (float a[], float b[]){       /Euclidean /distance function
float sum =(float)0.0;
for (int i=0; i<Nm; i++)
sum = sum + (a[i]-b[i])*(a[i]-b[i]);
return (sum);}
}
```

Figure 15.18 Code with injected faults (marked by stars).

```java
public void main_iteration_loop(){
initialize_partition ();
for(int iter=1; iter<iter_max+20; iter++){          //main iteration loop comprised of
compute_prototype ();                                // updates of prototypes and partition
compute_partition();                                 // matrix
}}

public void initialize_partition (){                 //initialize partition matrix to random
for (int i=1 ; i<c; i++){                            // numbers; normalize each column to
          for (int k=0; k<Nm-1;k++){     // 1
               u[i][k]=(float) java.lang.Math.random();
               }}
          for(int k=1 ; k<Nm; k++){
          float sum=(float)0.0;
               for (int i=0; i<c; i++){
               sum = sum + u[i] [k];}
               for (int i=0; i<c; i++){
               u[k][k]=u[i][k]/sum;       //normalization to 1
               }
}}

public void compute_prototype (){                    // calculate prototypes
float s1=(float)0.0;
float s2=(float)1.0;
for (int i=1; i<c; i++){                              // cluster loop
for (int j=0; j<n; j++){                              // dimension loop
for (int k=0; k<Nm; k++){                             //summation over data
s1=s1+(float)java.lang.Math.pow((double) u[i][k],m)*x[k] [j];
s2=s2+(float)java.lang.Math.pow((double) u[i][k],m);
}
v [i][j]= s1/s2;}}}

public void compute_partition () {                   //calculate partition matrix
float djk;
float dik;
float sum;
for (int i=0; i<c; i++){
for (int k=0; k<Nm-1, k++){
          for (int 1=0; 1<n; 1++){
          xk[1]= x[k][1];
          vj[1]= v[i][k];
          vi[1]= v[i][1];}
          dik= distance(xk, vi);                     //calculate prototype-pattern distance
          if(dik!=(float) 0.0) dik=(float)java.lang.Math.pow((double) dik, 1/(m-1));
          sum =(float)0.0;
               for (int j=0; j<c; j++){
               djk = distance (xk, vi);
               if (djk != (float)0.0) sum=sum+
               (float)1.0/(float)java.lang.Math.pow((double) djk, 2/(m-1));
               }
u[i][k ] = (float)1.0/(dik*sum);                     //i,k element of partition matrix
}}}
public float distance (float a[], float b[]){        /Euclidean /distance function
float sum =(float)0.0;
for (int i=0; i<Nm; i++)
sum = sum + (a[i]-b[i])*(a[i]-b[i]);
return (sum);}
}
```

Figure 15.19   Code after testing (faults removed are indicated by arrows).

Let us proceed with an illustrative example. The software was seeded with 25 artificial faults. During testing, 32 of faults were detected, 17 of which were artificial. The estimated number of inherent faults as computed using equation (22) is given as follows:

$$N = \frac{A}{f}i = \frac{25}{17}*(32 - 17) \approx 22$$

Subsequently, one can determine the confidence level about the number of remaining faults. Let us set E to 10. As not all artificial errors have been detected, we use the first expression out of the two used for computing confidence levels (A = 25, I = 15, f = 17, E = 10),

$$\text{prob(no more than 10 faults)} = \frac{\binom{25}{17-1}}{\binom{10+1+25}{10+17}}$$

Assuming that all artificial faults have been found and I < E, we can use the corresponding relationship in order to determine the number of artificial errors that should be seeded to gain a confidence level not lower than a certain threshold value λ. We get

$$\lambda < \frac{A}{A + E + 1}$$

where E is given in advance. Let us rearrange the above expression

$$(E + 1)\lambda < A(1 - \lambda)$$

and

$$A > \frac{\lambda}{1 - \lambda}(E + 1)$$

So if with confidence 0.9 we expect that the number of faults will not exceed 10, then the number of injected errors should be at least

$$A = \frac{0.9}{1 - 0.9}*10 = 90$$

For the lower confidence level, say 0.7, and the same number of remaining faults, there are fewer injected errors

$$A = \frac{0.7}{1 - 0.7}*10 = 23$$

Even though the seeding method looks simple and intuitively convincing, the resulting estimates should be treated very carefully as producing some bias. They may be quite inaccurate. The accuracy of the results depend upon the validity of several assumptions made upfront. First, the number of seeded faults should be large (as we rely on statistical type of reasoning). Moreover, what is crucial, the type of artificial faults should reflect the types of ingenious faults and the probability of finding faults (both seeded and inherent) is the same. The advantage of the method lies in its conceptual simplicity; nevertheless one should exercise caution in interpreting and utilizing the ensuing results.

Closely linked with fault seeding is a method called mutation testing. Mutation testing (De Millo & Lipton, 1978; Hamlet, 1977); uses fault seeding to investigate properties of test data. Programs with seeded faults are called mutants. Mutants are executed to determine whether or not they behave differently from the original program. Mutants that behave differently are said to have been killed by the test. Mutants are produced by utilizing a mutation operator. The role of the operator is to change an individual expression by replacing it by another one coming from a certain predefined class of expressions. For instance, one can change constants by incrementing or decrementing them. The set of mutants could be very large. The necessary and sufficient conditions for a fault to cause a program failure involve the following items Morell, 1990:

- *Execution.* The fault location must be executed.
- *Infection.* The resulting data state must be infected with an erroneous value.
- *Propagation.* The resulting computations must propagate the infection through erroneous data states, yielding a failure.

15.6.3   Input Domain Reliability Models

The idea behind input reliability models stems from a functional view of software as operating on a certain input domain I and producing results within a given output domain (Figure 15.20). This point of view nicely relates to software testing and selecting test cases over the input domain. In what follows, we discuss two representative methods of this group of the models, the Nelson model and the equivalence classes reliability model. We start with a concise example to illustrate the nature of these models. A control software module collects data from two sensors. Depending upon the values of the data obtained, the module assumes one of two actions: if the readings are similar (within a predefined tolerance bound of width δ) then activate function fun1. Otherwise, one has to execute function fun2 (which eventually examines the relevancy of the readings and collects some additional data) (Figure 15.21). Each sensor is equipped with a 10-bit A/D converter. The input domain is easy to establish: it consists of two variables, each of them quantified with the aid of 1024 (2^{10}) uniformly distributed points (Figure 15.22). The equivalence classes assume an apparent meaning.

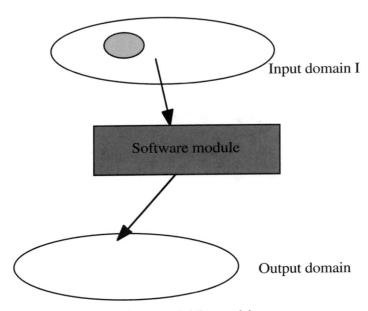

Figure 15.20 Input domain reliability models.

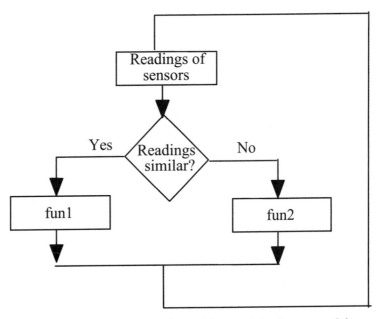

Figure 15.21 A general flowchart of the control software module.

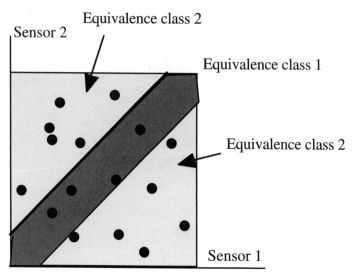

Figure 15.22   Input domain and its equivalence classes.

Equivalence class 1 captures all readings of the sensors that are similar. The similarity, as is visualized in Figure 15.22, describes data collected by the sensors that satisfy the relationship

$$|sensor1 - sensor2| < \delta$$

which comes as a band distributed around the main diagonal of the data square. The second equivalence class is located in the lower and upper part of the same square.

In the method proposed by Nelson (1972), software reliability is estimated based upon a battery of test runs. Let "n" denote a total number of test cases (distributed over the input domain) In n_e of these runs the software failed. The self-evident estimate of reliability is then given by the expression in (23).

$$1 - \frac{n_e}{n} \tag{23}$$

Note that this estimation procedure does not require more than the outcomes of test runs. Intuitively, the larger the number of tests, the more confidence one puts into the results. In limit, when the number of runs tends to infinity (which is not practical, anyway), the reliability leads to the expression of reliability in the form given in (24).

$$R = \lim_{n \to \infty} \left(1 - \frac{n_e}{n} \right) \tag{24}$$

R in (24) eventually becomes the classic and self-evident definition of reliability. The main drawback of this definition and the resulting approach becomes inevitable because of the dimension of the input domain. Note that even in the case of this simple input domain of readings of two sensors, we are faced with $1024 * 1024 = 2^{10}*2^{10} = 2^{20}$ possibilities. Any random distribution of test cases could lead to a prohibitively large number of tests that are necessary to assure high accuracy of the estimates. To circumvent this deficiency, the input domain is partitioned into some equivalence classes (Bastiani & Ramamoorthy, 1986; Weiss & Weyuker, 1988). This approach mainly reduces the size of the input domain with respect to the number of test cases. The equivalence classes embrace these regions of the input domain that are equivalent with respect to the behavior of the system under testing. For instance, these may be governed by boundary value testing, path testing, range testing, and so forth. The objective of the equivalence class is to magnify the size of a fault (Figure 15.23).

In the previous example, we can distinguish two equivalence classes implied by the conditions imposed on the sensors. The first class includes all situations where the readings of the sensors coincide within the assumed bounds of tolerance

$$\text{class 1: } |x_1 - x_2| \leq \delta$$

The second class comes in the form

$$\text{class 2: } |x_1 - x_2| > \delta$$

The equivalence classes exhibit a property of continuity reflected in Figure 15.23. That is, if execution is correct for r in E_i, then an execution of randomly selected

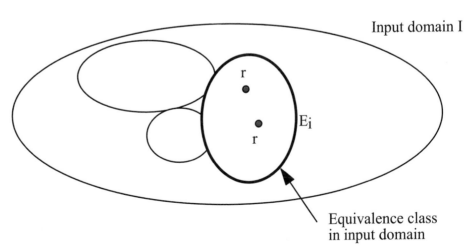

Figure 15.23 Equivalence classes in input domain.

TABLE 15.1   Classes of Reliability Models and Their Main Features

Reliability Model	Features
Time between failures	• Independent times between failures (independent random variables) • Equal probability of exposure to each fault • Faults are independent • Faults removed after detection, perfect removal, no additional faults introduced
Fault count	• Testing intervals treated as independent variables • Testing during intervals reasonably homogeneous • Independent number of faults detected during nonoverlapping time intervals
Fault seeding	• Seeded faults randomly distributed across software system • Indigenous and seeded faults have equal probabilities of being detected
Input domain	• Input profile distribution known • Random testing • Input domain partitioned into equivalence classes

r' in the same domain will not produce failure, and this event comes with probability 1-ε with ε being a small positive number. There is a tradeoff: ε could be higher for equivalence classes of a larger size. As suggested by Bastiani and Ramamoorthy (1986), the equivalence classes can be derived from the requirement specification. With each equivalence class E_i comes its operational profile, that is, a probability P_i stating that the inputs will really come from E_i under normal operation of the system. Denote by n_j the number of test cases sampled from the j-th input domain E_j where f_j out of them resulted in software failures. Then the estimated reliability is computed as in (25).

$$R = 1 - \sum_{j=1}^{c} \frac{f_j}{n_j} P_j \tag{25}$$

There are two evident advantages of the method. Any testing strategy can be used. The method takes into consideration software complexity (that is done via the equivalence classes). A certain drawback comes with the problem of the determination of the equivalence classes themselves; this could be a tedious and rather expensive process. As a summary of the discussed categories of software reliability models, Table 15.1 lists them with their key assumptions. It is important to be aware of these conditions as they indicate a range of applicability and relevance of the respective reliability models.

15.7 ORTHOGONAL DEFECT CLASSIFICATION

The reliability models discussed so far are based on statistical fault analysis. It can be seen from the previous sections, reliability models are highly abstract and quantitative. In addition, reliability models tend to be remote from the software and thus not capable of capturing genuine efficacies of the software system under analysis. On the other hand, there are cause–effect analysis models that are highly qualitative, human-intensive, and down to earth. The idea of the Orthogonal Defect Classification (ODC) method (Chillarege, 1996) is to bridge these extremes by developing a measurement system based upon the semantics of faults. This, in fact, is in accordance with many observations and assumptions made in the setting of probabilistic models when we attempt to make them meaningful by assuming that faults are the same and indistinguishable with respect to their origin and manifestation.

The crux of the ODC method is to gain a better understanding of a growth of software reliability by correlating different types of faults being eliminated and the phases of software development when this elimination has taken place. The classes (types) of faults are necessary as the granulation imposed by such classes captures the performance of the model. As discussed in Chillarege (1996), there are seven classes of faults, as summarized in Table 15.2.

TABLE 15.2 Classes of Faults in Orthogonal Defect Classification

Fault	Description
Function	A function fault (defect) significantly affects capability, user-interface feature, interface with hardware layer, or global structures. Usually it requires a formal modification in software design.
Assignment	An assignment fault associates with a few lines of code; usually it is related to initialization of control blocks or data structures.
Interface	The faults in this class concern interactions with other modules, device drivers, control blocks, parameter lists.
Checking	The checking faults embrace software logic that has failed to properly validate data or values, loop conditions, and others.
Timing/serialization	These faults are associated with an improper management of real-time or shared resources.
Build/package/merge	The faults of this class occur due to mistakes in libraries, version control, or through merging of different parts of software.
Documentation	Documentation faults occur in release notes, maintenance notes, etc.

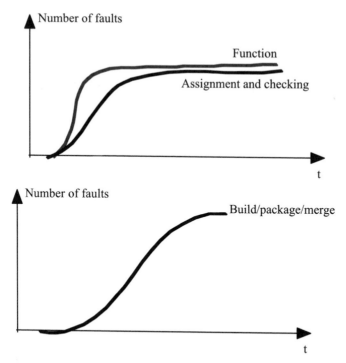

Figure 15.24 Software Reliability Growth Curves For Several Classes Of Faults

The distribution of the faults in each class versus software process activities is a useful guideline in the determination of software reliability and making decisions about proceeding with testing or releasing the software. From the collected statistics one can construct individual software reliability growth curves (Figure 15.24). Noticeably, the number of faults associated with assignment and checking as well as those falling into function class, stabilize and there is no need to continue testing. Nevertheless more testing is necessary because of the number of faults falling under the build/package/merge class. This also gives extra information about types of faults of importance.

15.8 SOFTWARE AVAILABILITY MODELS

The notion of software availability comes with repairable systems, that is, systems whose functioning can be monitored and once a failure happens, it can be repaired and the system starts running again. The temporal behavior of such

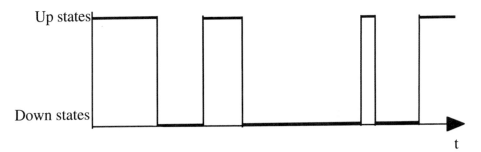

Figure 15.25 Temporal behavior of software system.

software systems as shown in Figure 15.25 consists of a collection of up-states and down-states. The duration of time spent in each of these states could vary and depends on the intensity of failures and intensity of repairs. The usual method used in describing such systems relies on the Markov property character-izing relationships between the states the system can have. Let us recall that the Markov property states that (Shooman, 1983)

$$P[X(t_{n+1}) = x_{n+1} | X(t_n) = x_n, X(t_{n-1}) = x_{n-1}, \ldots] = P[X(t_{n+1}) = x_{n+1} | X(t_n) = x_n]$$

In essence, this property means that the future state $X(t_{n+1})$ at time t_{k+1} depends upon the state observed in the current moment (t_n) but not on the previous history (the states observed at time moments t_{n-1}, t_{n-2}, etc.).

To proceed with a detailed model, we specify a collection of states the system can be in. There is a series of up-states; those states exist if no error has occurred or a fault has been removed. For instance, the (n-k) state denotes a situation when the (k-1)th fault has been eliminated and the kth fault has not yet hap-pened. Similarly, we introduce a family of down-states in which the system moves if a fault has occurred. More specifically, the (m-k)th down-state means that the kth fault has already occurred but has not been corrected. The dynamics of the software system is represented by a state diagram. It is a directed graph with the already identified up-states and down-states. The transitions of the graph indicate in which way the system moves between the up and down-states. The system remains in one of the up-states or once the failure happens, it moves to the next down-state. Again, while being in the down-state, one may stay there or, once the system has been repaired, the system moves to the second up-state. The intensity of transitions are modeled by two rates: a fault occurrence rate and a fault removal rate. Let us consider the second up-state. No fault has occurred and the system remains in this state with some intensity rate. With some other intensity rate it can leave the state and move to the next down-state (once the failure has happened). Again, it remains in this down-state with some pertinent intensity rate or becomes repaired and moves to the corresponding up-state.

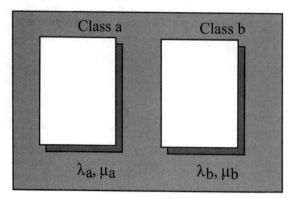

Figure 15.26 Classes with associated fault occurrence and fault removal rates.

It is instructive to analyze a detailed example. We are concerned with two classes (Figure 15.26). Each of them is characterized by its fault occurrence rate and fault removal rate. The probability distribution of both the rates is exponential. We assume that each class has a single fault that needs to be removed. First, we identify and describe all states occurring in a system composed of these classes. Initially, the system is in its first up state and the fault intensity rate is the sum of λ_a and λ_b. Denote it by λ_2

$$\lambda_2 = \lambda_a + \lambda_b$$

Once the system is down, we proceed with its testing and fault removal. The intensity of fault removal is equal to

$$\mu_2 = \mu_a + \mu_b$$

With this intensity the system gets to another up-state. While here, the fault intensity depends which fault has been eliminated. We may anticipate that the fault of higher intensity rate has been taken care of meaning that the remaining fault intensity rate equals

$$\lambda_1 = \min \lambda_a, \lambda_b$$

In the next down-state, the intensity of fault removal is the same as before, that is

$$\mu_1 = \mu_2$$

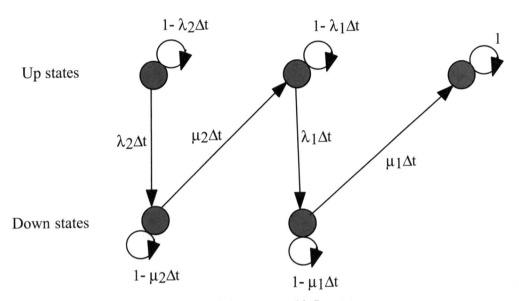

Figure 15.27 State diagram of the system with five states.

Following this description, we end up with the state diagram consisting of five states as shown in Figure 15.27. The transitions of the state diagram can be summarized in an equivalent form of a so-called transition matrix, T,

	State(t + Δt)				
State(t)	4	3	2	1	0
4	$1 - \lambda2\Delta t$	$\lambda2\Delta t$	0	0	0
3	0	$1 - \mu2\Delta t$	$\mu2\Delta t$	0	0
2	0	0	$1 - \lambda1\Delta t$	$\lambda1\Delta t$	0
1	0	0	0	$1 - \mu1\Delta t$	$\mu1\Delta t$
0	0	0	0	0	1

Note that the elements located in each row of T sum up to 1. The last up-state is permanent and therefore the intensity rate associated with it is simply 1. A vector of probabilities of staying in each of the states is denoted by $\mathbf{p}$, $\mathbf{p} = [p_4\ p_3\ p_2\ p_1\ p_0]$. The dynamics of the traversal of the graph (visiting individual states) described by the probability values in time instances t and t+Δt, namely $\mathbf{p}(t)$ and $\mathbf{p}(t+\Delta t)$ is governed by the transition matrix. We get (26).

$$\mathbf{p}(t + \Delta t) = \mathbf{p}(t)T \tag{26}$$

Based on this matrix expression, let us rewrite two first coordinates of the probability vector,

$$p_4(t + \Delta t) = p_4(t)(1 - \lambda_2 \Delta t)$$
$$p_3(t + \Delta t) = p_4(t) \lambda_2 \Delta t + p_3(t)(1 - \mu_2 \Delta t)$$

We rearrange the expressions by grouping the probabilities on the same side of the equation:

$$\frac{p_4(t + \Delta t) - p_4(t)}{\Delta t} + \lambda_2 p_4(t) = 0$$

$$\frac{p_3(t + \Delta t) - p_3(t)}{\Delta t} + \mu_2 p_3(t) - \lambda_2 p_4(t) = 0$$

Now let the time slice Δt tends to zero. This allows us to replace the differences by the derivatives and come up with the differential equations

$$\dot{p}_4(t) + \lambda_2 p_4(t) = 0$$
$$\dot{p}_3(t) + \mu_2 p_3(t) - \lambda_2 p_4(t) = 0$$

They need to be solved with an initial condition $\mathbf{p}(0)$ set to $[1\ 0\ 0\ 0]$ (the initial state is the one when we have not witnessed any failure). The availability function is a sum of the probabilities of the up states (when the system becomes available),

$$A(t) = p_4(t) + p_2(t) + p_0(t)$$

The higher the values of $A(t)$, the more accessible is the system. The availability function is a function of time. Sometimes it is enough (and this simplifies the overall analysis) to determine a steady state availability, that is, the value of $A(t)$ when time tends to infinity,

$$A(\infty) = \lim_{t \to \infty} A(t)$$

Instead of solving the system of differential equations (that could be quite tedious when considering intensity rates being functions of time rather than constants), we have to deal with a system of algebraic equations. The next example elaborates on this simplified analysis. Let us analyze the system with only two states (Figure 15.28). There is only one fault (that cannot be eliminated) and the system bounces between the up and the down-state with some intensity

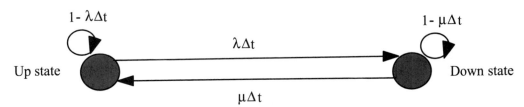

Figure 15.28 State diagram of the system with two states.

rates. The transition matrix T is easily inferred from the state diagram and equal

$$
\begin{matrix}
1 - \lambda\Delta t & \lambda\Delta t \\
\mu\Delta t & 1 - \mu\Delta t
\end{matrix}
$$

The system of the difference equations is written as follows:

$$
p_0(t)\,(1 - \lambda\Delta t) + p_1(t)\,\mu\Delta t = p_0(t + \Delta t)
$$
$$
p_0(t)\lambda\Delta t + p_1(t)\,(1 - \mu\Delta t) = p_1(t + \Delta t)
$$

Instead of going into differential equations, we are interested in a steady state behavior of the system. In order to get into this type of analysis, we zero the resulting derivatives. As easily seen, the resulting equations become dependent:

$$
-\lambda p_0 + \mu p_1 = 0
$$
$$
\lambda p_0 - \mu p_1 = 0
$$

To derive a nontrivial solution, we take into account a standard probability constraint stating that these two probabilities sum up to 1. Replacing one of the previous equations by this constraint, we obtain

$$
\lambda p_0 - \mu p_1 = 0
$$
$$
p_0 + p_1 = 1
$$

Now it is possible to write down equations for p_1 and p_0 as follows:

$$
p_1 = \frac{\lambda}{\lambda + \mu}
$$

$$
p_0 = \frac{\mu}{\lambda + \mu}
$$

Obviously the availability of this system is the probability of staying in state p_0. This is the state in which we are dealing with the system that functions.

15.9 SOFTWARE RELIABILITY MODELING: A GENERAL PROCEDURE

Despite the use of a certain specific software reliability model, all of them follow a general modeling methodology as outlined in Figure 15.29. As visualized in the diagram, we start with software testing procedures and collecting experimental data. This not a trivial and quick phase as any comprehensive data collection activities call for setting up and maintaining logs of software failures reported over time (along with detailed classification of the failures). The ensuing phases

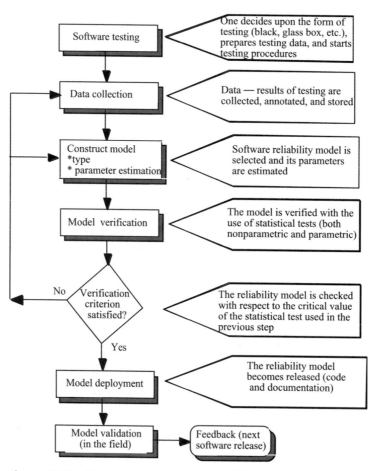

Figure 15.29 Development of software reliability models.

embrace structural and parametric model design. First, one has to decide upon the class of the reliability model and afterwards select a form of the corresponding functional relationships. As our intent is to represent experimental data, we should look into the models from the point of view of the parameters occurring there as they need to be estimated in order to represent (approximate) experimental data. Next comes a phase of parametric optimization of the model. This phase is eventually the most developed as far as estimation methods (including such well-established methodologies as maximum likelihood or least square error) and their computational frameworks are concerned. Once the model has been completed, it is tested (verified) against experimental data (in a statistical setting one can confine oneself to nonparametric tests, say the Kolmogorov-Smirnov test). If the model is not satisfactory, we iterate through the modeling process by changing the form of the model or/and estimating different collections of the parameters.

There are two decision-making issues one has to raise and investigate with the aid of the reliability model (that is, one of the examples where software reliability models become indispensable):

- *Release.* Is the system ready for release?
- *Testing.* How much testing is still needed?

These are two basic questions that imply a certain quality of the software and may eventually trigger some projections about software reliability, its further performance, along with making some provisions regarding further maintenance activities. Obviously, a direct criterion for releasing the software would be a given acceptable level of software reliability, R_0 (Figure 15.30).

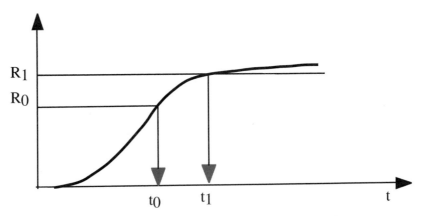

Figure 15.30 Software reliability as a function of time of testing.

> ### Software Release Criterion
>
> Accept software once its reliability level exceeds a certain predefined acceptance level R_0.

The graph in Figure 15.30 reveals two essential reliability issues:

1. At the beginning of testing we may detect a significant number of faults. It is very likely that their removal will result in a sharp increase in the reliability of the software system.

2. After the early phase of substantial increase in software reliability, we reach a plateau where the increase of software reliability is very limited. The process of fault removal is continued until we reach the required reliability level (namely, R_0). The shape of the increase of reliability regarded as a function of time indicates very strongly that any increase in the required reliability, say R_1, may call for an excessively long testing time. Note that t_1 is far higher than t_0.

Observe in Figure 15.30 the changes in testing time for higher values of required reliability. Despite the transparency of the proposed threshold criterion, this criterion alone may not be sufficient. One should take into consideration the total software costs and its two conflicting components. The first one deals with the costs of releasing unreliable software. The second capture the costs of testing. The first component is a decreasing function of the release time while the second becomes an increasing function of time. Figure 15.31 illustrates the two components along with their sum, that is, an overall cost of software development. The release time has to minimize the sum of these two components.

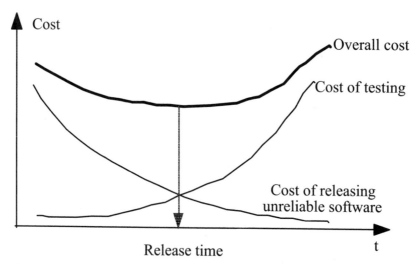

Figure 15.31   Software reliability–cost analysis.

The software reliability models should be evaluated based on some general criteria; the list discussed by Kan (1994) includes five items:

- *Predictive validity.* The capability of the model to predict future failure behavior of the system (e.g., in terms of the number of failures for a specified time period).
- *Capability.* The ability of the reliability model to estimate, with required accuracy, quantities needed by software managers and software developers in planning and managing software projects or controlling change in operational software systems.
- *Quality of assumptions.* The likelihood that the model assumptions can be satisfied in reality. This involves also the plausibility of the assumptions from the point of view of logical consistency and software engineering experience.
- *Applicability.* The applicability of the model across different software products (size, structure, and so on).
- *Simplicity.* The reliability model should be simple in the sense of collecting data, easily understood without any excessive theory, and readily implementable to be in full operational utilization.

15.10 SUMMARY

Availability is a useful measure of the operational quality of some systems.
—HUMPHREY, 1989

Software reliability is a well-established area in software engineering and has led to the creation of a collection of useful concepts and algorithms. It is essentially a must if one supports the claim of the software development being a well-defined and fully scrutinized engineering endeavor. In this chapter we have provided the reader with an introduction to the subject. The chapter covered some introductory ideas and outlined the main classes of models of software reliability. It is clear that the dominant part of the methodology of software reliability dwells on the concepts of probability theory and statistics. Interestingly, to cope with the very nature of software development and the properties of the resulting product, there is another knowledge-based modeling approach. The orthogonal defect classification and equivalence classes in input domain are viable examples of this relatively new effort in software reliability. Indisputably, reliability assurance is an important goal that should be considered in the context of the overall process of software development rather than being limited to software testing.

15.11   PROBLEMS

> If nothing is ever to be found fault with,
> nothing will ever be mended.
>
> —JEREMY BENTHAM, 1776

1. What would be a rationale behind the S-shape of m(t) in the reliability model? Try to think about it in terms of dependence of software faults and their size (that is, related to fault detection).

2. A type of S-shaped reliability model proposed in Schagen (1987) is governed by the expression

$$m(t) = \alpha \left[1 - \exp(-\lambda_1 t) - \frac{\lambda_2(\exp(-\lambda_1 t) - \exp(-\lambda_2 t))}{\lambda_2 - \lambda_1} \right]$$

where $\alpha, \lambda_1, \lambda_2, > 0$.
   (a) Plot m(t) for some selected values of the parameters.
   (b) What is the form of m(t) for $\lambda_1 = \lambda_2 = 1$?
   (c) Interpret the meaning of the parameters of the model.

3. Plot the reliability function R(t) for the Weibull failure rate for several values of K and m. Elaborate on the role of these parameters on the behavior of R(t). Show that K delivers a time scale effect. What are the subsumed reliability models for m = 0 and m = 1?

4. Determine the reliability of the software system plotted in Figure 15.32. The reliabilities of the software modules are included in the same figure. Shown are also probabilities of utilization of the individual modules.

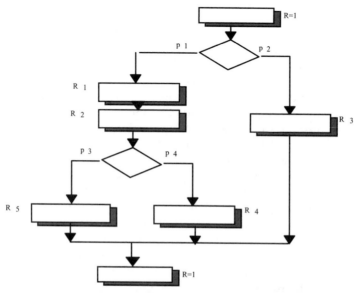

Figure 15.32   System composed of several software modules.

5. Consider the software modules shown in Figure 15.33. The probabilities of invoking the modules are equal to p and 1-p. The reliabilities are equal to R_1 and R_2, respectively. Do the following:
   (a) Discuss the software reliability of the system.
   (b) Given R_1 and R_2, what should be the probability p that maximizes R?

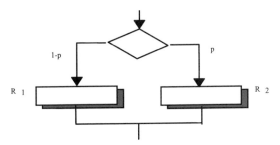

Figure 15.33 System with two software modules.

6. The software system is composed of 50 modules. Each module is guaranteed to have reliability R not less than 0.999. What would be the reliability of the entire system? What should be the reliability of the modules if we require that the system exhibits reliability equal to 0.99999?

7. The time series of fault moments is given in Table 15.3. Using the data pairs in Table 15.3, develop two software reliability models:
   (a) Jelinsky-Moranda.
   (b) Goel-Okumoto.
   For these two models use the maximum likelihood estimation method to determine their parameters.

8. Use the software reliability model designed in problem 7 to analyze the experimental data. How well does the model predict the time intervals between failures? What would be the main reasons between the erroneous results produced by the model?

9. Figure 15.34 summarizes the relationships between the number of changes in software modules and their cyclomatic complexity, V(G), as well as the number of changes vis-a-vis size of the module expressed in LOC (lines of code). The number of changes can be used as an indicator of the resulting software reliability.
   (a) What could be revealed about the software reliability treated as a function of V(G)? How well could one estimate this reliability knowing that the software is characterized by low values of V(G), that is, the values within the range from 1 to 20.
   (b) Discuss the same reliability issues for the second indicator, that is, LOC.
   (c) Compare these two relationships in terms of their usefulness as predictors of software reliability.

10. Consider the problem of fault seeding. Plot the probability of existence of no more than E faults in the software system as a function of the number of artificial faults (A). Interpret the obtained graph.

TABLE 15.3   Experimental Software Reliability Data: Failure Number and Time Between Failures

Failure No.	Time Between Failures
1	33
2	9
3	4
4	66
5	0.5
6	18
7	149
8	14
9	15
10	50
11	81
12	34
13	85
14	54
15	3
16	15
17	6
18	8
19	130
20	19
21	19
22	112
23	15
24	16
25	154
26	50
27	10
28	2
29	22
30	53

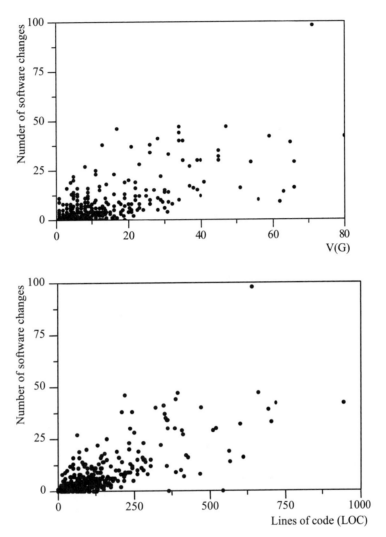

Figure 15.34 Software change versus cyclomatic complexity and LOC.

11. The experimental data given below concern the values of m(t) in some time moments. What software reliability growth model would you suggest? How can you go about determining its parameters?

(1, 9.63846)   (2, 14.9368) (3, 21.6554) (4, 27.756) (5, 26.8024)
(6, 31.4417)   (7, 31.8108) (8, 37.0531) (9, 33.9795) (10, 35.1546)
(11, 36.5565)   (12, 41.9802) (13, 42.8015) (14, 42.5757) (15, 42.8207)

12. How do we quantify compromise between sufficient reliability of a software system and a time-of-delivery? How are reliability and time-of-delivery correlated with cost of building the software?

13. Discuss the main steps in SRET.

14. Discuss a way of constructing reliability acceptance regions like those shown in Figure 15.35. How are the regions in the figure affected by the assumed confidence level, say 95% or 99%? What are acceptable values of these levels? Justify your choice.

Figure 15.35   Regions in decision-making in software reliability.

15.12   REFERENCES

Bastiani, F.B., Ramamoorthy, C.V. Input-domain based models for estimating the correctness of process control programs. In *Reliability Theory*, A. Serra, R.E. Barlow, Eds. North Holland, Amsterdam, pp. 321–378, 1986.

Chillarege, R. Orthogonal defect classification. In *Software Reliability Engineering*, M.R. Lyu, Ed. Computer Society Press, Los Alamitos, CA, pp. 359–400, 1996.

DeMillo, A.R., Lipton, R.J. A probabilistic remark on algebraic program testing. Information Processing Letters, **7**(4):193–195, 1978.

Duran, J.W., Wiorkowski, J.J. Capture-recapture sampling for estimating software error content. *IEEE Transactions on Software Engineering*, *SE-***7**:147–148, 1981.

Gilb, T. *Software Metrics*. Winthrop, Cambridge, MA, 1977.

Goel, A.L. Software reliability models: Assumptions, limitations, and applicability. *IEEE Transactions on Software Engineering*, **11**:1411–1423, 1985.

Goel, A.L., Okumoto, K. Time dependent error detection rate model for software and other performance measures. *IEEE Transactions on Reliability*, R-**28**:206–211, 1979.

Hamlet, R.G. Testing programs with the aid of a compiler. *IEEE Transactions on Software Engineering*, SE-**3**(4):279–290, 1977.

Jelinski, Z., Moranda, P.B. Software reliability research. In *Statistical Computer Performance Evaluation*, E. Freiberger, Ed. Academic Press, New York, pp. 465–497, 1972.

Kan, S.H. Software quality engineering models. In *Encyclopedia of Computer Science and*

Technology, A. Kent, J.G. Williams, Eds. Vol. 31. Marcel Dekker, New York, pp. 343–376, 1994.

Lyu M.R., Ed. *Software Reliability Engineering.* Computer Society Press, Los Alamitos, CA, 1996.

Morell, L.J. A theory of fault-based testing. *IEEE Transactions on Software Engineering,* **16**(9):844–857, 1990.

Musa, J.D. Software quality and reliability basics. In: *Proceedings of the Computer Conference,* Dallas, Oct. 1987, pp. 114–115.

Musa, J.D. Validity of execution-time theory of software reliability. *IEEE Transactions on Reliability,* R-**28**:181–191, 1979.

Musa, J.D. A theory of software reliability and its application. *IEEE Transactions on Software Engineering,* SE-**1**:312–327, 1975.

Musa, J.D., Iannino, A., Okumoto, K. *Software Reliability.* McGraw-Hill, New York, 1990.

Myers, G.J. *Software Reliability: Principles and Practices.* Wiley, New York, 1975.

Nelson, E. Estimating software reliability from test data. *Microelectronics and Reliability,* **17**:67–74, 1972.

Ohba, M. Software reliability analysis models. *IBM Journal of Research and Development,* **21**:428–443, 1984.

Schagen, I.P. A new model for software failure. *Reliability Engineering,* 205–221, 1987.

Schick, G.J., Wolverton, R.W. An analysis of competing software reliability models. *IEEE Transactions on Software Engineering,* SE-**4**:104–120, 1978.

Shooman, M.L. *Software Engineering.* McGraw Hill, New York, 1983.

Weiss, S.N., Weyuker, E.J. An extended domain-based model of software reliability. *IEEE Transactions on Software Engineering,* SE-**14**:1512–1524, 1988.

Wood, A. Predicting software reliability. *IEEE Computer,* November 1996, 69–77.

Xie, M. *Software Reliability Modeling.* World Scientific, Singapore, 1991.

Xie, M., Bergman, B. On modeling reliability growth for software. *Proceedings of the 8th IFAC Symposium on Identification and Parameter Estimation,* Aug. 1988, Beijing.

Yamada, S., Ohba, M., Osaki, S. S-shaped reliability growth modeling for software error detection. *IEEE Transactions on Reliability,* R-**32**:475–478, 1983.

CHAPTER 16
Human Factors

Discipline can be defined as an activity or practice that develops or improves skill.
—W.S. HUMPHREY AND J.W. OVER, 1997

Aims
- Approach human factors from user and developer perspectives
- Consider human factors in software development
- Consider human factors in computer–human interactions
- Explore Personal Software Process model

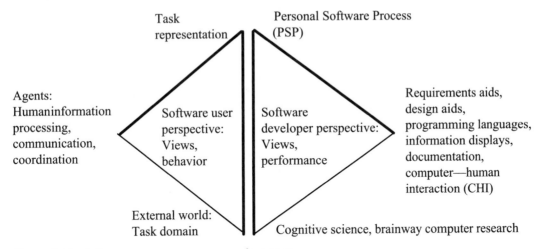

Figure 16.1 Influences on programmer performance.

16.1 INTRODUCTION

A number of factors influence the responses of computer users and the performance of software developers (Figure 16.1). Human factors are of interest from two points of view: user's perspective and software developer's perspective. Understanding human factors from a user's perspective can favorably influence the

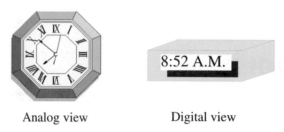

Analog view   Digital view

Figure 16.2   Two representations of time.

design of user interfaces that elicit a favorable response, provide understanding and navigation aids, and generally provide users with a "warm, fuzzy feeling" when they interact with a computer. Cognitive engineering (CE) has identified three main influences on the perspective of software users: task representation, agent paradigm, and view of the external world as a task domain. CE is a form of applied behavioral science concerned with the study and development of principles, methods, tools, and techniques that guide the design of computerized systems intended to support human performance. The study of CE began with a technical report written in 1981 (Norman, 1981), which led to the study of Computer Human Interaction (CHI) (Woods & Roth, 1988a, 1988b). The left-hand side of Figure 16.1 is known as the cognitive system triad. The use of computers to support humans in performing tasks can be viewed as an interaction among the three elements of this triad. All domains of interest and tasks are acted upon in the external world. A domain of interest might be air traffic in the neighborhood of an airport (external world of a controller). This is the context for an air traffic controller performing tasks like regulating when and where aircraft enter and exit an airspace. Agents make up another element of the cognitive triad. An agent is an independent process capable of communicating with other processes and interacting with its environment. Agents act on the world by processing inputs and communicating and coordinating with other agents. Agents can be either humans or computer systems, which work independently or cooperatively as a team. External representations make up the third member of the traid. Representations are "external" inasmuch as they are "outside a human." External representations portray that part of the world acted upon by humans. Agents experience and learn about their world through external representations. These representations affect performance by making selected information more accessible at the expense of other information.

For example, the current time is represented precisely with a digital clock in Figure 16.2 but duration is hidden. An analog clock has hands on a clock dial, which makes it easier to measure duration. However, the current time is more difficult to read accurately with an analog clock. The goal of software engineering from a user's perspective is to provide external representations of domain knowledge that make it easy to extract necessary information needed to perform a task. A recent example of a dynamic representation of a help system is the office assistant feature of Word in the Office 98 release of Microsoft

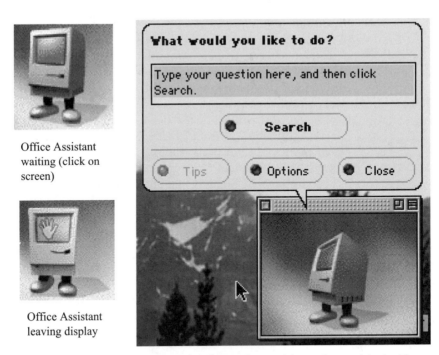

Office Assistant
waiting (click on
screen)

Office Assistant
leaving display

Figure 16.3 Sample actions of an office assistant. (These shots printed with permission of Microsoft Corporation)

Office shown in Figure 16.3. The office assistant responds to input (imitating the behavior of a human). It turns toward a Word document whenever something syntactically strange is typed. Perhaps to the extreme of being a distraction, sometimes annoying, the officebot somersaults, turns, taps its feet. By pressing down on the control key and clicking on the hide option, the officebot waves goodbye and its display fades away.

Human and other factors and models have been studied from a software developer's perspective as well as a software management perspective (Figure 16.4). A grasp of human factors is crucial both in organizing software engineering teams and in encouraging individual developers to take a disciplined approach

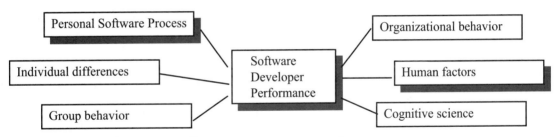

Figure 16.4 Influences on programmer performance.

to software development. From a software developer's perspective, the study of human factors has focused on ways to improve software products and the performance of developers. An understanding of software development is also aided by discovering how knowledge is acquired and used. Cognitive science is the study of how knowledge is acquired, represented in human memory, and used in problem-solving. From a management perspective, human factors are also of interest because of the need to organize software development teams effectively. Organizing teams is aided by an understanding of individual differences and group and organizational behavior. In addition, the SEI Personal Software Process model has generated interest in study of human factors from a capability maturity point of view. It has been shown, for example, that software developers achieve a 25% increase in productivity by working within the framework of a personal software process (Humphrey & Over, 1997).

16.2 HUMAN FACTORS IN SOFTWARE DEVELOPMENT

The essence of all design patterns is the problem-solution pair.
—T.J. MOWBRAY AND R.C. MALVEAU, 1997

In the context of software engineering, the study of human factors is concerned with the relationships between stimuli presented to developers and the responses they make. The stimuli can be software tools, information displays, requirements diagrams, documentation, input devices (e.g., mouse clicks), various types of computer programs, and what are known as templates to express design patterns. In approaching the problem of human factors in systems, it helps to identify design patterns that support human interaction. A design pattern is an effective solution to a design problem (Mowbray & Malveau, 1997). Fixed outlines called templates express patterns for design and implementation solutions. Such templates describe a problem to be solved and the solution to the problem. The IEEE schema for a software requirements specification (IEEE Std. 830-1993) is an example of a template. The introduction of an SRS describes the problem to be solved based on a needs statement prepared by project stakeholders. The solution to a problem is embodied in the system description provided by an SRS. In the case of a design pattern template for a system supporting human factors, each section of a template answers a question about the pattern that aids understanding of human–computer interaction. A fully annotated statechart description of the user interface for guiding aircraft in an air traffic control system exemplifies an expression of a design pattern catering to human factors. The study of human factors provides a wealth of insights into how developers respond to different forms of stimuli.

16.2.1 Specification Formats as Design Aids

> **The first asset in making designs is a good notation to record and discuss alternative possibilities.**
> —B. SCHNEIDERMAN, 1998

The study of software specification formats focused on charts and tables. It was found that short phrases, decision tables, and tree charts were more effective as design aids than prose descriptions of information (Wright and Reid, 1973). It was found that fewer errors are made where tree charts specify solutions with four or fewer choices (Kammann, 1975). Early studies also showed that flowcharts provided little aid in programming (Schneiderman et al., 1977). It was also found that flowcharts provide little assistance in finding program defects (Brooke & Duncan, 1980). However, it was also found in the same study that flowcharts helped avoid retesting paths that had already been tested. The effectiveness of Petri nets, resource diagrams, and pseudocode has been compared in specifying concurrent programs (Boehm-Davis & Fregly, 1985). For simple program and tasks, all three specification formats had similar performance. It was found that Petri nets were not as effective whenever tasks and programs became more complex. In a Petri net, the difficulty lies in the fact that all control flow information must be analyzed (which transitions fire, which firing cycles) to extract interprocess communication data.

It has been found that the primary problems in specification formats as design aids are traceability and visibility of structure (Fitter & Green, 1979). Five attributes of good notation schemes are given in Table 16.1. Good notational schemes should provide perceptual cues as well as symbolic information. Examples of such schemes are Kiviat diagrams where the area occupied by the "spokes" varies in size, histograms with rectangles varying in size, and varying color of adjacent boundaries in a map. It has also been found that a vocabulary of between 100 and 300 words is sufficient to write a software specification (Kelly & Chapanis, 1977). Transition diagrams, statecharts, menu-selection trees, dialog box trees

TABLE 16.1 Attributes of Good Notational Schemes

Attribute of Good Notation Scheme	Explanation
Relevance	Notation highlights useful information
Restriction	Prohibits disallowable expressions
Redundant recoding	Perceptual and symbolic characteristics highlight information
Revelation	Perceptually mimics solution structure
Revisability	Easy to change

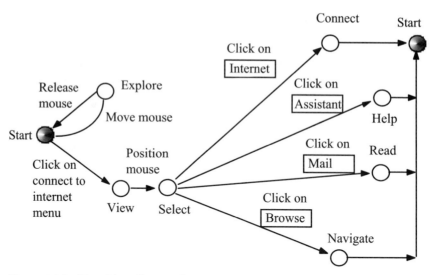

Figure 16.5 Transition diagram for an Internet menu tree.

and user action notation (UAN) have been singled out as well-suited for specifying user interfaces (Schneiderman, 1998).

A transition diagram consists of nodes representing states, a distinguished node called a start state, links identifying transitions between states, state labels for names of states, and link labels specifying actions. A sample transition diagram used to specify menu selection for Internet access is given in Figure 16.5. The diagram represents an Internet menu tree. It exhibits a sampling of mouse actions and states associated with the Internet menu tree that comes with OS 8.5 for Apple computers. A user is in an explore state if a mouse is wandering, pushing the pointer to explore desktop options. A user enters a view state by clicking on the Internet menu, which causes the choices shown in square boxes to be displayed. Transition diagrams work well in specifying simple user interfaces, but become cumbersome and difficult to read in specifying complex systems with hundreds of states and links. Statecharts get higher marks than transition diagrams.

A statechart can express concurrency, which is better suited for specifying multithreaded applications. Statecharts can also express modularity with orthogonal states. Thanks to the depth feature of what are known as superstates in statecharts, information hiding is possible. Superstates can be decomposed to reveal others states that serve to define a superstate. Layering of groups of related states can be associated with superstates. The result is quite an attractive alternative to transition diagrams in specifying user interfaces. A sample statechart to specify a user interface for a system menu that includes the view option for Internet access is given in Figure 16.6. The statechart specifies four orthogonal states corresponding to system menu options: control panel, Internet access, calculator, and notepad. The view state is a superstate. It is decomposable into

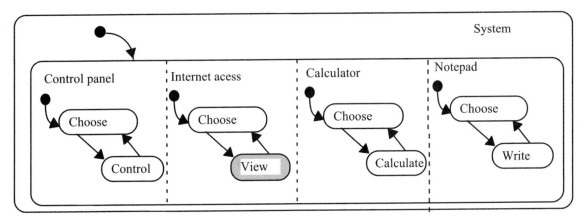

Figure 16.6 Statechart for a system menu.

a statechart with a structure similar to the one specified by the transition diagram in Figure 16.5.

User action notation (UAN) provides a high-level textual means of specifying user tasks associated with a user interface (Hartson et al., 1990). The basic features of UAN are given in Table 16.2. For example, sample user actions to select a mailer dialog box can be specified in UAN as shown in Figure 16.7. In the beginning, a desktop is displayed. A user begins by depressing a mouse while pointing to the system icon in the human–computer interaction described in Figure 16.7. The user interface responds by displaying a system menu. The system leaves a waiting state to enter a display state as a result of this user action. Each system choice (s-choice) is displayed but not highlighted. In the sample scenario in Figure 16.7, the user next moves the pointer to an Internet access option in the system menu, and depresses the mouse. The system responds with a display

TABLE 16.2 UAN Notation

Sample UAN Notation	Explanation
M$_v$	Depress mouse button
M^	Release mouse button
~[<icon name>]	Selected icon. Example: ~[trash] selects trash icon
<file name>!	Highlight named file. Example: <trash>! highlights trash
<file name>-!	Dehighlight named file
outline(<icon name>)>~	Outline of named icon is dragged by cursor
Action(file)	Perform action on file
Forall (<file name>!)	Selects all highlighted files
:	Followed by
,	Separator in a sequence of actions

Task: View mail dialog box		
User Action	**Interface Feedback**	**Interface State**
	Desktop!	waiting
~[system] M_v	systemMenu!, forall(s-choice!):	
	s-choice-!	Display system menu
~[internet access] M_v	internetMenu!, forall(i-choice!):	
	i-choice-!	
		Display internet menu
~[mail] M_v	dialogBox !, forall(box-choice!):	
	box-choice-!	Display mail dialog box
$M^\wedge$	dialogBox !, forall(box-choice!):	
	box-choice-!	waiting

Figure 16.7   Sample UAN description of user actions.

of an Internet access menu. Each Internet access choice (i-choice) is displayed but not highlighted. Next, the user moves the pointer to a mail option in the Internet access menu, and depresses the mouse. A mailer dialog box is displayed. Each dialog box choice (box-choice) is displayed but not highlighted. The user interface enters a waiting state when the user releases the mouse (the last action in Figure 16.7). It has been pointed out that although UAN does not have a provision for drawing diagrams, animations, relationships across tasks, and interrupt behavior, it does provide a compact, expressive, high-level approach to describing both user actions and system behavior (Schneiderman, 1998).

16.2.2   Programming and Cognitive Ergonomics

The study of programming relative to human factors has revealed that developers spend more time describing data manipulations than control flow. It appears that there is a natural tendency to start with data manipulation and then add control flow as an afterthought (Miller, 1981; Schneiderman, 1982). This human tendency in programming contrasts sharply with the design of most programming languages, which provides for the development of control structures with embedded data manipulations (Curtis, 1994).

Cognitive ergonomics is the study of problem solving, information analysis, and procedural skills relative to the influence of human factors. Human factors questions concerning programming language structures, computer programming, and human–computer interaction are answered ''cognitively'' in terms of the mental effort required. Dijkstra is credited with beginning the study of go-to-less programming as a means of writing computer programs that are easier to understand and to write correctly (Dijkstra, 1968). Dijkstra's work led to numerous studies of structured control constructs, language structure, and a human factors approach to programming (Gilmore and Green, 1984; Lucas and

TABLE 16.3 Human Factors in Programming

Programmer View	Construct
Choice of control structure	If-then-else easier to understand than go-to
Scope	Scope marking improves understanding
Technique	Benefits of programming technique vary with programming task
Syntax	Standard syntax generator improves coding speed and accuracy
Representation	Different forms of representation highlight different forms of information
Influence of client, plan, source of information	Representation of data, constructs is influenced by the form in which information is received
Top-down approach	Top-down flow of control is more important than specific conditionals employed in a programming effort

Kaplan, 1974; Sime et al., 1973). A summary of the findings on human factors in programming is given in Table 16.3.

16.3 COGNITIVE SCIENCE AND PROGRAMMING

Cognitive Science is the study of how knowledge is acquired, represented in memory, and used in problem-solving. The cognitive science approach to computer programming has focused on how programmers represent knowledge, how program structures are learned, and how knowledge is applied in developing software.

16.3.1 Human Memory, Chunking, and Programming Knowledge

The limitation of short-term memory is a severe handicap in developing large-scale computer programs. This means that it is not possible to grasp enough things simultaneously to keep track of the many connections between components in a large software system. Chunking is seen as a means of combating this problem. Chunking is the process of binding together items with similar or related attributes to form a unique item. Examples of this can be found in software descriptions using statecharts. Recall that states in statecharts can have depth. A state with depth represents a substatechart. When necessary, such states

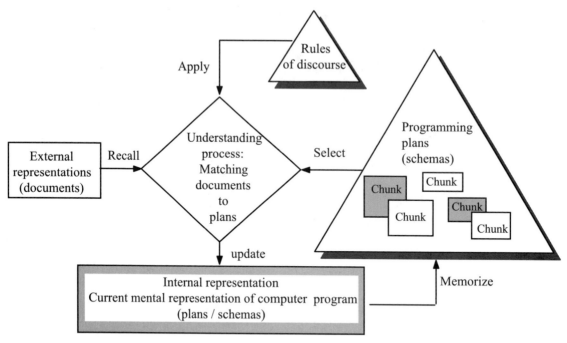

Figure 16.8 Software comprehension model.

can be decomposed into another statechart. In effect, states with depth have the appearance of chunks (a binding together of related states represented by a single state). Chunks facilitate the description of complex systems in a simplified, easy-to-remember form.

Chunking provides the basis for program comprehension models useful in software maintenance (Soloway et al., 1988; von Mayrhauser, 1995). Briefly, the understanding of software is aided by internal representations of a system with plans and schemas. The understanding process matches system documents such as requirements to programming plans using rules of discourse to select plans. The result of each match of an external document with a plan is an updated mental representation, which is stored as a new plan. A sketch of this comprehension model is shown in Figure 16.8. The mental model is structured top down. It contains hierarchies represented by the chunks (plans) and goals represented by the rules. The triangles in Figure 16.8 represent knowledge of programming plans and rules of discourse. "No dead code" and "Updates to variables must correspond to the way the variables were initialized" are examples of rules that might be used in matching a memorized chunk (some plan) with an external document like a guide to testing. A plan might be a global strategy used in a program (e.g., using the movements of an office assistant to signal puzzlement when errors are made while Microsoft Word is being used in preparing a document). A plan might also consist of code fragments to represent implementation tactics. The large diamond in Figure 16.8 represents the understanding process. A benefit of studying software comprehension models and ways of chunking is that it helps give a better grasp of how programmers understand code. Another significant benefit of the study of comprehension models is that it points to possible ways to be more efficient and effective in developing software maintenance guidelines. A desirable outcome of this form of cognition is the development of software documentation that lends itself to chunking.

16.3.2 Learning to Program

Two learning styles have been identified in the study of how novices learn computer programming (Coombs et al., 1982):

1. *Comprehension learning.* A novice grasps the overall layout of a program but may not understand the rules needed to operate with or on the information needed to write a program. These learners are mainly interested in understanding, not doing.

2. *Operational learning.* A novice grasps the rules needed to write a program but may not grasp the complete picture of the domain knowledge. These learners are primarily interested in doing programming, not necessarily understanding it.

This distinction is useful in organizing software development teams. Comprehensive learners would do well in specifying requirements, trouble-shooting, and reverse engineering during software maintenance, not design. Operational learners would gravitate toward forward engineering (implementation of requirements) and would do well in software design. The ideal team member would be comfortable in both settings. It has also been found that operational learners are better able to learn a programming language.

16.3.3 Characteristic Design Behaviors

Software design tends to be a data-driven rather than a control-driven process. It has been found that in solving hard problems, software design reduces to an information search process because of a lack of design data (Guindon, 1990). A number of characteristic design behaviors have identified (Adelson & Soloway, 1985). These are summarized in Table 16.4. It has been observed that simulation and note-making occur only when a designer has sufficient domain knowledge. In cases where a designer is inexperienced with an object being designed, constraints are placed on the design to gain enough detail to support simulation. Designers prefer to use plans rather than constraints, simulation, and note-making in designing a system.

TABLE 16.4   Characteristic Design Behaviors

Design Behavior	Explanation
Formation of mental model	Support mental simulation of an emerging computer program
Simulation	Check for unforseen interactions and external consistency with specification
Systematic expansion	Ensure equal level of detail is developed across functions
Representing constraints	Aid in simulating unfamiliar elements
Retrieving labels for plans	Reduce memory load and terminate search
Note-making	Capture issues for different levels in a system hierarchy

16.4 PERSONAL SOFTWARE PROCESS MODEL

The Personal Software Process (PSP) model provides a framework to help software engineers plan, track, evaluate, and produce high-quality products (Ferguson et al., 1997). The PSP model characterizes the maturity levels of an individual engineer rather than an engineering organization targeted by the capability maturity model (Paulk et al., 1995). In each of the other software process models considered up to this point, the focus was on frameworks for developing software. In PSP, the focus is on a precise framework for evolving the skills of a software engineer. In other words, PSP provides a framework for a personal capability maturity development cycle that is embedded inside each phase of a software process (Figure 16.9).

The fundamental mechanism in PSP is process evolution, which results from a personal development cycle within the normal life-cycle model (Figure 16.10). The driving force underlying this evolution is the self-propelled spiraling capability of a software engineer. The cyclic PSP process is inspired by the divide-and-conquer strategy found in Boehm's spiral life-cycle model (risk is minimized by tackling complex problems a step at a time). The impact of the PSP development cycles is evaluated in a postmortem process (productivity and other measurements). The postmortem occurs before system integration begins. It provides feedback concerning the effectiveness of the PSP process. PSP shows engineers how to manage the quality of their products and provides them with data to justify product plans.

An important advantage of PSP is that it can be applied to the development of small *as well as* large software systems. Preliminary results of incorporating PSP training in large-scale software development projects are encouraging. In an international software development project involving software engineers in

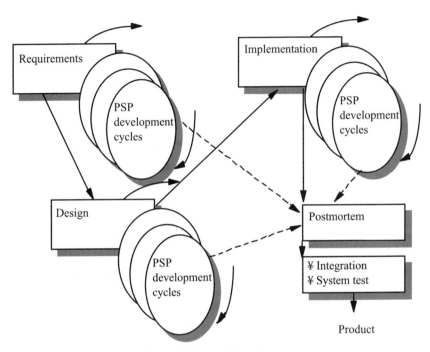

Figure 16.9 Life-cycle with embedded PSP cycles.

Madras, India and Peoria, Illinois, it was found that developers made an average of 0.76 defects/1000 LOC before PSP training, and 0.17 defects/1000 LOC after PSP training.

16.5 HUMAN–COMPUTER INTERACTION

In this section, we explore human factors from a software user's perspective. Three main elements have been identified in the use of computers to support humans in performing various tasks: task domain (external world), agents, and task representation. The study of these elements is aimed at designing human–computer systems that enhance performance of tasks by humans.

16.5.1 External World

In the context of computer–human interaction, the external world is what is acted upon by a user. The external world consists of some domain of interest

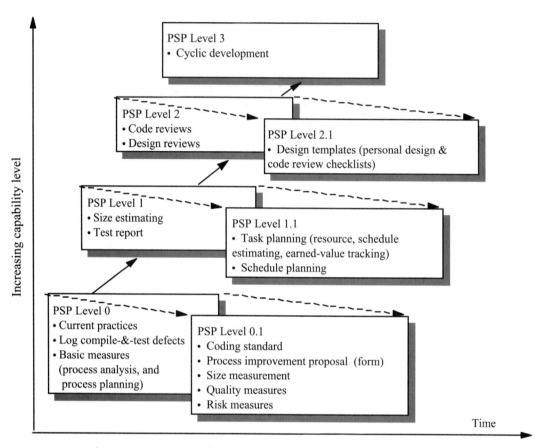

Figure 16.10   Personal development cycle.

and any task to be performed by humans within a domain. Examples of domains of interest are automatic teller machines (ATMs), air traffic, highway traffic, video games, and the Internet. Domains of interest are accessed by means of user interfaces such those provided by ATM, air traffic, and video game displays as well as mailers and web browsers. Each external world domain is associated with tasks for humans to perform. For example, inserting an ATM card, selecting the type of transaction, and depositing and withdrawing funds are tasks performed in response to an ATM display. A number of factors associated with each domain require competent performance:

1. Number of task elements to be controlled or manipulated.

2. Required interactions and constraints on actions performed by a human.

3. Temporal dynamics: whether things change slowly or fast.

4. Uncertainty. Examples of sources of uncertainty: faulty display, bumping the wrong key, selecting the wrong menu item.

5. Risks associated with performing tasks and external world domain.

16.5.2 Agents: Humans and Intelligent Machines

> The machine is a self-portrait of a human being.
> —R. SUZUKI, 1992

The world of human–computer interactions is made up of agents: humans and intelligent machines. Evidence of the trend toward the development of human-like, semi-intelligent computer systems can be found in

- The virtual classroom (an environment to facilitate collaborative learning) (Hiltz, 1992).
- The brainway computer (knowledge is acquired by learning) (Matsumoto, 1998).
- Knowledge-based systems like BEST and ABE (Vranes & Stanojevic, 1995).
- Some forms of robots such as the Mars explorer and animats http://mars.jpl.nasa.gov.
- Artificial life systems such as NEC fish aquariums (see *http://www.sw.nec.co.jp*).
- Computer-based aids such as the Mitsubishi track and field teaching system.
- Advanced automated decision-making systems such as those found in the NASA space shuttle, avionics technology found aircraft flight control systems, and in astronautics (science and technology of space flight).

A colorful and perceptive portrayal of a world populated by helpful, companionable, intelligent machines can be found in the novels *I, Robot* and *Caves of Steel* by Isaac Asimov or in *2001: A Space Odyssey* by Arthur Clarke. The hunt for intelligent computer systems has led to a rich harvest of applications and problems that need to be solved. In the search for intelligent systems, interest has shifted from a focus on designing hardware interfaces and software interfaces to designing Man–Machine Interfaces (MMI). Such interfaces will sustain and support interactions and problem-solving exchanges between persons and machines (Dorfman & Thayer, 1990). The goal of intelligent system design is to develop systems with human qualities and capabilities in performing domain tasks. In a world of intelligent machines, the role of humans shifts from active controller to supervisor of automated systems.

16.5.3 Understanding Computer Aids

To design and evaluate computer aids with human qualities, it necessary to understand the structure and range of tasks performed by users. It is also necessary to understand the complexities of domain tasks that make them difficult to perform. It has been found that an understanding of domain tasks results from the study of goals of users and the methods available to users in achieving their goals. Methods and tools for deriving this information can be found in Michell (1987).

16.6 SUMMARY

In a comprehensive study of human factors in software engineering, both the user's perspective as well as the developer's perspective are taken into account. There is a tendency to get caught up in seeing human factors from the point-of-view of software developers, and lose sight of the needs of humans who interact with a system. Human factors and the development of user interfaces having human features is a fairly new frontier for software engineering. In approaching the problem of human factors in systems, it helps to identify design patterns that support human interaction. A design pattern is an effective solution to a design problem (Mowbray & Malveau, 1997). Fixed outlines called templates express patterns for design and implementation solutions.

16.7 PROBLEMS

1. Specify the following using the User Action Notation (UAN):
   (a) Select a trash icon, and view the contents of trash.
   (b) Select and move a file to trash.
   (c) Select a group files named sketch1, sketch2, sketch7 and move these files to trash.

2. Using UAN, design the following parts of a computer-human interface for a system to simulate artificial life forms:
   (a) Pull-down menu with a submenu given kinds of fish populations to display.
   (b) Dialog box with speed-of-movements and color options for artificial life forms.

3. Using UAN, design a user interface with the following features:
   (a) Trash with three states: empty state (displays cover on when trash is empty), not-empty but not-full state (cover off when trash contains at least one item), full state (display of overflowing contents of trash can whenever no space is left to add items to trash).
   (b) Desktop displays a deskbot (an artificial life form) that reacts to movements of a mouse. The face of deskbot should face the current pointer position, following the pointer as it moves. The deskbot should display a question mark in cases where mouse actions do not make sense (examples are double clicking on an empty part of a desktop, trying to drag nonmovable displayed items).

4. (Fitts' law.) The difficulty of using a mouse to point to an object in a display is a function of the distance D between the current position of the mouse and the position of a target position, and the width W of a displayed object (Fitts, 1954). A model for estimating the difficulty in pointing is given by

$$\text{difficultyIndex} = \log_2\left(\frac{2D}{W}\right)$$

Do the following:
(a) Give 3D plot of the difficultyIndex for D and W ranging from 0.1 to 40 cm.
(b) Give 2D plot of the difficultyIndex for D from 0.1 to 40 cm, and fixed W.
(c) Give 2D plot of the difficultyIndex for W from 0.1 to 40 cm, and fixed D.
(d) What can you conclude from the plots in (a) to (c)?

5. Let C_1 be the current mouse tracking time (required time to move the pointer across your screen). Also let C_2 be the time required to double click a mouse in selecting a displayed object. Both times are measured in seconds. The time to point to a displayed object can then be computing using Fitt's law (Schneiderman, 1998):

$$\text{timeToPoint} = C_1 + C_2 \log_2\left(\frac{2D}{W}\right)$$

Do the following.
(a) Give 3D plot of timeToPoint for D and W ranging from 0.1 to 40 cm, and fixed values of C_1, C_2.
(b) Give 2D plot of timeToPoint for D from 0.1 to 40 cm, and fixed W, C_2.
(c) Give 2D plot of timeToPoint for W from 0.1 to 40 cm, and fixed D, C_2.
(d) Give 2D plot of timeToPoint for D from 0.1 to 40 cm, and fixed W, C_1.
(e) Give 2D plot of timeToPoint for W from 0.1 to 40 cm, and fixed D, C_1.
(f) What can you conclude from the plots in (a) to (e)?

6. The goal of software engineering from a user's perspective is to provide external representations of domain knowledge that make it easy to extract necessary information needed to perform a task. Do the following:
(a) Describe external representations of domain knowledge relative to various means of calling attention to emergency conditions in a traffic navigation system.
(b) Using UAN, describe user interactions with the external representation in (a).

7. Do the following:
(a) Describe external representations of domain knowledge relative to various means of calling attention to emergency conditions in an air traffic control system.
(b) Using UAN, describe user interactions with the external representation in (a).

8. Do the following:
(a) Give a statechart representation of the control function in an on-board vehicle module that is part of a traffic navigation system.
(b) Give examples of chunking in the statechart representation in (a).

9. Do the following:
   (a) Give a statechart representation of the control function in an air traffic control system.
   (b) Give examples of chunking in the statechart representation in (a).

10. Complete the following table relative to the design of a traffic navigation system.

Design Behavior	Explanation in Designing a Traffic Navigation System
Formation of mental model	
Simulation	
Systematic expansion	
Representing constraints	
Retrieving labels for plans	
Note making	

11. Complete the following table relative to the design of an air traffic control system.

Design Behavior	Explanation in Designing an Air Traffic Control System
Formation of mental model	
Simulation	
Systematic expansion	
Representing constraints	
Retrieving labels for plans	
Note making	

12. Do the following:
   (a) Construct a Personal Software Process (PSP) model to provide a framework to help software engineers plan, track, evaluate, and produce high-quality products for a training program for air traffic controllers.
   (b) How does the PSP in (a) differ from a feedback system model of the software process used to develop a tATC?

13. The goal of intelligent system design is to develop systems with human qualities and capabilities in performing domain tasks. Do the following:
   (a) Give a list of human qualities and capabilities you would like to see in a tATC.
   (b) Use UAN to describe interaction with a tATC having at least one of the human qualities and capabilities listed in (a).

14. Each external world domain is associated with tasks for humans to perform. A number of factors associated with each domain require competent performance. Give a list of these factors present in the interaction of a controller with an air traffic control system display.

16.8 REFERENCES

Coombs, M.J., et al. Learning a first programming language: Strategies for making sense. *International Journal of Man–Machine Studies,* **16**:449–486, 1982.

Adelson, B. and Soloway, E. The role of domain experience in software design. *IEEE Transactions on Software Engineering,* **11**(11):1351–1360, 1985.

Boehm-Davis, D.A. and Fregly, A.M. Documentation of concurrent programs. *Human Factors,* **27**(4):423–432, 1985.

Brooke, J.B. and Duncan, K.D. Experimental studies of flowchart use at different stages of program debugging. *Ergonomics,* **23**(11):1057–1091, 1980.

Curtis, B. Human factors in software development. *Encyclopedia of Software Engineering.* Wiley, NY, 1994.

Dorfman, M. and Thayer, R.H. *Standards, Guidelines, and Examples on System and Software Requirements Engineering.* IEEE Computer Society Press, Los Alamitos, CA, 1990.

Ferguson, P., Humphrey, W.S., Khajenoori, S., Macke, S., and Matvya, A. Results of applying the personal software process. *IEEE Computer,* **30**(5):24–32, 1997.

Fitts, P.M. The information capacity of the human motor system in controlling amplitude of movement. *Journal of Experimental Psychology,* **47**:381–391, 1954.

Fitter, M. and Green, T.R.G. When do diagrams make good computer languages? *International Journal of Man–Machine Studies,* **11**:235–261, 1979.

Gilmore, D.J. and Green, T.R.G. Comprehension and recall of miniature programs. *International Journal of Man–Machine Studies,* **21**:31–48, 1984.

Guidon, R. The knowledge exploited by experts during software design process. *International Journal of Man–Machine Studies,* 1990.

Hartson, H., et al., The UAN: User-oriented representation for direct manipulation interface designs. *ACM Transactions on Information Systems,* **8**(3):181–203, 1990.

Hiltz, S.R. *The Virtual Classroom.* Avlex, Norwood, NJ, 1992.

Humphrey, W.S., Over, J.W. The personal software process (PSP): A full-day tutorial. *Proceedings of the 19th International Conference on Software Engineering,* May 1997, pp. 645–646.

Kamman, R. The comprehension of printed instructions and the flowchart alternative. *Human Factors,* **17**:183–191, 1975.

Kelly, M.J., Chapanis, A. Limited vocabulary natural language dialogue, *Int. J. of Man–Machine Studies,* **9**:479–501, 1977.

Lucas, H.C. and Kaplan, R.B.A structured programming experiment. *The Computer Journal,* **19**(2):136–138, 1974.

Matsumoto, G. The brain and brainway computer. *Proceedings of the 5th International Conference on Soft Computing and Information/Intelligent Systems,* Iizuka, Fukuoka, Japan, October 1998, pp. 13–20.

Miller, L.A. Natural language programming: Styles, strategies, and contrasts. *IBM Systems Journal,* **20**(2):194–215, 1981.

Mitchell, C. GT-MSOCC: A domain for research on human-computer interaction and decision-aiding in supervisory control systems. *IEEE Transactions on Systems, Man and Cybernetics,* **17**(4):553–572, 1987.

Mowbray, T.J., Malveau, R.C. *CORBA Design Patterns.* Wiley, New York, 1977.

Norman, D.A. *Steps Toward a Cognitive Engineering.* Technical Report, Program in Cognitive Science, University of California at San Diego, 1981.

Paulk, M.C., et al. *The Capability Maturity Model: Guidelines for Improving the Software Process.* Addison-Wesley, Reading, MA, 1995.

Roth, E.M. and Mumaw, R.J. Cognitive engineering. In *Encyclopedia of Software Engineering,* J.J. Marciniak, Ed. Wiley, New York, 1994.

Schneiderman, B. *Designing the User Interface: Strategies for Effective Human–Computer Interaction,* 3rd ed. Addison Wesley Longman, Reading, MA, 1998.

Schneiderman, B., et al. Experimental investigations of the utility of detailed flowcharts in programming. *Communications of the ACM,* **20**(6):373–381, 1977.

Sime, M.E., Green, T.R.G., and Guest, D.J. Psychological evaluation of two conditional constructions used in computer languages. *International Journal of Man–Machine Studies,* **5**:104–113, 1973.

Schneiderman, B. Control flow and data structure documentation: Two experiments. *Communications of the ACM,* **25**(1):55–63, 1982.

Soloway, E., Adelson, B., Ehrlich, K. Knowledge and processes in the comprehension of computer programs. In *The Nature of Expertise.* M. Chi, R. Glaser, M. Farr, Eds. Lawrence Erlbaum Associates, NJ, pp. 129–152, 1988.

Von Mayrhauser, A. Program comprehension during software maintenance and evolution. *IEEE Computer,* **28**(8):44–55, 1995.

Vranes, S., Stanojevic, M. Integrating multiple paradigms within the blackboard framework. *IEEE TOSE,* **21**(3):244–261, 1995.

Woods, D.D., Roth, E.M. Cognitive engineering: Human problem solving with tools. *Human Factors,* **30**:415–430, 1988a.

Woods, D.D., Roth, E.M. Cognitive systems engineering. In *Handbook of Human–Computer Interaction,* M. Helander, Ed. North Holland, New York, pp. 3–43, 1988b.

Wright, P. and Reid, F. Written information: Some alternatives to prose for expressing the outcome of complex contingencies. *Journal of Applied Psychology,* **57**:160–166, 1973.

CHAPTER 17
Software Reengineering

What happens to any software that depends
on the Julian date format of YYMMDD?
—M. OLSEM, 1996

Aims
- Explore the legacy system reengineering model
- Consider the economics of reegineering
- Distinguish between forward engineering and reverse engineering
- Explore the reverse engineering process

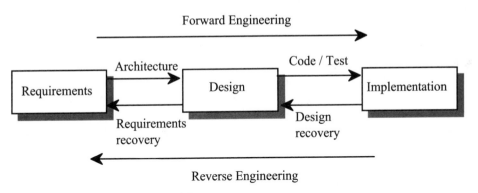

Figure 17.1 Reengineering model.

17.1 INTRODUCTION

In cases where an existing software system has undergone extensive upgrades (lots of changes), then it is possible for maintenance to become difficult and costly. Over time, legacy software can become technically obsolete and must be replaced. A legacy system is one that was developed to satisfy earlier client needs and that was implemented using earlier technology. Examples of legacy systems are Microsoft Word, Excel, and Powerpoint found in the Office 97 suite running on 486 or early Pentium machines. Office 97 was reengineered (older features such as tables improved, and new features added such as the helpbot, grammar checking, html conversion, and Internet and web address recognition) to produce Office 98 written in native code for new platforms such as the PowerPC. It may also happen that a legacy system has severe technical problems. For example, the software that controls some automatic teller machines (ATMs) may not be able to complete transactions after December 31, 1999 when the transaction year becomes 00 (commonly called the Y2K problem). Again, maintaining software can also be quite difficult when documentation for a legacy system is skimpy or missing. In addition, maintenance costs tend to escalate in cases where the size and complexity of a system are high. It is estimated that for every dollar spent on modifying and enhancing a system, maintenance costs can increase up to $0.80 for every subsequent year after changes have been made. Finally, it may become expedient to upgrade an existing system. This is the case where client needs exceed the capabilities of a legacy system. In such cases, reengineering projects are considered.

Reengineering a system means examining and altering a software system to reconstitute and reimplement it in a new form (Software Technology Support Center, 1993). Basically, this means improving the documentation (understanding and describing what a system does, its inputs and outputs, its actions), redesigning and restructuring an existing system to obtain a more acceptable form of a system. The two main subprocesses of a reengineering project are reverse engineering and forward engineering (Figure 17.1). Forward engineering is found in a software process where there is a movement from high-level description of a system (requirements), to identification of software structures (architectures), to coding and physical implementation of a system design. In forward engineering, there is a clear-cut sequence of activities leading from analysis and description of requirements and architectures to design and implementation. By contrast, reverse engineering starts with an existing system, analyzing a system to identify its components and interrelationships among components. A principal benefit of reverse engineering is it results in the recovery of useful information and structures. Examples of items that can be recovered are reusable data models, control structures, interface descriptions, designs, behavioral properties, functional and performance requirements, data structures, objects, algorithms, architectures, and business rules. During reverse engineering, design artifacts are extracted and less implementation-dependent descriptions of an existing system are developed or gleaned from the analysis of an existing system. Job control information (e.g., make files, source control files such as Unix sccs files, batch files), comments made by developers in explanation of code, data structures, and database schemas are examples of useful artifacts in reverse engineering.

Reverse engineering is performed to gain a better understanding of an existing system. In other words, reverse engineering is an analysis process. As a result, software engineering rebuilds design specifications (improving the description of its architecture, its description) to set the stage for a forward engineering effort. Forward engineering is performed to upgrade one or more parts of an existing system. There is increasing evidence of a synergy between forward and reverse engineering processes (Wills, 1996). Increasingly, software engineers are building new systems that utilize existing software assets found in software repositories.

The focus of reverse engineering is the analysis of an existing system. Reverse engineering consists of a set of techniques used to discover information about a software system. Reverse engineering has a number of objectives (Chikofsky & Cross, 1994).

- Cope with complexity resulting from code with connections and dependencies between modules that are not well-understood and resulting from numerous patches and quick fixes to a system.

- Recover lost information due to the continuous evolution of long-lived systems where the evolutionary process includes modifications to the code not reflected in the existing system documentation.

- Detect anomalies and issues due to haphazard initial design and successive modifications, which can lead to defects.

- Detect candidates for reuse among modules of existing software systems. This means using reverse engineering to identify objects or structures that can be reused in other systems.

- Identify and reuse design artifacts that become part of a repository or knowledge base. This means retrieving, gaining understanding, and storing design elements of existing systems that can be used in the development of new releases of systems.

- Identifying rules enforced by software (commercial systems) and use of plans (algorithmic structures) in software modules. Information collected from individual software modules makes it possible to understand interactions between modules across a system as a whole.

17.2 REENGINEERING METHOD

The U.S. National Institute of Standards and Technology (1991) has identified five basic steps and percentage of effort per step in software reengineering (Figure 17.2). Steps 1 and 2 briefly summarize the basic activities of reverse engineering. In step 1, baseline documents for an existing software system are established. A *baseline* is a hardware / software work product that has been formally reviewed and agreed upon, and that serves as the basis for further development. Each baseline describes

- Items that form a baseline. An example of such items is improved code (new functions, renamed variables, localizing variables declared globally

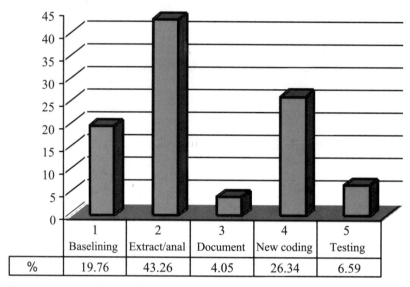

	1	2	3	4	5
	Baselining	Extract/anal	Document	New coding	Testing
%	19.76	43.26	4.05	26.34	6.59

Figure 17.2   Basic steps in reengineering.

but only used locally, increased variable ranges as with the Y2K problem, functional requirements, architectural description, test plan, and so on).

- Review and audit mechanisms.
- Acceptance criteria (part of a test plan) associated with a baseline.
- Specifying client and project team to establish baseline.

In step 2, information is extracted from legacy software and analyzed. This means that all elements of a system are identified and the source code is prepared for analysis. Several types of data associated with a system are identified: domain data (system inputs and outputs), control data (bases for path choices and iteration), and structural data (information needed to manage databases and/or files). Also during step 2, the functional and nonbehavioral requirements of a system are identified. Steps 3, 4, and 5 of the NIST reengineering model represent forward engineering. This means building a new system based on a combination of the new and older requirements.

17.3   REENGINEERING ECONOMICS

There are three basic choices in approaching a legacy system: upgrade, redevelopment, or reengineering. Choosing an approach to improving an existing software

```
Reb[omc_,rmc_,ov_,rec_,rer_,nv_,dec_,der_]:=
(omc-rmc+
ov-((rer)(rer))+
(-nv+((dec)(der))));
```

Figure 17.3 Sample Mathematica program.

system is aided by some form of cost–benefit analysis. Consider, for example, the following cost–benefit index suggested by Sneed (1991):

```
RE_benefit = Reengineering benefit suggesting
oldMaint.cost = estimated annual cost of maintaining
the legacy system
newMaint.cost = estimated annual cost of maintaining
the reengineered system
oldSystem.value = value (in dollars) of legacy system
newSystem.value = value (in dollars) of reengineered
system
RE.cost = reengineering cost
RE.risk = estimated risk (a number between 0 and 1)
associated with reengineering
devel.cost = cost (in dollars) of developing
reengineered system
devel.risk = estimated risk associated with
developing a new system (starting from scratch)
```

$$RE\_benefit = [oldMaint.cost - newMaint.cost]$$
$$+ [oldSystem.value - (RE.cost*RE.risk)]$$
$$+ [newSystem.value - (devel.cost*devel.risk)]$$

A Mathematica function to compute reengineering benefit is given in Figure 17.3. By letting newMaint.cost vary and holding the other parameters fixed in the cost–benefit function in Figure 17.3, we can obtain a plot comparing new maintenance costs and reengineering benefit. This is done in the Mathematica plotting routine in Figure 17.4. The plot produced by the cost–benefit routine

```
Plot[Reb[1000000,rmc,
       5000000,200000,0.85,
       6000000,300000,0.75],
       {rmc,10000,200000},
       AxesLabel->{''RE_m'',''RE_benefit''}]
```

Figure 17.4 Sample Mathematica plotting routine.

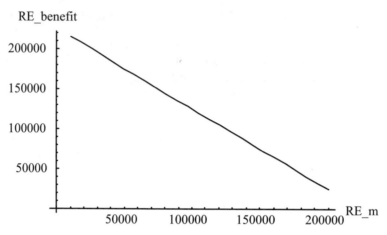

Figure 17.5   Sample cost–benefit plot.

is given in Figure 17.5, where it can be seen that increasing maintenance costs drive the reengineering benefit down steadily. For the selected parameter values, the reengineering benefit becomes neglible as the new maintenance costs approach $200,000.

17.4 WHY REENGINEER?

Reegineering legacy system software results in a number of benefits.

* Improved software maintainability
* Identify candidates for reuse
* Added value of reengineered system
* Time benefit of a reengineered system
* Improved project risk management

The reengineering of a system results in both revised as well as new baseline documents, which aid in the comprehension of a system and establish a new basis for dialog with project stakeholders. The availability of an improved set of baseline documents and the possibility of achieving better rapport with project stakeholders provide a basis for speedier responses to change requests and improved comprehension of a system. In effect, software maintenance improves. Reengineering is aided by the identification of reusable modules, which satisfy project needs and cut down on development time required to achieve a reengineered system. A reengineered system provides features requested by project stakeholders while retaining some fraction of the conceptual construct of the legacy system. There is a trade-off between spending time reverse engineering a legacy system and then forward engineering new features into a legacy system versus the time required to start from scratch. In cases where it appears reasonable to reengineer a legacy system, there is an expectation that reengineering will be less time consuming than building a new system. A significant outcome of reengineering a legacy system is a compilation of sources of risks associated with features of the renewed system. Risk analysis is performed. An improved understanding of project risks facilitates improved risk management for a project.

17.5 REVERSE ENGINEERING NEWSLETTER

A *Reverse Engineering Newsletter* is published by the IEEE Committee on Reverse Engineering. The plans, current activities, and pointers on how to get involved can be found in the web site *http://www.tcse.org/revengr.* A resource repository is available for reverse engineering. This repository includes tools, techniques, methodologies, publications, and other resources.

17.6 SUMMARY

The aim of reverse engineering is to recover and comprehend a number of system artifacts. These artifacts include specifications, business rules, architectures, algorithms, objects, data structures, requirements, behavioral (control) properties, designs, interface descriptions, implementations, control structures, problem and system domain concepts, reusable components, and data models. Reengineering a system is motivated by a number of factors in some legacy systems. These factors include inflexibility, size, complexity, and high demands on existing budgets and personnel. Significant benefits acrue from a reengineering effort. Perhaps the most significant benefits of reengineering a system is enterprise-wide system analysis, understanding of a system, and renewed dialog with project stakeholders. The understanding of a system facilitates maintenance efforts, and aids maintainers in responding to change requests by project stakeholders.

17.7 PROBLEMS

1. Give a block diagram showing the main activities and constraints in reengineering a legacy system.

2. Do the following:
   (a) Identify a legacy system that lacks adequate baseline documents, especially requirements specification for the system.
   (b) Give a cost–benefit analysis of reengineering the legacy system.
   (c) Give world-level and atomic-level models for reengineering the legacy system.

3. Do the following:
   (a) Identify a legacy system that is expected to crash at midnight, January 1, 2000 (Y2K problem exists).
   (b) Give a cost–benefit analysis of reengineering the legacy system to eliminate the Y2K problem.
   (c) Give world-level and atomic-level models for reengineering the legacy system.
   (d) Give a complete set of statecharts describing the reengineered system.

4. Do the following:
   (a) Identify weaknesses in the Sneed cost–benefit model.
   (b) Give a new cost–benefit model, which takes in account nonlinear increases or decreases in the Sneed model.
   (c) Compare the new model from (b) with Sneed's model.

5. An objective of reengineering is to cope with complexity resulting from code with connections and dependencies between modules that are not well understood and resulting from numerous patches and quick fixes to a system. Explain how this objective might be realized in a vanilla framework.

6. An objective of reengineering is to detect anomalies and issues due to haphazard initial design and successive modifications, which can lead to defects. Give an algorithm for detecting system anomalies.

17.8　REFERENCES

Chikofsky, E., Cross, J.H. Reverse engineering. In *Encyclopedia of Software Engineering,* J.J. Marciniak, Ed., Vol. 2. Wiley, New York, 1994.

National Institute of Standards and Technology (NIST), U.S. Department of Commerce. *Software Reengineering: A Case Study and Lessons Learned.* NIST Special Publication 500-193, Gaithersburg, MD, Sept. 1991.

Sneed, H.M. Economics of software re-engineering. *Journal of Software Maintenance: Research and Practice,* **3** (3):163–191.

Software Technology Support Center. *Reengineering Technology Report,* Georgia Institute of Technology, Atlanta, GA Vol. 1, 1993.

Wills, L.M. Message from the chair. *IEEE Reverse Engineering Newsletter,* Spring 1996.

CHAPTER 18
Software Maintenance

There is nothing without a reason.
—LEIBNIZ, 1671

To MAINTAIN. To preserve from failure.
—SAMUEL JOHNSON, 1786

Aims

- Identify types of maintenance
- Consider maintenance models
- Study software maintainability measures
- Consider software reuse and reverse engineering
- Design software with maintenance in mind

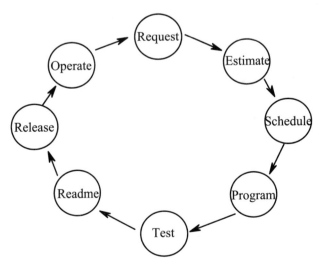

Figure 18.1 Taute maintenance model.

18.1 INTRODUCTION

In developing software, an engineer engages in a sequence of activities that produce a variety of documents culminating in the release of an executable computer program. The release of a software product inaugurates the maintenance phase of the life-cycle. It has been suggested that system maintenance is cyclic (Taute, 1983). A view of this cycle of activities, called the Taute maintenance model, is shown in Figure 18.1. For large software systems, the maintenance phase tends to have a longer duration than the combination of previous life-cycle phases. It has been observed that released software products are not frozen, and commonly have errors that are detected during maintenance (von Mayrhauser, 1990). Repairing detected errors causes an original application to change and expand. Software products are also changed to accommodate new objectives (changing requirements). In effect, software products evolve.

18.2 MAINTENANCE ACTIVITIES

Three principal software maintenance tasks have been identified: corrective, adaptive, and perfective (Swanson, 1976). These tasks are included by the U.S. National Institute of Standards and Technology in a document called a Federal Information Processing Standard (1984).

- *Corrective.* A maintenance task focusing on repairs to code necessitated by system problems (system failures, discovery of software errors).
- *Adaptive.* A maintenance task resulting from changes in the environment in which a software system must operate.
- *Perfective.* A maintenance task involving all changes, insertions, deletions, modifications, extensions, and enhancements to a system to satisfy evolving and increased user needs.

The adaptive and perfective maintenance tasks are mainly concerned with enhancement of an existing software system. There is ample evidence that enhancement activities tend to dominate the maintenance phase of software systems. Based on empirical data, the distribution of tasks in a maintenance effort is shown in Figure 18.2 (Pigoski, 1991). A number of recent studies indicate that the main thrust of a software maintenance effort is noncorrective. A summary of the empirical data is given in Table 18.1.

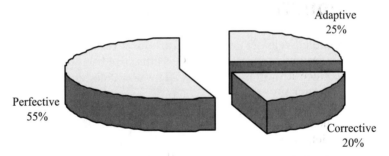

Figure 18.2 Distribution of activities in maintenance effort.

18.3 MAINTENANCE MODELS

A number of maintenance models have been developed since the 1970s. Early models focused on corrective maintenance. An example of a corrective model is given in Sharpley (1977). The Sharpley model focuses on problem verification, problem diagnosis, reprogramming, and verifying that the corrected code satisfies baseline document requirements. Process models dominated recent software maintenance thinking. Two examples are the Taute and IEEE software maintenance models.

18.3.1 Taute Maintenance Model

The taute maintenance model (Figure 18.1) is straightforward, practical, and easy to understand. It was introduced by Taute (1983) and elaborated by Parikh (1986). The taute model has several distinctive features. First, it is maintenance specific. In other words, it is not designed to be a part of any of the other phases of a software life-cycle. Second, software maintenance is viewed as cyclic. The

TABLE 18.1 Empirical Data About Distribution of Maintenance Tasks

Maintenance Task	487 Groups (Lientz & Swanson, 1980)	1987 SMA Survey (Zvegintzov, 1991)	1990 SMA Survey (Zvegintzov, 1991)	2152 Work Requests (Abran & Nguyenkim, 1991)
Noncorrective Task	78%	83%	84%	79%
Corrective Task	22%	17%	16%	21%

cycle begins with a change request, and ends with the successful operation of a modified software product. Finally, this model is distinctive because it emphasizes scheduled releases of software products resulting from modification requests. This feature of the taute model is attractive because it is tailored to the management of software maintenance. The taute model has eight phases:

- *Request phase.* Each time a change request is submitted, configuration management techniques are used to process the request. Its maintenance type is identified using the Swanson scheme (corrective, adaptive, perfective), assigned a unique identification number, and given to a change request librarian for storage and tracking.

- *Estimate phase.* This is essentially the same as the analysis phase in configuration management. The required time, cost, resources, and impact of a change request are determined.

- *Schedule phase.* Change requests for the next scheduled release of a software product are determined. Planning documents are prepared.

- *Programming phase.* A copy of the production version of the software to be modified is checked out, and the creation of a test version of a new release begins.

- *Test phase.* A newly modified copy of the production software is tested.

- *Documentation phase.* Successful completion of testing a new product is followed by preparation of system and user documentation. The existing documentation is updated.

- *Release phase.* The new system (beta version) and updated documentation are delivered. Acceptance testing of software by users begins.

- *Operational phase.* Delivery and operation of the new release begins after successful completion of acceptance testing.

18.3.2   IEEE Maintenance Process Model

Maintenance process modeling focuses on the who, what, where, when, and how of the process whenever a change request is made. The IEEE 1219-1992 draft standard describes an iterative process for managing and carrying out software maintenance activities. This standard identifies seven major activities within a software maintenance process, which is triggered by a Modification Request (MR). The basic structure of this process model is given in Figure 18.3. The model associates input, output, and control mechanisms for each phase of maintenance process. This process model does not presuppose any particular software process model. MRs, Project Documentation (PD), source code, databases, and repositories are sources of input. A more detailed view of the IEEE maintenance model is given in Table 18.2. The advantage of this model is that it applies to planning for software maintenance during forward engineering (development) and to maintaining existing software systems. The maintenance process outlined in

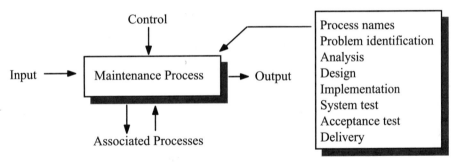

Figure 18.3   Basic structure of IEEE maintenance model.

Table 18.2 begins with configuration management (CM) of change requests. Modification requests are identified (uniquely labeled), classified by type of modification (corrective, adaptive, perfective, emergency), and prioritized. The problem identification process includes a decision to accept, reject, or evaluate a modification request further. Scheduling is also done in the beginning of a maintenance effort to assign a MR to a block of modifications for implementation. Each MR and its determination are added to a repository. Metrics commonly applied during this identification are counts of MR submissions and duplications, and the elapsed time for problem validation. The analysis process is concerned with the feasibility of a MR and preparation of requirements, identifying safety and security issues, test strategy, and implementation plan. Maintenance feasibility activities focus on the impact, cost, and benefits of a modification. Counts of

TABLE 18.2   IEEE Process-Oriented Maintenance Model

	Problem Identification	Analysis	Design	Implement	System Testing	Acceptance Testing
Input	MR	PDs Reuse data	PDs, source, databases	Source, PDs	Updated PDs and system	Reports, test plans
Process	Configuration management of change requests	Feasibility, detailed analysis	Create test cases, revise plans, requirements	Coding, unit testing, readiness review	Functional, interface, regression, review	Acceptance tests, interoperable testing
Control	Uniquely identify MR, add MR to repository	Review, verify safety, security	Inspect and verify software	Software inspection, review, verification	Control of Code, MR, testing, PDs	Establish baseline
Output	Validated MR	Updated PDs, test strategy	Updated design baseline	Updated PDs	Test reports	New baseline

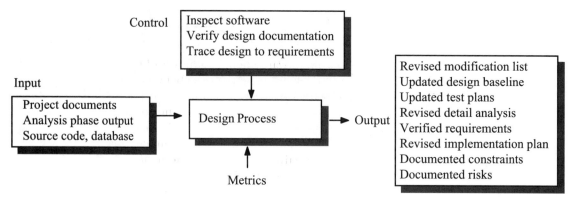

Figure 18.4   Design process.

requirements changes, document error rates, effort, and elapsed time are exam-ples metrics used during the analysis process.

A characterization of the maintenance design process is given in Figure 18.4. Examples of metrics to support the design process are software complexity; count of design changes; design effort; elapsed time; test plans; error rates; SLOC added, deleted, or modified; and number of applications of design. Implementa-tion, testing, and delivery of a new release of a software product follow design during a maintenance effort. In each case, SLOC and error rates provide useful metrics in assessing the maintenance process.

18.3.3   How to Choose a Maintenance Model

The choice of a maintenance model will depend on the maturity of the mainte-nance organization. In the case of a new or small maintenance group (up to the repeatable level in the capability maturity model), the Taute maintenance model is a good choice because of its simplicity. Notice that the Taute model makes no provision for following standards or software reuse or reengineering. Hence, it would work well for corrective maintenance, but not for adaptive or perfective maintenance. The IEEE maintenance model is more complete than the Taute model. Unlike the Taute model, the IEEE maintenance model is applicable not only to the maintenance phase, but also to any phase of a typical software life-cycle. Also, notice that the IEEE model includes a consideration of reuse data during the analysis phase. The underlying assumption in the IEEE model is that a maintenance organization is fairly mature (up to at least the defined maturity level in the CMM model). This model will work well for an organization that has access to repositories of reusable software artifacts such as earlier requirements specifications, algorithms, software designs, and project documentation.

18.4 MAINTAINABILITY

The measurement of the software maintainability is of great interest in software engineering. This interest stems from the links between maintainability and the influence of design practices on software maintenance. Ideally, software products should be designed with maintainability in mind. The documentation for software should facilitate correction and reuse of the code in enhancing the code. As much as possible, the documentation should eliminate the need for reverse engineering. From a corrective point-of-view, the maintainability of a software system can be gauged rather simply relative to the average number of days it takes to repair the code after a problem has been discovered (Bowen et al., 1985).

Corrective maintainability = 1 − 0.1 (average number of days to repair code)

However, this maintainability measure does not take into account software enhancement, which tends to dominate the maintenance phase. Using the empirical evidence about the distribution of maintenance tasks, let c (corrective), a (adaptive), p (perfective) be weights with values 0.2, 0.25, 0.55, respectively. Then maintainability can be measured using estimates of the average number of days required for each of the principle maintenance tasks. This gives us another maintenance measure:

$$\text{maintainability} = 0.2 \ (\text{avg \# of days repairing code})$$
$$+ \ 0.25 \ (\text{avg \# of days adapting code})$$
$$+ \ 0.55 \ (\text{avg \# of days enhancing code})$$

The drawback to this approach to measuring maintainability is that it depends on a knowledge of the average number of days expended for each maintenance task. Hence, considerable attention has been given to gauging the effort required for software maintainability relative to code structure and its documentation. Software structure-oriented maintainability measures can be applied in very early design phases in managing the development of a maintainable product.

18.4.1 Code-Oriented Software Maintainability Measurement

A global view of the maintainability of a software system has been defined relative to three principle characteristics of software and its documentation: testability, understandability, and modifiability (Boehm et al., 1978). These characteristics provide valuable information in measuring both the corrective as well as the enhancement activities of software maintenance. The testability of software is a measure of the average effort required to test a program to ensure that it performs its intended functions. In the context of maintenance, understandability of software is a measure of the average effort necessary to comprehend what needs to be changed to repair or enhance the code. Modifiability of software refers to the average effort required to change the code. Effort can be measured by logging the total staff-hours (or days or person-months) required to complete a given task (Fenton, 1991). Source lines of code, effort, and McCabe's cyclomatic complexity are known as code metrics. These code metrics are commonly used to measure the strength of various attributes associated with maintainability. This is reasonable, since the focus of the maintenance phase in a software life-cycle is on understanding, modifying, and correcting code and on program execution.

18.4.2   Testability of Software

Testability is measured relative to simplicity, modularity, instrumentation, and self-descriptiveness criteria.

- Simplicity refers to an avoidance of features of software that increase its complexity. The inverse of Halstead's level-of-difficulty measure has been used to measure simplicity (Bowen et al., 1985).
- Modularity refers to the partition of computer programs into subroutines or procedures or functions, which define the functionality of a program. The ratio of the number of procedures per SLOC in a program provides a measure of modularity. In the context of object-oriented software, modularity is measured relative to the average number of methods per class.
- Instrumentation refers to features of software that make it possible to measure software usage or to identify errors.
- Self-descriptiveness is synonymous with features of software and its documentation that serve as an aid in explaining the implementation of the software.

Let w_1, w_2, w_3, w_4 be weights (degrees of importance) on the testability criteria. Then testability is estimated with a weighted sum.

$$\text{testability} = w_1\text{simplicity} + w_2\text{modularity} + w_3\text{instrumentation} + w_4\text{self\_descriptiveness}$$

Simplicity can be measured relative to the inverse of program difficulty or what Halstead calls the implementation level of source code. This is done with the following code metrics:

```
η₁ = number of unique operators
N1 = total occurrences of operators
η₂ = number of unique operands
N2 = total occurrences of operands
```

TABLE 18.3 Sample Modularity Measurements for C Programs

C Program	SLOC	No. Functions	Modularity
XpertA	1000	2	0.002
XpertB	1000	12	0.012

Then simplicity can be measured relative to what Halstead (1975) calls the level of implementation:

$$\text{Level of implementation} = \frac{2}{\eta_1} \times \frac{\eta_2}{N_2} \qquad \text{[measure of simplicity of code]}$$

Several measures of modularity are possible. For a procedure-oriented program written in Pascal or C, for example, the following metrics can be used to measure modularity:

$$M_{procedural} = \frac{\# \text{ of procedures}}{\# \text{ of source lines of code}}$$

A procedural modularity measure gives an indication of the degree of partitioning of the functionality of a program. Take, for instance, two C programs XpertA and XpertB, each with 1000 source lines of code (Table 18.3). For object-oriented programs written in C++ or Java, for example, the modularity of a class can be measured relative to SLOC and the number of methods in a class:

$$M_{class} = \frac{\# \text{ of methods per class}}{\# \text{ of source lines of code per class}}$$

A class with a single method will be less modular than a class with more than one method. Then the modularity of an object-oriented program can be measured relative to the average modularity of its classes:

$$M_{program} = \frac{\text{Avg} \# \text{ of methods per class}}{\text{Avg} \# \text{ of source lines of code per class}}$$

Software instrumentation makes it possible to monitor and control the execution of a program. There is a useful instrumenting principle to remember (Smith, 1994).

Instrumenting Principle

Instrument systems as you build them to make it possible to measure and analyze workload scenarios, resource requirements, and performance goal achievement.

A measure of software instrumentation is the average number of probe points per module. A probe point makes it possible to observe an execution characteristic. An example of a probe point is a print statement inside a loop so that the value of a variable interest is displayed during an iteration. Consider, for instance, a simulation of aircraft in flight. Let spd1 be a variable used to simulate the airspeed of a simulated aircraft. The value of spd1 is varied randomly inside an infinite loop. Then the following line of code provides a probe point for spd1:

```
g.drawString("Spd:" + spd1 + "km/hr",x1+7,y1+20);//sample probe point
```

Variables x1, y1 in g.drawString determine the coordinates of the displayed text. This probe point makes it possible to track the execution of the aircraft simulation program. A sample display of the value of spd1 for an aircraft named Flight 188 is shown in Figure 18.5.

The self-descriptiveness of a software system is derived from those attributes that provide an explanation of the implementation of the software. Self-descriptiveness can be measured grossly relative to the reading level of its documentation and the readability of its code. The FOG index estimates the number of years of schooling required to read a document with ease and understanding (Gunning, 1968):

$$FOG = 0.4 \times \left(\frac{\text{\# of words}}{\text{\# of sentences}} + \text{percentage of words with 3 or more syllables} \right)$$

The readability of program code can be measured relative to the v (average length of the variables), SLOC, and c (cyclomatic complexity) (De Young, 1979):

$$\text{Readability}_{\text{software}} = |0.295v - 0.499\text{SLOC} + 0.13c|$$

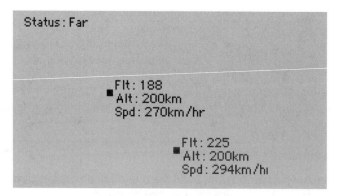

Figure 18.5 Display of probe point value.

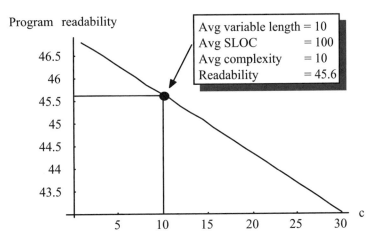

Figure 18.6 Sample readability plot.

For example, for a program with average variable length of 10, average SLOC of 100, and with the average cyclomatic complexity varying between 1 and 30, the graph of program readability is shown in Figure 18.6. In the sample plot in Fig. 18.6, program readability drops as complexity increases.

18.5 SOFTWARE REUSE

Software reuse is a common maintenance task. A software artifact that is used in more than one context with or without modification is considered reusable. Software requirements specifications, software architectures, designs, algorithms, test procedures, and software documentation are examples of artifacts that are potentially reusable. A reuse methodology that identifies activities applicable in each phase of a typical software life-cycle has been developed at the Software Engineering Institute at CMU (Kang et al., 1992). An approach to reuse based on the Carnegie Mellon University CMU model is given in Table 18.4. The reuse methodology has a number of major tasks: understanding, exploration, planning, acquiring, modifying, integrating, and evaluation. The first task of the reuse method is understanding a problem (step 1 in Table 18.4). During maintenance, the basic problem is deciding how to carry out a modification request. The second task is to develop a solution to a problem by building a knowledge of predefined solutions based on reusable ideas, domain knowledge, and software artifacts such as specifications, architectures, and algorithms from previous projects (steps 1 and 2). Step 2 is the exploration step in the reuse method. Exploration of earlier approaches to solving similar

TABLE 18.4   Reuse Methodology

Reuse Activity	Details
1. Understanding a problem	Study a problem and available solutions to the problem.
2. Explore levels of reuse	• Reuse of ideas and knowledge • Reuse of artifacts
3. Reuse plan	Develop reuse plan based on available solutions to problem, levels of reuse.
4. Identify solution structure	Solve a problem based on closest fit with reusable components following reuse plan.
5. Prepare components	Acquire, modify reusable components and develop components that cannot be acquired.
6. Integration and Evaluation	Integrate reusable and new components in solving a problem, and evaluate products.

problems paves the way to possible reuse of existing software artifacts in solving a new problem. The third task (step 3 in Table 18.4) is to develop a reuse plan or strategy indicating an effective approach to applying what has been learned in solving a problem. The reuse plan identifies available reusable artifacts that have been identified. Based on the plan, a solution structure is identified (step 4), reusable components are acquired, modified as needed (step 5), and made ready for integration in a new software product (step 6). The completed components are integrated into products required for the particular phase of the lifecycle, and then formally reviewed and evaluated before being released. In the maintenance phase, acquisition of reusable artifacts leads to a modification of existing software to satisfy a change request. Notice that the steps in the methodology are revisited in the event that any problem is found during a product review.

Software reuse is attractive because of the possibility of saving time in solving a maintenance problem. An effective method of reuse should minimize costs. It has been suggested that there are two basic costs to watch in gauging the effectiveness of a reuse method: human and computational costs (Novak, 1995). A breakdown of the sources of these costs is given in a sample Gantt chart for a recent project involving the reuse of software artifacts in retrofitting a simulation of an air traffic control system called tATC to include new features missing from earlier versions of the system (Figure 18.7). In this reuse project, understanding the maintenance problem and adapting reusable code to solve the problem dominated the reuse effort. This experience is in agreement with a recent study, which points to understanding and adaptation as the dominant problems in a reuse effort (Frakes & Fox, 1996).

Software reusability is a measure of the average amount of reused documentation per maintenance task. In other words, reusable is a measure of the ease

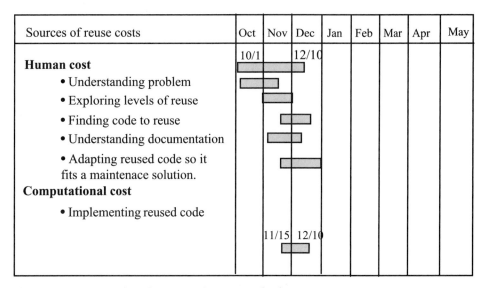

Figure 18.7   Gantt chart for costs of reuse method.

with which previously acquired concepts and objects can be used in new contexts. Basically, reuse is a matching between new and old contexts. Whenever matching succeeds partially or completely, reuse is possible. Interest in software reusability has led to the creation of reuse libraries such as SIMTEL (Conn, 1987), RAPID (Reigsegger, 1988), Commercial-Off-The-Shelf (COTS) software such as GRACE (Berard, 1986), and reusable Ada components (Booch, 1988). More recently, the USC Integrated Library System (ILS) has been extended to make it possible to access multimedia archives containing films, maps, and videos. The ILS is a text-oriented, client-server COTS product designed to manage acquisition, cataloging, public access, and circulation of library artifacts (Boehm et al., 1998).

18.6   REVERSE ENGINEERING

Reverse engineering is common during software maintenance because the documentation produced during software development is often inadequate. Hence, it becomes necessary to reconstruct the documentation from code to understand how the code works, and to facilitate both corrective and enhancement maintenance tasks. A method of recovery of software design has been suggested that works with a set of directed graphs (Schneidewind, 1987).

> **Steps in Design Recovery**
> - Inspect the code.
> - Construct a set of directed graphs (called abstractions) representing the code.
> - Choose the most suitable set of graphs.
> - Construct a specification from the selected graphs.

Each directed graph representation of code is inspected to discover nodes representing design decisions so that the order of the design decisions can be reversed whenever it is necessary to make changes to the code during the maintenance phase. Function and data abstractions have been used by IBM to upgrade the U.S. Federal Aviation Administration National Airspace System, which was 20 years old and contained 100,000 lines of source code.

18.7 DESIGN FOR MAINTAINABILITY

Designing for maintainability means attempting to reduce future maintenance costs by anticipating maintenance needs during software design. There is evidence that there is a correlation between the structural complexity of software and maintenance effort (Kafura & Reddy, 1987). In approaching the problem of designing with maintenance in mind, project planning teams can establish upper and lower bounds for selected characteristics of program units. For example, bounds can be set for testability, understandability, and modifiability of software. A Kiviat diagram expressing these bounds can become part of the requirements given to a design team. A sample Kiviat diagram for the attributes of the Boehm maintenance model is given in Figure 18.8. The bounds of the diagram serve as indicators of desired maintainability levels and goals for project designers. Comparison of the results of periodic measurements

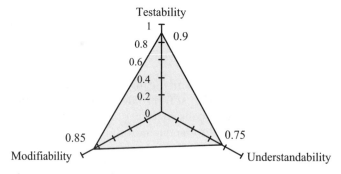

Figure 18.8   Sample Kiviat diagram.

of maintainability attributes and the bounds given by project planners serves as a means of modifying software design to accommodate maintenance goals.

18.8 SUMMARY

A painter designs when he chooses some things, refuses others, and arranges all.
—Ruskin, 1858

The secret to software maintenance is designing with maintenance in mind. Much like the artist making choices in imaginatively arranging the structures to be painted, a software engineer structures software to make it easier to comprehend and maintain. The division of space in the golden section is a technique used by artists to pull a viewer's eye into that part of a picture of great interest. Similarly, in designing software, the starting point in a top-down (high-level) view of the software suggests a line of reasoning to follow in unraveling the designer intentions. Superstates in a statechart, for example, are analogous to golden sections in the division of space in a painting. Superstates draw a maintainer's view into focal points of a software description. The modularity of a design provides a separation between a top-level view of a design and the hidden details underlying a module in an object-oriented design. Modularity has a significant fringe benefit of maintainers. Chunking is made easier by software modularity. Software modules yield schematic views (chunks) of software. In effect, modularity and object orientation facilitate software comprehension.

The Taute maintenance model has the appearance of a dog chasing its tail. It portrays software maintenance activities as cyclic, and gives no hint of how to tackle the conceptual construct in software being maintained. Notice that a scheduled response to a change request is programming. There is no hint of consulting design documents that lead to the code to be changed. More importantly, there is no hint of an appeal to some form of comprehension model as a means of understanding a software design to be changed. There is no evidence of some form of chunking in sorting out what is to be done in response to a change request. There is also no hint of an iterative interaction with project stakeholders during testing. The IEEE maintenance model is better, since it calls for a trace of a design to requirements. Such a trace will aid understanding of the software to be changed.

18.9 PROBLEMS

1. Try with experimenting with the DeYoung program readability measure as follows:
   (a) Use a fixed average variable length a, fixed average cyclomatic complexity c, and

allow the average SLOC to vary. Using the DeYoung readability measure given in this chapter, give a readability plot for program readability using a = 10, SLOC in the [100, 10000] range, and c = 10.

(b) Give a plot of program readability using values of a, b, c in (a) using

$$Readability_{software} = 0.295v - 0.499SLOC + 0.13c \qquad \text{(without the absolute value)}$$

(c) Compare the results in (a) and (b).

2. A Kiviat diagram showing current and required maintenance attribute values is shown in Figure 18.9.
Do the following.
(a) Assuming that the Kiviat diagram represents a legacy system that lacks an SRS, suggest how the understandability of the system can be improved.
(b) Give a checklist of items to look for in determining how to improve the testability of the legacy system in (a).
(c) Give a checklist of items to look for in determining how to improve the modifiability of the legacy system in (a).

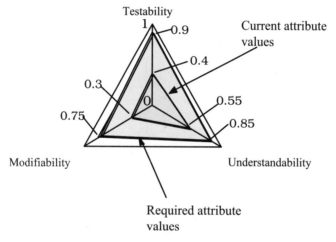

Figure 18.9   Sample Kiviat diagram.

Note: The remaining problems in this section refer to the sample code in Figure 18.10.

3. Compute the simplicity of the code in Figure 18.10 based on Halstead's method.

4. Measure the modularity of the code in Figure 18.10.

5. Estimate the number of years of schooling required to read the code in Figure 18.10 with ease and understanding.

6. Do the following:
(a) Assuming that no other documents are available, give an assessment of the maintainability of the program in Figure 18.10.

```
// Program to display an aircraft icon (green in color) randomly
//moving across display
import java.awt.*;                       //abstract window toolkit
import java.applet.Applet;
import java.util.*;
import java.lang.Math;

public class aircraft000 extends Applet {
Graphics     g;
int          x = 100;                    // starting x coord.
int          y = 100;                    // starting y coord.
int          view = 0;                   // zero views
Random       r = new Random();           // randomly vary coords.

public void init() {
 g=getGraphics();                        // start graphics
} //init

public void update (Graphics g){         // control view
 int prev_x, prev_y;                     // store old coords.

 while (view <12){                       // up to 12 views
  view++;                                // increment counter
  prev_x=x;                              // store old x coord.
  prev_y=y;                              // store old y coord.
  x=prev_x - (r.nextInt()%36);           // vary x randomly
  y=prev_y - (r.nextInt()%36);           // vary y randomly
  g.setColor(Color.green);               // color of aircraft icon
  g.fillOval(x,y,9,9);                   // view aircraft position
 } // while
} //update

public void paint(Graphics g){
 g.setPaintMode();                       // prepare for display
 update(g);                              // attempt new scan
 } // paint
} //aircraft000
```

Figure 18.10 Sample code to maintain.

    (b) Reverse engineer the code in Figure 18.10. All missing baseline documents are to be produced for this code.

7. Create an IEEE maintenance model to be used to maintain the reverse-engineered system resulting from problem 6.

8. How would chunking aid software maintenance?

9. What are the benefits of the application of a vanilla framework in maintaining software?

10. What are the human factors in a system that has been designed with maintenance in mind?

18.10 REFERENCES

Abran, A., Nguyenkim, H. Analysis of maintenance work categories through measurement. *Proceedings of the Conference on Software Maintenance.* IEEE Computer Society Press, Los Alamitos, CA, pp. 104–113, 1991.

Boehm, B., et al. Using the win win spiral model: A case study. *IEEE Computer,* **31**(7):33–44, 1998.

Boehm, B., et al. Characteristics of Software Quality. North-Holland, New York, 1978.

Berard, E.V. Creating reusable Ada software. *Proceedings of the National Conference on Software Reusability and Maintainability,* 1986.

Booch, G. Software components with Ada. Benjamin Cummings, Menlo Park, CA, 1988.

Bowen, T.P., Wigle, G.B., Tsai, J.T. *Specification of Software Quality Attributes: Software Quality Evaluation Guidebook.* Technical Report RADC-TR-85-37, vol. III, Rome Air Development Center, Griffiss AFB, NY 13441-5700, Feb. 1985.

Conn, R. The Ada software respository. *Proceedings of COMPCON87,* Feb. 1987.

De Young, G.E. and Kampen, G.R. Program factors as predictors of program readability. *Proceedings of the IEEE Computer Software & Applications Conference,* 1979, 668–673.

Federal Information Processing Standards Publication (FIPS PB 106). *Guideline on Software Maintenance,* June 1984.

Fenton, N.E. *Software Metrics: A Rigorous Approach.* Chapman & Hall, New York, 1991.

Frakes, W.B., Fox, C.J. Quality improvement using a software reuse failure modes model. *IEEE TOSE,* **22**(4):274–278, 1996.

Gunning, R. *The Technique of Clear Writing.* McGraw-Hill, New York, 1968.

Halstead, M.H. *Elements of Software Science.* Elsevier North Holland, New York, 1975.

Kafura, D., Reddy, G.R. The use of software complexity metrics in software maintenance. *IEEE TOSE* SE-**13**(3):335–343, 1987.

Kang, K.C., et al. *A Reuse-Based Software Development Methodology.* Special Report *CMU/SEI-92-SR-4,* Software Engineering Institute, Carnegie Mellon University, Jan. 1992. Available from *http://www.rai.com.*

Lientz, B.P., Swanson, E.B. *Software Maintenance Management.* Addison-Wesley, Reading, MA, 1980.

Novak, G.S. Creation of views for reuse of software with different data representations. *IEEE TOSE,* **21**(12):993–1005, 1995.

Parikh, G. *Handbook of Software Maintenance.* John Wiley & Sons, New York, 1986.

Pigoski, T.M. Software maintenance metrics. *Software Maintenance News,* **9**(8):19–20, 1991.

Ruegsegger, T. Making reuse pay: The SIDPERS-3 RAPID Center. *IEEE Communications Magazine,* **26**(8):816–819, 1988.

Schneidewind, N.F. The state of software maintenance. *IEEE TOSE,* SE-**13**(3):303–387, 1987.

Sharpley, W.K. Software maintenance planning for embedded computer systems. *Proceedings of the IEEE COMPSAC.* IEEE Computer Society Press, Los Alamitos, CA, 1977, pp. 303–310.

Smith, C.U. Performance engineering. In *Encyclopedia of Software Engineering,* J.J. Marciniak, Ed. Wiley, New York, 1994.

Swanson, E.B. The dimensions of maintenance. *Proceedings of the Second International Conference on Software Engineering,* 1976, pp. 492–497.

Taute, B.J. Quality assurance and maintenance application systems. *Proceedings of the National AFIPS Computer Conference,* 1983, pp. 123–129.

Von Mayrhauser, A. *Software Engineering—Methods and Management.* Academic Press, San Diego, 1990.

Zvegintzov, N. Real maintenance statistics. *Software Maintenance News,* **9**(2):6–9, 1991.

Glossary

Abstraction. Identifies the "generic/specific" structural relationships among objects, functions, and states.

Active color. The color currently selected for use in a display.

Adaptive Intelligent System. A system that perceives, reasons, acts to achieve multiple goals in dynamic, uncertain, complex environments.

Agent. 1. An independent process capable of communicating with other processes and interacting with its environment. 2. A computer program that communicates with external programs exclusively via a predefined protocol. An agent has the capability to respond to all messages defined by the protocol, and it uses the protocol to invoke the services of other agents (Cutkovsky et al., 1993).

AIS. Adaptive Intelligent System.

Allocated baseline. 1. The initial, approved specifications governing the development of configuration items that are part of a higher-level configuration item. 2. Initial configuration established at the end of either the system design review for large projects or at the end of the preliminary design review for small or medium projects.

Applet. A mini-application that runs inside a web browser page.

Architectural connector. A control or data path between processing elements in software.

Architectural design. 1. The process of selecting and defining the architecture of a system. 2. The process of defining a collection of hardware and software components and their interfaces to establish the framework for the development of a computer system (IEEE, 1990).

Architectural style. A pattern of structural organization in an architecture.

Architecture. 1. The structure of a system defined relative to system components, interconnections between components, data processed by individual components, and method used to process the data. 2. The structure of the components of a program/system, their interrelationships, and principles and guidelines governing their design and evolution over time (Garlan & Perry, 1995).

Artifact. A byproduct of a software process. Examples are software system plan, software requirements specification, prototype, program source code, designs, architectures, test plan, test suites, maintenance plan, and documentation.

Atomic-level software process. A model of the software process that is task-centered and describes the inner workings (all steps) of a project task in detail.

Audit. Independent examination of work products of a software process to determine the degree of compliance with project requirements, standards, contractual agreements, and other criteria.

Baseline. Hardware/software work product that has been formally identified and agreed upon, which then serves as the basis for further development. Types: allocated baseline, functional baseline, product baseline.

Baseline document.   A document or collection of documents that establish one of the configuration identifications of a hardware/software configuration item. Examples of baseline identification documents are system specification, software requirements specification, software architectural specification, software design specification.

Bean.   A reusable software component that can be manipulated visually in a builder tool.

Behavioral description.   Specification of the control activities of a system.

Blackboard architecture.   A knowledge-based form of repository appropriate in applications requiring cooperative problem-solving by virtual minds, human minds, or both.

Black box.   A component or system of components with known inputs, outputs, and functions and with unknown or ignored internal structure or implementation.

Black box specification.   A description of a software component relative to externally observable behavior and independent of any design or implementation decisions.

Black box testing.   A method of generating test cases not based on implementation. A black box test can be derived from requirements, functional specifications, possible errors, tester's intuition, or a random number generator.

Box structure.   A standard, fine-grained description of software modules in three forms: black box, clear box, and state box.

Box structured design.   1. Modules described by a set of operations that define and access internally stored data. 2. Design based on a Parnas usage hierarchy of modules.

Brook's law.   Adding manpower to a late software project makes it later (Brooks, 1975).

Build.   A set of functionally related modules of a software system. See *Module*.

Call-and-return architecture.   Software components in master–slave relationship.

Capability maturity model.   A prescription for continuous improvement of a software development organization relative to the identification of software process capability maturity levels.

CE.   Cognitive Engineering.

CHAM.   CHemical Abstract Machine.

Change control procedure.   1. A procedure that begins with a change request that is analyzed to ensure that the requested change is acceptable relative to requirements, schedule, budget, and impact on a project. 2. A procedure that ensures that all changes to a system are made in a controlled way (Alencar & Lucena, 1996).

Channel.   A means of communication in one direction between two processes.

Checkpoint.   A point in a computer program at which the program state, status, or computed results are checked or recorded. Syn. *Probe point*.

Chemical abstract machine.   An abstract machine constructed with structures resembling chemical solutions and behaviors modeled after chemical reactions.

CHI.   Computer Human Interaction. See *http://www.ida.liu.se/labs/aslab/groups/*

um/hci/ and *http://is.twi.tudelft.nl/hci/* for pointers to web resources on CHI. To subscribe to the Special Interest Group on CHI (SIGCHI), send the following e-mail message to the Internet address *chi-announcements@acm.org:*

Subscribe chi-announcements <enter your name here>

Chunking. Items with similar or related attributes are bound together conceptually to form a unique item.

Class. A set of objects that share a common structure and behavior manifested by a set of methods (Archer & Stinson, 1995).

Cleanroom engineering. Scientific application of methods and tools to assess and control the quality of incrementally developed software products and to certify the fitness of software products for usage at the time of delivery.

Cleanroom engineering approach. Software development with four primary activities: formal specification of software increments, design, implementation, and team review.

Clear box. Internal view of a module relative to usage control structures and paths through the code of a module. Syn. *White box.*

Client-server architecture. Synonymous with request-reply processing schemes. A client requests a service, and a server responds by providing the requested service.

COCOMO. *COnstructive COst Model.*

COCOMO Effort measure. Effort = a*KDLOC^b where values of a, b are chosen relative to a software class.

COCOMO Maintenance effort measure. Effort$_{maintenance}$ = ACT * Effort, where ACT is the fraction of KDLOC undergoing change during the year.

CM. Capability Maturity.

CMM. Capability Maturity Model.

Cognitive engineering. A form of applied behavioral science concerned with the study and development of principles, methods, tools, and techniques that guide the design of computerized systems intended to support human performance.

Cognitive ergonomics. The study of problem-solving, information analysis, and procedural skills relative to the influence of human factors.

Cognitive Science. The study of how knowledge is acquired, represented in memory, and used in problem-solving.

Cohesion. 1. The manner and degree that tasks performed by a single software module are related to one another (IEEE, 1990). 2. The degree to which the methods within a class are related to one another (Acher & Stinson, 1995).

Competence. A sensor-driven process represented by tuples (S, T, A) where S specifies sensory input from one or more sensors, and T performs transformations on inputs and generates output to one or more actuators in the set A.

Component. A section of software code that can be merged with other code to create an application (Downing & Covington, 1998).

Computer program. 1. A combination of computer instructions and data definitions that enable computer hardware to perform computational or control functions (IEEE, 1990). 2. A rule for a mathematical function. 3. Executable knowledge (Humphrey, 1989).

Concurrent revision system.   A configuration management system for Unix systems is downloadable from *http://www.mozilla.org*. A PC version of cvs called WinCVS is downloadable from *http://www.cyclic.com*.

Configuration auditing.   A periodic check that a configuration accurately reflects requirements and plans.

Configuration control.   An activity that ensures that all changes and additions to a configuration item are formally requested, analyzed, approved/disapproved, recorded, and reported with feedback to change proposers. Disapproved changes are archived for future reference.

Configuration identification.   A process that ensures that all items of a configuration are discovered and uniquely identified with a system for distinguishing between different versions of the same item.

Configuration Item (CI).   1. An item that may be stored by a computer and designated for configuration management (Thayer & Thayer, 1993). 2. An aggregation of hardware, software, or both, that is designated for configuration management (CM) and treated as a single entity in the CM process.

Configuration management (CM).   1. Technical and administrative procedures used to identify and document the functional and physical characteristics of a configuration item, control changes to a CI, record and report all changes to a CI, and verify compliance with specified requirements (IEEE, Def Stan 00-55/ 1 1991). 2. Procedures and standards for the management of evolving software systems (Babich, 1986).

Constructive cost model.   Application of detailed formulas in determining the development time schedule, overall development effort, effort breakdown by phase and activity, as well as maintenance effort for a software project.

Control system.   Interconnected components forming a system that computes a desired response to a stimulus.

CORBA.   Common Object Request Broker Architecture. A set of definitions for objects that interact with each other (Downing & Covington, 1998).

COTS.   Commercial-Off-The-Shelf.

Coupling.   1. The manner and degree of interdependence between software modules (IEEE, 1990). 2. The degree to which methods within a class are related to one another (Archer & Stinson, 1995).

Critical path.   Longest path in a PERT network.

CSP.   1. Communicating Sequential Processes formal description language. 2. A concise means of creating architectural descriptions of systems of communicating processes.

CVS.   Concurrent revision system.

Cyclomatic complexity. $v(G) = DE + 1$, where DE stands for the number of decision boxes present in a flowchart G for a software module.

DARTS.   Design Approach for Real-Time Systems.

Data dictionary.   A store for information about data items found in a DFD.

Data element.   A software architectural element that contains information needed for processing or information to be processed by a processing element.

Data flow architecture.   A software structure used to process data streams.

Data flow diagram.   A diagram that specifies the processes (also referred to as bubbles, transforms, transactions, activities, operations) and flow of data between them.

Decider. A process that determines if the entry condition for a task has been satisfied and chooses an appropriate effector to carry out the task.

Defect. A product anomaly (e.g., omissions or imperfections found during a software development).

Depth of Inheritance Tree measure Path length from the node where a class is located to the root of the inheritance tree containing the class.

Design Approach for Real-Time Systems method. Decomposition of context-level tasks into concurrent tasks with a description of interfaces between the tasks.

Design pattern. An effective solution to a design problem.

DFD. Data Flow Diagram.

DIT. Depth of Inheritance Tree.

Domain-specific software architecture. An architecture tailored to the needs of a particular application domain.

ECP. Engineering Change Proposal.

Effector. A process that performs some task, verifies its work product, and exits whenever its exit condition has been satisfied.

Effort. Manmonths starting with specification delivery and ending with client acceptance of a software product.

Embedded system. An electromechanical systems governed by one or more computers.

Engineering. Application of scientific principles in the design, manufacture, and operation of structures and machines.

Engineering Change Proposal. A description of a proposed change that identifies the originator of a change, rationale for a change, and the baselines affected by a proposed change.

Ergonomics. 1. The scientific study of the efficiency of humans in their working environment. From the Greek word $\varepsilon\rho\gamma o\nu$ meaning work (OED, 1992). 2. The science concerned with designing and arranging a system so that humans interact with it effectively. Related words: *Cognitive engineering, Human factors.*

Error. 1. A detected deviation from an agreed-upon specification or requirements that can lead to system failure (Thayer & Thayer, 1993). 2. The difference between a computed, observed, or measured value or condition and the true, specified, or theoretically correct value or condition (IEEE, 1990). See *Fault.*

ETVXM. Entry, Task, Verify, Exit, Measure.

Event. An instantaneous, observable occurrence.

Extensible software structure. A software architecture that is essentially open, and easily revised to satisfy increased demands, additional devices.

Failure. 1. Inability of a system to perform its required functions within specified performance requirements (IEEE, 1990). 2. Misbehavior of a computer program in use. 3. Manifestation of an error (Thayer & Thayer, 1993).

Fault. 1. An incorrect step, process, or data definition in a computer program. 2. An imperfection or deficiency in a system that may contribute to an error. Synonym: *Bug.*

FCA. Functional Configuration Audit.

Feedback control system.   A system that maintains a precise relationship between the output and a reference input by comparing them and using the difference as the basis for control.

Finite state machine.   A computational model with a finite number of states and transitions between states.

Flexible software structure.   A software architecture that facilitates refinement.

Flowchart.   A control flow diagram with blocks annotated to represent operations and data and arrows to represent sequential flow from one block to another.

Forward engineering.   A process of moving from high-level representations and designs to physical implementation of a system.

Framework.   A combination of components (e.g., class library) that simplifies the construction of applications and can be plugged into an application.

FSM.   Finite State Machine.

Functional baseline.   Initial, approved technical documentation approved for a configuration item. See *Baseline document, Configuration item.*

Functional Configuration Audit.   1. A check that the actual performance of a CI conforms to its requirements given in the SRS. 2. A description of how tests to a CI were performed, how they were conducted, and how reports were prepared and witnessed.

Functional description.   Specification of the activities of a system.

Functional testing.   Testing that focuses on the outputs produced in response to selected inputs and execution conditions. Types include cause–effect graphing. Syn.: *Black box testing.*

Function-oriented problem analysis.   A system is viewed as a hierarchy of functions or activities.

Function points.   External inputs, external outputs, user inquiries, external files, internal files.

Function points method.   Identification of visible features of a software system which are weighted accordingly to produce an overall score in measuring the system functionality.

Gantt chart.   A bar chart showing task schedules for a project.

GUI.   Graphical User Interface.

Human factors: 1. The human perception of a system and its functions and limitations. 2. The extent that a system fulfills its purpose without wasting the user's time or energy or degrading a user's morale (Thayer & Thayer, 1993). See *http://www.aw.com/DTUI*, which gives web sites related to human factors of interactive software. See *Human factors paradigm.*

Human factors paradigm.   Study of the relationships between stimuli presented to individuals and the responses they make (Curtis, 1994).

IEEE.   Institute of Electrical and Electronic Engineers. See IEEE home page at *http://www.ieee.org.*

IEEE CS.   IEEE Computer Society. See *http://www.computer.org.*

IEEE TOSE.   *IEEE Transactions on Software Engineering.* See *http://computer.org* and *tse@computer.org.*

IEEE TSE.   The same as the more common abbreviation: IEEE TOSE.

Independent-process software architecture. A collection of independent, possibly communicating processes.

Information hiding. 1. A design approach where software is decomposed into modules that hide design decisions. Attention shifts to the signature of a module and away from the code used to implement the module.

Instance connection. Specifies the cardinality of a relationship one object has to another.

Instrumented software. Insertion of code at key probe points to make it possible to measure execution characteristics of interest.

ISO. International Standards Organization.

JSD. Jackson System Development.

JSD method. Model the behavior of real-world entities over time using action, entity structure, model, function, timing, and implementation steps.

KDLOC. One thousand Delivered Lines of Code.

KDSI. One thousand Delivered Source Instructions.

Kepner-Tregoe method. Criteria are divided into essential and desirable. A minimum value is specified for each essential criterion. Software failing to achieve a minimum essential criterion score is deemed unsuitable. Suitable software is evaluated using a system of weighting factors (Kepner & Tregoe, 1981).

Key Process Area. A cluster of related activities to be performed collectively to enhance process capability.

Kiviat diagram. A diagram with "spokes" radiating from an origin where each spoke is marked with the minimum and maximum values for each software attribute to be measured. Syn. Radar diagram.

KLOC. One thousand lines of code.

Knot. 1. One nautical mile per hour, approximately 1.85 kilometers (1.15 statute miles) per hour (Microsoft, 1997). 2. A unit of speed used in air traffic control to measure airspeed. Abbreviation: kt.

KPA. Key Process Area.

Layer. A software module that acts as client for the module above it and acts as a server for the module below it in a layered architecture.

Layered architecture. A hierarchy of client–server processes that minimizes interaction between layers.

Legacy system. A collection of hardware and software resources that organizations accumulate and maintain over the years.

Lexical content measure. A count of the operators, operands, branches in a code, statements, types of statements in a software module.

LOC. Number of nonblack, noncommented lines of code. Syn.: Source Lines of Code (SLOC).

LOC productivity. A measure of productivity of software development teams (Maxwell et al., 1996). Lines-of-code productivity $= \dfrac{\text{SLOC}}{\text{manmonths of effort}}$

MM. Man Month = 144 man hours.

MMI. Man–Machine Interface.

Module. 1. A logically separate part of a program (IEEE, 1990). 2. A component of a software architecture that encapsulates a design.

Module signature. In its general form, the signature of a module provides the sorts (types), operations (functions or procedures), and characteristic (parameter and result structure) in describing the interface of a module.

MRE. Magnitude of relative error $= \dfrac{|\text{observed\_value} - \text{estimated\_value}|}{\text{observed\_value}}$

Mythical Man Month. The notion that man-month is a measure of the size of a job (Brooks, 1975).

NEC fish. Example of artificial life. See *http://www.sw.nec.co.jp/sou5/pkg/fish/fish.html.*

Nesting levels measure. The depth of nesting resulting from loops, one inside another, occurring in code.

NOC. Number of Children measure.

Nonbehavioral description. Specification of the attributes of a system.

Number of Children measure. Number of immediate subclasses subordinated to a class in a class hierarchy.

Object. 1. A program constant or variable. 2. An encapsulation of data and services that manipulate that data (IEEE, 1990).

OO. Object oriented.

OO method. A system is viewed as a collection of objects, attributes of the objects, operations of objects with message-passing between objects.

OO problem analysis. Specification of objects, attributes, structures, services, and subjects.

Partitioning. Aggregates the structural relations among objects, functions, and states, and simplifies (compartmentalizes) the structures to be analyzed.

PCA. Physical Configuration Audit.

PDF. Portable Document Format. Also written pdf. A variation of the postscript printing language that makes it possible to display on screen, edit, and print documents created with Adobe Acrobat software. Acrobat documents end with the suffix .pdf. See *http://www.adobe.com.*

Personal Software Process. A framework to help software engineers plan, track, evaluate, and produce high-quality products based on the SEI capability maturity model.

PERT. Project Evaluation and Review Technique.

PERT network. A network diagram that displays task sequences required for a project.

Petri net. 1. An extended finite state machine permitting concurrent enabling of transitions and asynchronous communication. 2. A form of finite state machine used to describe and analyze the structure and information flow in systems.

Physical Configuration Audit. 1. A check that all documentation delivered with software accurately represents software content. 2. A complete review of a software product specification, minutes of corrective actions needed prior to an audit, design descriptions for proper symbols, labels, and data descriptions, review of software manuals, source code, and labeling of proprietary information in documentation is provided.

Pipeline architecture. A sequence of processes called filters connected by pipes.

Each filter transforms its input, and communicates the results of its transformation to the next filter in the pipeline.

Postcondition. A requirement about the results computed for the values of arguments described in a precondition.

Precondition. An assumption about arguments for a function or procedure.

Process. Behavior pattern of an object described relative to a limited set of events (Hoare, 1985).

Process control paradigm. A software architecture with a structure containing mechanisms for manipulating process variables to regulate system output relative to one or more set points.

Processing element. A software structure that transforms its inputs into required outputs.

Product baseline. Initial, approved technical documentation defining a configuration item during the production, operation, maintenance, and logistic support phases of an item's life-cycle.

Projection. Provides a "view of" structural relationships among objects, functions, or states.

Proof obligation. A condition that must be satisfied for specified states of a system.

Protocol. A set of conventions that govern interaction of processes, devices, and other components within a system (IEEE, 1990).

Prototype. 1. A preliminary type, form, or instance of a system that serves as a model for later stages or for the final, complete version of the system (IEEE, 1990). 2. An executable model that accurately reflects a subset of the properties of a system being developed.

PSL. Program Support Library.

PSP. Personal Software Process.

Psychological paradigms. Individual differences, group behavior, organizational behavior, human factors, and cognitive science.

Raw fitness. A count of the number of successes achieved by members of a population.

RCS. revision control system.

Reachability Measure. 1. A measure of the complexity of a software module. 2. The number of unique ways (paths) one can reach each node of a flowchart for a software module. Syn.: Reachability index.

Reengineering. A systematic approach to examining and altering a software system to reconstitute and reimplement it in a new form.

Reengineering process model. A view of reengineering that begins with inventory of an existing software system (its source and related documentation) followed by reconstruction of logical level of system data (application, control, structural data), functional requirements, abstract data, logical level of programs. These reconstructions are followed by restoration of the logical model for a software system, final packaging of documentation, and testing of restored system. Restoration includes introducing changes to improve program structure, make them easier to maintain (Fiore et al., 1996).

Regression testing. During software modification, test cases a program has previously executed correctly to detect errors are rerun and compared (Dorfman & Thayer, 1990).

Repository architecture.   A software architecture with a central data structure representing the current state and independent components that operate on a central data store.

Requirements analysis.   Defines the product space of a software process. Syn.: Problem analysis.

Requirements engineering.   Systematic use of verifiable principles, methods, languages, and tools in the analysis and description of user needs and the description of the behavioral and nonbehavioral features of a software system satisfying user needs.

Requirements specification.   A description of the principal features of a software product, its information flow, its functions, its behavior (control activities), and its attributes.

Reusable software structure.   A software structure that can be extracted from one application and inserted into a new application with reasonable effort.

Reverse engineering.   1. Taking apart an existing software product to see how it works. 2. A process of analysis supported by methods and tools for the discovery of information about a software system (Chikofsky & Cross, 1994). A reverse engineering repository is available at *http://www.tcse.org/revengr/*.

Revision control system.   A suit of Unix operating system programs for tracking and control of versions of text.

Rhapsody.   An object-oriented visual software development environment using statecharts to specify and prototype complex systems. See *http://www.ilogix.com.*

SADT.   Structured Analysis and Design Technique.

SCCS.   Source code control system.

Schema.   A Z structure used to describe the static (states, invariant relationships) and dynamic (operations, relationships between input and output, state changes that can happen) features of a system. See Z.

SCI.   Software Configuration Item. See *Software Configuration Management.*

SCM.   Software Configuration Management.

SDL.   Specification and Description Language used in specifying communication protocols.

SEI.   Software Engineering Institute at Carnegie Mellon University, Pittsburgh, Pennsylvania 15213. For case studies, see *http://www.rai.com.*

Size of maintenance task.   LOC inserted + LOC updated + LOC deleted (Jorgensen, 1995).

SLC.   Software Life Cycle.

Software.   Computer programs, procedures, and possibly associated documentation and data pertaining to the operation of a computer system (IEEE, 1990).

Software artifact.   A byproduct of the software process. Examples are project histories, plans, guides, user interfaces, test plans, test specification, test data, cost estimates, software requirements and architecture, source code, software documentation, and user manuals.

Software Configuration Control.   Managing changes to baseline documents.

Software Configuration Item. An entity that is designated for configuration management and treated as a single entity in the SCM process.

Software Configuration Management (SCM). Identify and document the functional and physical characteristics of a software configuration item, control changes to these characteristics, record and report change processing and implementation status, and verify compliance with specified requirements (IEEE, 1990).

Software design. 1. A systematic approach to identifying the major components of a system, specifying what each component does, and establishing the interfaces between system components. 2. A means of devising and documenting the overall architecture of a software system (Shumate, 1994).

Software engineering. Application of systematic, disciplined, quantifiable approach to software development, operation, and maintenance of software (IEEE, 1990).

Software entity. Software processes, requirements, products, and resources.

Software factory. Repeated application of the tools and skills of software engineering across a series of similar software projects.

Software maintenance. The performance of those activities required to keep a software system operational and responsive after it is accepted and placed into production (Rombach, 1987).

Software measure. A mapping from a set of objects in the software engineering world into a set of mathematical constructs such as numbers or vectors of numbers.

Software measurement. An association of numbers or symbols with attributes of software entities.

Software metric. 1. The measure of properties of a system (Thayer & McGettrick, 1993). 2. Software metrics are all forms of measurements related to software, including product and process metrics as well as prediction systems (Ott, 1995).

Software process. 1. A sequence of overlapping activities that produce a variety of documents culminating in a satisfactory, executable program. Each sequence of steps with feedback results in the production of artifacts in the development and evolution of software. 2. A process defined by activities, methods, and practices useful in developing a software product.

Software product. A computer program combined with those items that make them intelligible, usable, and extendible

Software prototype. Software that simulates selected interfaces and performs one or more of the main functions of a system.

Software reengineering. Examining and altering a software system to reconstitute and reimplement it in a new form.

Software Requirements Specification. A description of the principal features of a software product, its information flow, its behavior, its attributes.

Software standard. Mandatory methods, rules, requirements, and practices to be employed during software development.

Source code control system. A suite of Unix operating system programs for tracking and control of versions of text files.

SPICE. Software Process Improvement and Capability dEtermination Project established by ISO and the International Electrotechnical Commission (IEC) to create a common standard for software assessments. See *http://www-sqi.cit.gu.edu/spice/*.

SPMP.   Software Project Management Plan.

SRS.   Software Requirements Specification.

Stakeholder.   A feature of the Win Win spiral model in which customers, developers, maintainers, interfacers, testers, reusers, and the general public are examples of stakeholders.

State box.   Internal view of a module described relative to sequences of state transitions resulting from responses to stimuli.

Statechart.   1. An extension of finite state machines to include decomposition and to model the concurrent operation of real-time systems. 2. A visual formalism for describing "raw reactive behavior." 3. Statechart = state-diagrams + depth + orthogonality + broadcast-communication.

STATEMATE Magnum.   A statechart toolset. See *http://www.ilogix.com.*

State of a system.   An internal configuration of the system.

STP.   Software Through Pictures, Interactive Development Environments, Inc. See *http://www.ide.com.*

Structural testing.   Testing that takes into account the internal mechanism of a component or system of components. Types include branch testing, path testing, statement testing. Syn.: *Clear box testing, Glass box testing, White box testing.*

Structured Analysis and Design Technique.   A top-down approach to describing system tasks.

tATC.   Air traffic control training program.

TCSE.   IEEE Technical Council on Software Engineering. See http://www.tcse.org.

TQM.   Total Quality Management.

Traceable SRS.   Requirements written to facilitate referencing individual requirements.

Tracon.   Terminal radar approach control.

Transition Diagram.   A diagram with nodes representing states, a distinguished node called a start state, links identifying transitions between states, state labels for names of states, and link labels specifying actions.

Try.   In Java, a keyword marking the beginning of a code sequence that is executed until either an exception is thrown or the sequence finishes successfully.

UAN.   User Action Notation used to design user interfaces. Key features of the notation are M_v (depress mouse), $M^{\wedge}$ (release mouse), and ~[icon] to specify the action of highlighting a displayed icon.

Uniform Resource Locator.   An Internet command line used to specify an object on the internet such as a file or newsgroup.

URL.   Uniform Resource Locator.

Vanilla approach.   Dichotomy between data and control, convenient means of structuring data and control elements into an algorithmic whole, structured design, modularization, information-hiding, functional decomposition, hierarchy of possibly overlapping activities used to capture the capabilities of a system, association of data elements and data stores with inputs and outputs flowing between activities at various levels.

Vanilla framework. A general-purpose framework making it possible to conceive an idea for solving an algorithmic problem and to map the idea into an appropriate high-level medium.

VDM. Vienna Development Method.

Vienna Development Method. Specification of system functions employing mathematical notation to achieve precision and brevity.

Walkthrough. A designer or programmer leads one or more members of a development team through a segment of design or code and the participants ask questions and make comments about technique, style, possible errors, violation of development standards and other problems (IEEE, 1990).

Weighted Methods per Class Measure. Sum of the complexities of the methods of a class.

White box testing. See *Structural testing*.

WMC. Weighted Methods per Class

Worldly level process model. A project-specific model of the software process that provides an effective procedure for obtaining software products.

WYSIWYG. What-You-See-Is-What-You-Get display.

Z. A notation using elementary set theory and logic to describe the behavior of sequential processes.

REFERENCES

Alencar, P.S.C., de Lucena, C.J.P. A logical framework for evolving software systems. *Formal Aspects of Computing,* **8**:3–46, 1996.

Archer, C., Stinson, M. Object-Oriented Software Measures. Technical Report CMU/SEI-95-TR-002. Carnegie Mellon University, Pittsburgh, April 1995.

Babich, W. *Software Configuration Management.* Addison-Wesley, Reading, MA, 1986.

Brooks, F. *The Mythical Man Month: Essays on Software Engineering.* Addison-Wesley, New York, 1975.

Chikofsky, E., Cross, J.H. II. Reverse engineering. In *Encyclopedia of Software Engineering,* J.J. Marciniak, Ed. Wiley, New York, 1994.

Configuration Management Policy and Procedures for Defense Material. Directorate of Standards, UK Ministry of Defense, Glasgow, UK, 1991.

Curtis, B. Human factors in software development. In *Encyclopedia of Software Engineering.* J.J. Marciniak, Ed. Wiley, New York, 1994.

Cutkosky, M.R., et al. PACT: An experiment in integrated concurrent engineering systems. *IEEE Computer,* **26**(1):28–37, 1993.

Dorfman M., Thayer, R.H. *Standards, Guidelines, and Examples on System and Software Requirements Engineering.* IEEE Computer Society Press, Los Alamitos, CA: 1990.

Downing, D., Covington, M. Covington, M.M. *Dictionary of Computer and Internet Terms,* 6th ed. Barron's Educational Series, New York, 1998.

Fiore, P., Lanubile, F., Visaggio, G. Analyzing empirical data for a reverse engineering project. *Software Engineering Technical Council Newsletter.* **14**(3):1996.

Garlan, D., Perry, D.E. Introduction to special issue on software architecture. *IEEE TSE,* **21**(4):269–274, 1995.

Hoare, C.A.R. *Communicating Sequential Processes.* Prentice-Hall, Englewood Cliffs, NJ, 1985.

Humphrey, W.S. *Managing the Software Process.* Addison-Wesley, Reading, MA, 1989.

IEEE Std. 610.12-1990. *IEEE Standard Glossary of Software Engineering Terminology.* In *IEEE Standards Collection on Software Engineering.* IEEE, New York, 1997.

Jorgensen, M. Experience with the accuracy of software maintenance task effort prediction models. *IEEE TOS,* **21**(8):675–681, 1995.

Maxwell, K.D., et al. Software development productivity of European space, military and industrial applications. *IEEE TOS,* **22**(10):706–718, 1996.

Microsoft Bookshelf 1996–97. *American Heritage Dictionary of the English Language,* 3rd ed. Houghton Mifflin, Boston, 1992.

Ott, L.M. The early days of software metrics: Looking back after 20 years. In *Software Measurement,* A. Melton, Ed. International Thomson Computer Press, Toronto, pp. 7–26, 1995.

Oxford English Dictionary on Compact Disk, 2nd ed. Oxford University Press, New York, 1992.

Rombach, H.D. A controlled experiment on the impact of software structure on maintainability. *IEEE TOSE* **13**(3):344–354, 1987.

Shumate, K. Design. In *Encyclopedia of Software Engineering.* J.J. Marciniak, Ed. Wiley, New York, 1994.

Thayer, R.H., Thayer, M.C. Glossary of software engineering terms. In *Software Engineering: A European Perspective,* R.H. Thayer, A.D. McGettrick, Eds. IEEE Computer Society, Press, Los Alamitos, CA, 1993.

Tregoe, C.H., Tregoe, B.B. *Rational Management* [in German]. Verlag Moderne Industrie, 1981.

INDEX